D0039665

Discover
China

Experience the best of China

This edition written and researched by

Damian Harper,
Piera Chen, Chung Wah Chow, David Eimer, Tienlon Ho,
Robert Kelly, Shawn Low, Emily Matchar, Daniel McCrohan, Phillip Tang

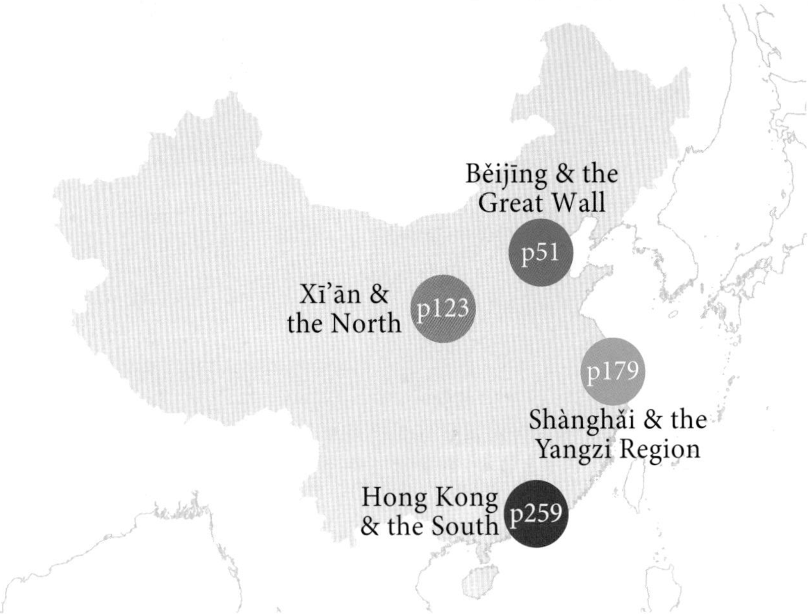

Běijīng & the
Great Wall

p51

Xī'ān &
the North

p123

p179

Shànghǎi & the
Yangzi Region

Hong Kong
& the South

p259

Contents

Plan Your Trip

Hong Kong & the South

Discover

Contents

Discover China

In Focus

Survival Guide

This is China

The central civilisation of the Far East and historically home to the dominant culture of the region, China is a traveller's treasure box: colossal palaces, sacred mountains, cliff-top temples, roaring metropolises, spectacular scenery and much, much more. A nation enjoying an exuberant and energetic coming of age, China is the country everyone's talking about.

China is modernising at a head-spinning pace.
But the slick skyscrapers, Lamborghini showrooms and Maglev trains are little more than dazzling baubles. Let's face it: the world's oldest continuous civilisation is bound to pull an artefact or two out of its hat. You won't bump into history at every turn, but travel selectively and rich seams of antiquity present themselves. Tumbledown chunks of the Great Wall, creaky historical residences, mist-wreathed and temple-strewn mountains, quaint villages and delightful water towns make travel in China both unique and astonishing.

China is vast.
So you must get outside: island-hop in Hong Kong, size up awesome sand dunes in Gānsù, trace the Great Wall as it meanders across mountain peaks, sail through awesome river gorges or cycle through otherworldly landscapes of karst peaks in Yángshuò. Ponder the desiccated enormity of the northwestern deserts and the preternatural mists of China's sacred mountains. Hike into a landscape richly flecked with seasonal shades, from the crimson leaves of autumn maples to the colourful azaleas of Huángshān in springtime or the ice-encrusted roofs of mountaintop Buddhist temples.

China is food obsessed.
Treat yourself and swap local Chinatown menus for the lavish Middle Kingdom cookbook: sample Peking duck, gobble down Lánzhōu noodles, sweat over spicy Sichuan dishes, and don't forget what's cooking in China's frontier lands – an excuse to get off the beaten path. Impress your friends as you *gānbēi* (down-in-one) the local firewater, sip a beer in a slick Běijīng bar or survey the Shànghǎi skyline through a raised cocktail glass. Culinary exploration is the most enticing aspect of Middle Kingdom travel: you'll return with stimulated taste buds and much-cherished gastronomic memories.

66
China is a traveller's treasure box...and the country everyone's talking about.
99

Lijiāng (p331)

China

RUSSIA

KAZAKHSTAN

KYRGYZSTAN

⊗ BISHKEK

Yīníng

Ürümqi

Kuqa

Kashgar

XĪNJIĀNG

Tashkurgan

ULAANBAATAR ☆

MONGOLIA

INNER MONGOLIA

Dūnhuáng ⑪ GĀNSÙ

⑭ Zhāngyè

Dégé Yínchuān

Wūhǎi

Zhōngwèi NÍNGXIÀ

Changtang Nature Preserve

QĪNGHǍI Qīnghǎi Lake

Xīníng

Xiàhé Lánzhōu

Shílín ⑰

Bǎojī

Lake Manasarovar

TIBET

Nam-tso

Ngal chu

NEPAL

KATHMANDU ⊕

Mt Everest ▲

Thimphu Valley

Lhasa

SÌCHUĀN

Lèshān ⑲ Chéngdū

④

Chóngqìng

☆ THIMPHU

BHUTAN

Shangri-la (Zhōngdiàn)

⑥ Lijiāng

Zūnyì

GUÌZHŌU

BANGLADESH

Xiàguān (Dàlǐ City)

Ānshùn

Guìyáng

DHAKA ☆

Téngchōng

Kūnmíng

Wēiníng

YÚNNÁN

ELEVATION

	6000m
	5000m
	4000m
	3000m
	2000m
	1000m
	500m
	0

MYANMAR (BURMA)

Jǐnghóng

Jǐngzhēn Měnglà

⊗ VIETNAM

20°N

90°E

Bay of Bengal

NAY PYI TAW ☆

HANOI ☆

LAOS

0 —— 500 km
0 —— 250 miles

THAILAND

VIENTIANE ☆

25
Top Highlights

1 Great Wall

2 Forbidden City, Běijīng

3 Terracotta Warriors, Xī'ān

4 Yangzi River cruise

5 Cruising Victoria Harbour, Hong Kong

6 Lìjiāng

7 The Bund, Shànghǎi

8 China's cuisine

9 Huángshān & Hui villages

10 Dragon's Backbone Rice Terraces

11 The Silk Road

12 Lí River & Yángshuò

13 Fújiàn *Tǔlóu*

14 Mògāo Caves, Dūnhuáng

15 Píngyáo

16 Fènghuáng

17 Labrang Monastery, Xiàhé

18 Wùyuán

19 Giant Panda Breeding Research Base, Chéngdū

20 *Hútòng*, Běijīng

21 Gǔlàng Yǔ

22 Canal towns

23 Yúngāng Caves

24 Wǔtái Shān

25 West Lake, Hángzhōu

25 China's Top Highlights

Great Wall

Spotting it from space is both tough and pointless: the only place you can truly put the Great Wall (p113) under your feet is in China. Select portions of the Great Wall according to taste: perfectly chiselled, dilapidated, stripped of its bricks, overrun with saplings, coiling splendidly into the hills or returning to dust. The fortification is a fitting symbol of those perennial Chinese traits: diligence, mass manpower, ambitious vision and engineering skill (coupled with a distrust of the neighbours).

1

Forbidden City, Běijīng

Běijīng's enormous palace (p66) is the be-all-and-end-all of dynastic grandeur, with its vast halls and splendid gates. No other place in China teems with so much history, legend and good old-fashioned imperial intrigue. You may get totally lost here but you'll always find something to write home about. The complex ranks among China's top three sights, boasting one of the land's most attractive admission prices and almost infinite value-for-money sightseeing.

Terracotta Warriors, Xī'ān

Standing silent guard over their emperor for more than 2000 years, the Terracotta Warriors (p141) are one of the most extraordinary archaeological discoveries ever made. It's not just that there are thousands of the life-sized figures lined up in battle formation; it's the fact that no two of them are alike, with every single one bearing a distinct expression. This is an army, but it's one made up of individuals. Gazing at these superbly sculpted faces brings the past alive in an utterly unique way.

The Best...
Places for Food

BĚIJĪNG
Ancestral home of Peking duck and a tantalising smorgasbord of Chinese and international food. (p97)

SHÀNGHǍI
Where else for hairy crab and a cornucopia of cuisine. (p213)

HONG KONG
First port of call for dim sum devotees. (p287)

MACAU
A mouth-watering and un-expected blend of Chinese, Asian, Portuguese and African culinary traditions. (p305)

XĪ'ĀN
Make the Muslim Quarter your first entree to China's scrumptious Silk Road cuisine. (p137)

The Best...
Modern Architecture

HONG KONG
A dramatic declaration of modernity, even more spectacular at night. (p271)

PŬDŌNG, SHÀNGHǍI
China's most iconic tower-scape thrusts up on the far side of the Huángpǔ River. (p201)

BĚIJĪNG
Architecture addicts will love the CCTV Building (p82) and the National Centre for the Performing Arts. (p105).

PEOPLE'S SQUARE, SHÀNGHǍI
The aptly named Tomorrow Sq building rockets into the clouds above Pǔxī. (p195)

Yangzi River Cruise

④

Snow, melting from the world's 'third pole' at the high-altitude Tibet–Qīnghǎi plateau, is the source of China's mighty, life-giving Yangzi. The country's longest river, it surges from west to east before pouring into the Pacific, reaching a crescendo at the Three Gorges, carved out over the millennia by the persistence of the powerful waters. The gorges are a magnificent spectacle and a Yangzi River cruise (p254) is a chance to hang up your travelling hat, take a seat and leisurely watch the drama unfold. Three Gorges (p254)

Cruising Victoria Harbour, Hong Kong

⑤

A whistle blows and your boat chugs forward. Beyond the waves, one of the world's most famous views unfolds: Hong Kong's skyscrapers in their steel and neon splendour, against a backdrop of mountains. You're on the Star Ferry (p286), a legendary service that's been carrying passengers between Hong Kong Island and Kowloon Peninsula since the 19th century. Victoria Harbour from Victoria Peak

Lìjiāng

The Naxi town of Lìjiāng (p331), in Yúnnán province, is one of China's most rewarding destinations for the ancient textures of ethnic minority life in its old town and the breathtaking beauty of Yúlóng Xuěshān (Jade Dragon Snow Mountain) rising over the town. While the old town itself can be crowded, an early rise is rewarded with quieter back alleys. Outside town almost limitless exploration beckons. Women in traditional dress, Lìjiāng

The Bund, Shànghǎi

More than just a city, Shànghǎi is the country's neon-lit beacon of change, opportunity and sophistication. With its sights set squarely on the not-too-distant future, Shànghǎi offers a taste of all the superlatives China can dare to dream up, from the world's highest observation deck to its largest underground theatre. Whether you're just pulling in after an epic 40-hour train trip from Xīnjiāng or it's your first stop, you'll find plenty to indulge in here. Start with the Bund (p196) – Shànghǎi's iconic riverfront area – where it all began. The Bund overlooking Pǔdōng

China's Cuisine

Say *zàijiàn* (goodbye) to that Chinatown schlock and *nǐhǎo* (hello) to a whole new world of food and flavour (p370). You'll certainly find dim sum, noodles and dumplings aplenty, but there's also the liquid fire of a Chóngqìng hotpot, Tibetan cuisine, or the adventurous flavours of Kashgar's night market. You'll see things you've never seen before, eat things you've never heard of and drink things that could lift a rocket into space. And that's just for starters. Dim sum cart, Guǎngzhōu (p308)

The Best...
Nightlife

HONG KONG
Natty music, dancing, drinking, tie-loosening and letting-down-of-hair. (p290)

MACAU
Romantic, elegant, European, charming, fun and a paradise for gamblers. (p306)

BĚIJĪNG
Běijīng's tirelessly rejuvenating clubs, bars and live-music venues should satisfy all comers. (p99)

SHÀNGHǍI
The name alone is synonymous with excess, hedonism and entertainment. (p215)

Huángshān & Hui Villages

Shrouded in mist and light rain more than 200 days a year and maddeningly crowded most of the time, Huángshān (p249) has an appeal that attracts millions of annual visitors. Perhaps it's the barren landscape, or an otherworldly vibe on the mountain. Mist rolls in and out at will; spindly bent pines stick out like lone pins across sheer, craggy granite faces. Not far from the mountain are the perfectly preserved Hui villages of Xīdì and Hóngcūn (p248). Unesco, Ang Lee and Zhang Yimou were captivated – you will be too. Lookout on Huángshān

9

The Best...
Places for
Karma

WǓTÁI SHĀN
A confluence of Buddhist magic, mountain air and alpine scenery. (p156)

MAHAYANA HALL, PǓNÍNG TEMPLE, CHÉNGDÉ
Feel Lilliputian alongside China's awesome Goddess of Mercy statue. (p121)

PO LIN MONASTERY, LANTAU, HONG KONG
The world's largest seated bronze Buddha statue. (p280)

LAMA TEMPLE, BĚIJĪNG
The most important Tibetan temple outside of the Roof of the World. (p72)

LABRANG MONASTERY, XIÀHÉ
Wreathed in devotion and visited by an incessant stream of Tibetan pilgrims. (p341)

Dragon's Backbone Rice Terraces

10

After a bumpy bus ride to the highland in northern Guǎngxī, you'll be dazzled by one of China's most archetypal and photographed landscapes: the splendidly named Dragon's Backbone Rice Terraces (p314). The region is a beguiling patchwork of minority villages, with sparkling layers of waterlogged terraced fields climbing the hillsides tenaciously. You'll be enticed into a game of village-hopping. The most invigorating walk between Píng'ān and Dàzhài villages offers spine-tingling views. After the summer rains, the fields glisten with reflections.

The Silk Road

11

There are other Silk Road cities in countries such as Uzbekistan and Turkmenistan, but it's really in China where you get the feeling of stepping on the actual Silk Road (p340). Travel by bus and experience the route as ancient traders once did – mile-by-mile, town-by-town. Kashgar (p344) is the ultimate Silk Road town and today remains a unique melting pot of peoples, with Jiāyùguān Fort (p342), a Great Wall fort framed by snow-capped mountains, marking the route. Xīnjiāng province

12

Lí River & Yángshuò

It's hard to exaggerate the beauty of Yángshuò (p316) and the Lí River that runs through it. The area is famed for classic, legendary images of China: mossy-green jagged limestone peaks provide a backdrop for weeping willow trees leaning over bubbling streams, wallowing water buffalos, and farmers sowing rice paddies. Ride a bamboo raft along the river and you'll understand why this stunning rural landscape has inspired painters and poets for centuries.

13

Fújiàn Tǔlóu

Rising up in colonies from the hilly borderlands of Fújiàn, Guǎngdōng and Jiāngxī, the stupendous *tǔlóu* round-houses (p325) house entire villages, even though occupant numbers are way down these days. The imposing and well-defended bastions of wood and earth – not all circular it must be added – were once mistaken by the CIA for missile silos. Do the right thing and spend the night in one: this is a vanishing way of life, the pastoral setting is quite superb and the architecture is unique.

Mògāo Caves, Dūnhuáng

Where China starts transforming into a lunar desertscape in the far west, the handsome oasis town of Dūnhuáng is a natural staging post for dusty Silk Road explorers. Mountainous sand dunes swell outside town while Great Wall fragments lie scoured by abrasive desert winds, but it is the magnificent caves at Mògāo (p343) that truly dazzle. Mògāo is the cream of China's crop of Buddhist caves – its statues are ineffably sublime and among the nation's most priceless cultural treasures.

14

The Best...
Outdoor Experiences

YÁNGSHUÒ
China's most photographed natural landscape verges on the idyllic. (p316)

HUÁNGSHĀN
Climb up into the spectral mists of China's most celebrated mountain. (p249)

COLOANE, MACAU
Gorgeous island retreat and one of Macau's most charming features. (p304)

LAMMA ISLAND, HONG KONG
Hong Kong: Gucci, skyscrapers, fake Rolexes and high population density. Not here though. (p291)

THE THREE GORGES
Flee urban China and be blown away by some stupendous geology. (p254)

The Best...
Great Wall Excursions

JIÀNKÒU
For the tumbledown, collapsing, wall-as-it-should-look, come here. (p115)

ZHUÀNGDÀOKŎU
Authentic sections of wall far away from the madding crowd. (p116)

JIĀYÙGUĀN FORT
Out in China's far west, pounded and scoured by the Gobi winds. (p342)

JĪNSHĀNLǏNG
Quite an expedition from Beijing, but the starting point of some exceptional hikes. (p116)

15

Píngyáo

Time-warped Píngyáo (p150), an intact, walled Chinese town with an unbroken sense of continuity to its Qing-dynasty heyday, is a true gem. Píngyáo ticks most of your China boxes with a flourish: imposing city walls, atmospheric alleys, ancient shopfronts, traditional courtyard houses, some excellent hotels and hospitable locals, all in a compact area. You can travel the length and breadth of China and not find another town like it. In fact, when you discover Píngyáo, you may never want to leave.

Above: Guanyin statue in Shuānglín Temple (p156); Left: Nan Dajie (p154)

ABOVE: KRZYSZTOF DYDYNSKI/GETTY IMAGES ©; LEFT: MARTIN MOOS/GETTY IMAGES ©

Fènghuáng

Houses perched precariously on stilts, ancestral halls, crumbling temples and gate towers set amid a warren of back alleys full of shops selling mysterious foods and medicines – it's enough on its own to make the ancient town of Fènghuáng (p319) an essential stop. Add in the seductive setting on either side of the Tuó River and the chance to stay at an inn right by the water, and you have one of the most evocative towns in China. The *diàojiǎolóu* (stilt houses) of Fènghuáng

KRZYSZTOF DYDYNSKI/GETTY IMAGES ©

Labrang Monastery, Xiàhé

If you can't make it to Tibet, visit this more accessible part of the historic Tibetan region of Amdo in Gānsù. Labrang Monastery (p341) in Xiàhé attracts legions of Tibetan pilgrims who perambulate single-mindedly around the monastery's prayer wheel–lined *kora* (pilgrim path). As a source of spiritual power, the monastery casts its spell far and wide, and with great hiking opportunities, plus an intriguing ethnic mix, it's in a fascinating corner of China.

Wùyuán

When urban China has finally taken its toll on your lungs and the countryside insists on exploration, come to Wùyuán (p253). The rural Jiāngxī landscape is a picture, the air is pure and the little villages that dot the scenery around Wùyuán are truly delightful. Find yourself a base in a village such as Little Lǐkēng and set out to explore from village to village along the old postal roads. You may have been to Shànghǎi and Běijīng, but your memories of Wùyuán might end up your best.

The Best...
History

BĚIJĪNG
China's leading city was capital to three imperial dynasties: the Yuan, Ming and Qing. (p62)

PÍNGYÁO
China's most sublime concentration of historical architecture. (p150)

XĪ'ĀN
Dynastic home of the Terracotta Warriors and end of the road for Silk Road traders. (p132)

FÚJIÀN TǓLÓU
Fortified, earthen round-houses that have housed minority groups, Hakka and Mǐnnán (Fujianese) people, for centuries. (p325)

FÈNGHUÁNG
Magnificent old Húnán architecture overlooking the Tuó River. (p319)

Giant Panda Breeding Research Base, Chéngdé

Chances of seeing a giant panda in the wilds of China are practically zilch, even if you're a motivated expert with time. You can catch a couple of specimens at China's penitentiary-like zoos, but that's hardly the same. The Giant Panda Breeding Research Base (p336) in Chéngdū isn't the wilds but neither is it a zoo, and with a population of almost 50 pandas, it's an excellent opportunity to see the giant panda in a setting approximating its natural habitat.

19

The Best...
Places for Photography

YÁNGSHUÒ
You can't go wrong with the subject matter: stupendous karst and river scenery. (p316)

LÙJIĀZUǏ, PǓDŌNG, SHÀNGHǍI
Stand among the dazzling night-time skyscrapers of Lùjiāzuǐ, point and shoot. (p201)

WEST LAKE, HÁNGZHŌU
Sunset on a clear day over the water is one of China's top sights. (p235)

CENTRAL DISTRICT, HONG KONG
Choose a night-time lookout on Tsim Sha Tsui and face due south for Hong Kong's most iconic vista. (p271)

Hútòng, Běijīng

20

To get under the skin of the capital, you need to get lost at least once in its enchanting, ancient *hútòng* (alleyways, p78), which are Běijīng's heart and soul. It's in these alleys that criss-cross the centre of the city that you'll discover the capital's unique street life. Despite its march into the 21st century, Běijīng's true charms – heavenly courtyard architecture, narrow lanes and a strong sense of community – are not high-rise. It's easy to find that out; just check into a courtyard hotel and the true Běijīng will be right on your doorstep. *Hútòng* in the Dōngchéng district, Běijīng

LONELY PLANET/GETTY IMAGES ©

Gǔlàng Yǔ

Linking Vietnam with North Korea, China's long coastline is dotted with the odd concession and the occasional colony where 19th-century foreign powers erected their buildings and embassy districts. Not the most famous, but perhaps the most charming of all, is Gǔlàng Yǔ (p323). A leisurely, car-free island of slowly decaying villa architecture and old churches, Gǔlàng Yǔ is an unexpected portrait of yesteryear European style and almost Mediterranean rhythms. Cable car, Gǔlàng Yǔ

Canal Towns

Partly due to their small size, the lovely water towns of Zhéjiāng and Jiāngsū have preserved their Ming- and Qing-dynasty architecture, despite being embedded in China's rapidly changing eastern seaboard. A tempting tableau of arched bridges, stone alleyways, ancient temples, canals and creaking architecture, the towns of Zhūjiājiǎo (p227), Sūzhōu (p228) and Tónglǐ (p233) are all easily accessible, offering a glimpse of a vanishing way of life. Canal boats, Zhūjiājiǎo

Yúngāng Caves

Buddhist art taken to sublime heights, these 5th century caves (p162) house some of the most remarkable statues in all of China. Carved out of the harsh yellow earth of Shānxī and surrounded by superb frescoes, the statues inside the caves represent the highpoint of the Tuoba people's culture and draw on influences from as far away as Greece and Persia. Marvel at how the pigment on some of them has miraculously survived 1500-odd years, and respect how potent they remain to followers of Buddhism.

23

The Best...
Shopping

HONG KONG
Retail hub and shoppers' paradise on the south China coast. (p291)

BĚIJĪNG
Great for clothes, arts and crafts, street markets and more. (p105)

SHÀNGHǍI
Shop your way around the French concession and see Shànghǎi's best side. (p219)

PÍNGYÁO
All sorts of items, from paper cuts to embroidered shoes, are sold in traditional-style shops. (p154)

Wǔtái Shān

Even though you have a chance of running headlong into snow as late as May, the mountain scenery and monastic disposition of Buddhist Wǔtái Shān (p156) is a fabulous north China experience. It's not the place for a quick in-and-out. Treat it as a spiritual retreat. Unwind, tune out completely from the chaos and noise of urban China and submit to some Buddhist mystery. After you've followed pilgrims and monks from temple to temple, set about exploring the rest of the vast mountain and turn up some of the oldest temple halls in China.

Xiāntōng Temple (p157), Wǔtái Shān

The Best...
Places for Ethnic Culture

LÌJIĀNG
Traditional Naxi village in the north of Yúnnán. (p331)

DÀLǏ
Excellent potential for exploration in the Bai heartland of Yúnnán. (p238)

KASHGAR
For strong flavours of Central Asia on the far northwest edge of China. (p344)

XIÀHÉ
In the ancestral Tibetan homelands of southwestern Gānsū, Xiàhé is rich in the shades of Tibet. (p341)

25

West Lake, Hángzhōu

China's most famous urban lake (p235) is one of the gems south of the mighty Yangzi River. In a charming vignette of traditional China pagodas rise on hills above the lake, willow branches hang limply over the water and boats float unhurriedly across a liquid expanse. This may be one of China's most-visited panoramas, but the lake is so large you always find space to admire the scenery and drift into a reverie. Try to spend an evening in Hángzhōu if you can, as the lake saves its best side for nightfall.

China's
Top Itineraries

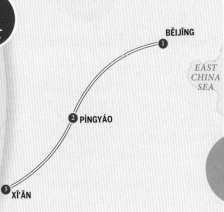

Běijīng to Xī'ān
The Northern Tour

1 WEEK

You can get loads done in a week. You'll need three days in Běijīng for the main sights and to walk on the Great Wall, followed by two days in China's most attractive walled town – Píngyáo – before continuing to the home of the Terracotta Warriors: Xī'ān.

BĚIJĪNG

EAST CHINA SEA

❷ PÍNGYÁO

❸ XĪ'ĀN

❶ Běijīng (p62)

To put China in immediate perspective, zero in on the very centre of town and size up both **Tiān'ānmén Square** and the **Forbidden City**. You'll need half a day for the **Summer Palace**, but find time for the bars and restaurants of **Nanluogu Xiang** and some *hútòng* exploration. Also book yourself a room in a **courtyard hotel** for doses of old Peking charm. Save a day for the **Great Wall** and half a day to appreciate the **Temple of Heaven**, but don't overlook the treasures of the **Poly Art Museum** or the **Lama Temple**.

BĚIJĪNG ➲ PÍNGYÁO

🚄 **4½ hours** D-class train from Běijīng west train station.

❷ Píngyáo (p150)

Try to have your Píngyáo accommodation booked in advance – then someone should meet you at Píngyáo Train Station. Wander the streets and alleys, enjoying their ancient textures, then explore the **Rìshēngchāng Financial House Museum**. The **city walls** are among the best preserved in China and the lovely old **City Tower** is a gem at the heart of town. Píngyáo's **Confucius Temple** contains the town's oldest surviving building, but perhaps its most appealing aspect is staying in one of the lovely courtyard hotels and seeing an authentic Chinese old town that refuses to modernise.

PÍNGYÁO ➲ XĪ'ĀN

🚄 **3½ hours** D-class train to Xī'ān north train station.

❸ Xī'ān (p132)

One of China's most renowned walled cities, Xī'ān is the Shaanxi home to the spellbinding **Terracotta Warriors** and a collection of significant **imperial tombs** that sprinkle the surrounding region. You'll want to climb the city's Ming-dynasty walls to recall Xī'ān's former epic grandeur, explore the **Muslim Quarter**, dine on the city's famous **Muslim cuisine**, admire Xī'ān's **Tang-dynasty pagodas** – which mark the town's zenith as Tang capital Cháng'ān – and explore the city's numerous and fascinating museums.

Hikers climb the Great Wall near Jīnshānlǐng (p116)

10 DAYS

Běijīng to Hángzhōu
The Capital Tour

After three days in Běijīng, chart your way southwest to Xī'ān and the Terracotta Warriors before recrossing China to Shànghǎi in the east via Luòyáng, with a detour to the Shàolín Temple, before concluding your journey next to West Lake in Hángzhōu.

① Běijīng (p62)

Běijīng is all about the **Forbidden City**, **Tiān'ānmén Square**, the **Temple of Heaven** and the **Great Wall**, as well as a crop of fine museums. To get under the city's skin, exploring Běijīng's ancient *hútòng* is essential – check into a courtyard hotel to immerse yourself in their charms. The **Summer Palace** is a rewarding excursion but try to make a detour to the **798 Art District**.

BĚIJĪNG ○ XĪ'ĀN

✈ **110 minutes** or 🚆 **5½ hours** G-class train from Běijīng west train station to Xī'ān north train station.

② Xī'ān (p132)

The former Tang-dynasty capital, today's Xī'ān is rapidly developing, but its venerable Ming-dynasty **city walls** are famous across China. Most visitors are here to see the awe-inspiring **Terracotta Warriors** outside town, however. The **Great Mosque** and the **Muslim Quarter** are reminders that this city marked the start of the Silk Road, while to the east of town rises the Taoist peak of **Huà Shān**, one of China's most sacred mountains.

XĪ'ĀN ○ LUÒYÁNG

🚆 **90 minutes** From Xī'ān north train station to Luòyáng Lóngmén station or 🚌 **Five hours**

③ Luòyáng (p146)

Former capital of 13 dynasties, Luòyáng today possesses little history beyond an intriguing **old town,** but the nearby **Lóngmén Caves** are one of China's most celebrated Buddhist grottoes. The **White Horse Temple** is China's oldest Buddhist temple, while a bus trip from Luòyáng brings you to the **Shàolín Temple**, birthplace of China's martial arts, and **Sōng Shān**, the central mountain of Taoism's five sacred peaks.

LUÒYÁNG ○ SHÀNGHǍI

✈ **One hour** or 🚆 **Nine hours**

④ Shànghǎi (p190)

Journey from China's ancestral heartland to Shànghǎi, the nation's financial capital. It's essential to spend time on the **Bund**, Shànghǎi's most august length of bombastic architecture. Try to book a terrace table at **M on the Bund** for lunch with a view. Take time to savour the **French Concession** and peruse the shops and traditional architecture of **Xīntiāndì** and **Tiānzǐfáng** before weighing up modern Chinese art at **M50**. Admire the **Yùyuán Gardens** and the **Shànghǎi Museum**.

SHÀNGHǍI ○ HÁNGZHŌU

🚆 **55 minutes** From Shànghǎi Hóngqiáo train station or 🚌 **2½ hours** From the Shànghǎi south long-distance bus station.

⑤ Hángzhōu (p235)

You can head down to Hángzhōu – former capital of the southern Song – as a day trip from Shànghǎi or spend the night. With its picture-postcard views and unhurried tempo, Hángzhōu's **West Lake** is perhaps the ideal conclusion to this itinerary: find yourself a lakeside bench or go on a boat trip.

Bronze Buddha in Qīnghéfāng Old Street (p240), Hángzhōu
GREG ELMS/GETTY IMAGES ©

Hong Kong to Xī'ān
South to North Highlights

After a few days in Hong Kong, journey to Guìlín for the region's beautiful karst landscape before heading to Fènghuáng and on to Yíchāng and a Three Gorges trip to Chóngqìng. Come to a halt in Xī'ān, via the Sìchuān capital, Chéngdū.

① Hong Kong (p270)

Hong Kong offers a wealth of sights and experiences: hop aboard the **Star Ferry** and climb **Victoria Peak** on the **Peak Tram** for views over the territory, go island-hopping to **Lantau** and **Lamma Islands** and glimpse another side to Hong Kong, while a day trip to **Macau** for good food, gorgeous ecclesiastical architecture and Portuguese charms is essential.

HONG KONG ➋ GUÌLÍN

✈ **90 minutes** From Hong Kong International Airport to Guìlín Liǎngjiāng International Airport or 🚍 **13 hours** Change trains in Guǎngzhōu.

② Guìlín (p311)

Guìlín is a useful base for more diverting excursions: take a boat down the Lí River to gorgeous **Yángshuò** and hike or cycle into some splendid karst countryside. Also plan a trip north to the glittering **Dragon's Backbone Rice Terraces**; plan on four to five hours for the Dàzhài to Píng'ān village hike.

GUÌLÍN ➋ FÈNGHUÁNG

🚌🚍 **14 hours** Train to Huáihuà (11 hours), then change to bus for Fènghuáng (three hours).

③ Fènghuáng (p319)

The funky riverside town of **Fènghuáng** is one of China's most attractive walled towns. Get your accommodation booked up front and aim to spend at least one night here, but consider longer stays.

FÈNGHUÁNG ➋ YÍCHĀNG

🚌🚍 **12 hours** Bus to Huáihuà (three hours) then train to Yíchāng east train station (nine hours).

④ Yíchāng & the Three Gorges (p254)

Situated on the Yangzi River – China's longest – Yíchāng has few sights, but it's the port of departure for hydrofoils and boats upstream through the **Three Gorges**. Boats go all the way to Chóngqìng, or you can take the bus from the port of Fèngjié.

YÍCHĀNG ➋ CHÉNGDŪ

🚢🚍🚍 **Eight hours** Hydrofoil to Fèngjié (four hours) then bus to Chóngqìng (four hours). Bullet train from Chóngqìng to Chéngdū (two hours) or 🚢🚍 **38 hours** Passenger boat to Chóngqìng; longer for tourist boats. Fast bullet train from Chóngqìng to Chéngdū (two hours).

⑤ Giant Panda Breeding Research Base (p336)

Make a morning visit to the **Giant Panda Breeding Research Base** 18km north of Chéngdū's city centre, which is home to a population of both giant and red pandas.

CHÉNGDŪ ➋ XĪ'ĀN

🚍 **13 to 18 hours** Sleeper train to Xī'ān or ✈ **70 minutes**

⑥ Xī'ān (p132)

The original remains of Tang capital Cháng'ān may be hard to discern under the roar of the modern city and its 20th century overlays, but Xī'ān's Tang-dynasty heritage survives in several pagoda and temple remains, while Ming history endures in its robust **city walls**. The city's undeniable highlight, however, vastly predates even the Tang: the **Terracotta Warriors** outside town.

Passengers on the Peak Tram (p279), Victoria Peak, Hong Kong
GREG ELMS/GETTY IMAGES ©

2 WEEKS

Shànghǎi to Hong Kong The Big Loop

This epic adventure takes you on a Yangzi region loop from Shànghǎi to Hong Kong, ticking off a roll call of the nation's most inimitable imperial sights, Buddhist treasures, breathtaking landscapes and ancient towns.

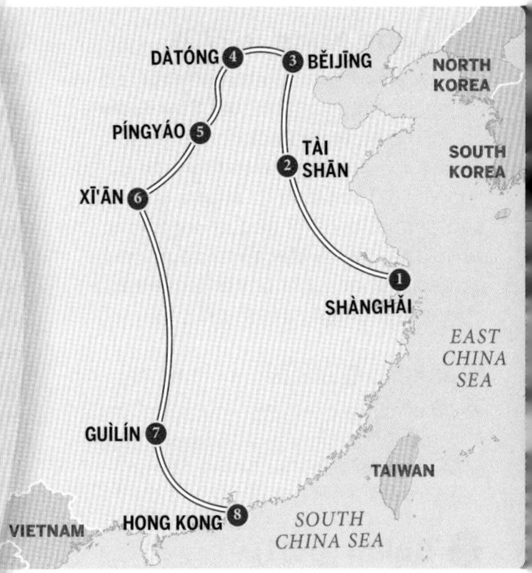

1 Shànghǎi (p190)

Where better to start this grand tour than in Shànghǎi – just south of the Yangzi River but roughly halfway down China's epic coastline. Spend a few days' sightseeing around the major sights: explore the **Bund,** the **French Concession** and the hallmark sights of **Pǔdōng**. Check out the excellent food and entertainment on offer: Shànghǎi has some of the best restaurants and bars in the nation.

SHÀNGHǍI ➔ TÀI SHĀN

Five to six hours Express train to Tài'ān train station or **12 hours**

2 Tài Shān (p156)

Explore the town of **Tài'ān**, visiting the **Dài Temple** before climbing the holy Taoist peak of Tài Shān. Try to spend the night on the mountain so you can catch the sunrise before descending the next day.

TÀI SHĀN ➔ BĚIJĪNG

Two hours or **Six hours**

3 Běijīng (p62)

China's 'northern capital' is a roll call of China's big sights: the **Forbidden City**, **Tiān'ānmén Square**, the **Great Wall** and the **Summer Palace**. Check into a courtyard hotel for a few nights to experience the city's adorable ***hútòng*** close up. Make sure you savour the city's outstanding restaurant options.

BĚIJĪNG ➔ DÀTÓNG

Four hours From Běijīng train station or **4½ hours** From Liùlǐqiáo long-distance bus station.

4 Dàtóng (p159)

Explore the city's recently restored **old town** but the top priority is the magnificent **Yúngāng Caves** outside town, one of China's most famous and colourful collections of Buddhist statuary and a stupendous chunk of artistic heritage.

DÁTÓNG ➔ PÍNGYÁO

Seven to eight hours or **Six hours** Via Tàiyuán, where you change bus.

Dim sum, Hong Kong (p287)
LONELY PLANET/GETTY IMAGES ©

dynasty **city wall**. Explore the city's Muslim Quarter, sample some of the local Silk Road cuisine, peruse the **Shaanxi History Museum** and, if you still have the energy, make a detour to the exhilarating Taoist mountain of **Huà Shān** east of town.

XĪ'ĀN ◐ GUÌLÍN

✈ Two hours or 🚌 28 hours

❼ Guìlín (p311)

On arrival in Guìlín, head immediately down to **Yángshuò** to explore the region's stunning karst landscape. Have a room booked at one of Yángshuò's hotels and spend a few days hiking and cycling around the region, journeying to nearby villages and settlements along the **Lí River**.

GUÌLÍN ◐ HONG KONG

✈ 90 minutes or 🚌 15 hours Change trains in Guǎngzhōu to Hung Hom from Guǎngzhōu east station.

❽ Hong Kong (p270)

The perfect conclusion to your China adventure: the former British colony of Hong Kong renowned for its dim sum, lovely islands, diverse heritage, stunning modern architecture and proximity to **Macau**. Take the **Peak Tram** up to **Victoria Peak**, explore Hong Kong Island's **Central district**, catch the **Star Ferry** over to **Tsim Sha Tsui** and gaze across Victoria Harbour for the illuminated night-time view over Central.

❺ Píngyáo (p150)

Come to a leisurely halt in this marvellous **old walled Shānxī town** where China's best collection of preserved, traditional homesteads creates a virtually immaculate portrait of old China. Check into an old courtyard hotel and explore the sights, making a few diversions out of town to visit nearby attractions, including the **Shuānglín Temple** and the **Wang Family Courtyard**.

PÍNGYÁO ◐ XĪ'ĀN

🚌 Three hours or 🚌 Seven hours

❻ Xī'ān (p132)

Fabled home of the **Terracotta Warriors** and start of the Silk Road, Xī'ān – like Píngyáo – is also enclosed by a Ming-

2 WEEKS

Běijīng to the Yangzi Region Via the Silk Road

Taking you from Běijīng to the Mògāo Caves in far northwest of China, this journey of a lifetime conveys you along the Silk Road to Xī'ān, via Tibetan borderlands, before charting a course to the Yangzi region cities of Hángzhōu and Sūzhōu, and finally coming to a halt in Shànghǎi.

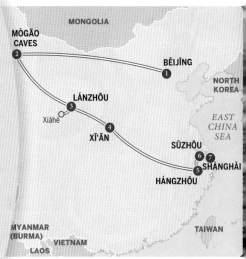

❶ Běijīng (p62)

Spend three days sizing up Běijīng and its epic sights, including **Tiān'ānmén Square**, the **Forbidden City**, the **Summer Palace** and the bars and restaurants of **Nanluogu Xiang**. Put aside a day for the **Great Wall** and half a day for the **Temple of Heaven**. Also make sure you get some *hútòng* exploration under your belt.

BĚIJĪNG ➲ MÒGĀO CAVES

✈ ➡ **Four hours** Fly to Dūnhuáng (April to October only), then bus to Mògāo Caves (30 minutes) or ➡➡➡ **26 hours** From Běijīng west train station to Liǔyuán (24 hours), then bus (two hours) to Dūnhuáng, change bus for Mògāo Caves (30 minutes).

❷ Mògāo Caves (p343)

Fly from Běijīng to Dūnhuáng in the distant northwest of China and journey out of town to visit the astonishing **Mògāo Caves**. China's grandest collection of Buddhist art, these caves are an incredible testament to the once splendid Buddhist civilisation that lay along the Silk Road.

MÒGĀO CAVES ➲ LÁNZHŌU

✈ **Two hours** from Dūnhuáng or ➡ **14 hours** from Dūnhuáng.

❸ Lánzhōu (p340)

If taking the train from **Dūnhuáng** consider stopping off en route in Jiāyùguān to visit **Jiāyùguān Fort** at the western end of the Great Wall (whose remains disappear in the Gobi Desert around here). Lánzhōu itself has little of interest, but it's the stopping-off point for the four-hour bus trips to **Labrang Monastery** in **Xiàhé**. A visit here is essential for travellers who want to get a taste of Tibet, and you can overnight in Xiàhé.

LÁNZHŌU ➲ XĪ'ĀN

✈ **One hour** or ➡ **Nine hours**

❹ Xī'ān (p132)

Put aside two days to fully explore Xī'ān – at the end of the Silk Road – so you can do justice to the **Terracotta Warriors**, **Big Goose Pagoda**, the **Shaanxi History Museum** and the **Muslim Quarter**.

Earthen fortress, Silk Road (p340)

FENG WEI PHOTOGRAPHY/GETTY IMAGES ©

HÁNGZHŌU ➔ SŪZHŌU

🚄 Two hours or 🚌 Two hours

❻ Sūzhoū (p228)

Start at the excellent **Sūzhōu Museum** before quietly exploring Sūzhōu's gardens, including the **Garden of the Master of the Nets** and the **Humble Administrator's Garden**. Sūzhōu's fascinating crop of temples includes the **North Temple Pagoda** and the **Temple of Mystery**. Further historical charm can be explored on **evening boat tours** in the outer canal.

SŪZHŌU ➔ SHÀNGHǍI

🚄 30 minutes or 🚌 90 minutes

XĪ'ĀN ➔ HÁNGZHŌU

✈ Two hours or 🚄 16 hours

❺ Hángzhōu (p235)

After dry and dusty Xī'ān, the moister and greener environs of Hángzhōu – former capital city of the southern Song dynasty – gives you a taste of China south of the Yangzi River. You won't have to stray too far from Hángzhōu's **West Lake** to fully enjoy the city, so book your accommodation as close to the water as possible. Hire a bike to cycle round the lakeside and along its causeways or seek divine inspiration at **Língyǐn Temple** and **Jìngcí Temple**. Pop down to **Qīnghéfāng Old Street** for some entertaining street stalls.

❼ Shànghǎi (p190)

Shànghǎi's most grandiose sight is the **Bund**, which faces skyscraper-encrusted Lùjiāzuǐ in **Pǔdōng** over the Huángpǔ River. You'll want to stroll along East Nanjing Road all the way to **People's Square** and the standout **Shànghǎi Museum**. The **French Concession** is the place for boutique shopping, dining, drinking and slow ambling past European architecture along leafy side streets, as well as the *shíkùmén* (stone-gate) architecture of **Xīntiāndì** and **Tiánzǐfáng**. Save Pǔdōng until last and visit the observation decks of the **Shànghǎi World Financial Center** for evening views of Shànghǎi before dinner and drinks on the **Bund**.

China Month by Month

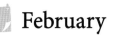

January

North China is a deep freeze but the cold in the south is far less bitter; preparations for the Chinese New Year get under way well in advance of the festival, which arrives any time between late January and March.

Spring Festival

The Chinese New Year is family-focused, with dining on dumplings and gift-giving of *hóngbāo* (red envelopes stuffed with money). Most families feast together on New Year's Eve, then China goes on a big week-long holiday. Expect fireworks, parades, temple fairs and lots of colour.

February

North China remains shockingly icy and dry but things are slowly warming up in Hong Kong and Macau. The Chinese New Year may be firing on all cylinders but sort out your tickets well in advance.

Monlam Great Prayer Festival

Held during two weeks from the third day of the Tibetan New Year and celebrated with spectacular processions across the Tibetan world, huge silk *thangka* (Tibetan sacred art) is unveiled and, on the last day, a statue of the Maitreya Buddha is conveyed around towns and monasteries; catch it in Xiàhé (p341).

Lantern Festival

Held 15 days after the spring festival, this celebration was traditionally a time when Chinese hung out highly decorated lanterns. Lantern-hung Píngyáo in Shānxī (p150) is an atmospheric place to soak up the festival (sometimes held in March).

February Lantern Festival, Shànghǎi
KEREN SU/GETTY IMAGES ©

March

China comes back to life after a long winter, although high-altitude areas remain glacial. The mercury climbs in Hong Kong and abrasive dust storms billow into Běijīng. Admission prices are still low-season.

⚫ Běijīng Book Bash

Curl up with a good book at the Bookworm cafe (p107) for Běijīng's international literary festival, and lend an ear to lectures from international and domestic authors. Also earmark Shànghǎi for its international literary festival in the Bund-side Glamour Bar or the Man Hong Kong International Literary Festival.

◉ Fields of Yellow

Delve into south Chinese countryside to be bowled over by a landscape saturated in bright yellow rapeseed. In some parts of China, such as lovely Wùyuán (p253) in Jiāngxī province, it's a real tourist draw.

April

Most of China is warm so it's a good time to be on the road, ahead of the May holiday period and before China's summer reaches its full power.

⚫ Tomb Sweeping (Qīngmíng) Festival

Now a three-day holiday period, this traditional festival around 5 April sees Chinese people taking a holiday to visit the tombs and graves of their ancestors. From a travel point of view, it can be a busy time to be on the road as train, bus and plane tickets are often in short supply.

⚫ Paean to Peonies

Wángchéng Park in Luòyáng (p146) bursts into full-coloured bloom with its peony festival: pop a flower garland on your head and join in the floral fun (but don't forget your camera).

⚫ Third Moon Festival

This Bai ethnic minority festival is an excellent reason to pitch up in the lovely north Yúnnán town of Dàlǐ (p328). It's a week of horse racing, singing and merrymaking at the end of April and the beginning of May.

◉ Formula 1

Petrol heads and aficionados of speed, burnt rubber and hairpin bends flock to Shànghǎi (p190) for some serious motor racing at the track near Āntíng. Get your hotel room booked early: it's one of the most glamorous events on the Shànghǎi calendar.

May

China is in full bloom in mountain regions such as Ānhuī province's Huángshān, where lovely azaleas flower. The first four days of May see China on vacation for one of the three big holiday periods, kicking off with Labour Day (1 May).

⚫ Great Wall Marathon

Experience the true meaning of pain (but get your Great Wall sightseeing done and dusted at the same time). Not for the infirm or unfit (or the cable-car fraternity). See www.great-wall-marathon.com for more details.

⚫ Buddha's Birthday in Xiàhé

A fascinating time to enjoy the Tibetan charms of Gānsù province's Xiàhé, when Buddhist monks make charitable handouts to beggars and the streets throng with pilgrims. Buddha's Birthday is celebrated on the 8th day of the fourth lunar month, usually in May.

rains' give Shànghǎi a serious soaking and the grasslands of Inner Mongolia and Qīnghǎi turn green.

✿ Torch Festival, Dàlǐ

The torch festival (huǒbǎ jié) in Dàlǐ (p328) is held on the 24th day of the sixth lunar month (normally July) and is likely to be the best photo op in the province. Flaming torches are paraded at night through homes and fields.

August

The temperature gauge of the 'three ovens' of the Yangzi region – Chóngqìng, Wǔhàn and Nánjīng – gets set to blow. Rainstorms hit Běijīng, which is usually way hotter than 40°C – so is Shànghǎi. So head uphill to Huángshān, Tài Shān, Éméi Shān or Huà Shān.

✿ Qīngdǎo International Beer Festival

Slake that chronic summer thirst with a round of beers and devour a plate of mussels in Shāndōng's best-looking port town, home of the Tsingtao beer brand.

September

Come to Běijīng and stay put – September is part of the fleetingly lovely tiāngāo qìshuǎng ('the sky is high and the air is fresh') autumnal season – it's an event in itself.

✿ Mid-Autumn Festival

Also called the moon festival, locals celebrate by devouring daintily prepared moon cakes – stuffed with bean paste, egg yolk, walnuts and more. With a full moon, it's a romantic occasion for lovers and a special time for families. It's on the 15th day of the eighth lunar month.

June

Most of China is hot and getting hotter. Once frozen areas, such as Jílín's Heaven Lake, are accessible, and nature springs instantly to life. The great peak season is cranking up.

✿ Dragon Boat Festival

Find yourself the nearest large river and catch all the waterborne drama of dragon boat races in this celebration of one of China's most famous poets. The Chinese traditionally eat zòngzi (triangular glutinous rice dumplings wrapped in reed leaves).

July

Typhoons can wreak havoc with travel itineraries down south, lashing the Guǎngdōng and Fújiàn coastlines. Plenty of rain sweeps across China: the big 'plum

😊 Confucius' Birthday

Head to the Confucius Temple in Qūfù (p16) f9or the 28 September birthday celebrations of axiom-quipping philosopher, sage and patriarch Confucius.

🪷 October

The first week of October can be hellish if you're on the road: the National Day week-long holiday kicks off, so everywhere is swamped. Go mid-month instead, when places will be deserted.

🦀 Hairy Crabs in Shànghǎi

Now's the time to sample delicious hairy crabs in Shànghǎi; they are at their best between October and December, when male and female crabs are eaten together with shots of lukewarm Shàoxīng rice wine.

😊 Miao New Year

Load up with rice wine and get on down to Guìzhōu for the ethnic festivities in the very heart of the minority-rich southwest.

🪷 November

Most of China is getting pretty cold as tourist numbers drop and holidaygoers begin to flock south for sun and the last pockets of warmth. Snow begins to fall on parts of north China and the northeast starts to get glacial.

👁 Macau Formula 3 Grand Prix

It's usually not hard to find a good reason to visit Macau at any time of the year, but if you wait until November you can tie it in with this celebrated motor-racing event in the former Portuguese territory.

Far left: **September** Preparing moon cakes for the Mid-Autumn Festival, Píngyáo; **Left: June** Dragon boat races, Hong Kong

(FAR LEFT) BRUCE BI/ GETTY IMAGES ©. (LEFT) RICHARD I'ANSON/GETTY IMAGES ©

Get Inspired

📖 Books

○ **Country Driving: A Chinese Road Trip** (2011) Peter Hessler's amusing and insightful journey behind the wheel around China's highways and byways.

○ **When a Billion Chinese Jump** (2010) Jonathan Watts' hefty account of China's environmental challenges.

○ **The Classic of the Way and Its Power** The seminal text of Taoism, penned by Laotzu and replete with ineffable insight.

○ **A Madman's Diary** (1918) Lu Xun's modernist horror story and powerfully influential work of modern literature.

🎞 Films

○ **The House of Flying Daggers** (2004) Zhang Yimou's vibrantly-coloured romantic martial arts epic.

○ **Still Life** (2006) Jia Zhangke's moving meditation on the impact of the construction of Three Gorges Dam on local lives.

○ **Chungking Express** (1994) Stylish and creative Hong Kong drama, from Wong Kar Wai.

○ **Raise the Red Lantern** (1991) Zhang Yimou's sumptuous and beautiful tragedy starring Gong Li.

🎵 Music

○ **Eagle** (2009) Mamer's unique take on Kazakh folk music from northwest Xīnjiāng province.

○ **Nothing to my Name** (Yiwu Suoyou; 1986) Cui Jian's gutsy rock milestone from a different age.

○ **Masterpieces of Chinese Traditional Music** (1995) Exquisite collection of traditional Chinese tunes.

○ **Lang Lang Live at Carnegie Hall** (2004) Astonishing display of virtuoso skill from China's leading pianist.

🔌 Websites

○ **Popup Chinese** (www.popupchinese. com) Resourceful podcasts (great for learning Chinese).

○ **Tea Leaf Nation** (www. tealeafnation.com) Chinese social media pickings

○ **ChinaSmack** (www. chinasmack.com) Human-interest stories, videos and perspectives on China.

Short on time?

These resources will give you an instant insight into the country.

Read *Wolf Totem* (2008) by Jiang Rong charts the clash between Han Chinese and Inner Mongolian culture.

Watch *In the Mood for Love* (2000) is Wong Kar Wai's gorgeously filmed romance set in 1962 Hong Kong.

Listen *The 1st Complete Collection from Faye Wong* by Faye Wong is the Hong Kong diva's definitive collection.

Log on Lost Laowai Click (www.lostlaowai.com) has reams of handy China info.

Taichi practitioners, Shànghǎi

Need to Know

Currency
Yuan (¥)

Languages
Mandarin and Cantonese

Visas
Needed for all visits to China except Hong Kong, Macau and 72-hour and under trips to Shànghǎi, Běijīng, Guǎngzhōu, Xī'ān, Hángzhōu, Guìlín, Chéngdū, Chóngqìng, Dàlián and Shěnyáng.

Money
Credit cards OK in big cities; elsewhere less widely accepted. ATMs in cities and towns.

Mobile Phones
Pay-as-you-go SIM cards can be bought locally for most mobile phones.

Wi-Fi
Wi-fi increasingly available in hotels, hostels, restaurants and bars.

Tipping
Small tip for hotel porters only.

For more information, see Survival Guide (p391).

When to Go

Warm to hot summers, mild winters
Mild to hot summers, cold winters
Mild summers, very cold winters
Desert, dry climate
Cold climate

Běijīng
GO Sep–Oct

Shànghǎi
GO Oct

Chéngdū
GO Mar–May

Guìlín
GO Apr–May

Hong Kong
GO Nov–Feb

High Season
(May–Aug)
○ Prepare for crowds at traveller hot spots, as well as summer downpours.

○ Accommodation prices peak during the May holiday period.

Shoulder Season
(Feb–Apr, Sep & Oct)
○ Expect warmer days in spring, cooler days in autumn (the optimum season for north China).

○ Accommodation prices rise during the October holiday period.

Low Season
(Nov–Feb)
○ Little domestic tourism, but busy and expensive at Chinese New Year.

○ It's bitterly cold in the north; only warm in the far south.

○ Expect to find far fewer tourist crowds at the top destinations.

Advance Planning

○ **Three months before** Start shopping for your flight and, in the high season, book your accommodation. Learn some basic Chinese phrases.

○ **One month before** Get your visa arranged.

○ **One week before** Book sleeper berths on trains, domestic air tickets if flying around China and tables in popular restaurants in Běijīng, Shànghǎi, Hong Kong or Macau.

Your Daily Costs

Budget less than ¥200

o Dorm beds: ¥40 to ¥60.

o Excellent, cheap hole-in-the-wall restaurants and food markets.

o Affordable internet access and bike hire.

o Some free museums.

Midrange ¥200 to ¥1000

o Double room in a midrange hotel: ¥200 to ¥600.

o Lunch and dinner in decent restaurants.

Top End more than ¥1000

o Double room in a high-end hotel: ¥600 or more.

o Lunch and dinner in excellent restaurants.

o Shopping at high-end shops.

Exchange Rates

Australia	A$1	¥4.87
Canada	C$1	¥5.02
Euro Zone	€1	¥7.10
Japan	¥100	¥5.27
New Zealand	NZ$1	¥4.70
UK	UK£1	¥9.61
USA	US$1	¥6.25

For current exchange rates see www.xe.com.

What to Bring

o **Passport** You'll need it to enter the country, register and hotels and buy train tickets.

o **Money belt** Petty theft is a small but significant risk on buses and at train stations.

o **Travel insurance** Essential.

o **A tablet or smartphone for wi-fi** For those long-distance bus journeys.

o **Mandarin phrasebook** English won't get you far, even on the beaten path.

o **Hiking or waterproof boots** You may not be able to find your shoe size in China.

Arriving in China

o **Běijīng Capital Airport**

Airport Express To subway lines 2, 10 and 13 every 10 minutes; 6am to 10.30pm.

Express Buses To central Běijīng every 10 to 20 minutes; 7am to 11pm.

Taxi ¥80 to ¥100; around 30 to 60 minutes into town.

o **Pǔdōng International Airport, Shànghǎi**

Maglev To Longyang Rd metro station every 20 minutes; 6.45am to 9.40pm.

Metro Line 2 45 minutes to People's Sq; 1¾ hours to Hóngqiáo Airport.

Buses Every 15 to 25 minutes; 6.30am to 11pm.

Taxi ¥160; one hour into Shànghǎi.

o **Hong Kong International Airport**

Airport Express To Hong Kong Station in Central every 12 minutes.

Buses To many Hong Kong destinations.

Taxi HK$300 to Central, luggage HK$5 per item.

Getting Around

o **Train** Extensive modern network covers the nation; high-speed trains connect many cities.

o **Bus** Extensive network; cheaper and slower than the train, but reaches some extra destinations.

o **Air** Numerous internal flights.

o **Car** Limited but growing options; roads chaotic.

o **Taxis** Cheap and plentiful in cities and big towns.

Sleeping

o **Hotels** Plentiful range from two- to five-star.

o **Youth hostels** Decent budget accommodation.

o **Guesthouses** Spartan budget accommodation.

o **Courtyard hotels** Charming converted historical residences in Běijīng; usually midrange.

o **Homesteads** Cheap, rural accommodation.

Be Forewarned

o **National holiday** First week October/first three days of May sights are swamped; hotel prices peak.

o **Spring festival** A week any time from late January to early March; transport tickets scarce.

o **Health** Drink bottled water.

Běijīng &
the Great
Wall

Běijīng is China's supreme historic capital. Other Chinese towns may trumpet lengthier histories, but none offers such tangible proof of its dynastic heritage or concocts the same imperial splendour. Yet Běijīng (the name means 'Northern Capital') is also the up-to-the-minute capital of a nation undergoing the greatest transformation that China – and the world – has ever witnessed. You'll encounter modernity and a switched-on, confident populace, but it's the backdrop of enchanting alleyways, imperial palaces and incense-wreathed temples that makes Běijīng so unique.

Shedding bricks willy-nilly into gullies and ravines, the Great Wall is China's standout ruin, careening haphazardly across Běijīng's undulating north. Even though its remains crumble across northern China, the wall is essentially synonymous with Běijīng, its most popular access point. To the east, the Héběi town of Chéngdé is home to a magnificent imperial resort and a delightful sprinkling of Qing-dynasty temples.

Meridian gate (p66), Forbidden City, Běijīng
MERTEN SNIJDERS/GETTY IMAGES ©

Great Wall, Bādálǐng (p117)
RICHARD I'ANSON/GETTY IMAGES ©

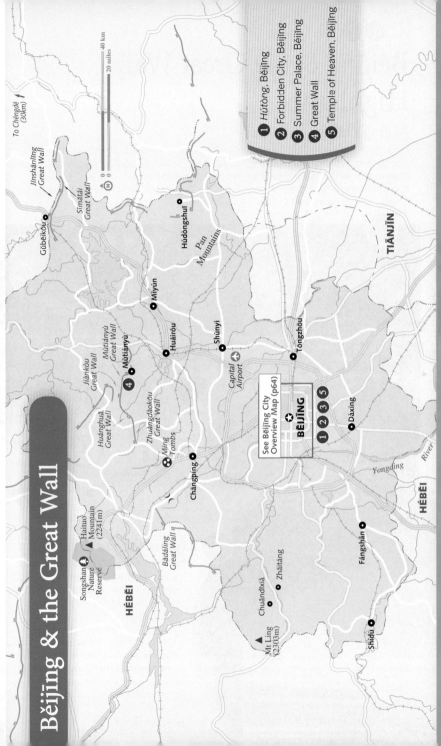

Běijīng & the Great Wall

1 Hútòng, Běijīng
2 Forbidden City, Běijīng
3 Summer Palace, Běijīng
4 Great Wall
5 Temple of Heaven, Běijīng

To Chéngdé (30km)

Jīnshānlǐng Great Wall

Sīmǎtái Great Wall

Gǔběikǒu

Hǔdòngshuǐ

Pan Mountains

Mìyún

Mùtiányù Great Wall

Huáiróu

Jiànkòu Great Wall

Mùtiányù

4

Huánghuā Great Wall

Zhuāngdàokǒu Great Wall

Shùnyì

Capital Airport

Tōngzhōu

TIĀNJĪN

Míng Tombs

Chāngpíng

See Běijīng City Overview Map (p64)

BĚIJĪNG
1 **2** **3** **5**

Dàxīng

Yongding River

HÉBĚI

Songshan Nature Reserve

Haituo Mountain (2241m)

HÉBĚI

Bādálǐng Great Wall

Chuāndǐxià

Mt Ling (2303m)

Zháitáng

Fángshān

Shídù

40 km
20 miles
N

Běijīng & the Great Wall Highlights

Běijīng's Hútòng

Hútòng (alleyways; p78) striate the geographic and cultural heart of traditional Běijīng. Homely and inviting, these charming thoroughfares are perfect for losing yourself in a slow-moving and crumbling universe of ancient alleys and historic lanes. The *hútòng* are also home to Běijīng's delightful and characteristic *sìhéyuàn* courtyard architecture, the Ming and Qing dynasty building blocks of the Peking of old.

2 Explore the Forbidden City

Home to two dynasties of emperors, the stupendous Forbidden City (p66) is Běijīng's other must-see sight after the meandering Great Wall. China's grandest piece of imperial heritage, the now-empty palace at the heart of Běijīng was once the source of imperial decrees and directives to the furthest-flung corners of the Chinese empire, until last orders were served by the Republic of China.

Wander Around the Summer Palace

Choose a sunny day for this magnificent regal encampment in the suburbs, and pack your camera for mouthwatering sunset views over sparkling Kūnmíng Lake. Prepare to hike – there are some outstanding walks. The Běijīng subway has done everyone a huge favour by plonking a station nearby so you can shuttle in at speed. Long Corridor (p91)

KEREN SU/GETTY IMAGES ©

RICHARD I'ANSON/GETTY IMAGES ©

Gallivant Along the Great Wall

China's best-known wall is easily reached from Běijīng where most of the remaining brick sections survive. Tourists surge to Bādálǐng (p117), but travellers earmark Jiànkòu (p115) or Zhuàngdàokǒu (p116) for their remoteness and the chance to see the masonry *au naturel*. You'll need to put aside a day at least for your trip and consider overnighting nearby for a multiday Great Wall adventure.

Marvel at the Temple of Heaven

OK, so it's not really a temple (p83) but the imperial architecture is astonishing and the surrounding park is huge enough to totally escape the hubbub of modern-day Běijīng. The Hall of Prayer for Good Harvests is the centrepiece, but get here early in the morning to catch practitioners of taichi. Put aside half a day to fully explore the sights. Taichi practitioners, Temple of Heaven Park

Běijīng & the Great Wall's Best...

Wining & Dining

○ **Lìqún Roast Duck Restaurant** Standout, top-of-the-range duck in a modest no-nonsense setting. (p99)

○ **Lost Heaven** For mouthwatering folk cuisine from the distant southwest province of Yúnnán. (p99)

○ **Crescent Moon Muslim Restaurant** Ever-moreish Uighur kebabs and lamb dishes. (p97)

○ **Brian McKenna @ The Courtyard** Mouth-watering fusion dishes accompany views of the Forbidden City wall and moat. (p98)

Architecture

○ **Forbidden City** China's grandest, largest and best-preserved array of imperial buildings. (p66)

○ **CCTV Building** Audacious chunk of gravity-defying cantilevered bravado. (p85)

○ **National Centre for the Performing Arts** Ultramodern counterpoint to the heavy-going Great Hall of the People. (p105)

○ **Summer Palace** Landscaped imperial summer retreat in the northwest of town. (p90)

Views

○ **Tiān'ānmén Square** Climb up the Gate of Heavenly Peace for choice views. (p76)

○ **Kūnmíng Lake, Summer Palace** Catch the lake at sunset. (p91)

○ **Jǐngshān Park** Supreme vistas right over the Forbidden City roofs. (p77)

○ **Jiànkòu Great Wall** For panoramas of the crumbling bastion clinging to precarious mountain ridges. (p115)

○ **Pǔtuózōngchéng Temple, Chéngdé** Climb to the top for some delicious views of the town. (p120)

Need to Know

Shopping

o **Nanluogu Xiang** Get your *hútòng* shopping and exploration done at the same time. (p106)

o **Bookworm** One of Běijīng's great literary institutions – great for literature and food. (p107)

o **Pānjiāyuán Market** Běijīng's ultimate emporium of knick-knacks and collectables. (p106)

o **Silk Market** Heaving multilevel bazaar of togs, silk and energetic haggling. (p107)

o **Shard Box Store** For a unique line in porcelain boxes. (p107)

ADVANCE PLANNING

o **One Month Before** Get your accommodation sorted and book your hotel room in Běijīng.

o **One Week Before** Book your train or air tickets out of Běijīng through your hotel or a local travel agent.

RESOURCES

o **Time Out** (www.timeout. com/beijing) Sharp, up-to-date listings.

o **The Beijinger** (www. thebeijinger.com) For restaurant, bar and club listings.

o **Air Quality Index China** (www.aqicn.org) Real time air pollution readings for Běijīng and other cities in China.

o **Popup Chinese** (www. popupchinese.com) Entertaining podcasts for learning Mandarin; Běijīng-based.

o **CTrip** (www.english. ctrip.com) Discounted hotels and ticketing; recommended.

GETTING AROUND

o **Train** From Capital Airport into town; high-speed trains from several stations to other points in China.

o **Subway** The best way to get around in town: fast, regular, dependable, extensive network.

o **Bus** To/from airport; extensive network around town (not user-friendly for Westerners); also long-distance.

o **Taxi** Ubiquitous, easy to hail, but Běijīng traffic is among the world's very worst.

o **Air** For long-distance flights.

BE FOREWARNED

o **Taxi Sharks** Avoid them at Capital Airport: join the taxi queue.

o **Crossing the Road** Cars can turn on red lights; traffic chaos reigns.

o **Scams** Avoid being taken to ultra-expensive teahouses, cafes and shops by English-speaking girls along Wangfujing Dajie and other spots.

o **Pedicabs** Avoid as you may be ripped off.

o **Pollution** Still bad and sometimes 'crazy bad'.

o **Language** English rarely used outside of tourist hotels and restaurants.

o **Hotels** Some cheap hotels don't take foreigners.

Left: Street food in Běijīng (p97)
Above: Tiān'ānmén Sq (p76)

Běijīng & the Great Wall Itineraries

These trips focus on Běijīng and the city's surrounding sights. You'll discover the Great Wall, while the longer tour lassos in the temple town of Chéngdé and a traditional village on the cusp of the Běijīng municipality.

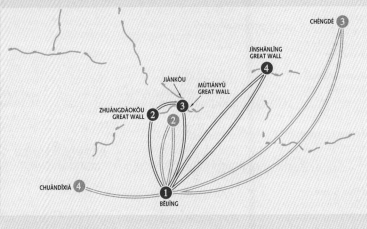

BĚIJĪNG TO THE GREAT WALL
HIGHLIGHTS TOUR

The kicking-off point for this tour is **❶ Běijīng** (p62), which warrants some determined exploration for its unequalled collection of sights. There's enough at the centre of town to swallow up a day's sightseeing, including the Forbidden City, the Gate of Heavenly Peace and Tiān'ānmén Sq. Try to have your accommodation sorted near Nanluogu Xiang so you can spend the night in a nearby *hútòng* courtyard hotel and dine locally. Rise early the next day for an expedition to the Great Wall. Putting aside an entire day is not unreasonable: you can hire a taxi with a driver to take you around two to three sections of wall; this way you could

compare the wall at **❷ Zhuàngdàokǒu Great Wall** (p116), **❸ Jiànkòu** (p115) and **Mùtiányù Great Wall** (p114). Alternatively, embark on a day trip to **❹ Jīnshānlǐng Great Wall** (p116) for its exhilarating hiking possibilities. Another option is to overnight at a hotel near the Great Wall to amplify the sense of adventure and allow more time the next day for continued exploration.

On day three, return to Běijīng to resume sightseeing in the capital. In the morning, set out to explore Běijīng's *hútòng* and earmark the afternoon for the Summer Palace: try to catch the sun setting over the hills west of Kūnmíng Lake.

 5 DAYS

BĚIJĪNG TO CHUĀNDĬXIÀ

CITY TO COUNTRY TOUR

Begin your journey in similar fashion to the Highlights Tour in ❶ **Běijīng** (p62), but put aside a bit of extra time for sightseeing around town so you can fully explore other sights, including the displays at the Poly Art Museum and Capital Museum, and perhaps detour to the 798 Art District to get a handle on modern Chinese art. Earmark the ❷ **Great Wall** (p113) for a day's exploration and consider hiring a taxi for a looping tour of its main areas as well as some of the lesser-known, more authentic chunks.

Take a train or a bus from Běijīng to ❸ **Chéngdé** (p117) for its imperial heritage and collection of Buddhist temples. It's worth spending the night in Chéngdé to fully savour the scenery and have time to properly explore the imperial resort of Bìshǔ Shānzhuāng. The standout temples, including Pǔníng Temple, which is home to a simply awesome statue of Guanyin, the Buddhist Goddess of Compassion, also need to be seen.

Return to Běijīng and catch a bus or take a taxi to ❹ **Chuāndĭxià** (p116), the ancient village in the southwest of the municipality. There are several homesteads where you can spend the night, introducing you to the bucolic charms of China's rural side.

Tower, Great Wall
GREG ELMS/GETTY IMAGES ©

Běijīng Walk

For historic charm along a manageable route through the city's traditional heartland, follow this easy tour exploring some of the hútòng *that branch off Běijīng's most famous alleyway, Nanluogu Xiang.*

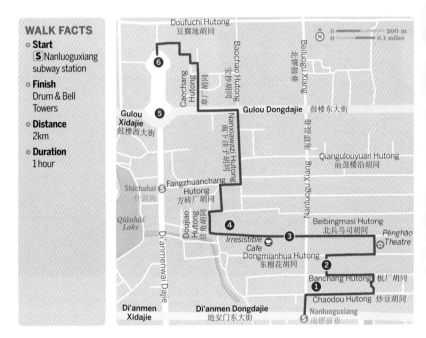

WALK FACTS

- **Start**
  S Nanluoguxiang subway station
- **Finish**
  Drum & Bell Towers
- **Distance**
  2km
- **Duration**
  1 hour

❶ Former Mansion of Seng Gelinqin

Exit Nanluoguxiang subway station and turn right into Chaodou Hutong (炒豆胡同). Starting at No 77, the next few courtyards once made up the former mansion of Seng Gelinqin, a Qing-dynasty army general. Note the enormous *bǎogǔshí* (drum stones) at the entranceway to No 77, followed by more impressive gateways at Nos 75, 69, 67 and 63. After No 53 turn left up an un-marked winding alleyway before turning left onto Banchang Hutong (板厂胡同).

❷ Hallway Gate

At No 19, turn right through a very unusual hallway gate, a connecting passageway which leads to Dongmianhua Hutong (东棉花胡同). Turn right here, then left down an unnamed alley, signposted to Pénghǎo Theatre Cafe.

❸ Mao'er Hutong

Turn left onto Beibingmasi Hutong (北兵马司胡同) and continue across Nanluogu Xiang (p106) into particularly historic Mao'er Hutong (帽儿胡同). Stop for a drink at Irresistible Cafe (p98) or just admire the entranceways to the charming old courtyards at Nos 5 and 11; both worth a peek if the gates are open.

④ Former Home of Wan Rong

Further on, No 37 was the former home of Wan Rong, who would later marry China's last emperor Puyi. Next, turn right down Doujiao Hutong (豆角胡同) and wind your way to Fangzhuanchang Hutong (方砖厂胡同) then Nanxiawazi Hutong (南下洼子胡同) with its small fruit and vegetable street market.

⑤ Drum Tower

Continue north to Gulou Dongdajie (鼓楼东大街), turn left and then, just before you reach the imperious red-painted Drum Tower (p80), turn right into Caochang Hutong (草厂胡同).

⑥ Bell Tower

Continue down the lane beside Sea View Cafe, then take the second left, where you'll see the magnificent grey-brick Bell Tower (p80) in front of you. Follow this wonderfully winding alley (parts of which have been slated for redevelopment) to the back of the Bell Tower, then walk around the tower to see how far the local government have got with their controversial plans to redevelop the Drum & Bell Square.

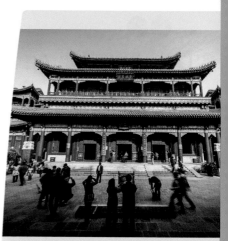

Běijīng In...

TWO DAYS

Stroll around the incense-filled courtyards of the **Lama Temple** (p72) before heading to laid-back **Confucius Temple** (p81). Embark on our Běijīng walking tour through the *hútòng* to the ancient **Drum Tower** (p80) and **Bell Tower** (p80) before finishing with dinner in **Lost Heaven** (p99). Get up early to enjoy the **Temple of Heaven Park** (p83) at its early-morning best. Grab a bite to eat in historic **Dashilar** (p90) before walking across **Tiān'ānmén Square** (p76) to explore the awe-inspiring **Forbidden City** (p66). Finish with roast duck at the **Lìqún Roast Duck Restaurant** (p99).

FOUR DAYS

Follow the itinerary above, but journey to the **Great Wall** (p113) on day three. Choose from a half-day jaunt at touristy **Bādálǐng** (p117) to strenuous hikes along unrestored sections such as **Zhuàngdàokǒu** (p116) or **Jiànkòu** (p115). On day four visit the **Summer Palace** (p90) or make a side trip to the **Old Summer Palace** (p93). Return for an early dinner so you have time to catch some **Peking opera** (p104) or **acrobatics** (p104) on your final evening.

Lama Temple (p72)

JUAN IGNACIO SÁNCHEZ LARA/GETTY IMAGES ©

Discover Běijīng & the Great Wall

BĚIJĪNG   北京

♩010 / POP 19.6 MILLION

Not only is Běijīng one of China's true ancient citadels, it's also a confident and increasingly modern capital that seems assured of its destiny to rule over China till the end of time.

Through its magnificent architecture – including numerous stretches of the Great Wall – visitors can trace every historical mood swing from Mongol times to the present day.

The city's denizens chat in Běijīnghuà – the gold standard of Mandarin – and marvel at their good fortune for occupying the centre of the known world. And yet for all its gusto, Běijīng dispenses with the persistent pace of Shànghǎi or Hong Kong.

History

Chinese historical sources date the earliest settlements in these parts from 1045 BC. In later centuries Běijīng was successively occupied by foreign forces: it was established as an auxiliary capital under the Khitan, nomadic Mongol people who formed China's Liao dynasty (907–1125). Later the Jurchens, Tungusic people originally from the Siberian region, turned the city into their Jin-dynasty (1115–1234) capital during which time the city was enclosed within fortified walls, accessed by eight gates.

In AD 1215 the army of the great Mongol warrior Genghis Khan razed Běijīng, an event that was paradoxically to mark the city's transformation into a powerful national capital.

The city came to be called Dàdū (大都; Great Capital), also assuming the Mongol

War memorial, Tiān'ānmén Square (p76)
TIM MAKINS/GETTY IMAGES ©

name Khanbalik (the Khan's town). By 1279, under the rule of Kublai Khan, grandson of Genghis Khan, Dàdū was the capital of the largest empire the world has ever known.

The basic grid of present-day Běijīng was laid during the Ming dynasty, and Emperor Yongle (r 1403–24) is credited with being the true architect of the modern city. Much of Běijīng's grandest architecture, such as the Forbidden City and the iconic Hall of Prayer for Good Harvests in Temple of Heaven Park, date from his reign.

The Manchu, who invaded China in the 17th century to establish the Qing dynasty, essentially preserved Běijīng's form. In the last 120 years of the Qing dynasty Běijīng, and subsequently China, was subjected to power struggles and invasions, and the ensuing chaos. The list is long: the Anglo-French troops who in 1860 burnt the Old Summer Palace to the ground; the corrupt regime of Empress Dowager Cixi; the catastrophic Boxer Rebellion; General Yuan Shikai; the warlords; the Japanese occupation of 1937; and the Kuomintang. Each and every period left its undeniable mark, although the shape and symmetry of Běijīng was maintained.

Modern Běijīng came of age when, in January 1949, the People's Liberation Army (PLA) entered the city. On 1 October of that year Mao Zedong proclaimed a 'People's Republic' from the Gate of Heavenly Peace to an audience of some 500,000 citizens.

Like the emperors before them, the communists significantly altered the face of Běijīng. The *páilóu* (decorative archways) were brought down and whole city blocks were pulverised to widen major boulevards. From 1950 to 1952, the city's magnificent outer walls were levelled in the interests of traffic circulation.

The past quarter of a century has transformed Běijīng into a modern city, with skyscrapers, shopping malls and an ever-expanding subway system.

If You Like…
Museums

If you enjoyed the Poly Art Museum (p92) and Capital Museum (p88), Běijīng has a host of eclectic and informative museums to keep you busy.

1 NATIONAL MUSEUM OF CHINA
(中国国际博物馆, Zhōngguó Guójì Bówùguǎn; Map p74; en.chnmuseum.cn; Guangchangdongce Lu, Tiān'ānmén Sq, 天安门，广场东侧路; audio guide ¥30, cafe coffee from ¥20, tea from ¥10, pastries & sandwiches ¥10-20; ⊙9am-5pm Tue-Sun, last entry 4pm; S Tiān'ānmén East) Běijīng's premier museum is housed in an immense 1950s building on the eastern side of Tiān'ānmén Sq, and is well worth visiting. The Ancient China exhibition on the basement floor is outstanding. You could easily spend a couple of hours in this exhibition alone. It contains dozens and dozens of stunning pieces, from prehistoric China through to the Qing dynasty, all displayed beautifully in modern, spacious, low-lit exhibition halls.

2 BĚIJĪNG POLICE MUSEUM
(北京警察博物馆, Běijīng Jǐngchá Bówùguǎn; Map p74; ☎8522 5018; 36 Dongjiaomin Xiang; adult ¥5, through ticket ¥20; ⊙9am-4pm Tue-Sun; S Qiánmén) Propaganda aside, riveting exhibits make this a fascinating exposé of Běijīng's *dà gài mào* (local slang for the constabulary). Learn how Běijīng's first Public Security Bureau (PSB) college operated from the Dōngyuè Temple in 1949 and find out how officers tackled the 'stragglers, disbanded soldiers, bandits, local ruffians, hoodlums and despots…' planted in Běijīng by the Kuomintang (KMT).

3 CHINA ART MUSEUM
(中国美术馆, Zhōngguó Měishùguǎn; Map p74; 1 Wusi Dajie; ⊙9am-5pm, last entry 4pm; S National Art Museum) This revamped museum has received a healthy shot of imagination and flair, with absorbing exhibitions from across China and abroad promising doses of colour and vibrancy. Běijīng's art-lovers have lapped up some top-notch presentations here, from the cream of Italian design to modern artworks from the Taipei Fine Arts Museum and exhibitions of paintings from some of China's ethnic minority groups.

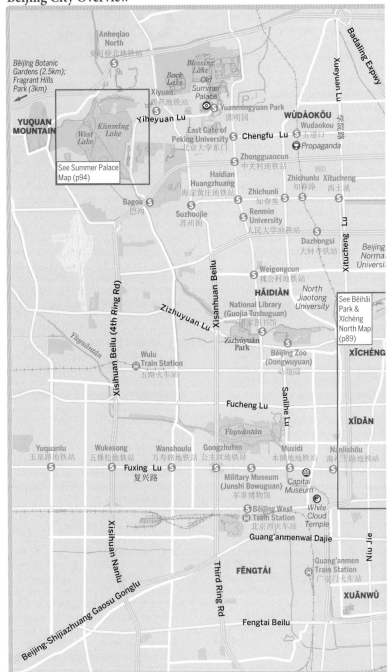

Anheqiao
North
安河桥北地铁站

Běijīng Botanic
Gardens (2.5km);
Fragrant Hills
Park (3km)

Back
Lake

Blessing
Lake

Old
Summer
Palace

Yuanmingyuan Park
圆明园

WŬDÀOKŎU

Xueyuan Lu

Badaling Expwy

Xiyuan
西苑地铁站

YUQUAN
MOUNTAIN

West
Lake

Kūnmíng
Lake

Yiheyuan Lu

East Gate of
Peking University
北京大学东门

Chengfu Lu

Wudaokou
五道口

Propaganda

See Summer Palace
Map (p94)

Zhongguancun
中关村地铁站

Zhichunlu Xitucheng
知春路   西土城

Haidian
Huangzhuang
海淀黄庄地铁站

Zhichunli
知春里

Xitucheng Lu

Bagou
巴沟

Suzhoujie
苏州街

Renmin
University
人民大学地铁站

Dazhongsi
大钟寺地铁站

Beijing
Norma.
Universi

Weigongcun
魏公村地铁站

HĂIDIÀN

North
Jiaotong
University

See Běihǎi
Park &
Xīchéng
North Map
(p89)

National Library
(Guojia Tushuguan)
国家图书馆

Yuyuántán

Zizhuyuan Lu

Xisanhuan Beilu

Zizhúyuán
Park

Běijīng Zoo
(Dongwuyuan)
动物园

XĪCHÉNG

Xishuan Beilu (4th Ring Rd)

Wulu
Train Station
五路火车站

Sanlihe Lu

Fucheng Lu

XĪDĀN

Yúyuántán

Yuquanlu
玉泉路地铁站

Wukesong
五棵松地铁站

Fuxing Lu
复兴路

Wanshoulu
万寿路地铁站

Gongzhufen
公主坟地铁站

Muxidi
木樨地地铁站

Nanlishilu
南礼士路地铁站

Military Museum
(Junshi Bowuguan)
军事博物馆

Capital
Museum

White
Cloud
Temple

Xishuan Nanlu

Běijīng West
Train Station
北京西火车站

Guang'anmenwai Dajie

Niu Jie

Third Ring Rd

FĒNGTÁI

Guang'anmen
Train Station
广安门火车站

XUĀNWŬ

Beijing-Shijiazhuang Gaosu Gonglu

Fengtai Beilu

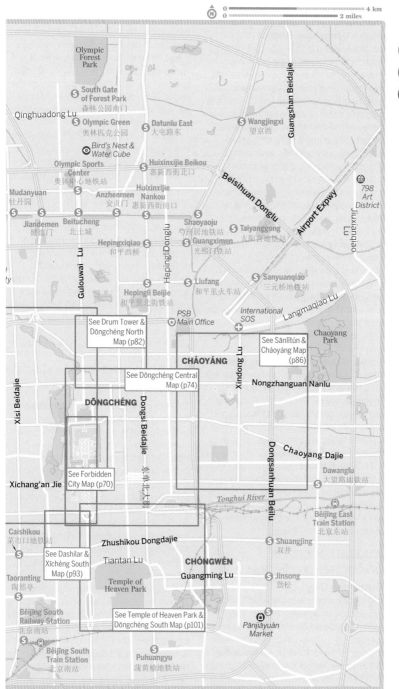

0 — 4 km
0 — 2 miles

Olympic Forest Park

Qinghuadong Lu

South Gate of Forest Park
森林公园南门

Olympic Green
奥林匹克公园

Datunlu East
大屯路东

Wangjingxi
望京西

Guangshan Beidajie

Bird's Nest & Water Cube

Olympic Sports Center
奥体中心地铁站

Huixinxijie Beikou
惠新西街北口

Beisihuan Donglu

798 Art District

Mudanyuan
牡丹园

Huixinxijie Nankou
惠新西街南口

Anzhenmen
安贞门

Airport Expwy

Jiuxianqiao Lu

Jiandemen
健德门

Beitucheng
北土城

Shaoyaoju
芍药居地铁站

Taiyanggong
太阳宫地铁站

Gulouwai Lu

Hepingxiqiao
和平西桥

Guangximen
光熙门铁站

Hepingli Xijie

Liufang
和平里火车站

Sanyuanqiao
三元桥地铁站

Hepingli Beijie
和平里北街铁站

Langmaqiao Lu

PSB Main Office

International SOS

Chaoyang Park

See Drum Tower & Dōngchéng North Map (p82)

See Sānlǐtún & Cháoyáng Map (p86)

CHÁOYÁNG

See Dōngchéng Central Map (p74)

Xindong Lu

Nongzhanguan Nanlu

Xisi Beidajie

DŌNGCHÉNG

Dongsi Beidajie
东四北大街

Chaoyang Dajie

See Forbidden City Map (p70)

Dongsanhuan Beilu

Dawanglu
大望路地铁站

Xichang'an Jie

Tonghui River

Běijīng East Train Station
北京东站

Caishikou
菜市口地铁站

Zhushikou Dongdajie

Shuangjing
双井

See Dashilar & Xīchéng South Map (p93)

Tiantan Lu

CHÓNGWÉN

Jinsong
劲松

Taoranting
陶然亭

Guangming Lu

Běijīng South Railway Station
北京南站

Temple of Heaven Park

Běijīng South Train Station
北京南站

See Temple of Heaven Park & Dōngchéng South Map (p101)

Pānjiāyuán Market

Puhuangyu
蒲黄榆地铁站

⊙ Sights

Historic **Dōngchéng District** (东城区; Dōngchéng Qū) is the largest of Běijīng's central districts and by far the most interesting for visitors. For convenience, we've split it into North, Central and South neighbourhoods. Dōngchéng Central has the lion's share of iconic sights, including the immense Forbidden City. A fascinating network of imperial *hútòng* (alleyways) fans out north and east from here. Dōngchéng North is also a fabulously historic, *hútòng*-rich neighbourhood, and arguably the most pleasant area in which to base yourself while in Běijīng. Dōngchéng South is dominated by the wonderful Temple of Heaven Park.

Cháoyáng District (朝阳区; Cháoyáng Qū) sprawls east from Dōngchéng and is home to the majority of Běijīng's foreign embassies, as well as most of its expat population. The area lacks history and character, but it does contain some of the capital's best modern restaurants, bars and shops, many of which centre on the area known as Sānlǐtún.

West of Dōngchéng, **Xīchéng District** (西城区; Xīchéng Qū) has strong historical links. We've split it into north and south neighbourhoods. The north includes the city's lovely central lakes – at Hòuhǎi and within the centuries-old Běihǎi Park. The south includes the backpacker-central neighbourhood of Dashilar.

Outlying **Hǎidiàn** (海淀区; Hǎidiàn Qū), is the capital's main university district – head to Wǔdàokǒu to tap into student life in Běijīng – but it also includes some great day-trip destinations, including the hugely attractive Summer Palace.

FORBIDDEN CITY & DŌNGCHÉNG CENTRAL

Forbidden City   Historic Site

(紫禁城; Zǐjìn Chéng; Map p70; 📞8500 7114; www.dpm.org.cn; admission Nov-Mar ¥40, Apr-Oct ¥60, Clock Exhibition Hall ¥10, Hall of Jewellery ¥10, audio tour ¥40; ⊙8.30am-4pm May-Sep, 8.30am-3.30pm Oct-Apr, closed Mon; Ⓢ Tiān'ānmén West or Tiān'ānmén East) Ringed by a 52m-wide moat at the very heart of Běijīng, the Forbidden City is China's largest and best-preserved collection of ancient buildings, and the largest palace complex in the world. So called because it was off limits for 500 years, when it was steeped in stultifying ritual and regal protocol, the otherworldly palace was the reclusive home to two dynasties of imperial rule until the Republic overthrew the last Qing emperor.

Today, the Forbidden City is prosaically known as the Palace Museum (故宫博物馆; Gùgōng Bówùguǎn), although most Chinese people simply call it Gù Gōng (故宫; ancient palace).

In former ages the price for uninvited admission was instant execution; these days ¥40 or ¥60 will do. Allow yourself the best part of a day for exploration or several trips if you're an enthusiast.

Guides – many with mechanical English – mill about the entrance, but the automatically activated audio tours are cheaper (¥40; more than 40 languages) and more reliable. Restaurants, a cafe, toilets and even ATMs can be found within the palace grounds. Wheelchairs (¥500 deposit) are free to use, as are pushchairs/strollers (¥300 deposit).

Entrance

Tourists must enter through **Meridian Gate** (午门; Wǔ Mén; Map p70), a massive U-shaped portal at the south end of the complex, which in former times was reserved for the use of the emperor. Gongs and bells would sound imperial comings and goings, while lesser mortals used lesser gates: the military used the west gate, civilians the east gate. The emperor also reviewed his armies from here, passed judgement on prisoners, announced the new year's calendar and oversaw the flogging of troublesome ministers.

Through Meridian Gate, you enter an enormous courtyard, and cross the **Golden Stream** (金水; Jīn Shuǐ) – shaped to resemble a Tartar bow and spanned by five marble bridges – on your way to the magnificent **Gate of Supreme Harmony** (太和门; Tàihé Mén; Map p70). This courtyard could hold an imperial

DAVID GEE/GETTY IMAGES ©

⭐ Don't Miss
Clock Exhibition Hall

The Clock Exhibition Hall is one of the unmissable highlights of the Forbidden City. Located in the Hall for Ancestral Worship (Fèngxiàn Diàn) – to the right after the Three Great Halls – the exhibition contains an astonishing array of elaborate timepieces, many of which were gifts to the Qing emperors from overseas. Many of the 18th-century examples were crafted by James Cox or Joseph Williamson (from London) and imported through Guǎngdōng from England; others are from Switzerland, America and Japan.

Exquisitely wrought and fashioned with magnificently designed elephants and other creatures, they all display astonishing artfulness and attention to detail. Standout clocks include the 'Gilt Copper Astronomy Clock' equipped with a working model of the solar system, and the automaton-equipped 'Gilt Copper Clock with a robot writing Chinese characters with a brush'. Time your arrival for 11am or 2pm to see the clock performance in which choice timepieces strike the hour and perform for wide-eyed children and adults.

NEED TO KNOW

钟表馆, Zhōngbiǎo Guǎn; Map p70; admission ¥10; ⊙8.30am-4pm summer, to 3.30pm winter

audience of 100,000 people. For an idea of the size of the restoration challenge, note how the crumbling courtyard stones are stuffed with dry weeds, especially on the periphery.

First Side Galleries
Before you pass through the Gate of Supreme Harmony to reach the Forbidden City's star attractions, veer off to the east

continued on p71

Forbidden City

WALKING TOUR

After entering through the imperious Meridian Gate, resist the temptation to dive straight into the star attractions and veer right for a peek at the excellent **Ceramics Gallery ❶** housed inside the creaking Hall of Literary Glory.

Walk back to the central complex and head through the magnificent Gate of Supreme Harmony towards the Three Great Halls: first, the largest – the **Hall of Supreme Harmony ❷**, followed by the **Hall of Middle Harmony ❸** and the **Hall of Preserving Harmony ❹**, behind which slopes the enormous Marble Imperial Carriageway.

Turn right here to visit the fascinating **Clock Exhibition Hall ❺** before entering the **Complete Palace of Peace & Longevity ❻**, a mini Forbidden City constructed along the eastern axis of the main complex. It includes the beautiful **Nine Dragon Screen ❼** and, to the north, a series of halls, housing some excellent exhibitions and known collectively as The Treasure Gallery. Don't miss the **Pavilion of Cheerful Melodies ❽**, a wonderful three-storey opera house.

Work your way to the far north of this section, then head west to the **Imperial Garden ❾**, with its ancient cypress trees and pretty pavilions, before exiting via the garden's West Gate (behind the Thousand Year Pavilion) to explore the **Western Palaces ❿**, an absorbing collection of courtyard homes where many of the emperors lived during their reign.

Exit this section at its southwest corner before turning back on yourself to walk north through the Gate of Heavenly Purity to see the three final Central Halls – the **Palace of Heavenly Purity ⓫**, the **Hall of Union ⓬** and the **Palace of Earthly Tranquility ⓭** – before leaving via the North Gate.

Water Vats
More than 300 copper and brass water vats dot the palace complex. They were used for fighting fires and in winter were prevented from freezing over by using thick quilts.

ENTRANCE/EXIT

You must enter through the south gate (Meridian Gate), but you can exit via south, north or east.

← ticket offices →

Guardian Lions
Pairs of lions guard important buildings. The male has a paw placed on a globe (representing the emperor's power over the world). The female has her paw on a baby lion (representing the emperor's fertility).

Kneeling Elephants

At the northern entrance of the Imperial Garden are two bronze elephants kneeling in an anatomically impossible fashion, which symbolise the power of the emperor; even elephants kowtowed before him.

Nine Dragon Screen

One of only three of its type left in China, this beautiful glazed dragon screen served to protect the Hall of Imperial Supremacy from evil spirits.

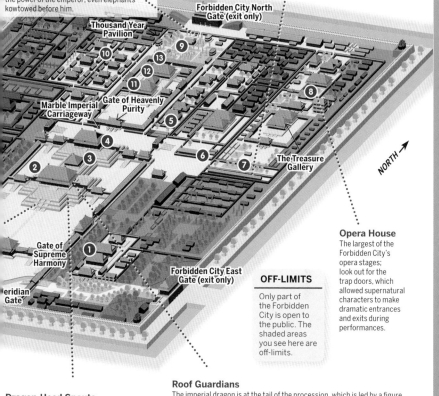

Forbidden City North Gate (exit only)

Thousand Year Pavilion

⑩ ⑬ ⑨
⑫
⑪

Marble Imperial Carriageway

Gate of Heavenly Purity

⑤

④

③
②

⑥ ⑦

⑧

The Treasure Gallery

NORTH →

Gate of Supreme Harmony

①

Meridian Gate

Forbidden City East Gate (exit only)

OFF-LIMITS

Only part of the Forbidden City is open to the public. The shaded areas you see here are off-limits.

Opera House

The largest of the Forbidden City's opera stages; look out for the trap doors, which allowed supernatural characters to make dramatic entrances and exits during performances.

Roof Guardians

The imperial dragon is at the tail of the procession, which is led by a figure riding a phoenix followed by a number of mythical beasts. The more beasts, the more important the building.

Dragon-Head Spouts

More than a thousand dragon-head spouts encircle the raised marble platforms at the centre of the Forbidden City. They were – and still are – part of the drainage system.

Forbidden City

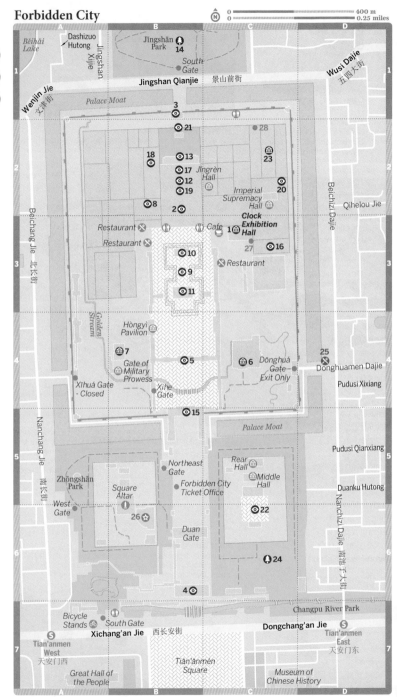

N

0 ———————————— 400 m
0 ———————————— 0.25 miles

Běihǎi Lake
Dashizuo Hutong
Jingshan Xijie
Jingshan Park 14
South Gate
Jingshan Qianjie 景山前街
Wusi Dajie 五四大街

Wenjin Jie 文津街
Palace Moat
3
21
18
13
28
Jingrèn Hall
17
12
19
Imperial Supremacy Hall
23
20
Běichízi Dajie
Qihelou Jie
8
2
Clock Exhibition Hall
Restaurant
Cafe
1
Restaurant
27
16
Běichang Jie 北长街
10
9
Restaurant
11
Golden Stream
Hòngyì Pavilion
7
5
6
Dōnghuá Gate – Exit Only
25
Donghuamen Dajie
Gate of Military Prowess
Xīhé Gate
Xīhuá Gate - Closed
Nanchang Jie 南长街
15
Palace Moat
Pudusi Xixiang
Pudusi Qianxiang
Zhōngshān Park
Northeast Gate
Rear Hall
Duanku Hutong
Square Altar
Forbidden City Ticket Office
Middle Hall
West Gate
26
22
Nanchizi Dajie 南池子大街
Duan Gate
24
4
Changpu River Park
Bicycle Stands
South Gate
Dongchang'an Jie
Tian'anmen West 天安门西
Xichang'an Jie 西长安街
Tian'anmen East 天安门东
Great Hall of the People
Tiān'ānmén Square
Museum of Chinese History

Forbidden City

continued from p67

and west of the huge courtyard to visit the Calligraphy and Painting Gallery inside the **Hall of Martial Valor** (武英殿; Wǔ Yīng Diàn; Map p70) and the particularly good Ceramics Gallery, housed inside the creaking **Hall of Literary Glory** (文化殿; Wén Huà Diàn; Map p70).

Three Great Halls

Raised on a three-tier marble terrace with balustrades are the Three Great Halls, the glorious heart of the Forbidden City. The recently restored **Hall of Supreme Harmony** (太和殿; Tàihé Diàn; Map p70) is the most important and largest structure in the Forbidden City. Built in the 15th century and restored in the 17th century, it was used for ceremonial occasions, such as the emperor's birthday, the nomination of military leaders and coronations. Inside the Hall of Supreme Harmony is a richly decorated **Dragon Throne** (龙椅; Lóngyǐ), from which the emperor would preside over trembling officials. The entire court had to touch the floor nine times with their foreheads (the custom known as kowtowing) in the emperor's presence. At the back of the throne is a carved Xumishan, the Buddhist paradise, signifying the throne's supremacy.

Behind the Hall of Supreme Harmony is the smaller **Hall of Middle Harmony** (中和殿; Zhōnghé Diàn; Map p70), which was used as the emperor's transit lounge. Here he would make last-minute preparations, rehearse speeches and receive close ministers. On display are two Qing-dynasty sedan chairs, the emperor's mode of transport around the Forbidden City. The last of the Qing emperors, Puyi, used a bicycle and altered a few features of the palace grounds to make it easier to get around.

The third of the Great Halls is the **Hall of Preserving Harmony** (保和殿; Bǎohé Diàn; Map p70), used for banquets and later for imperial examinations. The hall has no support pillars. To its rear is a 250-tonne marble imperial carriageway carved with dragons and clouds, which was transported into Běijīng on an ice path. The emperor used to be carried over this carriageway in his sedan chair as he ascended or descended the terrace. The outer housing surrounding the Three Great Halls was used for storing gold, silver, silks, carpets and other treasures.

A string of side halls on the eastern and western flanks of the Three Great Halls usually, but not always, house a series of excellent exhibitions, ranging from scientific instruments and articles of daily use to objects presented to the emperor by visiting dignitaries. One contains an interesting diorama of the whole complex.

RICHARD I'ANSON/GETTY IMAGES ©

⭐ Don't Miss
Lama Temple

If you only have time for one temple (the Temple of Heaven isn't really a temple) make it this one, where riveting roofs, fabulous frescoes, magnificent decorative arches, tapestries, carpentry, Tibetan prayer wheels, Tantric statues and a superb pair of Chinese lions mingle with dense clouds of incense.

The most renowned Tibetan Buddhist temple outside Tibet, the Lama Temple was converted to a lamasery in 1744 after serving as the residence of Emperor Yong Zheng. Today the temple is an active place of worship, attracting pilgrims from afar, some of whom prostrate themselves in submission at full length within its halls. Resplendent within the **Hall of the Wheel of the Law** (Fǎlún Diàn), the fourth hall from the entrance, is a substantial bronze statue of a benign and smiling Tsong Khapa (1357–1419), founder of the Gelugpa or Yellow Hat sect. The fifth hall, the **Wànfú Pavilion** (Wànfú Gé), houses a magnificent 18m-high statue of the Maitreya Buddha in his Tibetan form, clothed in yellow satin and reputedly sculpted from a single block of sandalwood. Each of the Bodhisattva's toes is the size of a pillow. The Wànfú Pavilion is linked by an overhead walkway to the Yánsuí Pavilion (Yánsuí Gé), which encloses a huge lotus flower that revolves to reveal an effigy of the Longevity Buddha. Don't miss the collection of bronze Tibetan Buddhist statues within the **Jiètái Lóu**. Most effigies date from the Qing dynasty, from languorous renditions of Green Tara and White Tara to exotic, Tantric pieces and figurines of the fierce-looking Mahakala. Also peruse the collection of Tibetan Buddhist ornaments within the **Bānchán Lóu**, another side hall, where an array of dorje (Tibetan sceptres), mandalas and Tantric figures are displayed along with an impressive selection of ceremonial robes in silk and satin.

NEED TO KNOW

雍和宫; Yōnghé Gōng; Map p82; 28 Yonghegong Dajie; admission ¥25, English audioguide ¥50; ⏱9am-4.30pm; S Yonghegong-Lama Temple

Lesser Central Halls

The basic configuration of the Three Great Halls is echoed by the next group of buildings. Smaller in scale, these buildings were more important in terms of real power, which in China traditionally lies at the back door.

The first structure is the **Palace of Heavenly Purity** (乾清宫; Qiánqīng Gōng; Map p70), a residence of Ming and early Qing emperors, and later an audience hall for receiving foreign envoys and high officials.

Immediately behind it is the **Hall of Union** (交泰殿; Jiāotài Diàn; Map p70), which contains a clepsydra – a water clock made in 1745 with five bronze vessels and a calibrated scale. There's also a mechanical clock built in 1797 and a collection of imperial jade seals on display. The **Palace of Earthly Tranquillity** (坤宁宫; Kūnníng Gōng; Map p70) was the imperial couple's bridal chamber and the centre of operations for the palace harem.

Imperial Garden

At the northern end of the Forbidden City is the **Imperial Garden** (御花园; Yù Huāyuán; Map p70), a classical Chinese garden with 7000 sq metres of fine landscaping, including rockeries, walkways, pavilions and ancient cypresses. Before you reach the **Gate of Divine Prowess** (神武门; Shénwǔ Mén; Map p70), the Forbidden City's north exit, and **Shùnzhēn Gate** (顺贞门; Shùnzhēn Mén; Map p70), which leads to it, note the pair of bronze elephants whose front knees bend in an anatomically impossible fashion, signifying the power of the emperor; even elephants would kowtow before him.

Complete Palace of Peace and Longevity

A mini Forbidden City, known as the **Complete Palace of Peace and Longevity** (宁寿全宫; Níng Shòu Quán Gōng; Map p70) was built in the northeastern corner of the complex, mimicking the structure of the great halls of the central axis. During the Ming dynasty this was where the empress dowager and the imperial concubines lived. Now it houses a series of quieter courtyard buildings, which contain a number of fine museum exhibitions, known collectively as the **Treasure Gallery** (珍宝馆, Zhēn Bǎo Guǎn; Map p70; entrance ¥10).

The complex is entered from the south – not far from the Clock Exhibition Hall. Just inside the entrance, you'll find the beautiful glazed **Nine Dragon Screen**

Carved ceiling, pavilion, Imperial Garden

Dōngchéng Central

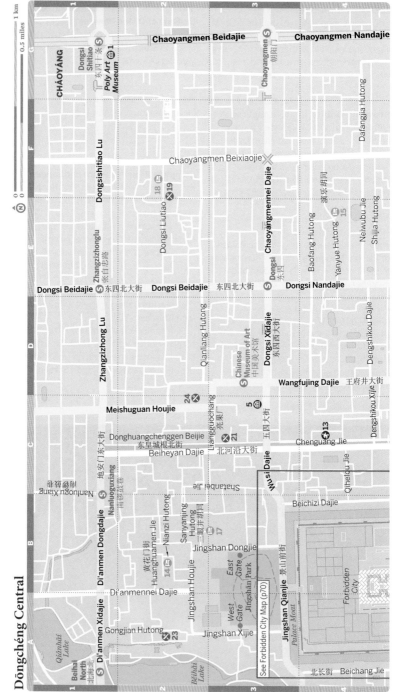

0.5 miles
1 km

CHÁOYÁNG

Dongsi Shitiao 🚇

Dongsi Shitiao 🚇 1
Poly Art Museum

Chaoyangmen Beidajie

Chaoyangmen Nandajie

🚇 Chaoyangmen 朝阳门

Dongsishitiao Lu

Dafangjia Hutong

Chaoyangmen Beixiaojie ✕

Chaoyangmennei Dajie

🚇 Dongsi 东四

18 🏨
✕ 19

Dongsi Liutiao

演乐胡同

15 🏨

Neiwubu Jie

Shijia Hutong

Baofang Hutong

Yanyue Hutong

Zhangzizhonglu

Zhangzizhong Lu

🚇 **Dongsi Beidajie** 东四北大街 **Dongsi Beidajie** 东四北大街 🚇 **Dongsi Nandajie**

Qianliang Hutong

Chinese Museum of Art 🚇
中国美术馆

Dongsi Xidajie
东四西大街

Dengshikou Dajie

Wangfujing Dajie 王府井大街

Dengshikou Xijie

Meishuguan Houjie
24 ✕

Liangguochang 亮果厂

5 🏨

13 🚇

Chenguang Jie

Donghuangchenggen Beijie
东皇城根北街

✕ 21

Wusi Dajie 五四大街

Beiheyan Dajie 北河沿大街

Qihelou Jie

Shatanbei Jie

🚇 Nanluoguxiang
南锣鼓巷

Nanluogu Xiang

Beichizi Dajie

Di'anmen Dongdajie
地安门东大街

Huangchuamen Jie
黄花门大街

Sanyanjing Hutong
三眼井胡同

17

Nianzi Hutong
碾子胡同

Jingshan Dongjie 景山东街

14 🏨

Jingshan Houjie

East Gate
景山前街

Jingshan Park
景山

See Forbidden City Map (p70)

Di'anmennei Dajie

Forbidden City

Qiánhǎi Lake

Běihǎi North
北海北

🚇 **Di'anmen Xidajie**

Gongjian Hutong

✕ 23

Jingshan Xijie

West Gate

Jingshan Qianjie 景山前街

Palace Moat

Forbidden City Moat

Běihǎi Lake

北长街 Beichang Jie

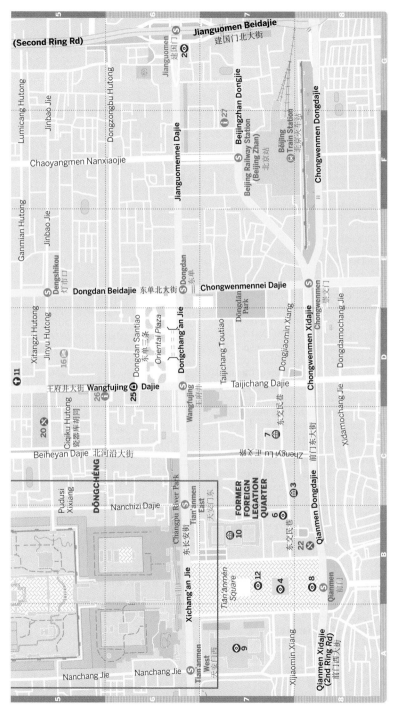

(Second Ring Rd)

Jianguomen Beidajie 建国门北大街
Jianguomen 建国门 2

Lumicang Hutong
Jinbao Jie
Dongzongbu Hutong
Chaoyangmen Nanxiaojie

Jianguomennei Dajie 建国门内大街

Beijingzhan Dongjie
27
Beijing Railway Station (Beijing Zhan) 北京站
Beijing Train Station 北京火车站

Chongwenmen Dongdajie

Ganmian Hutong
Jinbao Jie
Dengshikou 灯市口
Dongdan Beidajie 东单北大街
Dongdan 东单
Chongwenmennei Dajie

Xitangzi Hutong
Jinyu Hutong
Dongdan Santiao 东单三条
Oriental Plaza
16
Dongchang'an Jie
Dongdan Park
Chongwenmen 崇文门
Chongwenmen Xidajie

11

Dongdian Park
Taijichang Toutiao
Dongjiaomin Xiang
Dongdamochang Jie

王府井大街 Wangfujing 25 Dajie
26
Wangfujing 王府井
Taijichang Dajie

Ciqiku Hutong 瓷器库胡同
20

Xidamochang Jie

Beiheyan Dajie 北河沿大街
Zhengyi Lu 正义路
7 东文民巷

DONGCHÉNG
Pudusi Xixiang
Nanchizi Dajie
Changpu River Park
Tian'anmen East 天安门东
FORMER FOREIGN LEGATION QUARTER
6
3
Qianmen Dongdajie 前门东大街

Xichang'an Jie
东长安街
10
22
东文民巷

Tian'anmen Square
12
4
8
Qianmen 前门

Tian'anmen West 天安门西

9

Nanchang Jie
Nanchang Jie
Qianmen Xidajie (2nd Ring Rd) 前门西大街
Xijiaomin Xiang

Dōngchéng Central

(九龙壁; Jiǔlóng Bì; Map p70), one of only three of its type left in China.

Visitors then work their way north, exploring a number of peaceful halls and courtyards before being popped out at the **northern end (Map p70)** of the Forbidden City. Don't miss the **Pavilion of Cheerful Melodies** (畅音阁; Chàngyīn Gé; Map p70), a three-storey wooden opera house, which was the palace's largest theatre. Note the trap doors that allowed actors to make dramatic stage entrances.

Western and Eastern Palaces
About half a dozen smaller palace courtyards lie to the west and east of the Lesser Central Halls. They should all be open to the public, although at the time of research many of the eastern ones were closed for extensive renovation. It was in these smaller courtyard buildings that most of the emperors actually lived and many of the buildings, particularly those to the west, are decked out in imperial furniture. The **Hall of Mental Cultivation** (养心殿; Yǎng Xīn Diàn; Map p70) is a highlight, while the **Palace of Gathered Elegance** (储秀宫; Chǔ Xiù Gōng; Map p70) contains some interesting photos of the last emperor Puyi, who lived here as a child ruler at the turn of the 20th century.

Tiān'ānmén Square   Square
(天安门广场, Tiān'ānmén Guǎngchǎng; Map p74; ⑤ Tiān'ānmén West, Tiān'ānmén East or Qianmen) `FREE` Flanked by stern 1950s Soviet-style buildings and ringed by white perimeter fences, the world's largest public square (440,000 sq metres) is an immense flatland of paving stones at the heart of Běijīng. If you get up early, you can watch the flagraising ceremony at sunrise, performed by a troop of People's Liberation Army (PLA) soldiers drilled to march at precisely 108 paces per minute, 75cm per pace. The soldiers emerge through the Gate of Heavenly Peace to goosestep impeccably across Chang'an Jie; all traffic is halted. The same ceremony in reverse is performed at sunset.

Here one stands at the symbolic centre of the Chinese universe. The rectangular arrangement, flanked by halls to both east and west, to some extent echoes the layout of the Forbidden City: as such, the square employs a conventional plan that pays obeisance to traditional Chinese culture, but many of its ornaments and buildings are Soviet-inspired. Mao conceived the square to project the enormity of the Communist Party, and during the Cultural Revolution he reviewed parades of up to a million people here. The 'Tiān'ānmén Incident', in 1976, is the term given to the near-riot in the square that accompanied the death of Premier Zhou Enlai. Another million people jammed into the square to pay their last respects to Mao in the same year. Most infamously, in 1989 the army forced prodemocracy demonstrators out of the square. Hundreds lost their lives in the surrounding streets although, contrary to widespread belief, it is unlikely that anyone was killed in the square itself.

Despite being a public place, the square remains more in the hands of the government than the people; it is monitored by closed circuit TV cameras, Segway-riding police officers and plain-clothes officers. The designated points of access, security checks on entry and twitchy mood cleave Tiān'ānmén Sq from the city. A tangible atmosphere of restraint and authority reigns.

All this – plus the absence of anywhere to sit – means the square is hardly a place to chill out (don't whip out a guitar), but such is its iconic status that few people leave Běijīng without making a visit. In any case, there's more than enough space to stretch a leg and the view can be breathtaking, especially on a clear blue day or at nightfall when the area is illuminated.

Gate of
Heavenly Peace   Historic Site
(天安门, Tiān'ānmén; Map p70; admission ¥15, bag storage ¥2-6; ⏰8.30am-4.30pm; S Tiān'ānmén West or Tiān'ānmén East) Hung with a vast likeness of Mao Zedong, and guarded by two pairs of Ming stone lions, the double-eaved Gate of Heavenly Peace, north of Tiān'ānmén Sq, is a potent national symbol. Built in the 15th century and restored in the 17th century, the gate was formerly the largest of the four gates of the Imperial City Wall, and it was from this gate that Mao proclaimed the People's Republic of China on 1 October 1949. To-day's political coterie watches mass troop parades from here.

Front Gate   Historic Site
(前门, Qián Mén; Map p74; admission ¥20, audio guide ¥20; ⏰9am-4pm Tue-Sun; S Qianmen) Front Gate actually consists of two gates. The northernmost is the 40m-high

Zhèngyáng Gate (正阳门城楼; Zhèngyáng Mén Chénglóu), which dates from the Ming dynasty and which was the largest of the nine gates of the Inner City Wall separating the inner, or Tartar (Manchu) city from the outer, or Chinese city. With the disappear-ance of the city walls, the gate sits out of context, but it can be climbed for decent views of the square and of Arrow Tower, immediately to the south.

Chairman Mao
Memorial Hall   Mausoleum
(毛主席纪念堂, Máo Zhǔxí Jìniàntáng; Map p74; Tiān'ānmén Sq; bag storage ¥2-10, camera storage ¥2-5; ⏰7.30am-1pm Tue-Sun; S Tiān'ānmén West, Tiān'ānmén East or Qianmen) FREE Mao Zedong died in September 1976 and his memorial hall was constructed on the southern side of Tiān'ānmén Sq soon af-terwards. This squat, Soviet-inspired mau-soleum lies on Běijīng's north–south axis of symmetry on the footprint of Zhōnghuá Gate (Zhōnghuá Mén), a vast and ancient portal flattened during the communist development of Tiān'ānmén Sq. Mao is still revered across much of China, and you'll see some people reduced to tears here at the sight of his mummified corpse.

Former Foreign
Legation Quarter   Historic Buildings
(租界区; Map p74; S Chongwenmen, Qianmen or Wangfujing) The former Foreign Lega-tion Quarter, where the 19th-century foreign powers flung up their embassies, schools, post offices and banks, lies east of Tiān'ānmén Sq. Apart from the Běijīng Police Museum, the **former French Post Office** (Map p74; now a Sìchuān restau-rant), and some of the Legation Quarter buildings (now high-end restaurants and members clubs), you can't enter any of the buildings, but a stroll along the streets here (Dongjiaomin Xiang, Taijichang Dajie and Zhengyi Lu) gives you a hint of the area's former European flavour.

Jǐngshān Park   Park
(景山公园, Jǐngshān Gōngyuán; Map p70; Jingshan Qianjie; adult ¥2, in summer ¥5; ⏰6am-9.30pm; S Tiān'ānmén West, then bus 5) The dominating feature of Jǐngshān – among the city's finest parks – is one of central

Don't Miss
Běijīng's Hútòng

Běijīng's medieval genotype is most discernible down the city's leafy *hútòng* (胡同; narrow alleyways). Criss-crossing Běijīng within the Second Ring Rd, the *hútòng* link up into a huge and enchanting warren of one-storey dwellings and historic courtyard homes. Immersing yourself in the *hútòng* is an essential part of any visit to the capital and by far the best way to experience Běijīng street life.

Hiring a bike is by far the best way to explore this historic world. Organised tours are easy to find: *hútòng* rickshaw riders lurk in packs around the Drum & Bell Square and Qiánhǎi Lake, charging between ¥60 and ¥120 per person for a 45-minute or one-hour tour. Alternatively, Bike Běijīng (p114) does guided cycle tours.

History

After Genghis Khan's army reduced Běijīng to rubble, the new city was redesigned with *hútòng*. By the Qing dynasty more than 2000 passageways riddled the city, leaping to around 6000 by the 1950s; the figure has dwindled to somewhere above 1000. *Hútòng* nearly all run east–west so that the main gate faces south, satisfying feng shui (wind/water) requirements. This south-facing aspect guarantees sunshine and protection from negative principles amassing in the north. Old walled *sìhéyuàn* (traditional courtyard houses) are the building blocks of this delightful universe. Many are still lived in and hum with activity. Inside, scholar trees soar aloft, providing shade and a nesting ground for birds.

Famous Lanes

Venerable alleys include **Zhuanta Hutong** (砖塔胡同; Brick Pagoda Alley), dating from Mongol times and found west off Xisi Nandajie; and **Nanluogu Xiang**, which dates back 800 years and is now the best-known alley in town thanks to its emergence as a nightlife hub. Other *hútòng* survive in name only, such as 900-year-old **Sanmiao Jie** (三庙街; Three Temple St) in Xuānwǔ District, which dates back to the Liao dynasty (907–1125). Long cited as the oldest *hútòng* of them all, little is left of the ancient alley as its courtyard houses were demolished in 2009. See our *hútòng* walking tour for more pointers.

Finding the Hútòng

The most *hútòng*-rich neighbourhoods are in the centre and north of Dōngchéng District, closely followed by the northern part of Xīchéng District, especially the area around and to the west of Hòuhǎi Lakes. The *hútòng* immediately east and west of the Forbidden City were reserved for aristocrats and the city elite.

> **Local Knowledge**

Běijīng's Hútòng Don't Miss List

BY LI MEI, MEDIA AGENT/PLAYWRIGHT

1 NANLUOGU XIANG
Probably the best known tourist *hútòng* (alleyway), especially with young locals, this long north–south hub is a great blend of ancient and modern. Nanluogu Xiang's style stays close to the original low-rise grey brick, but the homes have been converted to shops, snack stalls, cafes and bars. It's crazy on weekends during daytime, with window-shoppers galore. Around 18 smaller *hútòng* run off Nanluogu Xiang; each one is worth a peek.

1 MAO'ER HUTONG
One of the streets off Nanluogu Xiang is this increasingly developed *hútòng* that provides a beautiful tree-lined walk to nearby Hòuhǎi Lakes tourist area. Most of its houses are still residential or privately owned, so it's really serene at night.

2 WUDAOYING HUTONG
A few years ago it was billed as the next place for *hútòng* hipsters, but it never really reached its potential. There are a few diamonds in the rough, however, and it's definitely worth a slow walk down. Some of the restaurants are popular with expats and it's conveniently located directly west of the Lama Temple.

3 FANGJIA HUTONG
A few streets south of Wudaoying Hutong, this was my pick several years back for the next big thing in Běijīng. There are some reasonable bars, galleries and shops along this once-quiet and residential (but now trendy) alley; the No 46 courtyard art complex with a theatre, cafes and hotel draws a young crowd.

4 DASHILAN WEST STREET
Southwest of Qiánmén, there's a long *hútòng* with a diverse mix of shops, Peking-duck restaurants, guesthouses and pretty much anything else you can think of. It's a little touristy near the main strip, but the further west you go, the better it gets. Like many *hútòng*, it ends in a bit of a maze, but getting lost is half the fun!

Běijīng's few hills; a mound that was created from the earth excavated to make the Forbidden City moat. Called Coal Hill by Westerners during Legation days, Jǐngshān also serves as a feng shui shield, protecting the palace from evil spirits – or dust storms – from the north. Clamber to the top for a magnificent panorama of the capital and princely views over the russet roofing of the Forbidden City.

Workers Cultural Palace   Park

(劳动人民文化宫, Láodòng Rénmín Wénhuà Gōng; Map p70; ☎tennis court 6512 2856; park entrance ¥2, tennis court per hour ¥80, Supreme Temple ¥10; ⏰6.30am-7.30pm, tennis court 6am-11.30pm; ⓢTiān'ānmén East) Despite the prosaic name and its location at the very heart of town, this reclusive park, between Tiān'ānmén Sq and the Forbidden City, is one of Běijīng's best-kept secrets. Few visitors divert here from their course towards the main gate of the Forbidden City, but this was the emperor's premier place of worship and contains the **Supreme Temple** (太庙, Tài Miào; Map p70; admission ¥10), with its beautifully carved interior roofing.

St Joseph's Church   Church

(东堂, Dōng Táng; Map p74; 74 Wangfujing Dajie; ⏰6.30am-5pm; ⓢDengshikou) FREE A crowning edifice on Wangfujing Dajie, and one of Běijīng's four principal churches, St Joseph's is known locally as Dōng Táng (East Cathedral). Originally built during the reign of Shunzhi in 1655, it was damaged by an earthquake in 1720 and reconstructed. The luckless church also caught fire in 1807, was destroyed again in 1900 during the Boxer Rebellion and restored in 1904, only to be shut in 1966. Now fully repaired, the church is a testament to the long history of Christianity in China.

Ancient Observatory   Observatory

(古观象台, Gǔ Guānxiàngtái; Map p74; Jianguomen Bridge, East 2nd Ring Rd; 二环东路建国门桥; Erhuandong Lu, Jianguomen Qiao; adult ¥20; ⏰9am-4.30pm Tue-Sun; ⓢJianguomen) This unusual former observatory is mounted on the battlements of a watchtower lying along the line of the old Ming City Wall and originally dates back to Kublai Khan's days, when it lay north of the present site.

Kublai, like later Ming and Qing emperors, relied heavily on astrologers to plan military endeavours. The present observatory – the only surviving example of several constructed during the Jin, Yuan, Ming and Qing dynasties – was built between 1437 and 1446 to facilitate both astrological predictions and seafaring navigation.

DRUM TOWER & DŌNGCHÉNG NORTH

Drum Tower   Historic Site

(鼓楼; Gǔlóu; Map p82; Gulou Dongdajie; admission ¥20, both towers through ticket ¥30; ⏰9am-5pm, last tickets 4.40pm; ⓢShichahai or Gulou Dajie) Along with the older-looking Bell Tower, which stands behind it, the magnificent redpainted Drum Tower used to be the city's official timekeeper, with drums and bells beaten and rung to mark the times of the day.

Originally built in 1272, the Drum Tower was once the heart of the Mongol capital of Dàdū, as Běijīng was then known. It was destroyed in a fire before a replacement was built, slightly to the east of the original location, in 1420. The current structure is a Qing-dynasty version of that 1420 tower.

You can climb the steep inner staircase for views of the grey-tiled rooftops in the surrounding *hútòng* alleys. But you can't view the Bell Tower as the north-facing balcony has been closed. It's well worth climbing the tower, though, especially if you can time it to coincide with one of the regular drumming performances, which are played out on reproductions of the 25 Ming-dynasty watch drums, which used to sound out across this part of the city. One of the original 25 drums, the **Night Watchman's Drum** (更鼓; Gēnggǔ), is also on display; dusty, battered and worn. Also on display is a replica of a Song-dynasty water clock, which was never actually used in the tower, but is interesting nonetheless.

The times of the **drumming performances**, which only last for a few minutes, are posted by the ticket office.

Bell Tower   Historic Site

(钟楼, Zhōnglóu; Map p82; Gulou Dongdajie; admission ¥20, both towers through ticket ¥30; ⏰9am-5pm, last tickets 4.40pm; ⓢShichahai

or Gulou Dajie) The modest, grey-stone structure of the Bell Tower is arguably more charming than its resplendent other half, the Drum Tower, after which this area of Běijīng is named. It also has the added advantage of being able to offer views of its sister tower from a balcony.

Along with the drums in the Drum Tower, the bells in the Bell Tower were used as Běijīng's official timekeepers throughout the Yuan, Ming and Qing dynasties, and on until 1924. The Bell Tower looks the older of the two, perhaps because it isn't painted. In fact both are of similar age. The Bell Tower was also built during the Mongol Yuan Dynasty, in 1272, and was rebuild in the 1440s after being destroyed in a fire. This current structure was built in 1745.

Like the Drum Tower, the Bell Tower can also be climbed up an incredibly steep inner staircase. But the views from the top are even better here, partly because the structure is set back more deeply into the surrounding *hútòng*, and partly because you can get great photos of the Drum Tower from its viewing balcony. Marvel too at the huge, 600-year-old, 63-tonne bell suspended in the pleasantly unrestored interior. Note how Chinese bells have no clappers but are instead struck with a stout pole.

Inside the tower on the ground floor (south side) is the **Bell Tower Tea House**, where you can sample a selection of Chinese teas (per person per hour ¥50) as well as buy tea and tea sets.

The Drum & Bell Sq, between the two towers, is a great people-watching area in which to while away some time even if you don't climb either of the two towers. There are a handful of excellent bars and cafes here too, some with rooftop views over the square. Both towers are lit up beautifully come evening. Note: the square was undergoing wholesale renovations at the time of research.

Confucius Temple & Imperial College Confucian Temple (孔庙、国子监, Kǒng Miào & Guózǐjiàn; Map p82; 13 Guozijian Jie; admission ¥30, audio guide ¥30; ☻8.30am-5.30pm; ⑤ Yonghegong-Lama Temple) An incense stick's toss away from the Lama Temple, China's second-largest Confucian temple had a refit in recent years, but the almost otherworldly sense of detachment is seemingly impossible to shift. A mood of impassiveness reigns and the lack of worship reinforces a sensation that time has stood still. However, in its tranquillity and reserve, the temple can be a pleasant sanctuary from Běijīng's often congested streets – a haven of peace and quiet.

Drum Tower
CHRISTIAN KOBER/GETTY IMAGES ©

Drum Tower & Dōngchéng North

Antediluvian *bìxì* (mythical tortoise-like dragons) glare from repainted pavilions while lumpy and ossified ancient cypresses claw stiffly at the Běijīng air. There's a stone 'forest' of 190 stelae recording the 13 Confucian classics in 630,000 Chinese characters at the temple rear. Also inscribed on stelae are the names of successful candidates of the highest level of the official Confucian examination system.

Next to the Confucius Temple, but within the same grounds, stands the **Imperial College**, where the emperor expounded the Confucian classics to an audience of thousands of kneeling students, professors and court officials – an annual rite. Built by the grandson of Kublai Khan in 1306, the former college was the supreme academy during the Yuan, Ming and Qing dynasties.

On the site is a marvellous, glazed, three-gate, single-eaved decorative archway called a *liúli páifāng* (glazed archway). The Biyong Hall beyond is a twin-roofed structure with yellow tiles surrounded by a moat and topped with a splendid gold knob. Its stupendous interior houses a vermillion and gold lectern.

Some of Běijīng's last remaining *páilóu* (decorated archways) bravely survive in the tree-lined street outside (Guozijian Jie) and the entire area of *hútòng* here is now dotted with small cafes, cute restaurants and boutique shops, making it an ideal place to browse in low gear. At the western end of Guozijian Jie stands a diminutive **Fire God Temple** (Huǒshén Miào; Map p82), built in 1802 and now occupied by Běijīng residents.

Drum Tower & Dōngchéng North

TEMPLE OF HEAVEN PARK & DŌNGCHÉNG SOUTH

Temple of Heaven Park   Park

(天坛公园, Tiāntán Gōngyuán; Map p101; ☏6701 2483; Tiantan Donglu; admission park/through ticket high season ¥15/35, low season ¥10/30, audio tour ¥40 (deposit ¥100); ⊙park 6am-8pm, sights 8am-5.30pm Apr-Oct, park 6am-8pm, sights 8am-5pm Nov-Mar; S Tiantandongmen) A tranquil oasis of peace and methodical Confucian design in one of China's busiest urban landscapes, the 267-hectare Temple of Heaven Park is absolutely unique. It originally served as a vast stage for solemn rites performed by the emperor of the time (known as the Son of Heaven), who prayed here for good harvests and sought divine clearance and atonement. Strictly speaking, it's an altar rather than a temple – so don't expect burning incense or worshippers.

Surrounded by a long wall and with a gate at each compass point, the arrangement is typical of Chinese parks, with the imperfections, bumps and wild irregularities of nature largely deleted and the harmonising hand of man accentuated in obsessively straight lines and regular arrangements. This effect is magnified by Confucian objectives, where the human intellect is imposed on the natural world, fashioning order and symmetry. The resulting balance and harmony have an almost haunting – but slightly claustrophobic – beauty. Police whir about in electric buggies as visitors stroll among old buildings, groves of ancient trees and birdsong. Around 4000 ancient, knotted cypresses (some 800 years old, their branches propped up on poles) poke towards the Běijīng skies within the grounds.

Seen from above, the temple halls are round and the bases square, in accordance with the notion 'Tiānyuán Dìfāng' (天圆地方) – 'Heaven is round, Earth is square'. Also observe that the northern rim of the park is semicircular, while its southern end is square. The traditional approach to the temple was from the south, via Zhāohēng Gate (昭亨门; Zhāohēng Mén); the north gate is an architectural afterthought. The highlight of the park, and an icon of Běijīng in its own right, is the **Hall of Prayer for Good Harvests** (祈年殿, Qínián Diàn; admission ¥20), an astonishing structure with a triple-eaved purplish-blue umbrella roof mounted on a three-tiered marble terrace. The wooden pillars (made from Oregon fir) support the ceiling without any nails or cement – for a building 38m high and 30m in diameter, that's quite an accomplishment. Embedded in the ceiling is a carved dragon, a symbol of the emperor. Built in 1420, the hall was reduced to carbon after being zapped by a lightning bolt during the reign of Guangxu in 1889; a faithful reproduction based on Ming architectural methods was erected the following year.

Běijīng City Walls

Had they been preserved – or even partially protected – rather than almost entirely obliterated in the ideological 1950s and '60s, Běijīng's mighty city walls and imposing gates would rank among China's top sights.

An epitaph for the city walls, the **Ming City Wall Ruins Park** (明城墙遗址公园, Míng Chéngqiáng Yízhǐ Gōngyuán; Map p101; Chongwenmen Dongdajie; ⏰24hr; Ⓢ Chongwenmen) runs next to a section of the Ming-era, inner-city wall along the entire length of the northern flank of Chongwenmen Dongdajie.

The park extends from the former site of Chōngwén Mén (one of the nine gates of the inner city wall) to the **Southeast Corner Watchtower** (东南角楼、红门画廊, Dōngnán Jiǎolóu & Hóngmén Huàláng; Map p101; ☎6527 0574; www.redgategallery.com; admission ¥10; ⏰8am-5.30pm; Ⓢ Jianguomen or Chongwenmen). The highly impressive interior has some staggering carpentry: huge red pillars surge upwards, topped with solid beams. An exhibition on the 2nd floor details the history of Běijīng's city gates and includes some fascinating old photographs.

Continuing south along an elevated imperial pathway, you soon reach the octagonal **Imperial Vault of Heaven** (皇穹宇; Huáng Qióng Yǔ), which was erected at the same time as the Round Altar, but with its shape echoing the lines of the Hall of Prayer for Good Harvests. The hall contained tablets of the emperor's ancestors, employed during winter solstice ceremonies.

Wrapped around the Imperial Vault of Heaven is **Echo Wall** (回音壁; Huíyīn Bì). A whisper can travel clearly from one end to your friend's ear at the other – unless a cacophonous tour group joins in (get here early for this one).

Immediately south of Echo Wall, the 5m-high **Round Altar** (圜丘; Yuán Qiū) was constructed in 1530 and rebuilt in 1740. Consisting of white marble arrayed in three tiers, its geometry revolves around the imperial number nine. Odd numbers possess heavenly significance, with nine the largest single-digit odd number. Symbolising heaven, the top tier is a huge mosaic of nine rings, each composed of multiples of nine stones, so that the ninth ring equals 81 stones. The stairs and balustrades are similarly presented in multiples of nine. Sounds generated from the centre of the upper terrace undergo amplification from the marble balustrades (the acoustics can get noisy when crowds join in).

Off to the eastern side of the Hall of Prayer for Good Harvests, and with a green-tiled tow-tier roof, the **Animal Killing Pavilion** (Zǎishēng Tíng) was the venue for the slaughter of sacrificial oxen, sheep, deer and other animals. Today it stands locked and passive but can be admired from the outside. Stretching out from here runs a **Long Corridor** (Cháng Láng), where locals sit out and deal cards, listen to the radio, play keyboards, practise Peking opera, try dance moves and kick hacky-sacks. Just north of here is a large and very popular exercise park.

In the west of the park, sacrificial music was rehearsed at the **Divine Music Administration** (Shényuè Shǔ), while wild cats inhabit the dry moat of the green-tiled **Fasting Palace** (Zhāi Gōng).

Běijīng Railway Museum   Museum
(北京铁路博物馆, Běijīng Tiělù Bówùguǎn; Map p101; ☎6705 1638; 2a Qianmen Dongdajie, 前门东大街2a号; admission ¥20; ⏰9am-5pm Tue-Sun; Ⓢ Qianmen) Located in the historic former Qiánmén Railway Station, which once connected Běijīng to Tiānjīn, this museum offers an engaging history of the development of the capital and China's railway system, with plenty of photos and models. Its lack of space, though, means it doesn't have many actual trains, although there is a

life-size model of the cab of one of China's high-speed trains to clamber into (¥10).

SĀNLǏTÚN & CHÁOYÁNG

Dōngyuè Temple   Taoist Temple
(东岳庙, Dōngyuè Miào; Map p86; 141 Chaoyangmenwai Dajie; adult ¥10, with guide ¥40; ⊘7.30am-5.30pm Apr-Oct, 8.30am-4.30pm Nov-Mar, closed Mon year-round; [S]Chaoyangmen or Dongdaqiao) Dedicated to the Eastern Peak (Tài Shān) of China's five Taoist mountains, the morbid Taoist shrine of Dōngyuè Temple is an unsettling, albeit fascinating, experience and one of the capital's most unique temples. An active place of worship tended by top-knotted Taoist monks, the temple's roots go all the way back to the Yuan dynasty. A visit here takes you into a world entirely at odds with the surrounding glass and steel high-rises.

Rìtán Park   Park
(日坛公园, Rìtán Gōngyuán; Ritan Lu; admission free; ⊘6am-9pm; [S]Chaoyangmen or Jianguomen) Meaning 'Altar of the Sun', Rìtán (pronounced 'rer-tan') is a real oasis in the heart of Běijīng's business district. Dating back to 1530 and one of a set of imperial parks which covered each compass point –

others include the Temple of Heaven and Temple of Earth (Dìtán Park) – the altar is now little more than a raised platform. But the surrounding park is beautifully landscaped and a great place to tune out from the surrounding mayhem.

CCTV Building   Architecture
(央视大楼, Yāngshì Dàlóu; Map p86; 32 Dongsanhuan Zhonglu; [S]Jintaixizhao) Shaped like an enormous pair of trousers, and known locally as Dà Kùchǎ (大裤衩), or Big Underpants, the astonishing CCTV Tower is an architectural fantasy that appears to defy gravity. It's made possible by an unusual engineering design which creates a three-dimensional cranked loop, supported by an irregular grid on its surface. Designed by Rem Koolhaas and Ole Scheeren, the building is an audacious statement of modernity (despite its nickname) and a unique addition to the Běijīng skyline.

Bird's Nest & Water Cube   Architecture
(国家体育场、国家游泳中心, Guójiā Tǐyùchǎng & Guójiā Yóuyǒng Zhōngxīn; Bird's Nest ¥50, Water Cube ¥30; ⊘9am-5pm Nov-Mar, 9am-6.30pm Apr-Oct; [S]Olympic Sports Centre) Seven years

Pavilion, Rìtán Park

NORA TEJADA/GETTY IMAGES ©

BĚIJĪNG & THE GREAT WALL

PSB Main Office
(900m)

Xiangheyuan Lu

Dongzhimenwai Xiejie

River

International
SOS (200m)

中路

Sanlitun
Dongliujie

SĀNLǏTÚN
EMBASSY
AREA

Dongzhimenwai Xiaojie

Liangma

Sanlitun Xiwujie

Dongzhimen ⑤
东直门

Dongzhimenwai Dajie

CHÁOYÁNG

Xinzhong Jie

Chunxiu Lu

Xindong Lu

Sanlitun Beilu

Sanlitun Lu

Sanlitun
Dongsijie

11 ⑪ Sanlitun
③ Dongsanjie

Dong'erhuan
Lu
(East 2nd Ring Rd)
东二环

Dongzhong Jie

Xingfucun Lu

Běijīng
Tourist
Information
Center 13

8 ⑨

10 12
⑩⑫

Dongsi
Shitiao ⑤
东四十条

Gongrentiyuchang Beilu

⑨9

Nansanlitun Lu

Ⓧ
6

Workers
Stadium

Baijiazhuang

Chaoyangmen Beidajie

Gongrentiyuchang Xilu

Gongrentiyuchang Donglu

Gongrentiyuchang Nanlu

工人体育场东路

Chaoyangmen ⑤
朝阳门

Chaoyangmenwai Dajie
朝阳门外大街

2
ⓟ

Chaoyang Beilu

Chaoyang Dajie

Jianguomen Beidajie

Chaowaishichang Jie

JIÀNGUÓMÉNWÀI
EMBASSY
AREA

Lumicang Hutong

Ritan Beilu

14 ⑭

Dongdaqiao Lu

Guandongdian Nanjie

Yabao Lu

Ritan Lu

Ritan Donglu

Rìtán
Park

Ritan
Dong'erjie

Guanghua Lu

Guanghua Lu

Dongzongbu Hutong

Ritan Lu

Jianhua Lu

Xiushui Beijie

Xiushui Dongjie

⑤

Xiushui Nanjie

17

Jianguomen ⑤
建国门

Jianguomenwai Dajie
建国门外大街

15 ⑮

7 Ⓧ

⑤ Yonganli
永安里

4 ⑭

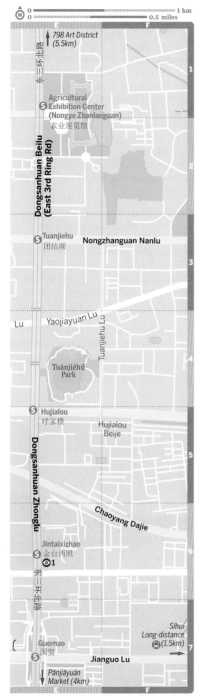

Sānlǐtún & Cháoyáng

after the 2008 Olympics, walking around the Olympic Sports Centre midweek is rather like being stuck in a district of Brasilia or one of those zombie movies where humans have all but been wiped out. A few events are staged at the signature National Stadium, known colloquially as the Bird's Nest (鸟巢; Niǎocháo), but it mostly stands empty and security staff and optimistic street vendors outnumber visitors. Nevertheless, it remains an iconic, if forlorn, piece of architecture.

BĚIHǍI PARK & XĪCHÉNG NORTH

Běihǎi Park   Park

(北海公园, Běihǎi Gōngyuán; Map p89; ☎6403 1102; admission high/low season ¥10/5, through ticket high/low season ¥20/15; ☉park 6am-9pm, sights until 5pm; Ⓢ Xisi or Nanluogu Xiang) Běihǎi Park, northwest of the Forbidden City (p66), is largely occupied by the North Sea (běihǎi), a huge lake that freezes in winter and blooms with lotuses in summer. Old folk dance together outside temple halls and come twilight, young couples cuddle on benches. It's a restful place to stroll around, rent a rowing boat in summer and watch calligraphers practising characters on paving slabs with fat brushes and water.

The site is associated with Kublai Khan's palace, Běijīng's navel before the arrival of the Forbidden City. All that survives of Khan's court is a large jar made of green jade in the **Round City** (团城; Tuánchéng; Map p89), near the southern entrance. Also within the Round City is the **Chengguang Hall** (Chéngguāng Diàn), where a white jade statue of Sakyamuni from Myanmar (Burma) can be found, its arm wounded by the allied forces that swarmed through Běijīng in 1900 to quash the Boxer Rebellion. At the time of writing, the Round City was closed to visitors.

Attached to the North Sea, the South (Nánhǎi) and Middle (Zhōnghǎi) Seas to the south lend their name to Zhōngnánhǎi (literally 'Middle and South Seas'), the heavily-guarded compound less than a mile south of the park where the Chinese Communist Party's top leadership live.

Topping **Jade Islet** (琼岛; Qióngdǎo) on the lake, the 36m-high Tibetan-style **White Dagoba** (白塔; Báitǎ; Map p89) was built in

1651 for a visit by the Dalai Lama, and was rebuilt in 1741. Climb up to the dagoba via the **Yǒng'ān Temple** (永安寺; Yǒng'ān Sì).

Xītiān Fánjìng (西天梵境; Western Paradise; Map p89), situated on the northern shore of the lake, is a lovely temple (admission to which is included in the park ticket). The nearby **Nine Dragon Screen** (九龙壁; Jiǔlóng Bì; Map p89), a 5m-high and 27m-long spirit wall, is a glimmering stretch of coloured glazed tiles depicting coiling dragons, similar to its counterpart in the Forbidden City. West, along the shore, is the pleasant **Little Western Heaven** (小西天; Xiǎo Xītiān), a further shrine.

Capital Museum   Museum
(首都博物馆, Shǒudū Bówùguǎn; Map p64; ☏6339 3339; www.capitalmuseum.org.cn; 16 Fuxingmenwai Dajie; ⊙9am-5pm Tue-Sun; Ⓢ Muxidi) FREE Behind the riveting good looks of the Capital Museum are some first-rate galleries, including a mesmerising collection of ancient Buddhist statues and a lavish exhibition of Chinese porcelain. There is also an interesting chronological history of Běijīng, an exhibition that is dedicated to cultural relics of Peking opera, a fascinating Běijīng Folk

Běihǎi Park

ZHAOLINGHE/GETTY IMAGES ©

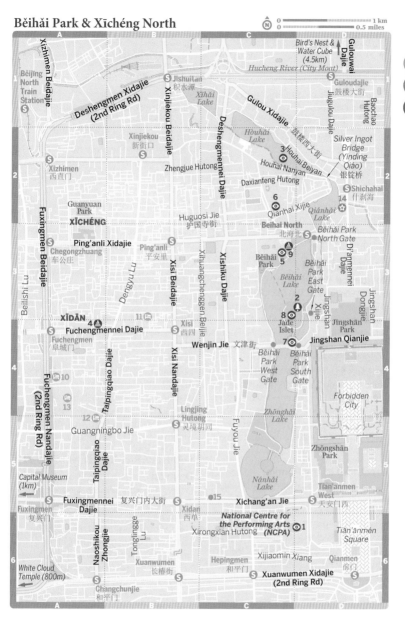

Customs exhibition, and displays of ancient bronzes, jade, calligraphy and paintings.

Hòuhǎi Lakes
Lakes

(后海, Hòuhǎi; Map p89; S Shichahai, Nanluogu Xiang or Jishuitan) FREE Also known as Shíchàhǎi (什刹海) but mostly just referred to collectively as 'Hòuhǎi', the Hòuhǎi Lakes are comprised of three lakes: Qiánhǎi (Front Lake), Hòuhǎi (Back Lake) and Xīhǎi (West Lake). Together they are one of the capital's

Běihǎi Park & Xīchéng North

favourite outdoor spots, heaving with locals and out-of-towners in the summer especially, and providing great people-spotting action.

Prince Gong's Residence   House, Historic Building
(恭王府, Gōngwáng Fǔ; Map p89; ☑8328 8149; 14 Liuyin Jie; admission ¥40, tours incl short opera show & tea ceremony ¥70; ⊙7.30am-4.30pm Mar-Oct, 8am-4pm Nov-Mar; Ⓢ Ping'anli) Reputed to be the model for the mansion in Cáo Xuěqín's 18th-century classic *Dream of the Red Mansions,* this historic courtyard home is one of Běijīng's largest private residential compounds. It remains one of the capital's more attractive retreats, decorated with rockeries, plants, pools, pavilions and elaborately carved gateways, although it can get very crowded with tour groups.

Great Hall of the People   Parliament
(人民大会堂, Rénmín Dàhuìtáng; Map p74; adult ¥30, bag deposit ¥2-5; ⊙8.30am-3pm (times vary); Ⓢ Tiān'ānmén West) On the western side of Tiān'ānmén Sq, on a site previously occupied by Taichang Temple, the Jinyiwei (Ming-dynasty secret service) and the Ministry of Justice, the Great Hall of the People is the venue of the legislature, the National People's Congress (NPC). The 1959 architecture is monolithic and intimidating, and a fitting symbol of China's huge bureaucracy.

Miàoyīng Temple White Dagoba   Buddhist Temple
(妙应寺白塔, Miàoyīng Sì Báitǎ; Map p89; ☑6616 0211; 171 Fuchengmennei Dajie; adult ¥20; ⊙9am-5pm Tue-Sun; Ⓢ Fuchengmen, then bus 13, 101, 102 or 103 to Baita Si) Originally built in 1271, the Miàoyīng Temple slumbers beneath its huge, distinctive, chalk-white Yuán-dynasty pagoda, which towers over the surrounding *hútòng*. It was, when it was built, the tallest structure in Dàdū (the Yuan-dynasty name for Běijīng), and even today it is the tallest Tibetan-style pagoda in China.

White Cloud Temple   Taoist Temple
(白云观, Báiyún Guàn; Map p64; ☑6346 3887; 9 Baiyunguan Jie; adult ¥10; ⊙8.30am-4.30pm; Ⓢ Muxidi) White Cloud Temple, once the Taoist centre of northern China, was founded in AD 739, although most of the temple halls date from the Qing dynasty. It's a lively, huge and fascinating complex of shrines and courtyards, tended by Taoist monks with their hair gathered into topknots.

DASHILAR & XĪCHÉNG SOUTH

Dashilar   Historic Shopping Street
(大栅栏, Dàzhàlan; Map p93; Ⓢ Qianmen) This centuries-old shopping street, also known as Dazhalan Jie, is just west of Qianmen Dajie. While a misjudged makeover has sadly robbed it of much of its charm, many of the shops have been in business here for hundreds of years and still draw many locals. Some specialise in esoteric goods – ancient herbal remedies, hand-made cloth shoes – and most make for intriguing window shopping.

SUMMER PALACE & HǍIDIÀN

Summer Palace   Historic Site
(颐和园, Yíhé Yuán; Map p94; 19 Xinjian Gongmen; ticket ¥20, through ticket ¥50, audio guide ¥40; ⊙7am-7pm, sights 8am-5pm summer, 8.30am-

4.30pm winter; S Xiyuan or Beigongmen) As mandatory a Běijīng sight as the Great Wall or the Forbidden City, the Summer Palace was the playground for emperors fleeing the suffocating summer torpor of the old imperial city. A marvel of design, the palace – with its huge lake and hilltop views – offers a pastoral escape into the landscapes of traditional Chinese painting. It merits an entire day's exploration, although a (high-paced) morning or afternoon exploring the temples, gardens, pavilions, bridges and corridors may suffice.

The domain had long been a royal garden before being considerably enlarged and embellished by Emperor Qianlong in the 18th century. He marshalled a 100,000-strong army of labourers to deepen and expand **Kūnmíng Lake** (昆明湖; Kūnmíng Hú), and reputedly surveyed imperial navy drills from a hilltop perch.

Anglo-French troops vandalised the palace during the Second Opium War (1856–60). Empress Dowager Cixi launched into a refit in 1888 with money earmarked for a modern navy; the marble boat at the northern edge of the lake was her only nautical concession. Foreign troops, angered by the Boxer Rebellion, had another go at torching the Summer Palace in 1900, prompting further restoration work. By 1949 the palace had once more fallen into disrepair, eliciting a major overhaul.

Glittering Kūnmíng Lake swallows up three-quarters of the park, overlooked by **Longevity Hill** (万寿山; Wànshòu Shān). The principal structure is the **Hall of Benevolence and Longevity** (仁寿殿; Rénshòu Diàn; Map p94), by the east gate, housing a hardwood throne and attached to a courtyard decorated with bronze animals, including the mythical qílín (a hybrid animal that only appeared on earth at times of harmony). Unfortunately, the hall is barricaded off so you will have to peer in.

An elegant stretch of woodwork along the northern shore, the **Long Corridor** (长廊; Cháng Láng; Map p94) is trimmed with a plethora of paintings, while the slopes and crest of Longevity Hill behind are adorned with Buddhist temples. Slung out uphill on a north–south axis, the **Buddhist Fragrance Pavilion** (佛香阁; Fóxiāng Gé; Map p94) and the **Cloud Dispelling Hall** (排云殿; Páiyún Diàn; Map p94) are linked by corridors. Crowning the peak is the **Buddhist Temple of the Sea of Wisdom** (智慧海; Zhìhuì Hǎi; Map p94) tiled with effigies of Buddha, many with obliterated heads.

Kūnmíng Lake

GAVIN HELLIER/GETTY IMAGES ©

GETTY IMAGES ©

⭐ Don't Miss
Poly Art Museum

This small but exquisite museum displays a glorious array of ancient bronzes from the Shang and Zhou dynasties, a magnificent high-water mark for bronze production. Check out the intricate scaling on the '*Zūn* vessel in the shape of a Phoenix' (佣季凤鸟尊) or the '*Yǒu* with Divine Faces' (神面卣), with its elephant head on the side of the vessel. The detailed animist patterns on the *Gangbo You* (榽柏卣) are similarly vivid and fascinating.

NEED TO KNOW

保利艺术博物馆, Bǎolì Yìshù Bówùguǎn; Map p74; ☎ 6500 8117; www.polymuseum. com; 9th fl, Poly Plaza, 14 Dongzhimen Nandajie; admission ¥20, audio guide ¥10; ⊙ 9.30am-5pm, closed Sun; Ⓢ Dongsi Shitiao

Cixi's **marble boat** (清晏船; Qīngyuàn Chuán; Map p94) sits immobile on the north shore, south of some fine **Qing boathouses** (船坞; chuán wù; Map p94). When the lake is not frozen, you can traverse Kūnmíng Lake by ferry to **South Lake Island** (南湖岛; Nánhú Dǎo), where Cixi went to beseech the **Dragon King Temple** (龙王庙; Lóngwáng Miào; Map p94) for rain in times of drought. A graceful 17-arch bridge spans the 150m to the eastern shore of the lake. In warm weather, pedal boats are also available from the dock.

Try to do a circuit of the lake along the West Causeway to return along the east shore (or vice versa). It gets you away from the crowds, the views are gorgeous and it's a great cardiovascular workout. Based on the Su Causeway in Hángzhōu, and lined with willow and mulberry trees, the causeway kicks off just west of the boathouses. With its delightful hump, the grey and white marble Jade Belt Bridge dates from the reign of emperor Qianlong and crosses the point where the **Jade River** (Yùhé) enters the lake (when it flows).

Towards the North Palace Gate, **Sūzhōu Street** (苏州街; Sūzhōu Jiē) is an entertaining and light-hearted diversion of riverside walkways, shops and eateries, which are designed to mimic the famous Jiāngsū canal town.

Old Summer Palace   Historic Site
(圆明园, Yuánmíng Yuán; Map p64; 28 Qinghua Xilu; adult ¥10, through ticket ¥25, map ¥6; ⏰7am-6pm; Ⓢ Yuanmingyuan) Located northwest of the city centre, the Old Summer Palace was laid out in the 12th century. The ever-capable Jesuits were later employed by Emperor Qianlong to fashion European-style palaces for the gardens, incorporating elaborate fountains and baroque statuary. In 1860, during the Second Opium War, British and French troops torched and looted the palace, an event forever inscribed in Chinese history books as a low point in China's humiliation by foreign powers.

🍄 Activities

**Happy Magic
Water Park**   Swimming
(水立方嬉水乐园, Shuǐlìfāng Xīshuǐ Lèyuán; Olympic Green, off Beichen Lu, 北辰路奥林匹克公园内; water park entrance adult/child ¥200/160, swimming only ¥50; ⏰10am-8pm; Ⓢ Olympic Green) Unlike most of the 2008 Olympics venues, Běijīng's National Aquatics Centre, aka the Water Cube, has found a new lease of life post-Olympics. The otherworldly, bubble-like structure now houses Běijīng's largest indoor water park. It's a fave with children, who can negotiate neon plastic slides, tunnels, water jets and pools, all set alongside elaborate, surreal underwater styling.

🛏 Sleeping

Hútòng-rich Dōngchéng North is Běijīng's most pleasant neighbourhood to stay in, although Dōngchéng Central has some great digs too. Dashilar, in Xīchéng South, is ground zero for budget backpackers, although there are good hostels throughout the capital.

If you want familiar Western-friendly luxury, international five-star hotel chains are well represented in Běijīng and include:

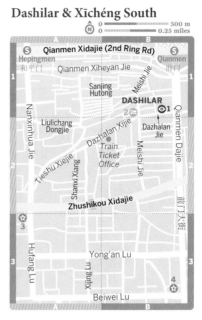

Dashilar & Xīchéng South

Ⓢ Sights
1 Dashilar B1

🛏 Sleeping
2 Qiánmén Hostel B1

🎭 Entertainment
3 Húguǎng Guild Hall A3
4 Tiānqiáo Acrobatics Theatre B3

Hilton (北京王府井希尔顿酒店, Běijīng Wángfǔjǐng Xī'ěrdùn Jiǔdiàn; Map p74; ☎5812 8888; www.wangfujing.hilton.com; Xiaowei Hutong, 王府井东大街校尉胡同, off Wangfujing Dongdajie; d ¥1550; 🚗❄@🛜❄; Ⓢ Wangfujing)

Hyatt (柏悦酒店, Bóyuè Jiǔdiàn; Map p86; ☎8567 1234; www.beijing.park.hyatt.com; 2 Jianguomenwai Dajie, 建国门外大街2号; r ¥2500-6500, China Bar cocktails from ¥70; ⏰China Bar 4pm-1am; 🚗❄@🛜❄; Ⓢ Guomao)

InterContinental (北京金融街洲际酒店; Běijīng Jīnróngjiē Zhōujì Jiǔdiàn; Map p89; ☎5852 5888; www.ihg.com; 11 Financial St; 金融街11号; r from ¥1500)

93

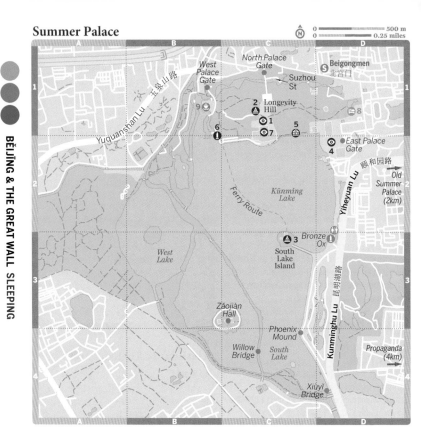

Ritz-Carlton (北京金融街丽嘉酒店; Běijīng Jīnróngjiē Lìjiā Jiǔdiàn; Map p89; ☏6601 6666; www.ritzcarlton.com; 1 Jinchengfang Dongjie; 金城坊东街1号; r from ¥2000)

Westin (金茂北京威斯汀大饭店; Jīnmào Běijīng Wēisītīng Dàfàndiàn; Map p89; ☏6606 8866; www.starwoodhotels.com; 9 Jinrong Dajie; 金融大街乙9号; from ¥1500)

FORBIDDEN CITY & DŌNGCHÉNG CENTRAL

City Walls Courtyard   Hostel $$

(城墙旅舍, Chéngqiáng Lǚshè; Map p74; ☏6402 7805; www.beijingcitywalls.com; 57 Nianzi Hutong, 碾子胡同57号; dm/s/tw ¥100/240/480; ❋@🛜; Ⓢ Nanluoguxiang) This quiet hostel is on the pricey side for sure, but it's still an attractive choice because of its peaceful courtyard atmosphere and fabulous *hútòng* location – authentically hidden

away from more touristy areas in one of the city's most historic neighbourhoods. All rooms have private bathrooms.

Jǐngshān Garden Hotel   Courtyard Hotel $$

(景山花园酒店; Jǐngshān Huāyuán Jiǔdiàn; Map p74; ☏8404 7979; www.jingshangardenhotel.com; 68 Sanyanjing Hutong, off Jingshan Dongjie; 景山东街,三眼井胡同68号; r ¥650-750; ❋@🛜) This delightful, unfussy, two-storey guesthouse has bright spacious rooms surrounding a large, peaceful, flower-filled courtyard. First-floor rooms are pricier, but brighter than the ground-floor ones, and some have views of Jǐngshān Park from their bathrooms. Walking down Sanyuanjing Hutong from the direction of Jǐngshān Park, turn right down the first alleyway, and the hotel is at the end.

Summer Palace

Red Capital Residence   Courtyard Hotel $$$

(新红资客栈, Xīnhóngzī Kèzhàn; Map p74;
8401 8886, 8403 5308; www.redcapitalclub.
com.cn; 9 Dongsi Liutiao, 东四六条9号; r ¥1050
incl breakfast; ❄ @ ᗰ; S Zhangzizhonglu)
Dressed up with Liberation-era artefacts
and established in a gorgeous Qing-dynasty
courtyard, this tiny but unique guesthouse –
owned by American activist and author
Laurence Brahm – offers a heady dose of
nostalgia for a vanished age. Make your
choice from three rooms decked out with
paraphernalia that wouldn't look out of
place in a museum.

Côté Cour   Courtyard Hotel $$$

(北京演乐酒店, Běijīng Yǎnyuè Jiǔdiàn; Map
p74; 6523 3958; www.hotelcotecourbj.com; 70
Yanyue Hutong, 演乐胡同70号; d/ste incl breakfast ¥1166/1995; ❄ @ ᗰ; S Dengshikou) With a
calm, serene atmosphere and a lovely magnolia courtyard, this 14-room *hútòng* hotel
makes a charming place to rest your head.
The decor is exquisite – especially in the
suite – and there's plenty of space to relax in
the courtyard or on the extensive rooftop –
perfect for a candle-lit evening drink.

DRUM TOWER & DŌNGCHÉNG NORTH

Peking Youth Hostel   Hútòng Hostel $$

(北平国际青年旅社, Běipíng Guójì Qīngnián
Lǚshè; Map p82; 8403 9098; pekinghostel@
vip.163.com; 113 Nanluogu Xiang, 南锣鼓巷113号;
dm/tw from ¥180/500; ❄ @ ᗰ; S Nanluogu-

xiang) Slick, colourful, but rather cramped
rooms are located round the back of the
flower-filled Peking Cafe, which opens out
onto Nanluogu Xiang. Prices reflect the
location rather than the size or quality of
the rooms, or the quality of the service
(staff can be a bit slack, especially in the
busy cafe), but this is a sound choice
nevertheless.

Courtyard 7   Courtyard Hotel $$$

(四合院酒店, Sìhéyuàn Jiǔdiàn; Map p82;
6406 0777; www.courtyard7.com; 7 Qiangu-
louyuan Hutong, off Nanluogu Xiang; 鼓楼东大
街南锣鼓巷前鼓楼苑胡同7号; r ¥900-1500;
❄ @; S Nanluoguxiang) Immaculate rooms,
decorated in traditional Chinese furniture face onto a series of different-sized,
400-year-old courtyards, which over the
years have been home to government ministers, rich merchants and even an army
general. Despite the historical narrative,
rooms still come with modern comforts
such as underfloor heating, broadband
internet, wi-fi, and cable TV.

SĀNLĪTÚN & CHÁOYÁNG

Opposite House Hotel   Boutique Hotel $$$

(瑜舍; Yúshè; Map p86; 6417 6688; www.
theoppositehouse.com; Bldg 1, Village, 11 Sanlitun
Lu, 三里屯路11号院1号楼; r ¥2300-3100;
⊜ ❄ @ ᗰ ᕊ; S Tuanjiehu) With see-all
open-plan bathrooms, American oak bath-
tubs, lovely mood lighting, underfloor heating, sliding doors, complimentary beers,
TVs on extendable arms and a metal basin

Accommodation Price Indicators

The price ranges for accommodation
in the Běijīng & the Great Wall
chapter are as follows:

$ less than ¥400 (for a standard
room)

$$ ¥400 to ¥1000

$$$ more than ¥1000

Detour:
798 Art District

A vast area of disused factories built by the East Germans, **798 Art District** (798 艺术新区, Qī Jiǔ Bā Yìshù Qū; Map p64; cnr Jiuxianqiao Lu & Jiuxianqiao Beilu; 酒仙桥路; 🕙galleries 10am-6pm, most closed Mon; 🚌403 or 909), also known as Dà Shānzi (大山子), is Běijīng's leading concentration of contemporary art galleries. The voluminous factory workshops are ideally suited to art galleries that require space for multimedia installations and other ambitious projects. You could easily spend half a day wandering around the complex.

From Exit C of Dongzhimen subway station, take Bus 909 (¥2) for about 6km northeast to Dashanzi Lukou Nan (大山子路口南), where you'll see the big red 798 sign. Buses run until 8.30pm.

A further extensive colony of art galleries can be found around 3km northeast of 798 Art District at **Cǎochǎngdì** (草场地). Bus 909 continues here.

swimming pool, this trendy Swire-owned boutique hotel is top-drawer chic. The location is ideal for shopping, restaurants and drinking. It has no obvious sign. Just walk into the striking green glass cube of a building and ask.

St Regis Luxury Hotel **$$$**
(北京国际俱乐部饭店, Běijīng Guójì Jùlèbù Fàndiàn; Map p86; 🖀6460 6688; www.stregis.com/beijing; 21 Jianguomenwai Dajie, 建国门外大街21号; r from ¥4100; ➡️❄️@🛜🏊; S Jianguomen) An extravagant foyer, thorough professionalism and tip-top location make the St Regis a marvellous, if costly, five-star choice, although 40% discounts are often

available. Sumptuous and soothing rooms ooze comfort, 24-hour butlers are at hand to fine-tune your stay, while Chinese and Italian restaurants offer some of Běijīng's finest dining experiences. Shamefully, wi-fi access is ¥80 per day.

BĚIHǍI PARK & XĪCHÉNG NORTH

Red Lantern House
West Yard Courtyard Hotel **$**
(红灯笼, Hóng Dēnglóng; Map p89; 🖀6617 0870; 12 Xisi Beiertiao, 西四北二条12号; s ¥280, d & tw ¥360, ste ¥450; ❄️@🛜; S Xisi) Previously the most engaging of the Red Lantern brood, West Yard was closed for wholesale renovations at the time of research, but it will be open again by the time you read this. It was set around two lovely, quiet courtyards, and the rooms were thoughtfully and comfortably furnished in an old-Běijīng style. Book ahead. To find it, walk north on Xisi Beidajie from Xisi metro; it's two *hútòng* up on the left.

DASHILAR & XĪCHÉNG SOUTH

Qiánmén Hostel Hostel **$**
(前门客栈, Qiánmén Kèzhàn; Map p93; 🖀6313 2369, 6313 2370; www.qianmenhostel.net; 33 Meishi Jie, 煤市街33号; 6-8 bed dm ¥70, 4-bed dm ¥80, with/without bathroom d & tw ¥280/240, tr ¥380/300; ❄️@🛜; S Qianmen) A five-minute trot southwest of Tiān'ānmén Sq, this heritage hostel with a cool courtyard offers a relaxing environment with able staff. The rooms are simple and not big but, like the dorms, they are clean, as are the shared bathrooms, and all were being upgraded at the time of writing. There's a decent cafe to hang out in too.

SUMMER PALACE & HǍIDIÀN

Aman at
Summer Palace Heritage Hotel **$$$**
(颐和安缦, Yíhé Ānmàn; Map p94; 🖀5987 9999; www.amanresorts.com; 1 Gongmen Qianjie, 宫门前街1号; r ¥4000, courtyard r ¥5200, ste ¥6400; ➡️❄️@🛜🏊; S Xiyuan) Hard to fault, this exquisite hotel is a candidate for best in Běijīng. It's located around the corner from the Summer Palace – parts of the hotel date back to the 19th century and were used to house distinguished guests waiting

for audiences with Empress Dowager Cixi. Superbly appointed rooms are contained in a series of picture-perfect pavilions set around courtyards.

🍴 Eating

Běijīng has a staggering 60,000 restaurants, and between them they cater to all tastes and all budgets.

FORBIDDEN CITY & DŌNGCHÉNG CENTRAL

Zuǒ Lín Yòu Shè   Beijing $

(左邻右舍褡裢火烧; Map p74; 50 Meishuguan Houjie, 美术馆后街50号; dumplings per liang ¥6-7, dishes ¥10-30; ⊙11am-9.30pm; ⓢNational Art Museum) This small, no-frills restaurant focuses on Běijīng cuisine. The speciality is *dālian huǒshāo* (褡裢火烧), golden-fried finger-shaped dumplings stuffed with all manner of savoury fillings; we prefer the pork ones, but there are lamb, beef and veggie choices too. They are served by the *liǎng* (两), with one *liǎng* equal to three dumplings, and they prefer you to order at least two *liǎng* (二两; *èr liǎng*) of each filling to make it worth their while cooking a batch.

Crescent Moon Muslim Restaurant   Xinjiang $

(新疆弯弯月亮维吾尔穆斯林餐厅, Xīnjiāng Wānwānyuèliàng Wéiwú'ěr Mùsīlín Cāntīng; Map p74; 16 Dongsi Liutiao Hutong, 东四六条胡同16号, 东四北大街; dishes from ¥18; ⊙11am-11pm; ⓢDongsi Shitiao) You can find a Chinese Muslim restaurant on almost every street in Běijīng. Most are run by Huí Muslims, who are Hàn Chinese, rather than ethnic-minority Uighurs from the remote western province of Xīnjiāng. Crescent Moon is the real deal – owned and staffed by Uighurs, it attracts many Běijīng-based Uighurs and people from Central Asia, as well as a lot of Western expats.

Dōnghuámén Night Market   Street Food $

(东华门夜市, Dōnghuámén Yèshì; Map p74; Dong'anmen Dajie, 东安门大街; snacks ¥5-15; ⊙4-10pm; ⓢWangfujing) A sight in itself, the bustling night market near Wangfujing Dajie is a veritable food zoo: lamb, beef and chicken skewers, corn on the cob, smelly *dòufu* (tofu), cicadas, grasshoppers, kidneys, quail eggs, snake, squid, fruit, porridge, fried pancakes, strawberry kebabs, bananas, Inner Mongolian cheese, stuffed eggplants, chicken hearts, pita bread

798 Art District

If You Like…
Hútòng Cafes

If you like Běijīng's *hútòng* and cafes, combine the two in the city's cute alleyway wi-fi cafes. There are dozens of excellent ones, particularly in and around the *hútòng* of Dōngchéng North.

1 IRRESISTIBLE CAFE
(诱惑咖啡厅, Yòu Huò Kāfēitīng; Map p82; 14 Mao'er Hutong, 帽儿胡同14号; ⊙11am-midnight, closed Mon & Tue; 🛜) Large courtyard. Czech beers. Good, healthy food.

2 CAFE CONFUCIUS
(秀冠咖啡, Xiù Guàn Kāfēi; Map p82; 25 Guozijian Jie, 国子监街25号; ⊙8.30am-8.30pm; 🛜) Buddhist themed. Very friendly.

3 ESSENCE
(萃饮咖啡, Cuìyǐn Kāfēi; Map p82; 47 Zhonglouwan Hutong, off Drum & Bell Square; 钟鼓楼广场, 钟楼湾胡同47号; ⊙10am-10pm) Top-quality coffee. Small roof terrace with Drum Tower views.

4 THREE TREES COFFEE
(三棵树; Sān Kē Shù; Map p82; 89 Nanluogu Xiang; 南锣鼓巷89号; ⊙9.30am-10pm) Cosy Bohemian retreat from Nanluogu Xiang's shopping frenzy.

stuffed with meat, shrimps – and that's just the start.

Little Yúnnán   Yunnan $$
(小云南; Xiǎo Yúnnán; Map p74; 📞6401 9498; 28 Donghuang Chenggen Beijie, 东皇城根北街28号; mains ¥20-60; ⊙10am-10pm) Run by young, friendly staff and housed in a cute courtyard conversion, Little Yúnnán is one of the more down-to-earth Yúnnán restaurants in Běijīng. The main room has a rustic feel to it, with wooden beams, flooring and furniture. The tables up in the eaves are fun, and there's also some seating in the small open-air courtyard by the entrance.

Brian McKenna @ The Courtyard   Fusion $$$
(马克南四合轩, Mǎkènán Sìhéxuān; Map p70; 📞6526 8883; www.bmktc.com; 95 Donghuamen Dajie, 东华门大街95号; set menus from ¥588; ⊙11.30am-2.30pm & 6-10pm; Ⓢ Tiān'ānmén East or Dengshikou) This 10-year-old classic of the Běijīng fine-dining scene has been given a new lease of life by UK-born chef Brian McKenna. Courtyard still enjoys its peerless location, housed in a Qing-dynasty building beside the Forbidden City moat, but McKenna has revamped both the interior (there are more tables with a view of the moat now) and the menu (with some innovative new creations, such as his chocolate terracotta warrior).

DRUM TOWER & DŌNGCHÉNG NORTH

Yáojì Chǎogān   Beijing $
(姚记炒肝店; Map p82; 311 Gulou Dongdajie, 鼓楼东大街311号; mains ¥8-20; ⊙6am-10.30pm; Ⓢ Shichahai) Proper locals' joint, serving Běijīng dishes in a noisy, no-nonsense atmosphere. The house speciality is *chǎogān* (炒肝; pig's liver stew; ¥6 to ¥9). This is also a good place to try *zhá guànchang* (炸灌肠; garlic-topped deep-fried crackers; ¥6) and *má dòufu* (麻豆腐; spicy tofu paste; ¥10).

Yī Lóng Zhāi   Xinjiang $
(伊隆斋; Map p82; cnr Mao'er Hutong & Doujiao Hutong, 帽儿胡同和豆角胡同的路口; mains ¥15-30; ⊙11am-midnight; Ⓢ Shichahai) Bright and boisterous, this no-frills restaurant specialises in the Turkic-influenced cuisine of Xīnjiāng province, in west China. So expect lots of tasty lamb dishes. The *kǎo yáng tuǐ* (烤羊腿; grilled leg of lamb; ¥25) is excellent, as are the *yáng ròu chuàn* (羊肉串; lamb skewers; ¥3). There's also a good selection of noodle dishes (¥12 to ¥18) in the photo menu.

Dàlǐ Courtyard   Yunnan $$$
(大理, Dàlǐ; Map p82; 📞8404 1430; 67 Xiaojing-chang Hutong, Gulou Dongdajie, 鼓楼东大街小经厂胡同67号; set menu ¥150; ⊙midday-2pm & 6-10.30pm; Ⓢ Andingmen) The charming *hútòng* setting in a restored courtyard

makes this one of Běijīng's more pleasant places to eat, especially in summer (in winter they cover the courtyard with an unattractive temporary roof). It specialises in the subtle flavours of Yúnnán cuisine. There's no menu. Instead, you pay ¥150 (drinks are extra), and enjoy whatever inspires the chef that day. He rarely disappoints.

TEMPLE OF HEAVEN PARK & DŌNGCHÉNG SOUTH

Lost Heaven   Yunnan $$$
(花马天堂, Huāmǎ Tiāntáng; Map p74; ✆8516 2698; 23 Qianmen Dongdajie, 前门东大街23号; dishes from ¥68; ⏰11am-2pm, 5.30pm-10.30pm; Ⓢ Qianmen) The Běijīng branch of the famed Shànghǎi restaurant, Lost Heaven specialises in the folk cuisine of Yúnnán province. While the spices have been toned down, the flavours remain subtle and light and are guaranteed to transport you to China's balmy southwest. The location in the elegant former Legation Quarter is an added bonus, and there's an outside terrace for the summer.

Lìqún Roast Duck Restaurant   Peking Duck $$$
(利群烤鸭店, Lìqún Kǎoyādiàn; Map p101; ✆6702 5681, 6705 5578; 11 Beixiangfeng Hutong, 前门东大街正义路南口北翔凤胡同11号; roast duck for 2/3 people ¥255/275; ⏰10am-10pm; Ⓢ Qianmen) As you walk in to this compact courtyard restaurant, you're greeted by the fine sight of rows of ducks on hooks glowing in the ovens. The delectable duck on offer is so in demand that it's essential to call ahead to reserve both a bird and a table (otherwise, turn up off-peak and be prepared to wait an hour).

Qiánmén Quánjùdé Roast Duck Restaurant   Peking Duck $$$
(前门全聚德烤鸭店, Qiánmén Quánjùdé Kǎoyādiàn; Map p101; ✆67011379; 30 Qianmen Dajie, 前门大街30号; roast duck ¥296; ⏰11am-1.30pm, 4.30-8pm; Ⓢ Qianmen) The most popular branch of Běijīng's most famous destination for duck – check out the photos of everyone from Fidel Castro to Zhang Yimou. The duck, while not the best in town, is roasted in ovens fired by fruit-tree wood,

which means the birds have a unique fragrance, as well as being juicy, if slightly fatty.

SĀNLǏTÚN & CHÁOYÁNG

Nàjiā Xiǎoguǎn   Imperial $$
(那家小馆; Map p86; ✆6567 3663; 10 Yong'an Xili, off Jianguomenwai Dajie, Chunxiu Lu, 建国门外大街永安西里10号; mains ¥40-90; ⏰11.30am-9pm; Ⓢ Yong'anli) There's a touch of the traditional Chinese teahouse to this excellent restaurant, housed in a reconstructed two-storey interior courtyard, and bubbling with old-Peking atmosphere. The menu is based on an old imperial recipe book known as the *Golden Soup Bible*, and the dishes are consistently good (and fairly priced considering the quality).

BĚIHǍI PARK & XĪCHÉNG NORTH

Royal Icehouse   Shandong $$
(皇家冰窖小院; Huángjiā Bīngjiào Xiǎoyuàn; Map p74; ✆6401 1358; 5 Gongjian Wuxiang, Gongjian Hutong; 恭俭胡同5巷5号; mains ¥30-60; ⏰11.30am-2pm & 5.30-9.30pm) Tucked away in the *hútòng* running alongside the east wall of Běihǎi Park, this intriguing restaurant is located inside one of the city's former royal ice houses – where, before the days of refrigeration, massive blocks of ice were stored for use in the imperial court during summer.

 Drinking

There are three top spots for a night out in Běijīng (and others you can explore). **Sānlǐtún** (三里屯), loud, brash and

Ghost Street

Hopping at weekends and one of Běijīng's busiest and most colourful restaurant strips at virtually any hour, **Ghost St** (簋街; Guǐ Jiē) is the English nickname for this spirited section of Dongzhimennei Dajie, where scores of restaurants converge to feed legions of locals and out-of-towners. It's always open so you'll always be able to get fed. Take the subway to Běixīnqiáo, and walk east.

relatively expensive, is where expats and Chinese party-goers come when they want to drink all night long.

Dōngchéng North is a more laid back area than Sānlǐtún with its historic *hútòng* housing smaller bars – some in converted courtyards – that are better for a drink and a chat, rather than a dance.

At **Hòuhǎi Lakes** (后海) there's a noisy but undoubtedly fun strip of bars, located attractively on the banks of Hòuhǎi and Qiánhǎi Lakes in Xīchéng North. It's more popular with Chinese drinkers than foreigners, and dead in winter.

Fangjia Hutong (方家胡同), a largely residential lane south of the Confucius Temple, has recently become another drinking hotspot with quirky, laidback bars similar to those found in the Dōngchéng North area.

DRUM TOWER & DŌNGCHÉNG NORTH

Great Leap Brewing   Bar, Brewery

(大跃啤酒, Dàyuè Píjiǔ; Map p82; www.greatleap brewing.com; 6 Doujiao Hutong, 豆角胡同6号; beer per pint ¥25-50; ⏰2pm-midnight; Ⓢ Shicha-hai) Běijīng's original microbrewery, this refreshingly simple courtyard bar, run by American beer enthusiast Carl Setzer, is housed in a hard-to-find, but beautifully renovated, 100-year-old Qing-dynasty

courtyard and serves up a wonderful selection of unique ales made largely from locally sourced ingredients. Sip on familiar favourites such as pale ales and porters or choose from China-inspired tipples such as Honey Ma, a brew made with lip-tingling Sìchuān peppercorns.

El Nido   Bar

(59号酒吧, Wǔshíjiǔ Hào Jiǔbā; Map p82; 59 Fangjia Hutong, 方家胡同59号; beers from ¥10; ⏰6pm-late; Ⓢ Andingmen) Friendly pint-sized bar, with more than 100 types of imported beer. There's no drinks menu; just dive into the fridge and pick out whichever bottles take your fancy. Prices for the foreign beers start at ¥30, while Harbin beer costs just ¥10 a bottle. There's also some imported liquor, including a number of different types of absinthe.

Zá Jiā   Bar

(杂家; Map p82; www.zajia.cc; Hóng Ēn Temple, Doufuchi Hutong, 豆腐池胡同宏恩观; ⏰1pm-2am; Ⓢ Guloudajie) Built into the entrance gate of Hóng Ēn Guàn (宏恩观), a 600-year-old former Taoist temple – most of which is now a household goods market – beautiful Zá Jiā is a cafe by day (coffee from ¥25), bar by night (beer from ¥20). The interior is as cool as it is unique, with split-level seating reaching up into the eaves, and the atmosphere is friendly and relaxed.

Mao Mao Chong Bar   Bar

(毛毛虫, Máo Máo Chóng; Map p82; 12 Banchang Hutong, 板厂胡同12号; beers from ¥35, cocktails ¥40-50; ⏰7pm-midnight, closed Mon & Tue; Ⓢ Nanluoguxiang) This small but lively expat favourite has a rustic interior, good-value cocktails and a no-smoking policy. Its pizzas (¥40 to ¥65) also get rave reviews.

Mài   Bar

(麦; Map p82; 40 Beiluogu Xiang, 北锣鼓巷40号; cocktails from ¥45, beers from ¥30; ⏰6pm-2am; Ⓢ Guloudajie) This area's first proper cocktail bar, Mài is funky, friendly and housed in a beautifully renovated part of an old courtyard building. Most importantly, though, the manager mixes very good cocktails.

Temple of Heaven Park & Dōngchéng South

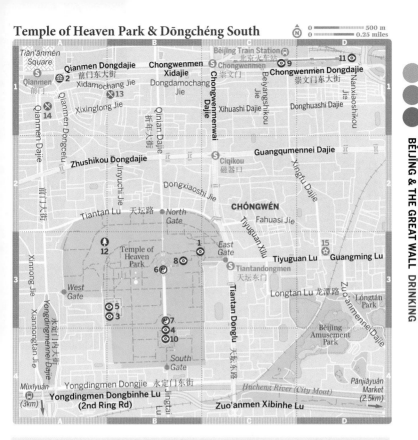

Temple of Heaven Park & Dōngchéng South

◉ Sights

1 Animal Killing Pavilion B3
2 Bĕijīng Railway Museum A1
3 Divine Music Administration B3
4 Echo Wall B4
5 Fasting Palace B3
6 Hall of Prayer for Good Harvests B3
7 Imperial Vault of Heaven B3
8 Long Corridor B3
9 Ming City Wall Ruins Park C1
10 Round Altar B4
11 Southeast Corner Watchtower &
    Red Gate Gallery D1
12 Temple of Heaven Park A3

◆ Eating

13 Lìqún Roast Duck Restaurant B1
14 Qiánmén Quánjùdé Roast Duck
    Restaurant A1

◆ Entertainment

15 Red Theatre D3

SĀNLǏTÚN & CHÁOYÁNG

Apothecary   Cocktail Bar
(酒术, Jiǔ Shù; Map p86; ☏5208 6040; www.
apothecarychina.com; 3rd fl Nali Patio, 81 Sanlitunbei
Lu, 三里屯北路81号那里花园3层; cocktails from
¥65; ◷6pm-late; 🛜; 🅂Tuanjiehu) A candidate
for the city's best cocktail bar, Apothecary's
blend of lovingly mixed drinks – including
ingenious in-house creations – and a
sophisticated but laid-back atmosphere has
spawned an increasing number of imitators
around town. Few, though, can match Apothecary's attention to detail – the history of
each drink is detailed on the menu – or the
quality of the cocktails.

101

Below: Běijīng opera performer; **Right:** Performance at the Mao Livehouse

Migas Bar Bar
(米家思, **Mǐ Jiā Sī; Map p86; ☎5208 6061; 6th fl Nali Patio, 81 Sanlitunbei Lu,** 三里屯北路**81**号那里花园**6**层**; beer from ¥30, cocktails from ¥60, mains from ¥98; ⏰noon-2.30pm & 6-10.30pm, bar 6pm-late; 📶; S Tuanjiehu)** A good-quality Spanish restaurant, cosy bar and enticing roof terrace are three reasons why Migas remains one of the most popular venues in the area. During summer, the terrace offers cocktails and city views and is jammed at weekends. There are DJs on Fridays and live music on Tuesdays, while the separate restaurant is almost as busy most evenings.

✪ Entertainment

FORBIDDEN CITY & DŌNGCHÉNG CENTRAL

Forbidden City Concert Hall Classical Music
(中山公园音乐堂, **Zhōngshān Gōngyuán Yīnyuè Táng; Map p70; ☎6559 8285; Zhōngshān Park,** 中山公园内**; tickets ¥30-880; ⏰performances 7.30pm; S Tiān'ānmén West)** Located on the eastern side of Zhōngshān Park, this is a wonderfully romantic venue for performances of classical and traditional Chinese music. It's also the best acoustically.

DRUM TOWER & DŌNGCHÉNG NORTH

Jiāng Hú Live Music
(江湖酒吧, **Jiāng Hú Jiǔbā; Map p82; 7 Dongmianhua Hutong,** 东棉花胡同7号**; admission ¥30-50; ⏰7pm-2am, closed Mon; S Nanluoguxiang)** One of the coolest places to hear Chinese indie and rock bands, Jiāng Hú, run by a trombone-playing, music-loving manager, is housed in a small courtyard and packs in the punters on a good night. Intimate, cool, and a decent spot for a drink in a courtyard, even when no bands are playing. Beers from ¥25.

Yúgōng Yíshān Live Music
(愚公移山**; Map p82; ☎6404 2711; www.yugongyishan.com; 3-2 Zhangzizhong Lu, West Courtyard,** 张自忠路**3-2,** 号段祺瑞执政府旧址西院;

admission from ¥50; ⏰7pm-2am; S Zhangzizhonglu) Reputedly one of the most haunted places in Běijīng, this historic building has been home to Qing-dynasty royalty, warlords and the occupying Japanese army in the 1930s. You could probably hear the ghosts screaming if it wasn't for the array of local and foreign bands, solo artists and DJs who take to the stage here every week.

Mao Livehouse Live Music
(光芒, Guāngmáng; Map p82; 111 Gulou Dongdajie, 鼓楼东大街111号; admission from ¥60, beers from ¥20; ⏰8pm-late; S Shichahai) This midsized venue, opposite the northern entrance to Nanluogu Xiang, is large enough to give the many gigs it hosts a sense of occasion, but small enough to feel intimate. The decor is functional and the sound tight. All sorts of bands play here, but if they're from overseas, the entrance price can be sky-high.

TEMPLE OF HEAVEN PARK & DŌNGCHÉNG SOUTH

Red Theatre Acrobatics
(红剧场, Hóng Jùchǎng; Map p101; ☎6714 2473; 44 Xingfu Dajie, 幸福大街44号; tickets ¥200-680; ⏰performances 5.15pm & 7.30pm; S Tiantandongmen) The daily show here is *The Legend of Kung Fu,* which follows one boy's journey to becoming a warrior monk. Slick, high-energy fight scenes are interspersed with more soulful dance sequences, as well as plenty of 'how do they do that' balancing on spears and other body-defying acts. To find the theatre, look for the all-red exterior set back from the road.

SĀNLǏTÚN & CHÁOYÁNG

Vics Club
(威克斯, Wēikèsī; Map p86; ☎5293 0333; Workers Stadium, North Gate, Gongrentiyuchang Beilu, 工人体育场北路，工人体育场北门; entry Sun-Thu ¥50, Fri & Sat ¥100; ⏰8.30pm-5am; S Dongsi Shitiao) Not the most sophisticated nightclub, but a favourite with the young (and older and sleazy) crowd for many years now, which makes it some sort of an institution. The tunes are mostly standard R&B and hip-hop and there's an infamous ladies night on Wednesdays (free drinks for women before midnight). If you can't score here, you never will.

BĚIHĂI PARK & XĪCHÉNG NORTH

East Shore Jazz Café Jazz
(东岸, Dōng'àn; Map p89; ☎8403 2131; 2 Shichahai Nanyan, 地安门外大街 什刹海南沿2号楼
2层, 地安门邮局西侧, 2nd fl; beers from ¥30,
cocktails from ¥45; ☺3pm-2am; Ⓢ Shichahai)
Cui Jian's saxophonist, whose quartet
plays here, opened this chilled venue just
off Di'anmen Waidajie and next to Qiánhǎi
Lake. It's a place to hear the best local
jazz bands, with live performances from
Wednesdays to Sundays (from 10pm), in a
laid-back, comfortable atmosphere.

DASHILAR & XĪCHÉNG SOUTH

Húguǎng Guild Hall Peking Opera
(湖广会馆, Húguǎng Huìguǎn; Map p93; ☎6351
8284; 3 Hufang Lu, 虎坊桥路3号; tickets
¥180-680, opera museum ¥10; ☺performances
8pm, opera museum 9am-5pm; Ⓢ Caishikou)
The most historic and atmospheric place
in town for a night of Peking opera. The
interior is magnificent, coloured in red,
green and gold, and decked out with tables
and a stone floor, while balconies surround
the canopied stage. Opposite the theatre
there's a very small opera museum
displaying operatic scores, old catalogues
and other paraphernalia.

Tiānqiáo Acrobatics Theatre Acrobatics
(天桥杂技剧场, Tiānqiáo Zájì Jùchǎng; Map p93;
☎6303 7449; 95 Tianqiao Shichang Lu Jie, 天桥
市场街95号; tickets ¥180-380; ☺performances
5.30pm & 7.15pm; Ⓢ Taranting) West of the
Temple of Heaven Park, this 100-year-old
theatre offers one of Běijīng's best acrobatic displays, a one-hour show performed by
the Běijīng Acrobatic Troupe. Less touristy
than the other venues, the theatre's small
size means you can get very close to the
action. The high-wire display is awesome.
The entrance is down the eastern side of
the building.

SUMMER PALACE & HĂIDIÀN

Propaganda Club
(Map p64; ☎8286 3991; Huaqing Jiayuan, 华
清嘉园; ☺8.30pm-5.30am; Ⓢ Wudaokou)
Wǔdàokǒu's student crew are drawn to

Dolls

FELIX RIOUX/GETTY IMAGES ©

LONELY PLANET/GETTY IMAGES ©

⭐ Don't Miss
National Centre for the Performing Arts (NCPA)

Critics have compared this building to an egg (although it looks more like a massive mercury bead), while modernists love it to bits. The NCPA, also known as the National Grand Theatre, is a surreal location in which to catch a show.

NEED TO KNOW
国家大剧院, Guójiā Dàjùyuàn; Map p89; ☎ 6655 0000; www.chncpa.org/ens; admission ¥30, concert tickets ¥100-400; ⊗9am-5pm Tue-Sun; Ⓢ Tiān'ānmén West

this unprepossessing but long-running club for its cheap drinks, hip-hop sounds and the chance for cultural exchange with the locals. Entry is free. It's 100m north of the east gate of Huaqing Jiayuan.

🔒 Shopping

With much of the nation's wealth concentrated in Běijīng, shopping has become the favourite pastime of the young and the rising middle class in recent years.

FORBIDDEN CITY & DŌNGCHÉNG CENTRAL

Wangfujing Dajie   Shopping Street
(王府井; Map p74; Ⓢ Wangfujing) Prestigious, but these days rather old-fashioned, this part-pedestrianised shopping street not far from Tiān'ānmén Sq, is generally known as Wángfǔjǐng. It boasts a strip of stores selling well-known, midrange brands, and a number of tacky souvenir outlets. At its south end, **Oriental Plaza** is a top-quality, modern shopping mall. Further north, just before the pedestrianised

DAN HERRICK/GETTY IMAGES ©

⭐ Don't Miss
Pānjiāyuán Market

Hands down the best place in Běijīng to shop for *yìshù* (arts), *gōngyì* (crafts) and *gǔwán* (antiques). Some stalls open every day, but the market is at its biggest and most lively on weekends, when you can find everything from calligraphy, Cultural Revolution memorabilia and cigarette ad posters, to Buddha heads, ceramics, Qing dynasty–style furniture and Tibetan carpets.

NEED TO KNOW

潘家园古玩市场, Pānjiāyuán Gǔwán Shìchǎng; Map p64; West of Panjiayuan Qiao, 潘家园桥西侧; ⏰8.30am-6pm Mon-Fri, 4.30pm-6pm Sat & Sun; ⑤Panjiayuan

section ends, is the well-stocked **Foreign Languages Bookstore**.

DRUM TOWER & DŌNGCHÉNG NORTH

Nanluogu Xiang Shopping Street
(南锣鼓巷; Map p82; ⑤Nanluoguxiang) The wildly popular historical *hútòng* of Nanluogu Xiang contains an eclectic mix of clothes and gifts, sold in trendy boutique shops, alongside dozens of cute cafes, bars and restaurants. It's an extremely pleasant

place to shop for souvenirs, but avoid summer weekends if you can, when it gets unfeasibly busy.

SĀNLĬTÚN & CHÁOYÁNG

Sānlĭtún Village Shopping Mall
(Map p86; 19 Sanlitun Lu, 三里屯路19号; ⏰10am-10pm; ⑤Tuanjiehu) This eye-catching collection of midsized malls is a shopping and architectural highlight of this part of the city. The Village – known officially as Taikooli (Tàigǔlǐ; 太古里) – looms over what was once a seedy strip of dive bars

and has transformed the area into a hot-spot for locals and foreigners alike. There are two parts to the complex (Map p86), **South Village** and **North Village**.

Bookworm
Cafe $$

(书虫, Shūchóng; Map p86; 📞6586 9507; www.beijingbookworm.com; Bldg 4, Nansanlitun Lu, 南三里屯路4号楼; mains from ¥60; ⏰9am-midnight; 📶; Ⓢ Tuanjiehu) A combination of a bar, cafe, restaurant and library, the Bookworm is a Běijīng institution and one of the epicentres of the capital's literary life. Much more than just an upmarket cafe, there are 16,000-plus books here you can browse while sipping your coffee. The food is reasonably priced, if uninspired, but there's a decent wine list.

Shard Box Store
Jewellery

(慎德阁, Shèndégé; Map p86; 📞8561 8358; 4 Ritan Beilu, 日坛北路4号; ⏰9am-7pm; Ⓢ Dongdaqiao) Using porcelain fragments from Ming- and Qing-dynasty vases that were destroyed during the Cultural Revolution, this fascinating family-run store creates beautiful and unique shard boxes, bottles and jewellery. The boxes range from the tiny (¥25), for storing rings or cufflinks, to the large (¥780). It also repairs and sells jewellery, mostly sourced from Tibet and Mongolia.

Silk Market
Clothing, Souvenirs

(秀水市场; Xiùshuǐ Shìchǎng; Map p86; 14 Dongdaqiao Lu; 东大桥路14号; ⏰9.30am-9pm; Ⓢ Yong'anli) The six-storey Silk Market is more upmarket than it once was, but remains jammed with fake clothing, bags, electronics and jewellery, despite some vendors being hit by lawsuits from top-name brands tired of being counterfeited on such a huge scale. The silk, which you'll find on the 3rd floor, is one of the few genuine items on sale here.

Sānlǐtún Yashow Clothing Market
Clothing, Souvenirs

(三里屯雅秀服装市场; Sānlǐtún Yǎxiù Fúzhuāng Shìchǎng; Map p86; 58 Gongrentiyuchang Beilu; 工体北路58号; ⏰10am-8.30pm; Ⓢ Tuanjiehu) Five floors of anything you might need and a favourite with expats and visitors. Basement: shoes, handbags and suitcases. Big Shoes is useful if you're struggling to find suitably sized footwear. First floor: coats and jackets. Second floor: shirts, suits and ladies wear. Third floor: silk, clothes. Fourth floor: carpets, fabrics, jewellery, souvenirs and toys. Bargain hard here.

DASHILAR & XĪCHÉNG SOUTH

Liulichang Xijie
Antiques

(琉璃厂, Liúlíchǎng) Běijīng's premier antique street, not far west of Dashilar, is worth wandering along for its quaint, albeit dressed-up, age-old village atmosphere and (largely fake) antiques. Alongside ersatz Qing monochrome bowls and Cultural Revolution kitsch, you can also rummage through old Chinese books, paintings, brushes, ink and paper.

Prepare yourself for pushy sales staff and stratospheric prices. If you want a chop (carved seal) made, you can do it here. At the western end of Liulichang Xijie, a collection of ramshackle stalls flog bric-a-brac, Buddhist statuary, Cultural Revolution pamphlets and posters, fake Tang-dynasty *sāncǎi* (three-colour porcelain), shoes for bound feet, silks, handicrafts, Chinese kites, swords, walking sticks, door knockers, etc.

Con 'Artists' & Tea Merchants

Beware of pesky 'art students' and English students around Wangfujing Dajie, Tiān'ānmén Sq and other tourist areas. They drag Western visitors to exhibitions of overpriced art or extortionate tea ceremonies; the latter may cost ¥2000 or more. If approached by over-friendly girls wanting to speak English, refuse to go to a place of their choosing.

ℹ Information

Maps

English-language maps of Běijīng can be grabbed for free at most big hotels and branches of the Běijīng Tourist Information Center.

Medical Services

International SOS (国际SOS医务诊所, Guójì SOS Yīwù Zhěnsuǒ; Map p64; 🖉 24hr alarm centre 6462 9100, clinic appointments 6462 9199, dental appointments 6462 0333; www.internationalsos.com; Suite 105, Wing 1, Kunsha Bldg, 16 Xinyuanli, off Xin Donglu, Cháoyáng; ⊙9am-8pm Mon-Fri, 9am-6pm Sat & Sun) Offering 24-hour emergency medical care, with a high-quality clinic with English-speaking staff. Dental check up ¥930; medical consultation ¥1240.

Money

ATMs (取款机; qǔkuǎnjī) accepting international cards are in abundance, including at the airport.

Foreign currency and travellers cheques can be changed at large branches of the Bank of China, CITIC Industrial Bank, Industrial & Commercial Bank of China (ICBC), HSBC, the airport and hotel money-changing counters.

Public Security Bureau

PSB Main Office (北京公安局出入境管理处, Běijīngshì Gōng'ānjú Chūrùjìng Guǎnlǐchù;

Map p64; 🖉 8402 0101, 8401 5292; 2 Andingmen Dongdajie, Dōngchéng; ⊙8.30am-4.30pm Mon-Sat) The Foreign Affairs Branch of the local PSB – the police force – handles visa extensions. The visa office is on the 2nd floor, accessed from the north second ring road. You can also apply for a residence permit here.

Tourist Information

Hotels often have tourist information desks, but the best travel advice for independent travellers is usually dished out at youth hostels.

Běijīng Tourist Information Centers (北京旅游咨询, Běijīng Lǚyóu Zīxún Fúwù Zhōngxīn; ⊙9am-5pm) Běijīng train station (Map p74; 🖉 6528 4848; 16 Laoqianju Hutong) Capital Airport (🖉 6459 8148; Terminal 3, Capital Airport) Wangfujing Dajie (Map p74; 269 Wangfujing Dajie, 王府井大街269号, Wángfǔjǐng; ⊙9am-9pm) English skills are limited and information is basic, but you can grab a free tourist map of town and handfuls of free literature; some offices also have train ticket offices.

ℹ Getting There & Away

As the nation's capital, getting to Běijīng is straightforward. Rail and air connections link the city to virtually every point in China, and fleets of buses head to abundant destinations from Běijīng.

Běijīng south train station (p110)

Taken for a Ride

A well-established illegal taxi operation at the airport attempts to lure weary travellers into a ¥300-plus ride to the city, so be on your guard. If anyone approaches you offering a taxi ride, ignore them and insist on joining the queue for a taxi outside.

Air

Běijīng has direct air connections to most major cities in the world.

Daily flights connect Běijīng to every major city in China. There should be at least one flight a week to smaller cities throughout China.

For good deals, check the following websites:

C-trip (www.ctrip.com)

eLong (www.elong.net)

Travel Zen (www.travelzen.com)

eBookers (www.ebookers.com)

If for some reason you can't get online, you can also purchase tickets in person at the Civil Aviation Administration of China (中国民航, Zhōngguó Mínháng, Aviation Bldg, 民航营业大厦, Mínháng Yíngyè Dàshà; Map p89; ☏ 6656 9118, domestic 6601 3336, international 6601 6667; 15 Xichang'an Jie; ⏱ 8.30am-6pm).

You can make enquiries for all airlines at Běijīng's Capital Airport (p111). Call ☏ 6454 1100 for information on international and domestic arrivals and departures.

Bus

No international buses serve Běijīng, but there are plenty of long-distance domestic routes from the city's numerous long-distance bus stations.

Sìhuì long-distance bus station (四惠长途汽车站; Sìhuì chángtú qìchēzhàn) is in the east of town, 200m east of Sihui subway station. Destinations include:

Chéngdé 承德 ¥56 to ¥74, four hours, frequent (5.10am to 5.30pm)

Liùlǐqiáo long-distance bus station (六里桥长途站; Liùlǐqiáo chángtúzhàn) is in the southwest

of town, one subway stop from Běijīng West Train Station. Destinations include:

Chéngdé 承德 ¥85, 4 hours, frequent (5.40am to 6.40pm)

Dàtóng 大同 ¥100 to ¥132, 4½ hours, frequent (7.10am to 6pm)

Luòyáng 洛阳 ¥129 to ¥149, 10 hours, six daily (8.30am to 10pm)

Shíjiāzhuāng 石家庄 ¥75 to ¥90, 3½ hours, frequent (6.30am to 8.55pm)

Xī'ān 西安 ¥259, 12 hours, one daily (5.45pm)

Zhèngzhōu 郑州 ¥129 to ¥149, 8½ hours, nine daily (8.30am to 8.30pm)

Train

Increasingly, ticket sellers at the three main stations speak a bit of English, but don't bank on it.

Almost all hotels and hostels can buy train tickets for you, for a small commission, of course. Official train ticket offices (火车票代售处; huǒchēpiào dàishòuchù) are dotted around town and charge a very reasonable ¥10 commission per ticket.

China DIY Travel (www.china-diy-travel.com; commission $10 per ticket) is transparent and reliable, and can pre-book train tickets for you, China-wide.

Běijīng train station (北京站; Běijīng Zhàn) is the most central of Běijīng's four main train stations, and is linked to the subway system.

Typical fares (hard sleeper unless indicated) include:

Dàtóng 大同 K-series, ¥99 to ¥107, six hours (frequent)

Shànghǎi 上海 T-series, soft-sleeper ¥476 to ¥497, 14 hours (7.33pm)

Běijīng west train station (西站; Xī Zhàn) is gargantuan, accommodating fast Z series trains, such as the following (fares are soft-sleeper unless indicated):

Lánzhōu 兰州 Z- and T-series, hard-sleeper ¥322 to ¥388, 17 hours (five trains daily)

Xī'ān 西安 G-series, 2nd-class seat ¥515, five to six hours (seven trains daily)

Xī'ān 西安 Z- and T-series, hard-sleeper ¥254 to ¥288, 11 to 12 hours (eight trains daily)

Detour:
Fragrant Hills Park & Botanic Gardens

Within striking distance of the Summer Palace are Běijīng's Western Hills (西山; Xī Shān), another former villa-resort of the emperors.

The section closest to Běijīng is known as **Fragrant Hills Park** (香山公园, Xiāng Shān Gōngyuán; summer/winter ¥10/5, through ticket ¥15; ⏱6am-7pm; 🚌331, Ⓢ Xiyuan or Yuanmingyuan). Scramble up the slopes to the top of **Incense-Burner Peak** (Xiānglú Fēng), or take the **chairlift** (one way/return ¥60/120, 9.30am to 3.30pm).

From the peak there's an all-encompassing view of the countryside, and you can leave the crowds behind by hiking further into the Western Hills. Běijīngers flock here in autumn when the maple leaves saturate the hillsides in great splashes of red.

Near the north gate of Fragrant Hills Park, but still within the park, is the excellent **Azure Clouds Temple** (Bìyún Sì; adult ¥10; ⏱8am-4.30pm), which dates back to the Yuan dynasty.

About 1km northeast of Fragrant Hills Park and exploding with blossom in spring is the well-tended **Botanic Gardens** (北京植物园, Běijīng Zhíwùyuán; adult ¥5; through ticket ¥50; ⏱6am-8pm summer (last entry 7pm), 7.30am-5pm winter (last entry 4pm); 🚌331, Ⓢ Xiyuan or Yuanmingyuan). Containing a rainforest house, the standout **Běijīng Botanical Gardens Conservatory** (Běijīng Zhíwùyuán Wēnshì; admission with through ticket; ⏱8am-4.30pm) bursts with 3000 different varieties of plants.

About a 15-minute walk from the front gate (follow the signs), but within the grounds of the gardens, is the **Sleeping Buddha Temple** (Wòfó Sì; adult ¥5, or entry with through ticket; ⏱8am-4.30pm summer, 8.30am-4pm winter). The temple, first built during the Tang dynasty, houses a huge reclining effigy of Sakyamuni weighing 54 tonnes.

At the time of writing it was expected that sometime after 2015 the subway will extend here via the Summer Palace and Botanic Gardens.

Kowloon (Hong Kong) 九龙 ¥584 to ¥611, 24 hours (train Q97, 1.08pm)

Other typical train fares for hard-sleeper tickets include:

Chéngdū 成都 T- and K-series, ¥389 to ¥486, 26 to 31 hours (9am, 11.08am, 6.29pm and 9.52pm)

Chóngqìng 重庆 T- and K-class trains, ¥389 to ¥456, 25 to 30 hours (five daily)

Guǎngzhōu 广州 T- and K-class trains, ¥426 to ¥456, 21 hours (five daily)

Guìyáng 贵阳 T- and K-series, ¥465 to ¥487, 29 hours (3.58pm and 4.57pm)

Kūnmíng 昆明 T-series, ¥536 to ¥575, 38 hours (06.26am and 4.31pm)

Ürümqi 乌鲁木齐 T-series, ¥536 to ¥585, 34 hours (10.01am and 3.18pm)

Yíchāng 宜昌 K-series, ¥310 to ¥331, 21½ hours (11.11pm)

Běijīng south train station (南站; Nán Zhàn) is ultra modern, accommodating very high speed 'bullet' trains to destinations such as Tiānjīn, Shànghǎi, Hángzhōu and Qīngdǎo. Sample fares:

Hángzhōu 杭州 G-series, 2nd-class seat ¥538 to ¥629, six hours (frequent)

Qīngdǎo 青岛 G- and D-series, 2nd-class seat ¥249 to ¥314, five hours (frequent)

Shànghǎi (Hóngqiáo station) 上海虹桥 G-class trains, 2nd-class seat, ¥553, 5½ hours (frequent)

Sūzhōu 苏州 G-series, 2nd-class seat ¥523, five hours (frequent)

Běijīng north train station (北站; Běi Zhàn) is a short walk north of Xizhimen subway station, and is much smaller. Destinations include:

Bādálǐng Great Wall 八达岭 Hard-seat ¥6, 75 minutes (frequent)

ℹ Getting Around

To/From Capital Airport

The **Airport Express** (机场快轨, jīchǎng kuàiguǐ; Map p86; one way ¥25), also written as ABC (Airport Běijīng City), is quick and convenient and links Terminals 2 and 3 to Běijīng's subway system at Sanyuanqiao station (Line 10) and Dongzhimen station (Lines 2 and 13). Trains leave every few minutes. Train times are as follows: Terminal 3 (6.21am to 10.51pm); Terminal 2 (6.35am to 11.10pm); Dōngzhímén (6am to 10.30pm).

A taxi (using its meter) should cost ¥80 to ¥100 from the airport to the city centre, including the ¥10 airport expressway toll; bank on 30 minutes to one hour to get into town. Join the taxi ranks and ignore approaches from drivers. When you get into the taxi, make sure the driver uses the meter (打表; dǎ biǎo). It is also useful to have the name of your hotel written down in Chinese to show the driver. Very few drivers speak English.

There are 11 different routes for the airport **shuttle bus** (机场巴士, jīchǎng bāshì; one way ¥15-24) including those listed below. They all leave from all three terminals and run from around 5am to midnight.

Line 1 To Fāngzhuāng (方庄), via Dàbéiyáo (大北窑) for the CBD (国贸; guó mào)

Line 3 To Běijīng train station (北京站; Běijīng Zhàn), via Dōngzhímén (东直门), Dōngsìshítiáo (东四十条) and Cháoyángmén (朝阳门)

Line 7 To Běijīng west train station (西站; Xī Zhàn)

Line 10 To Běijīng south train station (南站; Nán Zhàn)

To/From Nányuàn Airport

The very small **Nányuàn Airport** (南苑机场, Nányuàn Jīchǎng, NAY; ☏6797 8899; Jingbeixi Lu, Nányuàn Zhèn, Fēngtái District, 丰台区南苑镇警备西路, 警备东路口) south of the city, feels more like a provincial bus station than an airport, but it does service quite a few domestic routes.

The **shuttle bus** (机场巴士; jīchǎng bāshì) goes to Xīdàn (西单; ¥18; 1½ hours; 9am to last flight arrival), from where you can pick up the subway.

A taxi costs around ¥60 to the Tiān'ānmén Sq area.

Subway

Massive, and getting bigger every year, the **Běijīng subway system** (地铁, dìtiě; www.bjsubway.com; per trip ¥2; ⊙6am-11pm) is modern, easy to use and cheap. Get hold of a **travel card** (交通一卡通, jiāotōng yīkǎtōng; refundable deposit ¥20) if you don't fancy queuing for tickets each time you travel. The card won't make subway trips any cheaper, although it will get you a 60% discount on all bus journeys within the municipality of Běijīng.

Taxi

Taxis (出租车; chūzūchē) are everywhere, although finding one can be a problem during rush hour and rainstorms.

Flag fall is ¥13, and lasts for three kilometres. After that it's ¥2 per kilometre. Drivers also add a small flat-rate fuel surcharge (usually ¥1). Rates increase slightly at night.

Drivers rarely speak any English so it is important to have the name and address of where you want to go written down in Chinese characters. And always remember to keep your hotel's business card on you so you can get home easily at the end of the night.

By law, taxi drivers must use their meter (打表; dǎ biǎo). If they refuse, get out and find another cab to catch. The exception is for long, out-of-town trips to, for example, the Great Wall, where prices are agreed (but not paid for!) beforehand.

Car

The Vehicle Administration Office (p412) on the 1st floor of Terminal 3 at Běijīng's Capital Airport – look out for the 'Traffic Police' sign – issues temporary driving licences for use within the Běijīng municipality.

Applicants must be between the ages of 18 and 70 and must hold a temporary Chinese visa (of three months or less). The straightforward procedure takes about 30 minutes and costs ¥10.

Bus

Běijīng's buses (公共汽车; gōnggòng qìchē) have always been numerous and dirt cheap (from ¥1), but they're now becoming easier to use for non-Chinese-speaking visitors, with swipe cards, announcements in English, and bus stop signs written in Pīnyīn as well as Chinese characters.

If you use a travel card, you get 60% discount on all journeys. Useful routes include:

2 Qianmen, north on Dongdan Beidajie, Dongsi Nandajie, Dongsi Beidajie, Lama Temple, Zhonghua Minzu Yuan (Ethnic Minorities Park), Asian Games Village

Taxis and Car Hire

Miles Meng (📞137 1786 1403; www.beijingenglishdriver.com) Friendly, reliable, English-speaking driver. See his blog for prices.

Mr Sun (孙先生, Sūn Xiānsheng; 📞136 5109 3753) Only speaks Chinese but is reliable and can find other drivers if he's busy. Round trips to the Wall from ¥600.

Hertz (赫兹, Hèzī; Map p86; 📞5739 2000, 800 988 1336; www.hertz.cn; ⏰8am-8pm Mon-Fri, 9am-6pm Sat-Sun) Has an office at Terminal 3 of Běijīng airport. Self-drive hire cars (自驾; *zìjià*) from ¥230 per day, with ¥10,000 deposit. Car with driver (代驾; *dàijià*) from ¥660 per day.

5 Déshèngmén, Di'anmen, Běihǎi Park, Xihuamen, Zhongshan Park, Qianmen

20 Běijīng south train station, Tiānqiáo, Dashilar, Tiān'ānmén Sq, Wángfǔjǐng, Dongdan, Běijīng train station

52 Běijīng west train station, Muxidi, Fuxingmen, Xīdān, Gate of Heavenly Peace, Dongdan, Běijīng train station, Jianguomen

103 Běijīng train station, Dengshikou, China Art Gallery, Forbidden City (north entrance), Běihǎi Park, Fuchengmen, Běijīng Zoo

AROUND BĚIJĪNG

Ming Tombs 十三陵

The Unesco-protected Ming Tombs (十三陵; Shísān Líng) is the final resting place for 13 of the 16 Ming-dynasty emperors and makes for a fascinating half-day trip. The scattered tombs – each a huge temple-like complex, guarding an enormous burial mound at its rear – back onto the southern slopes of Tiānshòu Mountain. Only three of the 13 tombs are open to the public, and only one has had its underground burial chambers excavated, but what you are able to see is impressive, and leaves you wondering just how many priceless treasures must still be buried here.

Cháng Líng (长陵; admission ¥50, audio guide ¥50), the resting place of the first of the 13 emperors to be buried here, contains the body of Emperor Yongle (1360–1424), his wife and 16 concubines, and is the largest, most impressive and most important of the tombs. Seated upon a three-tiered marble terrace, the standout structure in the complex is the **Hall of Eminent Favours** (灵恩殿; Líng'ēn Diàn), containing a recent statue of Yongle, various artefacts excavated from Dìng Líng, and a breathtaking interior with vast *nánmù* (cedar wood) columns. You can climb the **Soul Tower** (明楼; Míng Lóu) at the back of the complex for fine views of the surrounding hills.

Dìng Líng (定陵; admission ¥65, audio guide ¥50), the resting place of Emperor Wanli (1563–1620) and his wife and concubines, is at first less impressive than Cháng Líng because many of the halls and gateways have been destroyed. But this is the only tomb where you can climb down into the burial chambers.

Zhāo Líng (昭陵; admission ¥35) is the smallest of the three, and many of its buildings are recent rebuilds. The tomb, which is the resting place of Emperor Longqing (1537–1572), is located at the end of the small and eerily quiet village of Zhāolíng Cūn (昭陵村).

Spirit Way (神道; Shéndào; admission ¥35) is the original road leading to the tombs. Commencing from the south with a triumphal triple archway, known as the **Great Palace Gate** (大宫门; Dàgōng Mén), the road (now a pedestrianised pathway) passes through **Stele Pavilion** (碑亭; Bēi Tíng), which contains a giant *bìxì* bearing the largest stelae in China. A guard of 12 sets of stone animals and officials awaits.

ℹ️ Getting There & Away

Bus 872 (¥9, one hour, 7.10am-7.10pm) leaves regularly from the north side of the **Déshèngmén Gateway** (德胜门) and passes all the sights, apart from Zhāo Líng, before terminating at Cháng Líng, the main tomb. Last bus back is at 6pm.

It's easy to bus-hop once you're here: get off the 872 at Da Gong Men (大宫门) bus stop, and walk through the triple-arched Great Palace Gate (大宫门) that leads to Spirit Way. After walking the length of Spirit Way, catch bus 67 from Hu Zhuang (胡庄) bus stop (the first bus stop on your right) to its terminus at Zhāo Líng (¥1); walk straight on through the village to find the tomb. Then, coming back the way you came, catch another 67, or walk (2km; left at the end of the road, then left again) to Dìng Líng, from where you can catch bus 314 to Cháng Líng (¥1).

THE GREAT WALL
长城

China's greatest engineering triumph and must-see sight, the Great Wall (长城; Wànlǐ Chángchéng) wriggles haphazardly from its scattered Manchurian remains in Liáoníng province to wind-scoured rubble in the Gobi desert and faint traces in the unforgiving sands of Xīnjiāng.

The most renowned and robust examples undulate majestically over the peaks and hills of Běijīng municipality –

and these are the sections we focus on in this chapter – but the Great Wall can be realistically visited in many northern China provinces.

GREAT WALL HISTORY

The 'original' wall was begun more than 2000 years ago during the Qin dynasty (221–207 BC), when China was unified under Emperor Qin Shi Huang. Separate walls that had been constructed by independent kingdoms to keep out marauders were linked together. The effort required hundreds of thousands of workers, many of whom were political prisoners, and 10 years of hard labour under General Meng Tian.

Ming engineers made determined efforts to revamp the eroding bastion, facing it with some 60 million cubic metres of bricks and stone slabs.

Mao Zedong encouraged the use of the wall as a source of free building material, a habit that continues unofficially today.

Without its cladding, lengthy sections have dissolved to dust and the barricade might have vanished entirely without the tourist industry.

Spirit Way, Ming Tombs

TIM GRAHAM/GETTY IMAGES ©

VISITING THE WALL

Tours run by hostels, or by specialist tour companies, are far preferable to those run by ordinary hotels or state-run travel companies, as they tend to cater more to the needs of adventurous Western travellers and don't come with any hidden extras, such as a side-trip to the Ming Tombs (a common add-on) or a tiresome diversion to a gem factory or a traditional Chinese medicine centre. Independent companies, which run trips to the wall that we like, include the following:

Běijīng Sideways   Tours
(www.beijingsideways.com) For trips in a motorbike sidecar.

Bespoke Běijīng   Tours
(www.bespokebeijing.com) High-end trips and tours.

Bike Běijīng   Cycling
(康多自行车租赁, Kāngduō Zìxíngchē Zūlìn; Map p74; ☎ 6526 5857; www.bikebeijing.com; 34 Donghuangchenggen Nanjie, 东皇城根南街34 号; ⏰9am-6pm; ⑤China Museum of Art) Rents a range of good-quality bikes, including mountain bikes (¥200), road bikes (¥400)

and ordinary city bikes (¥100), and runs guided bike tours around the city (half-day tours from ¥300 per person) and beyond, including trips to the Great Wall (¥900 to ¥1800 per person).

China Hiking   Tours
(www.chinahiking.cn) Affordable hiking and camping trips run by a Chinese–Belgian couple.

....

Mùtiányù   慕田峪

Mùtiányù (慕田峪; Mùtiányù Chángchéng; adult/student ¥45/25; ⏰7am-6.30pm, winter 7.30am-5.30pm), 90km northeast of Běijīng, is a recently renovated stretch of wall, which sees a lot of tourists and is fairly easy to reach from Běijīng. It's also well set up for families, with a cable car, a chair lift and a hugely popular toboggan ride. Famed for its Ming-era guard towers and excellent views, this 3km-long section of wall is largely a recently restored Ming dynasty structure that was built upon an earlier northern Qi-dynasty edifice.

Mùtiányù section of the Great Wall

EMAD ALJUMAH/GETTY IMAGES ©

Escape To The Great Wall

As well as the usual accommodation options in this Great Wall section the following luxury digs offer some exclusivity beside more remote parts of China's best-known icon.

Commune by the Great Wall (长城脚下的公社, Chángchéng Jiǎoxià de Gōngshè; ☎ 8118 1888; www.communebythegreatwall.com; r from ¥2500; ✹ @ ☎ ⛷) is seriously expensive, but the cantilevered geometric architecture, location and superb panoramas are simply standout. Positioned at the Shuǐguān Great Wall, off the Badaling Hwy, the Kempinski-managed Commune may have a proletarian name but the design and presentation are purely for the affluent. Take out another mortgage and treat yourself – this is the ultimate view, with a room.

Doing its own thing miles from civilisation, **Red Capital Ranch** (新红资避暑山庄, Xīnhóngzī Bìshǔshānzhuāng; ☎ 8401 8886, 8403 5308; www.redcapitalclub.com.cn; 28 Xiaguandi Village, 怀柔县雁栖镇下关地村28号, Yanxi; r from ¥1050 incl breakfast; ✹ @ ⛷) is *the* Běijīng escapist option. Ten individually styled villas are housed in a Manchurian hunting lodge on a 20-acre estate. If the mountain setting – complete with Great Wall remains running through the estate – doesn't dissolve your stress, the Tibetan Tantric Space Spa will.

ℹ Getting To Mùtiányù

From Dongzhimen Wai bus stand (东直门外车站; Dōngzhímén Wài chēzhàn), bus 867 makes a special detour to Mùtiányù twice every morning (¥16, 2½ hours, 7am and 8.30am, 15 March to 15 November only) and returns from Mùtiányù twice each afternoon (2pm and 4pm). Otherwise, you need to go via the town of Huáiróu (怀柔). From Dongzhimen transport hub (Dōngzhímén shūniǔzhàn) take bus 916快 (the character is 'kuài', and means 'fast') to Huáiróu (¥12, one hour, 6.30am to 7.30pm). Get off at Míngzhū Guǎngchǎng (明珠广场) bus stop (ignore touts that try to lure you off the bus before that), then take the first right to find a bunch of minivans waiting to take passengers to Mùtiányù (per person ¥10-20, 30 minutes). Return minivans start drying up from around 6pm. The last 916快 back to Běijīng leaves Huáiróu at around 7pm.

Jiànkòu 箭扣

For stupefyingly gorgeous hikes along perhaps Běijīng's most incomparable section of 'wild wall', head to the rear section of the **Jiànkòu** (后箭扣长城, Hòu Jiànkòu Chángchéng; admission ¥20), accessible from the town of Huáiróu. But this is completely unrestored wall, so it is both dangerous and, strictly speaking, illegal to hike along it. Make sure you wear footwear with very good grips, and never attempt to traverse this section in the rain, particularly during thunderstorms.

From the drop off at Xīzhàzi Village (西栅子村; Xīzhàzi Cūn), it's a one-hour walk uphill to the wall, along a narrow dirt path which climbs through a beautiful pine forest. From here turn east to hike all the way to Mùtiányù (two hours), from where you can easily pick up transport back to Huáiróu, or even to Běijīng.

ℹ Getting To Jiànkòu

From Dongzhimen Transport Hub (Dōngzhímén Shūniǔzhàn) take bus 916快 to Huáiróu (¥11, one hour, 6.30am to 7.30pm). Get off at Nanhuayuan Sanqu (南花园三区) bus stop, then walk straight ahead about 200m (crossing one road), until you get to the next bus stop, which is called Nanhuayuan Siqu (南花园四区). The H21 bus from here to Shuǐ Chángchéng (水长城) stops at Zhuàngdàokǒu (¥8, one hour, every 30 minutes until 6.30pm). The last 916快 bus from Huáiróu back to Běijīng leaves Huáiróu at around 7pm.

Detour:

Chuāndǐxià

Nestled in a valley 90km west of Běijīng and overlooked by towering peaks, the Ming-dynasty village of **Chuāndǐxià** (川底下) is a gorgeous cluster of historic courtyard homes with old-world charm. The backdrop is lovely: terraced orchards and fields with ancient houses and alleyways rising up the hillside. Two hours is more than enough to wander around the village because it's not big, but staying the night allows you to soak up its historic charms without the distraction of all those day-trippers. There are Maoist slogans to track down, and temples in the surrounding hills, but the main attractions here are the courtyard homes and the steps and alleyways that link them up.

Restaurant and guesthouse signs are clearly labelled in English, so places are easy to spot. Your best bet is to simply wander round and find what best suits you. Most restaurants have English menus. Specialities here include walnuts, apricots and roast leg of lamb.

Bus 892 leaves from a bus stop 200m west of Pingguoyuan subway station (come out of Exit D and turn right) and goes to Zhāitáng (斋堂; ¥16, two hours, 6.30am-5.50pm), from where you'll have to take a taxi (¥20) for the last 6km to Chuāndǐxià. The last bus back leaves Zhāitáng at 5pm. If you miss that you're looking at around ¥200 for a taxi back to Pingguoyuan.

Zhuàngdàokǒu 撞道口

The small village of Zhuàngdàokǒu (撞道口), 80km north of Běijīng, and just over the hill from Huánghuā Chéng, has access to a rarely visited and completely unrestored section of 'wild wall'. It's also possible to hike over to Huánghuā Chéng on a restored section from here, although surprisingly few people do this, considering how straightforward it is.

The bus should drop you off at the far end of Zhuàngdàokǒu village, where the road crosses a small stream. Pick up some water and snacks at the small shop near here, then turn right and follow the lane along the stream and then up behind the houses until it meets a rocky pathway that leads up the wall. Once at the wall (20 minutes), turn right for a one-hour walk along a restored, but very steep section of wall that eventually leads down to the road at Huánghuā Chéng, via some fabulous viewpoints. Or turn left to commence a two-hour hike along a crumbling stretch of shrub-covered wall towards Shuǐ Chángchéng. You'll see almost no one on this unrestored section and the going can get tricky, so take extra care here.

ⓘ Getting To Zhuàngdàokǒu

From Dongzhimen Transport Hub (Dōngzhímén Shūniǔzhàn) take bus 916快 to Huáiróu (¥11, one hour, 6.30am to 7.30pm). Get off at Nanhuayuan Sanqu (南花园三区) bus stop, then walk straight ahead about 200m (crossing one road), until you get to the next bus stop, which is called Nanhuayuan Siqu (南花园四区). The H21 bus from here to Shuǐ Chángchéng (水长城) stops at Zhuàngdàokǒu (¥8, one hour, every 30 minutes until 6.30pm). The last 916快 bus from Huáiróu back to Běijīng leaves Huáiróu at around 7pm.

Jīnshānlǐng 金山岭

The **Jīnshānlǐng** (金山岭长城; Jīnshānlǐng Chángchéng; ☏ 0314 883 0222; summer/winter ¥65/55) section of the Great Wall is a completely restored stretch, but it's so far from Běijīng that it sees far fewer tourists than other fully restored sections. It contains some unusual features such as Barrier Walls (walls within the Wall), and each watchtower comes with an inscription, in English, detailing the historic significance of that part of the Wall. Hiking (in either direction) on the restored section of the Wall here is straightforward. There's an east gate and a west gate (about 2km apart), which means you can do a round trip (90 minutes) without backtracking; from the east gate, turn right at the Wall to find the west gate, then right again once back down on the road. If you need it, there's a **cable car** (缆车, lǎn chē; one way/return trip ¥30/50) by the west gate ticket office.

❶ Getting To Jīnshānlǐng

A direct bus takes you from Wangjing West subway station (Line 13) to a point about 30 minutes walk from the Jīnshānlǐng east-gate ticket office. Come out of Exit C of the subway station and look over your right shoulder to see the red sign for the 'Tourist Bus to Jinshanling Great Wall' (金山岭 长城旅游班车; Jīnshānlǐng Chángchéng lǚyóu bānchē), from where there are half-hourly buses to Jīnshānlǐng (¥32, 90 minutes, 7.30am-4pm). From the bus drop-off point (a service station on a highway), walk back under the highway and keep going for about 2km to the east-gate ticket office. Note, when you return (turn right out of the east gate area), the bus will pick up passengers from the same side of the highway it dropped you off at; not from the side which has a police station beside it. Last bus back leaves the service station at 4.20pm.

Bādálǐng 八达岭

The mere mention of its name sends a shudder down the spine of hardcore wall walkers, but **Bādálǐng** (八达岭长城; Bādálǐng Chángchéng; adult/student ¥45/25; ⏰6am-7pm summer, 7am-6pm winter), 70km northwest of Běijīng, is the easiest part of the Wall to get to and as such, if you are really pushed for time, this may be your only option. It ticks all the iffy Great Wall boxes in one flourish: souvenir stalls, T-shirt flogging hawkers, restaurants, heavily restored brickwork, little authenticity, guardrails and mobs of sightseers.

There is a **cable car** (缆车, lǎn chē; one way/return ¥80/100; ⏰8am-4.30pm) as well as disabled access.

❶ Getting To Bādálǐng

Local Bus

The 877 (¥12, one hour, 6am to 5pm) leaves for Bādálǐng from the northern side of the Déshèngmén gateway (德胜门), about 500m east of Jishuitan subway station. It goes to east car park at Bādálǐng. From there, walk uphill a little, turn left through a covered souvenir-shop strip, then left again.

Train

Getting here by train is the cheapest and most enjoyable option. Bādálǐng train station is a 1km-walk downhill from the west car park; come out of the train station and turn left. Morning trains (¥6, 70-80 minutes) leave from Běijīng north train station (北京北站; Běijīng běizhàn), which is connected to Xizhimen subway station, at the following times from Tuesday to Thursday: 6.12am, 8.34am, 10.57am and 12.42pm; and at the following times from Friday to Monday: 6.12am, 7.58am, 9.02am, 10.57am and 1.14pm and 1.35pm.

CHÉNGDÉ 承德

Chéngdé might look like an unremarkable provincial town at first glance, but it has an extraordinary history as the summer playground of the Qing-dynasty emperors.

History

In 1703, when an expedition passed through the Chéngdé valley, Emperor Kangxi was so enamoured with the surroundings that he had a hunting lodge built, which gradually grew into the summer resort. Rèhé – or Jehol (Warm River; named after a hot spring here) – as Chéngdé was then known, grew in importance and the Qing court began to spend more time here, sometimes up to several months a year, with some 10,000 people accompanying the emperor on his seven-day expedition from Běijīng.

The emperors also convened with the border tribes in Chéngdé – undoubtedly more at ease here than in Běijīng – who

Below: Building at the Imperial Villa; **Right:** Bìshǔ Shānzhuāng or the Imperial Villa

(BELOW) CREDIT LINE© HENRY WESTHEIM /GETTY IMAGES ©; (RIGHT) TIBOR BOGNAR/GETTY IMAGES ©

posed the greatest threats to the Qing frontiers: the Mongols, Tibetans, Uighurs and, eventually, Europeans. The resort reached its peak under Emperor Qianlong (r 1735–96), who commissioned many of the outlying temples to overawe visiting leaders.

The Emperor Xianfeng died here in 1861, permanently warping Chéngdé's feng shui and tipping the imperial villa towards long-term decline.

◉ Sights

Skirting the northern and eastern walls of the Bìshǔ Shānzhuāng, the **Eight Outer Temples** (外八庙; *wài bā miào*) were, unusually, designed for diplomatic rather than spiritual reasons. Some were based on actual Tibetan Buddhist monasteries but the emphasis was on appearance: smaller temple buildings are sometimes solid, and the Tibetan facades (with painted windows) are often fronts for traditional Chinese temple interiors. The surviving temples and monasteries were all built between 1713 and 1780; the prominence given to Tibetan Buddhism was as much for the Mongols (fervent Lamaists) as the Tibetan leaders.

Bìshǔ Shānzhuāng   Historic Site
(避暑山庄; Imperial Villa; Lizhengmen Dajie; admission Apr-Oct ¥120, Nov-Mar ¥90; ☺palace 7am-6pm Apr-Oct, 8am-5.30pm Nov-Oct) The imperial summer resort is composed of a main palace complex and vast park-like gardens, all enclosed by a handsome 10km-long wall. The entrance price is steep (as it is with all the main sights in Chéngdé), and it gets packed with tourists here in summer, but the splendid gardens provide ample opportunity to take a quiet walk away from the crowds.

A huge spirit wall shields the resort entrance at Lizhengmen Dajie. Through **Lìzhèng Gate** (丽正门; Lìzhèng Mén), the **Main Palace** (正宫; Zhèng Gōng) is a series of nine courtyards and five elegant, unpainted halls,

with a rusticity complemented by towering pine trees. The wings in each courtyard have various exhibitions (porcelain, clothing, weaponry), and most of the halls are decked out in period furnishings.

The first hall is the refreshingly cool **Hall of Simplicity and Sincerity**, built of an aromatic cedar called *nánmù*, and displaying a carved throne draped in yellow silk. Other prominent halls include the emperor's study (Study of Four Knowledges) and living quarters (Hall of Refreshing Mists and Waves). On the left-hand side of the latter is the imperial bedroom. Two residential areas branch out from here: the empress dowager's **Pine Crane Palace** (松鹤斋; Sōnghè Zhāi), to the east, and the smaller **Western Apartments**, where the concubines (including a young Cixi) resided.

Exiting the Main Palace brings you to the gardens and forested hunting grounds, with landscapes borrowed from famous southern scenic areas in Hángzhōu, Sūzhōu and Jiāxīng, as well as the Mongolian grasslands.

The double-storey **Misty Rain Tower** (烟雨楼; Yānyǔ Lóu), on the northwestern side of the main lake, served as an imperial study. Further north is the **Wénjīn Pavilion** (文津阁; Wénjīn Gé), built in 1773. Don't miss the elegant 250-year-old **Yǒngyòusì Pagoda** (永佑寺塔; Yǒngyòusì Tǎ) which soars above the fragments of its vanished temple in the northeast of the complex.

Most of the compound is taken up by lakes, hills, forests and plains. There are magnificent views of some of the outlying temples from the northern wall.

Just beyond the Main Palace is the start-point for **bus tours of the gardens** (环山车; huánshān chē; one hour, including three short stops; per person ¥50). Further on you'll find a place for **boat-rental** (出租小船; chūzū xiǎochuán; per hr ¥50-90, deposit ¥300).

Almost all of the forested section is closed from November to May because of fire hazard in the dry months, but you can still wander around the rest of the park.

Tourists can exit by any of the gates, but can only buy tickets to enter at Lìzhèng Gate.

119

Pǔtuózōngchéng Temple
Buddhist Temple

(普陀宗乘之庙, **Pǔtuózōngchéng Zhīmiào; Shizigou Lu; admission Apr-Oct ¥80, Nov-Mar ¥60;** 8am-6pm Apr-Oct, 8.30am-5pm Nov-Mar) Chéngdé's largest temple is a not-so-small replica of Lhasa's Potala Palace and houses the nebulous presence of Avalokiteshvara (Guanyin). A marvellous sight on a clear day, the temple's red walls stand out against its mountain backdrop. Enter to a huge stele pavilion, followed by a large triple archway topped with five small stupas in red, green, yellow, white and black.

Temple of Sumeru, Happiness & Longevity
Buddhist Temple

(须弥福寿之庙, **Xūmífúshòu Zhīmiào; Shizigou Lu; admission Apr-Oct ¥80, Nov-Mar ¥60;** 8am-6pm Apr-Oct, 8.30am-5pm Nov-Mar) This huge temple was built in honour of the sixth Panchen Lama, who stayed here in 1781. Incorporating Tibetan and Chinese architectural elements, it's an imitation of the Panchen's home monastery Tashilhunpo in Shigatse, Tibet. Note the eight huge, glinting dragons (each said to weigh over 1000kg) that adorn the roof of the main hall. The admission price includes entry to the neighbouring Pǔtuózōngchéng Temple.

Pǔlè Temple
Buddhist Temple

(普乐寺, **Pǔlè Sì; admission incl Hammer Rock ¥50;** 8am-5.30pm Apr-Oct, 8.30am-4.30pm Nov-Mar) This peaceful temple was built in 1776 for the visits of minority envoys (Kazakhs among them). At the rear of the temple is the unusual Round Pavilion, reminiscent of the Hall of Prayer for Good Harvests at Běijīng's Temple of Heaven Park. Inside is an enormous wooden mandala (a geometric representation of the universe).

Pǔyòu Temple
Buddhist Temple

(普佑寺, **Pǔyòu Sì;** 8am-6pm) Housed within the grounds of Pǔníng Temple, on the east side, this temple is dilapidated and missing its main hall, but it has a plentiful contingent of merry gilded *luóhàn* in the side wings, although a fire in 1964 incinerated many of their confrères. Entry is covered by the ticket for Pǔníng Temple.

Sleeping

Chéngdé has an unremarkable and expensive range of tourist accommodation. Hotel room prices increase at the weekend and during the holiday periods.

Huìlóng Hotel
Hotel $$

(会龙大厦酒店; **Huìlóng Dàshà Jiǔdiàn;** 0314 761 0360, 0314 252 8119; Huilong Plaza, Xinjuzhai, Chezhan Lu, 车站路新居宅会龙大厦; **tw from ¥260;**) Formerly Ming's Dynasty Hostel, this well turned-out budget hotel is good value. It no longer has its youth-hostel perks (common area, reliable travel advice), but some staff do speak English, and the rooms are very comfortable and well-equipped for the price (TV, wi-fi, modern bathroom).

Mountain Villa Hotel
Hotel $$$

(山庄宾馆, **Shānzhuāng Bīnguǎn;** 0314 209 5500; 11 Lizhengmen Dajie, 丽正门路11号; common/standard/deluxe ¥380/780/980;) This huge hotel offers pole position for a trip to Bìshǔ Shānzhuāng. The standard and deluxe rooms are super smart, and are discounted to ¥580 and ¥680 respectively. The common/standard rooms are in a building out the back, but are tattier than cheaper rooms in other hotels.

Eating

Dà Qīng Huā
Dumplings $

(大清花; 241 Chezhan Lu, 车站路241号; **mains from ¥20;** 10.30am-9.30pm;) The finest dumpling house in Chéngdé, this excellent establishment has a big choice of juicy *jiǎozi* (boiled dumplings; ¥14-28 per serving) with some unusual fillings, including veg options and pan-fried dumplings. There's a huge range of other dishes too.

Information

Bank of China (中国银行, **Zhōngguó Yínháng;** 4 Dutongfu Dajie) Also on Xinsheng Lu and Lizhengmen Dajie; 24-hour ATMs.

Public Security Bureau (PSB, 公安局, **Gōng'ānjú;** 0314 202 2352; 9 Wulie Lu; 8.30am-5pm Mon-Fri)

RICHARD MANIN/GETTY IMAGES ©

⭐ Don't Miss
Pǔníng Temple

With its squeaking prayer wheels and devotional intonations of its monks, Chéngdé's only active temple was built in 1755 in anticipation of Qianlong's victory over the western Mongol tribes in Xīnjiāng. Supposedly modelled on the earliest Tibetan Buddhist monastery (Samye), the first half of the temple is distinctly Chinese (with Tibetan buildings at the rear).

NEED TO KNOW
普宁寺; Pǔníng Sì, Puningsi Lu; admission Apr-Oct ¥80, Nov-Mar ¥60; ⊗8am-6pm Apr-Oct, 8.30am-5pm Nov-Mar

❶ Getting There & Away

Bus

Buses for Chéngdé leave Běijīng hourly from Liùlǐqiáo bus station (¥85, four hours, 5.40am-6.40pm). Buses from Chéngdé leave every half-hour for Běijīng (¥85, four hours, 6.20am-6.40pm) from the train station car park.

Buses from Chéngdé's east bus station (汽车东站; qìchē dōngzhàn), 8km south of town, include:

Běijīng ¥85, four hours, every 20 minutes (6am to 6pm)

Dàlián ¥224, 13 to 14 hours, 3pm

Train

The three fastest trains to Chéngdé from Běijīng train station (hard seat ¥35-40) take 4½ to five hours and leave at 7.56am, 12.20pm and 2.03pm. Returning, they leave Chéngdé at 5.45am, 7.45am and 7.15pm.

❶ Getting Around

A taxi from the train station to the Bìshǔ Shānzhuāng should cost around ¥10.

Buses 13, 24 and 29 link East Bus Station with the train station; 13 and 29 carry on to Guāndì Temple.

Xī'ān & the North

A monumental trail of antiquity extends across north China.

Affluent urban Chinese may roll their eyes at the mention of earthy Hénán, yet the province's heritage takes us back to China's earliest days. Neighbouring Shaanxi boasts a similar pedigree, when Emperor Qin Shi Huang buried Confucian scholars alive, torched their literature and left the Terracotta Warriors to posterity. Furthermore, the Shaanxi capital Xī'ān marked the beginning and end of the Silk Road, evolving into a cosmopolitan, bustling Tang capital.

Nearby Shānxī province is a traveller's dream. If you only visited Píngyáo and jetted home, you may assume China was bursting with picture-perfect, ancient walled settlements. The mountain vastness of Wǔtái Shān reveals a Buddhist leaning that finds further expression in the astonishing Buddhist cave sculpture at Yúngāng.

East towards the Yellow Sea, Shāndōng's ancient bedrocks are Confucius, the Yellow River and sacred Tài Shān, while the breezy port of Qīngdǎo will blow the north China dust from your hair.

Street, Píngyáo (p150)
MARTIN MOOS/GETTY IMAGES ©

Hired bicycle, Xī'ān City Walls (p136)

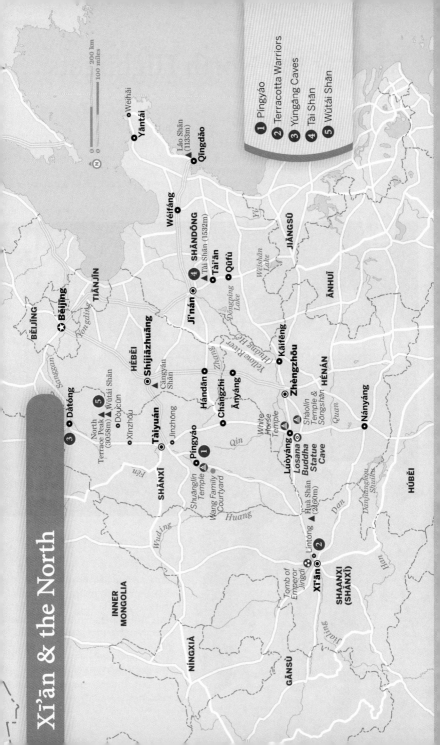

Xī'ān & the North

1	Píngyáo
2	Terracotta Warriors
3	Yúngāng Caves
4	Tài Shān
5	Wǔtái Shān

Wēihǎi

Yāntái

Láo Shān (1133m)
Qīngdǎo

Wéifāng

SHĀNDŌNG

4 Tài Shān (1532m)
Tài'ān

Qūfù

JIĀNGSŪ

Jǐ'nán

Weìshān Lake

Dōngping Lake

Yellow River (Huáng Hé)

BĚIJĪNG

TIĀNJĪN

Bĕijīng

Yongding

HÉBĚI

Shíjiāzhuāng

Kāifēng

Zhèngzhōu

HÉNÁN

ĀNHUĪ

Dàtóng

Sanggan

Wǔtái Shān

5 North Terrace Peak (3058m)
Dòucūn

Xinzhōu

Cāngyán Shān

Zhāng

Hándān

Chángzhì

Ānyáng

Shàolín Temple & Sōngshān

Nányáng

Quàn

SHĀNXĪ

Tàiyuán

Jīnzhōng

Píngyáo 1

Qín

White Horse Temple

Luòyáng

Losana Buddha Statue Cave

HÚBĚI

Fén

Shuānglín Temple

Wang Family Courtyard

Huáng

Wǔjìng

Dan

Huà Shān (2160m)

Lìntóng

Xī'ān 2

SHAANXI (SHĂNXĪ)

Tomb of Emperor Jǐngdì

Dānjiāngkŏu Shuĭkù

Hàn

INNER MONGOLIA

NÍNGXIÀ

GĀNSÙ

Jiālíng

300 km
100 miles

N

Xī'ān & the North Highlights

Potter Around Píngyáo

Reaching Píngyáo (p150) is like stepping through a wormhole to a distant age. The almost immaculate town walls, courtyard houses and charming alleyways brim with history and heritage. There are few, if any, walled towns in China that are so well preserved. It may be busy and flooded with visitors almost round the clock, but it's not hard to eke out some of the most exquisite street views in the land. Nan Dajie (p154)

❷ Marvel at the Terracotta Warriors

Gazing out from the millennia on the outskirts of Xī'ān, the silent Terracotta Warriors (p141) stand as one of China's most awe-inspiring artistic milestones, embodying the towering creativity of Qin-dynasty craftsmen. Yet they also represent the overarching megalomania of the emperor whose unexcavated tomb they guard, a mausoleum inside which – legends attest – flowed rivers of mercury.

Wonder at Yúngāng Caves

The ancient Buddhist statuary (p162) at
Yúngāng is one of China's three great
collections of cave art. Despite being
scoured by pollution and weathering,
the statues retain much pigmenta-
tion. The vast seated Buddha in
Cave 20 may be the drawcard, but
the entire galaxy of effigies is magnificent. The eagle-eyed can even
track down graffiti from the Cultural
Revolution and iconoclastic contributions from other eras.

Watch the Sunrise from Tài Shān

China's most-climbed mountain is also
its holiest Taoist peak; the easternmost of
the five Taoist mountains. In ancient times
the Chinese believed that the sun began
its daily journey from Tài Shān (p166). Emperors climbed Tài Shān in search of divine
blessing while today's sprightly octogenar-
ians bound up the steps, propelled by faith
(or belief in the adage that you'll live to 100
if you climb the mountain).

Temple Trekking in Wǔtái Shān

Mountainous home to the Bodhisattva of
Wisdom, the monastic enclave of Táihuái in
Wǔtái Shān (p156) harbours an extraordinary number of temples, and the surrounding peaks are sprinkled with yet more. The
five peaks are one of China's four holiest
Buddhist mountains and worshippers converge from across the land; the scenery and
spiritual focus forming an alluring magic.

Tǎyuàn Temple (p157)

Xī'ān & the North's Best...

Buddhist Culture

○ **Yúngāng Caves** A Sutra in stone and one of China's most supreme Buddhist treasures. (p162)

○ **Xiǎntōng Temple, Wǔtái Shān** Alluring Buddhist temple decorated with magnificent architecture. (p157)

○ **Lóngmén Caves** A master class in Buddhist statuary. (p149)

○ **Shuānglín Temple** A riveting collection of elegantly painted statues from the Song and Yuan dynasties. (p156)

Cuisine

○ **Muslim Quarter, Xī'ān** Follow your nostrils, snacking on Silk Road staples. (p139)

○ **Sānjiěmèi Jiǎozi** Save your dumpling fix for this excellent Xī'ān restaurant. (p137)

○ **Lǎo Sūn Jiā** Celebrated old-timer serving classic Shǎnxī fare. (p137)

○ **Qīngdǎo** Some of the best seafood and kebabs in north China. (p175)

Places to Stay

○ **Sofitel, Xī'ān** At the apex of luxury in Xī'ān. (p136)

○ **Hàn Táng House** Excellent beds, tidy and prim rooms in Xī'ān. (p135)

○ **Jing's Residence** Highly sophisticated and stylish Píngyáo courtyard accommodation – traditional meets modern. (p153)

○ **Runaway Youth Hostel** All the more reason to head into the sacred hills of Wǔtái Shān. (p158)

Need to Know

Scenery

- **Huà Shān** Pine trees, hair-raising ascents and awesome views from Taoism's sacred western mountain. (p143)

- **Wǔtái Shān** Astonishing Shānxī mountain panorama sprinkled with Buddhist temples. (p156)

- **Tài Shān** Sunrise panoramas from Taoism's holiest peak. (p166)

- **Qīngdǎo** Balmy Shāndōng coastline with superb views of the Yellow Sea. (p172)

- **City Walls**, **Xī'ān** Clamber up for excellent views over the city. (p136)

ADVANCE PLANNING

- **One Month Before** Get your accommodation sorted and book your hotel rooms.

- **One Week Before** Book your onward train or air tickets to and from the region through your hotel or a local travel agent.

RESOURCES

- **Xianease** (www. xianease.com) Info-packed Xī'ān expat website.

- **My Red Star** (www. myredstar.com) Qīngdǎo listings and entertainment guide.

- **That's Qīngdǎo** (www. thatsqingdao.com) Online Qīngdǎo guide with listings and news clips.

- **Mount Tài Shān** (www. mount-tai.com.cn) Official website of Tài Shān.

GETTING AROUND

- **Train** Your best bet for getting around between towns and cities conveniently and at speed.

- **Air** Good connections within the region and nationwide.

- **Long-Distance Bus** Extensive and reasonably efficient network throughout the region.

- **Taxis** Your primary means of transport within town.

- **Local Bus** Extensive network within town but not foreigner-friendly.

BE FOREWARNED

- **Language** English skills are rudimentary in most parts.

- **Fake Monks** Guard against fake monks asking for alms and donations.

- **Ticket Price Hikes** Admission ticket prices for top sights regularly go up.

- **Pollution** Air quality in some big towns can be shocking.

- **Weather** Cold weather or snow may make high-altitude destinations out of reach or uncomfortable to visit.

Left: Buddha, Yúngāng Caves (p162);
Above: Muslim Quarter (p139), Xī'ān
(LEFT) MARTIN MOOS/GETTY IMAGES ©;
(ABOVE) MARTIN MOOS/GETTY IMAGES ©

Xī'ān & the North Itineraries

These tours encompass the highlights of north China, from the Terracotta Warriors to Buddhist caves at Lóngmén and Yúngāng to the ancient town of Píngyáo, and on via Wǔtái Shān to the clement port city of Qīngdǎo.

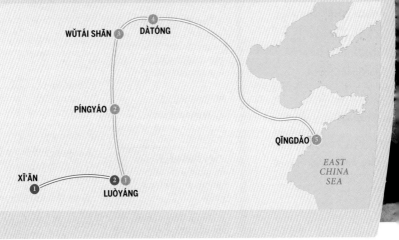

WǓTÁI SHĀN ③   DÀTÓNG ④

PÍNGYÁO ②

QĪNGDǍO ③

XĪ'ĀN ①   ②①
LUÒYÁNG

EAST CHINA SEA

XĪ'ĀN TO LUÒYÁNG

5 DAYS

TERRACOTTA WARRIORS, WARRIOR MONKS

Devote two days to exploring the diverse sights of the Shaanxi (Shǎnxī) capital ❶**Xī'ān** (p132), including the outstanding Terracotta Warriors, the Ming city walls, the city's rare collection of Tang-dynasty pagodas, its atmospheric Muslim Quarter, fascinating museums and the excellent choice of restaurants, where you can sample the scrumptious local Muslim cuisine. If you have more time on your hands and an adventurous streak, consider journeying east to the further-flung Taoist mountain of Huà Shān (where you can spend the night) or an exploration of the scattered imperial tombs and temples around Xī'ān. Then jump

aboard an express train to ❷**Luòyáng** (p146) to overnight and visit the old town and the astonishing Lóngmén Caves, one of China's most significant collections of Buddhist statuary, outside town. The White Horse Temple, also in the Luòyáng outskirts, is China's oldest Buddhist temple. A short detour by bus to the legendary birthplace of *gōngfū* (kung fu), the Shàolín Temple, is also recommended for anyone with either an interest in Buddhism or the mystery of China's *wǔshù* (martial arts). Visiting the Shàolín Temple is also an opportunity to explore the surrounding Taoist mountain of Sōng Shān, another of China's most sacred Taoist sites.

LUÒYÁNG TO QĪNGDǍO

OLD TOWNS & GERMAN BEER

1 WEEK

After seeing the sights of ❶ **Luòyáng** (p146) head north into Shānxī province to spend a few days in the delightful walled town of ❷ **Píngyáo** (p150). Journey out to some of the sights beyond Píngyáo, but spend most of your time enjoying the age-old textures of the ancient city walls and low-rise architecture. Then make your way north again to the Buddhist mountain fastness of ❸ **Wǔtái Shān** (p156), but don't attempt this in winter. In summer, buses run from Wǔtái Shān to ❹ **Dàtóng** (p159), which you can also reach from Píngyáo via Tàiyuán, the provincial capital of Shānxī. Visit the astounding Yúngāng Caves outside

town to compare them with the effigies of Lóngmén. To reach ❺ **Qīngdǎo** (p172) – far away on the coast of the Shāndōng peninsula – take an overnight train direct from Dàtóng or go via Běijīng and then catch an express D train or G train. Alternatively, fly from Tàiyuán. Qīngdǎo is a fetching terminus: with its beaches, robust German architecture, historical churches and excellent seafood, the Shāndōng port city is a relaxing place to hang your travelling hat. The city is also the home of Tsingtao beer – so raise a glass to your travels!

Terracotta Warriors (p141)
KRZYSZTOF DYDYNSKI/GETTY IMAGES ©

131

Discover Xī'ān & the North

Bicycle commuters passing the Bell Tower, Xī'ān
GREG ELMS/GETTY IMAGES ©

XĪ'ĀN   西安

029 / POP 6.5 MILLION

Xī'ān's fabled past is a double-edged sword. Primed with the knowledge that this legendary city was once the terminus of the Silk Road and a melting pot of cultures and religions, as well as home to emperors, courtesans, poets, monks, merchants and warriors, visitors can feel let down by the roaring, modern-day version. But even though Xī'ān's glory days ended in the early 10th century, many elements of ancient Cháng'ān, the former Xī'ān, are still present.

The Ming-era city walls remain intact, vendors of all descriptions still crowd the narrow lanes of the warren-like Muslim Quarter, and there are enough places of interest to keep even the most diligent amateur historian busy.

Must-sees include the Terracotta Warriors, the Tomb of Emperor Jingdi, and the Muslim Quarter, but set time aside for the city walls, pagodas and museums.

◎ Sights

INSIDE THE CITY WALLS

Great Mosque   Mosque
(清真大寺, Qīngzhēn Dàsì; Huajue Xiang, 化觉巷; admission Mar-Nov ¥25, Dec-Feb ¥15, Muslims free; ⏱8am-7.30pm Mar-Nov, to 5.30pm Dec-Feb) One of the largest mosques in China and a fascinating blend of Chinese and Islamic architecture. The present buildings are mostly Ming and Qing, though the mosque was founded in the 8th century. Arab influences extend from the central minaret (cleverly disguised as a pagoda) to the enormous turquoise-roofed prayer hall (not open to visitors)

at the back of the complex, and elegant calligraphy gracing most entryways.

Forest of Stelae Museum
Museum

(碑林博物馆, Bēilín Bówùguǎn; www.beilin-museum.com; 15 Sanxue Jie, 三学街15号; admission Mar-Nov ¥75, Dec-Feb ¥50; ☺8am-6.45pm Mar-Nov, to 5.45pm Dec-Feb, last admission 45min before closing) Housed in Xī'ān's Confucius Temple, this museum holds more than 1000 stone stelae (inscribed tablets), including the nine Confucian classics and some exemplary calligraphy. The highlight is the fantastic sculpture gallery (across from the gift shop), which contains animal guardians from the Tang dynasty, pictorial tomb stones and Buddhist statuary. To get to the museum, follow Shuyuan Xiang east from the South Gate.

Bell Tower & Drum Tower
Historic Site

Now marooned on a traffic island, the **Bell Tower** (钟楼, Zhōng Lóu; admission ¥35, combined Drum Tower ticket ¥40; ☺8.30am-9.30pm Mar-Oct, to 6.30pm Nov-Feb, last admission 30min before closing) sits at the heart of Xī'ān and originally held a large bell that was rung at dawn, while its alter ego, the **Drum Tower** (鼓楼, Gǔ Lóu; Beiyuanmen; admission ¥35, combined Bell Tower ticket ¥40; ☺8.30am-9.30pm Mar-Oct, to 6.30pm Nov-Feb, last admission 30min before closing), marked nightfall. Both date from the 14th century but the Drum Tower was renovated in 1740 while the Bell Tower was moved and reconstructed in 1582 using the same beams and fixtures from where it stood two blocks west.

Musical performances, included in the ticket price, are held inside each at 9.10am, 10am, 11am, 3pm, 4pm and 5pm. Enter the Bell Tower through the underpass on the north side.

OUTSIDE THE CITY WALLS

Xī'ān is one of the few cities in China where the old city walls are still standing. Built in 1370 during the Ming dynasty, the 12m-high walls are surrounded by a dry moat and form a rectangle with a perimeter of 14km.

Shaanxi History Museum
Museum

(陕西历史博物馆, Shǎnxī Lìshǐ Bówùguǎn; 91 Xiaozhai Donglu, 小寨东路91号; ☺8.30am-6pm Tue-Sun Apr-Oct, last admission 4.30pm, 9.30am-5pm Tue-Sun Nov-Mar, last admission 4pm) **FREE** Shaanxi's museum has plenty of overlap with Xī'ān's surrounding sights but makes for a comprehensive stroll through ancient Cháng'ān. Most exhibits include illuminating explanations in English. Look for the four original terracotta warrior statues on the ground floor. Go early and expect to queue for at least 30 minutes. Bring your passport to claim your free ticket.

Big Goose Pagoda
Buddhist Temple

(大雁塔, Dàyàn Tǎ; Yanta Nanlu, 雁塔南路; admission to grounds ¥50, entry into pagoda ¥40; ☺8am-7pm Apr-Oct, to 6pm Nov-Mar) This pagoda, Xī'ān's most famous landmark, 4km southeast of the South Gate, dominates the surrounding modern buildings. One of China's best examples of a Tang-style pagoda (squarish rather than round), it was completed in AD 652 to house the Buddhist Sutras brought back from India by the monk Xuan Zang. His travels inspired one of the best-known works of Chinese literature, *Journey to the West.*

Xī'ān Museum
Museum

(西安博物院, Xī'ān Bówùyuàn; www.xabwy.com; 76 Youyi Xilu, 友谊西路76号; ☺8.30am-7pm Wed-Mon) **FREE** Housed in the pleasant grounds of the Jiànfú Temple is this museum featuring relics unearthed in Xī'ān over the years. There are some exquisite ceramics from the Han dynasty, as well as figurines, an exhibition of Ming-dynasty seals and jade artefacts. Don't miss the basement, where a large-scale model of ancient Xī'ān gives a good sense of the place in its former pomp and glory.

Temple of the Eight Immortals
Taoist Temple

(八仙庵, Bāxiān Ān; Yongle Lu, 永乐路; admission ¥3; ☺7.30am-5.30pm Mar-Nov, 8am-5pm Dec-Feb) Xī'ān's largest Taoist temple dates back to the Song dynasty and is still an active place of worship. Supposedly built on the site of an ancient wine shop, it was

Xi'ān

Xī'ān

constructed to protect against subterranean divine thunder. Scenes from Taoist mythology are painted around the courtyard. Empress Cixi, the mother of the last emperor, stayed here in 1901 after fleeing Běijīng during the Boxer Rebellion. Bus 502 runs close by the temple (eastbound from Xi Xinjie).

🛏 Sleeping

Shūyuàn Youth Hostel   Hostel $
(书院青年旅舍, Shūyuàn Qīngnián Lǚshè; ☎029 8728 0092; www.hostelxian.com; 2 Shuncheng Nanlu Xiduan, 南门里顺城南路西段2号; dm ¥40-60, s/d ¥160/180; 🌐@📶; Ⓜ Yong Ningmen) The longest-running hostel in Xī'ān, Shūyuàn is a converted residence with beautiful courtyards near the South Gate. The cafe serves excellent food and the lively bar in the basement (guests get a free beer voucher) is a popular locals/travellers meeting spot. Rooms are simple but clean and the staff is switched on to the needs of travellers.

Hàn Táng House   Hostel $$
(汉唐驿青年旅舍, Hàntáng Yì Qīngnián Lǚshè; ☎029 8738 9765; www.itisxian.com; 32 Nanchang Xiang, 南长巷32号; ◷dm/s/d/tr ¥60/168/268/338; 🍴🌐@📶; Ⓜ Zhonglou (Bell Tower)) A hybrid of sorts, this place

has dorms and the vibe of a youth hostel but the look and feel of a three-star hotel. The spotless rooms are decked out with high-quality dark-wood furnishings, slab floors and some of the most comfortable beds in China. It's located down a residential street off Nanxin Jie.

Jano's Backpackers   Hostel $$
(杰诺庭院背包旅舍, Jíenuò Tíingyuàn Bèibāo Lǚshè; ☎029 8725 6656; www.xian-backpackers.com; 69 Shuncheng Nanlu Zhongduan, South Gate, 南门顺城南路中段69号; dm ¥50-60, r without bathroom ¥120, with bathroom ¥220-260, ste ¥320-390; 🌐@📶; Ⓜ Yong Ningmen) Set in a little faux hútòng (narrow alleyway) with artist galleries and cafes nearby,

---

Accommodation Price Indicators

The price ranges for sleeping in Xī'ān & the North region are as follows:

- **$** less than ¥190
- **$$** ¥190 to ¥400
- **$$$** more than ¥400

CHRISTIAN KOBER/GETTY IMAGES ©

⭐ Don't Miss
Xī'ān City Walls

Xī'ān is one of the few cities in China where the old city walls are still standing. Built in 1370 during the Ming dynasty, the 12m-high walls are surrounded by a dry moat, forming a rectangle with a perimeter of 14km. Most sections have been restored or rebuilt, and it is possible to walk the entirety of the walls in a leisurely four hours.

NEED TO KNOW
城墙, Chéngqiáng; admission ¥54; ⊙8am-8.30pm Apr-Oct, to 7pm Nov-Mar

Jano's is a pleasant place to escape bustling Xī'ān (though street-facing rooms get pub noise). Rooms are well-maintained and decorated in traditional style, including some with *kang* (heatable beds). Despite the name, it feels more like a small boutique hotel rather than a backpacker hangout. Staff speak English

Sofitel   Hotel $$$
(索菲特人民大厦, Suǒfēitè Rénmín Dàshà; ☏029 8792 8888; sofitel@renminsquare.com; 319 Dong Xinjie, 东新街319号; d/ste ¥1760/3150; ➡❄@☎; ⓂZhonglou, Bell Tower) Xī'ān's self-proclaimed 'six-star' hotel is undoubtedly the most luxurious choice in the city and has a soothing, hushed atmosphere.

The bathrooms are top-notch. Cantonese, Japanese and Moroccan restaurants are on-site, as well as a South American–themed bar. Reception is in the east wing. Room rates change daily, so you can score a deal when business is slow.

Bell Tower Hotel   Hotel $$$
(西安钟楼饭店, Xī'ān Zhōnglóu Fàndiàn; ☏029 8760 0000; www.belltowerhtl.com; 110 Nan Dajie, 南大街110号; d ¥850-1080; ❄@; ⓂZhonglou, Bell Tower) Slap in the centre of downtown, this state-owned four-star place is comfortable and handy for the airport bus stop. Some rooms have a bird's-eye view of the Bell Tower and all are spacious and comfortable with cable TV and ADSL inter-

net connections. Low-season discounts up to 30%.

Jano's Backpackers   Hostel $$

(杰诺庭院背包旅舍, Jíenuò Tínyuàn Beībāo Lŭshè; ☏029 8725 6656; www.xian-backpackers. com; 69 Shuncheng Nanlu Zhongduan, South Gate, 南门顺城南路中段69号; dm ¥50-60, r without bathroom ¥120, with bathroom ¥220-260, ste ¥320-390; ✳@🛜; Ⓜ Yong Ningmen) Set in a little faux *hútòng* (narrow alleyway) with artist galleries and cafes nearby, Jano's is a pleasant place to escape bustling Xī'ān (though street-facing rooms get pub noise). Rooms are well-maintained and decorated in traditional style, including some with *kang* (heatable beds). Despite the name, it feels more like a small boutique hotel rather than a backpacker hangout. Staff speak English.

🍴 Eating

Hit the Muslim Quarter for fine eating in Xī'ān. Common dishes here are *májiàng liángpí* (麻酱凉皮; cold noodles in sesame sauce), *fĕnzhēngròu* (粉蒸肉; chopped mutton fried in a wok with ground wheat), *ròujiāmó* (肉夹馍; fried pork or beef in pitta bread, sometimes with green peppers and cumin), *càijiāmó* (菜夹馍; the vegetarian version of *ròujiāmó*) and the ubiquitous *ròuchuàn* (肉串; kebabs).

Best of all is the delicious *yángròu pàomó* (羊肉泡馍), a soup dish that involves crumbling a flat loaf of bread into a bowl and adding noodles, mutton and broth.

A good street to wander for a selection of more typically Chinese restaurants is Dongmutou Shi, east of Nan Dajie.

Sānjiĕmèi Jiăozi   Dumplings $

(三姐妹饺子, Three Sisters Dumplings; ☏029 8725 2129; 140 Dongmutou Shi, 东木头市140号; dumplings ¥13-23; ⏰11am-2.30pm & 5-9.30pm; 🏃) Weary diners with dumpling fatigue, let the rustic Three Sisters reinspire you with a twist on classics, well done. Try succulent carrot and lamb dumplings blanketed in crisp peanuts and fried chives. Or for vegetarians, the winning texture of dry and marinated tofu (yes, two types) with the zing of crunchy coriander and a lashing of chilli. Picture menu.

Dĭng Dĭng Xiāng   Chinese $

(顶顶香; 130 Nanyuanmen, 南院门130号; dishes ¥18-58; ⏰10am-10pm; 🏃) This is what modern Xī'ān is all about. A clean, cafe atmosphere over four floors with aspirational snaps of Europe in scattered picture frames on the walls while a lively well-dressed crowd peers down onto the street, drinking beer and eating Chinese classics such as hotpots with generous servings. The extensive English picture menu includes excellent veg options.

Jamaica Blue   Cafe $$

(蓝色牙买加, Lánsè Yámăijiā; 32 Nanchang Xiang, 南长巷32号; dishes ¥32-49; ⏰8am-11pm; 🛜) This Australia-based cafe has washed up in a little alley in Xī'ān, serving up excellent sandwiches, wraps, Western-style breakfast, pastas, desserts and reliable coffee. Has a friendly English-speaking staff, wi-fi, games and quasi-Irish pub atmosphere. Live music is played nightly from 9pm to 11pm.

Lăo Sūn Jiā   Shaanxi $$

(老孙家; ☏029-8240 3205; 5th fl, 364 Dong Dajie, 东大街364号5层; dishes ¥12-49; ⏰8am-9.30pm) Xī'ān's most famous, upmarket restaurant (with more than 100 years of history) is well known for its speciality dish – steaming bowls of *yángròu pàomó*. The catch here is that the patron is responsible for ripping up the bread before the chefs add the soup. The soup is an acquired taste for most people but the experience is fun.

Eating Price Indicators

The price ranges for eating in Xī'ān are as follows:

- **$** less than ¥30
- **$$** ¥30 to ¥60
- **$$$** more than ¥60

🍷 Drinking

The main bar strip is Defu Xiang, close to the South Gate.

Old Henry's Bar
Bar

(老亨利酒吧, Lǎohēnglì Jiǔbā; 48 Defu Xiang, 德福巷48号; ⏰8pm-3am; 📶) A small bar with a pub vibe and live music in the evenings. Always busy and has outside seating.

The Belgian
Bar

(比利时咖啡酒吧, Bǐlìshí Kāfēi Jiǔbā; 69 Shuncheng Nanlu, 顺城南路中段69号; ⏰7pm-3am) A laid-back Western-style bar stocked with around 40 types of imported Belgian beers and pub grub like burgers and fries. The little alley where it sits is developing as a pub street so it's fun to hang out on the patio and people-watch.

⭐ Entertainment

Some travellers enjoy spending the evening at the **fountain and music show** (Dayan Ta Bei Guangchang, 大雁塔北广场; ⏰9pm Mar-Nov, 8pm Dec-Feb) on Big Goose Pagoda Sq; the largest such 'musical fountain' in Asia. Xī'ān also has a number of dinner-dance shows, which are normally packed out with tour groups.

1+1
Club

(壹加壹俱乐部, Yījiāyī Jùlèbù; 2nd fl, Heping Yinzuo Bldg, 118 Heping Lu, 和平银座二楼405号; ⏰7pm-late) The ever-popular 1+1 is a neon-lit maze of a place that pumps out slightly cheesy party tunes well into the early hours. Hip, it is not.

Tang Dynasty
Dinner Show

(唐乐宫, Tángyuè Gōng; 📞029 8782 2222; www.xiantangdynasty.com; 75 Chang'an Beilu, 长安北路75号; performance with/without dinner ¥500/220) The most famous dinner theatre in the city stages an over-the-top spectacle with Vegas-style costumes, traditional dance, live music and singing. It's dubbed into English. Buses can take you to the theatre 1.5km directly south of the South Gate, or walk five minutes south of South Shaomen metro.

Shaanxi Grand Opera House
Dinner Show

(陕歌大剧院, Shǎngē Dàjùyuàn; 📞029 8785 3295; 165 Wenyi Beilu, 文艺北路165号; performance with/without dinner ¥298/198) Also known as the Tang Palace Dance Show, this is cheaper and less flashy than other dinner-dance shows in town. Wenyi Lu starts south of the city walls. You can get a better price by buying your ticket through a reputable hostel or hotel.

🔒 Shopping

A good place to search out gifts is the Muslim Quarter, where prices are generally cheaper than elsewhere.

Xiyang Shi is a narrow, crowded alley running north of the Great Mosque where terracotta warriors, Huxian farmer paintings, shadow puppets, lanterns, tea ware, Mao memorabilia and T-shirts are on offer. Serious shoppers should also visit the **Northwest Antique Market** (西北古玩城, Xīběi Gǔwán Chéng; Dong Xinjie (Shuncheng Donglu), 东新街 (顺城东路北段); ⏰10am-5.30pm), by the Zhongshan Gate.

There's a much smaller antique market by the Temple of the Eight Immortals on Sunday and Wednesday mornings.

ℹ️ Information

The English-language magazine *Xianese* (www.xianese.com) is available in some hotels and restaurants that cater to tourists.

Bank of China (中国银行, Zhōngguó Yínháng) Juhuayuan Lu (38 Juhuayuan Lu; ⏰8am-8pm); Nan Dajie (29 Nan Dajie; ⏰8am-6pm) You can exchange cash and travellers cheques and use the ATMs at both of these branches.

Public Security Bureau (PSB, 公安局, Gōng'ānjú; 2 Keji Lu; ⏰8.30am-noon & 2-6pm Mon-Fri) This is on the southeast corner of Xixie 7 Lu. Visa extensions take five working days. To get there from the Bell Tower, take bus K205 and get off at Xixie 7 Lu.

ℹ️ Getting There & Away

Air

Most hostels and hotels and all travel agencies sell airline tickets.

JULIET COOMBE/GETTY IMAGES ©

Don't Miss
Muslim Quarter

The backstreets leading north from the Drum Tower have been home to the city's Hui community (Chinese Muslims) for centuries.

The narrow lanes of the Muslim Quarter (回族区) are full of butcher shops, sesame-oil factories, smaller mosques hidden behind enormous wooden doors, men in white skullcaps and women with their heads covered in coloured scarves. It's a great place to wander and is especially atmospheric at night.

China Eastern Airlines (中国东方航空公司, **Zhōngguó Dōngfāng Hángkōng; ☎029 8208 8707; 64 Xi Wulu; ⏲8am-9pm)** operates most flights to and from Xī'ān. Daily flights include Běijīng (¥840), Chéngdū (¥630), Guǎngzhōu (¥890), Shànghǎi (¥1260) and Ürümqi (¥2060). On the international front, China Eastern has flights from Xī'ān to Hong Kong (¥1640), Seoul, Bangkok, Tokyo and Nagoya.

Bus

The **long-distance bus station** (长途汽车站; chángtú qìchēzhàn) is opposite Xī'ān's train station. Note that buses to Huà Shān (6am to 8pm) depart from in front of the train station.

Other bus stations around town where you may be dropped off include the **east bus station** (城东客运站, **chéngdōng kèyùnzhàn; Changle Lu,** 长乐路) and the **west bus station** (城西客运站, **chéngxī kèyùnzhàn; Zaoyuan Donglu,** 枣园东路). Both are located outside the Second Ring Rd. A taxi into the city from either bus station costs between ¥15 and ¥20.

Buses from Xī'ān's long-distance bus station go to:

Luòyáng ¥107.50, five hours (10am, 12pm, 1pm and 3pm)

Píngyáo ¥160, six hours (8am, 9.30am, 10.30am, 12.30pm and 4.30pm)

Buses from Xī'ān's east bus station go to:

Huà Shān one way ¥40.50, two hours, hourly (7.30am to 7pm)

Train

Xī'ān's **main train station** (Xī'ān Huǒchē Zhàn) is just outside the northern city walls. Xī'ān's **north**

train station *(Běi Huǒchē Zhàn)* is used by D- and G-class high-speed trains.

Most hotels and hostels can get you tickets (¥40 commission); there's also an **advance train ticket booking office** (代售火车票, Dàishòu Huǒchēpiào; Nan Dajie; 南大街; ⏱8.50am-noon & 1.30-4.30pm) in the ICBC Bank's south entrance.

All prices listed below are for hard/soft sleeper tickets.

Běijīng West first/second class ¥826/517, 5½ hours, 10 daily

Chéngdū ¥195/302, 16½ hours

Chóngqìng ¥179/275, 11 hours

Guìlín ¥372/587, 28 hours

Lánzhōu ¥171/261, seven to nine hours

Luòyáng ¥101/156, five hours

Píngyáo ¥120/189, nine hours

Shànghǎi ¥312/490, 14 to 20 hours

Ūrümqi ¥466/737, 28 to 35 hours

ⓘ Getting Around

Xī'ān's Xiányáng Airport is about 40km northwest of Xī'ān. Shuttle buses run every 20 to 30 minutes from 5.40am to 8pm between the airport and the Melody Hotel. Taxis into the city charge more than ¥100 on the meter. Taxi flagfall is ¥6.

If you can cope with the congested roads, bikes are a good alternative and can be hired at the youth hostels.

The Xī'ān metro system (西安地铁; Xī'ān dìtiě) started up in 2011 with Line 2, followed by Line 1 in 2013 and Line 3 planned for 2015. Rides cost ¥2 to ¥4 depending on distance. Useful stations on Line 2 include Běihuǒchē Zhàn (north train station) and Xiǎozhài (near the Shaanxi History Museum). Line 1 has a stop at the Bànpō Neolithic Village.

AROUND XĪ'ĀN

The plains surrounding Xī'ān are strewn with early imperial tombs, many of which have not yet been excavated. But unless you have a particular fascination for burial sites, you can probably come away satisfied after visiting a couple of them.

Left: Army of Terracotta Warriors; **Below:** Dragon lantern, Spring Festival
(LEFT) KRZYSZTOF DYDYNSKI/GETTY IMAGES ©; (BELOW) PAN HONG/GETTY IMAGES ©

The Army of Terracotta Warriors is obviously the most famous site, but it's really worth the effort to get to the Tomb of Emperor Jingdi as well.

Tourist buses run to almost all of the sites from in front of Xī'ān Train Station, with the notable exception of the Tomb of Emperor Jingdi.

◉ Sights

EAST OF XĪ'ĀN

Army of Terracotta Warriors
Historic Site

(兵马俑, Bīngmǎyǒng; www.bmy.com.cn; admission Mar-Nov ¥150, students ¥75, Dec-Feb ¥120, students ¥60; ⊙8.30am-5.30pm Mar-Nov, to 5pm Dec-Feb) The Terracotta Army isn't just Xī'ān's premier site, but one of the most famous archaeological finds in the world. This subterranean life-size army of thousands has silently stood guard over the soul of China's first unifier for more than two millennia. Either Qin Shi Huang was terrified of the vanquished spirits awaiting him in the afterlife, or, as most archaeologists believe, he expected his rule to continue in death as it had in life – whatever the case, the guardians of his tomb today offer some of the greatest insights we have into the world of ancient China.

Tomb of Qin Shi Huang
Historic Site

(秦始皇陵, Qín Shǐhuáng Líng; admission free with Terracotta Warrior ticket; ⊙8am-6pm Mar-Nov, to 5pm Dec-Feb) In its time this tomb must have been one of the grandest mausoleums the world had ever seen. Historical accounts describe it as containing palaces filled with precious stones, underground rivers of flowing mercury and ingenious defences against intruders. The tomb reputedly took 38 years to complete, and required a workforce of 700,000 people. It is said that the artisans who built it were buried alive within, taking its secrets with them.

141

Emperor Jingdi

A Han-dynasty emperor influenced by Taoism, Jingdi (188–141 BC) based his rule upon the concept of *wúwéi* (nonaction or noninterference) and did much to improve the life of his subjects: he lowered taxes greatly, used diplomacy to cut back on unnecessary military expeditions and even reduced the punishment meted out to criminals. The contents of his tomb are particularly interesting, as they reveal more about daily life than martial preoccupations – a total contrast with the Terracotta Army.

The site has been divided into two sections: the museum and the excavation area. The museum holds a large display of expressive terracotta figurines (more than 50,000 were buried here), including eunuchs, servants, domesticated animals and even female cavalry on horseback.

Inside the tomb are 21 narrow pits, some of which have been covered by a glass floor, allowing you to walk over the top of ongoing excavations and get a great view of the relics. In all, there are believed to be 81 burial pits here.

To get here, take Xīān metro Line 2 to the station Shitushuguan. Outside exit D take bus 4 (¥1) to the tomb, which leaves at 8.30am, 9.30am, 10.30am, noon, 1.30pm, 3.00pm, 4.00pm and 5.00pm, returning to Xīān at 9am, noon, 4pm and 5pm. Alternatively, you can take a tour (around ¥160), usually arranged by the guesthouses. The tomb is 20 minutes from the airport, so makes an easy stop off by taxi.

Bànpō Neolithic Village
Ancient Village

(半坡博物馆, Bànpō Bówùguǎn; admission Mar-Nov ¥65, Dec-Feb ¥45; ⏰8am-6pm) Bànpō is the earliest example of the Neolithic Yangshao culture, which is believed to have been matriarchal. The village appears to have been occupied from 4500 BC until around 3750 BC. The excavated area is divided into three parts: a pottery manufacturing area, a residential area complete with moat, and a cemetery.

This village is of enormous importance for Chinese archaeological studies, but unless you're desperately interested in the subject it can be an underwhelming visitor experience.

NORTH & WEST OF XĪĀN

Tomb of Emperor Jingdi
Tomb

(汉阳陵, Hàn Yánglíng; admission Mar-Nov ¥90, Dec-Feb ¥65; ⏰8.30am-7pm Mar-Nov, to 6pm Dec-Feb) This tomb, which is also referred to as the Han Jing Mausoleum, Liu Qi Mausoleum and Yangling Mausoleum, is easily Xīān's most underrated highlight. If you only have time for two sights, then it should be the Army of Terracotta Warriors and this impressive museum and tomb. Unlike the warriors, though, there are relatively few visitors here so you have the space to appreciate what you're seeing.

Imperial Tombs
Historic Sites

A large number of imperial tombs (皇陵, huáng líng) dot the Guānzhōng plain around Xīān. They are sometimes included on tours from Xīān, but most aren't so remarkable as to be destinations in themselves. By far the most impressive is the **Qián Tomb** (乾陵, Qián Líng; admission incl other imperial tombs Mar-Nov ¥45, Dec-Feb ¥25; ⏰8am-6pm), where China's only female emperor, Wu Zetian (AD 624–705), is buried with her husband Emperor Gaozong, whom she succeeded.

🅣 Tours

One-day tours allow you to see all the sights around Xīān more quickly and conveniently than if you arranged one yourself. Itineraries differ somewhat, but there are two basic tours: an Eastern Tour and a Western Tour.

Most hostels run their own tours, but make sure you find out what is included (admission fees, lunch, English-speaking guide) and try to get an exact itinerary, or you could end up being herded through the Terracotta Warriors before you have a chance to get your camera out.

Huà Shān   华山

One of Taoism's five sacred mountains, the granite domes of Huà Shān used to be home to hermits and sages. There are knife-blade ridges and twisted pine trees clinging to ledges as you ascend, while the summits offer transcendent panoramas of green mountains and countryside stretching away to the horizon.

◉ Sights & Activities

There are three ways up the mountain to the **North Peak** (北峰; Běi Fēng), the first of five summit peaks. Two of these options start from the eastern base of the mountain, at the cable-car terminus. The first option is handy if you don't fancy the climb: an Austrian-built **cable car** (one way/return ¥80/150; ⊙7am-7pm) will lift you to the North Peak in eight scenic minutes.

The second option is to work your way to the North Peak under the cable-car route. This takes a sweaty two hours, and two sections of 50m or so are quite literally vertical, with nothing but a steel chain to grab onto and tiny chinks cut into the rock for footing.

The third option is the most popular, but it's still hard work. A 6km path leads to the North Peak from the village of Huà Shān, at the base of the mountain (the other side of the mountain from the cable car). It usually takes between three and five hours to reach the North Peak via this route. The first 4km up are pretty easy going, but after that it's all steep stairs.

The village at the trailhead is a good place to stock up on water and snacks. These are also available at shops on the trail but prices double and triple the further you head up the mountain.

If you want to carry on to the other peaks, then count on a minimum of eight hours in total from the base of Huà Shān. If you want to spare your knees, then another option is to take the cable car to the North Peak and then climb to the other peaks, before ending up back where you started. It takes about four hours to complete the circuit in this fashion and it's still fairly strenuous. Huà Shān has a reputation for being dangerous,

♥ If You Like...
Sacred Mountains

If you like the Taoist peak of Huà Shān, north China frequently crumples into spectacular mountain ranges. Many, but by no means all, have been requisitioned by Taoists and Buddhists who have left their slopes littered with temples and myth.

1 **WǓDĀNG SHĀN**
(武当山; admission ¥140, bus ¥100, audio guide ¥30) Birthplace of the 'soft' martial art of taichi, Wǔdāng Shān is deeply venerated by Taoist monks and nuns who make a continuous pilgrimage to its slopes. Located in northwest Húběi province; the nearest train station is Wǔdāng Shān.

2 **HÉNG SHĀN**
(衡山) Héng Shān is the northernmost peak of Taoism's five holy mountains. The cliff-clinging Hanging Monastery is its most celebrated highlight. Southeast of Dàtóng.

3 **SŌNG SHĀN**
(嵩山) Sōng Shān is best known for the Buddhist Shàolín Temple, although the mountain is itself – paradoxically perhaps – the central peak of China's five Taoist mountains. Located southeast of Luòyáng; all buses from Luòyáng to the Shàolín Temple reach Sōng Shān.

especially when the trails are crowded, or if it's wet or icy, so exercise caution.

But the scenery is sublime. Along **Blue Dragon Ridge** (苍龙岭; Cānglóng Lǐng), which connects the North Peak with the **East Peak** (东峰; Dōng Fēng), **South Peak** (南峰; Nán Fēng) and **West Peak** (西峰; Xī Fēng), the way has been cut along a narrow rock ridge with impressive sheer cliffs on either side.

There is accommodation on the mountain, most of it basic and overpriced, but it does allow you to start climbing in the afternoon, watch the sunset and then spend the night, before catching the sunrise from either the East Peak or South Peak. Some locals make the climb at night, using torches (flashlights).

Admission is ¥180 (students ¥90). To get to either cable car (suǒdào), take a taxi from the village to the ticket office (¥10) and then a shuttle bus (one way/ return to North cable car ¥20/40, to West cable car ¥40/80) the rest of the way.

🛌 Sleeping

You can either spend the night in Huà Shān village or on one of the peaks. Take your own food or eat well before ascending, unless you like to feast on instant noodles and processed meat – proper meals are very pricey on the mountain. Don't forget a torch and warm clothes. Bear in mind that prices for a bed triple during public holidays. The hotels on the mountain are basic; there are no showers and only shared bathrooms.

IN HUÀ SHĀN VILLAGE:

Míngzhū Jiǔdiàn   Hotel $$
(明珠酒店; ☎0913 436 9899; Yuquan Donglu, 玉泉東路, Huà Shān village; s & d ¥238-281; ❄ 🛜) Located in Huà Shān village at the main intersection, this Chinese two-star hotel has clean, modern rooms with wi-fi. Discounts of 30% available outside peak holiday travel times.

Left: Héng Shān (p143); **Below:** Pagoda at sunset
(LEFT) CHEN XIAOBO/GETTY IMAGES ©; (BELOW) KEREN SU/GETTY IMAGES ©

Huáyuè Kuài Jié Jiŭdiàn
Hotel **$**

(华岳快捷酒店; ☎ 0913 436 8555; Yuquan Donglu, 玉泉路, Huà Shān village; s & d ¥150; ✆) Clean and simple rooms with OK bathrooms make this an obvious option for budget travellers. It's on Yuquan Lu at the bottom of the hill near the main intersection.

ON THE MOUNTAIN:

West Peak Hostel
Hostel **$**

(西峰旅社, Xīfēng Lǚshè; dm ¥100) Rustic and basic, but also the friendliest place on the mountain. It shares its premises with an old Taoist temple.

Wǔyúnfēng Fàndiàn
Hotel **$$**

(五云峰饭店; dm ¥100-180, tr/d ¥220/300) This basic hotel is along the Black Dragon Ridge and on a hillside, not a peak. A good choice mostly if you're planning on doing a circuit of the rear peaks the next day, or want to catch the sunrise at the East or South Peak.

Dōngfēng Bīnguǎn
Hotel **$$**

(东峰宾馆; dm ¥150-220, tr/d ¥280/340) The top location on the East Peak for watching the sun come up also has the best restaurant.

North Peak Hotel
Hotel **$$**

(北峰饭店, Běifēng Fàndiàn; ☎ 157 1913 6466; dm ¥100, d ¥260-280) The busiest of the peak hotels.

❶ Getting There & Away

From Xī'ān to Huà Shān, catch one of the private buses (¥36, two hours, 6am to 8pm) that depart when full from in front of Xī'ān train station. You'll be dropped off on Yuquan Lu, which is also where buses back to Xī'ān leave from 7.30am to 7pm. Coming from the east, try to talk your driver into dropping you at the Huà Shān highway exit if you can't find a direct bus. Don't pay more than ¥10 for a taxi into Huà Shān village.

Buddha statues, Lóngmén Caves (p149)

KRZYSZTOF DYDYNSKI/GETTY IMAGES ©

There are few buses (if any) going east from Huà Shān; pretty much everyone catches a taxi to the highway and then flags down buses headed for Yùnchéng, Tàiyuán or Luòyáng.

LUÒYÁNG 洛阳

Capital of 13 dynasties until the Northern Song dynasty shifted its capital to Kāifēng in the 10th century, Luòyáng was one of China's true dynastic citadels. It's hard today to conceive that Luòyáng was once the very centre of the Chinese universe and the eastern capital of the great Tang dynasty. The heart of the magnificent Sui-dynasty palace complex was centred on the point where today's Zhongzhou Lu and Dingding Lu intersect in a frenzy of traffic.

Nearby, the magnificently sculpted Lóngmén Caves by the banks of the Yī River (Yī Hé) remain one of China's most prized Buddhist treasures and the annual peony festival, centred on Wángchéng Park in April, is colourful fun.

◉ Sights & Activities

Luòyáng Museum   Museum
(洛阳市博物馆, Luòyáng Shì Bówùguǎn; www.lymuseum.com; Nietai Lu, 聂泰路; audio tour ¥40; ☺9am-4.30pm Tue-Sun) **FREE** This huge new museum, situated out of the action south of the river, has exhilarating displays across two huge floors and is one of the few places to get ancient Luòyáng in any kind of perspective. There's an absorbing collection of Tang-dynasty three-colour *sāncǎi* porcelain, and the city's rise is traced through dynastic pottery, bronzeware and other magnificent objects.

Old Town   Historic Site
(老城区, lǎochéngqū) Any Chinese city worth its salt has an old town. Luòyáng's is east of the rebuilt **Lijīng Gate** (丽京门, Lìjīng Mén), where a maze of narrow and winding streets yield up old courtyard houses and the occasional creaking monument, including the old **Drum Tower** (鼓楼, Gǔ Lóu), rising up at the east end of Dong Dajie (东大街) and the lovely brick **Wenfeng Pagoda** (文峰塔, Wénfēng Tǎ),

originally built in the Song dynasty. The rest of Dong Dajie is a hubbub of local life, with hairdressers, noodle stalls and tradesmiths clustering within crumbling old houses.

Wángchéng Park   Park
(王城公园, Wángchéng Gōngyuán; Zhongzhou Zhonglu; admission park ¥15, park & zoo ¥25, park, zoo & cable car ¥30, after 7pm ¥15, peony festival ¥55) One of Luòyáng's indispensable green lungs, this park is the site of the annual **peony festival**; held in April, the festival sees the park flooded with colour, floral aficionados, photographers, girls with garlands on their heads and hawkers selling huge bouquets of flowers. Unfortunately, the park is home to a decrepit zoo for which you're forced to pay an admission charge. There's also an amusement park (rides ¥15 to ¥20).

🛏 Sleeping

Christian's Hotel   Boutique Hotel $$$
(克丽司汀酒店, Kèlìsītīng Jiǔdiàn; 📞 6326 6666; www.5xjd.com; 56 Jiefang Lu, 解放路56号; d incl breakfast ¥1390; ❄ @) This boutique hotel scores points for its variety of rooms, each one with a kitchen and dining area, large plush beds, flat-screen TVs, and mini-bar. Do you go for the room with the dark rich tones or the one with the white walls and circular bed? Regardless, you'll be thanking Christian each time you step into the room. Efficient staff rounds out the experience.

🡢 Detour:
Shàolín Temple

In Taoism, Sōng Shān is regarded as the central mountain, symbolising earth (tǔ) among the five elements and occupying the axis directly beneath heaven. Despite this Taoist affiliation, the mountains are also home to one of China's most famous and legendary Zen (Chan) Buddhist temples, the **Shàolín Temple** (少林寺, Shàolín Sì; 📞 6370 2503; admission ¥100; ⏱ 7.30am-5.30pm). You could spend an entire day or two here, as there are other smaller temples to visit and peaks to hike up and around.

The Shàolín Temple's claim to fame, gōngfū (kung fu) based on varying animals and insects, was reputedly the result of a monk named Damo developing a set of exercises for monks to keep fit.

Many buildings, such as the main **Daxiong Hall** (大雄宝殿; Dàxióng Bǎodiàn; reconstructed in 1985) were levelled by fire in 1928. Among the oldest structures at the temple are the **decorative arches** and **stone lions**, outside the main gate. At the rear, the **West Facing Hall** (西方圣人殿; Xīfāng Shēngrén Diàn) contains floor depressions, apocryphally the result of generations of monks practising their stance work, and huge colour frescoes.

The **Pagoda Forest** (少林塔林; Shàolín Tǎlín), a cemetery of 248 brick pagodas, is worth visiting if you get here ahead of the crowds. At 1512m above sea level and reachable on the **Sōngyáng Cableway** (Sōngyáng Suǒdào; ¥60 return, 20 minutes), **Shàoshì Shān** (少室山) is the area's tallest peak.

To reach the Shàolín Temple, take a minibus from Luòyáng (¥19.50, 1½ hours) to the drop-off.

🍴 Eating

Qiánmén Kǎoyā Dàjiǔdiàn
Peking Duck $$

(前门烤鸭大酒店; ☎6395 3333; cnr Zhongzhou Donglu & Minzu Jie; half/whole duck ¥70/138, other dishes from ¥28; ⏰10am-2pm & 5-9pm) This efficient and smart choice serves up rich and tasty roast duck (烤鸭; *kǎoyā*), cooked by an army of white-clad chefs. There are other vegetable and meat dishes on the menu but why bother?

ℹ Information

Bank of China (中国银行, Zhōngguó Yínháng; ⏰8am-4.30pm) Most branches have ATMs that take international cards. The Zhongzhou Xilu office exchanges travellers cheques. There's also a branch on the corner of Zhongzhou Lu and Shachang Nanlu. Another branch just west of the train station has foreign-exchange services.

Industrial & Commercial Bank of China (CBC, 工商银行, Gōngshāng yínháng; 228 Zhongzhou Zhonglu) Huge branch; foreign exchange and 24-hour ATM.

Public Security Bureau (PSB, 公安局, Gōng'ānjú; ☎6393 8397; cnr Kaixuan Lu & Tiyuchang Lu; ⏰8am-noon & 2-5.30pm Mon-Fri) The exit-entry department (出入境大厅, Chūrùjìng Dàtīng) is in the south building.

ℹ Getting There & Away

Air

You would do better to fly into or out of Zhèngzhōu. Daily flights operate to Běijīng (¥860, 1½ hours), Shànghǎi (¥890, 1½ hours), Guǎngzhōu (¥1410) and other cities. Obtain tickets through hotels or Ctrip (http://english. ctrip.com).

Bus

Regular departures from the **long-distance bus station** (一运汽车站, yīyùn qìchēzhàn; 51 Jinguyuan Lu) diagonally across from the train station include the following:

Shàolín Temple ¥19.50, 1½ hours, every 30 minutes (5.20am to 4pm)

Xī'ān ¥71-79, four hours, hourly

Buses to similar destinations also depart from the friendly and less frantic **Jīnyuǎn bus station** (锦远汽车站; Jīnyuǎn qìchēzhàn), just west of the train station.

Train

Luòyáng's **Luòyáng Lóngmén station** (洛阳龙门站; Lùoyáng Lóngmén Zhàn) over the river in the south of town has D and G trains. The regular **train station** (洛阳火车站; Lùoyáng Huǒchē Zhàn) has regional and long-distance trains.

From Lùoyáng Lóngmén Station:

Běijīng west G train 2nd/1st class ¥368/589, 4 hours

Shànghǎi D train 2nd/1st class ¥264/765, nine hours

Gōngfū exponents, Shàolín Temple (p147)
NANCY BROWN/GETTY IMAGES ©

DIGITAL VISION./GETTY IMAGES ©

⭐ Don't Miss
Losana Buddha Statue Cave

The most physically imposing and magnificent of all the Lóngmén Caves, this vast cave (奉先寺; Fèngxīan Sì) was carved during the Tang dynasty between AD 672 and 675; it contains the best examples of sculpture, despite evident weathering and vandalism.

In contrast to the other-worldly effigies of the Northern Wei, many Tang figures possess a more fearsome ferocity and muscularity, most noticeable in the huge guardian figure in the north wall.

The 17m-high seated central Buddha is said to be Losana, whose face is allegedly modelled on Tang empress and Buddhist patron Wu Zetian, who funded its carving.

Xī'ān north G train 2nd/1st class ¥175/280, two hours, regular

ℹ Getting Around

The airport is 12km north of the city. Bus 83 (¥1, 30 minutes) runs from the parking lot to the right as you exit the train station. A taxi from the train station costs about ¥35.

Taxis are ¥5 at flag fall, making them good value and a more attractive option than taking motor-rickshaws, which will cost you around ¥4 from the train station to Wángchéng Sq.

Around Luòyáng

LÓNGMÉN CAVES   龙门石窟

A Sutra in stone, the epic achievement of the **Lóngmén Caves** (龙门石窟, Lóngmén Shíkū; admission ¥120, English-speaking guide ¥150; ⏱7.30am-4.30pm & 7-10.30pm summer, 8am-4pm & 7-10.30pm winter) was first undertaken by chisellers from the Northern Wei dynasty, after the capital was relocated here from Dàtóng in AD 494. During the next 200 years or so, more than 100,000 images and statues of Buddha and his disciples emerged from more than a kilometre of limestone cliff wall along the Yī River (Yī Hé).

In the early 20th century, many effigies were beheaded by unscrupulous collectors or simply extracted whole, many ending up abroad in such institutions as the Metropolitan Museum of Art in New York, the Atkinson Museum in Kansas City and the Tokyo National Museum. Weather has also played its part, wearing smooth the faces of many other statues.

The caves are scattered in a line on the west and east sides of the river. Most of the significant Buddhist carvings are on the west side, but a notable crop can also be admired after traversing the bridge to the east side.

The Lóngmén Caves are 13km south of Luòyáng and can be reached by taxi (¥30) or bus 81 (¥1.50, 40 minutes) from the east side of Luòyáng's train station. The last bus 81 returns to Luòyáng at 8.50pm. Buses 53 and 60 also run to the caves.

West Side

Three Bīnyáng Caves   Cave
(宾阳三洞, Bīnyáng Sān Dòng) Work began on the Three Bīnyáng Caves during the Northern Wei dynasty. Despite the completion of two of the caves during the Sui and Tang dynasties, statues here all display the benevolent expressions that characterised Northern Wei style. Traces of pigment remain within the three large grottoes and other small niches honeycomb the cliff walls. Nearby is the **Móyá Three Buddha Niche** (摩崖三佛龛, Móyá Sānfó Kān), with seven figures that date to the Tang dynasty.

Ten Thousand Buddha Cave   Cave
(万佛洞, Wànfó Dòng) South of Three Bīnyáng Caves, the Tang-dynasty Ten Thousand Buddha Cave dates from AD680. In addition to its namesake galaxy of tiny bas-relief Buddhas, there is a fine effigy of the Amitabha Buddha. Note the red pigment on the ceiling.

East Side
When you have reached the last cave on the west side, cross the bridge and walk back north along the east side. The lovely **Thousand Arm and Thousand Eye Guanyin** (千手千眼观音龛; Qiānshǒu Qiānyǎn Guānyīn Kān) in Cave 2132 is a splendid bas-relief dating to the Tang dynasty, revealing the Goddess of Mercy framed in a huge fan of carved hands, each sporting an eye. Further is the large **Reading Sutra Cave** (看经寺洞; Kàn Jīng Sìdòng), with a carved lotus on its ceiling and 29 *luóhàn* (or *arhats* – noble ones who have achieved enlightenment) around the base of the walls.

WHITE HORSE TEMPLE

Although its original structures have largely been replaced and it is likely older temples have vanished, this active **monastery** (白马寺, Báimǎ Sì; admission ¥50; ⏱7am-6pm) is regarded as the first surviving Buddhist temple erected on Chinese soil, originally dating from the 1st century AD.

When two Han-dynasty court emissaries went in search of Buddhist scriptures, they encountered two Indian monks in Afghanistan; the monks returned to Luòyáng on two white horses carrying Buddhist Sutras and statues. The impressed emperor built the temple to house the monks; it is also their resting place. In the **Hall of the Heavenly Kings**, Milefo (the future Buddha) laughs from within an intricately carved cabinet featuring more than 50 dragons writhing across the structure. The standout **Qíyún Pagoda** (齐云塔; Qíyún Tǎ), an ancient 12-tiered brick tower, is a pleasant five-minute walk through a garden and across a bridge. The temple is 13km east of Luòyáng, around 40 minutes away on bus 56 from the Xīguān (西关) stop. Bus 58 from Zhongzhou Donglu in the old town also runs here.

PÍNGYÁO 平遥

📞0354 / POP 450,000

China's best-preserved ancient walled town, Píngyáo is fantastic. This is the

Píngyáo

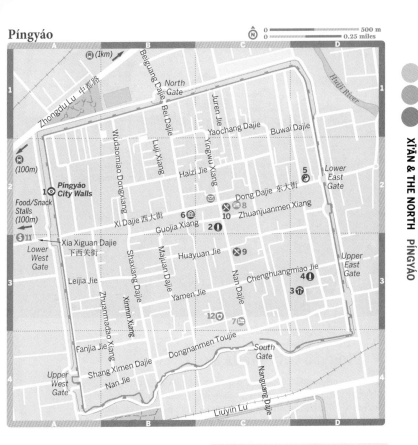

China of your dreams: red-lantern–hung lanes set against night-time silhouettes of imposing town walls, elegant courtyard architecture, ancient towers poking into the north China sky, and an entire brood of creaking temples and old buildings.

History

Already a thriving merchant town during the Ming dynasty, Píngyáo's ascendancy came during the Qing era when merchants created the country's first banks and cheques to facilitate the transfer of vast amounts of silver from one place to another. The city escaped the shocking reshaping much loved by communist town planners, and almost 4000 Ming- and Qing-dynasty residences remain within the city walls.

Píngyáo

CHINA PHOTOS/STRINGER/GETTY IMAGES ©

⭐ Don't Miss
Píngyáo City Walls

The magnificent **city walls** (城墙; chéng qiáng), which date from 1370, are unmissable. At 10m high and more than 6km in circumference, they are punctuated by 72 watchtowers, each containing a paragraph from Sunzi's *The Art of War*. Píngyáo's **city gates** (城门; chéngmén) are fascinating and are some of the best preserved in China; the **Lower West Gate** (Fèngyì Mén; Phoenix Appearing Gate) has a section of the original road, deeply grooved with the troughs left by cartwheels (also visible at the South Gate).

◉ Sights

It's free to walk the streets, but you must pay ¥150 to climb the city walls or enter any of the 18 buildings deemed historically significant. Tickets are valid for three days.

Rìshēngchāng Financial House Museum
Museum

(日升昌, Rìshēngchāng; 38 Xi Dajie, 西大街 38号; ◉8am-7pm) Not to be missed, this museum began life as a humble dye shop in the late 18th century before its tremendous success as a business saw it transform into China's first draft bank (1823), eventually expanding to 57 branches nationwide. The museum has nearly 100 rooms, including offices, living quarters and a kitchen, as well as several old cheques.

Confucius Temple
Confucian Temple

(文庙, Wén Miào; ◉8am-7pm) Píngyáo's oldest surviving building is **Dàchéng Hall** (大成殿; Dàchéng Diàn), dating from 1163 and found in the Confucius Temple, a huge complex where bureaucrats-to-be came to take the imperial exams.

City Tower
Tower

(市楼, Shì Lóu; Nan Dajie; ◉8am-7pm) Snap a photo before passing under the tallest building in the old town en route to other sites. Sadly, you can no longer climb its stone steps for city views.

Qīngxū Guàn
Taoist Temple

(清虚观; Dong Dajie; ☺8am-7pm) Shānxī dust has penetrated every crevice of the 10 halls that make up this impressive Taoist temple. But that only adds to its ancient aura; it dates back to the Tang dynasty.

Nine Dragon Screen
Wall

(九龙壁, Jiǔlóng Bì; Chenghuangmiao Jie) The old **Píngyáo Theatre** (大戏堂; Dàxì-táng) has now been converted into a hotel's banquet hall but is fronted by this magnificent stone wall.

🛏 Sleeping

Most of the old-town hotels are conversions of old courtyard homes, and finding a bed for the night is not hard. Most hotels and hostels will do pick-ups from the train or bus stations.

Harmony Guesthouse
Courtyard Hotel $

(和义昌客栈, Héyìchāng Kèzhàn; ☎0354 568 4952; www.py-harmony.com; 165 Nan Dajie, 南大街165号; dm ¥50-60, r ¥120 & 280; ❄@🛜) The dorms and rooms in these two neatly preserved 300-year-old Qing courtyards, as well as in a smaller courtyard down a neighbouring alley, could use an up-date. However, the English-speaking husband and wife team offer good local information and common areas are cosy. The hostel also offers tours, ticketing, bike rental (¥10 per day), laundry and pick-up.

Jing's Residence
Courtyard Hotel $$$

(锦宅, Jǐn Zhái; ☎0354 584 1000; www.jingsresidence.com; 16 Dong Dajie, 东大街16号; r ¥1500-3200; ❄@🛜) With the super-hushed atmosphere that's unique to the most exclusive (and expensive) hotels, Jing's is a soothing blend of old Píngyáo and modern flair that's squarely aimed at upmarket Western travellers. At 260 years

Píngyáo's Don't Miss List

BY YANG MAOLIN, PÍNGYÁO LOCAL

1 CITY WALL
I love the city wall around Píngyáo. The Ming-dynasty ramparts are all around you as you enter town. From the earliest days, residents have clambered onto the fortification, especially during spring festival when they dress in their finest. It's always satisfying to look out over town and compare the bricks and tiles of Píngyáo with the view beyond.

2 SHUĀNGLÍN TEMPLE
Local people really revere Shuānglín Temple. On the eighth day of the fourth month (on the lunar calendar), worshippers flock to the temple to light incense and worship Buddha. Some pray to Guanyin for peace; others pray to the Money God for lucrative business; others still entreat Niangniang for a son or daughter.

3 NAN DAJIE
Píngyáo's best-known street – 440m-long Nan Dajie – forms the commercial heart of town and symbolises Píngyáo. Most of the buildings here date to the Ming and Qing dynasties, presenting a genteel and well-preserved portrait of old Píngyáo.

4 CITY TOWER
You must visit the 300-year-old City Tower on Nan Dajie for a perspective of the town. With its Qing-dynasty tablets, iron bell and original Qing-dynasty murals adorning the eastern and western walls, views over the old town are excellent.

5 PÍNGYÁO BEEF
When you've finished sightseeing, try some of Píngyáo's exquisite tender beef, which enjoys a nationwide reputation. When the Empress Dowager passed through Píngyáo, she enjoyed the local beef so much it was elevated to the status of an imperial dish. Look out for *zhōnghuá lǎozìhào niúròu* (Chinese old-style beef) – a locally prepared beef.

Below: Buddha statue; **Right:** Street and Ming-dynasty pagoda
(BELOW) NANCY BROWN/GETTY IMAGES ©; (RIGHT) YANN LAYMA/GETTY IMAGES ©

old the former home of a Qing-dynasty silk merchant is sleek and well finished with polished service from the English-speaking staff.

Eating & Drinking

Déjūyuán Shanxi $

(Petit Resto; 德居源; 82 Nan Dajie; mains from ¥25; ⏰8.30am-10pm) Traveller friendly, but no worse for that, this welcoming and popular little restaurant has a simple and tasty menu (in English) of northern Chinese dishes, such as dumplings (¥15), as well as all the local faves. Try the famed Píngyáo beef (¥42) or the mountain noodles (¥12). Cold dishes start at ¥8.

Sakura Cafe Cafe, Bar $$

(櫻花屋西餐酒吧, Yīnghuāwū Xīcān Jiǔbā; 6 Dong Dajie; dishes from ¥35, beers from ¥15; ⏰9.30am-midnight; 📶) This dark and moody cafe-bar attracts both locals and foreigners with its daily food and drink specials. It does decent if pricey pizzas (from ¥55), burgers, as well as breakfast, coffee, beers and cocktails. There's another equally popular branch at 86 Nan Dajie.

Shopping

Part of Píngyáo's charm lies in its peeling and weatherbeaten shopfronts, yet to be mercilessly restored. **Nan Dajie** is stuffed with wood-panelled shops selling ginger sweets (marvel at vendors pulling the golden sugary ginger mass into strips), moon cakes, Píngyáo snacks, knick-knacks, Cultural Revolution memorabilia, jade, shoes, slippers and loads more.

Information

All guesthouses and hostels have internet and wi-fi access.

工商银行, Gōngshāng Yínháng; Xia Xiguan Dajie)
Has an ATM

Public Security Bureau (PSB, 公安局,
Gōng'ānjú; ☏0354 563 5010; off Yamen Jie;
☺8am-noon & 3-6pm Mon-Fri)

ℹ Getting There & Away

Bus

Píngyáo's **bus station** (汽车新站; qìchēxīnzhàn)
has buses to Tàiyuán (¥26, two hours, frequent,
6.30am to 7.40pm), Líshí (¥44, two hours,
8.30am and 12.30pm), Chángzhì (¥79, three
hours, 7.50am and 1.40pm) and the Qiao's Family
Courtyard (¥26, 45 minutes, half hourly).

Train

Tickets for trains (especially to Xī'ān) are tough
to get in summer, so plan ahead. Your hotel/
hostel should be able to help. Trains depart for the
following destinations:

Běijīng D train ¥161, 4½ hours, two daily

Dàtóng hard seat/sleeper ¥62/123, seven to
eight hours, four daily

Tàiyuán ¥18, 1½ hours, frequent

Xī'ān D train ¥136, three hours, four daily

ℹ Getting Around

Píngyáo can be easily navigated on foot or bicycle
(¥10 per day). Rickshaws run to the train and bus
stations for ¥10.

Around Píngyáo

Most hostels and guesthouses will
arrange transport to the surrounding
sights.

WANG FAMILY
COURTYARD   王家大院

More castle than cosy home, this Qing-
dynasty **former residence** (王家大院;
Wángjiā Dàyuàn; admission ¥66; ☺8am-7pm) is
grand and has been very well maintained (note the wooden galleries still
fronting many of the courtyard buildings). Its sheer size, though, means that

155

the seemingly endless procession of courtyards (123 in all) becomes a little repetitive. Behind the castle walls are interesting and still-occupied **cave dwellings** (窑洞; yáodòng), while in front of the complex is a Yuan-dynasty **Confucius Temple** (文庙, Wén Miào; admission ¥10), with a beautiful three-tiered wooden pagoda.

Two direct buses (8.20am and 2.40pm) leave from Píngyáo bus station. Regular buses go to Jièxiū (介休; ¥7, 40 minutes), where you can change to bus 11 (¥4, 40 minutes), which terminates at the complex. The last bus back to Jièxiū leaves at 6pm.

SHUĀNGLÍN TEMPLE 双林寺

Within easy reach of Píngyáo, this **Buddhist temple** (双林寺, Shuānglín Sì; admission ¥40; ⏱8.30am-6.30pm) surrounded by cornfields, houses a number of rare, intricately carved Song- and Yuan-era painted statues. The interiors of the Sakyamuni Hall and flanking buildings are especially exquisite. A rickshaw or taxi from town will cost ¥40 to ¥50 return, or you could cycle the 7km here (although expect to swallow coal truck dust if you do).

WŬTÁI SHĀN 五台山

The gorgeous mountainous, monastic enclave of Wŭtái Shān (Five Terrace Mountains) is Buddhism's sacred northern range and the earthly abode of Manjusri (文殊; Wénshū), the Bodhisattva of Wisdom. Chinese students sitting the ferociously competitive *gāokǎo* (university entrance) exams troop here for a nod from the learned bodhisattva, proffering incense alongside saffron-robed monks and octogenarian pilgrims. A powerful sense of the divine holds sway in Wŭtái Shān, emanating from the port-walled monasteries – the principal sources of spiritual power – and finding further amplification in the sublime mountain scenery.

There's a steep ¥218 entrance fee for the area – including a mandatory ¥50 'sightseeing bus' ticket (旅游观光车票; lǚyóu guānguāng chēpiào) for transport within the area, which is valid for three days. Some of the more popular temples charge an additional small entrance fee.

Avoid Wŭtái Shān during the holiday periods and high-season weekends; temperatures are often below zero from October to March and roads can be impassable.

History

It's believed that by the 6th century there were already 200 temples in the area, although all but two were destroyed during the official persecution of Buddhism in the 9th century.

⊙ Sights

Enclosed within a lush valley between the five main peaks is an elongated, unashamedly touristy town, called **Táihuái** (台怀) but which everyone simply calls Wŭtái Shān. It's here that you'll find the largest concentration of temples, as well as all the area's hotels and tourist facilities. The five main peaks are **north** (北台顶; běitái dǐng), **east** (东台顶; dōngtái dǐng), **south** (南台顶; nántái dǐng), **west** (西台顶; xītái dǐng) and **central** (中台顶; zhōngtái dǐng).

Climate

Wŭtái Shān is at high altitude and powerful blizzards can sweep in as late as May and as early as September. Winters are freezing and snowbound; the summer months are the most pleasant, but always pack a jacket, as well as suitable shoes or boots for rain, as temperatures fall at night.

KARL JOHAENTGES/GETTY IMAGES ©

⭐ Don't Miss
Xiăntōng Temple

Xiăntōng Temple – the largest temple in town – was erected in AD 68 and was the first Buddhist temple in the area. It comprises more than 100 halls and rooms. The **Qiānbō Wénshū Hall** contains a 1000-armed, multifaced Wenshu, whose every palm supports a miniature Buddha. The squat brick **Beamless Hall** (无梁殿; Wúliáng Diàn) holds a miniature Yuan-dynasty pagoda, remarkable statues of contemplative monks meditating in the alcoves and a vast seated effigy of Wenshu.

NEED TO KNOW
显通寺, Xiăntōng Sì; ⏱ 6am-6pm

More than 50 temples lie scattered in town and across the surrounding countryside, so knowing where to start can be a daunting prospect. Most travellers limit themselves to what is called the **Táihuái Temple Cluster** (Táihuái Sìmiàoqún; 台怀寺庙群), about 20 temples around Táihuái itself, among which Tǎyuàn Temple and Xiăntōng Temple are considered the best. You could spend weeks exploring the mountain area, investigating temple after temple.

Tǎyuàn Temple   Buddhist Temple
(塔院寺, Tǎyuàn Sì; admission ¥10; ⏱ 6am-6pm)
At the base of **Spirit Vulture Peak** (灵鹫峰; Língjiù Fēng), the distinctive white stupa rising above, Tǎyuàn Temple is the most prominent landmark in Wǔtái Shān and virtually all pilgrims pass through here to spin the prayer wheels at its base or to prostrate themselves, even in the snow. Even Chairman Mao did his tour of duty, staying in the **Abbot Courtyard** in 1948.

OTHER SIGHTS

You can continue exploring the cluster of temples north beyond Xiǎntōng Temple. **Yuánzhào Temple** (圆照寺; Yuánzhào Sì) contains a smaller stupa than the one at Tǎyuàn Temple.

A 10-minute walk south down the road, **Shūxiàng Temple** (殊像寺; Shūxiàng Sì) can be reached up some steep steps beyond its spirit wall by the side of the road. The temple contains Wǔtái Shān's largest statue of Wenshu riding a lion.

For great views of the town, you can hike, take a chairlift (one way/return ¥50/85) or ride a horse (¥50) up to the temple on **Dàiluó Peak** (黛螺顶, Dàiluó Dǐng; admission ¥8), on the eastern side of Qīngshuǐ River (清水河; Qīngshuǐ Hé).

For even better views of the surrounding hills, walk 2.5km south to the isolated, fortress-like **Nánshān Temple** (南山寺; Nánshān Sì), which sees far fewer tour groups than the other temples and has beautiful stone carvings.

Sleeping

Most accommodation is fairly basic. You can find real cheapies without showers in the north of the village.

Runaway Youth Hostel Hostel **$** (五台山Runaway国际青年旅舍, Runaway Guójì Qīngnián Lǚshě; ☎186 3604 2689, 0354 654 9505; 648984355@qq.com; dm ¥50, d & tw ¥128-148; ⊗closed Oct-Apr; @🛜) The Húběi owner Zhou Jin is a passionate traveller who set up this hostel with his local wife in a quiet southwestern section of the mountain. Enter via a cosy lounge area (equipped with an Xbox) that leads up to clean hotel-standard private rooms and rooftop bunk rooms, all en suite.

Ask about organised hikes and mountain-bike rides, several to the peaks.

Eating

Loads of small family-run restaurants are tucked away behind hotels and down small alleys off the main strip.

Information

Bring cash, as there's nowhere to change money and ATMs only accept Chinese cards.

Getting There & Away

Bus

Buses from Wǔtái Shān bus station (汽车站; qìchē zhàn):

Běijīng ¥145, five hours, 9am and 2pm

Dàtóng ¥75, four hours, three daily (8.30am 1pm and 2pm, summer only)

Hanging Monastery ¥65, three hours, one daily (8.30am)

Tàiyuán ¥74, five hours, hourly (6.30am to 4pm)

Gate and walls of Luo Hou Monastery, Wǔtái Shān

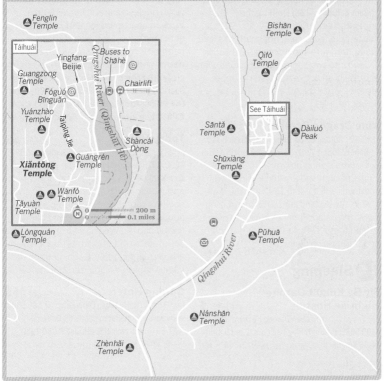

Buses to **Shāhé** (¥25, 1½ hours, hourly, 8am to 5pm) leave from the car park by the chairlift to Dàiluó Peak.

Train

The station known as Wǔtái Shān is actually 50km away in the town of Shāhé (砂河) from where you can get a minibus taxi the rest of the way from around ¥70. An example route and fare is for Běijīng (seat ¥50, six to seven hours, two daily).

DÀTÓNG 大同

Its coal-belt setting and socialist-era refashioning have robbed Dàtóng of much of its charm. The city has, however, ploughed mountains of cash – an estimated ¥50 billion – into a colossal renovation program of its old quarter. But even without its pricey facelift, Dàtóng still cuts it as a coal-dusted heavyweight in China's increasingly competitive tourist challenge. The city is the gateway to the awe-inspiring Yúngāng Caves, one of China's most outstanding Buddhist treasures, as well as close to the photogenic Hanging Monastery.

⊙ Sights

Much of Dàtóng's **old town** (老城区; lǎochéngqū) has been levelled to restore what was there before. Illogical for sure, but this is China. The renovations were ongoing at the time of writing, with Red Flag Sq completely inaccessible and the area around the Drum Tower (鼓楼; Gǔ Lóu) re-emerging as a twee 'Ye Olde Qing Quarter'.

Huáyán Temple
Buddhist

(华严寺, Huáyán Sì; Huayan Jie; admission ¥80; ⏰8am-6.30pm; 🚌38) Built by the Khitan during the Liao dynasty (AD 907–1125), this temple faces east, not south (it's said the Khitan were sun worshippers) and is divided into two separate complexes. One of these is an active monastery (upper temple), while the other is a museum (lower temple).

Nine Dragon Screen
Wall

(九龙壁, Jiǔlóng Bì; Da Dongjie; admission ¥10; ⏰8am-6.30pm) With its nine beautiful multicoloured coiling dragons, this 45.5m-long, 8m-high and 2m-thick Ming-dynasty spirit wall was built in 1392. It's the largest glazed-tile wall in China and an amazing sight; the palace it once protected belonged to the 13th son of a Ming emperor and burnt down years ago.

🛌 Sleeping

Fly By Knight Datong Highrise Hostel
Hostel $

(夜奔大同客栈; Yèbēn Dàtóng Kèzhàn; ☎130 4109 5935; datongfbk@gmail.com; 22nd fl, Unit 14, 15 Yingbin Xijie, 迎宾西街15号22楼14室 (桐

城中央); dm ¥80-140, s & tw shared bathroom ¥150-180, d en suite ¥200; 🛜) China's (possibly) priciest hostel is housed within a modern apartment located 1.5km west of the old town. Neat Ikea-furnished bedrooms have been converted into dorms and private rooms. Bathrooms are clean and the English-speaking staff are friendly. The hostel is a ¥10 cab ride from the bus station and old town, and ¥15 from the train station.

Today Hotel
Hotel $$

(今日商务酒店, Jīnrì Shāngwù Juǐdiàn; ☎537 9800; 1029 Weidu Dadao; 魏都大道1029号; d & tw ¥219; ❄🛜) This chain hotel located opposite the train station has large and spotless rooms with wooden-panelled flooring (no icky carpets), good bathrooms and is a great spot to decamp after you stumble out of the train station from an overnight journey. Get a room on the higher floor to escape the street noise.

Garden Hotel
Hotel $$$

(花园大饭店, Huāyuán Dàfàndiàn; ☎586 5888; www.gardenhoteldatong.com; 59 Da Nanjie, 大南街59号; d & tw incl breakfast ¥1080-1380; ☺❄@🛜) The large impeccable rooms

Nine Dragon Screen

WARWICK KENT/GETTY IMAGES ©

at this hotel feature goose-down quilts, carved rosewood bed frames, reproduction antique furnishings and superb bathrooms. It has an attractive atrium, Latin American and Chinese restaurants, plus excellent staff. The impressive breakfast spread includes good espresso coffee. Significant discounts (even in high season) knock prices as low as ¥310, making it one of the best-value hotels in China.

Eating

Tónghé Dàfàndiàn
Chinese $

(同和大饭店; Zhanqian Jie; dishes ¥16-40; ☺11am-2pm & 6-9pm) This very popular, bright and cheery spot next to the Hongqi Hotel may look a little intimidating with its big round tables better suited to functions, but solo diners can also pull up a chair. There's a huge range of tasty, well-presented dishes on the picture menu, suiting all budgets.

Information

Agricultural Bank of China (ABC; 中国农业银行; Zhōngguó Nóngyè Yínháng; Da Nanjie) ATM and money exchange.

Public Security Bureau (PSB, 公安局出入境接待处, Gōng'ānjú Chūrùjìng Jiēdàichù; ☎206 1833; 11 fl, Hualin Xintiandi, Weidu Dadao, 花林新天地, 11楼, 魏都大道; ☺9am-noon & 3-5.30pm Mon-Fri)

Getting There & Away

Air
Located 20km east of the city, Dàtóng's small airport has flights to Běijīng (¥450, one hour), Shànghǎi (¥1450, 2½ hours) and Guǎngzhōu (¥1650, 4½ hours). No public transport goes to the airport. A taxi costs around ¥50.

Bus
Minibuses also run to some of the destinations listed below from outside the train station. Buses from the south bus station (新南站; xīnnán zhàn), located 9km from the train station depart for:

If You Like...
City Walls

If you like the city walls of Píngyáo (p150) and Xī'ān (p136), north China has other towns ringed by ramparts. Their survival usually signifies further historical remains.

1 ZHÈNGDÌNG
(城墙, Chéngqiáng) Walled Zhèngdìng has an outstanding collection of temples, including Lóngxīng Temple which houses an astonishing bronze colossus of Guanyin. From Shíjiāzhuāng, take bus 30 (¥2) from beside the former train station to the south bus station (南焦客运站, Nánjiāo Kèyùnzhàn), then take bus 177 (¥2, one hour, 6.50am to 8.50pm), which passes through South Gate and the other temples before reaching Lóngxīng Temple.

2 KĀIFĒNG
Once the prosperous capital of the Northern Song, the walled town of Kāifēng has an alluring crop of temples and pagodas. West of Zhèngzhōu, Kāifēng is on the railway line between Xī'ān and Shànghǎi, with several high speed trains passing through.

3 JĪMÍNGYÌ
(东门, Dōng Mén) Whipped by dust storms in spring, Jīmíngyì (140km northwest of Běijīng) is China's oldest remaining post station. The town walls still stand (although sections have collapsed); ascend the East Gate for fine views. Jīmíngyì can be reached from the small mining town of Xià Huāyuán (下花园), 5km away. To get to Xià Huāyuán, take bus 880 (2½ hours, ¥32; with travel card ¥24) from beside Déshèngmén Gateway in Běijīng. Then take a minivan (per person ¥1.50) to the local bus station (汽车站; qìchēzhàn), then take the small bus to Shāchéng (沙城), which goes past Jīmíngyì (5 minutes, ¥3). Three trains (10.40am, 2.37pm and 2.41pm) leave each day from Běijīng west train station to Xià Huāyuán. The cheapest and quickest is the 2.37pm (¥10, 3 hours). Come out of the train station and turn right to walk to Jīmíngyì (4km) or flag down the Shāchéng bus (¥3).

Detour:
Hanging Monastery

Built precariously into the side of a cliff, the Buddhist **Hanging Monastery** (Xuánkōng Sì; admission ¥130; ☉8am-7pm summer) is made all the more stunning by its long support stilts. The halls have been built along the contours of the cliff face, connected by rickety catwalks and narrow corridors, which can get very crowded in summer.

Buses travel here from Dàtóng's main bus station (¥31, two hours). Most will transfer passengers to the monastery into a free taxi for the last 5km from Húnyuán (浑源). Heading back, you'll be stung for ¥20 for a taxi (per person) to Húnyuán. If you want to go on to Mùtǎ, there are frequent buses from Húnyuán (¥14, one hour), or shared taxis make the run from the monastery car park for ¥50 per person (when full).

Běijīng ¥128, four hours, hourly (7.10am to 4.10pm)

Wǔtái Shān ¥75, 3½ hours, two daily (8.30am, 9am and 2pm; summer only)

Buses from the **main bus station** (大同汽车站, Dàtóng qìchēzhàn; ☏246 4464; Xinjian Nanlu):

Hanging Monastery ¥31, two hours, half-hourly (6.30am to 11am)

Train

Train departures from Dàtóng include the following:

Běijīng hard seat/sleeper ¥54/108, six hours, 11 daily

Píngyáo hard seat/sleeper ¥68/129, seven to eight hours, four daily

Xī'ān hard seat/sleeper ¥117/230, 16½ hours, one daily (4.40pm)

ⓘ Getting Around

Taxi flagfall is ¥7.

Around Dàtóng

YÚNGĀNG CAVES   云冈石窟

One of China's most superlative examples of Buddhist cave art, these 5th-century **caves** (Yúngāng Shíkū; 0352 302 6230; admission ¥150; ☉8.30am-5.30pm summer) are ineffably sublime. With 51,000 ancient statues, they put virtually everything else in the Shānxī shade.

Carved by the Turkic-speaking Tuoba, the Yúngāng Caves draw their designs from Indian, Persian and even Greek influences that swept along the Silk Road. Work began in AD 460, continuing for 60 years before all 252 caves, the oldest collection of Buddhist carvings in China, had been completed.

Despite weathering, many of the statues at Yúngāng still retain their gorgeous pigment, unlike the slightly more recent statues at Lóngmén Caves. Note that worshippers still pray here, too. A number of the caves were once covered by wooden structures, but many of these are long gone, although **Caves 5**, **6**, **7** and **8** are fronted by wooden temples.

Some caves contain intricately carved square-shaped pagodas, while others depict the inside of temples, carved and painted to look as though made of wood. Frescoes are in abundance and there are graceful depictions of animals, birds and angels, some still brightly painted, and almost every cave contains the 1000-Buddha motif (tiny Buddhas seated in niches).

Eight of the caves contain enormous Buddha statues; the largest can be found in **Cave 5**, an outstanding 17m-high, seated effigy of Sakyamuni with a gilded face. The frescos in this cave are badly scratched, but note the painted vaulted ceiling. Bursting with colour, **Cave 6** is also stunning, resembling a set from an *Indiana Jones* epic with legions of Buddhist angels, bodhisattvas and other figures. In the middle of the cave, a square block pagoda connects with the ceiling, with Buddhas on each side over two levels.

Chronic weathering has afflicted **Cave 7** (carved between AD 470 and 493) and **Cave 8**, both scoured by the Shānxī winds. Atmospheric pollution has also taken its toll.

Caves 16 to **20** are the earliest caves at Yúngāng, carved under the supervision of monk Tanyao. Examine the exceptional quality of the carvings in **Cave 18**; some of the faces are perfectly presented. **Cave 19** contains a vast 16.8m-high effigy of Sakyamuni. The Maitreya Buddha is a popular subject for Yúngāng's sculptors, for example in the vast seated form in **Cave 17** and **Cave 13**; the latter statue has been defaced with graffiti by workers from Hohhot and other miscreants.

Cave 20 is similar to the Ancestor Worshipping Cave at Lóngmén, originally depicting a trinity of Buddhas (the past, present and future Buddhas). The huge seated Buddha in the middle is the representative icon at Yúngāng, while the Buddha on the left has somehow vanished. Many caves in the western end of Yúngāng have Buddhas with their heads smashed off, as in **Cave 39**.

Most of the caves come with good English captions, but there's also a free audio guide in English (¥100 deposit). Note that photography is permitted in some caves but not in others.

ⓘ Getting There & Away

Take the 云冈 double decker bus (¥2, 45 minutes) from outside the train station to its terminus. Buses run every 10 to 15 minutes. A taxi is ¥40 each way.

Climbing Tài Shān (p166)

PEROUSSE BRUNO/GETTY IMAGES ©

TÀI'ĀN   泰安

Gateway to Tài Shān's sacred slopes, Tài'ān's tourist industry has been in full swing since before the Ming dynasty.

Though there's not much to see outside of the magnificent Dài Temple, you will need the better part of a day for the mountain, so spending the night here or at the summit is advised.

⊙ Sights

Dài Temple   Taoist Temple

(岱庙; Dài Miào; www.daimiao.cn/English; Daimiao Beijie Lu; adult/child ¥30/15; ⊙8am-6pm summer, to 5pm winter) This magnificent Taoist temple complex is where all Tài'ān roads lead, being the traditional first stop on the pilgrimage route up Tài Shān.

The grounds are an impressive example of Song-dynasty (960–1127) temple construction with features of an imperial palace, though other structures stood here 1000 years before that.

🛏 Sleeping

Tàishān International Youth Hostel   Hostel **$**

(太山国际青年旅舍; Tàishān Guójì Qīngnián Lüshè; ☑628 5196; 65 Tongtian Jie; 通天街65号; dm ¥50-70, s & d ¥188; ❄@🛜; 🖵1, 4, 7, 8, 17) Tài'ān's first youth hostel has clean spartan rooms with pine furnishings and old propaganda posters. Bike rental, free laundry and a bar on the 4th floor make this a pleasant experience. Look for the pair of arches just off Tongtian Jie. Discounts get rooms down to ¥128.

Yùzuò Hotel   Hotel **$$$**

(御座宾馆; Yùzuò Bīnguǎn; ☑826 9999; www.yuzuo.cn; 50 Daimiao Beilu; 岱庙北路50号; s & d ¥780, ste ¥1680; ❄🛜; 🖵4, 6) This pretty hotel next to the Dài Temple's north gate was purposely kept to two storeys out of respect for its neighbour. Deluxe rooms are decked out in imperial style; cheaper rooms are rather ordinary. The attached bakery and restaurants serve Taoist food (12 courses ¥168 per person). Discounts of 50% make this a good deal.

Sunrise on the sacred mountain of Tài Shān

O. LOUIS MAZZATENTA/GETTY IMAGES ©

Detour:
Tiānzhú Peak Route 天烛峰景区

The route up the back of Tài Shān (p166) from the Tiānzhú Peak Scenic Area (Tiānzhú Fēng Jǐngqū) offers a rare chance to ascend the mountain without crowds. It's mostly ancient forest and peaks back there, so take the central route down for the man-made sights.

Get an early start; the bus ride takes 45 minutes, and the climb itself can take upwards of five hours.

It's 5.4km from the trailhead to the **Rear Rocky Recess cable car** (后石坞索道; Hòu Shíwù suǒdào; ☑0538 833 0765; one way ¥20; ◷8.30am-4pm Apr-Oct, closed 16 Oct-15 Apr), which takes you from the back of the mountain to the **North Gate to Heaven cable car stop** (北天门索道站; Běi Tiānmén suǒdào zhàn) and offers views of Tiānzhú Peak – when it's running. Call in advance.

🍴 Eating

The **night market** (yè shì; ◷5.30pm-late) on the Nai River's east bank has many hotpot stalls. Vendors on **Běixīn Snack Street** (北新小吃步行街; Běixīn Xiǎochī Bùxíng Jiē) set up carts for lunch (except Saturday) and dinner.

Ā Dōng de Shuǐjiǎo   Chinese $
(阿东的水饺; ☑139 5489 8518; 31 Hongmen Lu; mains from ¥20; ◷9am-10pm; 🌶) This centrally located restaurant serves up northern Chinese staples including shuǐjiǎo (水饺; dumplings). There are a wide range of fillings including lamb (羊肉; yángròu; ¥34 per jīn – enough for two) and vegetarian tofu (豆腐; dòufu; ¥18 per jīn). The English menu is challenging, so be prepared to point.

ⓘ Information

Bank of China (中国银行; Zhōngguó Yínháng; 116 Tongtian Jie; ◷8.30am-4.30pm) Currency exchange and 24-hour ATM accepts foreign cards.

Public Security Bureau (PSB; 公安局; Gōng'ānjú; ☑827 5264; cnr Dongyue Dajie & Qingnian Lu; ◷visa office 8.30am-noon & 1-5pm Mon-Fri, or by appointment) The visa office (出入境管理处) is on the east side of the shiny grey building.

ⓘ Getting There & Away

Bus

The **long-distance bus station** (长途汽车站; chángtú qìchēzhàn; ☑218 8777; cnr Tài'shān Dalu & Longtan Lu), also known as the old station (lǎo zhàn), is just south of the train station. Buses regularly depart for these destinations:

Qīngdǎo ¥126, 5½ hours, five daily (6am, 8am, 8.40am, 2.30pm and 4pm)

Qūfù ¥23, one hour, every 30 minutes (7.20am to 5.20pm)

Train

Two train stations service this region. **Tài Shān train station** (泰山火车站; ☑688 7358; cnr Dongyue Dajie & Longtan Lu) is the most central, but express trains only pass through **Tài'ān train station** (泰安火车站; ☑138 0538 5950; Xingaotiezhan Lu), sometimes referred to as the new station (xīn zhàn), 9km west of the town centre.

Some regular trains departing from Tài Shān train station:

Qīngdǎo K seat ¥70, five to seven hours, hourly (12.28am to 2.52pm)

Qūfù K seat ¥19, 1½hours, two daily (6.05am and 10.50am)

Some express trains departing from Tài'ān train station:

Běijīng D/G seat ¥214, 2 hours, hourly (7.48am to 9.21pm)

Qīngdǎo G seat ¥149, three hours, one daily (11.14am, 12.54pm, 3.10pm, 5.14pm, 5.46pm and 6.32pm)

Shànghǎi G seat ¥374, 31½hours, every 30 minutes (7.24am to 7.45pm)

❶ Getting Around

Taxis cost ¥6 to ¥7 for the first 3km and ¥1.50 (slightly more at night) per kilometre thereafter.

TÀI SHĀN 泰山

📞0538

Sacred mountains are a dime a dozen in China, but in the end the one that matters most is **Tài Shān** (泰山; www.taishangeopark. com; adult/student & senior Feb-Nov ¥127/60, Dec-Jan ¥102/50). It is said if you climb this Taoist mountain, you'll live to 100.

Qin Shi Huang, the First Emperor, chose Tài Shān's summit to proclaim

the unified kingdom of China in 219 BC. Seventy-one other emperors and countless figures including Du Fu and Mao Zedong have also left their marks on the mountain.

Autumn, when humidity is low, is the best time to visit; while early October onwards has the clearest weather. In winter temperatures dip below freezing and most summit hotels have no hot water.

◉ Sights & Activities

There are three routes up the mountain to its highest peak, 1533m above sea level, that can be followed on foot: the **central route** (historically the Emperor's Route (御道; Yù Dào), winding 8.9km from base to summit, gaining 1400m of elevation; the **western route**, which follows the bus route; and the less travelled **Tiānzhú Peak route** (天烛峰景区) trail up the back of the mountain.

The central and western routes converge at the halfway point (Midway Gate to Heaven), from where it's another 3.5km up steep steps to the summit.

If this sounds like too much for your knees, take a minibus to Midway Gate to Heaven and then a cable car to South Gate to Heaven near the summit, and then a bus back down.

Weather can change suddenly and the summit can be very cold, windy and wet, so bring warm layers and rain gear. You can buy rain ponchos and at the top, rent overcoats (¥30).

As with all Chinese mountain hikes, viewing the sunrise is considered an integral part of the experience.

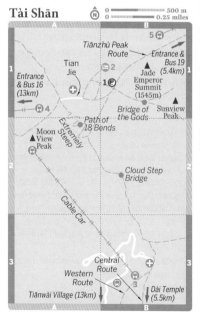

Tài Shān

◉ Sights
1 Azure Clouds Temple...........................B1

🛏 Sleeping
2 Shénqì Hotel B1

❶ Transport
3 Main Cable Car....................................B3
4 Peach Blossom Park Cable Car..........A1
5 Rear Rocky Recess Cable Car............B1

CENTRAL ROUTE 中路

This has been the main route up the mountain since the 3rd century BC, and over the past two millennia a bewildering number of bridges, trees, rivers, gullies, inscriptions, caves, pavilions and temples have become famous sites in their own right. Figure on at least four hours to get to the top.

Purists begin with a south–north perambulation through Dài Temple in Tài'ān, 1.7km south of the trailhead, in accordance with imperial tradition, but there is no shame in starting at the bus stop by **Guandi Temple** (关帝庙; Guāndì Miào; admission ¥10), the first of many dedicated to the Taoist protector of peace.

Passing **First Gate of Heaven** (一天门; Yītiān Mén; 987m) marks the start of the actual ascent, though the **ticket office** (售票处; Shòupiào Chù; ☎0538 806 6077; ⏲24hr) is further still. The **Red Gate Palace** (红门宫; Hóng Mén Gōng; admission ¥5; ⏲8am-5pm) is the first of a series of temples dedicated to Bixia, the compassionate daughter of the god of Tài Shān.

Take a detour into the **Geoheritage Scenic Area** (地质园区; Dìzhí Yuánqū) for a look at unusual radial rock formations that mesmerised Confucius himself. Back on the main path is the **Buddhist Dǒumǔ Hall** (斗母宫; Dǒumǔ Gōng), first constructed in 1542 under the more magical name 'Dragon Spring Nunnery'.

The **Midway Gate to Heaven** (中天门; Zhōng Tiān Mén) marks the point where some travellers, seeing the stairway disappearing into the clouds, turn heel for the cable car. Don't give up!

If you decide to catch a ride, the **main cable car** (空中索道; kōngzhōng suǒdào; one way/return ¥100/200; ⏲7.30am-6.30pm 16 Apr-15 Oct, 8.30am-5pm 16 Oct-15 Apr) is near the Midway Gate to Heaven. Be warned: peak season and weekend queues can take two hours. You'll pass **Opposing Pines Pavilion** (对松亭; Duìsōng Tíng) and then finally reach the arduous **Path of 18 Bends** (十八盘,Shíbāpán), a 400-metre near vertical ascent to the mountain's false summit; climbing it is performed in slow motion as legs turn to lead.

The final stretch takes you to the **South Gate to Heaven** (南天门; Nán Tián Mén), the third celestial gate, which marks the beginning of the summit area. Bear right along Tian Jie, the main strip, and pass through the gate to reach the sublimely

Summit, Tài Shān

KRZYSZTOF DYDYNSKI/GETTY IMAGES ©

perched **Azure Clouds Temple** (碧霞祠; Bìxiá Cí; ⏱8am-5.15pm) FREE.

The Taoist **Qīngdì Palace** (青帝宫; Qīngdì Gōng) is right before the fog- and cloud-swathed **Jade Emperor Temple** (玉皇顶; Yùhuáng Dǐng), which stands at the Jade Emperor Summit (1545m).

The main sunrise vantage point is the **North Pointing Rock** (拱北石; Gǒngběi Shí); if you're lucky, visibility extends more than 200km to the coast.

WESTERN ROUTE 西路

The most popular way to ascend the mountain is by bus (¥30) via the western route. If you walk, the poorly marked footpath and road often intercept or coincide.

The western route treats you to a variety of scenic orchards and pools. The main attraction along this route is **Black Dragon Pool** (黑龙潭; Hēilóng Tán), just below **Longevity Bridge** (长寿桥; Chángshòu Qiáo).

At the mountain's base, **Pervading Light Temple** (普照寺; Pǔzhào Sì; admission ¥5; ⏱8am-5.30pm), a Buddhist temple dating from the Southern and Northern dynasties (420–589), offers a serene end to the hike.

🛏 Sleeping & Eating

Rates provided below don't apply to holiday periods, when they can triple.

There is no food shortage on Tài Shān; the central route is dotted with stalls and restaurants, but prices rise as you do.

Shénqì Hotel   Hotel $$$
(神憩宾馆; Shénqì Bīnguǎn; ☎0538 822 3866; fax 0538 826 3816; s & d ¥1200-1800, ste ¥6000; ❄ @) The only hotel on the actual summit and prices reflect that. The priciest mountain-view, standard rooms have new everything and were the first on the mountain with hot water in the winter. The restaurant serves Taoist banquet fare (from ¥26).

ℹ Getting There & Away

Bus 3 (¥2) connects the Tài Shān central route trailhead to the western route trailhead at Tiānwài village via the Tài Shān train station.

Bus Y2 (游2; ¥3) and bus 19 (¥2) connect from Caiyuan Dajie across from the train station to the Tiānzhú Peak trailhead. The last bus returns to Tài'ān at 5pm.

ⓘ Getting Around

From Tiānwài village, minibuses (¥30 each way) depart every 20 minutes (or when full) for the 13km journey to Midway Gate to Heaven, halfway up Tài Shān, from 4am to 8pm in peak season and from 7am to 7pm in low season.

QŪFÙ 曲阜

☏0537 / POP 302,805

Hometown of the great sage Confucius and his descendants the Kong clan, Qūfù is a testament to the importance of Confucian thought in imperial China.

⊙ Sights

The principal sights, Confucius Temple, Confucius Mansion and Confucius Forest, are known collectively as *Sān Kǒng* or Three Kongs. The **main ticket office** (售票处; *shòupiàochù*) is at the corner of Queli Jie and Nanma Dao, east of the Confucius Temple's main entrance. You can buy admission to individual sights, but the **combination ticket** (¥150), grants

access to all three plus free or half-price entry to a number of other Confucius-related sights, including **Confucius Cave** (夫子洞, Fūzǐ Dòng) about 30km southeast of Qūfù on Ni Shān. This is where, according to legend, a frighteningly ugly Confucius was born, abandoned, cared for by a tiger and an eagle before his mother realised he was sent from heaven and decided to care for him.

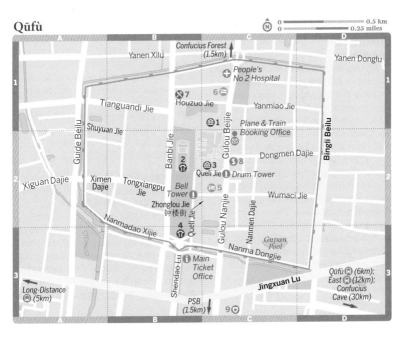

Qūfù

Below: Ceremonial guard, Qūfù ; **Right:** Qūfù city walls
(BELOW) CHRISTIAN KOBER/GETTY IMAGES ©; (RIGHT) KEREN SU/GETTY IMAGES ©

Confucius Temple
Confucian Temple

(孔庙; Kǒng Miào; admission included in combination ticket or ¥90; ☺8am-5.10pm) China's largest imperial building complex after the Forbidden City began as Confucius' three-room house. After his death in 478 BC, the Duke of the Lǔ state consecrated his simple abode as a temple. Everything in it, including his clothing, books, musical instruments and a carriage, was perfectly preserved. The house was rebuilt for the first time in AD 153, kicking off a series of expansions and renovations in subsequent centuries. By 1012, it had four courtyards and over 300 rooms. An imperial-palace-style wall was added. After a fire in 1499, it was rebuilt to its present scale.

Confucius Mansion
Museum

(孔府; Kǒng Fǔ; admission included in combination ticket or ¥60; ☺8am-5.15pm) Next to Confucius Temple is this maze of living quarters, halls, studies and more studies. The mansion buildings were moved from the temple grounds to the present site in 1377 and vastly expanded into 560 rooms in 1503. More remodelling followed, including reconstruction following a devastating fire in 1885.

Confucius Forest
Cemetery

(孔林; Kǒng Lín; admission included in combination ticket or ¥40; ☺8am-5.20pm) About 2km north of town on Lindao Lu is the peaceful Confucius Forest, a cemetery of pine and cypress covering 200 hectares bounded by a 10km-long wall. Confucius and more than 100,000 of his descendants have been buried here for the past 2000 years, a tradition still ongoing.

🛏 Sleeping

Qūfù International Youth Hostel   Hostel $

(曲阜国际青年旅舍; Qūfù Guójì Qīngnián Lǚshè; 📞0537 441 8989; www.yhaqf.com; Gulou Beijie; 鼓楼北街北首路西; dm/tw/tr ¥45/128/158; ❄@🛜) The best deal in town, this friendly hostel at the north end of Gulou Beijie has rooms so clean you can smell the fresh linen. There's bike rental, ticket bookings and a cafe-bar (cocktails from ¥18) serving Chinese and Western fare. Dorms have four to eight beds and share a nice bathroom. Only fault? Hot water can be scarce in the mornings.

Quèlǐ Hotel   Hotel $$$

(阙里宾舍; Quèlǐ Bīnshè; 📞0537 486 6400; www.quelihotel.com; 15 Zhonglou Jie; 钟楼街15号; incl breakfast s ¥398-598, d/ste ¥568/2288; ❄🛜) The four-star Quèlǐ was once the fanciest hotel in town. A recent refurb dusted off the fading photos of the visit-ing dignitaries on the walls, but some rooms are still nicer than others. Look first. Discounts of 20%.

🍴 Eating

Restaurants skip the pageantry nowa-days but for still less formal fare, head to the area around **Shendao Lu** (south of Confucius Temple) or the **night market** (夜市, yèshì), off Wumaci Jie, east of Gu-lou Nanjie. At night, the **Muslim Quarter** comes alive outside the western gate on Xiguan Dajie (西关大街).

Mù'ēn Lóu Halal Food & Drink   Muslim $

(穆恩楼清真餐飲; Mù'ēn Lóu, Qīngzhēn Cānyǐn; 📞0537 448 3877; Houzuo Jie; mains ¥15-60; ⏰8.30am-1.30pm & 5-8.30pm) A friendly Hui family runs this simple place behind the Confucius Mansion, serving house spe-cialities like beef spiced with cumin, star anise and turmeric (南前牛肉; nánqián niúròu piàn; ¥68) and tongue-numbing spicy tofu (麻辣豆腐; málà dòufu; ¥12).

Information

ATMs accepting foreign cards are along or just off Gulou Beijie.

Bank of China (中国银行; **Zhōngguó Yínháng;** 96 Dongmen Dajie; ◷8.30am-4.30pm) Foreign exchange and ATM.

Public Security Bureau (PSB; 公安局; Gōng'ānjú; ☑0537 443 0007; 1 Wuyutai Lu; 舞 零台路1号; ◷8.30am-noon & 2-6pm Mon-Fri) About 1.5km south of the city walls. Can help with initial paperwork for lost passports, but for more you'll have to go to Jíníng (济宁).

Getting There & Away

Bus

Qūfú's **long-distance bus station** (长途汽车站; **chángtú qìchēzhàn; ☑0537 441 2554; Yulong Lu & Yulan Lu;** 裕隆路与玉兰路) is 3km west of the city walls. **Left luggage** (¥2; ◷6am-6pm) is available here. Buses depart for:

Qīngdǎo ¥134, five hours, five daily (8.30am, 9.30am, 1.30pm, 2.20pm and 4.40pm)

Tài'ān ¥23, 1½ hours, every 30 minutes

Train

Trains are the most convenient transport. Catch express trains at the **east train station** (高铁 东火车站; ☑0537 442 1571), 12km east of the walled city. **Qūfú train station** (曲阜火车站; ☑0537 442 1571; Dianlan Lu) is closest to the walled city (6km east) but only regular trains stop there. If tickets are sold out, try **Yānzhōu train station** (兖州火车站; ☑0537 346 2965; Beiguan Jie), 16km west of Qūfú, which is on the Běijīng–Shànghǎi line and has more frequent regular trains.

Some express trains departing from **east train station:**

Běijīng G seat ¥244/409, 2½ hours, frequently (7.26am to 9.01pm)

Qīngdǎo G seat ¥179, 3½ hours, six daily (9.11am, 2.49pm, 4.54pm, 5.25pm, 5.43pm)

Shànghǎi G seat ¥344/584, 3½ hours, frequently (7.53am to 8.11pm)

Air

The Jìníng Qūfù Airport is 80km southwest of Qūfú's old town and connects to Běijīng (¥617, 1½ hour), Chéngdū (¥1167, 2 hours), Guǎngzhōu (¥877, 2½ hours), Shànghǎi (¥868, 2 hours), Xi'an (¥674, 55 minutes), and a handful of other cities. There are no direct buses to Qūfú, however, so flying into Jì'nán can be more convenient.

Getting Around

Bus K01 connects the long-distance bus station to Qūfù's main gate (¥2) and the east train station (¥3). A taxi from within the walls is about ¥40 to the east train station and ¥20 to the long-distance bus station. Bus 1 (¥2) traverses old town along Gulou Beijie to Confucius Forest.

Ubiquitous pedicabs (¥6 to ¥8 within Qūfù; ¥10 to ¥20 outside the walls) are the most pleasant way to get around.

Minibuses (¥5 to ¥7) connect the main gate to Yǎnzhōu train station from 6.30am to 5.30pm, otherwise a taxi costs about ¥50.

QĪNGDǍO 青岛

☑0532 / POP 3.5 MILLION

Offering a breath of fresh air to those emerging from the polluted urban interior, Qīngdǎo is a rare modern city that has managed to preserve some of its past. The winding cobbled streets and red-capped hillside villas are captivating. Qīngdǎo is rapidly expanding into a true multidistrict city, but for now, most of the fun is in or around **Shìnán district** (市南 区), the strip of land along the sea.

History

Before catching the acquisitive eye of Kaiser Wilhelm II, Qīngdǎo was a harbour and fishing village known for producing delicious sea salt. Its excellent strategic location was not lost on the Ming dynasty, which built a defensive battery – nor on the Germans who wrested it from them in 1897.

In 1914 the Japanese took over after a successful joint Anglo-Japanese naval bombardment of the city. The city reverted to Chinese rule in 1922 but the Japanese seized it again in 1938 in the Sino-Japanese War and held it until the end of WWII.

◎ Sights

Governor's House Museum
Museum

(青岛德国总督楼旧址博物馆; Qīngdǎo Déguó Zǒngdū Lóu Jiùzhǐ Bówùguǎn; ☏0532 8286 8838; 26 Longshan Lu; admission summer/winter ¥20/13, multilingual audio tour ¥10; ⏰8.30am-5.30pm; ☒1, 221) East of Signal Hill Park stands one of Qīngdǎo's best examples of concession-era architecture – the former German governor's residence constructed in the style of a German palace. The building's interior is characteristic of Jugendstil, the German arm of art nouveau, with some German and Chinese furnishings of the era.

Protestant Church
Church

(基督教堂; Jīdū Jiàotáng; 15 Jiangsu Lu; admission ¥10; ⏰8.30am-5.30pm; ☒1, 221, 367) On a street of German buildings, this copper-capped church was designed by Curt Rothkegel and built in 1908. The interior is simple and Lutheran in its sparseness, apart from some carvings on the pillar cornices. You can climb up to inspect the clock mechanism (Bockenem 1909).

St Michael's Cathedral
Church

(天主教堂; Tiānzhǔ Jiàotáng; ☏0532 8286 5960; 15 Zhejiang Lu; admission ¥10; ⏰8.30am-5pm Mon-Sat, 10am-5pm Sun; ☒1, 221, 367) Up a hill off Zhongshan Lu looms this grand Gothic- and Roman-style edifice. Completed in 1934, the church spires were supposed to be clock towers, but Chancellor Hitler cut funding of overseas projects and the plans were scrapped.

Huāshí Lóu
Historic Building

(花石楼; Huāshí Lóu; ☏0532 8387 2168; 18 Huanghai Lu; admission ¥8.50; ⏰9am-6pm; ☒26, 231, 604) This granite and marble villa built in 1930 was first the home of a Russian aristocrat, and later the German governor's hunting lodge. It is also known as the 'Chiang Kaishek Building', as the generalissimo secretly stayed here in 1947. While most of the rooms are closed, you can clamber up two narrow stairwells to the turret for a great view.

View over Qīngdǎo

MIRAGEC/GETTY IMAGES ©

Qīngdǎo

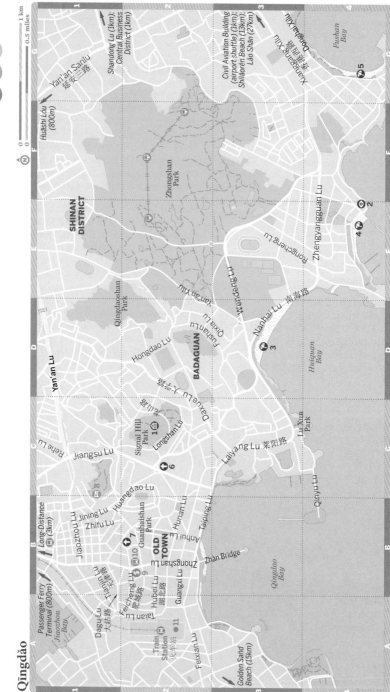

Ⓝ 0 _____ 1 km
0 _____ 0.5 miles

G
Yan'an Sanlu
延安三路

Dōnghǎi Xīlù
东海西路

Fúshān Bay

Xiānggǎng Xīlù
香港西路

Civil Aviation Building
(airport shuttle) (1km);
Shílǎorén Beach (13km);
Lǎo Shān (27km)

Shandong Lu (1km);
Central Business
District (1km)

Huāshí Lóu
(800m)

F
Zhongshan Park

SHINAN DISTRICT

Zhengyangguan Lu

Rongcheng Lu

E
Qīngdǎoshan Park

Yan'an Lu

Hongdao Lu

BADAGUAN

Fúshan Lu

Qíxia Lu

Wendeng Lu

Nanhai Lu 南海路

Huìquán Bay

D
Rehe Lu

Jiangsu Lu

Signal Hill Park

Longshan Lu

Dàxué Lu 大学路

Laiyang Lu 莱阳路

Lu Xun Park

Qínyú Lu

C
Huangdao Lu

Jining Lu
Zhifu Lu

Guanhaishan Park

Húnan Lu

Ānhui Lu

Taiping Lu

Zhan Bridge

B
Long-Distance (3km)

Jiaozhou Lu

Feicheng Lu

OLD TOWN

Zhongshan Lu

Hubei Lu 湖北路

Guangxi Lu

Qīngdǎo Bay

A
Passenger Ferry
Terminal (800m)

Jiaozhou Bay

Dagu Lu
大沽路

Tianjin Lu 天津路

Taian Lu

Train Station
火车站

Feixian Lu

Golden Sand
Beach (15km)

Qīngdǎo

No 1 Bathing Beach
Beach

(第一海水浴场; Dì Yī Hǎishuǐ Yùchǎng; 🚌304)
South of tree-lined Bādàguān, No 1 Bathing Beach is a very popular spot, perhaps for its snack stalls and kiddie toy selection, but more likely for its muscle beach.

No 2 Bathing Beach
Beach

(第二海水浴场; Dì Èr Hǎishuǐ Yùchǎng; 🚌214)
Once reserved only for the likes of Mao and other state leaders, this sheltered cove just east of Bādàguān has calm waters good for a swim. Take bus 214 directly, or bus 26 to the Wǔshèngguān (武胜关) stop to first wander past the villas and sanitoriums scattered in Bādàguān's wooded headlands down to the sea.

No 3 Bathing Beach
Beach

(第三海水浴场; Dì Sān Hǎishuǐ Yùchǎng; 🚌26, 202) On the eastern side of Tàipíng Cape in Bādàguān is this cove with dedicated swim lanes, paddle boats and gentle waves.

Shíláorén Beach
Beach

(石老人海水浴场; Shíláorén Hǎishuǐ Yùchǎng; 🚌301) On the far east side of town in Láo Shān district, this 2.5km-long strip of clean sand is Qīngdǎo's largest beach and has the highest waves in town (decent for bodyboarding). The 'Old Stone Man' from which the beach gets its name is the rocky outcrop to the east. Take bus 301 (¥2, 50 minutes) or a taxi (¥45) from Old Town.

🛏 Sleeping

Kǎiyuè Hostelling International
Hostel $

(凯越国际青年旅馆; Kǎiyuè Guójì Qīngnián Lǚguǎn; 🌙0532 8284 5450; kaiyuehostel@126.com; 31 Jining Lu; 济宁路31号; dm ¥55-75, r without bathroom ¥70-150, with bathroom ¥100-300; ❄🛜) This hostel in a historic church at Sifang Lu and Jining Lu has a lively congregation. They come to worship in the slick new bar and restaurant (Jinns' Café), which serves great pizza (from ¥55) and desserts on the ground floor. The rooms above need the equivalent revamp, though dorms are clean.

China Community Art & Culture
Hotel $$$

(老转村公社文华艺术酒店; Lǎozhuǎncūn Gōngshè Wénhuá Yìshù Jiǔdiàn; 🌙0532 8576 8776; 8 Minjiang Sanlu; 闽江三路8号; s from ¥288, d from ¥598, ste ¥1008; 🚌228, 402, 604) With silk lanterns illuminating the hallways, ceramic bowls serving as sinks, wood-floor showers and antique furnishings, each sumptuously decorated room in this polished hotel in the heart of Dōngbù has the feel of a courtyard residence. There's a fantastic restaurant on the premises. Discounts of 10%. Some English spoken.

🍴 Eating

For the city's staple seafood, stick to the streets.

China Community Art & Culture
Shandong, Sichuanese $$

(老转村公社文华艺术酒店; Lǎozhuǎncūn Gōngshè Wénhuá Yìshù Jiǔdiàn; 🌙0532 8077 6776; 8 Minjiang Sanlu; mains from ¥48, eight-course set meal ¥68; ⏰11.30am-10pm; 🚌228, 312) This lovely restaurant next to its namesake hotel is in a stylised Hakka roundhouse (the sort once mistaken by the CIA for missile silos). The kitchen turns out sumptuous regional cuisine from Shāndōng and Sìchuān. Everything from

Below: No 2 bathing beach (p175); **Right:** Qīngdǎo

(BELOW) MARTIN MOOS/GETTY IMAGES ©; (RIGHT) KEN STRAITON/GETTY IMAGES ©

the mushrooms to water for the tea is locally sourced from Láo Shān.

Information

Emergency

Public Security Bureau (PSB; 公安局; **Gōng'ānjú; ☎general hotline 6657 0000, visa inquiries 6657 3250, ext 2860; 272 Ningxia Lu;** 宁夏路272号; **⏲9am-noon & 1.30-5pm Mon-Fri)** Take bus 301 from the train station to the Xiāoyáo Lù (逍遥路) stop and cross the street to the terracotta-coloured building with the flag on top.

Money

ATMs are easy to find in Qīngdǎo.

Bank of China (中国银行; **Zhōngguó Yínháng; 68 Zhongshan Lu;** 中山路68号; **⏲9am-5pm Mon-Sat)** On Zhongshan Lu at Feicheng Lu in Old Town. Also in the tower at the intersection of Fuzhou Nanlu and Xianggang Zhonglu in the CBD. Branches have currency exchange and 24-hour ATMs.

Tourist Information

Skip the travel agencies and consult with one of the city's excellent hostels for travel advice. Also check out **Qingdaonese** (www.qingdaonese.com) for event listings or pick up a copy of **Red Star magazine** (www.myredstar.com) in hotels, bars and western restaurants.

Getting There & Away

Air

Qīngdǎo's **Liúting International Airport** (**☎booking & flight status 0532 8471 5139, hotline 96567; www.qdairport.com)** is 30km north of the city.

Bus

Among Qīngdǎo's many bus stations, the **long-distance bus station** (长途汽车站; **chángtú qìchēzhàn; ☎400 691 6916; 2 Wenzhou Lu)** in the Sìfāng (四方区) district, north of most tourist sights, best serves most travellers.

Train

Buy tickets at the **train station** (**☎0532 9510 5175; 2 Tai'an Lu)**, which has a hectic 24-

hour ticket office on the east side (bring your passport).

Express trains regularly depart for:

Běijīng South D/G seat ¥249/314, 4½ to 5 hours, 13 daily (5.32am to 5.07pm)

Qūfù G seat ¥179, three hours, three daily (6.23am, 8.31am, 4.21pm)

Shànghǎi G train ¥596/1014, 6½ hours, four daily (6.55am, 9.26am, 1.55pm and 4.35pm)

Tài'ān G seat ¥149, three hours, four daily (6.57am, 9.19am, 9.32am, 2.38pm)

ℹ Getting Around

To/From the Airport

Bright blue **airport shuttles** (机场巴士; **jīchǎng bāshì**; ☏0532 8286 0977; tickets ¥20) follow three routes through town. Shuttles leave hourly from the train station's south lot and then **Airlines Inn** (航空快线商务酒店; ☏96567; 77 Zhongshan Lu) in Old Town from 5.30am to 8.40pm; the **Civil Aviation Building** (民航大厦; 30 Xianggang Xilu) across from the Carrefour from 6am to 9pm; and the CBD's **Century Mandarin Hotel** (世纪文化酒店; 10 Haijiang Lu) from 6.45am to 4.45pm. A taxi to/from Shìnán district is ¥80 to ¥120.

Public Transport

Outside the train station, red double-decker sightseeing buses (unlimited ¥30, per stop ¥10; hourly) head to all the biggies: Bus 1 passes sights along the water going east to Láo Shān from 9am to 3pm, last return at 5pm.

The first line of the highly anticipated underground metro, scheduled to open in late 2015, will ease some of Qīngdǎo's gridlock.

Taxi

Flag fall is ¥9 or ¥12 for the first 6km and then ¥2.10 (slightly more at night) per kilometre thereafter, plus a ¥1 fuel surcharge.

Shànghǎi & the Yangzi Region

You can't see the Great Wall from space, but you'd have a job missing Shànghǎi. Don't come here for dusty imperial tombs or creaking old palaces; Shànghǎi doesn't do those. Come instead for crisp modernity, youthful vigour, funky art deco architecture, gorgeous French Concession streetscapes, rocketing skyscrapers and charming 19th-century *shíkùmén* (stone-gate) buildings. You could also simply come for its restaurants and bars – and rarely feel short-changed.

Shànghǎi lies at the end of the mighty and turbulent Yangzi River (Cháng Jiāng), which traces its source back to the Tibet–Qīnghǎi plateau in China's high-altitude west. Within easy reach of Shànghǎi are the ancient Yangzi region's canal towns that dot the lushly watered landscape. Hángzhōu's fabulous West Lake is a speedy train trip away, but many travellers will want to climb Huángshān (the fabled Yellow Mountains), savour the gardens of Sūzhōu, explore the delightful landscape around Wùyuán or float on a boat through the magnificent Three Gorges.

Qībǎo (p207)

East Nanjing Road (p195)

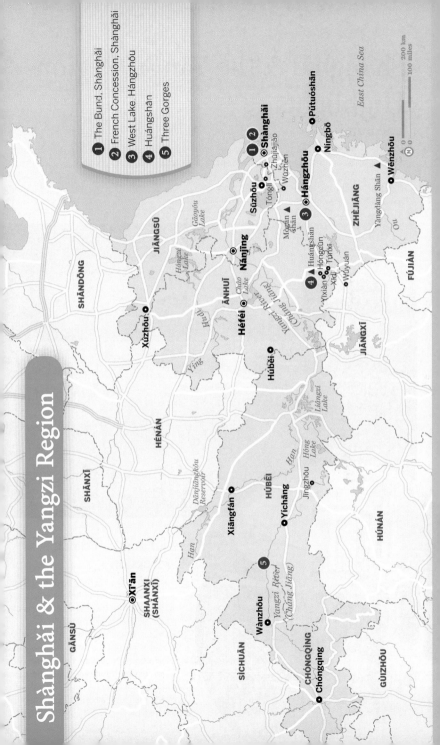

Shànghǎi & the Yangzi Region

1 The Bund, Shànghǎi
2 French Concession, Shànghǎi
3 West Lake Hángzhōu
4 Huángshān
5 Three Gorges

East China Sea

200 km
100 miles

GĀNSÙ

SHAANXI
(SHĂNXĪ)

Xī'ān

SHĀNXĪ

HÉNÁN

SHĀNDŌNG

Xúzhōu

JIĀNGSŪ

Gāoyóu
Lake

Hóngzé
Lake

Nánjīng

Chán
Lake

ĀNHUĪ

Héféi

Huái

Yíng

Húběi

Yangzi River
(Cháng Jiāng)

Mógàn
Shān

Sūzhōu
Tónglǐ

Wūzhèn

Zhūjiājiǎo

1 2 Shànghǎi

Hángzhōu 3

Pǔtuóshān

Níngbō

Wēnzhōu

ZHÈJIĀNG

Yàndàng Shān

Ōu

FÚJIÀN

JIĀNGXĪ

Huángshān 4
Hóngcūn
Yìxiàn Tūnxī
Xīdì

Wùyuán

Dānjiāngkǒu
Reservoir

Hàn

Xiāngfán

HÚBĚI

Yíchāng

Jīngzhōu

Hóng
Lake

Liángzǐ
Lake

HÚNÁN

Yangzi River
(Cháng Jiāng)

Wànzhōu

SÌCHUĀN

5

CHÓNGQÌNG

Chóngqìng

GUÌZHŌU

Shànghǎi & the Yangzi Region Highlights

The Bund

Mainland China's most iconic foreign concession–era architectural backdrop and streetscape is Shànghǎi's supreme standout sight. From neoclassical bombast to art deco elegance, the Bund (p196) is a sweeping curve of stone and brick wreathed in nostalgia for a vanished age. The riverfront promenade facing the Bund is also *the* vantage point for the most mind-blowing views in town: the nocturnal neonscape of Lùjiāzuǐ.

2 Savouring the French Concession

The Pǔdōng skyline may be Shànghǎi's most iconic motif, but it's low on culture. That is kept for the French Concession (p200), Shànghǎi's romantic, chic quarter. The city doesn't attract many bohemians, but the ones it snares make the French Concession their home. From art deco apartment blocks to modish restaurants, funky bars, little boutiques and leafy back lanes, the French Concession is the place to be.

Wandering Around West Lake

3

China's archetypal city lake in Hángzhōu (p235) is surrounded by a tranquilising tableau of pagodas, lilting willows, select temple architecture and some really excellent hotel options. Few urban panoramas in China are so seductively presented and the lake truly comes into its own at night when couples wander arm-in-arm round the shore or perch themselves on lakeside benches.

JOHN BORTHWICK/GETTY IMAGES ©

4

Hiking up Huángshān

When China's most otherworldly mountain rises up from a spectral sea of mist and fog it may make other top sights on your itinerary seem banal by comparison. Huángshān (p249) may not be one of China's holy mountains, but the views – in the right weather conditions – are preternaturally sublime. If you only have time for one mountain in China, make it this one.

5

Drifting Through the Three Gorges

Apocryphally the work of the Great Yu – that mythical Chinese tamer of floods – the Three Gorges (p254) are the most dramatic scenic wonders along China's longest river, the Yangzi. A hydrofoil could do the trick for the speedy highlights version; otherwise, take your pick from a choice of vessels to entirely disengage from road, rail or plane travel for three or four days and savour the scenery. Little Three Gorges (p255)

Shànghǎi & the Yangzi Region's Best…

Escapes

○ **Huángshān** Count the steps up to the top of Heavenly Capital Peak. (p249)

○ **Hui villages** Hike between the villages of south Ānhuī province. (p248)

○ **West Lake** Tranquil, leisurely, dreamy and inviting. (p235)

○ **Wùyuán** Immerse yourself in the magic of the Jiāngxī countryside. (p253)

○ **Three Gorges Cruise** China's most famous river journey. (p254)

Wining & Dining

○ **Fu 1039** Shànghǎi cuisine in a villa setting. (p215)

○ **Flair** Definitive neonscape of nocturnal Lùjiāzuǐ. (p217)

○ **Jian Guo 328** First-rate French Concession choice for Shanghainese dishes. (p214)

○ **Vue** Views from a north Bund vantage point. (p217)

○ **Green Tea Restaurant** Culinary heaven a chopstick's toss from Hángzhōu's West Lake. (p241)

Beds

○ **Park Hyatt** Seriously snazzy, and not just the views. (p212)

○ **Ritz-Carlton Shanghai Pudong** Hyper-stylish and elegant rooms. (p212)

○ **Astor House Hotel** Grand old perch on the wrong side of Wàibáidù Bridge. (p208)

○ **Urbn** Carbon-neutral, nifty and serene. (p211)

○ **Waterhouse at South Bund** *The* place to stay by the Cool Docks. (p210)

○ **Four Seasons Hotel Hángzhōu** Unruffled tranquility next to West Lake. (p240)

Need to Know

Buildings

○ **Shànghǎi Tower** This is the city's – and China's – most sky-scraping edifice. (p201)

○ **French Concession** The city's best villa architecture, art deco and *shíkùmén* buildings. (p200)

○ **Fairmont Peace Hotel** The jewel in Shànghǎi's art deco crown. (p208)

○ **Tónglǐ** Age-old canal town architecture. (p233)

○ **Sūzhōu Museum** Jiāngnán garden architecture brought up to date. (p228)

○ **Hóngcūn & Xīdì** Magnificent examples of Hui village architecture. (p248)

ADVANCE PLANNING

○ **One Month Before** Get accommodation sorted and hotel rooms booked.

○ **One Week Before** Book onward train or air tickets out of Shànghǎi and through the region via your hotel or a local travel agent.

RESOURCES

○ **Time Out Shanghai** (www.timeoutshanghai. com) Authoritative entertainment listings.

○ **City Weekend** (www. cityweekend.com.cn/ shanghai) Listings website.

○ **Shanghaiist** (www. shanghaiist.com) Entertainment and news blog.

○ **SmartShanghai** (www. smartshanghai.com) Food, fun and frolicking; good entertainment coverage.

○ **Shanghai Street Stories** (www. shanghaistreetstories. com) Fascinating blog from Sue Anne Tay on the heritage, society and culture of changing Shànghǎi.

○ **CTrip** (www.english. ctrip.com) Discounted hotels and ticketing; recommended.

GETTING AROUND

○ **Metro** Extensive, efficient and fast system reaching all major sights and Pǔdōng International Airport.

○ **Bus** Extensive urban network; nonuser-friendly for foreign travellers.

○ **Long-distance Bus** For reaching regional destinations.

○ **Maglev** Links Pǔdōng International Airport with the Shànghǎi metro.

○ **Train** Efficient high-speed rail system out of Shànghǎi and beyond.

○ **Air** For regional and more long-distance flights.

○ **Boat** For journeys along the Three Gorges.

○ **Taxi** Good value and dependable for getting around town.

BE FOREWARNED

○ **Scams** Guard against English-speaking girls on Shànghǎi's Bund pressing you to visit extortionately priced tea ceremonies.

○ **Taxi Sharks** At Pǔdōng International Airport.

○ **Language** English rarely used outside of tourist hotels and restaurants.

○ **Museums** Some shut on Monday.

t: Wū Gorge (p255), Three Gorges;
ove: Huángshān (p249)

(LEFT) KRZYSZTOF DYDYNSKI/GETTY IMAGES ©;
(ABOVE) DIANA MAYFIELD/GETTY IMAGES ©

Shànghǎi & the Yangzi Region Itineraries

Five days is enough for Hángzhōu and the standout canal towns of Jiāngsū; in a week the mountain panoramas of Zhèjiāng and Ānhuī, including Huángshān and the sacred island of Pǔtuóshān, are within reach.

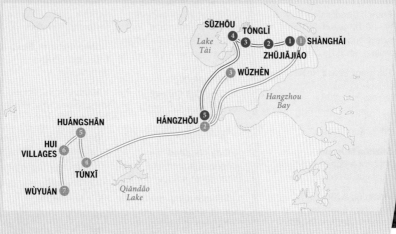

SHÀNGHǍI TO HÁNGZHŌU
WATER TOWNS & WEST LAKE

After you have seen the sights in swinging **❶ Shànghǎi** (p190), jump on a bus to the nearby picturesque canal town of **❷ Zhūjiājiǎo** (p227) for a day trip. Wander through the village's charming streets, popping into temples and churches, crossing humpbacked bridges that vault the waters and snacking as you go. If you want, spend the night in Zhūjiājiǎo and continue by bus to the delightful water town of **❸ Tónglǐ** (p233) in Jiāngsū province, or spend the night in Tónglǐ. Explore the old town, pop into Tónglǐ's Chinese Sex Culture Museum, take a boat tour along the canal and admire the Tuìsī Garden and the Ming-dynasty

Gēnglè Táng estate. From Tónglǐ it's a short bus journey to **❹ Sūzhōu** (p228) for a day's exploration of the top sights, including the eye-catching Sūzhōu Museum, the Garden of the Master of the Nets, the Humble Administrator's Garden, the town's canal views and temple vistas. **❺ Hángzhōu** (p235) is another short hop away by high-speed train and constitutes a delightful terminus, with several days of unhurried sightseeing opportunities around the good-looking West Lake and beyond, and the option to return to Shànghǎi by either bus or train.

SHÀNGHǍI TO HUÁNGSHĀN
CITY TO COUNTRYSIDE

From ❶ **Shànghǎi** (p190), take the fast train to ❷ **Hángzhōu** (p235) for several days' sightseeing around stunning West Lake, taking in Língyǐn Temple and some of the fantastic restaurants in town. Check into a hotel near West Lake to amplify the charms of the area. From Hángzhōu, grab a bus to ❸ **Wūzhèn** (p245), a charming canal town in Zhèjiāng, where you can also spend the night. Returning to Hángzhōu, jump on a bus to ❹ **Túnxī** (p247) en route to the stunning mountain panoramas of ❺ **Huángshān** (p249), China's fabled mountain of mists and photogenic pine trees. Aim to spend a night on the moun-

tain so you can catch the famous sunrise from the peak and descend the next morning. After clambering down Huángshān, return to terra firma to explore the surrounding ❻ **Hui villages** (p248) around Túnxī, including Hóngcūn and Xìdì, where you can also spend the night to maximise the charms of the region. If you've taken to the tempo of China's rural villages, consider a side trip into Jiāngxī province to hike through the adorable countryside around ❼ **Wùyuán** (p253), before hopping on a bus back to Shànghǎi.

Sū Causeway (p237), West Lake, Hángzhōu
KEREN SU/GETTY IMAGES ©

187

Shànghǎi Walk

This walk begins in Hóngkǒu, where the American Settlement was established in 1848, before crossing Sūzhōu Creek to follow the river before guiding you past the magnificent concession buildings of Yuanmingyuan Rd.

WALK FACTS

- **Start** Broadway Mansions
- **Finish** Rockbund Art Museum
- **Distance** 800m
- **Duration** 45 minutes

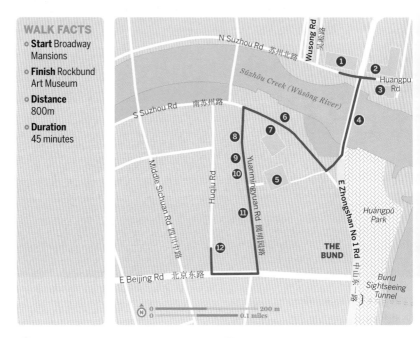

① Broadway Mansions

First stop is the Orwellian brick pile of Broadway Mansions (1934), originally an apartment block that later became a favourite with military officers and journalists because of its commanding views over the harbour. The Japanese occupied the building from 1937 until the end of WWII (it's a hotel today).

② Astor House Hotel

Not far from here is this marvellous old hotel (p208), first established in 1846 as the Richards Hotel. It was Shànghǎi's most prestigious hotel until the completion of the Cathay Hotel in 1929, and from 1990 to 1998 its ballroom served as the location of the Shànghǎi Stock Exchange.

③ Russian Consulate

Across the street is the original red-roofed Russian Consulate, built in the 19th century and still in use today.

④ Wàibáidù Bridge

Head south over Wàibáidù Bridge (which replaced the wooden Garden Bridge in 1907). This was the first steel bridge in China, over which trams used to glide. Wàibáidù Bridge was entirely removed in 2008 for cleaning and restoration.

⑤ Former British Consulate

From here, cross the street to the grounds of the former British Consulate (1873), whose manicured gardens are also home to the former consul's residence (1884). The consulate was one of the first foreign buildings to go up in Shànghǎi in 1852, although the original was destroyed in a fire in 1870.

6 Former Shànghǎi Rowing Club & 7 Former Union Church

Continue west past the former Shànghǎi Rowing Club (1905) – noting the old filled-in swimming pool alongside it and the former Union Church (1886) on the other side of the street – to arrive at the restored Yuanmingyuan Rd.

8 Yuanmingyuan Road

This impressive and fabulously restored street was once home to several godowns – buildings that served as both warehouses and office space.

9 China Baptist Publication Society

Some buildings were shared by traders and missionaries, such as the China Baptist Publication Society, whose Gothamesque offices at No 187 (1932) were designed by the prolific Ladislas Hudec.

10 Lyceum Building

Further along is the Italian Renaissance Lyceum Building (1927), the former home of the Lyceum Theatre, set up by foreign residents in Shànghǎi.

11 Missions Building & Other Buildings

Other historic buildings along Yuanmingyuan Rd include the multidenominational Missions Building (1924; No 169), the lovely YWCA Building (1932; No 133) and the red-brick Yuanmingyuan Apartments (No 115).

12 Royal Asiatic Society Building

Turn onto Huqiu Rd to end the tour at the Royal Asiatic Society building (1933), once Shànghǎi's first museum and now housing the excellent Rockbund Art Museum (p191).

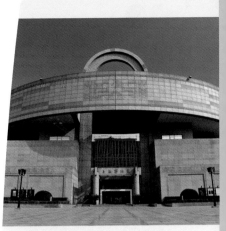

Shànghǎi In...

ONE DAY

Rise to the early morning riverside scenes on the **Bund** (p196) as the city stirs. Embark on the Shànghǎi walking tour around the area and then stroll down East Nanjing Rd to **People's Square** (p195) and the **Shànghǎi Museum** (p195). After dumplings on **Huanghe Rd food street** (p215), hop on the metro to **Pǔdōng** (p201). Explore the fun and interactive **Shànghǎi History Museum** (p204), then take a high-speed lift to the observation deck in the **Shànghǎi World Financial Center** (p202). Stomach rumbling? Time for dinner in the French Concession (p214), followed by a nightcap on the Bund if you want to go full circle.

TWO DAYS

Pre-empt the crowds with an early start at **Yùyuán Gardens** (p205) before poking around for souvenirs on **Old Street** (p205) and wandering the alleys. Next stop is **Xīntiāndì** (p200) for lunch, then grab a taxi to **Tiánzǐfáng** (p206) for the afternoon, before another **French Concession** (p214) dinner. Got a second wind? Catch the acrobats, hit the clubs or unwind with a traditional Chinese massage.

Discover Shànghǎi & the Yangzi Region

SHÀNGHǍI 上海

♪021 / POP 24 MILLION

One of the country's most massive and vibrant cities, Shànghǎi somehow typifies modern China while being unlike anywhere else in the land. Shànghǎi *is* real China, but – rather like Hong Kong or Macau – just not the China you had in mind.

This is a city of action, not ideas. You won't spot many Buddhist monks contemplating the dharma, oddball bohemians or wild-haired poets handing out flyers, but skyscrapers will form before your eyes. Shànghǎi is best seen as an epilogue to your China experience: submit to its charms after you've had your fill of dusty imperial palaces and bumpy 10-hour bus rides.

History

As the gateway to the Yangzi River (Cháng Jiāng), Shànghǎi (the name means 'by the sea') has long been an ideal trading port. However, although it supported as many as 50,000 residents by the late 17th century, it wasn't until after the British opened their concession here in 1842 that modern Shànghǎi really came into being.

The British presence in Shànghǎi was soon followed by that of the French and Americans, and by 1853 Shànghǎi had overtaken all other Chinese ports. Built on the trade of opium, silk and tea, the city also lured the world's great houses of finance, which erected grand palaces of plenty. Shànghǎi also became a byword for exploitation and vice; its countless opium dens, gambling joints and brothels

Pavilion on West Lake (p235), Hángzhōu

ANDREAS BRANDL / GETTY IMAGES ©

managed by gangs were at the heart of Shànghǎi life. Guarding it all were the American, French and Italian marines, British Tommies and Japanese bluejackets.

Exploited in workhouse conditions, crippled by hunger and poverty, sold into slavery, and excluded from the high life and the parks created by the foreigners, the poor of Shànghǎi had a voracious appetite for radical opinion. The Chinese Communist Party (CCP) was formed here in 1921 and, after numerous setbacks, 'liberated' the city in 1949.

Shànghǎi became a colourless factory town and political hotbed, and was the power base of the infamous Gang of Four during the Cultural Revolution.

Shànghǎi's long slumber came to an abrupt end in 1990, with the announcement of plans to develop Pǔdōng, on the eastern side of the Huángpǔ River. Since then Shànghǎi's burgeoning economy, leadership and intrinsic self-confidence have put it miles ahead of other Chinese cities. Its bright lights and opportunities have branded Shànghǎi a mecca for Chinese (and foreign) economic migrants. In 2010, 3600 people squeezed into every square kilometre, compared with 2588 per sq km in 2000 and by 2014, the city's population had leaped to a staggering 24 million.

If You Like…
Shànghǎi Museums

If you liked Shànghǎi Museum (p195), the city has a riveting choice of museums and exhibition spaces.

1 ROCKBUND ART MUSEUM
(上海外滩美术馆; Shànghǎi Wàitān Měishùguǎn; Map p198; www.rockbundartmuseum. org; 20 Huqiu Rd; 虎丘路20号; adult ¥15; ⏰10am-6pm Tue-Sun; Ⓜ East Nanjing Rd) Housed in the former Royal Asiatic Society building, once Shànghǎi's first museum, this space behind the Bund focuses on contemporary Chinese art, with rotating exhibits year-round. One of the city's top modern-art venues, the building's interior and exterior are sublime. Check out the art deco eight-sided *bāguà* (trigram) windows at the front, a synthesis of Western modernist style and traditional Chinese design.

2 SHÀNGHǍI URBAN PLANNING EXHIBITION HALL
(上海城市规划展示馆; Shànghǎi Chéngshì Guīhuà Zhǎnshìguǎn; Map p198; 100 Renmin Ave, entrance on Middle Xizang Rd; 人民大道100号; adult ¥30; ⏰9am-5pm Tue-Sun, last entry 4pm; Ⓜ People's Square) Some cities romanticise their past; others promise good times in the present, only in China are you expected to visit places that haven't been built yet. The highlight here is the 3rd floor, where you'll find an incredible model layout of the megalopolis-to-be, plus a dizzying virtual 3-D wraparound tour. There are also photos and maps of historic Shànghǎi.

3 SHÀNGHǍI MUSEUM OF CONTEMPORARY ART (MOCA SHÀNGHǍI)
(上海当代艺术馆; Shànghǎi Dāngdài Yìshùguǎn; Map p198; www.mocashanghai.org; People's Park; 人民公园; admission adult/student ¥50/25; ⏰10am-6pm Mon-Thu, 9am-7pm Fri-Sun; Ⓜ People's Square) This non-profit museum collection has an all-glass home to maximise natural sunlight, a tip-top location in People's Park and a fresh, invigorating approach to exhibiting contemporary artwork. Exhibits are temporary only; check the website to see what's on. On the top floor is a funky restaurant and bar with a terrace.

Don't Miss
The Bund

Symbolic of colonial Shànghǎi, the Bund (Wàitān) was the city's Wall St, a place of feverish trading and fortunes made and lost. Originally a towpath for dragging barges of rice, the riverfront was gradually transformed into a grandiose sweep containing the most powerful banks and trading houses in town.

Map p198

East Zhongshan No 1 Rd; 中山东一路

M East Nanjing Rd

⊘ 24 hours

What's in a Name?

The Bund gets its Anglo-Indian name from the embankments built up to discourage flooding (a *band* is an embankment in Hindi). There's some debate over how to say the word, though given its origins, it's likely the correct pronunciation is 'bunned', not 'booned'.

Promenade

The Bund today has emerged as a designer retail and restaurant zone, and the city's most exclusive boutiques, restaurants, bars and hotels see the Bund as the only place to be. The optimum activity is to simply stroll, contrasting the bones of the past with the futuristic geometry of Pǔdōng's skyline. The Bund promenade begins at Huángpǔ Park; you can follow it 1km to the Bund's south end at the Meteorological Signal Tower. It's accessible around the clock, but is at its best in the early morning, when locals are out practising taichi, or in the early evening, when both sides of the river are lit up and the romance of the waterfront reaches a crescendo.

Huángpǔ Park

China's first public **park** (黄浦公园; Huángpǔ Gōngyuán; Map p198; **M** East Nanjing Rd) was laid out in 1886 by a Scottish gardener shipped out to Shànghǎi especially for that purpose. The park achieved lasting notoriety for its apocryphal 'No Dogs or Chinese allowed' sign. Located at the northern end of the Bund, the park's anachronistic **Monument to the People's Heroes** (Map p198) hides the entrance to the **Bund History Museum** (外滩历史纪念馆; Wàitān Lìshǐ Jìniànguǎn; Map p198; ◎9am-4.30pm Mon-Fri) FREE, which contains a collection of old maps and photographs.

River Cruise

The Bund's monumental facades presented an imposing – if strikingly un-Chinese – view for those arriving in the busy port. For a glimpse of how it might have looked, take a river cruise departing from the docks in either Pǔxī or Pǔdōng.

The Bund Don't Miss List

BY HAN YUQI, ART DIRECTOR, IMAGETUNNEL

1 HISTORIC ALLURE

When I was small, my dad would take me to the Bund. I really wanted to ride the trams with 'plaits' (electric cables), which are no more. The old vessels that pulled in here and the winged statue of the Goddess of Peace have likewise disappeared. I love the Customs Building, HSBC Bank building, Fairmont Peace Hotel and the overlooked Meteorological Signal Tower, which resembles an old film set!

2 NOSTALGIA

What does the Fairmont Peace Hotel (p208) – then known as Sassoon House and the tallest building on the Bund courtesy of Shànghǎi's most successful adventurer, Victor Sassoon – mean today? Several years ago I went to listen to the Peace Hotel Old Jazz Band and it came to me: Shànghǎi is a modern legend.

3 YUANMINGYUAN ROAD

When admiring the 33 buildings along the bank of the Huángpǔ River, turn into Yuanmingyuan Rd and you'll be even more blown away. You may not know each building's story; you'll be moved by their sheer style and sense of historical drama. I call this street the 'back garden of the Bund!'

4 ROMANCE

Starting at Wàibáidù Bridge, the 'Bund Sweetheart's Wall' is a concrete flood barrier. From the 1970s it became Shànghǎi's most romantic dating spot partly due to its scenic charms but more because Shànghǎi people had such limited living space! On China's 'Valentine's Day' (seventh day of the seventh month), if you pass by the bridge it's a sea of couples among all the lights.

5 NINGBO ROAD

If you're feeling peckish, I recommend heading to Ningbo Rd – just a few minutes' walk from the Bund – for restaurants offering tasty and good-value food. If the weather's good, take a seat outside at twilight and take in its sensations.

Shànghǎi City Overview

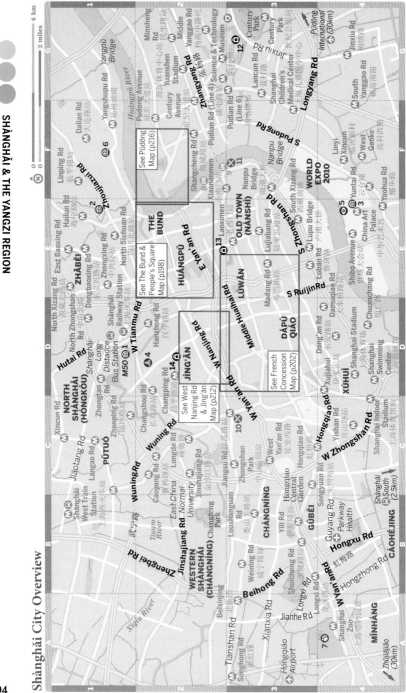

Shànghǎi City Overview

◉ Sights

Broadly, central Shànghǎi is divided into two areas: Pǔxī (west of the Huángpǔ River) and Pǔdōng (east of the Huángpǔ River). The historical attractions and charm are in Pǔxī, where Shànghǎi's personality lives: the Bund (officially called East Zhongshan No 1 Rd) and the former foreign concessions, the principal shopping districts, and Shànghǎi's trendiest clusters of bars, restaurants and nightclubs. Pǔdōng – the location of the financial district and the famous Shànghǎi skyline – is a very recent creation, with sights falling in the observation deck/skyscraping towers/museums arena.

THE BUND 外滩

The area around the Bund is the tourist centre of Shànghǎi and is the city's most famous mile.

East Nanjing Road   Architecture
(南京东路; Nánjīng Dōnglù; Map p198; Ⓜ East Nanjing Rd) Linking the Bund with People's Sq is East Nanjing Rd, once known as Nanking Rd. The first department stores in China opened here in the 1920s, when the modern machine-age – with its new products, automobiles, art deco styling and newfangled ideas – was ushered in. A glowing forest of neon at night, it's no longer the cream of Shànghǎi shopping, but its pedestrian strip remains one of the most famous and crowded streets in China.

PEOPLE'S SQUARE 人民广场

Once the site of the Shànghǎi Racecourse, People's Sq is the modern city's nerve centre. Overshadowed by the dramatic form of **Tomorrow Square** (明天广场; Míngtiān Guǎngchǎng), the open space is peppered with museums, performing arts venues and leafy People's Park.

Shànghǎi Museum   Art Museum
(上海博物馆; Shànghǎi Bówùguǎn; Map p198; www.shanghaimuseum.net; 201 Renmin Ave; 人民大道201号; ⊙9am-5pm; Ⓜ People's Square) FREE This must-see museum escorts you through the craft of millennia and the pages of Chinese history. It's home to one of the most impressive collections in the land: take your pick from the archaic green patinas of the Ancient Chinese Bronzes Gallery through to the silent solemnity of the Ancient Chinese Sculpture Gallery; from the exquisite beauty of the ceramics in the Zande Lou Gallery to the measured and timeless flourishes captured in the Chinese Calligraphy Gallery.

OLD TOWN & SOUTH BUND 南市

Known to locals as Nán Shì (Southern City), the Old Town is the most traditionally Chinese part of Shànghǎi, bar Qībǎo. Its oval layout still reflects the footprint of its 16th-century walls, erected to keep marauding Japanese pirates at bay. On the South Bund, the **Cool Docks** (时尚老码头; Shíshàng Lǎomǎtóu) is a kind of riverside Xīntiāndì-lite, with *shíkùmén* (low-rise tenement buildings built in the early 1900s) houses and converted warehouses.

The Bund

The best way to get acquainted with Shànghǎi is to take a stroll along the Bund. The waterfront was the seat of colonial power from the mid-19th century onward, and the city's landmark hotels, banks and trading houses all established themselves here, gradually replacing their original buildings with even grander constructions as the decades passed.

The Bund had its golden age in the 1920s and '30s before the turmoil of war and occupation brought an end to the high life enjoyed by Shànghǎi's foreign residents. Mothballed during the communist era, it's only in the past 15 years that the strip has sought to rekindle its past glory, restoring one heritage building after another. Today, it has become China's showcase lifestyle destination, and many of the landmarks here house designer restaurants, swish cocktail bars and the flagship stores of some of the world's most exclusive brands.

Once you've wandered the promenade and ogled at the Pǔdōng skyline opposite, return

Hongkong & Shanghai Bank Building (1923)
Head into this massive bank (☉9am-4.30pm Mon-Fri) to marvel at the beautiful mosaic ceiling, featuring the 12 zodiac signs and the world's (former) eight centres of finance.

North China Daily News Building (1924)
Known as the 'Old Lady of the Bund', the *News* ran from 1864 to 1951 as the main English-language newspaper in China. Look for the paper's motto above the central windows.

Russo-Chinese Bank Building (1902)

Custom House (1927)
One of the most important buildings on the Bund, Custom House was capped by the largest clock face in Asia and 'Big Ching', a bell modelled on London's Big Ben.

Former Bank of Communications (1947)

Bund Public Service Centre (2010)

TOP TIP

The promenade is open around the clock, but it's at its best in the early morning, when locals are out practising taichi, or in the early evening, when both sides of the river are lit up and the majesty of the waterfront is at its grandest.

to examine the Bund's magnificent facades in more detail and visit the interiors of those buildings open to the public.

This illustration shows the main sights along the Bund's central stretch, beginning near the intersection with East Nanjing Road. The Bund is 1km long and walking it should take around an hour. Head to the area south of the Hongkong & Shanghai Bank Building to find the biggest selection of prominent drinking and dining destinations.

Former Palace Hotel (1909)

Now known as the Swatch Art Peace Hotel (an artists' residence and gallery, with a top-floor restaurant and bar), this building hosted Sun Yatsen's 1911 victory celebration following his election as the first president of the Republic of China.

Bank of China (1942)

This unusual building was originally commissioned to be the tallest building in Shànghǎi, but, probably because of Victor Sassoon's influence, wound up being one metre shorter than its neighbour.

CHRISTOPHER PITTS

Former Bank of Taiwan (1927)

Former Chartered Bank Building (1923)

Reopened in 2004 as the upscale entertainment complex Bund 18, the building's top-floor Bar Rouge is one of the Bund's premier late-night destinations.

CHRISTOPHER PITTS

GREG ELMS/GETTY ©

Fairmont Peace Hotel (1929)

Originally built as the Cathay Hotel, this art deco masterpiece was the place to stay in Shànghǎi and the crown jewel in Sassoon's real estate empire.

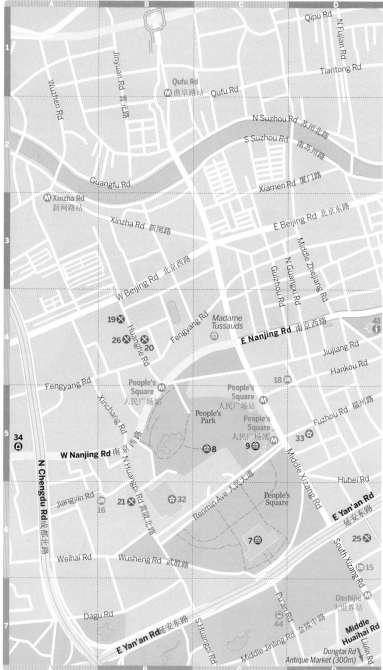

SHÀNGHǍI & THE YANGZI REGION

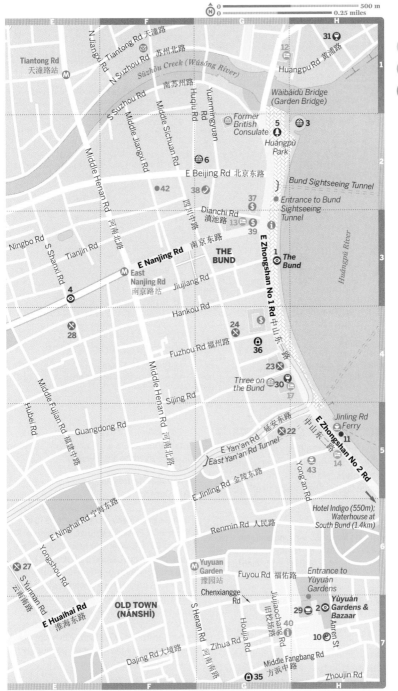

0 | 500 m
0 | 0.25 miles

31

Huangpu Rd 黄浦路

Tiantong Rd
天潼路站

N Jiangxi Rd

Tiantong Rd 天潼路

S Suzhou Rd

Sūzhōu Creek (Wúsōng River)

南苏州路:

Wàibáidù Bridge
(Garden Bridge)

Yuanmingyuan Rd

Middle Jiangxi Rd

Middle Sichuan Rd

Huqiu Rd

Former British Consulate

5

3

Middle Henan Rd

6

Huángpǔ Park

河南北路

E Beijing Rd 北京东路

42

38

S Shanxi Rd

Tianjin Rd

Ningbo Rd

四川中路

37

Dianchi Rd
滇池路

13

39

Bund Sightseeing Tunnel

Entrance to Bund Sightseeing Tunnel

E Nanjing Rd

南京东路

THE BUND

1 The Bund

East Nanjing Rd
南京路站

E Zhongshan No 1 Rd 中山东一路

Jiujiang Rd

Huángpǔ River

4

Hankou Rd

28

24

Fuzhou Rd 福州路

36

Middle Henan Rd

Sijing Rd

23

Three on the Bund

30

17

Middle Fujian Rd 福建中路

Hubei Rd

Guangdong Rd

河南北路

Jinling Rd
Ferry

11

E Yan'an Rd 延安东路

22

East Yan'an Rd Tunnel

14

E Jinling Rd 金陵东路

43

Yong'an Rd

E Ninghai Rd 宁海东路

Renmin Rd 人民路

Hotel Indigo (550m);
Waterhouse at
South Bund (1.4km)

Yongshou Rd

27

S Yunnan Rd

E Huaihai Rd 淮海东路

Yuyuan Garden
豫园站

Fuyou Rd 福佑路

Entrance to Yùyuán Gardens

云南南路

Chenxiangge Rd

OLD TOWN
(NÁNSHÌ)

S Henan Rd

旧校场路

29

Jiujiaochang Rd

40

2

Yùyuán Gardens & Bazaar

Anren St

10

Houjia Rd

Zihua Rd

河南南路

Dajing Rd 大境路

35

Middle Fangbang Rd
方浜中路

Zhoujin Rd

199

The Bund & People's Square

FRENCH CONCESSION 法租界

Once home to the bulk of Shànghǎi's adventurers, revolutionaries, gangsters, prostitutes and writers, the French Concession is the most graceful part of the city.

Xīntiāndì
Area

(新天地; Map p202; www.xintiandi.com; 2 blocks btw Taicang, Zizhong, Madang & South Huangpi Rds; 太仓路与马当路路口; M South Huangpi Rd, Xintiandi) With its own namesake metro station, Xīntiāndì has been a Shànghǎi icon for a decade or more. An upscale entertainment and shopping (see p221) complex modelled on traditional alleyway (lòngtáng) homes, this was the first development in the city to prove that historic architecture makes big commercial sense. Elsewhere that might sound like a no-brainer, but in 21st-century China, where bulldozers were always on standby, it came as quite a revelation.

Propaganda Poster
Art Centre
Museum

(宣传画年画艺术中心; Map p202; Shànghǎi Xuānchuánhuà Yìshù Zhōngxīn; ☑ 6211 1845; Room B-OC, President Mansion, 868 Huashan Rd; 华山路868号B-OC室; admission ¥20; ☉ 10am-5pm; M Shanghai Library) If phalanxes of red tractors, bumper harvests, muscled peasants and lantern-jawed proletariats fire you up, this small gallery in the bowels of a residential block should intoxicate. The collection of 3000 original posters from the 1950s, '60s and '70s – the golden age of Maoist poster production – will have you weak-kneed.

WEST NANJING ROAD & JÌNG'ĀN 南京西路、静安

Lined with sharp top-end shopping malls, clusters of foreign offices and a dense crop of embassies and consulates, West Nanjing Rd is where Shànghǎi's streets are paved with gold, or at least Prada and Gucci.

Jade Buddha Temple
Buddhist Temple

(玉佛寺; Yùfó Sì; Map p194; cnr Anyuan & Jiangning Rds; 安远路和江宁路街口; admission high/low season ¥20/10; ⏰8am-4.30pm; 🚌19 from Broadway Mansions along Tiantong Rd, MⒸhangshou Rd) One of Shànghǎi's few active Buddhist monasteries, this temple was built between 1918 and 1928. The highlight is a transcendent Buddha crafted from pure jade, one of five shipped back to China by the monk Hui Gen at the turn of the 20th century. In February, during the Lunar New Year, the temple is very busy, as some 20,000 Chinese Buddhists throng to pray for prosperity.

Jìng'ān Temple
Buddhist Temple

(静安寺; Jìng'ān Sì; 1686-1688 West Nanjing Rd; 南京西路1686-1688号; admission ¥50;

⏰7.30am-5pm; MⒿing'an Temple) Its roof work an incongruous, shimmering mirage amid West Nanjing Rd's soaring skyscrapers, Jing'an Temple is a much-restored sacred portal to the Buddhist world that partially, at least, underpins this metropolis of 24 million souls. There are fewer devotees than at the neighbourhood's popular Jade Buddha Temple, but over a decade's restoration has fashioned a workable temple at the very heart of Shànghǎi. Its spectacular position among the district's soaring skyscrapers makes for eye-catching photos while the temple emits an air of reverence.

PǓDŌNG 浦东新区

On the east side of the Huángpǔ River, the colossal concrete and steel Pǔdōng New Area (Pǔdōng Xīnqū) is best known for the skyscraper-stuffed skyline of Lùjiāzuǐ, one of China's most photographed panoramas.

Shànghǎi Tower
Notable Building

(上海中心大厦; Shànghǎi Zhōngxīn Dàshà; Map p216; www.shanghaitower.com.cn; cnr Middle Yincheng & Huayuanshiqiao Rds; MⓁujiazui) China's tallest building dramatically

---

Shànghǎi for Children

Shànghǎi isn't exactly at the top of most kids' holiday wish lists, but the new Disney theme park in Pǔdōng (estimated completion date 2015) will no doubt improve its future standing. Recommended for kids:

◦ **Observation decks** at Shànghǎi Tower (p201), Shànghǎi World Financial Center (p202) or Jīnmào Tower (p203)

◦ **Shànghǎi History Museum** (p204)

◦ **Acrobatics show** (p216)

◦ **Bus tours** (p223)

◦ **Shànghǎi Zoo** (上海动物园; Shànghǎi Dòngwùyuán; Map p194; 📞6268 7775; www.shanghaizoo.cn; 2381 Hongqiao Rd; 虹桥路2381号; adult/child ¥40/20, tour buggy trips ¥15; ⏰6.30am-6pm Apr-Sep, to 5pm Oct-Mar; 👶; MⓈhanghaiZoo) As Chinese zoos go, this is just about the best there is.

Note that, in general, 1.4m (4ft 7in) is the cut-off height for children's tickets. Children under 0.8m (2ft 7in) normally get in for free.

French Concession

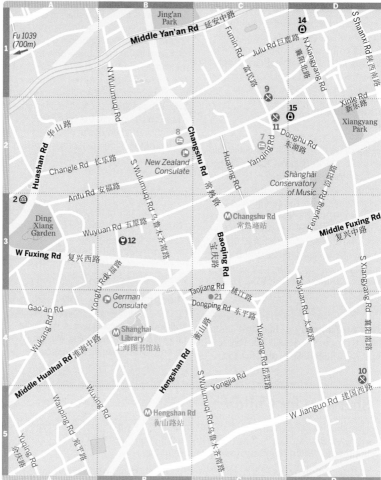

Jing'an Park

Fu 1039
(700m)

Middle Yan'an Rd 延安中路

Julu Rd 巨鹿路

N Xiangyang Rd 襄阳北路

S Shaanxi Rd 陕西南路

Fumin Rd 富民路

14

N Wulumuqi Rd

9

Xinle Rd 新乐路

15

Xiangyang Park

Huashan Rd 华山路

Changle Rd 长乐路

Changshu Rd 常熟路

8

New Zealand Consulate

Huating Rd

11

7

Yanqing Rd

Donghu Rd 东湖路

S Wulumuqi Rd 乌鲁木齐南路

Anfu Rd 安福路

Shànghǎi Conservatory of Music

Fenyang Rd 汾阳路

2

Ding Xiang Garden

Wuyuan Rd 五原路

12

Changshu Rd
常熟路站

Middle Fuxing Rd
复兴中路

Baoqing Rd 宝庆路

W Fuxing Rd 复兴西路

S Xiangyang Rd 襄阳南路

Yongfu Rd 永福路

German Consulate

Taojiang Rd

桃江路

21

Dongping Rd 东平路

Taiyuan Rd 太原路

Gao'an Rd

Shanghai Library
上海图书馆站

Hengshan Rd

Yueyang Rd 岳阳路

10

Wukang Rd

S Wulumuqi Rd 乌鲁木齐南路

Yongjia Rd 永嘉路

W Jianguo Rd 建国西路

Wanping Rd

Wuxing Rd

Hengshan Rd
衡山路站

Yuqing Rd 余庆路

---

twists skywards from the firmament of Lùjiāzuǐ. The 121-storey, 632m-tall Gensler-designed Shànghǎi Tower topped out in August 2013 and was set to fully open in 2015. The spiral-shaped tower will house office space, entertainment venues, retail outlets, a conference centre, a luxury hotel and 'sky lobbies'. The gently corkscrewing form – its nine interior cylindrical units wrapped in two glass skins – is the world's second-tallest building, at the time of writing.

Shànghǎi World Financial Center
Notable Building

(上海环球金融中心; Shànghǎi Huánqiú Jīnróng Zhōngxīn; Map p216; ☎5878 0101; http://swfc-shanghai.com; 100 Century Ave; 世纪大道100 号; observation deck adult 94th, 97th & 100th fl ¥120/180, child under 140cm ¥60/90; ☺8am-11pm, last entry 10pm; Mː Lujiazui) Although trumped by the adjacent Shànghǎi Tower as the city's most stratospheric building, the awe-inspiring 492m-high Shànghǎi World Financial Center is an astonishing

SHÀNGHǍI & THE YANGZI REGION SHÀNGHǍI

202

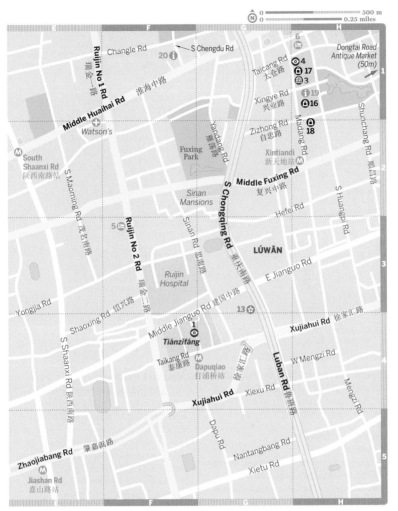

sight, even more so come nightfall when its 'bottle opener' top dances with lights. There are three observation decks here on levels 94, 97 and 100, with head-spinningly altitude-adjusted ticket prices and wow-factor elevators thrown in.

Jīnmào Tower   Building
(金茂大厦; Jīnmào Dàshà; Map p216; ☑5047 5101; 88 Century Ave; 世纪大道88号; adult/student/child ¥120/90/60; ⊙8.30am-9.30pm; Ⓜ Lujiazui) Resembling an art deco take

on a pagoda, this crystalline edifice is a beauty and by far the most attractive of the Shànghǎi World Financial Center (SWFC), Shànghǎi Tower, Jīnmào Tower triumvirate. It's essentially an office block with the high-altitude **Grand Hyatt** (金茂君悦大酒店; Jīnmào Jūnyuè Dàjiǔdiàn; Map p216; ☑5049 1234; www.shanghai.grand. hyatt.com; Jinmao Tower; d from ¥2000-2450; ✳ @ 🛰 🛋; Ⓜ Lujiazu) renting space from the 53rd to 87th floors. You can zip up in the elevators to the 88th-floor

French Concession

observation deck, accessed from the separate podium building to the side of the main tower (aim for dusk for both day and night views).

Shànghǎi History Museum
Museum

(上海城市历史发展陈列馆; Shànghǎi Chéngshì Lìshǐ Fāzhǎn Chénlièguǎn; Map p216; ☎5879 8888; Oriental Pearl TV Tower basement; admission ¥35, English audio tour ¥30; ◷8am-9.30pm; ⓂLujiazui) The entire family will enjoy this informative museum with a fun presentation on old Shànghǎi. Learn how the city prospered on the back of the cotton trade and junk transportation, when it was known as 'Little Sūzhōu'. Life-sized models of traditional shops are staffed by realistic waxworks, amid a wealth of historical detail, including a boundary stone from the International Settlement and one of the bronze lions that originally guarded the entrance to the HSBC bank on the Bund.

China Art Palace
Museum

(中华艺术宫; Zhōnghuá Yìshùgōng; Map p194; 205 Shangnan Rd; 上南路205号; ◷9am-5pm Tue-Sun; ⓂChina Art Museum) **FREE** This 160,000 sq metre five-floor modern-art museum has invigorating international exhibitions, and the inverted red pyramid building is a modern icon of Shànghǎi; however, the permanent Chinese art collection is prosaic and there's lots of propaganda. Occasional quality surfaces, such as *Virgin* (初潮的处女) by Xiang Jing, a moving, tender and comic sculptural work depicting awakening sexuality, while the Shànghǎi and Paris gallery looks absorbingly at the influence of impressionism on Shànghǎi art.

Oriental Pearl TV Tower
Building

(东方明珠广播电视塔; Dōngfāng Míngzhū Guǎngbō Diànshì Tǎ; Map p216; ☎5879 1888; ◷8am-10pm, revolving restaurant 11am-2pm & 5-9pm; ⓂLujiazui) Love it or hate it, it's hard

JEREMY WOODHOUSE/GETTY IMAGES ©

⭐ Don't Miss
Yùyuán Gardens & Bazaar

With their shaded alcoves, glittering pools churning with fish, pavilions, pines sprouting wistfully from rockeries, and roving packs of Japanese tourists, these gardens are one of Shànghǎi's premier sights – but become overpoweringly crowded at weekends.

The spring and summer blossoms bring a fragrant and floral aspect to the gardens, especially in the luxurious petals of its Magnolia grandiflora, Shànghǎi's flower. Other trees include the Luohan pine, bristling with thick needles, willows, gingkos, cherry trees and magnificent dawn redwoods. The Pan family, rich Ming-dynasty officials, founded the gardens, which took 18 years (1559–77) to be nurtured into existence before bombardment during the Opium War in 1842. The gardens took another trashing during French reprisals for attacks on their nearby concession by Taiping rebels. Restored, they are a fine example of Ming garden design.

Next to the garden entrance is the **Húxīntíng Teahouse** (湖心亭; Húxīntíng; Map p198; Tea upstairs/downstairs: ¥50/35; ⏰8.30am-9.30pm), once part of the gardens and now one of the most famous teahouses in China.

The adjacent bazaar may be tacky, but it's good for a browse if you can handle the push and pull of the crowds and vendors. The nearby Taoist **Temple of the Town God** (城隍庙; Chénghuáng Miào; Map p198; Yùyuán Bazaar, off Middle Fangbang Rd; admission ¥10; ⏰8.30am-4.30pm; Ⓜ Yuyuan Garden) is also worth visiting. Just outside the bazaar is **Old Street** (老街; Lǎo Jiē; Map p198; Middle Fangbang Rd; 方浜中路; Ⓜ Yuyuan Garden), known more prosaically as Middle Fangbang Rd, a busy street lined with curio shops and teahouses.

NEED TO KNOW

豫园、豫园商城; Yùyuán & Yùyuán Shāngchéng; Map p198; Anren Jie; 安仁街; admission low/high season ¥30/40; ⏰8.30am-5.30pm, last entry at 5pm; Ⓜ Yuyuan Garden

KYLIE MCLAUGHLIN/GETTY IMAGES ©

⭐ Don't Miss
Tiánzǐfáng

Xīntiāndì and Tiánzǐfáng are based on a similar idea – an entertainment complex housed within a warren of traditional *lòngtáng* (alleyways) – but when it comes to genuine charm and vibrancy, Tiánzǐfáng is the one that delivers. This community of design studios, wi-fi cafes and boutiques (see p219) is the perfect antidote to Shànghǎi's oversized malls and intimidating skyscrapers. With some families still residing in neighbouring buildings, a community mood survives.

NEED TO KNOW

田子坊; Map p202; www.tianzifang.cn; Taikang Rd; 泰康路; M Dapuqiao

to be indifferent to this 468m-tall poured-concrete tripod tower, especially at night, when it dazzles. Sucking in streams of visitors, the Deng Xiaoping–era design is inadvertently retro, but socialism with Chinese characteristics was always cheesy back in the day. The highlight is the excellent Shànghǎi History Museum (p204), in the basement. You can queue up for views of Shànghǎi, but there are better views elsewhere and the long lines are matched by a tortuous ticketing system.

Riverside Promenade   Waterfront

(滨江大道; Bīnjiāng Dàdào; Map p216; ⌚6.30am-11pm; M Lujiazui) Hands down the best stroll in Pǔdōng. The sections of promenade alongside Riverside Ave on the eastern bank of the Huángpǔ River offer splendid views to the Bund across the way. Choicely positioned cafes look out over the water.

Mercedes-Benz Arena   Arena

(梅赛德斯奔驰文化中心; Méisàidésī Bēnchí Wénhuà Zhōngxīn; Map p194; www.mercedes-benz

arena.com) Galactically styled UFO structure of an arena at the 2010 World Expo site.

NORTH SHÀNGHǍI (HÓNGKǑU) 虹口

Originally the American Settlement before the Japanese took over, Hóngkǒu also welcomed thousands of Jewish refugees fleeing persecution.

Ohel Moishe Synagogue
Museum

(摩西会堂; Móxī Huìtáng; Map p194; 62 Changyang Rd; 长阳路62号; admission ¥50; ⊙9am-5pm, last entry 4.30pm; MDalian Rd) Built by the Russian Ashkenazi Jewish community in 1927, this synagogue lies in the heart of the 1940s Jewish ghetto. Today, it houses the synagogue and the **Shànghǎi Jewish Refugees Museum**, with exhibitions on the lives of the approximately 20,000 Central European refugees who fled to Shànghǎi to escape the Nazis. There are English-language tours every 45 minutes (9.30am to 4.15pm).

1933
Historic Building

(上海1933老场坊; Shànghǎi 1933 Lǎochǎngfáng; Map p194; 10 Shajing Rd; 沙泾路10号; MHailun Rd) This vast concrete former abattoir is one of Shànghǎi's unique buildings, today converted to house boutiques, bars, shops and restaurants. An extraordinary place built around a central core, its structure is a maze of flared columns, sky-bridges (across which cattle would be led to slaughter), ramps, curved stairwells – and jostling photo opportunities. The shops are not of much interest, but a well-positioned branch of trendy Noodle Bull makes the most of its concrete setting.

WEST SHÀNGHǍI

Qībǎo
Village

(七宝; 2 Minzhu Rd, Mǐnháng district; 闵行区民主路2号; admission high/low season ¥45/30; ⊙sights 8.30am- 4.30pm; MQibao) When you tire of Shànghǎi's incessant quest for modernity, this tiny town is only a hop, skip and metro ride away. An ancient settlement that prospered during the Ming and Qing dynasties, it is littered with traditional historic architecture, threaded by small, busy alleyways and cut by a picturesque canal. If you can somehow blot out the crowds, Qībǎo brings you the flavours of old China along with huge doses of entertainment.

🚩 Tours

Huángpǔ River Cruise
Cruise

(黄浦江游览; Huángpǔ Jiāng Yóulǎn; Map p198; 219-239 East Zhongshan No 2 Rd; 中山东二路219-239号; tickets ¥128; MEast Nanjing Rd) The Huángpǔ River offers intriguing views of the Bund, Pǔdōng and riverfront activity. The night cruises are arguably more scenic, though boat traffic during the day is more interesting – depending on when you go, you'll pass an enormous variety of craft, from freighters, bulk carriers and roll-on roll-off ships to sculling sampans and massive floating TV advertisements.

Most cruises last 90 minutes and include not one, but two trips up to the International Cruise Terminal and back.

Pearl Dock
Cruise

(明珠码头; Míngzhū Mǎtou; Map p216; 1 Century Ave; tickets ¥100) Boat tours on the Huángpǔ River operate from the Pearl Dock, next to the Oriental Pearl TV Tower (p204).

Insiders Experience
Driving Tour

(☎138 1761 6975; www.insidersexperience.com; from ¥800) Fun motorcycle-sidecar tours of the city for up to two passengers, setting off from the Andaz in Xīntiāndì (but can pick up from anywhere, at extra cost).

🛏 Sleeping

In general, hotels fall into five main categories: luxury skyscraper hotels, historic old villa and apartment block hotels, boutique hotels, Chinese chain hotels, and hostels. There's also a handful of B&Bs, though these are relatively scarce.

Rack rates are listed here, but discounts are standard outside holiday periods. For hotel bookings, the online agencies **Ctrip** (http://english.ctrip.com) and **Elong** (www.elong.net) are good choices.

Below: The Bund (p196); **Right:** Taichi practitioners
(BELOW) KEREN SU/GETTY IMAGES ©; (RIGHT) GRANT FAINT/GETTY IMAGES ©

THE BUND & PEOPLE'S SQUARE

Astor House Hotel
Historic Hotel **$$$**

(浦江饭店; Pǔjiāng Fàndiàn; Map p198; ☎ 6324 6388; www.astorhousehotel.com; 15 Huangpu Rd; 黄浦路15号; d/tw ¥1280-1680, 'celebrity' r ¥2080, ste ¥2800-4800; ❄ @ ☎; Ⓜ Tiantong Rd) Stuffed with history (and perhaps a ghost or two), this august old-timer shakes up an impressive cocktail from select ingredients: a location just off the Bund; old-world, Shànghǎi-era charm; great discounts; and colossal rooms. The original polished wooden floorboards, corridors and galleries pitch the mood somewhere between British public school and Victorian asylum.

Fairmont Peace Hotel
Historic Hotel **$$$**

(费尔蒙和平饭店; Fèi'ěrméng Hépíng Fàndiàn; Map p198; ☎ 6321 6888; www.fairmont.com; 20 East Nanjing Rd; 南京东路20号; d ¥2300-3800;

❄ ☎ ☎; Ⓜ East Nanjing Rd) If anywhere in town fully conveys swish 1930s Shànghǎi, it's the old Cathay, rising imperiously from the Bund. Renamed the Peace Hotel in the 1950s and reopened in 2010 after a protracted renovation, it's reaffirmed its position as one of the city's most iconic hotels. Rooms are decked out in art deco elegance, from light fixtures down to coffee tables.

Marvel Hotel
Hotel **$$**

(商悦青年会大酒店; Shāngyuè Qīngniánhuì Dàjiǔdiàn; Map p198; ☎ 3305 9999; www. marvelhotels.com.cn; 123 South Xizang Rd; 西藏南路123号; d ¥1080-1280, ste ¥1580; ❄ @ ☎; Ⓜ Dashijie) Occupying the former YMCA building (1931) just south of People's Sq, the Marvel is one of the city's better midrange hotels. Beyond the chintzy corridors, the brown and cream rooms offer a reassuring degree of style. The building resembles Běijīng's Southeast Corner Watchtower (although the blurb compares

it to Qiánmén), with a traditional hammer-beam ceiling.

Yangtze Boutique Shanghai
Boutique Hotel $$$
(朗廷扬子精品宾馆; Lǎngtíng Yángzǐ Jīngpǐn Bīnguǎn; Map p198; ☎6080 0800; www.theyangtzehotel.com; 740 Hankou Rd; 汉口路740号; d ¥1300-1800; ✱ 🛰; Ⓜ People's Square) Originally built in the 1930s, this art deco gem has been splendidly refurbished. In addition to period decor, rooms feature deep baths, glass-walled bathrooms (with Venetian blinds) and even tiny balconies – a rarity in Shànghǎi. Check out the sumptuous stained-glass oblong and recessed skylight in the lobby, above a deco-style curved staircase.

Les Suites Orient
Luxury Hotel $$$
(东方商旅酒店; Dōngfāng Shānglǚ Jiǔdiàn; Map p198; ☎6320 0088; www.lessuitesorient.com; 1 East Jinling Rd; 金陵东路1号; d ¥1900, with river view ¥2050, ste ¥2350, with river view ¥2500; ✱ @ 🛰 ⛵; Ⓜ Yuyuan Garden) Located at the southern edge of the Bund, Les Suites Orient is notable as the only hotel on the strip offering standard rooms (Bund Studio) with fantastic river and Bund vistas – in some rooms even the bathtub gets a view. It's housed in a modern 23-storey tower, with hardwood floors and minimalist design adding to the appealingly chic interior. Excellent service.

Accommodation Price Indicators

The price ranges for accommodation in Shànghǎi only are as follows:

- ○ $ less than ¥500
- ○ $$ ¥500 to ¥1300
- ○ $$$ more than ¥1300

Waldorf Astoria
Luxury Hotel $$$

(华尔道夫酒店; Huáěr Dàofū Jiǔdiàn; Map p198; ☏ 6322 9988; www.waldorfastoriashanghai.com; 2 East Zhongshan No 1 Rd; 中山东一路2号; d/ste ¥3100/4600; ❄@🛜🏊; Ⓜ East Nanjing Rd) Grandly marking the southern end of the Bund is the former Shànghǎi Club (1910), once the Bund's most exclusive gentlemen's hang-out. The 20 original rooms here have been reconverted to house the Waldorf Astoria's premium suites, six of which look out onto the Huángpǔ River. Behind this heritage building is a new hotel tower, with 252 state-of-the-art rooms.

Mingtown E-Tour Youth Hostel
Hostel $

(明堂上海青年旅舍; Míngtáng Shànghǎi Qīngnián Lǚshè; Map p198; ☏ 6327 7766; 57 Jiangyin Rd; 江阴路57号; dm ¥50, d without/with bathroom ¥160/260, tw ¥240; ❄@🛜; Ⓜ People's Square) One of Shànghǎi's best youth hostels, E-tour has fine feng shui, a historic alleyway setting and pleasant rooms. But it's the tranquil courtyard with fish pond and the superb split-level bar-restaurant with comfy sofas that really sell it; plus there's a free pool table and plenty of outdoor seating on wooden decking.

OLD TOWN & SOUTH BUND

Waterhouse at South Bund
Boutique Hotel $$

(水舍时尚设计酒店; Shuǐshè Shíshàng Shèjì Jiǔdiàn; Map p194; ☏ 6080 2988; www.waterhouseshanghai.com; 1-3 Maojiayuan Rd, Lane 479, South Zhongshan Rd; 中山南路479弄毛家园路1-3号; d ¥1100-2800; ❄🛜; Ⓜ Xiaonanmen) There are few cooler places to base yourself in Shànghǎi than this awfully trendy 19-room, four-storey South Bund converted 1930s warehouse right by the Cool Docks. Gazing out onto supreme views of Pǔdōng (or into the crisp courtyard), the Waterhouse's natty rooms (some with terrace) are swishly dressed. Service can be wanting, though, and it's isolated from the action.

Hotel Indigo
Hotel $$$

(英迪格酒店; Yīngdígé Jiǔdiàn; Map p194; www.hotelindigo.com; 585 East Zhongshan No 2 Rd; 中山东二路585号; ❄🛜🏊; Ⓜ Xiaonanmen)

Boutiques, French Concession

LONELY PLANET/GETTY IMAGES ©

With its quirkily designed lobby – chairs like birdcages; tree branches trapped in cascades of glass jars; sheets of metal riveted to the wall; modish, sinuously shaped furniture; and funky ceiling lights – towering Hotel Indigo is a stylish South Bund choice. Chic and playful guestrooms are about colourful cushions and whimsical designs, with lovely rugs and spotless bathrooms.

FRENCH CONCESSION

Langham Xīntiāndì
Luxury Hotel $$$

(新天地朗廷酒店; Xīntiāndì Lǎngtíng Jiǔdiàn; Map p202; ☏2330 2288; xintiandi.langham hotels.com; 99 Madang Rd, French Concession East; 马当路99号; r/ste ¥1600/1840; ❀☎☒; Ⓜ South Huangpi Rd) Xīntiāndì has become a magnet for luxury hotels, and they don't come much nicer than this one. Its 357 rooms all feature huge floor-to-ceiling windows, plenty of space to spread out in, and an attention to the minute details that make all the difference: Japanese-style wooden tubs in suites, heated bathroom floors, internet radio and white orchids.

Magnolia Bed & Breakfast
B&B $$

(Map p202; ☏138 1794 0848; www.magnoliabnb shanghai.com; 36 Yanqing Rd, French Concession West; 延庆路36号; r ¥702-1296; ❀@☎; Ⓜ Changshu Rd) Opened by Miranda Yao of the cooking school **The Kitchen at...** (☏6433 2700; www.thekitchenat.com; Ⓜ Changshu Rd), this cosy little five-room B&B is located in a 1927 French Concession home. It's Shànghǎi all the way, with an art deco starting point followed by comfort and stylish design. While rooms are on the small side, they are high-ceilinged and bright. It's a true labour of love.

Quintet
B&B $$

(Map p202; ☏6249 9088; www.quintet-shanghai. com; 808 Changle Rd, French Concession West; 长乐路808号; d incl breakfast ¥850-1200; ☺❀☎; Ⓜ Changshu Rd) This chic B&B has six beautiful double rooms in a 1930s townhouse that's not short on character.

Some of the rooms are small, but each is decorated with style, incorporating modern luxuries such as large-screen satellite TVs and laptop-sized safes, with more classic touches such as wood-stripped floorboards and deep porcelain bathtubs.

InterContinental Shanghai Ruijin Hotel
Historic Hotel $$$

(上海瑞金洲际酒店; Shànghǎi Ruìjīn Zhōují Jiǔdiàn; Map p202; ☏6472 5222; www.ihg.com; 118 Ruijin No 2 Rd, French Concession East; 瑞金二路118号; standard/executive d ¥1320/2310; ❀@☎; Ⓜ South Shaanxi Rd) The InterContinental group has acquired this historic 238-guestroom garden estate, which includes Building No 1, a 1919 red-brick mansion and former residence of Benjamin Morris, one-time owner of *North China Daily News*. Dark-wood panelled corridors lead to enormous, pleasantly appointed rooms. The architecture and the park-like gardens are lovely. The staff's spoken English is fitful.

WEST NANJING ROAD & JÌNG'ĀN

Urbn
Boutique Hotel $$$

(☏5153 4600; www.urbnhotels.com; 183 Jiaozhou Rd; 胶州路183号; r from ¥1500; ❀; Ⓜ Changping Rd) China's first carbon-neutral hotel not only incorporates recyclable materials and low-energy products where possible, it also calculates its complete carbon footprint – including staff commutes and delivery journeys – and offsets it by donating money to environmentally friendly projects. Open-plan rooms are beautifully designed with low furniture and sunken living areas exuding space.

Le Tour Traveler's Rest
Hostel $

(乐途静安国际青年旅舍; Lètú Jing'ān Guójì Qīngnián Lǚshè; ☏6267 1912; www.letour shanghai.com; 319 Jiaozhou Rd; 胶州路319号; dm ¥70, d ¥260-280, tr/q ¥360/360; ❀@☎; Ⓜ Changping Rd) Housed in a former towel factory, this fabulous youth hostel leaves most others out to dry. You'll pass a row of splendid *shíkùmén* (stone-gate houses) on your way down the alley to get here. The old-Shànghǎi textures continue once inside, with red-brick walls and reproduced

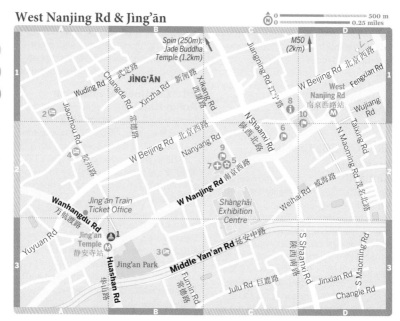

stone gateways above doorways leading to simple but smart rooms and six-person dorms (shared bathrooms).

Púlì
Luxury Hotel $$$

(璞丽酒店; Púlì Jiǔdiàn; ☏ 3203 9999; www. thepuli.com; 1 Changde Rd; 常德路1号; d from ¥3880; ❄ 🛜 ⚞; Ⓜ Jing'an Temple) With open-space rooms divided by hanging silk screens and an understated beige-and-mahogany colour scheme accentuated by the beauty of a few well-placed orchids, the Púlì is an exquisite choice. The Zen calm and gorgeous design of this 26-storey hotel make another strong case for stylish skyscrapers. Book ahead for discounts of up to 60%.

PǓDŌNG

Ritz-Carlton Shanghai Pudong
Luxury Hotel $$$

(上海浦东丽思卡尔顿酒店; Shànghǎi Pǔdōng Lìsī Kǎ'ěrdùn Jiǔdiàn; Map p216; ☏ 2020 1888; www.ritzcarlton.com; Shànghǎi IFC, 8 Century Ave; 世纪大道8号; d from ¥2800; ❄ @ 🛜 ⚞; Ⓜ Lujiazui) From the stingray-skin effect

wallpaper in the lift to its exquisite accommodation and stunning alfresco bar, the deliciously styled 285-room Ritz-Carlton in the Shànghǎi IFC is a peach. The beautifully designed rooms – a blend of feminine colours, eye-catching art deco motifs, chic elegance and dramatic Bund-side views – are a stylistic triumph.

Park Hyatt
Luxury Hotel $$$

(柏悦酒店; Bóyuè Jiǔdiàn; Map p216; ☏ 6888 1234; www.parkhyattshanghai.com; Shànghǎi World Financial Center, 100 Century Ave; 世纪大道100号世界金融中心; d from ¥2500; ❄ @ 🛜 ⚞; Ⓜ Lujiazui) Spanning the 79th to 93rd floors of the towering Shànghǎi World Financial Center, this soaring hotel sees Pǔdōng's huge buildings (bar the Shànghǎi Tower) dwarfing into Lego blocks as lobby views graze the tip of the Jīnmào Tower. Smaller than the Grand Hyatt, it's a subdued but stylish 174-room affair with a deco slant, high-walled corridors of brown-fabric and grey-stone textures.

West Nanjing Rd & Jìng'ān

🍴 Eating

In true Shànghǎi style, today's restaurant scene is a reflection of the city's craving for outside trends and tastes, whether it's Hunanese spice or French foie gras.

THE BUND & PEOPLE'S SQUARE

Lost Heaven
Yunnan **$$**

(花马天堂; Huāmǎ Tiāntáng; Map p198; ☎6330 0967; www.lostheaven.com.cn; 17 East Yan'an Rd; 延安东路17号; dishes ¥50-210; ⏰noon-2pm & 5.30-10.30pm; Ⓜ East Nanjing Rd) Lost Heaven might not have the views that keep its rivals in business, but why go to the same old Western restaurants when you can get sophisticated Bai, Dai and Miao folk cuisine from China's mighty southwest? Specialities are flowers (banana and pomegranate), wild mushrooms, chillies, Burmese curries, Bai chicken and superb *pǔ'ěr* (pu-erh) teas, all served up in gorgeous Yúnnán-meets-Shànghǎi surrounds.

Shànghǎi Grandmother
Chinese **$**

(上海姥姥; Shànghǎi Lǎolao; Map p198; ☎6321 6613; 70 Fuzhou Rd; 福州路70号; dishes ¥25-55; ⏰10.30am-9.30pm; Ⓜ East Nanjing Rd) This packed eatery is within easy striking distance of the Bund and cooks up all manner of home-style dishes. You can't go wrong with the classics here: braised eggplant in soya sauce, Grandmother's braised pork, crispy duck, three-cup chicken and *mápó dòufu* (tofu and pork crumbs in a spicy sauce) rarely disappoint.

Yúxìn Chuāncài
Sichuanese **$**

(渝信川菜; Map p198; ☎6361 1777; 5th fl, Huasheng Tower, 399 Jiujiang Rd; 九江路399号华盛大厦5楼; dishes ¥20-98; ⏰11am-2.30pm & 5-9.30pm; 📶; Ⓜ East Nanjing Rd) In the top league of Shànghǎi's best Sìchuān restaurants, Yúxìn is a dab hand in the arts of blistering chillies and numbing peppercorns. All-stars include the 'mouthwatering chicken' starter (口水鸡; *kǒushuǐ jī*), or opt for the simply smoking spicy chicken (辣子鸡; *làzǐ jī*), the crispy camphor tea duck (half/whole ¥38/68) or catfish in chilli oil.

M on the Bund
European **$$$**

(米氏西餐厅; Mǐshì Xīcāntīng; Map p198; ☎6350 9988; www.m-restaurantgroup.com/mbund/home.html; 7th fl, 20 Guangdong Rd; 广东路20号7楼; mains ¥128-288, 2-course set lunch ¥188, light lunch menu ¥118; Ⓜ East Nanjing Rd) M exudes a timelessness and level of sophistication that eclipses the razzle-dazzle of many other upscale Shànghǎi restaurants. The menu ain't radical, but that's the question it seems to ask you – is breaking new culinary ground really so

---

Eating Price Indicators

The price ranges for eating out in Shànghǎi are as follows:

o **$** less than ¥60

o **$$** ¥60 to ¥160

o **$$$** more than ¥160

crucial? Crispy suckling pig and a chicken tajine with saffron are, after all, simply delicious just the way they are.

OLD TOWN & SOUTH BUND

Kebabs on the Grille   Indian $$
(Map p194; ☑6152 6567; No 8, Cool Docks, 505 South Zhongshan Rd; 中山南路505号老码头8号; mains ¥45-125, set lunch Mon-Fri ¥58; ☺11am-10.30pm; Ⓜ Xiaonanmen; 🏄) This immensely popular and busy Cool Docks restaurant is a genuine crowd-pleaser, and has alfresco seating by the pond outside. The Boti mutton (barbecued lamb pieces) is fantastic. There's a delicious range of tandoori dishes, live table-top grills, vegetarian choices, smooth and spicy daal options, plus an all-you-can-eat Sunday brunch (¥150). Another central branch can be found west of **People's Square** (Map p198; ☑3315 0132; 227 North Huangpi Rd, inside Central Plaza; 黄陂北路227号; dishes ¥60-90, set lunch ¥48-58; Ⓜ People's Square).

Char   Steak $$$
(恰餐厅; Qià Cāntīng; Map p194; ☑3302 9995; www.char-thebund.com; 29th-31st fl, Hotel Indigo, 585 East Zhongshan No 2 Rd; 中山东二路585号29-31fl; steaks from ¥438, burgers ¥298, mains from ¥188; ☺6-10pm; 🛜; Ⓜ Xiaonanmen) Char has become a Shànghǎi steakhouse sensation. Park yourself on a sofa against the window or in a comfy chair facing Lùjiāzuǐ for optimum views. Or keep one eye on the open kitchen to see how your Tajima Wagyu rib-eye steak, grilled black cod or seafood tower is coming along. There's a choice of six different steak knives. Book ahead.

The views continue in spectacular fashion from the terrace of the supremely chilled-out upstairs **bar** (恰酒吧; Qià Jiǔbā; Map p194; www.char-thebund.com; 30th fl, Hotel Indigo, 585 East Zhongshan No 2 Rd; 中山东二路585号30楼; ☺5pm-1.30am Mon-Thu, to 2.30am Fri & Sat, 2pm-1am Sun; Ⓜ Xiaonanmen).

FRENCH CONCESSION

Jian Guo 328   Shanghainese $
(Map p202; 328 West Jianguo Rd; 建国西路328号; mains from ¥12; ☺11am-9.30pm; Ⓜ Jiashan Rd) Frequently crammed, this boisterous two-floor MSG-free spot tucked away on Jianguo Rd does a roaring trade on the back of fine Shànghǎi cuisine. You can't go wrong with the menu, but for pointers the deep-fried spare ribs feature succulent pork in a crispy coating while the eggplant in casserole is a rich, thick and thumb-raising choice, high on flavour.

Food stalls
ANDREW ROWAT/GETTY IMAGES ©

Food Streets

With a prime central location near People's Park, **Huanghe Road** (黄河路美食街; Huánghé Lù Měishí Jiē; Map p198; M People's Square) covers all the bases from cheap lunches to late-night post-theatre snacks. It's best for dumplings – get 'em fried at **Yang's Fry Dumplings** (小杨生煎馆; Xiǎoyáng Shēngjiān Guǎn; Map p198; 97 Huanghe Rd; 黄河路97号; 4 dumplings ¥6; ⏱6.30am-8.30pm; M People's Square) or served up in bamboo steamers across the road at **Jiājiā Soup Dumplings** (佳家汤包; Jiājiā Tāngbāo; Map p198; 90 Huanghe Rd; 黄河路90号; ⏱7am-10pm).

Yunnan Road (云南路美食街; Yúnnán Lù Měishí Jiē; Map p198; M Dashijie) has some interesting speciality restaurants and is just the spot for an authentic meal after museum-hopping at People's Sq. Look out for Shaanxi specialities at No 15 and five-fragrance dim sum at **Wǔ Fāng Zhāi** (五芳斋; Map p198; 28 Yunnan Rd; 云南路28号; ⏱7am-10pm).

Noodle Bull   Noodles $

(牡牛面; Hěnniú Miàn; Map p202; ☎6170 1299; Unit 3b, 291 Fumin Rd; 富民路291号3b室; noodles ¥28-35; ⏱11am-midnight; 🛜; M Changshu Rd, South Shaanxi Rd; 🍴) Noodle Bull is the bees-knees: far cooler than your average street-corner noodle stand (minimalist concrete chic and funky bowls), inexpensive, and boy is that broth slurpable. It doesn't matter whether you go vegetarian or for the roasted beef noodles (¥38), it's a winner both ways. Vegetarians can zero in on the carrot-and-cucumber-sprinkled sesame-paste noodles (¥32), which are divine. The cherry on the cake? No MSG. Enter on Changle Rd.

Bǎoluó Jiǔlóu   Shanghainese $$

(保罗酒楼; Map p202; ☎6279 2827; 271 Fumin Rd; 富民路271号; dishes ¥58; ⏱11-3am; M Changshu Rd, Jing'an Temple) Gather up some friends to join the Shanghainese at this expanded, highly popular Fumin Rd venue. It's a great place to get a feel for Shànghǎi's famous buzz. Try the excellent baked eel (保罗烤鳗; bǎoluó kǎomán) or pot-stewed crab and pork.

WEST NANJING ROAD & JÌNG'ĀN

Fu 1039   Shanghainese $$$

(福一零三九; Fú Yào Líng Sān Jiǔ; Map p194; ☎5237 1878; 1039 Yuyuan Rd; 愚园路1039 号; dishes ¥60-108; M Jiangsu Rd) Set in a three-storey 1913 villa, Fu attains an old-fashioned charm. Foodies who appreciate sophisticated surroundings and Shanghainese food on par with the decor, take note – Fu is a must. The succulent standards won't disappoint: the smoked fish starter and stewed pork in soy sauce are recommended, with the sautéed chicken and mango, and the sweet-and-sour Mandarin fish a close second.

PǓDŌNG

South Beauty   Sichuanese, Cantonese $

(俏江南; Qiào Jiāngnán; Map p216; ☎5047 1817; 10th fl, Superbrand Mall, 168 West Lujiazui Rd; 陆家嘴西路168号正大广场10楼; dishes from ¥20; ⏱11am-10pm; M Lujiazui) This smart restaurant with vermilion leather furniture and silky white table cloths on the 10th floor of the Superbrand Mall cooks up classic dishes from fiery Chóngqìng, Chéngdū and the south. The scorching boiled beef with hot pepper in chilli oil (¥48) opens the sweat pores, while the piquant *mápó dòufu* (¥38) arrives in a scarlet oily sauce. Divine.

🍷 Drinking

Shànghǎi is awash with watering holes, their fortunes cresting and falling with the vagaries of the latest vogue.

Pŭdōng

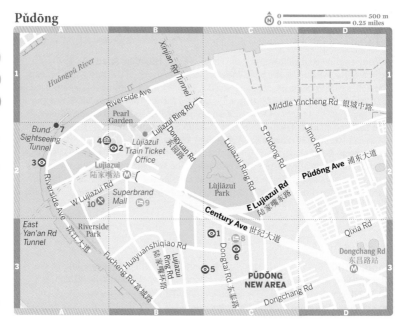

THE BUND & PEOPLE'S SQUARE

Long Bar
Bar

(廊吧; Láng Bā; Map p198; ☎6322 9988; 2 East Zhongshan No 1 Rd; 中山东一路2号; ⊙4pm-1am Mon-Sat, 2pm-1am Sun; ☎; ☒East Nanjing Rd) For a taste of colonial-era

Shànghǎi's elitist trappings, you'll do no better than the Long Bar. This was once the members-only Shànghǎi Club, whose most spectacular accoutrement was a 34m-long wooden bar. Foreign businessmen would sit here according to rank, comparing fortunes, with the taipans (foreign heads of business) closest to the view of the Bund.

New Heights
Bar

(新视角; Xīn Shìjiǎo; Map p198; ☎6321 0909; 7th fl, Three on the Bund, 3 East Zhongshan No 1 Rd; 中山东一路3号7楼; ⊙11.30-1.30am; ☒East Nanjing Rd) The most amenable of the big Bund bars, this splendid roof terrace has the choicest angle on Pŭdōng's hypnotising neon performance. There's always a crowd, whether for coffee, cocktails or meals (set meals from ¥188).

FRENCH CONCESSION

Apartment
Bar

(Map p202; ☎6437 9478; www.theapartment-shanghai.com; 3rd fl, 47 Yongfu Rd; 永福路47 号; ⊙5pm-late; ☎; ☒Shanghai Library) This trendy loft-style bar is designed to pull in the full spectrum of 30-something professionals, with a comfort-food menu; a dance space and lounge zone; a retro bar room; and topping it all a terrace for views and the summer BBQ action.

Bell Bar
Bar

(Map p202; www.bellbar.cn; Tiánzǐfáng, back door No 11, Lane 248, Taikang Rd; 泰康路248弄11号后门田子坊; ⌚11-2am; 🛜; Ⓜ Dapuqiao) This eccentric, unconventional boho haven is a delightful Tiánzǐfáng hideaway, with creaking, narrow wooden stairs leading to a higgledy-piggledy array of rooms to the tucked-away attic slung out above. Expect hookah pipes, mismatched furniture, warped secondhand paperbacks and a small, secluded mezzanine for stowaways from the bedlam outside. It's in the second alley (Lane 248) on the right.

PŮDŌNG

Flair
Bar

(Map p216; 58th fl, Ritz-Carlton Shanghai Pudong, 8 Century Ave; 世纪大道8号58楼; cocktails ¥90; ⌚5-2am; 🛜; Ⓜ Lujiazui) Wow your date with Shànghǎi's most intoxicating nocturnal visuals from the 58th floor of the Ritz-Carlton, where Flair nudges you that bit closer to the baubles of the Oriental Pearl TV Tower. If it's raining, you'll end up inside, but that's OK as the chilled-out interior is supercool and there's a minimum price (¥400) for sitting outside.

NORTH SHÀNGHǍI (HÓNGKǑU)

Vue
Bar

(非常时髦; Fēicháng Shímáo; Map p198; 32nd & 33rd fl, Hyatt on the Bund, 199 Huangpu Rd; 外滩茂悦大酒店黄浦路199号32-33楼; ⌚6pm-1am; Ⓜ Tiantong Rd) Extrasensory nocturnal views of the Bund and Pǔdōng from the Hyatt on the Bund with an outdoor Jacuzzi to go with your raised glasses of bubbly or Vue martinis (vodka and mango purée).

⭐ Entertainment

LIVE MUSIC

Fairmont Peace Hotel Jazz Bar
Jazz

(爵士吧; Juéshì Bā; Map p198; ☎6138 6883; 20 East Nanjing Rd; 南京东路20号费尔蒙和平饭店; ⌚5.30pm-2am, live music from 7pm; Ⓜ East Najing Rd) Shànghǎi's most famous hotel

Acrobats, Shànghǎi Centre Theatre (p218)

features Shànghǎi's most famous jazz band, a septuagenarian sextet that's been churning out nostalgic covers such as 'Moon River' and 'Summertime' since the dawn of time. There's no admission fee, but you'll need to sink a drink from the bar (draught beer starts at ¥70, a White Lady is ¥98).

MAO Livehouse
Live Music

(Map p202; www.mao-music.com; 3rd fl, 308 South Chongqing Rd; 重庆南路308号3楼; M Dapuqiao) One of the city's best and largest music venues, MAO is a stalwart of the Shànghǎi music scene, with acts ranging from rock to pop to electronica. Check the website for schedules and ticket prices.

NIGHTCLUBS

Shelter
Club

(Map p202; 5 Yongfu Rd; 永福路5号; ⏰9pm-4am Wed-Sat; M Shanghai Library) The darling of the underground crowd, Shelter is a reconverted bomb shelter where you can count on great music, cheap drinks and a nonexistent dress code. They bring in a fantastic line-up of international DJs and hip-hop artists; the large barely lit dance area is the place to be. Cover for big shows is usually around ¥30.

CLASSICAL MUSIC, OPERA & THEATRE

Shànghǎi Centre Theatre
Acrobatics

(上海商城剧院; Shànghǎi Shāngchéng Jùyuàn; ☎6279 8948; Shànghǎi Centre, 1376 West Nanjing Rd; 南京西路1376号; tickets ¥180, ¥240 & ¥300; M Jing'an Temple) The Shànghǎi Acrobatics Troupe has popular performances here most nights at 7.30pm. It's a short but fun show and is high on the to-do list of most first-time visitors. Buy tickets a couple of days in advance from the ticket office on the right-hand side at the entrance to the Shànghǎi Centre.

Shànghǎi Grand Theatre
Classical Music

(上海大剧院; Shànghǎi Dàjùyuàn; Map p198; ☎6386 8686; www.shgtheatre.com; 300 Renmin Ave; 人民广场人民大道300号; M People's Square) Shànghǎi's state-of-the-art concert venue hosts everything from Broadway musicals to symphonies, ballets, operas

Dongtai Road Antique Market

and performances by internationally acclaimed classical soloists. There are also traditional Chinese music performances here. Pick up a schedule at the ticket office.

Yìfū Theatre — Chinese Opera

(逸夫舞台; Yìfū Wǔtái; Map p198; ☎6322 5294; www.tianchan.com; 701 Fuzhou Rd; 人民广场福州路701号; tickets ¥30-280; Ⓜ People's Square) One block east of People's Sq, this is the main opera theatre in town and recognisable by the huge opera mask above the entrance. The theatre presents a popular program of Běijīng, Kun and Yue (Shaoxing) opera. A Běijīng opera highlights show is performed several times a week at 1.30pm and 7.15pm; pick up a brochure at the ticket office.

🔒 Shopping

From megamalls to independent boutiques and haute couture, Shànghǎi is once again at the forefront of Chinese fashion and design.

THE BUND & PEOPLE'S SQUARE

Sūzhōu Cobblers — Accessories

(上海起想艺术品; Shànghǎi Qǐxiǎng Yìshùpǐn; Map p198; Unit 101, 17 Fuzhou Rd; 福州路17号101室; ⏱10am-6.30pm; Ⓜ East Nanjing Rd) Right off the Bund, this cute boutique sells exquisite hand-embroidered silk slippers, bags, hats and clothing. Patterns and colours are based on the fashions of the 1930s, and as far as the owner, Huang Mengqi, is concerned, the products are one of a kind. Slippers start at ¥480 and the shop can make to order.

OLD TOWN

Yùyuán Bazaar (p205) is a frantic sprawl of souvenir shops with some choice gift-giving ideas and quality handicrafts, from painted snuff bottles to paper and leather silhouette cuttings, delightful Chinese kites, embroidered paintings, and clever palm and finger paintings, but sadly the hard sell is off-putting. Shops along nearby Old St (p205) are more ye olde, selling everything under the Shànghǎi sun from calligraphy to teapots, memorabilia,

woodcuts, reproduction 1930s posters and surreal 3D dazzle photos of kittens.

Dongtai Road Antique Market — Souvenirs

(东台路古玩市场; Dōngtái Lù Gǔwán Shìchǎng; Map p194; ☎5582 5254; Dongtai Rd; 东台路; ⏱9am-6pm; Ⓜ Laoximen) A block west of South Xizang Rd, this market street has more than 100 stalls strewn along both Dongtai Rd and Liuhekou Rd. It's a long sprawl of miniature terracotta warriors, Guanyin figures, imperial robes, walnut-faced luóhàn (arhat) statues, twee lotus shoes, helicopter pilot helmets and Mao-era knick-knacks, but generally only recent stuff such as art deco (and later) ornaments are genuine.

FRENCH CONCESSION

The French Concession is where it's at for shoppers; there are boutiques on almost every corner.

Tiánzǐfáng — Clothing, Souvenirs

(田子坊; Map p202; Lane 210, Taikang Rd; 泰康路210弄; Ⓜ Dapuqiao) Burrow into the lǐlòng (alleys) here for a rewarding haul of creative boutiques, selling everything from hip jewellery and yak-wool scarves to retro communist dinnerware. **Shànghǎi 1936** (Map p202; Unit 110, No 3, Lane 210, Taikang Rd; ⏱10am-8pm; Ⓜ Dapuqiao) is the place to pick up a tailored wàitào (Chinese jacket) or qípáo (cheongsam; figure-hugging Chinese dress); it also has a nearby **men's store** (Map p202; Unit 910, No 9, Lane 210, Taikang Rd; ⏱10am-8pm; Ⓜ Dapuqiao).

Further along is **Harvest** (Map p202; Rm 18, Bldg 3, Lane 210, Taikang Rd; 泰康路210弄3号楼118室田子坊; ⏱9.30am-8pm; Ⓜ Dapuqiao), which sells Miao embroidery from southwest China, and the courtyard at No 7, Lane 210 (aka the Yard): here, look for Himalayan jewellery and tapestries at **Joma** (Map p202; Unit 6, No 7, Lane 210, Taikang Rd; 泰康路210弄7号-6田子坊; Ⓜ Dapuqiao) and local fashion designers at **La Vie** (生; Shēng; Map p202; ☎6445 3585; The Yard, No 7, Lane 210, Taikang Rd; 泰康路210弄7号13室; ⏱10.30am-8.30pm; Ⓜ Dapuqiao). For funky ceramics, cloisonné and lacquer, stop by excellent **Pilingpalang**

ZHANG PENG/GETTY IMAGES ©

⭐ Don't Miss
M50

Edgier Běijīng still dominates the art scene, but swanky Shànghǎi's own gallery subculture is centred on this complex of industrial buildings down graffiti-splashed Moganshan Rd. Although the artists who originally established the M50 enclave are long gone, it's worth putting aside a half-day to poke around the galleries. There's a lot of mass-produced commercial prints, but there are also some challenging and innovative galleries. Most galleries are open from 10am to 6pm; some close on Monday.

NEED TO KNOW
M50创意产业集聚区; M50 Chuàngyì Chǎnyè Jíjùqū; Map p194; 50 Moganshan Rd; 莫干山路50号; Ⓜ Shanghai Railway Station

(噼吟啪啷; Map p202; http://pilingpalang.com; No 220, Lane 210, Taikang Rd; 泰康路210弄22号田子坊; ⊙10am-9pm; Ⓜ Dapuqiao). Pop into colourful **Link Shanghai** (搭界; Dājiè; Map p202; www.olinksh.com; No 5, Lane 248, Taikang Rd; 泰康路248弄5号田子坊; ⊙10.30am-9pm; Ⓜ Dapuqiao) for imaginative artwork and books, and **Shanghai Code** (上海密码; Shànghǎi Mìmǎ; Map p202; No 9, Lane 274, Taikang Rd; 泰康路274弄9号田子坊; ⊙2.30-9.30pm; Ⓜ Dapuqiao) for vintage spectacle frames. You'll find 1960s propaganda prints and old calendar posters at **Unique**

uniquehillgallery.com; No 10, Lane 210, Taikang Rd; 泰康路210弄10号田子坊; ⊙9am-10pm; Ⓜ Dapuqiao). The vibrant and colourful selection of crafts at **Esydragon** (Map p202; ☎ 021 6467 4818; No 51, Lane 210, Taikang Rd; 泰康路210弄51号田子坊; Ⓜ Dapuqiao) makes for excellent gifts; **Zhēnchálín Tea** (臻茶林; Zhēnchálín; Map p202; No 13, Lane 210, Taikang Rd; 泰康路210弄13号田子坊; ⊙10am-8.30pm; Ⓜ Dapuqiao) has Chinese herbal teas in nifty packaging. Other stand-out stores are **Chouchou Chic** (Map p202; No

5, Lane 248, Taikang Rd; 泰康路248弄5号; **M**Dapuqiao) and **Urban Tribe** (Map p202; No 14, Lane 248, Taikang Rd; 泰康路248弄14号; **M**Dapuqiao).

Xīntiāndì
Clothing, Accessories

(新天地; Map p202; www.xintiandi.com; 2 blocks btwn Taicang, Zizhong, Madang & South Huangpi Rds; 太仓路与马当路路口; **M**South Huangpi Rd, Xintiandi) There are few bargains to be had at Xīntiāndì, but even window-shoppers can make a fun afternoon of it here. The North Block features embroidered accessories at **Annabel Lee** (安梨家居; Ānlí Jiājū; Map p202; Xīntiāndì North Block, Bldg 3; 太仓路181弄新天地北里3号楼; ⊙10.30am-10.30pm; **M**South Huangpi Rd, Xintiandi), high-end fashion from **Shanghai Tang** (上海滩; Shànghǎi Tān; Map p202; Xīntiāndì North Block, Bldg 15; 太仓路181弄新天地北里15号楼; **M**South Huangpi Rd) and home furnishings at **Simply Life** (逸居生活; Yìjū Shēnghuó; Map p202; ☎6387 5100; Xīntiāndì North Block, Unit 101, 159 Madang Rd; 马当路159号新天地北里101单元; ⊙10.30am-10pm; **M**South Huangpi Rd, Xintiandi) as well as a few scattered souvenir shops. The South Block has not one, but two malls,

including **Xīntiāndì Style** (新天地时尚; Xīntiāndì Shíshàng; Map p202; 245 Madang Rd; 马当路245号).

NuoMi
Clothing

(糯米; Nùomǐ; Map p202; www.nuomishanghai.com; 196 Xinle Rd; 新乐路196号; ⊙11am-10pm; **M**Changshu Rd) This Shànghǎi-based label seems to do everything right: gorgeous dresses made from organic cotton, silk and bamboo; eye-catching jewellery fashioned from recycled materials; a sustainable business plan that gives back to the community; and even an irresistible line of kids' clothes.

Brocade Country
Handicrafts

(锦绣纺; Jǐnxiù Fǎng; Map p202; 616 Julu Rd; 巨鹿路616号; ⊙10am-7.30pm; **M**South Shaanxi Rd) Peruse an exquisite collection of minority handicrafts from China's southwest, most of which are second-hand (ie not made for the tourist trade) and personally selected by the owner Liu Xiaolan, a Guìzhōu native. Items for sale include embroidered wall hangings (some of which were originally baby carriers), sashes, shoes and hats, as well as silver jewellery.

Sūzhōu Cobblers (p219)

LONELY PLANET/GETTY IMAGES ©

JÌNG'ÀN

Spin   Ceramics
(旋; Xuán; Map p194; 360 Kangding Rd; 康定路
360号; ⏰11am-8pm; M Changping Rd) High
on creative flair, Spin brings Chinese
ceramics up to speed with its oblong
teacups, twisted sake sets and all manner of cool plates, chopstick holders,
and 'kung fu' and 'exploded pillar' vases.
Pieces are never overbearing, but trendily
lean towards the whimsical, geometric,
thoughtful and elegantly fashionable.

Amy Lin's Pearls   Pearls
(艾敏林氏珍珠; Àimǐn Línshì Zhēnzhū; Map
p198; Room 30, 3rd fl, 580 West Nanjing Rd; 南
京西路580号3楼30号; ⏰10am-8pm; M West
Nanjing Rd) The most reliable retailer of
pearls of all colours and sizes. Both freshwater pearls (from ¥80), including prized
black Zhèjiāng pearls (from ¥3000),
and saltwater pearls (from ¥200) are
available here. The staff speaks English
and will string your selection for you. This
place sells jade and jewellery, too.

PǓDŌNG

AP Xīnyáng Fashion & Gifts
Market   Souvenirs
(亚太新阳服饰礼品市场; Yàtài Xīnyáng Fúshì
Lǐpǐn Shìchǎng; Map p194; ⏰10am-8pm; M Science & Technology Museum) This mammoth
underground market by the Science &
Technology Museum metro station is
Shànghǎi's largest collection of shopping
stalls. There's tons of merchandise and
fakes, from suits to moccasins, glinting
copy watches, Darth Vader toys, jackets,
Lionel Messi football strips, T-shirts, Indian saris, Angry Birds bags, Bob Marley
Bermuda shorts, Great Wall snow globes:
everything under the sun.

ℹ Information

Free English and bilingual maps of Shànghǎi are
available at airports, tourist information and
service centres, bookshops and many hotels.

Medical Services

Huashan Worldwide Medical Center (华山
医院国际医疗中心; Huáshān Yīyuàn Guójì
Yīliáo Zhōngxīn; ☎6248 3986; www.sh-hwmc.
com.cn; ⏰8am-10pm) Hospital treatment and
outpatient consultations are available at the
8th-floor foreigners' clinic of Huàshān Hospital,
with 24-hour emergency treatment on the 15th
floor in building 6.

Parkway Health (以极佳医疗保健服
务; Yǐjíjiā Yīliáo Bǎojiàn Fúwù; ☎24hr
hotline 6445 5999; www.parkway
health.cn) Seven locations around
town including Hóngqiáo (以
极佳医疗保健服务; Yǐjíjiā
Yīliáo Bǎojiàn Fúwù; Map p194;
Unit 30, Mandarine City,
788 Hongxu Rd; 虹许路
788号30室) and Jing'an
(以极佳医疗保健服
务; Yǐjíjiā Yīliáo Bǎojiàn
Fúwù; Suite 203, Shànghǎi
Centre, 1376 W Nanjing
Rd; 南京西路1376号203
室) Offers comprehensive
private medical care from
internationally trained
physicians and dentists.

Amy Lin's Pearls
KYLIE MCLAUGHLIN/GETTY IMAGES ©

Going for a Ride

Tickets for the handy hop-on, hop-off open-top **City Sightseeing Buses** (都市 观光; Dūshì Guānguāng; ☏40082 06222; www.springtour.com; tickets ¥30; ⏱9am-8.30pm summer, to 6pm winter) last 24 hours and are, besides touring Shànghǎi's highlights, a great way to get around the city centre and Pǔdōng. A recorded commentary runs in eight languages: just plug in your earphones (supplied). Buses have their own stops across central Shànghǎi, including the Bund, the Old Town and People's Sq. **Big Bus Tours** (上海观光车; Shànghǎi Guānguāngchē; ☏6351 5988; www. bigbustours.com; adult/child US$48/32) also operate hop-on, hop-off bus services, lassoing in the top sights along 22 stops across two routes. Tickets are valid for 48 hours and include a one-hour boat tour of the Huángpǔ River plus admission to the 88th-floor observation tower of the Jīnmào Tower.

Members can access after-hours services and an emergency hotline.

Money

Almost every hotel has money-changing counters. Most tourist hotels, upmarket restaurants and banks accept major credit cards. Twenty-four hour ATMs are everywhere; most accept major cards.

Bank of China (中国银行; Zhōngguó Yínháng; Map p198; The Bund; ⏱9am-noon & 1.30-4.30pm Mon-Fri, 9am-noon Sat) Right next to the Fairmont Peace Hotel. Tends to get crowded, but is better organised than Chinese banks elsewhere around the country (it's worth a peek for its grand interior). Take a ticket and wait for your number. For credit-card advances, head to the furthest hall (counter No 2).

Tourist Information

Your hotel should be able to provide you with maps and most of the tourist information you require.

Public Security Bureau (PSB; 公安局; Gōng'ānjú; Map p194; ☏2895 1900; 1500 Minsheng Rd; 民生路1500号; ⏱9am-5pm Mon-Sat) Visa extensions in Shànghǎi are available from the PSB.

Shànghǎi Call Centre (☏962 288) This toll-free English-language hotline is possibly the most useful telephone number in Shànghǎi – it can even give your cab driver directions if you've got a mobile phone.

Shanghai Information Centre for International Visitors (Map p202; ☏6384 9366; Xīntiāndì South Block, Bldg 2, Xingye Rd; ⏱10am-10pm) Useful Xīntiāndì information centre.

Tourist Information & Service Centre (旅游 咨询服务中心; Lǚyóu Zīxún Fúwù Zhōngxīn; Map p198; ☏6357 3718; 518 Jiujiang Rd; 九江路518 号; ⏱9.30am-8pm)

Websites

- **Shanghaiist** (www.shanghaiist.com)
- **Smart Shanghai** (www.smartshanghai.com)
- **Time Out** (www.timeoutshanghai.com)
- **City Weekend** (www.cityweekend.com.cn/ shanghai)

ℹ️ Getting There & Away

Shànghǎi is straightforward to reach. With two airports, rail and air connections to places all over China, and buses to destinations in adjoining provinces and beyond, it's a handy springboard to the rest of the land.

Air

Shànghǎi has international flight connections to most major cities, many operated by China Eastern, which has its base here.

All international flights (and a few domestic flights) operate out of **Pǔdōng International Airport** (PVG; 浦东国际机场; Pǔdōng Guójì Jīchǎng; ☏6834 1000, flight information 96990; www.shairport.com), with most (but not all) domestic flights operating out of **Hóngqiáo International Airport** (SHA; 虹桥国际机场; Hóngqiáo Guójì Jīchǎng; ☏5260 4620, flight information 6268 8899; www.shairport.com; Ⓜ Hongqiao Airport Terminal 1, Hongqiao Airport Terminal 2) on Shànghǎi's western outskirts. If you are making an onward domestic connection from Pǔdōng, it is essential that you find out whether the domestic flight leaves from Pǔdōng or Hóngqiáo, as the latter will require *at least* an hour to cross the city.

Daily (usually several times) domestic flights connect Shànghǎi to major cities in China:

Běijīng ¥1300, 1½ hours

Chéngdū ¥1700, two hours and 20 minutes

Guǎngzhōu ¥1300, two hours

Guìlín ¥1250, two hours

Qīngdǎo ¥800, one hour

Xī'ān ¥1350, two hours

You can buy air tickets almost anywhere, including at major hotels, travel agencies and online websites such as ctrip.com and elong.net. Discounts of up to 40% are standard.

Boat

Domestic boat tickets can be bought from travel agents in the **domestic boat tickets shop** (Map p198; ☑ 6308 9822; 21 East Jinling Rd, 金陵东路 21号; ☉ 9am-6pm; Ⓜ East Nanjing Rd) on East Jinling Rd.

The **China-Japan International Ferry Company** (中日国际轮渡有限公司; Zhōngguó Guójì Lúndù Yǒuxiàn Gōngsī; ☑ 6595 6888, 6325 7642; www.chinajapanferry.com; 18th fl, Jin'an Bldg, 908 Dongdaming Rd, 东大明路908 号金岸大厦; tickets from ¥1300, plus ¥150 fuel surcharge) has staggered departures weekly to either Osaka or Kobe in Japan on Saturdays at 12.30pm.

The **Shànghǎi International Ferry Company** (☑ 6595 8666; www.shanghai-ferry.co.jp/ english/; 15th fl, Jin'an Bldg, 908 Dongdaming Rd, 东大明路908号金岸大厦; tickets from ¥1300, plus ¥150 fuel surcharge) has departures to Osaka on Tuesdays at 11am.

Both ferry companies are located in the **Jin'an Building** (908 Dongdaming Rd; 东大明路908号金 岸大厦), north of the Bund. Fares on all boats (44 hours) range from ¥1300 in an eight-bed dorm to ¥6500 in a deluxe twin cabin. Reservations are recommended in July and August. Passengers must be at the harbour three hours before departure to get through immigration. All vessels depart from the **Shànghǎi Port International**

Cruise Terminal (上海港国际客运中心; Shànghǎi Gǎng Guójì Kèyùn Zhōngxīn; Gaoyang Rd, 高阳路).

Bus

Shànghǎi has several long-distance bus stations, though, given the traffic gridlock, it's best to take the train when possible.

The vast **Shànghǎi south long-distance bus station** (上海长途客运南站; Shànghǎi Chángtú Kèyùn Nánzhàn; ☑ 5436 2835; www.ctnz.net; 666 Shilong Rd; Ⓜ Shanghai South Railway Station) serves cities in south China, including:

Hángzhōu (main bus station at Jiǔbǎo, Hángzhōu north bus station and Hángzhōu south bus station) ¥68, two hours, regular (7.10am to 7.20pm)

Sūzhōu (south and north bus stations) ¥38, 1½ hours, regular (6.27am to 7.30pm)

Túnxī/Huáng Shān ¥135, six hours, nine daily

Wùyuán ¥210, five hours, two daily (9.32am & 6.52pm)

Wūzhèn ¥51, two hours, 11 daily (7.15am to 6.17pm)

The massive **Shànghǎi long-distance bus station** (上海长途汽车客运总站; Shànghǎi Chángtú Qìchē Kèyùn Zǒngzhàn; Map p194; ☑ 6605 0000; www.kyzz.com.cn; 1666 Zhongxing Rd; 中兴路1666号; Ⓜ Shanghai Railway Station), north of Shànghǎi Train Station, has buses to destinations as far away as Gānsù province and Inner Mongolia. Regular buses run to Sūzhōu (frequent) and Hángzhōu (frequent), as well as Nánjīng (12 daily) and Běijīng (¥311, 4pm).

Train

Many parts of the country can be reached by direct train from Shànghǎi. The city has three useful stations: the main **Shànghǎi railway station** (上海火车站; Shànghǎi Huǒchē Zhàn; ☑ 6317 9090; 385 Meiyuan Rd; Ⓜ Shanghai Railway Station), the **Shànghǎi south railway station** (上海南站; Shànghǎi Nánzhàn; ☑ 9510 5123; 200 Zhaofeng Rd) and **Shànghǎi Hóngqiáo railway station** (上海虹桥站; Shànghǎi Hóngqiáo Zhàn; Ⓜ Hongqiao Railway Station) near Hóngqiáo International Airport. Most trains depart from the main station, though for some southern destinations, like Hángzhōu, they leave from Shànghǎi South. International trains for Kowloon in Hong Kong leave from the main train station. The Hóngqiáo train station is for new express trains (many Nánjīng and Sūzhōu trains leave from here) and serves as the terminus for the Shànghǎi–Běijīng G class express. Wherever you're going, make sure to get your tickets as early as possible.

There are several ways to purchase tickets: at the station (generally stressful), via your hotel or a travel agency (much easier but expect a commission charge), or at train ticket offices around town.

You will need your passport to buy tickets. Alternatively, tickets can be purchased for a small commission (¥5) from one of the numerous train ticket offices (火车票预售处; huǒchēpiào yùshòuchù) around town: **Bund** (Map p198; 384 Middle Jiangxi Rd; 江西中路384号; ⊙8am-8pm); **Jìng'ān** (77 Wanhangdu Rd; 万航渡路77 号; ⊙8am-5pm); **French Concession** (Map p202; 12 Dongping Rd; ⊙8am-noon & 1-6pm Mon-Fri, 9am-noon & 1-5.30pm Sat & Sun); **Pǔdōng** (Map p216; 1396 Lujiazui Ring Rd; 陆家嘴环路1396号; ⊙8am-7pm).

Prices and times listed are always for the fastest train. Slower, less expensive trains have not been listed. Some trains leaving from Shànghǎi train station are as follows:

Běijīng (D class) seat/sleeper ¥309/696, eight to 11½ hours, three daily

Hángzhōu (G class) 2nd/1st class ¥93/148, 1½ hours, four daily

Hong Kong hard/soft sleeper ¥471/732, 18½ hours, one daily (6.20pm)

Huángshān seat/hard sleeper ¥93/174, 11½ hours, two daily

Sūzhōu (G class) 2nd/1st class ¥40/60, 30 minutes, frequent

Xī'ān North (D class) seat/sleeper ¥338/834, 16 to 20 hours, 10 daily

Some trains leaving from Shànghǎi south train station are:

Hángzhōu ¥29, 2½ to three hours, frequent

Some trains leaving from Hóngqiáo train station are:

Běijīng (G class) 2nd/1st class ¥553/933, 5½ hours, very regular (7am to 7.55pm)

Hángzhōu (G class) 2nd/1st class ¥73/117, one hour, very regular (6.20am to 10.36pm)

Qīngdǎo (G class) 2nd/1st class ¥518/818, 6½ hours, four daily

Sūzhōu (G class) 2nd/1st class ¥39/59, 30 minutes, regular

Sūzhōu north (G class) 2nd/1st class ¥34/64, 23 minutes, very regular

Pond, Jade Buddha Temple (p201)

ⓘ Getting Around

The best way to get around Shànghǎi is the metro, which now reaches most places in the city, followed by cabs. Buses (¥2) are tricky to use unless you are a proficient Mandarin speaker.

To/From the Airport

Pǔdōng International Airport handles most international flights and some domestic flights. There are four ways to get from the airport to the city: taxi, Maglev train, metro and bus.

Taxi rides into central Shànghǎi cost around ¥160 and take about an hour; to Hóngqiáo International Airport it costs around ¥200. Regular buses run to Sūzhōu (¥84) and Hángzhōu (¥100).

The bullet-fast and time-saving Maglev train (www.smtdc.com) runs from Pǔdōng International Airport to its terminal in Pǔdōng in just eight minutes, from where you can transfer to the metro (Longyang Rd station) or take a taxi (¥40 to People's Sq). Economy single/return tickets cost ¥50/80, but show your same-day air ticket and it's ¥40 one way. Children under 1.2m travel free (taller kids are half price). Trains depart every 20 minutes from roughly 6.45am to 9.40pm.

Metro Line 2 runs from Pǔdōng International Airport to Hóngqiáo Airport, passing through central Shànghǎi. From Pǔdōng Airport it takes about 75 minutes to People's Sq (¥7) and 1¾ hours to Hóngqiáo Airport (¥8).

There are also numerous **airport buses**, which take between one and 1½ hours to run to their destinations in Pǔxī. Buses leave from the airport roughly every 15 to 25 minutes from 6.30am to 11pm; they go to the airport from roughly 5.30am to 9.30pm (bus 1 runs till 11pm). The most useful buses are airport bus 1 (¥30), linking Pǔdōng International Airport with Hóngqiáo International Airport, and airport bus 2 (¥22), linking Pǔdōng International Airport with the Airport City Terminal (上海机场城市航站楼; Shànghǎi Jīchǎng Chéngshì Hángzhàn Lóu) on West Nanjing Rd, east of Jìng'ān Temple.

Hóngqiáo International Airport is 18km from the Bund, a 30- to 60-minute trip. Most flights now arrive at Terminal 2, connected to the city centre via metro Lines 2 and 10 (30 minutes to People's Sq). Terminal 1 is connected to the centre of town by line 10; shuttle buses run regularly (6am to 11pm) between both terminals, taking 13 minutes. Airport bus 1 (¥30, 6am to 9.30pm) runs to Pǔdōng International Airport; bus 941 (¥6) links Hóngqiáo Airport with Shànghǎi Main Train Station. Taxis cost ¥70 to ¥100 to central Shànghǎi.

Public Transport

Ferry The Jinling Rd Ferry (金陵路轮渡站; Jīnlíng Lù Lúndù Zhàn) runs between the southern end of the Bund and the Dongchang Rd dock in Pǔdōng. Ferries (¥2) run roughly every 15 minutes from 7am to 10pm. The Fuxing Rd Ferry (复兴路轮渡站; Fùxìng Lù Lúndù Zhàn) runs from Fuxing Rd north of the Cool Docks in the South Bund to Dongchang Rd as well. Ferries (¥2) run every 10 to 20 minutes from around 5am to 11pm.

Metro The Shànghǎi metro system (www.shmetro.com), indicated by a red M, currently runs to 14 lines after a huge expansion, with further lines and extensions under construction. Lines 1, 2 and 10 are the most useful for travellers. Single-fare tickets cost ¥3 to ¥10 depending on distance, sold from coin and note-operated bilingual automated machines (and from booths at some stations); keep your ticket until you exit.

Transport cards are available from information desks and can also be used in taxis and on most buses. Sold at metro stations and some convenience stores, cards can be topped up with credit and used on the metro, most buses and in taxis. One-day (¥18) and three-day metro (¥45) passes are also sold from information desks.

Metro maps are available at most stations; the free tourist maps also have a small metro map printed on them. Check out www.shmetro.com for a map of the metro network.

Taxi

Shànghǎi's taxis are reasonably cheap, hassle-free and easy to flag down outside rush hour, although finding a cab during rainstorms is impossible. Flag fall is ¥14 (for the first 3km) and ¥18 at night (11pm to 5am).

Companies include:

Bāshì (巴士; ☎96840) Green-coloured Bāshì is one of Shànghǎi's major taxi companies.

Qiángshēng (强生; ☎6258 0000) Gold-coloured Qiángshēng taxis is one of the main taxi companies in Shànghǎi.

AROUND SHÀNGHǍI

Zhūjiājiǎo   朱家角

Thirty kilometres west of Shànghǎi, **Zhūjiājiǎo** (www.zhujiajiao.com/en; optional ticket incl entry to 4/8/9 sights ¥30/60/80) is easy to reach and charming – as long as your visit does not coincide with the arrival of phalanxes of tour buses.

What survives of this historic canal town today is a charming tableau of Ming- and Qing-dynasty alleys, bridges and *gǔzhèn* (古镇; old town) architecture; its alleyways steeped in the aroma of *chòu dòufu* (stinky tofu).

On the west side of the recently built City God Temple bridge stands the **City God Temple** (城隍庙; Chénghuáng Miào; Caohe Jie, 漕河街; admission ¥10; ⏱7.30am-4pm), moved here in 1769 from its original location in Xuějiābāng. Further north along Caohe St (漕河街), running alongside the canal, is the **Yuánjīn Buddhist Temple** (圆津禅院; Yuánjīn Chányuàn; Caohe Jie, 漕河街; admission ¥5;

⏱8am-4pm) near the distinctive **Tài'ān Bridge** (泰安桥; Tài'ān Qiáo). Also hunt down the **Qing dynasty Post Office** (admission ¥5).

Of Zhūjiājiǎo's quaint ancient bridges, the standout **Fàngshēng Bridge** (放生桥; Fàngshēng Qiáo) is the most photogenic. First built in 1571, the five-arched bridge was originally assembled with proceeds from a monk's 15 years of alms gathering.

You can jump on boats for comprehensive tours of town at various points, including Fàngshēng Bridge. Tickets are ¥60/120 per boat for the short/long tour; speed boats (¥40) also run from the bridge for 30-minute trips.

To overnight, a charming choice is the **Cǎo Táng Inn** (草堂客栈; Cǎotáng Kèzhàn; ☎021 5978 6442; 31 Dongjing Jie; 东井街31号; dm ¥100, d ¥300-320; ❉@🛜), not far from Fàngshēng Bridge. Book ahead.

To get to Zhūjiājiǎo, head to the **Pu'an Rd Bus Station** (普安路汽车站, Pǔ'ān Lù Qìchē Zhàn; Map p198; Pu'an Lu; 普安路; MDashijie) just south of People's Sq, and hop on the pink and white Hùzhū Gāosù Kuàixiàn bus (沪朱高速快线; ¥12,

Canal in Zhūjiājiǎo

DANITA DELIMONT/GETTY IMAGES ©

one hour, every 20 minutes from 6am to 10pm, less frequently in low season) direct to the town.

Sūzhōu 苏州

📞 0512 / POP 1.3 MILLION

Historically, Sūzhōu was synonymous with high culture and elegance, and generations of artists, scholars, writers and high society in China were drawn by its exquisite art forms and the delicate beauty of its gardens.

You could easily spend an enjoyable several days wandering through gardens, visiting some excellent museums, and exploring some of Sūzhōu's surviving canal scenes, pagodas and humpbacked bridges.

⦿ Sights & Activities

Sūzhōu Museum   Museum
(苏州博物馆, Sūzhōu Bówùguǎn; 204 Dongbei Jie; 东北街204号; audioguide ¥30; ⊙9am-5pm; 🚌Y5) FREE An architectural triumph, this IM Pei–designed museum is a modern interpretation of a Sūzhōu garden, a confluence of water, bamboo and clinical geometry. Inside is a fascinating array of jade, ceramics, wooden carvings, textiles and other displays, all with good English captions. Look out for the boxwood statue of Avalokiteshvara (Guanyin), dating from the republican period. No flip-flops.

Humble Administrator's Garden   Gardens
(拙政园, Zhuōzhèng Yuán; 178 Dongbei Jie; 东北街178号; high/low season ¥70/50, audioguide free; ⊙7.30am-5.30pm) First built in 1509, this 5.2-hectare garden is clustered with water features, a museum, a teahouse and at least 10 pavilions such as 'the listening to the sound of rain' and 'the faraway looking' pavilions – hardly humble, we know. The largest of the gardens, it's often considered to be the most impressive. With zigzagging bridges, pavilions, bamboo groves and fragrant lotus ponds, it should be an ideal place for a leisurely stroll, but you'll be battling crowds for right of way.

West Garden Temple   Gardens
(西园寺, Xīyuán Sì; Xiyuan Lu; 西园路; admission ¥25; ⊙8am-5pm; 🚌Y1, Y3) This magnificent temple, with its mustard-yellow walls and gracefully curved eaves, was burnt to the ground during the Taiping Rebellion and rebuilt in the late 19th century. Greeting you as you enter the stunning **Arhat Hall** (罗汉堂; Luóhàn Táng) is an amazing four-faced and thousand-armed statue of Guanyin. Beyond lie mesmerising and slightly unnerving rows of 500 glittering luóhàn (arhats – monks who have achieved enlightenment and passed to nirvana at death) statues, each unique and near life-size.

Pingjiang Lu   Street
(平江路; Ⓜ Lindun Lu or Xiangmen) While most of the town canals have been sealed and paved into roads, the pedestrianised Pingjiang Lu offers clues to the Sūzhōu of yesteryear. On the eastern side of the city, this canal-side road has whitewashed local houses, many now converted to guesthouses, teahouses or trendy cafes selling overpriced beverages, sitting comfortably side-by-side. Duck down some of the side

Sūzhōu

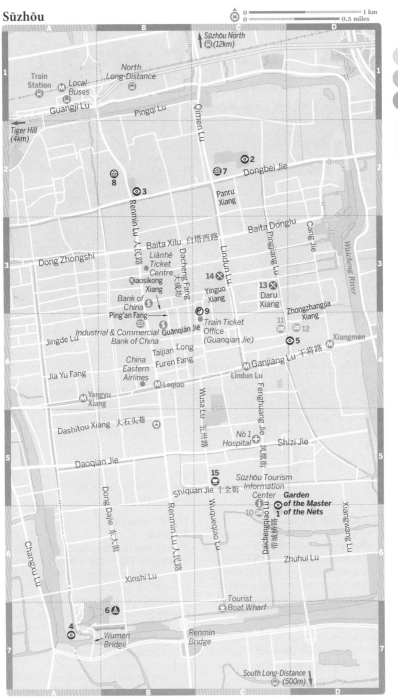

N
0 ——————— 1 km
0 ——————— 0.5 miles

Train Station
Local Buses
Guangji Lu
North Long-Distance
Pingqi Lu
Qimen Lu
Sūzhōu North (12km)

Tiger Hill (4km)

2
7
Dongbei Jie

8
3
Panru Xiang

Baita Dongbu
Cang Jie
Baita Xilu 白塔西路
Dong Zhongshi
Liánhé Ticket Centre
Dacheng Fang 大成坊
Lindun Lu
Pingjiang Lu
Waicheng River

Qiaosikong Xiang
14
Yinguo Xiang
13
Daru Xiang
Zhongzhangjia Xiang

Bank of China
Ping'an Fang
9
Train Ticket Office (Guanqian Jie)
11
12

Industrial & Commercial Bank of China
Guānqián Jiē
5
Xiangmen

Jingde Lu
Taijian Long
Furen Fang
Ganjiang Lu 干将路

Jia Yu Fang
China Eastern Airlines
Lindun Lu

Yangyu Xiang
Leqiao
Wusai Lu 五井路
Fenghuang Jie 凤凰街

Dashitou Xiang 大石头巷
No 1 Hospital
Shizi Jie

Daoqian Jie

Dong Dajie 东大街
15
Shiquan Jie 十全街
Sūzhōu Tourism Information Center
Garden of the Master of the Nets
1
10

Renmin Lu 人民路
Wuquequ Lu
Daichengqiao Lu 带城桥路
Xiangwang Lu

Changxu Lu
Xinshi Lu
Zhuhui Lu

6
Wumen Bridge
Tourist Boat Wharf
Renmin Bridge
4

South Long-Distance (500m)

DEA / C. DANI-I. JESKE/GETTY IMAGES ©

⭐ Don't Miss
Garden of the Master of the Nets

Off Shiquan Jie in Sūzhōu, this **pocket-sized garden** (网师园, Wǎngshī Yuán; high/low season ¥30/20; 🕑7.30am-5pm) is considered one of the best preserved in the city. It was laid out in the 12th century, went to seed and was later restored in the 18th century as part of the home of a retired official turned fisherman (hence the name).

streets that jut out from the main path for a glimpse at slow-paced local life.

Sūzhōu Silk Museum   Museum
(苏州丝绸博物馆, Sūzhōu Sīchóu Bówùguǎn; 2001 Renmin Lu; 人民路2001号; 🕑9am-5pm; Ⓜ Sūzhōu Train Station) FREE By the 13th century Sūzhōu was the place for silk production and weaving, and the Sūzhōu Silk Museum houses fascinating exhibitions detailing the history of Sūzhōu's 4000-year-old silk industry. Exhibits include a section on silk-weaving techniques and silk fashion through the dynasties, while you can amble among mulberry shrubs outdoors. You can also

see functioning looms and staff at work on, say, a large brocade.

North Temple Pagoda   Pagoda
(北寺塔; Běisì Tǎ; 1918 Renmin Lu; 人民路1918号; admission ¥25; 🕑7.45am-5pm) The tallest pagoda south of the Yangzi River, the nine-storey North Temple Pagoda dominates the northern end of Renmin Lu. Part of **Bào'ēn Temple** (报恩寺; Bào'ēn Sì), you can climb the pagoda (塔; tǎ) for sweeping views of hazy modern-day Sūzhōu.

The complex goes back 1700 years and was originally a residence; the current reincarnation dates back to the

17th century. Off to one side is **Nánmù Guānyīn Hall** (楠木观音殿; *Nánmù Guānyīn Diàn*), which was rebuilt in the Ming dynasty with some features imported from elsewhere.

Pán Gate Scenic Area   Landmark

(盘门, Pán Mén; 1 Dong Dajie; admission Pán Gate only/with Ruìguāng Pagoda ¥25/31; ⏱7.30am-6pm; 🚌Y2) This stretch of the city wall, straddling the outer moat in the southwest corner of the city has Sūzhōu's only remaining original coiled gate, **Pán Gate**, which dates from 1355. This overgrown double-walled **water gate** was used for controlling waterways, with defensive positions at the top.

From the gate, you can view the exquisite arched **Wúmén Bridge** (Wúmén Qiáo) to the east, the long moat and the crumbling **Ruìguāng Pagoda** (瑞光塔; Ruìguāng Tǎ; Dong Dajie; admission ¥6), constructed in 1004.

Temple of Mystery   Taoist Temple

(玄妙观, Xuánmiào Guàn; Guanqian Jie; 观前街; admission ¥10; ⏱7.30am-5pm; Ⓜ Lindun Lu or Leqiao) Lashed by electronic music from the shops alongside, the Taoist Temple of Mystery stands in what was once Sūzhōu's old bazaar, a rowdy entertainment district with travelling showmen, acrobats and actors. The temple dates from 1181 and is the sole surviving example of Song architecture in Sūzhōu.

The complex contains several elaborately decorated halls, including the huge **Sānqīng Diàn** (三清殿; Three Purities Hall), which is supported by 60 pillars and capped by a double roof with upturned eaves.

 Tours

Each evening 55-minute **boat tours** (¥120; ⏱6pm to 8.30pm) wind their way around the outer canal. Tickets can be bought at the port near Renmin Bridge, which shares the same quarters with the **Grand Canal boat ticket office** (划船售票处; Huáchuán Shòupiàochù).

🛏 **Sleeping**

Píngjiāng Lodge   Boutique Hotel $$$

(苏州平江客栈, Sūzhōu Píngjiāng Kèzhàn; ☎6523 2888; www.pingjianglodge.com; 33 Niujia Xiang, 钮家巷33号; d ¥988-1588, ste ¥1888-2588; ❄@; Ⓜ Xiangmen or Lindun Lu) Capturing the white-washed walls, canal-side Sūzhōu aesthetic, this 17th-century, traditional courtyard building has well-kept gardens and 51 rooms bedecked in traditional furniture. Rooms at the pointy end are suites with split-level living spaces; standard rooms are a bit bashed and could do with new carpets. Staff speak (faltering) English. Discounts of up to 50% are available.

Sūzhōu Mingtown Youth Hostel   Hostel $

(苏州明堂青年旅舍, Sūzhōu Míngtáng Qīngnián Lǚshè; ☎6581 6869; 28 Pingjiang Lu, 平江路28号; 6-bed dm ¥50, rm ¥125-185; ❄@; Ⓜ Xiangmen or Lindun Lu) This well-run youth hostel with a Thai sleeping Buddha at the door, has a charming lobby and rooms and dorms with dark wooden 'antique' furniture. The only downside is that rooms aren't soundproof and hot water can misfire. There's free internet, free laundry, and bike rental. Rooms are around ¥20 pricier on Friday and Saturday.

Garden Hotel   Hotel $$$

(苏州南园宾馆, Sūzhōu Nányuán Bīnguǎn; ☎6778 6778; www.gardenhotelsuzhou.com; 99 Daichengqiao Lu; 带城桥路99号; r from ¥1558; ➖@🛜) Within huge, green grounds, the very popular and recently redone five-star Garden Hotel has lovely, spacious and attractively decorated accommodation. Washed over with Chinese instrumental *pípá* music, the lobby is a picture of Sūzhōu, with a clear pond, grey bricks and white walls. Serene stuff and an oasis of calm.

 Eating

Plentiful restaurants can be found along Guanqian Jie, especially down the road from the Temple of Mystery.

Pingvon
Teahouse $

(品芳, Pínfāng; 94 Pingjiang Lu; dishes from ¥6) A cute little teahouse perched beside one of Sūzhōu's most popular canal-side streets, Pingvon serves up excellent dumplings and delicate little morsels on small plates. The tea rooms upstairs are more atmospheric. Try the pine nuts and pumpkin soup (¥6) and the crab *xiǎolóngbāo* (steamed dumplings; ¥10 a portion). Picture menu.

Yăba Shēngjiān
Dumplings $

(哑巴生煎; 12 Lindun Lu; dumplings ¥12 for eight; ⏱5.30am-6.30pm) With great clouds of steam rising from the kitchen, this 60-year-old institution mainly flogs noodles but its handmade *shēngjiān bāo* (生煎包; pan-fried dumplings), stuffed with juicy pork, are outstanding and flavour-packed. During lunch hours expect to queue for 30 minutes just to order! Protocol: get a ticket, join the line, snag a table and enjoy.

🍷 Drinking

Bookworm
Cafe, Bar

(老书虫, Lǎo Shūchóng; 77 Gunxiu Fang; 滚绣坊77号; ⏱9-1am) Běijīng's Bookworm wormed its way down to Sūzhōu, although the book selection isn't as good as Běijīng's. The food is crowd pleasing (lots of Western options) and the cold beers include Tsingtao and Erdinger. There are occasional events and books you can borrow or buy. Just off Shiquan Jie.

⭐ Entertainment

Garden of the Master of the Nets
Music

(网师园, Wǎngshī Yuán; tickets ¥100) From March to November, music performances are held nightly from 7.30pm to 9.30pm for tourist groups at this garden. Don't expect anything too authentic.

ℹ️ Information

Major tourist hotels have foreign-exchange counters.

Bank of China (中国银行, Zhōngguó Yínháng; 1450 Renmin Lu) Changes travellers cheques and foreign cash. There are ATMs that take international cards at most larger branches of the Bank of China.

Industrial & Commercial Bank of China (工商银行, Gōngshāng Yínháng; 222 Guanqian Jie) 24-hour ATM facilities.

Public Security Bureau (PSB, 公安局, Gōng'ānjú; ☎ext 20593, 6522 5661; 1109 Renmin Lu) Can help with emergencies and visa problems. The visa office is about 200m down a lane called Dashitou Xiang.

Sūzhōu Tourism Information Center (苏州旅游咨询中心, Sūzhōu Lǚyóu Zīxún Zhōngxīn; ☎6530 5887; www.classicsuzhou.com; 101 Daichengqiao Lu; 带城桥路101号) This branch is just north of the Garden Hotel; there are several other branches in town including at bus stations. Can help with booking accommodation and tours.

ℹ️ Getting There & Away

Air

Sūzhōu does not have an airport, but **China Eastern Airlines** (东方航空公司, Dōngfāng Hángkōng Gōngsī; ☎6522 2788; 115 Ganjiang Lu) can help with booking flights out of Shànghǎi. Buses leave here frequently between 6.20am and 4.50pm for Hóngqiáo International Airport (¥53) and Pǔdōng International Airport (¥54) in Shànghǎi.

Bus

Sūzhōu has three long-distance bus stations and the two listed are the most useful. Tickets for all buses can also be bought at the **Liánhé Ticket Centre** (联合售票处; Liánhé Shòupiàochù; ☎6520 6681; 1606 Renmin Lu; ⏱bus tickets 8.30-11.30am & 1-5pm; train tickets 7.30-11am & noon-5pm).

The principal station is the **north long-distance bus station** (汽车北站; Qìchē Běizhàn; ☎6577 6577; 29 Xihui Lu; 西汇路29号) at the northern end of Renmin Lu, next to the train station: A sample journey:

Hángzhōu ¥74, two hours, regular services

The **south long-distance bus station** (汽车南站; Qìchē Nánzhàn; cnr Yingchun Lu & Nanhuan Donglu) has buses to:

Hángzhōu ¥74, two hours, every 20 minutes

Shànghǎi ¥34, 1½ hours, every 30 minutes

Train

Sūzhōu is on the Nánjīng–Shànghǎi express G line. Trains stop at either the more centrally located **Sūzhōu train station** (苏州站; Sūzhōu Zhàn) or the new **Sūzhōu north train station** (苏州北站; Sūzhōu Běizhàn), 12km north of the city centre. Book train tickets on the 2nd floor of the Liánhé Ticket Centre. There's also a **ticket office** along Guanqian Jie across from the Temple of Mystery. Services include:

Běijīng South 2nd/1st class ¥524/884, five hours, 15 daily

Shànghǎi 2nd/1st class ¥40/60, 25 minutes, frequent

🛈 Getting Around

Bicycle

Riding a bike is the best way to see Sūzhōu, though nutty drivers and traffic in the city centre can be nerve jangling.

You can rent a bike from most hostels in Sūzhōu.

Public Transport

Bus Sūzhōu has some convenient tourist buses that visit all sights and cost ¥2. They all pass by the train station:

Bus Y5 Goes around the western and eastern sides of the city and has a stop at Sūzhōu Museum.

Bus Y2 Travels from Tiger Hill and Pán Gate and along Shiquan Jie.

Buses Y1 & **Y4** Run the length of Renmin Lu.

Bus 80 Runs between the two train stations.

Metro Sūzhōu metro line 1 runs along Ganjiang Lu, connecting Mùdú in the southwest with Zhongnan Jie in the east and running through the Culture & Expo Centre and Times Square, in the Sūzhōu Industrial Park. Line 2 runs north–south from Sūzhōu north railway station

to Baodaiqiaonan in the south, via Sūzhōu train station.

Taxi

Fares start at ¥10 and drivers generally use their meters. Pedicabs hover around the tourist areas and can be persistent (¥5 for short rides is standard).

....

Around Sūzhōu

TÓNGLǏ   同里

📞 0512

This lovely **old town** (老城区, Lǎochéngqū; 📞 6333 1140; admission ¥100, free after 5.30pm), only 18km southeast of Sūzhōu, boasts rich, historical canal-side atmosphere and weather-beaten charm. You can reach Tónglǐ from either Sūzhōu or Shànghǎi, but aim for a weekday visit.

The admission fee to the town includes access to the following sights, except the Chinese Sex Culture Museum.

Canal bridge, Tónglǐ
JOHN W BANAGAN/GETTY IMAGES ©

⦿ Sights

Chinese Sex Culture Museum
Museum

(中华性文化博物馆, Zhōnghuá Xìngwénhuà Bówùguǎn; admission ¥20; ☉9am-5.30pm)
This private museum, located east of Tuìsī Garden, is quietly housed in a historic but disused girls' school campus and you won't miss it. Despite occasionally didactic and inaccurate pronouncements ('there were globally three abnormal sexual phenomena: prostitution, foot-binding and eunuchs'), it's fascinating, and ranges from the penal (sticks used to beat prostitutes, chastity belts) and the penile (Qing-dynasty dildos), to the innocent (small statues of the Goddess of Mercy) and the positively charming (porcelain figures of courting couples).

The setting – with a lovely garden and courtyard – is stunning.

Gēnglè Táng
Historic Building

(耕乐堂; ☉9am-5.30pm) There are three old residences in Tónglǐ that you'll pass at some point and the most pleasant is this elegant and composed Ming-dynasty estate with 52 halls spread out over five courtyards in the west of town. The build-ings have been elaborately restored and redecorated with paintings, calligraphy and antique furniture while the black-brick faced paths, osmanthus trees and cooling corridors hung with *mǎdēng* lanterns (traditional Chinese lanterns) conjure up an alluring charm.

Tuìsī Garden
Gardens

(退思园, Tuìsī Yuán; ☉9am-5.30pm) This beautiful 19th-century garden in the east of the Old Town delightfully translates as the 'Withdraw and Reflect Garden', so named because it was a Qing government official's retirement home. The 'Tower of Fanning Delight' served as the living quarters, while the garden itself is a meditative portrait of pond water churning with koi, rockeries and pavilions, caressed by traditional Chinese music.

Pearl Pagoda
Pagoda

(珍珠塔, Zhēnzhū Tǎ; ☉9am-5.30pm) In the north of town, this compound dates from the Qing dynasty. Inside, you'll find a large residential complex decorated with Qing-era antiques, an ancestral hall, a garden and an opera stage. It gets its name from a tiny pagoda draped in pearls.

Figurine, Chinese Sex Culture Museum

👉 Tours

Slow-moving **six-person boats** (¥90 for 25 minutes) ply the waters of Tónglǐ's canal system.

🛏 Sleeping

Guesthouses are plentiful, with basic rooms starting at about ¥100.

Zhèngfú Cǎotáng
Boutique Hotel **$$**

(正福草堂; ☑ 6333 6358; www.zfct.net; 138 Mingqing Jie, 明清街138号; s ¥480, d ¥680, ste ¥1380; ❄ @ 🛜) *The* place to stay in town. Each one unique, the 14 deluxe rooms and suites are all aesthetically set with Qing-style furniture and antiques, with four-poster beds in some. Facilities like bathrooms and floor heating are ultramodern.

Tongli International Youth Hostel
Hostel **$**

(同里国际青年旅舍; Tónglǐ Guójì Qīngnián Lǔshè; ☑ 6333 9311; 10 Zhuhang Jie, 竹行街10号; dm ¥55, r from ¥110; ❄ @ 🛜) This youth hostel has two locations. The main one, slightly off Zhongchuan Beilu and near Zhongchuan Bridge, is 300m west of Zhèngfú Cǎotáng hotel. With a charming wooden interior, rooms here have traditional furniture (some with four-poster beds), oozing old-China charm. The lobby area is attractive, decked out with international flags and sofas draped in throws.

ℹ Getting There & Away

From Sūzhōu, take a bus (¥8, 50 minutes, every 30 minutes) at the south long-distance bus station for Tónglǐ. Grab an electric cart (¥5) from beside the Tongli bus station to the Old Town, or you can walk it in about 15 minutes.

Twelve daily buses (¥32) leave Tónglǐ bus station for Shànghǎi and there are frequent buses to Zhōuzhuāng (¥2 to ¥6, 30 minutes).

Hángzhōu 杭州

☑ 0571 / POP 6.16 MILLION

One of China's most illustrious tourist drawcards, Hángzhōu's dreamy West Lake panoramas and fabulously green and hilly environs can easily lull you into long sojourns. Eulogised by poets and applauded by emperors, the lake has intoxicated the Chinese imagination for aeons.

HISTORY

Hángzhōu's history dates back to the start of the Qin dynasty (221 BC). Marco Polo passed through in the 13th century, calling Hángzhōu Kinsai and noting in astonishment that Hángzhōu had a circumference of 100 miles, its waters vaulted by 12,000 bridges.

Hángzhōu flourished after being linked with the Grand Canal in AD 610 but fully prospered after the Song dynasty was overthrown by the invading Jurchen, who captured the Song capital Kāifēng, along with the emperor and the leaders of the imperial court, in 1126. The remnants of the Song court fled south, finally settling in Hángzhōu and establishing it as the capital of the southern Song dynasty. Hángzhōu's wooden buildings made fire a perennial hazard; among major conflagrations, the great fire of 1237 reduced some 30,000 residences to piles of smoking carbon.

With 10 city gates by Ming times, Hángzhōu took a hammering from Taiping rebels, who besieged the city in 1861 and captured it; two years later the imperial armies reclaimed it.

Few monuments survived the devastation; much of what can be seen in Hángzhōu today is of fairly recent construction.

👁 Sights & Activities

West Lake
Lake

(西湖; Xīhú) The unashamed tourist brochure hyperbole extolling West Lake is almost justified in its shrill accolades. The very definition of classical beauty in China, West Lake is mesmerising and methodical prettification has weaved some cunning magic: pagoda-topped hills rise over willow-lined waters as boats drift slowly through a vignette of leisurely charm. With history heavily repackaged, it's not that

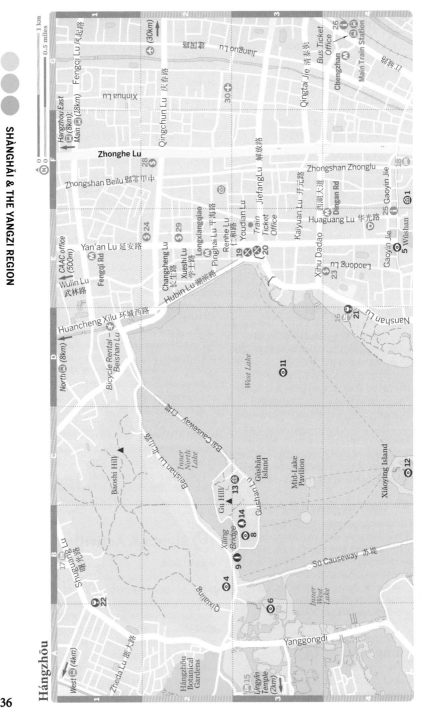

Hángzhōu

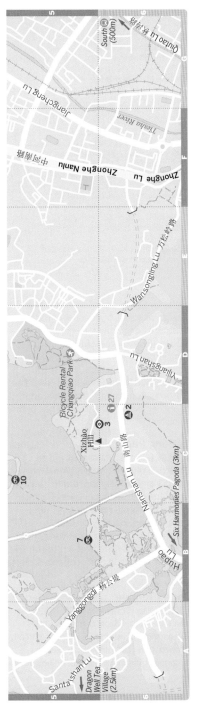

authentic – not by a long shot – but it's still a grade-A cover version of classical China.

Originally a lagoon adjoining the Qiántáng River, the lake didn't come into existence until the 8th century, when the governor of Hángzhōu had the marshy expanse dredged. As time passed, the lake's splendour was gradually cultivated: gardens were planted, pagodas built, and causeways and islands were constructed from dredged silt.

Celebrated poet Su Dongpo himself had a hand in the lake's development, constructing the **Sū Causeway** (苏堤; *Sūdī*) during his tenure as local governor in the 11th century. It wasn't an original idea – the poet-governor Bai Juyi had already constructed the **Bái Causeway** (白堤; *Báidī*) some 200 years earlier. Lined by willow, plum and peach trees, today the traffic-free causeways with their half-moon bridges make for restful outings.

Lashed to the northern shores by the Bái Causeway is **Gūshān Island** (孤山岛; *Gūshān Dǎo*), the largest island in the lake and the location of the **Zhèjiāng Provincial Museum** (浙江省博物馆; Zhèjiāng Shěng Bówùguǎn; 25 Gushan Lu; 孤山路25号; audioguide ¥10; ◎9am-5pm Tue-Sun) FREE and **Zhōngshān Park** (中山公园; Zhōngshān Gōngyuán). The island's buildings and gardens were once the site of Emperor Qianlong's 18th-century holiday palace and gardens. Also on the island is the intriguing **Seal Engravers Society** (西泠印社; Xīlíng Yìnshè; ◎9am-5.30pm) FREE, dedicated to the ancient art of carving the name seals (chops) that serve as personal signatures.

The northwest of the lake is fringed with the lovely **Qūyuàn Garden** (曲院风荷; Qūyuàn Fēnghé), a collection of gardens spread out over numerous islets and renowned for their fragrant spring lotus blossoms. Near Xīlíng Bridge (Xīlíng Qiáo) is **Su Xiaoxiao's Tomb** (苏小小墓; Sū Xiǎoxiǎo Mù), a 5th-century courtesan who died of grief while waiting for her lover to return. It's been said that her ghost haunts the area and the tinkle of the bells on her gown are audible at night.

Hángzhōu

The smaller island in the lake is **Xiǎoyíng Island** (小瀛洲; Xiǎoyíng Zhōu), where you can look over at **Three Pools Mirroring the Moon** (三潭印月; Sāntán Yìnyuè), three small towers in the water on the south side of the island; each has five holes that release shafts of candlelight on the night of the mid-autumn festival. From Lesser Yíngzhōu Island, you can gaze over to **Red Carp Pond** (花港观鱼; Huāgǎng Guānyú), home to a few thousand red carp.

Impromptu opera singing and other cultural activities may suddenly kick off around the lake, and if the weather's fine don't forget to earmark the east shore for sunset over West Lake photos. **Impression West Lake** is a spectacular evening performance on the lake waters near the Yue Fei Temple, usually starting at either 7.15pm or 7.45pm.

The best way to get around the lake is by bike. Tourist buses Y1 and Y2 also run around West Lake.

Mausoleum of General Yue Fei
Temple

(岳庙; Yuè Fēi Mù; Beishan Lu; admission ¥25; ⊙7am-6pm) This temple is more mean-ingful for Chinese patriots, rather than foreign visitors. Commander of the southern Song armies, General Yue Fei (1103–42) led successful battles against northern Jurchen invaders in the 12th century. Despite initial successes, he was recalled to the Song court, where he was executed, along with his son, after being deceived by the treacherous prime minister Qin Hui.

Léifēng Pagoda
Pagoda

(雷峰塔, Léifēng Tǎ; Nanshan Lu; 南山路; adult/child ¥40/20; ⊙8am-8.30pm Mar-Nov, 8am-5.30pm Dec-Feb) Topped with a golden spire, the eye-catching Léifēng Pagoda can be climbed for fine views of West Lake. The original pagoda, built in AD 977, collapsed in 1924. During renovations in 2001, Buddhist scriptures written on silk were discovered in the foundations, along with other treasures.

Jìngcí Temple
Buddhist Temple

(净慈寺; Jìngcí Sì; Nanshan Lu; 南山路; admission ¥10; ⊙6am-5.15pm summer, 6.30am-4.45pm winter) The serene yet monastically active Chan (Zen) Jìngcí Temple was originally built in AD 954 and is now fully restored. The splendid first hall contains the massive, foreboding Heavenly Kings and an elaborate red and gold case encapsulating Milefo (the future Buddha) and Weituo (protector of the Buddhist temples and teachings). The main hall – the **Great Treasure Hall** – contains a vast seated effigy of Sakyamuni (Buddha).

Língyǐn Temple   Buddhist Temple
(灵隐寺; Língyǐn Sì; Lingyin Lu; 灵隐路; grounds ¥35, grounds & temple ¥65; ◷7am-5pm) Hángzhōu's most famous Buddhist temple, Língyǐn Temple was built in AD 326, but has been destroyed and restored no fewer than 16 times. During the Five Dynasties (AD 907–960) about 3000 monks lived here. The Hall of the Four Heavenly Kings is astonishing, with its four vast guardians and an ornate cabinet housing Milefo (the future Buddha). The **Great Hall** contains a magnificent 20m-high statue of Siddhartha Gautama (Sakyamuni), sculpted from 24 blocks of camphor wood in 1956 and based on a Tang-dynasty original.

Behind the giant statue is a startling montage of Guanyin surrounded by 150 small figures, including multiple *luóhàn* (arhat), in a variety of poses. The earlier hall collapsed in 1949, crushing the Buddhist statues within, so it was rebuilt and the statue conceived. The Hall of the Medicine Buddha is beyond.

The walk up to the temple skirts the flanks of **Fēilái Peak** (Fēilái Fēng; Peak Flying from Afar), magically transported here from India according to legend. The Buddhist carvings (all 470 of them) lining the riverbanks and hillsides and tucked away inside grottoes date from the 10th to 14th centuries. To get a close-up view of the best carvings, including the famed 'laughing' Maitreya Buddha, follow the paths along the far (east) side of the stream.

There are several other temples near Língyǐn Temple that can be explored, including **Yǒngfú Temple** and **Tāoguāng Temple**.

Behind Língyǐn Temple is the **Northern Peak** (Běi Gāofēng), which can be scaled by **cable car** (up/down/return ¥30/20/40). From the summit there are sweeping views across West Lake and the city.

West Lake

RAY WISE/GETTY IMAGES ©

Bus K7 and tourist bus Y2 (both from the train station), and tourist bus Y1 from the roads circling West Lake, go to the temple.

Qīnghéfāng Old Street   Street
(清河坊历史文化街; Qīnghéfāng Lìshǐ Wénhuà Jiē; Hefang Jie; 河坊街) At the south end of Zhongshan Zhonglu is this touristy, crowded and bustling pedestrian street, with makeshift puppet theatres, tea-houses and gift and curio stalls, selling everything from stone teapots to boxes of *lóngxūtáng* (龙须糖; dragon whiskers sweets), ginseng and silk. It's also home to several traditional medicine shops, including the **Húqìngyú Táng Chinese Medicine Museum** (中药博物馆; Zhōngyào Bówùguǎn; 95 Dajing Xiang; admission ¥10; ⏱8.30am-5pm), which is an actual dispensary and clinic.

🛏 Sleeping

Hángzhōu's hotels have expanded in recent years across all budgets; youth hostels are now plentiful. Book well ahead in the summer months, at weekends and during the busy holiday periods.

Street, Hángzhōu

Four Seasons Hotel
Hángzhōu   Hotel $$$
(杭州西子湖四季酒店; Hángzhōu Xīzihú Sìjì Jiǔdiàn; ☎0571 8829 8888; www.fourseasons.com/hangzhou; 5 Lingyin Lu, 灵隐路5号; d ¥3800, ste from ¥8200; 😊❄@🛜🏊) More of a resort than a hotel, the fabulous 78-room, two-swimming pool Four Seasons enjoys a seductive position in lush grounds next to West Lake. Low-storey buildings and villas echo traditional China, a sensation amplified by the osmanthus trees, ornamental shrubs, ponds and tranquillity.

Tea Boutique Hotel   Hotel $$$
(杭州天伦精品酒店; Hángzhōu Tiānlún Jīngpǐn Jiǔdiàn; ☎0571 8799 9888; www.teaboutiquehotel.com; 124 Shuguang Lu, 曙光路124号; d from ¥1098, ste ¥2280; 😊❄@🛜) The simply but effectively done wood-sculpted foyer area with its sinuously shaped reception is a presage to the lovely accommodation at this hotel where a Japanese-minimalist mood holds sway among celadon teacups, muted colours and – interestingly for China – a Bible in each room.

BEST VIEW STOCK/GETTY IMAGES ©

Wúshānyì International Youth Hostel
Hostel $

(吴山驿国际青年旅社; Wúshānyì Guójì Qīngnián Lǚshè; ☑ 0571 8701 8790; 22 Zhongshan Zhonglu, 中山中路22号; dm ¥55 rm ¥158-178 d/tr/q ¥248-268/298/358; ❄@🛜) With a healthy mix of Chinese and Western travellers, this quiet, unhurried and comfy hostel has clean rooms and excellent, helpful staff plus a charmingly tucked-away location off Qinghefang Jie (and not too far from West Lake either). There are female dorms available (¥65) and cheap attic tatami rooms. Note that prices for non-dorm rooms go up by at least ¥30 on Friday and Saturday.

Mingtown Youth Hostel
Hostel $

(明堂杭州国际青年旅社; Míngtáng Hángzhōu Guójì Qīngnián Lǚshè; ☑ 0571 8791 8948; 101-11 Nanshan Lu; 南山路101-11号; dm/s/d, ¥65/200/295; ❄🛜) With its pleasant lakeside location, this friendly and highly popular hostel is often booked out so reserve well ahead. It has a relaxing cafe/bar, offers ticket booking, internet access, rents bikes and camping gear, and is attractively decked out with orchids.

🍴 Eating

Hángzhōu's most popular restaurant street is Gaoyin Jie, parallel to Qīnghéfāng Old St, a long sprawl of restaurants brashly lit up like casinos at night and aimed at visitors.

Green Tea Restaurant
Hángzhōu $

(绿茶; Lǜchá; 250 Jiefang Lu, 解放路250号; mains from ¥20; ⏰10.30am-11pm; Ⓜ Longxiangqiao) Often packed, this excellent Hángzhōu restaurant has superb food. With a bare brick finish and decorated with rattan utensils and colourful flower-patterned cushions, the dining style is casual. The long paper menu (tick what you want) runs from salty and more-ish pea soup (¥18), to gorgeous eggplant claypot (¥20), lip-smacking Dōngpō Chicken (¥48) and beyond. Seven branches in town.

Grandma's Kitchen
Hángzhōu $

(外婆家; Wàipójiā; 3 Hubin Lu, 湖滨路3号; mains ¥6-55; ⏰lunch & dinner; Ⓜ Longxiangqiao) Besieged by enthusiastic diners, this restaurant cooks up classic Hángzhōu favourites; try the hóngshāo dōngpō ròu (红烧东坡肉; braised pork), but prepare to wait for a table. There are several other branches in town.

🍷 Drinking

For drinking, Shuguang Lu north of West Lake is the place; a brash clutch of lesser bars also operates opposite the China Academy of Art on Nanshan Lu (南山路).

Maya Bar
Bar

(玛雅酒吧; Mǎyǎ Jiǔbā; 94 Baishaquan, Shuguang Lu; 曙光路白沙泉94号; ⏰10-2am) Jim Morrison, Kurt Cobain, Mick Jagger, Bob Dylan, the Beatles and a mural of a shaman/spirit warrior watch on approvingly from the walls of this darkly lit and rock-steady bar. Just as importantly, the drinks are seriously cheap; Tuesdays and Thursdays see Tsingtao and Tiger dropping to ¥10 a pint (¥20 at other times), and a DJ from 9.30pm.

Eudora Station
Bar

(亿多瑞站; Yìduōruìzhàn; 101-107 Nanshan Lu; 南山路101-107号; ⏰9-2am) A fab location by West Lake, roof terrace aloft, outside seating, a strong menu and a sure-fire atmosphere conspire to make this welcoming watering hole a great choice. There's sports TV, live music, a ground-floor terrace, a good range of beers, and barbecues fire up on the roof terrace in the warmer months.

ℹ️ Information

Money

Bank of China - Laodong Lu (中国银行, Zhōngguó Yínháng; 177 Laodong Lu; ⏰9am-5pm) Offers currency exchange plus 24-hour ATM.

Public Security Bureau

Public Security Bureau (PSB; 公安局; Gōng'ānjú Bànzhèng Zhōngxīn; ☑ 0571 8728

0600; 35 Huaguang Lu; ⏱8.30am-noon & 2-5pm Mon-Fri) Can extend visas.

Tourist Information

Asking at, or phoning up, your hostel or hotel for info can be very handy.

Hángzhōu Tourist Information Centre (杭州旅游咨询服务中心; Hángzhōu Lǚyóu Zīxún Fúwù Zhōngxīn; ☎0571 8797 8123; Léifēng Pagoda, Nanshan Lu; ⏱8am-5pm) Provides basic travel info, free maps and tours. Other branches include Hángzhōu train station and 10 Huaguang Lu, just off Qīnghéfāng Old Street.

ⓘ Getting There & Away

Air

Hángzhōu has flights to all major Chinese cities (bar Shànghǎi) and international connections to Hong Kong, Macau, Tokyo, Singapore and other destinations.

One place at which to book air tickets is the **Civil Aviation Administration of China** (CAAC; 中国民航; Zhōngguó Mínháng; ☎0571 8666 8666; 390 Tiyuchang Lu; ⏱7.30am-8pm).

Bus

All four bus stations are outside the city centre; tickets can be conveniently bought for all stations from the **bus ticket office** (长途汽车售票处; Chángtú Qìchē Shòupiàochù; Chengzhan Lu; 城站路; ⏱6.30am-5pm) right off the exit from Hángzhōu's main train station.

Buses from the huge **main bus station** (客运中心站; Kèyùn Zhōngxīn; ☎0571 8765 0678; Jiubao Zhijie; 九堡直街) at Jiǔbǎo, in the far northeast of Hángzhōu (and linked to the centre of town by metro, a taxi will cost around ¥60) include:

Huángshān (scenic zone) ¥98 to ¥110, four hours, five daily

Níngbō ¥62, two hours, regular

Shànghǎi ¥68, 2½ hours, regular

Sūzhōu ¥71, two hours, regular

Wūzhèn ¥27 to ¥30, one hour, 16 daily

Left: Futuristic architecture, Hángzhōu; **Below:** Market seller
(LEFT) ANDY BRANDL/GETTY IMAGES ©: (BELOW) MAHAUX PHOTOGRAPHY/GETTY IMAGES ©

Buses from the north bus station (汽车北站; Qìchē Běizhàn; 766 Moganshan Lu) include:

Sūzhōu ¥72, two hours, regular

Tónglǐ ¥62, two hours, three daily

Buses for **Huángshān** (¥98 to ¥110, four hours, five daily) leave from the west bus station (汽车西站; Qìchē Xīzhàn; 357 Tianmushan Lu).

Train

The easiest way to travel to Hángzhōu from Shànghǎi is on the high-speed G class train to Hángzhōu main train station (杭州火车站; Hángzhōu Huǒchēzhàn; ☎0571 8762 2362; Chengzhan Lu; 城站路) east of West Lake, while high-speed trains zip to numerous other cities.

Daily G class high-speed trains from Hángzhōu main train station include:

Běijīng south 2nd/1st class ¥629/1056, 6½ hours, two daily

Shànghǎi Hóngqiáo 2nd/1st class ¥78/124, 55 minutes, first/last 6.10am/8.26pm, regular

Sūzhōu 2nd/1st class ¥118 to ¥184, 1½ hours, two daily

Daily D class high-speed trains from Hángzhōu main train station include:

Shànghǎi Hóngqiáo 2nd/1st class ¥49/60, one hour 10 minutes, eight daily

Sūzhōu 2nd/1st class ¥75/91, two hours, two daily

G class trains running from the huge new Hángzhōu east train station (杭州东站; Hángzhōu Dōngzhàn; Dongning Lu; 东宁路), linked to the centre of town by metro, include:

Běijīng south 2nd/1st class ¥537/907, six hours, 12 daily

Shànghǎi Hóngqiáo 2nd/1st class ¥74/118, one hour, regular

Sūzhōu 2nd/1st class ¥112/179, 1½ hours, three daily

243

ⓘ Getting Around

To/From the Airport

Hángzhōu's airport is 30km from the city centre; taxi drivers ask around ¥100 to ¥130 for the trip. Shuttle buses (¥20, one hour) run every 15 minutes between 5.30am and 9pm from the CAAC office (also stopping at the train station).

Bicycle

The best way to rent a bike is to use the **Hángzhōu Bike Hire Scheme** (☏0571 8533 1122; www.hzzxc.com.cn; ¥200 deposit, ¥100 credit; ◷6.30am-9pm Apr-Oct, 6am-9pm Nov-Mar). Stations (2700 in total) are dotted in large numbers around the city, in what is the world's largest network. Apply at one of the booths at numerous bike stations near West Lake; you will need your passport as ID. Fill in a form and you will receive a swipe card, then swipe the pad at one of the docking stations till you get a steady green light, free a bike and Bob's your uncle.

Return bikes to any other station (ensure the bike is properly docked before leaving it). The first hour on each bike is free, so if you switch bikes within the hour, the rides are free. The second hour on the same bike is ¥1, the third is ¥2 and after that it's ¥3 per hour.

Youth hostels also rent out bikes, but these are more expensive.

Public Transport

Bus Hángzhōu has a clean, efficient bus system and getting around is easy (but roads are increasingly gridlocked). 'Y' buses are tourist buses; 'K' is simply an abbreviation of '*kōngtiáo*' (air-con). Tickets are ¥2 to ¥5. The following are popular bus routes:

Bus K7 Usefully connects the main train station to the western side of West Lake and Língyǐn Temple.

Tourist bus Y2 Goes from the main train station, along Beishan Lu and up to Língyǐn Temple.

Metro Hángzhōu's new metro line 1 (tickets ¥2 to ¥7; first/last train 6.06am/11.32pm), runs from the southeast of town, through the main train station, the east side of West Lake and on to the east train station, the main bus station and the northeast of town. Line 2 is expected to start service in 2016, while other lines are planned.

Taxi

Metered Hyundai taxis are ubiquitous and start at ¥10; figure on around ¥20 to ¥25 from the main train station (queues can be horrendous, though) to Hubin Lu.

···

Around Hángzhōu

MÒGĀNSHĀN 莫干山
☏0572

A blessed release from the suffocating summer torpor roasting north Zhèjiāng, this **hilltop resort** (admission ¥80) was developed by 19th-century Europeans from Shànghǎi and Hángzhōu during the concession era, in the style of Lúshān and Jīgōngshān in Hénán. Cool in summer and sometimes smothered in spectral fog, Mògānshān is famed for its scenic, forested views, towering bamboo and stone villa architecture; the mountain remains a weekend bolt hole for expat *tàitai* (wives) fleeing the simmering lowland heat.

◎ Sights & Activities

The best way to enjoy Mògānshān is to wander the forest paths and stone steps, taking in the architecture en route. There's Shànghǎi gangster **Du Yuesheng's old villa** (杜月笙别墅; Dù Yuèshēng Biéshù), which is now a hotel, Chiang Kai-shek's lodge, a couple of churches (375 Moganshan and 419 Moganshan) and other villas linked (sometimes tenuously) with the rich and famous, including the **house** (毛主席下榻处; Máo Zhǔxí Xiàtàchù; 126 Moganshan) where Chairman Mao rested his chubby limbs.

Containing **Tǎ Mountain** (塔山; Tǎshān) in the northwest, the **Dà Kēng Scenic Area** (大坑景区; Dàkēng Jǐngqū) is great for rambling.

🛏 Sleeping

Mògānshān is full of hotels of varying quality, most housed in crumbling villas. Room prices peak at weekends (Friday to

Sunday); if you come off-season (eg early spring) you can expect good discounted rates, but be warned that many hotels either shut up shop or close for renovation over the winter.

Mògānshān House 23 Hotel $$$

(莫干山杭疗23号; Mògānshān Hángliáo 23 Hào; ✆0572 803 3822; www.moganshanhouse23. com; 23 Moganshan; 莫干山23号; d & tw weekday/weekend ¥900/1200; @ 🛜) This restored villa bursts with period charm, from art deco–style sinks, black-and-white tiled bathroom floors, wooden floorboards and the original staircase to a lovely English kitchen. It's also kid friendly with a family room, baby chairs and swings in the garden. With only six rooms, book well in advance, especially for weekend stays (when it's a minimum two-night stay).

Naked Stables
Private Reserve Villas $$$

(✆021 6431 8901; www.nakedretreats.cn; 37 Shangxiazhuang, Lanshukeng Village, Fatou, 筏头乡兰树坑村上下庄37号; earth hut ¥2600, 2-/3-/4-room tree-top villas from ¥7200/9000/1200; ❄ @ ⛷) 🍃 For unbridled escapism, head for these luxurious and beautifully situated mod-con-equipped tree-top villas and earth huts within a 24-hectare resort in Mògānshān. Expect serene forest views, infinity pools, a spa and wellness centre, and heaps of eco brownie points.

Le Passage
Mohkan Shan Hotel $$$

(莫干山里法国山居; Mògānshānlǐ Fǎguóshānjū; ✆0572 805 2958; www.lepassagemoganshan. com; Xiānrénkēng Tea Plantation, Zǐlǐng Village, 紫岭村仙人坑茶厂; d/tr/q ¥4800/5800/6800; ➖ 🛜 ⛷) 🍃 Le Passage is a lovely and kid-friendly 38-room country-house hotel ensconced within a Mògānshān tea plantation. Rooms and bathrooms are big on period charm, with high ceilings. Rates are cheaper per night for a two-evening stay. Pick-up service from Shànghǎi (¥1300) and Hángzhōu (¥500) provided. There's a wine cellar, of course.

✖ Eating

Yinshan Jie has a number of restaurants and hotels with restaurants.

Mògānshān Lodge International $$

(马克的咖啡厅; Mǎkè de Kāfēitīng; ✆0572 803 3011; www.moganshanlodge.com; Songliang Shanzhuang, off Yinshan Jie; ⏰8.30am-11pm, Thu-Tue; 🛜) This elegantly presented villa, up some steps from Yinshan Jie, does decent enough breakfasts, bacon sandwiches, lunches and coffee, but dinner's the main meal (phone ahead to find out what's the choice of the day), and travel advice is dispensed. Serves only coffee (no meals) on Tuesdays.

ℹ Information

The main village (Mògānshān Zhèn) is centred on Yinshan Jie (荫山街), where you will find China Post (40 Moganshan; ⏰8.30-11am & 1-4pm), a branch of the PSB (opposite the post office) and several hotels.

ℹ Getting There & Away

Wǔkāng (武康; also known as Déqīng; 德清) is the jumping-off point for Mògānshān. From Hángzhōu's north bus station, buses leave for Wǔkāng (¥15, one hour, every 30 minutes) from 6.20am to 7pm; in the other direction, buses run every 30 minutes from 6.30am till 7pm. Don't take a sānlúnchē as they will drop you at the foot of the mountain.

From Wǔkāng minivans run to the top of Mògānshān for around ¥80; a taxi will cost around ¥80 to ¥100. Buses from Shànghǎi south bus station run four times a day to Wǔkāng (¥63 to ¥75, four hours, 7.55am, 9.25am, 1.25pm and 2.55pm).

WŪZHÈN 乌镇

✆0573

Like Zhōuzhuāng and other water towns in southern Jiāngsū, Wūzhèn's charming network of waterways and access to the Grand Canal once made it a prosperous place for its trade and production of silk.

Below: Canal boats; Right: Restaurant
(BELOW) ZHANG PENG/GETTY IMAGES ©; (RIGHT) ZHANG PENG/GETTY IMAGES ©

⊙ Sights

With its old bridges, ancient temples, age-old residences, museums and canal-side Ming- and Qing-dynasty architecture, Wūzhèn (www.wuzhen.com.cn) is an appetising and photogenic if over-commercialised slice of old China.

The old town is divided into two areas: **Dōngzhà** (东栅; ¥100; east scenic zone) and **Xīzhà** (西栅; ¥120, ¥80 after 5pm; west scenic zone), with a combined ticket for both areas (¥150). Buy your ticket at the **main visitor centre** (入口; Rùkǒu; Daqiao Lu; ⊙8am-5.30pm), where money exchange and an ATM can be found; you can also take a boat from here across the lake.

The main street of Dōngzhà scenic zone, Dongda Jie, is a narrow path paved with stone slabs and flanked by wooden buildings. Some of these are workshops, such as the **Sānbái Wine Workshop** (三白酒坊; Sānbái Jiǔfáng), an actual distillery churning out a pungent rice wine ripe for the sampling.

Mao Dun's Former Residence   Historic Building

(茅盾故居; Máo Dùn Gùjū; Guanqian Jie; 观前街; ⊙8am-5pm) Near the entrance to the Dōngzhà scenic zone, Mao Dun's Former Residence was the home of the revolutionary writer and author of Spring Silkworms and Midnight. His great-grandfather, a successful merchant, bought the house in 1885 and it's a fairly typical example from the late Qing dynasty.

Huìyuán Pawn House   Historic Building

(汇源当铺; Huìyuán Dàngpù; Changfeng Jie; ⊙8am-5pm) The Huìyuán Pawn House was once a famous pawnshop that eventually expanded to branches in Shànghǎi.

Sleeping

Wūzhèn
Guesthouse
Guesthouse **$**

(☎0573 873 1666; 137 Xizha Jie; 西栅街137号; r from ¥300; ❊) In the Xīzhà scenic zone, this is a centralised collection of canal-side B&Bs along Xi Dajie and on the other side of the water, run by families where you are then given a well-presented room with air-con, telephone and bathroom. Non-river rooms are the cheapest. To identify accommodation, look for the characters 民宿.

Wisteria Youth
Hostel
Hostel **$**

(紫藤国际青年旅社; Zǐténg Guójì Qīngnián Lüshè; ☎0573 8873 1088; 43 Sizuo Jie; 丝作街 43号; 4-/6-/8-bed dm ¥100/80/60) This OK place has a nice location on a lovely square opposite the Yida Silk Workshop on the far side of Renji Bridge, but only has dorm rooms. Wi-fi largely in lobby only.

ⓘ Getting There & Away

From Hángzhōu, buses (¥29, one hour, hourly from 6.35am to 6.15pm) run regularly to Wūzhèn from the main bus station.

From Shànghǎi, buses (¥49, two hours, hourly 7am to 6pm) run from the Shànghǎi south bus station. Four buses (¥34) also run between Wūzhèn and Sūzhōu train station.

Túnxī 屯溪

☎0559 / POP 77,000

Ringed by low-lying hills, the old trading town of Túnxī (also called Huángshān Shì) is the main springboard for trips to Huángshān and the surrounding Huīzhōu villages.

🛏 Sleeping

Hui Boutique
Hotel
Boutique Hotel **$$**

(黄山徽舍品酒店, Huángshān Huīshèpǐn Jiǔ-diàn; ☎235 2003; 3 Lihong Xiang, 老街李洪 巷3号; s/tw/d/f ¥450/450/570/690; ❊ 🛜)

Tucked down an alley off Old St, this hotel blends boutique chic and traditional style with a restored Qing-dynasty building setting. Dark rooms are attractively decked out with antique furnishings and modern toilets, with 40% discounts online softening the tariff.

Eating

Měishí Rénjiā
Hui $

(美食人家; 247 Lao Jie; dishes ¥7-60; ⊙ 10.30am-late) At the official entrance to Lao Jie, this bustling restaurant – spread over two floors and hung with traditional Chinese *mǎdēng* lanterns – is a perennial favourite. Size up the range of dishes on display – *húndūn* (wontons; dumpling soup), *jiǎozi* (stuffed dumplings), *bāozi* (steamed buns stuffed with meat or vegetables), noodles, claypot and more – then have them cooked up.

Information

Bank of China (中国银行, Zhōngguó Yínháng; cnr Xin'an Beilu & Huangshan Xilu; ⊙8am-5.30pm) Changes travellers cheques and major currencies; 24-hour ATM.

Public Security Bureau (PSB, 公安局, Gōng'ānjú; ☑251 2929; 1st fl, 108 Changgan Donglu; ⊙8am-noon & 2.30-5pm) For visa extensions and police assistance.

Getting There & Away

Air
Daily flights from **Huángshān City Airport** (黄山市飞机场; Huángshānshì Fēijīchǎng):
Běijīng ¥1090, 2½ hours, two daily
Guǎngzhōu ¥960, 1½ hours, two daily
Hong Kong ¥2470, 1¾ hours, three times a week
Shànghǎi ¥580, one hour, one daily

Bus
The **long-distance bus station** (客运总站; kèyùn zǒngzhàn; Qiyun Dadao) is roughly 2km west of the train station on the outskirts of town. Destinations include the following:
Hángzhōu ¥85, three hours, hourly (6.50am to 5.50pm)

Shànghǎi ¥132, five hours, 11 daily (last bus 6pm)
Sūzhōu ¥132, six hours, two daily (6am and 11am)
Wùyuán ¥34, two hours, three daily (8.10am, 9am & 12.30pm)

Buses to Huángshān go to the main base at Tāngkǒu (¥18, one hour, frequent, 6am to 5pm) and on to the north entrance, Tàipíng (¥20, two hours). There are also minibuses to Tāngkǒu (¥18) from in front of the train station.

Inside the bus station (to the right as you enter) is the separate **Huángshān Tourist Distribution Centre** (黄山市旅游集散中心; Lǚyóu Jísàn Zhōngxīn; ☑252 4798; Qiyun Lu, 齐云路; ⊙7.30am-6pm) with special tourist buses to popular destinations. Return buses operate hourly from 8am to 4pm, with a break from noon to 1pm. Destinations include:
Hóngcūn ¥14.50, 1½ hours
Xīdì ¥12.50, one hour

Train
Train connections are abysmal. Trains from Běijīng (¥181 to ¥510, 20 hours, 9.21am), Shànghǎi (¥110 to ¥265, 13 hours, 8.45pm and 10.06pm) and Nánjīng (¥70 to ¥159, six to 7½ hours, nine daily) stop at Túnxī (generally called Huángshān Shì; 黄山市).

Getting Around
Taxis are ¥5 at flag fall, with the 5km taxi ride to the airport costing about ¥30.

Around Túnxī

Xīdì
Historic Site

(西递; admission ¥104) Typical of the elegant Huīzhōu style, Xīdì's 124 surviving buildings reflect the wealth and prestige of the prosperous merchants who settled here. Its Unesco World Heritage Site status means Xīdì, located 54km northwest of Túnxī, enjoys a lucrative tourist economy, yet it remains a picturesque tableau of slender lanes, cream-coloured walls topped with horse-head gables, roofs capped with dark tiles, and doorways ornately decorated with carved lintels.

Hóngcūn
Village

(宏村; admission ¥104) Dating to the southern Song dynasty, the delightful village and Unesco World Heritage Site of Hóngcūn, 11km northeast of Yīxiàn, has crescent-shaped **Moon Pond** (月沼, Yuè Zhǎo) at its heart and is encapsulated by **South Lake** (南湖, Nán Hú), **West Stream** (西溪, Xī Xī) and **Léigǎng Mountain** (雷岗山, Léigǎng Shān). Founding village elders of the Wang (汪) clan consulted a feng shui master and the village was remodelled to suggest an ox, with its still-functioning waterway system representing its entrails.

ℹ Getting There & Around

Bus Tourist buses run directly to Xīdi (¥12.50, one hour) and then to Hóngcūn (¥14.50, 1½ hours) from the Túnxī long-distance bus station's tourist centre, leaving hourly from 8am to 4pm, with a break at noon. Otherwise, catch a local bus from the long-distance bus station to Yīxiàn (¥13, one hour, frequent, 6am to 5pm), the transport hub for public transport to the surrounding villages.

Bicycle A great way to explore the surrounding countryside is via bikes (出租自行车; chūzū zìxíngchē; per 4hr ¥5 to ¥15), found on the modern street opposite Hóngcūn's Hóngjì Bridge (宏际桥; Hóngjì Qiáo).

....

Huángshān 黄山

☑ 0559

When its archetypal granite peaks and twisted pines are wreathed in spectral folds of mist, Huángshān's idyllic views easily nudge it into the select company of China's top 10, nay, top five, sights.

◎ Sights & Activities

Buses from Túnxī (Huángshān Shì) drop you off in Tāngkǒu, the sprawling town at the foot of Huángshān. A base for climbers, this is the place to stock up on supplies (maps, raincoats, food, money), store your excess luggage and arrange onward transport.

ASCENDING & DESCENDING THE MOUNTAIN

Regardless of how you ascend **Huángshān** (admission Mar-Nov ¥230, Dec-Feb

Climbing Huángshān

¥150, child 1.2-1.4m ¥115, under 1.2m free), you will be stung by the dizzying entrance fee. You can pay at the eastern steps near the **Yúngŭ Station** (云谷站; Yúngŭ Zhàn) or at the **Mercy Light Temple Station** (慈光阁站; Cíguāng Gé Zhàn), where the western steps begin. Shuttle buses (¥19) run to both places from Tāngkŏu.

Three basic routes will get you up to the summit: the short, hard way (eastern steps); the longer, harder way (western steps); and the very short, easy way (cable car). The eastern steps lead up from the Yúngŭ Station; the western steps lead up from the carpark near Mercy Light Temple. It's possible to do a 10-hour circuit going up the eastern steps and then down the western steps in one day, but you'll have to be slightly insane and in good shape, and you'll definitely miss out on some of the more spectacular, hard-to-get-to areas.

Most travellers do opt to spend more than one night on the summit to explore all the various trails.

Make sure to bring enough water, food, warm clothing and rain gear before climbing. Bottled water and food prices increase the higher you go.

Eastern Steps   Hiking
A medium-fast climb of the 7.5km eastern steps from Yúngŭ Station (890m) to **White Goose Ridge** (白鹅峰, Bái'é Fēng; 1770m) can be done in 2½ hours. The route is pleasant, but lacks the awesome geological scenery of the western steps. In spring wild azalea and *weigela* add gorgeous splashes of colour to the wooded slopes. Much of the climb is comfortably shaded and although it can be tiring, it's a doddle compared with the western steps.

Western Steps   Hiking
The 15km western steps route has some stellar scenery, but it's twice as long and strenuous as the eastern steps, and much easier to enjoy if you're clambering down rather than gasping your way up. If you take the cable car up the mountain, just do this in reverse. The western steps descent begins at the **Flying Rock** (飞来石, Fēilái Shí), a boulder perched on an outcrop 30 minutes

A footpath along the western route of Huángshān

Huángshān

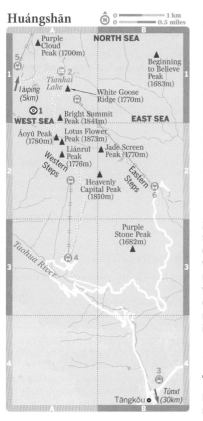

0 ————— 1 km
0 ————— 0.5 miles

Huángshān

海; Běihǎi) sunrise is a highlight for those staying overnight. **Refreshing Terrace** (清凉台; Qīngliáng Tái) is five minutes' walk from Běihǎi Hotel and attracts sunrise crowds. Lucky visitors are rewarded with the luminous spectacle of *yúnhǎi* (literally 'sea of clouds'): idyllic pools of mist that settle over the mountain, filling its chasms and valleys with fog.

🛏 Sleeping & Eating

TĀNGKǑU 汤口

Mediocre midrange hotels line Tāngkǒu's main strip, Feicui Lu; remember to look at rooms first and ask for discounts before committing.

Pine Ridge Lodge　　　　　Hotel **$**
(黄山天客山庄, Huángshān Tiānkè Shānzhuāng; ☏1377-761 8111; Scenic Area South Gate, 风景区南门; r incl breakfast ¥120-150; ❄) Wayne, the friendly English-speaking owner, likens it to a lodge in Aspen...in reality, the place isn't so much a ski lodge but a very decent midrange hotel. The in-house restaurant serves great local food. Rooms include return transfers to/from the Tāngkǒu bus station.

Zhōngruìhuáyì Hotel　　　Hotel **$$$**
(中瑞华艺大酒店, Zhōngruìhuáyì Dàjiǔdiàn; ☏556 6888, 556 8222; South Gate, 南大门; r from ¥780; ❄) This white four-star hotel on the west side of the river on the

from Běihǎi Hotel, and goes over **Bright Summit Peak** (光明顶, Guāngmíng Dǐng; 1841m), from where you can see **Áoyú Peak** (鳌鱼峰, Áoyú Fēng; 1780m), which resembles two turtles!

Yúngǔ Cable Car　　　　Cable Car
(云谷索道, Yúngǔ Suǒdào; one way Mar-Nov ¥80, Dec-Feb ¥65; ⏱7am-4.30pm) Shuttle buses (¥19) ferry visitors from Tāngkǒu to the cable car. Either arrive very early or late (if you're staying overnight) as long queues are the norm. The new cable-car station has shortened the three-hour queues to nothing more than 45 minutes.

ON THE SUMMIT

More than a few visitors spend several nights on the peak, and the North Sea (北

Huángshān access road has the most expensive and pleasant rooms in Tāngkǒu. Staff can help with bus and flight bookings and there's a free shuttle bus to the bus station.

THE SUMMIT 山顶

Ideally, Huángshān visits include nights on the summit. Note that room prices will rise on Saturday and Sunday, and are astronomical during major holiday periods.

Běihǎi Hotel   Hotel $$$
(北海宾馆, Běihǎi Bīnguǎn; ☎ 558 2555; www. hsbeihaihotel.com; dm ¥360, d ¥1680; @ 🛜) Located north of White Goose Ridge, the four-star Běihǎi comes with professional service, money exchange, cafe and 30% discounts during the week. Larger doubles with private bathroom have older fittings than the smaller, better-fitted-out doubles (same price). There are ¥1280 doubles in the three-star compound on a hill across the main square. Although it's the best-located hotel, it's also the busiest and lacks charm.

ℹ️ Information

Tāngkǒu

Bank of China (中国银行, Zhōngguó Yínháng; Yanxi Jie; ⏰8am-5pm) Southern end of Yanxi Jie.

Public Security Bureau (PSB, 公安局, Gōng'ānjú; ☎556 2311) Western end of the bridge.

On the Mountain

Bank of China (中国银行, Zhōngguó Yínháng; ⏰8-11am & 2.30-5pm) Changes money and has an ATM that accepts international cards. Opposite Běihǎi Hotel.

Police Station (派出所, pàichūsuǒ; ☎558 1388) Beside the bank.

ℹ️ Getting There & Away

Buses from Túnxī (aka Huángshān Shì) take around one hour to reach Tāngkǒu from either the long-distance bus station (¥18, one hour, frequent, 6am to 5pm) or the train station (¥18, departures when full, 6.30am to 5pm, may leave as late as 8pm in summer). Buses back to Túnxī from Tāngkǒu are plentiful, and can be flagged down on the road to Túnxī (¥18). The last bus back leaves at 5.30pm.

Tāngkǒu has two bus stations. When getting into Tāngkǒu, you will be dropped at the **south long-**

Flying Rock (p250), Huángshān

Climate

Summer (July and August) is the rainy season, though storms can blow through fairly quickly. Autumn (September to October) is generally considered to be the best travel period. Even at the height of summer, average temperatures rarely rise above 20°C at the summit, so come prepared.

distance station (南大门换乘分中心; nándàmén huànchéng fēnzhōngxīn). When coming down the mountain, you may be dropped at the east long-distance bus station (东岭换乘分中心; dōnglíng huànchéng fēnzhōngxīn), east of the town centre and within walking distance from Feicui Lu. Major destinations include:

Hángzhōu ¥100, 3½ hours, seven daily

Shànghǎi ¥140, 6½ hours, five daily

Yìxiàn ¥13, one hour, four daily (stops at Hóngcūn and Xīdì)

ⓘ Getting Around

Official tourist shuttles run between the two long-distance bus stations and the hot springs area (¥11), Yúngǔ station (云谷站, Yúngǔ Zhàn; Eastern Steps; ¥19) and Mercy Light Temple station (慈光阁站, Cíguānggé zhàn; Western Steps; ¥19), departing every 20 minutes from 6am to 5.30pm; though they usually wait until enough people are on board. A taxi to the eastern or western steps will cost ¥50; to the hot springs area ¥30.

Wùyuán 婺源

 0793 / POP 81,200

The countryside around Wùyuán is home to some of southeastern China's most immaculate views. Parcelled away in this hilly pocket is a scattered cluster of picturesque Huīzhōu villages, where old China remains preserved in enticing panoramas of ancient bridges, glittering rivers and stone-flagged alleyways.

Despite lending its name to the entire area, Wùyuán itself is a far-from-graceful town and most travellers will need no excuses before immersing themselves in the region's tantalising bucolic charms way out beyond the shabby suburbs.

ⓘ Getting There & Away

Wùyuán bus station (婺源汽车站; Wùyuán qìchēzhàn) is about 2km west of town. Some services include:

Hángzhōu ¥140, 3½ hours, 9.10am, 1.30pm & 4.30pm

Shànghǎi south ¥210, six hours, 9.50am & 10.30am

Túnxī ¥46, 2½ hours, 8.20am & 1.20pm

Services from the smaller **north bus station** (北站; Běizhàn) include:

Guānkēng ¥23, 2½ hours, 7am, 8.30am, 11am & 2.30pm

Lìkēng ¥6, 20 minutes, half-hourly (6.30am to 5.20pm)

Lǐngjiǎo ¥20, 90 minutes, 8am, 9.20am, 10.30am, 1.30pm & 3.10pm

Qīnghuá (via Sīkǒu) ¥10, 30 minutes, half-hourly (7am to 5pm)

Xiǎoqī ¥15, one hour, hourly (6.30am to 3.30pm)

Around Wùyuán

Wùyuán has become a massively popular destination with domestic tourists in the past few years. Avoid public holidays and, if possible, weekends.

There are two main ticketing options: either a **five-day pass** (¥210), which grants you admission to 12 villages/scenic areas, or **single tickets** (¥60) at each village.

Lesser-known villages, such as Guānkēng, Lǐngjiǎo, Qìngyuán and Chángxī, are free to visit.

ⓘ Getting Around

Transport throughout the region can be frustrating as villages are spaced apart and are not always linked by reliable bus connections. Hiring a *módī* (摩的; motorbike), taxi or minivan in either Wùyuán or Qīnghuá is easier than getting a bus. Motorbikes can go as low as ¥120 (plus lunch for your driver) for a full day, which should give you enough time to get to four or five villages. Taxis and minivans generally start out asking around ¥300 for a full day, but they may go as low as ¥200 when business is slow.

CRUISING THE YANGZI

Few river panoramas have inspired as much awe as the **Three Gorges** (三峡; Sānxiá). For as long as many Yangzi boat hands can remember, the Three Gorges have been a member of the prestigious China Tour triumvirate, rubbing shoulders with the Terracotta Warriors and the Great Wall.

The Route

Apocryphally the handiwork of the Great Yu, a legendary architect of the river, the gorges – Qútáng, Wū and Xīlíng – commence just east of Fèngjié in Chóngqìng province and level out west of Yíchāng in Húběi province, a distance of around 200km.

The route can be travelled in either direction, but most passengers journey downstream from Chóngqìng.

Chóngqìng to Wànzhōu 重庆 – 万州

Passing the drowned town of Fúlíng (涪陵), the first port of call is at **Fēngdū** (丰都), 170km from Chóngqìng city. Long nicknamed the **City of Ghosts** (鬼城; Guǐchéng), the town is just that: inundated in 2009, its residents were moved across the river. This is the stepping-off point for crowds to clamber up **Míng Shān** (名山; Míng Shān; admission ¥120, cable car ¥20), with its theme-park crop of ghost-focused temples.

Drifting through the county of Zhōngzhōu, the boat takes around three hours to arrive at **Shíbǎozhài** (石宝寨, Stone Treasure Stockade; admission ¥50; ⏰8am-4pm) on the northern bank of the river. A 12-storey, 56m-high wooden pagoda built on a huge, river-water-encircled rock bluff, the structure originally dates back to the reign of Qing-dynasty emperor Kangxi (1662–1722).

Most morning boats moor for the night at partially inundated **Wànzhōu** (万州; also called Wànxiàn). Travellers aiming to get from A to B as fast as possible while taking in the gorges can skip the Chóngqìng to Wànzhōu section by hopping on a three-hour bus and then taking either the hydrofoil or a passenger ship from the Wànzhōu jetty.

Little Three Gorges
JOHN BORTHWICK/GETTY IMAGES ©

The Effects of the Three Gorges Dam

The dwarfing chasms of rock, sculpted over aeons by the irresistible volume of water, are the Yangzi River's most fabled length. Yet the construction of the controversial and record-breaking **Three Gorges Dam** (三峡大坝; Sānxiá Dàbà) cloaked the gorges in as much uncertainty as their famous mists: have the gorges been humbled or can they somehow shrug off the rising waters? The peaks are not as towering as they once were, nor are the flooded chasms through which boats travel as narrow and pinched. The effect is more evident to seasoned boat hands or repeat visitors. For first-timers the gorges still put together a dramatic show.

Wànzhōu to Yíchāng 万州-宜昌

Boats departing from Wànzhōu soon pass the relocated **Zhāng Fēi Temple** (张飞庙, Zhāngfēi Miào; admission ¥40), where short disembarkations may be made.

The ancient town of **Fèngjié** (奉节), capital of the state of Kui during the periods known as the 'Spring and Autumn' (722–481 BC) and 'Warring States' (475–221 BC), overlooks Qútáng Gorge, the first of the three gorges. The town – where most ships and hydrofoils berth – is also the entrance point to half-submerged **White King Town** (白帝城, Báidìchéng; admission ¥120), where the King of Shu, Liu Bei, entrusted his son and kingdom to Zhu Geliang, as chronicled in *The Romance of the Three Kingdoms*.

Qútáng Gorge (瞿塘峡; Qútáng Xiá) – also known as Kui Gorge (夔峡; Kuí Xiá) – rises dramatically into view, towering into huge vertiginous slabs of rock, its cliffs jutting out in jagged and triangular chunks. The shortest and narrowest of the three gorges, 8km-long Qútáng Gorge is over almost as abruptly as it starts, but is considered by many to be the most awe-inspiring.

After Qútáng Gorge the terrain folds into a 20km stretch of low-lying land before boats pull in at the riverside town of **Wūshān** (巫山), situated high above the river. Many boats stop at Wūshān for five to six hours so passengers can transfer to smaller tour boats for trips along the **Little Three Gorges** (小三峡, Xiǎo Sānxiá; tickets ¥200) on the Dàníng River (大宁河; Dàníng Hé).

Wū Gorge (巫峡; Wū Xiá) – the Gorge of Witches – is stunning, cloaked in green and carpeted in shrubs, its cliffs frequently disappearing into ethereal layers of mist. About 40km in length, its towering cliffs are topped by sharp, jagged peaks on the northern bank.

At 80km, **Xīlíng Gorge** (西陵峡; Xīlíng Xiá) is the longest and perhaps least impressive gorge; sections of the gorge in the west have been submerged.

Apart from some of the top-end luxury cruises, most tour boats no longer pass through the monumental **Three Gorges Dam** (p255). The passenger ferries and hydrofoils tend to finish (or begin) their journey at **Tàipíng Creek Port** (太平溪港; Tàipíngxī Gǎng), upstream from the dam. From here, two types of shuttle bus wait to take you into Yíchāng (one hour). Ordinary tourist boats tend to use **Máopíng Port** (茅坪港; Máopíng Gǎng), from where you can at least see the dam, and which is also connected to Yíchāng via shuttle buses.

BOATS

There are four categories of boats: luxury cruises, tourist boats, passenger ships and hydrofoil.

Luxury Cruises 豪华游轮

The most luxurious passage is on international-standard cruise ships (háohuá yóulún), where maximum comfort and visibility accompany a leisurely agenda. Trips typically depart Chóngqìng mid-evening and include shore visits to all the major sights (Three Gorges Dam, Little Three Gorges et al), allowing time to tour the attractions (often secondary to the scenery). Cabins have air-con, TV (perhaps satellite), fridge/minibar and sometimes more. The average duration for such a cruise is three nights and three to four days.

Tourist Boats 普通游轮

Typically departing from Chóngqìng at around 9pm, ordinary tourist cruise ships (pǔtōng yóulún) usually take just under 40 hours to reach Yíchāng (including three nights on board). Some boats stop at all the sights; others stop at just a few (or even none at all). They are less professional than the luxury tour cruises and are aimed more at domestic travellers (Chinese food, little spoken English):

Special class (特等; tèděng) ¥1780, two-bed cabin

1st class (一等; yīděng) ¥1440, two-bed cabin

2nd class (二等; èrděng) ¥1150, four-bed cabin

3rd class (三等; sānděng) ¥1000, six-bed cabin

Passenger Ships 客船

Straightforward passenger ships (kè chuán) are cheap, but can be disappointing because you sail through two of the gorges in the dead of night. Stops are frequent, but hasty, and they pass by the tourist sights. Journeys between Chóngqìng and Yíchāng take around 36 hours; between Fèngjié and Yíchāng,

around 12 hours. Toilets are shared, and soon get pretty grotty.

Chóngqìng to Yíchāng:

1st class (一等; yīděng) ¥884, twin cabin

2nd class (二等; èrděng) ¥534, twin cabin

3rd class (三等; sānděng) ¥367, four- to six-bed dorm

4th class (四等; sìděng) ¥224, eight-bed dorm

Fèngjié to Yíchāng:

1st class ¥343

2nd class ¥212

3rd class ¥147

4th class ¥119

Hydrofoil 快艇

Yangzi River hydrofoils (kuài tǐng) are a dying breed. There are now just three per day and they only run between Fèngjié and Yíchāng. Regular buses, though, connect Fèngjié with Chóngqìng (¥160, five hours, 7.30am to 8.30pm) so this is still a quick and reasonably convenient way of seeing the Three Gorges.

Hydrofoils are passenger vessels and are not geared towards tourists, so there's no outside seating. Visibility is OK (albeit through Perspex windows), but if you stand by the door you can get a good view. Hydrofoils make regular but very brief stops at towns along the river for embarkation and disembarkation.

At the time of research, times of departure and prices for tickets bought at the relevant port's official ticket office were as follows (note, the Yíchāng times of departure are for the free shuttle buses which leave from Yíchāng's old port before connecting with the hydrofoils, which leave from a newer port 45km upstream):

Yíchāng to Fèngjié ¥245, four to five hours (7.20am, 9.50am and 1.20pm)

Fèngjié to Yíchāng ¥235, four to five hours (8.30am, 11am and 2pm)

If you get stuck for the night in Fèngjié, **Fènggǎng Bīnguǎn** (奉港宾馆; ☏ 023 5683 4333; tw & d from ¥80), attached to the ferry port, has large clean rooms, some with river views.

TICKETS

In Chóngqìng or Yíchāng, most hotels, hostels and travel agents can sell you a trip on either the luxury cruise ships or the ordinary tourist boats. In either city, passenger ferry tickets have to be bought at the ferry port ticket halls, which also sell ordinary tourist boat tickets. For the hydrofoil, you can buy westbound tickets in Yíchāng from the Three Gorges Tourist Centre, at the old ferry port. Eastbound tickets must be bought at the ticket hall in Fèngjié, where the hydrofoil starts its journey. You can no longer buy hydrofoil tickets in Chóngqìng.

The price of your ticket will include the one-hour shuttle bus ride to/from the old ferry port in the centre of Yíchāng from/to one of the two newer ferry ports, about 45km upstream, where almost all boats now leave from or terminate at.

Chóngqìng

Harbour Plaza
Travel Centre
Travel Agency

(海逸旅游中心; Hǎiyì Lǔyóu Zhōngxīn; ☏ 6373 5664; 3rd fl, Harbour Plaza, Wuyi Lu; ⏱ 8am-10pm; Ⓜ Jiāochǎngkǒu) Staff here are helpful, speak English and can book air tickets and arrange Three Gorges cruises.

Chóngqìng Ferry
Port Ticket Hall
Ferry Port

(重庆港售票大厅; Chóngqìnggǎng Shòupiào Dàtīng; ⏱ 7am-10pm) Is the cheapest place to buy ordinary tourist boat tickets, and the only place that sells passenger ferry tickets. No English spoken.

Yíchāng

China International
Travel Service
Tours

(CITS, 中国国际旅行社, Zhōngguó Guójì Lǔxíngshè; ☏ 0717 625 3088; Yunji Lu; ⏱ 8am-6pm) Sells luxury cruises to Chóngqìng (from ¥2800) and tourist boat tickets to Chóngqìng (¥880 to ¥900), but not hydrofoil tickets. Some English spoken.

Three Gorges
Tourist Centre
Ferry Tickets

(三峡游客中心, Sānxiá Yóukè Zhōngxīn; ☏ 0717 696 6116; Yanjiang Dadao, 沿江大道; ⏱ 7am-8pm) Commission-free, so cheaper than CITS. Sells hydrofoil tickets to Fèngjié (¥245) plus passenger ferry tickets to various destinations between Yíchāng and Chóngqìng. Minimal English spoken, but staff members are helpful. Enter the modern tourist centre (no English sign) and head to the ticket counters at the far right of the building.

Yangtze River
International Travel
Ferry Tickets

(宜昌长江国际旅行社, Yíchāng Chángjiāng Guójì Lǔxíngshè; ☏ 0717 692 1808; ⏱ 7am-8pm) Marginally cheaper than CITS for ordinary tourist boat tickets to Chóngqìng (from ¥890). Also sells luxury cruises. Housed inside the Three Gorges Tourist Centre, but has a separate desk beside the passenger boat ticket counters.

Fèngjié

Fèngjié Ferry Port
Ticket Hall
Ferry Port

(奉节港售票厅, Fèngjié Gǎng Shòupiàotīng) Sells passenger ferry tickets in either direction, plus hydrofoil tickets to Yíchāng (¥235). Don't expect to be able to board tourist boats from here because tickets are usually sold out in Chóngqìng or Yíchāng.

Hong Kong & the South

Hong Kong is more than just a snappy-looking and convenient international gateway to China: in many ways it is China – and always has been – in its language, cooking, people and folk traditions. The mellifluous singsong sounds of Cantonese are everywhere on the harbour breeze, as is the aroma of dim sum. But British rule lent Hong Kong something distinctive, most evidently in its vigorous cosmopolitanism and open-mindedness. Across the water, Macau is equally special: call it China with Portuguese characteristics.

Over the border, southern China ranges across a tantalising spectrum of landscapes, from the picture-perfect karst peaks of Yángshuò to the spectacular roundhouse-dotted hills of southwest Fújiàn, the ancient and good-looking Húnán river town of Fènghuáng and the gentrified island retreat of Gǔlàng Yǔ, offshore from Xiàmén and facing Taiwan.

Central district, Hong Kong Island (p271), Hong Kong

Big Buddha, Lantau Island (p280)
GREG ELMS/GETTY IMAGES ©

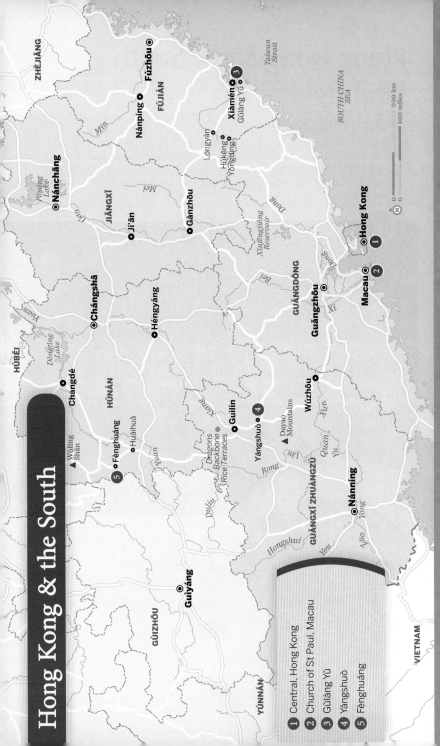

Hong Kong & the South

ZHĒJIĀNG

Fúzhōu ◎

FÚJIÀN

Nánpíng ●

Lóngyán ●
Húkēng ●
Yóngdìng ●

Xiàmén ◎ ❸
Gǔlàng Yǔ

Taiwan
Strait

SOUTH CHINA
SEA

Mǐn

Nánchāng ◎

Póyáng
Lake

JIĀNGXĪ

Jǐ'ān ●

Gàn

Gànzhōu ●

Méi

Xīnfēngjiāng
Reservoir

Dōng

Hong Kong ◎ ❶

Macau ◎ ❷

GUǍNGDŌNG

Guǎngzhōu ◎

Dōng

Xī

250 km

100 miles

N

HÚBĚI

Yuán

Dòngtíng
Lake

Chángdé ●
Chángshā ◎

HÚNÁN

Héngyáng ●

Bēi

Wǔfēng
Shān ▲

Fènghuáng ●
Huáihuà ●

❺

Yuán

Xiāng

Dragons
Backbone
Rice Terraces

Guìlín ●

Yángshuò ●
❹

Dàyáo
Mountains ▲

Wúzhōu ●

Xún

Rong

Liǔ

Quán

Yù

GUǍNGXĪ ZHUÀNGZÚ

Nánníng ◎

Yǒng

Dūliǔ

Hóngshuǐ

You

Zuǒ
Yǒu

GUÌZHŌU

Guìyáng ◎

YÚNNÁN

VIETNAM

❶ Central, Hong Kong
❷ Church of St Paul, Macau
❸ Gǔlàng Yǔ
❹ Yángshuò
❺ Fènghuáng

Hong Kong & the South Highlights

Central, Hong Kong

Every traveller takes in Hong Kong's glittering and pulsing business hub, Central (p271), which is also home to the Peak Tram, historic buildings, skyrocketing towers and the most superlative wining and dining in south China. The best introduction is on the wide-angled approach aboard the Star Ferry, while the night-time vista from Tsim Sha Tsui (pictured) is simply awesome.

1

Ruins of the Church of St Paul

2

South China's most sublime architectural ruin, the facade of the Church of St Paul (p299), is an almost mandatory pilgrimage for heathens and faithful alike. Macau isn't short of churches, but this staggering edifice – gorgeously illuminated at night – has its own unique magic and story to tell. Macau's casinos and big-spending gamblers are bywords for the ex-Portuguese territory, but this is its most poignant and enduring icon.

Amble Around Gǔlàng Yǔ

Xiàmén saves its best treasures offshore. It's only a matter of miles to the Taiwan-controlled island of Jīnmén, and the overseas connection doesn't finish there. A short boat trip from Xiàmén, Gǔlàng Yǔ's (p323) colonial-era architecture and European layout is a perfect restorative for anyone inured to the numbing socialist planning of Chinese towns. The island is small and compact, but get your room booked early; it's a popular bolthole.

DIANA MAYFIELD/GETTY IMAGES ©

Explore Yángshuò

For some travellers the town of Yángshuò (p316) is a turn-off: Western food, colloquial-English-speaking support staff and backpackers aplenty. But this is more than made up for by the surrounding, unbelievably lovely karst peaks: possibly *the* last word in iconic Chinese landscapes. And vices aside, the town is loads of fun, and for anyone who has travelled at length around China, its sheer energy and commercial vitality is an impressive display.

Discover Fènghuáng

With its classic riverine setting, brooding gate towers, ancient temples and riverside rooms precariously supported on stilts, this lovely Húnán walled town (p319) is a superlative slice of old China. Get lost down Fènghuáng's old lanes, size up the covered Hóng Bridge and pick up all manner of souvenirs from streetside ethnic-minority hawkers; but try to book a room in advance (it's popular with Chinese tourists).

Hong Kong & the South's Best...

Lodgings

○ **Upper House** Elegant and composed boutique hotel on Hong Kong Island. (p284)

○ **Peninsula Hong Kong** Top drawer luxury, fine views, colonial style. (p286)

○ **Pousada de Mong Há** For a hilltop perspective of the Macau peninsula. (p305)

○ **Secret Garden** Fantastic getaway in a small village location near the Yùlóng River. (p317)

○ **White House** Elegantly decked-out boutique choice in Guìlín. (p312)

Wining & Dining

○ **Luk Yu Tea House** The place to yum cha in Central, Hong Kong. (p288)

○ **Delicious Kitchen** The signature honey-glazed pork chop explains the queues. (p287)

○ **António** Fine Portuguese fare makes waves on Macau's Taipa Island. (p306)

○ **Alfonso III** Outstanding Macanese cuisine on the south China coast. (p305)

○ **Pure Lotus Vegetarian Restaurant** Zen calm, veggie karma, excellent food. (p318)

Architecture

○ **Hong Kong Island** From colonial elegance to stratospheric towers. (p271)

○ **Macau** A rich seam of ecclesiastical architecture and Portuguese-era grandeur. (p297)

○ **Fènghuáng** Charming vistas of traditional riverside Chinese architecture and bridges. (p319)

○ **Yǒngdìng** Awesome earth *tǔlóu* (roundhouses) rising up from the Fújiàn countryside. (p325)

Scenic Exploration

o **Gǔlàng Yǔ** Graceful south China island enclave of European villas and church architecture. (p323)

o **Dragon's Backbone Rice Terraces** Hike glittering rice terraces. (p314)

o **Yángshuò** Hire a bike and delve into the idyllic landscape of the southwest. (p316)

o **Yǒngdìng** Hike around the Fújiàn countryside in search of Hakka *tǔlóu*. (p325)

o **Lamma** Hike across this Hong Kong island. (p291)

o **Taipa** & **Coloane** Explore Macau's islands. (p304)

Need to Know

ADVANCE PLANNING

o **One Month Before** Get your hotel room booked; get your visa sorted.

o **Two Weeks Before** Book tickets for entertainment events.

o **One Week Before** Book a table at Hong Kong or Macau restaurants.

RESOURCES

o **Hong Kong Tourism Board** (www. discoverhongkong.com) Very efficient and useful website.

o **HK Magazine** (http://hk-magazine.com) Hong Kong listings and entertainment; free magazine available from restaurants, bars and hotels.

o **Time Out** (www.timeout. com.hk) Informative entertainment website; look out for the hard copy from newsstands.

o **bc Magazine** (www. bcmagazine.net) Hong Kong entertainment magazine; free hard copy.

GETTING AROUND

o **Airport Express** The fastest way into town from Hong Kong International Airport.

o **MTR** Hong Kong's metro system is very fast and highly efficient.

o **Boats** Ply the waters of Hong Kong and Macau.

o **Train** Trains criss-cross the entire southern region.

o **Air** Planes service the region and China, and fly to international destinations from Hong Kong.

o **Local Bus** The Hong Kong and Macau bus system is efficient; urban buses elsewhere are not foreigner-friendly.

o **Long-distance Buses** Serve numerous destinations across the region.

BE FOREWARNED

o **Summer Heat** Hot and very humid in Hong Kong and Macau, with lots of rain.

o **Museums** Some museums in Hong Kong close for a weekday, sometimes Tuesday (often Monday in Macau).

o **Language** English-language skills are poor outside of Hong Kong and Yángshuò.

o **Touts** Highly annoying in drawcard destinations such as Yángshuò.

Left: Yángshuò (p316);
Above: Largo do Senado (p297), Macau
(LEFT) SARA-JANE CLELAND/GETTY IMAGES ©;
(ABOVE) MANFRED GOTTSCHALK/GETTY IMAGES ©

Hong Kong & the South Itineraries

From dynamic Hong Kong, these tours take you via Macau to the spectacular karst scenery of Yángshuò to the rice terraces of northern Guǎngxī and on to sedate Xiàmén and the robust earthen buildings of Fújiàn province.

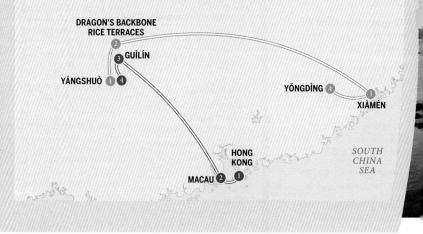

DRAGON'S BACKBONE RICE TERRACES

GUÌLÍN

YÁNGSHUÒ

YǑNGDÌNG

XIÀMÉN

HONG KONG

SOUTH CHINA SEA

MACAU

5 DAYS

HONG KONG TO YÁNGSHUÒ

COSMOPOLITAN CITYSCAPE, KARST CAPITAL

Start your journey in ❶**Hong Kong** (p270), which is overflowing with sights. Explore Hong Kong Island's Central district, ride the Peak Tram up to Victoria Peak, pay your respects in the Man Mo Temple along Hollywood Rd, hop aboard one of the island's antique trams, and pop across Victoria Harbour to Tsim Sha Tsui aboard the Star Ferry. Dining on dim sum will be a culinary highlight of your Hong Kong experience, so make the most of the restaurants in this book. Speed across the water to ❷**Macau** (p297) to explore the ex-Portuguese territory, including the ruins of the Church of St Paul, Monte Fort, Macau Museum of Art and the Mandarin's House,

and enjoy some mouthwatering Macanese food. Don't overlook the islands of Taipa and Coloane. Fly from Macau to ❸**Guìlín** (p311) in Guǎngxī province. Do some sightseeing in town before jumping aboard a boat down the Lí River to ❹**Yángshuò** (p316). You'll drift past an astonishing panorama of verdant karst peaks en route, a landscape that becomes almost impossibly dreamy around Yángshuò. Spend a few days in Yángshuò, to hike through the surrounding karst countryside – the opportunities for exploration are almost endless – or turn your hand to some rock climbing or hop on a bike to pedal around the region.

YÁNGSHUÒ TO YǑNGDÌNG
RURAL IDYLLS, ROUNDHOUSES

1 WEEK

From ❶ **Yángshuò** (p316) return to Guìlín and make a diversion north to the ❷ **Dragon's Backbone Rice Terraces** (p314) to hike from the village of Dàzhài to Píng'ān past jaw-dropping vistas of sparkling terraced rice fields. Spend a night in one of the charming guesthouses in Dàzhài, Tiántóuzhài or Píng'ān before returning to Guìlín to take a flight to ❸ **Xiàmén** (p321) in Fújiàn province. Basing yourself on the charming, carless island of Gǔlàng Yǔ is the way to go; you'll need to have some accommodation prebooked, and hop on a ferry with your suitcases to check in. Gǔlàng Yǔ is worth careful exploration and is tailor-made for slow and lazy apprecia-

tion. You may find there is little reason to leave the island – except perhaps for a visit to the Nánpǔtuó Temple – until it's time for an excursion to the Fújiàn *tǔlóu* (roundhouses) of ❹ **Yǒngdìng** (p325) and Nánjìng. These colossal – usually round but sometimes oval or rectangular – earthen buildings are essentially fortified villages for the (usually Hakka Chinese) families who dwell in them. Do spend the night in one if you have time – it's easy to find a room and it's a unique and unforgettable experience.

Lǐ River, Yángshuò (p316)
MERTEN SNIJDERS/GETTY IMAGES ©

Hong Kong Walk

This walk takes you through Hong Kong Island's historic and indefatigable Central district, guiding you past some of the territory's most iconic, impressive and dramatic architecture.

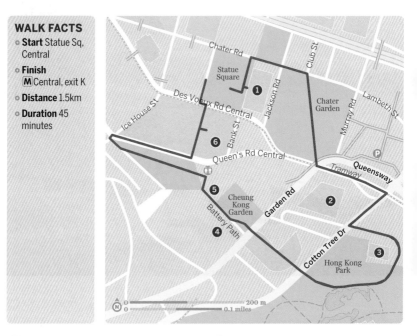

WALK FACTS
- **Start** Statue Sq, Central
- **Finish** Ⓜ Central, exit K
- **Distance** 1.5km
- **Duration** 45 minutes

❶ Legislative Council Building

Begin the walk at Statue Sq (p275) and take in the handsome outline of the neoclassical Legislative Council Building, one of the few colonial-era survivors in the area and the seat of Hong Kong's modern legislature. Built in 1912 from granite quarried on Stonecutter's Island, during WWII it was the headquarters of the Kempeitai, the Japanese version of the Gestapo.

❷ Bank of China Tower

Walk southwest through Chater Garden and cross over Garden Rd to the angular, modern lines of the Bank of China Tower (p275), completed in 1990 and offering amazing views from the 43rd floor.

❸ Flagstaff House Museum of Tea Ware

Duck into Hong Kong Park (p275) for the free Flagstaff House Museum of Tea Ware displaying valuable pots, cups and other elegant tea ware. Sample some of China's finest teas in the serene cafe.

❹ St John's Cathedral

From here take elevated walkways west over Cotton Tree Dr, through Citybank Plaza, over Garden Rd and through Cheung Kong Garden to St John's Cathedral, dating from 1849. It is a modest building to earn the title of cathedral, especially with the towering corporate cathedrals now surrounding it, but it is an important historic Hong Kong monument all the same. Services have been held here continuously since the church opened, except in 1944, when the Japanese Imperial Army used it as a social club.

⑤ Former French Mission Building

Follow Battery Path to Ice House St past the Former French Mission Building, a charming structure built for the Russian consul in Hong Kong in the 1860s and extensively rebuilt in 1917. It served as the headquarters of the provisional colonial government after WWII.

⑥ HSBC Building

Cross over Ice House St and walk right (east) along Queen's Rd Central to the HSBC building (p271) and up the escalator (if it's open) to the large airy atrium. Walk through the ground-floor plaza to pat Stephen and Stitt, the two lions guarding the exit to Des Voeux Rd Central. The closest Central Mass Transit Railway (MTR) station entrance is a short distance to the north along the pedestrian walkway between Statue Sq and Prince's Building.

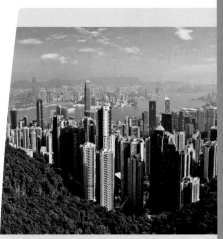

Hong Kong In...

ONE DAY

Catch the **Peak Tram** (p279) up to Victoria Peak for views of the city, stopping in **Central** (p271) for lunch on the way down. Follow our Hong Kong walking tour for a guide around this imposing and historic district. Head to **Man Mo Temple** (p275)for a taste of spirituality before hopping aboard the **Star Ferry** (p286) across Victoria Harbour to Kowloon. Enjoy the views across to Hong Kong Island from **Tsim Sha Tsui East Promenade** (p277) as you stroll to the riveting **Museum of History** (p278). After dinner in Tsim Sha Tsui, take the MTR back to Hong Kong Island for drinks in **Lan Kwai Fong** (p290) or **Soho** (p290).

TWO DAYS

In addition to the above, you could go to **Aberdeen** (p277) for a boat ride, then to **Ap Lei Chau** (p277) for seafood and shopping. Alternatively, journey to the **Po Lin Monastery** (p280) on Lantau or walk across breezy **Lamma Island** (p291). After dark, make your way to the **Temple Street Night Market** (p278) for sightseeing, shopping and street food before rounding off the day with a drink in **Ozone** (p290), Asia's highest bar.

View of Hong Kong from Victoria Peak
MELISSA TSE/GETTY IMAGES ©

Discover Hong Kong & the South

At a Glance

o **Hong Kong Island** (p271) Home of glittering Central district and Victoria Peak.

o **Kowloon** (p277) High-density shopping and tourist warren.

o **Macau** (p297) Gorgeous slice of yester-century Portugal with island escapes.

o **Xiàmén** (p321) Gateway to Gǔlàng Yǔ and Hakka territory.

o **Yángshuò** (p316) Backpacker mecca and karst wonderland.

HONG KONG

✏️ 852 / POP 7 MILLION

Like a shot of adrenalin, Hong Kong quickens the pulse. Skyscrapers march up jungle-clad slopes by day and blaze neon by night across a harbour criss-crossed by freighters and motor junks. Above streets teeming with traffic, five-star hotels stand next to ageing tenement blocks.

The very acme of luxury can be yours, though enjoying the city need not cost the earth. The HK$2 ride across the harbour must be one of the world's best-value cruises. A meander through a market offers similarly cheap thrills. You can also escape the crowds – just head for one of the city's many country parks.

History

Until European traders started importing opium into the country, Hong Kong was an obscure backwater in the Chinese empire. The British developed the trade aggressively, and by the start of the 19th century traded this 'foreign mud' for Chinese tea, silk and porcelain.

China's attempts to stamp out the opium trade gave the British the pretext they needed for military action. Gunboats were sent in. In 1841 the Union flag was hoisted on Hong Kong Island and the Treaty of Nanking, which brought an end to the so-called First Opium War, ceded the island to the British crown 'in perpetuity'.

At the end of the Second Opium War in 1860, Britain took possession of Kowloon peninsula, and in 1898 a 99-year lease was granted for the New Territories.

View from Victoria Peak
WICHIANDUANGSRI/GETTY IMAGES ©

In 1984 Britain agreed to return what would become the Special Administrative Region (SAR) of Hong Kong to China in 1997, on the condition it would retain its free-market economy and its social and legal systems for 50 years.

Climate

Hong Kong rarely gets especially cold, but it's worth packing something at least a little bit warm between November and March. Between May and mid-September temperatures in the mid-30s combined with stifling humidity can turn you into a walking sweat machine. This time is also the wettest, accounting for about 80% of annual rainfall, partly due to typhoons. The best time to visit Hong Kong is between mid-September and February.

⊙ Sights

Hong Kong comprises four main areas: Hong Kong Island, Kowloon, the New Territories (NT) and the Outlying Islands. More than 70% of Hong Kong is mountains and forests, with most of it in the New Territories.

HONG KONG ISLAND

Central is where high finance meets haute couture, and mega deals are closed in towering skyscrapers. To the west is historically rich Sheung Wan, while Admiralty with its few but excellent offerings lies to the east. East of Admiralty is Wan Chai, which features skyscrapers in the north and old neighbourhoods in the south. Neon-clad Causeway Bay lies to the east.

HSBC Building Building
(滙豐銀行總行大廈; Map p282; www.hsbc.com.hk/1/2/about/home/unique-headquarters; 1 Queen's Rd Central, Central; ☉ escalator 9am-4.30pm Mon-Fri, 9am-12.30pm Sat; M Central, exit K) FREE Make sure you have a close-up look at the stunning headquarters of what is now HSBC (formerly the Hongkong & Shanghai Bank) headquarters, designed by British

♥ If You Like…
Hong Kong Temples

If you liked the Man Mo Temple (p275), Hong Kong has a host of other smoky shrines dedicated to colourful Taoist and Buddhist deities.

1 PAK TAI TEMPLE
(北帝廟; Map p288; 2 Lung On St, Wan Chai; ☉8am-5pm; M Wan Chai, exit A3) A stroll up Stone Nullah Lane takes you to a majestic Taoist temple built in 1863 to honour a god of the sea, Pak Tai. It is the largest temple on Hong Kong Island. The main hall contains a 3m-tall copper likeness of Pak Tai cast in the Ming dynasty.

2 SIK SIK YUEN WONG TAI SIN TEMPLE
(嗇色園黃大仙祠; ☎ 2327 8141, 2351 5640; www.siksikyuen.org.hk; 2 Chuk Yuen Village, Wong Tai Sin; donation HK$2; ☉7am-5.30pm; M Wong Tai Sin, exit B2) An explosion of pillars, roofs, flowers, lattice work and incense, this busy temple hosts all walks of Hong Kong life, from pensioners to parents and professionals. Some come to pray, others to divine the future with chim – bamboo 'fortune sticks' that are shaken from a box to the ground and read by a fortune-teller.

3 TIN HAU TEMPLE
(天后廟; Map p274; ☎ 2385 0759; www.ctc.org.hk; cnr Temple St & Public Square St, Yau Ma Tei; ☉ 8am-5pm; M Yau Ma Tei, exit C) This large, incense-filled sanctuary built in the 19th century is one of Hong Kong's most famous Tin Hau (Goddess of the Sea) temples. The public square is Yau Ma Tei's communal heart where fishers once laid out hemp ropes next to the Chinese banyans that today shade chess players.

4 CHI LIN NUNNERY
(志蓮淨苑; ☎ 2354 1888; www.chilin.org; 5 Chi Lin Dr, Diamond Hill; ☉nunnery 9am-4.30pm, garden 6.30am-7pm; M Diamond Hill, exit C2) FREE One of the most beautiful built environments in Hong Kong, this large Buddhist complex, dating from the 1930s, was rebuilt completely out of wood (and not a single nail) in the style of the Tang dynasty in 1998. It's a serene place, with lotus ponds, bonsai tea plants and bougainvillea, and silent nuns delivering offerings of fruit and rice to Buddha or chanting behind intricately carved screens.

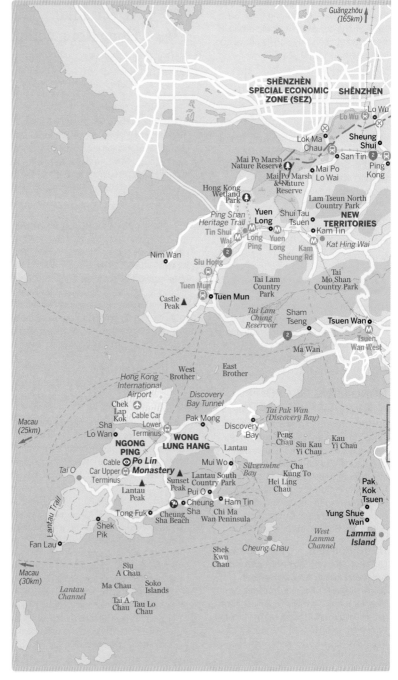

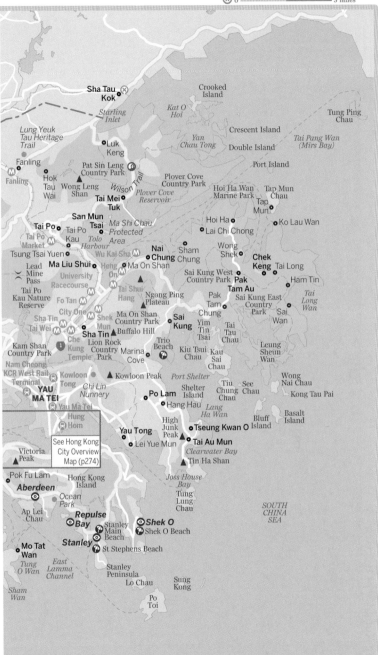

0 ———————————— 10 km
0 ———————————— 5 miles

Sha Tau Kok
Crooked Island
Tung Ping Chau
Starling Inlet
Kat O Hoi
Lung Yeuk Tau Heritage Trail
Crescent Island
Tai Pang Wan (Mirs Bay)
Fanling
Luk Keng
Yan Chau Tong
Double Island
Port Island
Fanling
Hok Tau Wai
Pat Sin Leng Country Park
Wong Leng Shan
Plover Cove Country Park
Hoi Ha Wan Marine Park
Tap Mun Chau
Tai Mei Tuk
Wilson Trail
Plover Cove Reservoir
Hoi Ha
Tap Mun
San Mun Tsai
Ma Shi Chau Protected Area
Hoi Ha
Ko Lau Wan
Tai Po
Tai Po Kau
Tolo Harbour
Lai Chi Chong
Tai Po Market
Wu Kai Sha
Nai Chung
Sham Chung
Wong Shek
Chek Keng
Tai Long
Tsung Tsai Yuen
Ma Liu Shui
Heng On
Ma On Shan
Lead Mine Pass
University
Sai Kung West Country Park
Pak Tam Au
Ham Tin
Tai Po Kau Nature Reserve
Racecourse
Tai Shui Hang
Ngong Ping Plateau
Pak Tam Chung
Sai Kung East Country Park
Tai Long Wan
Fo Tan
City One
Ma On Shan Country Park
Sai Kung
Yim Tin Tsai
Tai Tau Chau
Sai Wan
Sha Tin
Tai Wai
Shek Mun
Che Kung Temple
Buffalo Hill
Lion Rock Country Park
Trio Beach
Kiu Tsui Chau
Kau Sai Chau
Leung Sheun Wan
Kam Shan Country Park
Marina Cove
Nam Cheong
Kowloon Tong
Kowloon Peak
Port Shelter
Tiu Chung Chau
See Chau
Wong Nai Chau
KCR West Rail Terminal
Chi Lin Nunnery
Shelter Island
Kong Tau Pai
YAU MA TEI
Po Lam
Lang Ha Wan
Bluff Island
Basalt Island
Yau Ma Tei
Hang Hau
Hung Hom
High Junk Peak
Tseung Kwan O
See Hong Kong City Overview Map (p274)
Yau Tong
Tai Au Mun
Victoria Peak
Lei Yue Mun
Clearwater Bay
Pok Fu Lam
Hong Kong Island
Tin Ha Shan
Aberdeen
Ocean Park
Joss House Bay
Ap Lei Chau
Tung Lung Chau
SOUTH CHINA SEA
Repulse Bay
Stanley Main Beach
Shek O
Shek O Beach
Mo Tat Wan
Stanley
St Stephens Beach
Tung O Wan
East Lamma Channel
Stanley Peninsula
Lo Chau
Sung Kong
Sham Wan
Po Toi

Hong Kong City Overview

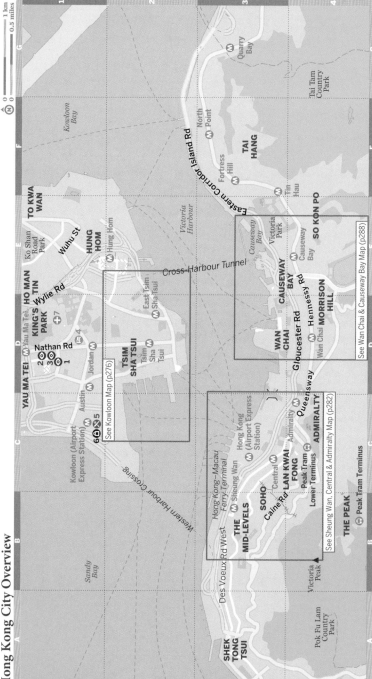

architect Sir Norman Foster in 1985. The building is a masterpiece of precision, sophistication and innovation. And so it should be. On completion in 1985 it was the world's most expensive building (it cost upward of US$1 billion).

Man Mo Temple — Taoist Temple

(文武廟; Map p282; ☎ 2540 0350; 124-126 Hollywood Rd, Sheung Wan; ⊙ 8am-6pm; 🚌 26) **FREE** One of Hong Kong's oldest temples and a declared monument, atmospheric Man Mo Temple is dedicated to the gods of literature ('Man'), holding a writing brush, and of war ('Mo'), wielding a sword. Built in 1847 during the Qing dynasty by wealthy Chinese merchants, it was, besides a place of worship, a court of arbitration for local disputes when trust was thin between the Chinese and the colonialists. Oaths taken at this Taoist temple (often accompanied by the ritual beheading of a rooster) were accepted by the colonial government.

Bank of China Tower — Building

(中銀大廈, BOC Tower; Map p282; 1 Garden Rd, Central; Ⓜ Central, exit K) The awesome 70-storey Bank of China Tower designed by IM Pei rises from the ground like a cube, and is then successively reduced, quarter by quarter, until the south-facing side is left to rise on its own. The public viewing gallery (open 8am to 6pm weekdays) on the 43rd floor offers panoramic views of Hong Kong. Some geomancers believe the four prisms are negative symbols; being the opposite of circles, these triangles

contradict what circles suggest – money, union and perfection.

Hong Kong Park — Park

(香港公園; Map p282; ☎ 2521 5041; www.lcsd. gov.hk/parks/hkp/en/index.php; 19 Cotton Tree Dr, Admiralty; ⊙ park 6am-11pm; 👬; Ⓜ Admiralty, exit C1) **FREE** Designed to look anything but natural, Hong Kong Park is one of the most unusual parks in the world, emphasising artificial creations such as its fountain plaza, conservatory, waterfall, indoor games hall, playground, taichi garden, viewing tower, museum and arts centre. For all its artifice, the eight-hectare park is beautiful in its own weird way and, with a wall of skyscrapers on one side and mountains on the other, makes for some dramatic photographs.

Happy Valley Racecourse — Horse Racing

(跑馬地馬場; Map p288; www.hkjc.com/home/ english/index.asp; 2 Sports Rd, Happy Valley; admission HK$10; ⊙ 7pm-10.30pm Wed Sep-Jun; 🚇 Happy Valley) An outing at the races is one of the quintessential Hong Kong things to do, especially if you happen to be around during one of the weekly Wednesday evening races here. The punters pack into the stands and trackside, cheering, drinking and eating, and the atmosphere is electric.

Hong Kong Zoological & Botanical Gardens — Park

(香港動植物公園; Map p282; www.lcsd.gov.hk/ parks; Albany Rd, Central; ⊙ terrace gardens 5am-10pm, greenhouse 9am-4.30pm; 👬; 🚌 3B, 12) **FREE** Built in the Victorian era, this garden has a welcoming collection of fountains, sculptures and greenhouses, plus a zoo and some fabulous aviaries. Along with exotic vegetation, some 160 species of bird reside here. The zoo is surprisingly comprehensive, and is also one of the world's leading centres for the captive breeding of endangered species. Albany Rd divides the gardens, with the plants and aviaries to the east, close to Garden Rd, and most of the animals to the west.

Statue Square — Square

(皇后像廣場; Map p282; Edinburgh Pl, Central; Ⓜ Central, exit K) This leisurely square used

Kowloon

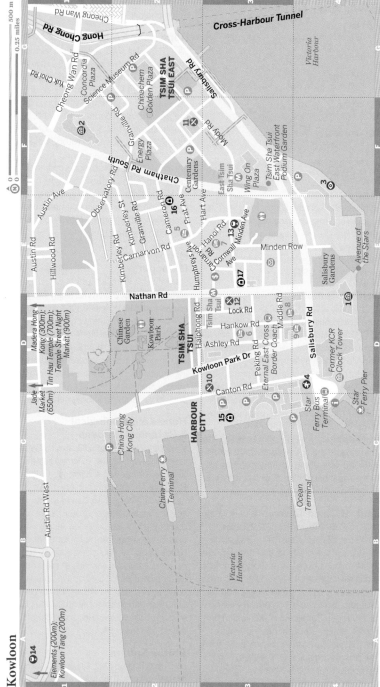

Cross-Harbour Tunnel

Victoria Harbour

TSIM SHA TSUI EAST

Concordia Plaza

Science Museum Rd

Chinachem Golden Plaza

Energy Plaza

Cheong Wan Rd

Yuk Choi Rd

Hong Chong Rd

Cheong Wan Rd

Salisbury Rd

Mody Rd

Granville Rd

Chatham Rd South

Centenary Gardens

East Tsim Sha Tsui

Wing On Plaza

Tsim Sha Tsui East Waterfront Podium Garden

Observatory Rd

Austin Ave

Austin Rd

Hillwood Rd

Kimberley Rd

Kimberley St

Granville Rd

Cameron Rd

Prat Ave

Hart Ave

Hanoi Rd

Minden Ave

Minden Row

Carnarvon Rd

Humphreys Ave

Cornwall Ave

Minden Row

Avenue of the Stars

Salisbury Gardens

Nathan Rd

Haiphong Rd

Tsim Sha Tsui

Lock Rd

Hankow Rd

Ashley Rd

Peking Rd

Middle Rd

Salisbury Rd

TSIM SHA TSUI

Kowloon Park Dr

Chinese Garden

Kowloon Park

Canton Rd

Eternal East Cross Border Coach

Former KCR Clock Tower

Star Ferry Pier

HARBOUR CITY

China Hong Kong City

China Ferry Terminal

Star Ferry Bus Terminal

Ocean Terminal

Victoria Harbour

Austin Rd West

Elements (200m); Kowloon Tong (200m)

Jade Market (650m); Tin Hau Temple (700m); Temple Street Night Market (900m)

Madera Hong Kong (300m)

500 m
0.25 miles

Kowloon

to house effigies of British royalty. Now it pays tribute to a single sovereign – the founder of HSBC. In the northern area (reached via an underpass) is the **Cenotaph** (和平紀念碑; Map p282; Chater Rd), built in 1923 as a memorial to Hong Kong residents killed during the two world wars. On the south side of Chater Rd, Statue Sq has a pleasant collection of fountains and seating areas, with tiling that's strangely reminiscent of a 1980s municipal washroom.

Victoria Park   Park
(維多利亞公園; Map p288; www.lcsd.gov.hk/en/ls_park.php; Causeway Rd, Causeway Bay; ⊙6am or 7am-11pm; Ⓜ Tin Hau, exit B) FREE Victoria Park is the biggest patch of public greenery on Hong Kong Island. The best time to go is on a weekday morning, when it becomes a forest of people practising the slow-motion choreography of taichi. The park becomes a flower market a few days before the Chinese New Year. It's also worth a visit during the **Mid-Autumn Festival**, when people turn out en masse carrying lanterns.

Stanley   Village
This crowd pleaser is best visited on weekdays. **Stanley Market** (赤柱市集; Stanley Village Rd; ⊙9am-6pm; Ⓠ6, 6A, 6X or 260) is a maze of alleyways that has bargain clothing (haggling a must!). **Stanley Main Beach** is for beach-bumming and windsurfing. With graves dating back to 1841, **Stanley Military Cemetery** (赤柱軍人墳場; ☎2557 3498; Wong Ma Kok Rd; ⊙8am-5pm; Ⓠ14, 6A), 500m south of the market, is worth a visit.

Aberdeen   Village
Aberdeen's main attraction is the typhoon shelter it shares with sleepy **Ap Lei Chau** (Ⓔ Ap Lei Chau), where the sampans of Hong Kong's boat-dwelling fisherfolk used to moor. On weekday evenings, you may spot dragon boat teams practising here. The best way to see the area is by sampan. A half-hour tour of the typhoon shelter costs about HK$55 per person. Embark from **Aberdeen Promenade**.

Repulse Bay   Beach
(淺水灣; Ⓠ6, 6A, 6X, 260) The long beach with tawny sand at Repulse Bay is visited by Chinese tourist groups year-round and, needless to say, packed on weekends in summer. It's a good place if you like people-watching. The beach has showers and changing rooms and shade trees at the roadside, but the water is pretty murky.

Shek O Beach   Beach
(Ⓠ9 from Shau Kei Wan MTR station, exit A3) Shek O beach has a large expanse of sand, shady trees to the rear, showers, changing facilities and lockers for rent.

KOWLOON

Tsim Sha Tsui (TST), known for its dining and shopping options, is Hong Kong's most eclectic district, with the glamorous only a stone's throw from the pedestrian, and a population comprising Chinese, South Asians, Africans, Filipinos and Europeans.

Tsim Sha Tsui East
Promenade   Harbour
(尖沙嘴東部海濱花園; Map p276; Salisbury Rd, Tsim Sha Tsui; Ⓜ Tsim Sha Tsui, exit E) One

of the finest city skylines in the world has to be that of Hong Kong Island, and the promenade here is one of the best ways to get an uninterrupted view. It's a lovely place to stroll around during the day, but it really comes into its own in the evening, during the nightly **Symphony of Lights** (🕑8-8.20pm), a spectacular sound-and-light show involving 44 buildings on the Hong Kong Island skyline. The new **Deck 'n Beer** bar located here is a great spot to have an alfresco, waterside drink (weather permitting).

Hong Kong Museum
of History   Museum

(香港歷史博物館; Map p276; 📞2724 9042; http://hk.history.museum; 100 Chatham Rd South, Tsim Sha Tsui; adult/concession HK$10/5, Wed free; 🕑10am-6pm Mon & Wed-Sat, to 7pm Sun; 🚻; Ⓜ Tsim Sha Tsui, exit B2) For a whistle-stop overview of the territory's archaeology, ethnography, and natural and local history, this museum is well worth a visit, not only to learn more about the subject but also to understand how Hong Kong presents its stories to the world. 'The Hong Kong Story' takes visitors on a fascinating walk through the territory's past via eight galleries, starting with the natural environment and prehistoric Hong Kong – about 6000 years ago, give or take a lunar year – and ending with the territory's return to China in 1997.

Hong Kong Museum
of Art   Museum

(香港藝術館; Map p276; 📞2721 0116; http://hk.art.museum; 10 Salisbury Rd, Tsim Sha Tsui; adult/concession HK$10/5, Wed free; 🕑10am-6pm Mon-Fri, to 7pm Sat & Sun; 🚢Star Ferry, Ⓜ East Tsim Sha Tsui, exit J) This excellent museum has seven galleries spread over six floors, exhibiting Chinese antiquities, fine art, historical pictures and contemporary Hong Kong art. Highlights include the Xubaizhi collection of paintings and calligraphy, contemporary works, ceramics and other antiques from China. Audio guides are available for HK$10. Refer to the tour schedule in the lobby for free English-language tours.

Temple Street
Night Market   Market

(廟街夜市; Map p274; Yau Ma Tei; 🕑6-11pm; Ⓜ Yau Ma Tei, exit C) The liveliest night market in Hong Kong, Temple St extends from Man Ming Lane in the north to Nanking St in the south and is cut in two by the

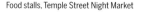

Food stalls, Temple Street Night Market

JENNY JONES/GETTY IMAGES ©

ANTHONY COLLINS/GETTY IMAGES ©

⭐ Don't Miss
Peak Tram

The Peak Tram is not really a tram but a cable-hauled funicular railway that has been scaling the 396m ascent to the highest point on Hong Kong Island since 1888. It is thus the oldest form of public transport in the territory.

The Peak Tram runs every 10 to 15 minutes from 7am to midnight. Octopus cards (see p295) can be used.

NEED TO KNOW

Map p282; ☎2522 0922; www.thepeak.com.hk; Lower Terminus 33 Garden Rd, Central; one-way/return adult HK$28/40, seniors over 65 & child 3-11yr HK$11/18; ☺7am-midnight

---

Tin Hau Temple complex. While you may find better bargains further north in New Kowloon, and certainly over the border in Shēnzhèn, it is still a good place to go for the bustling atmosphere and the smells and tastes on offer from the *dai pai dong* (open-air street stall) food.

Jade Market   Market
(玉器市場; Map p274; Battery St & Kansu St, Yau Ma Tei; ☺10am-6pm; ⓜYau Ma Tei, exit C)
The covered Jade Market, split into two parts by Battery St, has hundreds of stalls selling all varieties and grades of jade. But unless you really know your nephrite from

your jadeite, it's not wise to buy expensive pieces here.

Yuen Po Street Bird Garden
& Flower Market   Park, Market
(園圃街雀鳥花園, 花墟; Yuen Po St & Boundary St, Mong Kok; ☺7am-8pm; ⓜPrince Edward, exit B1) In this enchanting corner of Mong Kok, you will find a handful of old men out 'walking' their caged songbirds. Stick around long enough and you should see birds being fed squirming caterpillars with chopsticks. There are also feathered creatures for sale, along with elaborate cages carved from teak. Adjacent to the garden

is the **flower market** (Flower Market Rd), which theoretically keeps the same hours, but only gets busy after 10am.

NEW TERRITORIES

Occupying 747 sq km of Hong Kong's land mass, the New Territories is a combination of housing estates and some unspoiled rural areas.

Ping Shan
Heritage Trail   Outdoors

(屏山文物徑; ☑2617 1959; ☺ancestral halls 9am-1pm & 2-5pm, Tsui Sing Lau 9am-1pm & 2-5pm, closed Tue; Ⓜ West Rail Tin Shui Wai, exit E) Hong Kong's first ever heritage trail features historic buildings belonging to the Tangs, the first and the most powerful of the 'Five Clans'. Highlights of the 1km trail include Hong Kong's oldest pagoda (Tsui Sing Lau) a magnificent ancestral hall, a temple, a study hall, a well and a gallery inside an old police station that was built by the British as much to monitor the coastline as to keep an eye on the clan.

Kat Hing Wai   Village

(吉慶圍; 🚌64K) This tiny village is 500 years old and was walled during the early years of the Ming dynasty (1368–1644). It contains just one main street, off which a host of dark and narrow alleyways lead. There are quite a few new buildings and retiled older ones in the village. A small temple stands at the end of the street. Visitors are asked to make a donation when they enter the village; put the money in the coin slot by the entrance.

OUTLYING ISLANDS

Lantau is the largest island in Hong Kong and is ideal for a multiday excursion to explore its trails and villages, and to enjoy the beaches. Mui Wo is the arrival point for ferries from Central, and Tung Chung is connected by MTR.

Po Lin Monastery
& Big Buddha   Buddhist Monastery

(寶蓮禪寺; ☑2985 5248; Lantau; ☺9am-6pm) Po Lin is a huge Buddhist monastery and temple complex that was built in 1924.

Today, it seems more of a tourist honeypot than a religious retreat, attracting hundreds of thousands of visitors a year, and is still being expanded. Most of the buildings you'll see on arrival are new, with the older, simpler ones tucked away behind them.

Tai O   Village
(🚌 1 from Mui Wo, 11 from Tung Chung, 21 from Ngong Ping) On weekends, droves of visitors trek to the far-flung west coast of Lantau to see a fascinating way of life. Here in Tai O, historical home to the Tanka boat people, life is all about the sea. Houses are built on stilts above the ocean, sampans ply the dark-green waterways, and elderly residents still dry seafood on traditional straw mats and make the village's celebrated shrimp paste.

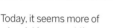 **Activities**

The Hong Kong Tourism Board (HKTB) offers a range of fun and free activities, from feng shui classes to sunset cruises to taichi sessions. For a list of what's on, visit www.discoverhongkong.com.

HIKING

Hong Kong is an excellent place to hike, and the numerous trails on offer are all very attractive. The four main ones are **MacLehose Trail**, **Wilson Trail**, **Lantau Trail** and **Hong Kong Trail**. The famous **Dragon's Back Trail** is scenic and relatively easy. For more information check out www.hkwalkers.net.

👉 **Tours**

Star Ferry (Map 282; ☎ 2118 6201; www.star ferry.com.hk/tour) runs a one-hour Harbour Tour covering calling points at Tsim Sha Tsui, Central and Wan Chai. You can get your tickets at the piers.

There are a number of tours run by the **HKTB** (QTS; ☎ 2806 2823; www.qtshk.com), including:

281

HKTB Island Tour   Bus Tour
(half-/full day HK$350/490) Includes Man Mo
Temple, the Peak, Aberdeen, Repulse Bay
and Stanley Market.

Hong Kong Dolphinwatch   Cruise
(香港海豚觀察; Map p276; ☎2984 1414; www.
hkdolphinwatch.com; 15th fl, Middle Block, 1528A
Star House, 3 Salisbury Rd, Tsim Sha Tsui; adult/
child HK$420/210; ☉cruises Wed, Fri & Sun)

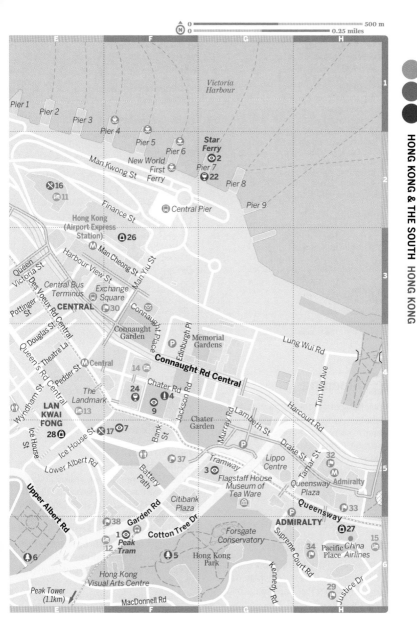

Hong Kong Dolphinwatch was founded in 1995 to raise awareness of Hong Kong's wonderful pink dolphins and promote responsible ecotourism. It offers 2½-hour cruises to see them in their natural habitat every Wednesday, Friday and Sunday year-round. About 97% of the cruises result in the sighting of at least one dolphin; if none are spotted, passengers are offered a free trip.

Sheung Wan, Central & Admiralty

🛏 Sleeping

Hong Kong offers the full gamut of accommodation, from cell-like spaces to palatial suites in some of the world's finest hotels. The rates listed here are the rack rates.

Most hotels are on Hong Kong Island between Central and Causeway Bay, and either side of Nathan Rd in Kowloon, where you'll also find the largest range of budget places. All hotels and some budget places add 13% in taxes to the listed rates.

HONG KONG ISLAND

Most of Hong Kong Island's top-end hotels are in Central and Admiralty, while Wan Chai and Sheung Wan cater to the mid-range market.

Helena May   Hotel $
(梅夫人婦女會主樓; Map p282; ☏2522 6766; www.helenamay.com; 35 Garden Rd, Central; s/d HK$510/670, studios per month HK$15, 520-20,230; 🚌23) If you like the peninsula's colonial setting but not its price tag, this grand dame could be your cup of

tea. Founded in 1916 as a social club for single European women in the territory, the Helena May is now a private club for women of all nationalities and a hotel with 43 creaky but charming rooms.

Y-Loft Youth
Square Hostel   Hostel $$
(☏3721 8989; www.youthsquare.hk; 238 Chai Wan Rd, Chai Wan; tw/tr low season HK$700/900, high season HK$1200/1800, ste HK$3000; @🛜; Ⓜ Chai Wan, exit A) If you don't mind trading 20 extra minutes on the MTR for an excellent budget option, you'll be rewarded with large, clean and cheerful rooms atop a community youth centre in Chai Wan (not Wan Chai!). Popular with students from mainland China on semesters abroad, the vibe here is more upscale dormitory than backpacker hostel.

Upper House   Boutique Hotel $$$
(Map p282; ☏2918 1838; www.upperhouse.com; 88 Queensway, Pacific Pl, Admiralty; r/ste from HK$4500/12,000; @🛜; Ⓜ Admiralty, exit F) Every corner of this boutique hotel spells

zen-like serenity – the understated lobby, the sleek eco-minded rooms, the elegant sculptures, the warm and discreet service and the manicured lawn where guests can join free yoga classes. Other pluses include a free and 'bottomless' minibar, and easy access to the Admiralty MTR station.

Mandarin Oriental
Luxury Hotel $$$

(文華東方酒店; Map p282; ☑2522 0111; www.mandarinoriental.com/hongkong/; 5 Connaught Rd, Central; r HK$5300-7400, ste HK$8000-65,000; @ 🛜 🛋; M Central, exit J3) The venerable Mandarin has historically set the standard in Asia and continues to be a contender for the top spot, despite competition from the likes of the Four Seasons. The styling, service, food and atmosphere are stellar throughout and there's a sense of gracious, old-world charm. The sleek **Landmark Oriental** (Map p282; ☑2132 0088; www.mandarinoriental.com/landmark; 15 Queen's Rd, Central; r HK$3500-6800, ste HK$9300-45,000; @ 🛜 🛋), just across the way, offers modern luxury, but with a business vibe.

Four Seasons
Luxury Hotel $$$

(四季酒店; Map p282; ☑3196 8888; www.fourseasons.com/hongkong; 8 Finance St, Central; r HK$4800-8100, ste HK$9800-65,000; @ 🛜 🛋; M Hong Kong, exit F) The Four Seasons arguably edges into top place on the island for its amazing views, pristine service, and its location close to the Star Ferry Pier, Hong Kong station, and Sheung Wan. Also on offer are palatial rooms, a glorious pool and spa complex, and award-winning restaurants **Caprice** (Map p282; ☑3196 8888; www.fourseasons.com/hongkong; set lunch/dinner from HK$540/1740; ⏱noon-2.30pm & 6-10.30pm; 🛜) and Lung King Heen (p289).

KOWLOON

Kowloon has an incredible array of accommodation: from the Peninsula, the 'grand dame' of hotels, to its infamous neighbour, Chungking Mansions, plus plenty in between.

Hop Inn on Hankow
Hostel $

(Map p276; ☑2881 7331; www.hopinn.hk; 19-21 Hankow Rd, flat A, 2nd fl, Hanyee Bldg, Tsim Sha Tsui; s HK$410-530, d & tw HK$520-790, tr HK$650-980, q HK$1020-1200; @ 🛜; M Tsim Sha Tsui, exit C1) This nonsmoking hostel has a youthful vibe and nine spotless and dainty rooms, each sporting illustrations by a different Hong Kong artist. The rooms without windows are quieter than the ones that have them. The other branch **Hop Inn on Carnarvon** (Map p276; ☑2881 7331; www.hopinn.hk; 33-35 Carnarvon Rd, 9th fl, James S Lee Mansion, Tsim Sha Tsui; s HK$410-530, d & tw HK$520-790, tr HK$650-980, q HK$1020-1200; 🛜; M Tsim Sha Tsui, exit A2) has newer rooms in an older building. Both branches offer free in-room wi-fi and will help to organise China visas.

Salisbury
Hotel $$

(香港基督教青年會; Map p276; ☑2268 7888; www.ymcahk.org.hk; 41 Salisbury Rd, Tsim Sha Tsui; dm HK$300, s/d/ste from HK$1000/1200/2200; @ 🛜 🛋; M Tsim Sha Tsui, exit E) If you can manage to book a room at this fabulously located place, you'll be rewarded with professional service and excellent exercise facilities. Rooms and suites are comfortable but simple, so keep your eyes on the harbour: that view would cost you five times as much at the Peninsula next door. The dormitory rooms are a bonus but restrictions apply.

Madera Hong Kong
Boutique Hotel $$

(木的地酒店; Map p274; ☑2121 9888; www.hotelmadera.com.hk; 1-9 Cheong Lok St, Yau Ma Tei; r HK$1200-4000, ste HK$4200-$9000; M Jordan, exit B1) A spirited addition to

Accommodation Price Indicators

The price ranges for accommodation in Hong Kong are as follows:

- **$** less than HK$900
- **$$** HK$900 to HK$1500
- **$$$** more than HK$1500

TRAVELASIA/GETTY IMAGES ©

⭐ Don't Miss
Star Ferry

You can't say you've 'done' Hong Kong until you've taken a ride on a Star Ferry, that wonderful fleet of electric-diesel vessels with names suc *Morning Star*, *Celestial Star* and *Twinkling Star*. Try to take your first trip on a clear night from Kowloon to Central. It's not half as dramatic in the opposite direction.

NEED TO KNOW

天星小輪; Map p282; ☎2367 7065; www.starferry.com.hk; adult HK$2.50-3.40, child HK$1.50-2.10; ⏱every 6-12min, 6.30am-11.30pm

Kowloon's midrange options, Madera is close to the Temple Street Night Market (p278) and the Jordan MTR station. The decent-sized rooms come in neutral tones accented with the bold, vibrant colours of Spanish aesthetics. Madera (meaning 'wood') also has a ladies' floor, a hypo-allergenic floor, and a tiny but adequate gym room.

Peninsula
Hong Kong   Luxury Hotel $$$

(香港半島酒店; Map p276; ☎2920 2888; www.peninsula.com; Salisbury Rd, Tsim Sha Tsui; r/ste from HK$4080/7880; @ 🛜 🛖; M Tsim Sha Tsui, exit E) Lording it over the southern tip of

Kowloon, Hong Kong's finest hotel exudes colonial elegance. Your dilemma will be how to get here: landing on the rooftop helipad or arriving in one of the hotel's 14-strong fleet of Rolls Royce Phantoms. Some 300 classic European-style rooms sport wi-fi, CD and DVD players, as well as marble bathrooms.

Hyatt Regency
Tsim Sha Tsui   Luxury Hotel $$$

(尖沙咀凱悅酒店; Map p276; ☎2311 1234; http://hongkong.tsimshatsui.hyatt.com; 18 Hanoi Rd, Tsim Sha Tsui; s/d/ste from HK$1200/4200/3600; @ 🛜 🛖; M Tsim Sha Tsui, exit D2) Top marks to this classic that oozes understated elegance and composure. Rooms are plush and relatively spacious with those on the upper floors commanding views over the city. Black-and-white photos of Tsim Sha Tsui add a thoughtful touch to the decor. The lobby gets crowded at times, but the helpful and resourceful staff will put you back at ease.

Eating

One of the world's greatest food cities, Hong Kong offers culinary excitement whether you're spending HK$20 on a bowl of noodles or megabucks on haute cuisine. At most of the eateries listed here, reservations are strongly advised, especially for dinner.

HONG KONG ISLAND

The island's best range of cuisines is in Central, Sheung Wan and Wan Chai.

Delicious Kitchen

Shanghainese **$**

(Map p288; ☑️2577 7720; 9-11B Cleveland St, Causeway Bay; meals HK$40-100; 🕙11am-11pm; Ⓜ️Causeway Bay, exit E) ☑️ The Shanghainese rice cooked with shredded Chinese cabbage is so good at this *cha chaan tang* (tea house) that fashionistas are tripping over themselves to land a table here. It's best with the legendary honey-glazed pork chop. Fat, veggie-stuffed wontons and perfectly crispy fried tofu are also winners.

22 Ships
Tapas **$$**

(Map p288; ☑️2555 0722; www.22ships. hk; 22 Ship St, Wan Chai; tapas HK$68-178; 🕙noon-3pm & 6-11pm; Ⓜ️Wan Chai, exit B2) The star of the recent crop of new tapas restaurants to open in Hong Kong, this tiny, trendy spot is packed from open to close. But the long wait (the restaurant doesn't take reservations) is worth it for exquisite, playful small plates by much-buzzed-about young British chef Jason Atherton.

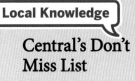

Local Knowledge

Central's Don't Miss List

BY JONATHAN SILVER, LAWYER

1 STAR FERRY & LAN KWAI FONG
When I take guests around, we first hop aboard the Star Ferry (p286) for a trip across the harbour from Tsim Sha Tsui to Central. Central's lights are spectacular at night. If you've time to spare, stop for a quick beer at **Pier 7** (Map p282; ☑️2167 8377; www.cafedecogroup.com; Shop M, Roof Viewing Deck, Central Pier 7, Star Ferry Pier, Central; 🕙9am-midnight, happy hour 6-9pm; 🛜; Ⓜ️Hong Kong, exit A1) before hitting the bars and clubs of Lan Kwai Fong.

2 PEAK TRAM
Rub shoulders with tourists and wealthy residents on the Peak Tram (p279). The train leans 27 degrees at times during its ascent up Victoria Peak, so ensure you claim a seat before take-off. Stop at Peak Tower for a coffee (or ice cream) or a stroll around the shops, and admire perhaps Hong Kong's best views (clouds permitting).

3 TRAM TO SHEUNG WAN
Journey back in time on a Hong Kong tram (p297) from Central to Sheung Wan or Happy Valley. Squeeze up the front of the top deck for the best vantage point, but prepare early for disembarking – after 16 years, I am still amazed by the number of people who cram into one small tram and I still can't fight past the old ladies to get off.

4 SEVVA
Look for the lift serving only the 25th floor in the lobby of Princes Building. Sevva (p290) is something of a secret oasis: the tree-lined outdoor area has stunning 360-degree views over Central and the old Mandarin Oriental hotel. Its honeycomb cream cake is hard to beat – order it to go, too.

5 PMQ
The Former Hollywood Road Police Married Quarters (www.pmq.org.hk) on the corner of Hollywood Road and Aberdeen Street has an über-cool vibe all of its own. This former school (which Dr Sun Yatsen attended) and junior police officers' married quarters was given a new lease of life in 2014. The site now houses studios, workshops, a performance venue, shops, bars and restaurants galore. Stop here for an alternative arts performance followed by a home brewed beer and a meal.

Wan Chai & Causeway Bay

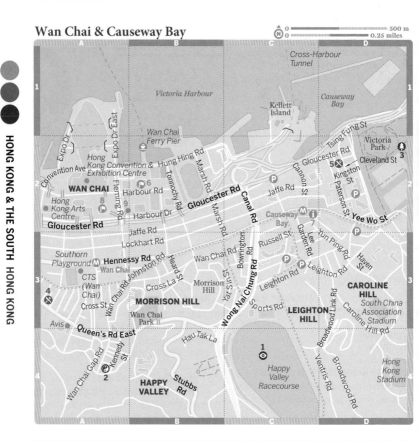

Wan Chai & Causeway Bay

Luk Yu Tea
House Cantonese, Dim Sum **$$**
(陸羽茶室; Map p282; ☎2523 5464; 24-26
Stanley St, Lan Kwai Fong; meals HK$300; ⊙7am-
10pm, dim sum to 5.30pm; 🚻; Ⓜ Central, exit D2)
This gorgeous teahouse (c 1933), known
for its masterful cooking and Eastern art
deco decor, was the haunt of opera artists,
writers and painters (including the creator
of one exorbitant ink-and-brush gracing a

wall), who came to give recitals and discuss
the national fate. Today, some of the wait-
ers who served the tousled glamourati
will pour your tea in the same pleasantly
irreverent manner.

Life
Cafe Vegetarian, International **$**
(Map p282; ☎2810 9777; www.lifecafe.com.hk; 10
Shelley St, Soho; meals HK$100; ⊙noon-10pm;

⏴📶🚬; M Central, exit D1) Right next to the Central–Mid-Levels Escalator, Life is a vegetarian's dream, serving organic vegan salads, guilt-free desserts, and tasty dishes free of gluten, wheat, onion, garlic – you name it – over three floors stylishly decked out in reclaimed teak and recycled copper-domed lamps. The ground-floor counter has goodies to take away.

Lung King Heen
Cantonese, Dim Sum $$$

(龍景軒; Map p282; 🖀3196 8888; www.four seasons.com/hongkong; 8 Finance St, Four Seasons Hotel, Central; set lunch/dinner HK$500/1560; ⏱noon-2.30pm & 6-10.30pm; 📶; M Hong Kong, exit E1) The world's first Chinese restaurant to receive three stars from the Michelin people, still retains them. The Cantonese food, though by no means peerless in Hong Kong, is excellent in both taste and presentation, and when combined with the harbour views and the impeccable service, provides a truly stellar dining experience. The signature steamed lobster and scallop dumplings sell out early.

KOWLOON

There's plenty of choice in both cuisine and budget, especially in Tsim Sha Tsui. More local places can be found further north.

Ziafat
Middle Eastern, Indian $

(Map p276; 🖀2312 1015; 81 Nathan Rd, 6th fl, Harilela Mansion, Tsim Sha Tsui; meals HK$80-200; ⏱noon-midnight; 🚬; M Tsim Sha Tsui, exit R) This halal restaurant serves up decent Arabic and Indian fare like falafel, lentil soup, kebabs and curries. It's in a weary, post-WWII building alongside budget guesthouses, but the restaurant is clean, quiet and humbly furnished with Arabic art. You can also smoke shisha here.

Dong Lai Shun
Chinese $$

(東來順; Map p276; 🖀2733 2020; www.rghk.com. hk; 69 Mody Rd, B2, the Royal Garden, Tsim Sha Tsui; meals HK$250-1500; ⏱11.30am-2.30pm & 6pm-10.30pm; 📶📶; M East Tsim Sha Tsui, exit P2) Besides superbly executed northern Chinese dishes, the phonebook of a menu here also features Shanghainese, Sichuanese, and Cantonese favourites. But Dong Lai

Shun is best known for its mutton hotpot which involves dunking paper-thin slices of mutton into boiling water and eating it with sesame sauce. The atmosphere is a little formal but the service is warm.

Kowloon Tang
Chinese, Dim Sum $$

(九龍廳; Map p274; 🖀2811 9398; www.kowloon tang.com; 1 Austin Rd W, Shop R002-003, Civic Square, 3rd fl, Roof Deck, Elements mall; meals HK$300-2000; ⏱noon-10.30pm; 📶; M Kowloon, exit U3) Sophisticated Kowloon Tang serves impeccable Cantonese dishes, including a few Dong Guan classics, a laudable Peking duck, and an impressive selection of Western-style desserts in an art deco–inspired setting, reminiscent of its cousin across the harbour, **Island Tang** (港島廳; Map p282; 🖀2526 8798; www.islandtang.com; 9 Queen's Rd Central, Shop 222, Galleria, Central; set lunch from HK$308, dinner from HK$400; ⏱noon-2.30pm & 6-10.30pm; 📶; M Central, exit D1).

Din Tai Fung
Taiwanese, Noodles $$

(鼎泰豐; Map p276; 🖀2730 6928; www. dintaifung.com.hk; 30 Canton Rd, Shop 130, 3rd fl, Silvercord, Tsim Sha Tsui; meals HK$120-300; ⏱11.30am-10.30pm; 📶; M Tsim Sha Tsui, exit C1) Whether it's comfort food or a carb fix you're craving, the juicy Shanghai dumplings and hearty northern-style noodles at this Taiwanese chain will do the trick. Queues are the norm and it doesn't take reservations, but service is excellent. DTF has one Michelin star.

Eating Price Indicators

The price ranges for eating in Hong Kong are as follows:

- **$** less than HK$200
- **$$** HK$200 to HK$400
- **$$$** more than HK$400

🍷 Drinking

Lan Kwai Fong (LKF) in Central is synonymous with nightlife in Hong Kong, attracting everyone from expat and Chinese suits to travellers. Soho, along the Central–Mid-levels Escalator, is another popular drinking and dining area.

HONG KONG ISLAND

Globe   Pub
(Map p282; 📞2543 1941; www.theglobe.com.hk; 45-53 Graham St, Soho; ⊙10am-2am, happy hour to 8pm; MCentral, exit D1) Besides an impressive list of 150 imported beers, including 13 on tap, the Globe serves T8, the first cask-conditioned ale brewed in Hong Kong. Occupying an enviable 370 sq metres, the bar has a huge dining area with long wooden tables and comfortable banquettes.

Club 71   Bar
(Map p282; 67 Hollywood Rd, basement, Soho; ⊙3pm-2am Mon-Sat, 6pm-1am Sun, happy hour 3-9pm; 🚌26, MCentral, exit D1) This friendly

bar with a bohemian vibe is named after a protest march on 1 July 2003. It's a favourite haunt of local artists and activists who come for the beer and music jamming sessions. In the garden out front, revolutionaries plotted to overthrow the Qing dynasty a hundred years ago. Enter from the alley next to 69 Hollywood.

Sevva   Cocktail Bar
(Map p282; 📞2537 1388; www.sevva.hk; 10 Chater Rd, 25th fl, Prince's Bldg, Central; ⊙noon-midnight Mon-Thu, to 2am Fri & Sat; 📶; MCentral, exit H) If there was a million-dollar view in Hong Kong, it'd be the one from the balcony of ultra-stylish Sevva – skyscrapers so close you can see their arteries of steel, with the harbour and Kowloon in the distance. At night it takes your breath away. To get there though, you have to overcome expensive drinks and patchy service.

KOWLOON

Butler   Cocktail Bar
(Map p276; 📞2724 3828; 30 Mody Rd, 5th fl, Mody House, Tsim Sha Tsui; cover HK$200, snacks HK$30; ⊙6.30pm-3am Mon-Fri, 6.30pm-2am Sat & Sun; MEast Tsim Sha Tsui, exit N2) A cocktail and whisky heaven hidden in the residential part of TST. You can flip through its whisky magazines as you watch bartender Uchida create magical concoctions with the flair and precision of a master mixologist in Ginza. We loved the cocktails made from fresh citruses. A discreet and welcome addition to the TST drinking scene.

Ozone   Bar
(Map p276; 📞2263 2263; www.ritzcarlton.com; 1 Austin Rd, 118th fl, ICC, Tsim Sha Tsui; ⊙5pm-1am Mon-Wed, to 2am Thu, to 3am Fri, 3pm-3am Sat, noon-midnight Sun; 📶; MKowloon, exit U3) Ozone is the highest

bar in Asia. The imaginative interiors, created to evoke a cyberesque Garden of Eden, have pillars resembling chocolate fountains in a hurricane and a myriad of refracted glass and colour-changing illumination. Equally dizzying is the wine list, with the most expensive bottle selling for over HK$150,000. Offers potential for a once-in-a-lifetime experience, in more ways than one.

⭐ Entertainment

To find out what's on, pick up a copy of **HK Magazine** (http://hk-magazine.com), an entertainment listings magazine. It's free, appears on Friday and can be found in restaurants, bars and hotels. For more comprehensive listings buy the fortnightly **Time Out** (www.timeout.com.hk) from newsstands. Also worth checking out is the freebie **bc magazine** (www.bcmagazine.net).

The main ticket providers, **Urbtix** (☎ 2734 9009; www.urbtix.hk; ⏰ 10am-8pm), **Cityline** (☎ 2317 6666; www.cityline.com.hk) and **Hong Kong Ticketing** (☎ 3128 8288; www.hkticketing.com; ⏰ 10am-8pm), have among them tickets to every major event in Hong Kong. Book online or by phone.

LIVE MUSIC

Peel Fresco   Jazz
(Map p282; ☎ 2540 2046; www.peelfresco.com; 49 Peel St, Soho; ⏰ 5pm-late Mon-Sat; 🚌 13, 26, 40M) Charming Peel Fresco has live jazz six nights a week, with local and overseas acts performing on a small but spectacular stage next to teetering faux-Renaissance paintings. The action starts around 9.30pm, but go at 9pm to secure a seat.

GAY & LESBIAN VENUES

Hong Kong's premier lesbian organisation, **Les Peches** (☎ 9101 8001; lespechesinfo@yahoo.com) has monthly events for lesbians, bisexual women and their friends.

Propaganda   Gay Club
(Map p282; ☎ 2868 1316; 1 Hollywood Rd, lower ground fl, Central; ⏰ 9pm-4am Tue-Thu, to 6am Fri & Sat, happy hour 9pm-1.30am Tue-Thu; Ⓜ Central, exit D2) Hong Kong's default gay dance club

Detour:
Hong Kong Islands

Laid-back Lamma has decent beaches, excellent walks and a cluster of restaurants in **Yung Shue Wan** (榕樹灣; ⛴ Yung Shue Wan) and **Sok Kwu Wan** (索罟灣; ⛴ Sok Kwu Wan). A fun day involves taking the ferry to Yung Shue Wan, walking the easy 90-minute trail to Sok Kwu Wan and settling in for lunch at one of the seafood restaurants beside the water.

Dumbbell-shaped **Cheung Chau** (⛴ Cheung Chau), with a harbour filled with fishing boats, a windsurfing centre, several temples and some waterfront restaurants, also makes a fun day out.

and meat market; cover charge (HK$120 to HK$160) applies on Friday and Saturday. Enter from Ezra's Lane.

🔒 Shopping

It's not the bargain destination it was, but Hong Kong is crammed with retail space, making it a delight for shoppers. If you prefer everything under one roof, some of the sleeker options are: **IFC Mall** (Map p282; ☎ 2295 3308; www.ifc.com.hk; 8 Finance St; Ⓜ Hong Kong, exit F), **Pacific Place** (太古廣場; Map p282; ☎ 2844 8988; www.pacificplace.com.hk; 88 Queensway, Admiralty; Ⓜ Admiralty, exit F), **Elements** (圓方; Map p274; www.elements hk.com; 1 Austin Rd W, West Kowloon; ⏰ 11am-9pm; Ⓜ Kowloon, exit U3) and **Harbour City** (Map p276; www.harbourcity.com.hk; 3-9 Canton Rd; Ⓜ Tsim Sha Tsui, exit C1).

If you're looking for antiques and curios, Central's **Hollywood Road** should be your first stop, while cheaper **Cat Street**, also in Central, specialises in younger (ie retro) items such as Mao paraphernalia.

mah-jong tile sets, designed in a modern chinoiserie style.

For cheap attire, browse at **Jardine's Bazaar** (渣甸街) in Causeway Bay, **Johnston Road** in Wan Chai or the **Ladies Market** (通菜街, 女人街, Tung Choi St; ⏰noon-11.30pm; Ⓜ Mong Kok, exit D3) in Mong Kok, Kowloon.

HONG KONG ISLAND

Central and Causeway Bay are the main shopping districts on Hong Kong Island.

Shanghai Tang   Clothing, Homeware
(上海灘; Map p282; ☎2525 7333; www. shanghaitang.com; 1 Duddell St, Shanghai Tang Mansion, Central; ⏰10.30am-8pm; Ⓜ Central, exit D1) This elegant four-level store is the place to go if you fancy a body-hugging *qípáo* (cheongsam) with a modern twist, a Chinese-style clutch or a lime-green mandarin jacket. Custom tailoring is available; it takes two weeks to a month and requires a fitting. Shanghai Tang also stocks cushions, picture frames, teapots, even

KOWLOON

Premier Jewellery   Jewellery
(愛寶珠寶有限公司; Map p276; ☎2368 0003; 50 Nathan Rd, Shop G14-15, ground fl, Holiday Inn Golden Mile Shopping Mall, Tsim Sha Tsui; ⏰10am-7.30pm Mon-Sat, to 4pm Sun; Ⓜ Tsim Sha Tsui, exit G) This third-generation family firm is directed by a qualified gemmologist and is one of our favourite places to shop. The range isn't huge but if you're looking for something particular, give Premier Jewellery a day's notice and a selection will be ready in time for your arrival. Staff can also help you design your own piece.

Initial   Clothing
(Map p276; www.initialfashion.com; 48 Cameron Rd, Shop 2, Tsim Sha Tsui; ⏰11.30am-11.30pm; Ⓜ Tsim Sha Tsui, exit B2) This attractive shop and cafe carries stylish, multifunctional urbanwear with European and Japanese

HONG KONG & THE SOUTH HONG KONG

influences. The clothes created by local designers are complemented by imported shoes, bags and costume jewellery.

ℹ Information

Emergency

Fire, Police & Ambulance (☎999)

Medical Services

Medical care is of a high standard in Hong Kong, though private hospital care is costly. The emergency telephone number for an ambulance is ☎999.

Hospitals with 24-hour emergency services:

Queen Elizabeth Hospital (伊利沙伯醫院; **Map p274**; ☎2958 8888; 30 Gascoigne Rd, Yau Ma Tei) Public hospital in Kowloon.

Money

ATMs are available throughout Hong Kong, including at the airport. Banks have the best exchange rates, but some levy commissions of HK$50 or more per transaction. Opening hours are 9am to 4.30pm or 5.30pm Monday to Friday and 9am to 12.30pm Saturday.

You can change money in most banks and any authorised moneychanger. The latter usually open well into the evening.

Telephone

All phone numbers have eight digits (except ☎800 toll-free numbers) and no area codes. Local calls are free on private phones and cost HK$1 for five minutes on pay phones.

A phonecard, available at convenience stores, will let you make international direct-dial calls. A SIM card (from HK$50) with prepaid call time will connect you to the local mobile phone network.

Tourist Information

Hong Kong Tourism Board (香港旅遊發展局, HKTB; ☎visitor hotline 2508 1234; www.discoverhongkong.com; ⊙hotline 9am-6pm) runs a website, visitor hotline and Visitor Information and Service Centres:

Hong Kong International Airport HKTB Centres (Chek Lap Kok; ⊙7am-11pm) There are centres in Halls A and B on the arrivals level in Terminal 1 and the E2 transfer area.

Detour: Mai Po Marsh Nature Reserve

This 380-hectare wildlife reserve in **Deep Bay** (米埔自然保護區; ☎2471 3480; www.wwf.org.hk; Mai Po, Sin Tin, Yuen Long; admission HK$120; ⏰9am-5pm; 🚌76K from Sheung Shui East Rail or Yuen Long West Rail stations) is home to a plethora of flora and fauna, including 380 species of migratory and resident birds. Three-hour English tours (HK$70) leave the visitor centre at 9.30am, 10am, 2pm and 2.30pm on weekends and public holidays. Take bus 76K from Fanling or Sheung Shui MTR East Rail stations.

Hong Kong Island HKTB Centre (港島旅客諮詢及服務中心; Map p288; Peak Piazza; ⏰9am-9pm)

Kowloon HKTB Centre (香港旅遊發展局; Star Ferry Concourse, Tsim Sha Tsui; ⏰8am-8pm)

Museum Pass This pass allows multiple entries to all museums mentioned in this chapter and is available from the participating museums – see www.discoverhongkong.com/eng/attractions/museum-major.html.

Travel Agencies

China Travel Service (中國旅行社, CTS; Map p282; ☎2522 0450; www.ctshk.com; 77 Queen's Rd, ground fl, China Travel Bldg; ⏰9am-6pm Mon-Fri, 9am-7.30pm Mon-Sat, 9.30am-5pm Sun)

Websites

Discover Hong Kong (www.discoverhongkong.com) A good general resource if you're seeking inspiration with lots of pictures.

Lonely Planet (www.lonelyplanet.com/hong-kong) Destination information, bookings, traveller forum and more.

Time Out (www.timeout.com.hk) An authoritative fortnightly guide and listings of what's on.

🛈 Getting There & Away

Air

More than 100 airlines operate between Hong Kong International Airport (HKIA; p408) and some 160 destinations around the world.

That said, bargain airfares between Hong Kong and mainland China are few, as the government regulates the prices. If you're prepared to travel to Guǎngzhōu or Shēnzhèn, in Guǎngdōng province, you can find much cheaper flights.

Bus

You can reach virtually any major destination in Guǎngdōng province by bus (HK$100 to HK$220):

CTS Express Coach (Map p282; ☎2764 9803; http://ctsbus.hkcts.com)

Trans-Island Limousine Service (☎3193 9333; www.trans-island.com.hk) Mainland destinations from Hong Kong include Dōngguǎn, Fóshān, Guǎngzhōu, Huìzhōu, Kāipíng, Shēnzhèn's Bǎoān airport and Zhōngshān.

Train

For schedules and prices, see www.mtr.com.hk.

Immigration formalities at Hung Hom station must be completed before boarding, including checking your visa for China; arrive at the station 45 minutes before departure.

Tickets can be booked at CTS, East Rail stations in Hung Hom, Mong Kok, Kowloon Tong and Sha Tin, and MTR Travel at Admiralty station; tickets booked with a credit card by phone (☎2947 7888) must be collected at least one hour before departure.

Trains to Guǎngzhōu, Shànghǎi, Běijīng and Zhàoqìng depart daily from Hung Hom station (HK$190 to HK$1191).

🛈 Getting Around

Hong Kong's public transport system is fast, convenient, relatively inexpensive and easy to use with the Octopus card payment system.

To/From the Airport

Airport Express (☎2881 8888; www.mtr.com.hk; HK$100/90/60 per 24/21/13min from Central/Kowloon/Tsing Yi) Fastest and costliest public route to the airport; most airlines allow Airport Express passengers to check in at Central or Kowloon stations between 5.30am and 12.30am one day to 90 minutes before departure. At Hong Kong International Airport there is a left-luggage office (☎2261 0110; level 3, Terminal 2; per hr/day HK$12/140; ☺5.30am-1.30am) on Level 3 of Terminal 2.

Bus fares to the airport are HK$21 to HK$45. See Transport on the www.hkairport.com website for details.

A taxi to Central is about HK$300 plus luggage charge of HK$5 per item.

Bicycle

In quiet areas of the Outlying Islands or New Territories, a bike can be a lovely way of getting around.

Car & Motorcycle

Driving in Hong Kong isn't for the faint-hearted. But if you are determined to see Hong Kong under your own steam try Avis (Map p288; ☎2890 6988; www.avis.com.hk; 183 Queen's Rd E, Hopewell Centre, Wan Chai; Ⓜ Wan Chai, exit B2) which has Honda Civics with unlimited kilometres.

Public Transport

Passes

No more rummaging in your bag for small change:

Airport Express Travel Pass (HK$220/300) Three consecutive days of unlimited travel on the MTR and one or two trips on the Airport Express.

MTR Tourist Day Pass (HK$55) Unlimited travel on the MTR for 24 hours.

Octopus Card (☎2266 2222; www.octopuscards.com) The Octopus Card is a rechargeable 'smart card' valid on the MTR and most forms of public transport in Hong Kong. It also allows you to make purchases at retail outlets across the territory (such as convenience stores and supermarkets). The card costs HK$150 (HK$70 for children and seniors), which includes a HK$50 refundable deposit and HK$100 worth of travel. Octopus fares are about 5% cheaper than ordinary fares on the MTR. You can buy one and recharge at any MTR station.

Buses

Hong Kong's bus system will get you almost anywhere. Exact change or an Octopus card is required. The HKTB has leaflets on major bus routes.

City Bus (☎2873 0818)

First Bus (☎2136 8888; www.nwstbus.com.hk)

HKIA to China the Fast Way

You can head straight from Hong Kong International Airport (HKIA) to Macau and airports in Shēnzhèn and Guǎngzhōu. The following companies (all with counters at HKIA Terminal 2) have buses going to points in southern China (Fóshān HK$230, Guǎngzhōu HK$250 and Shēnzhèn airport HK$130):

○ **CTS Express Coach** (p294)

○ **Eternal East Cross Border Coach** (Map p276; ☎3760 0888, 3412 6677; 4-6 Hankow Rd, 13th fl, Kai Seng Commercial Centre; ☺7am-8pm)

○ **Trans-Island Limousine Service** (p294)

○ **Skypier** (☎2215 3232) Links HKIA with Macau and six Pearl River Delta destinations by a fast ferry service. Travellers can board ferries without clearing Hong Kong customs and immigration.

○ **Chu Kong Passenger Transportation Co** (☎2858 3876; www.cksp.com.hk) Has ferries from HKIA to Shēnzhèn airport (HK$220, 40 minutes, eight daily, 10.15am to 6.30pm) and to Macau, Shékǒu, Dōngguǎn, Zhūhǎi and Zhōngshān.

○ **TurboJet** (Map p282; ☎2859 3333; www.turbojet.com.hk) Has services to Macau (HK$159, one hour, eight daily, 10am to 10pm).

Kowloon Motor Bus (KMB; ☎2745 4466; www.kmb.hk)

New Lantau Bus (☎2984 9848; www.newlantaobus.com)

Major bus stops and stations:

Central Bus Terminus (Map p282; Exchange Sq) Gets you to the southern side of the island: buses 6, 6A and 260 leave for Stanley and Repulse Bay; buses 70 and 70P for Aberdeen.

Admiralty Above Admiralty MTR station: gets you to the southern side of the island.

Star Ferry Pier (Map p276) Has buses to Hung Hom station and points in eastern and western Kowloon.

Public Light Bus

Better known as 'minibuses', these 16-seaters come in two varieties:

With red roof/stripe Fares HK$2 to HK$22; supplement bus services. Get on or off almost anywhere – just yell 'ni do, m gói' (here, please); Octopus card accepted on certain routes.

With green roof/stripe Operate on more than 350 set routes and make designated stops; Octopus card accepted on all routes.

Ferry

Cross-Harbour Ferry The Star Ferry (www.starferry.com.hk) operates on two routes: Central–Tsim Sha Tsui and Wan Chai–Tsim Sha Tsui.

Outlying Islands Ferry See schedules at ferry piers and ferry company websites, or ask for a pocket-sized timetable. Most ferries depart from the Outlying Islands Piers close to the IFC building in Central. The main companies are:

Hong Kong & Kowloon Ferry Co (HKKF; ☎2815 6063; www.hkkf.com.hk) Serves Lamma.

New World First Ferry (NWFF; Map p282; ☎2131 8181; www.nwff.com.hk) Services to Cheung Chau, Peng Chau and Lantau; an inter-island service connects the three.

Train

The Mass Transit Railway (MTR; ☎2881 8888; www.mtr.com.hk; fares HK$4-25) runs 10 lines; buy tickets or use Octopus cards (slightly cheaper). The MTR also runs overland services on two main lines and two smaller lines, offering transport to the New Territories. Left-luggage lockers in major MTR train stations, including Hung Hom station.

East Rail From Hung Hom station in Kowloon to Lo Wu and Lok Ma Chau (HK$36-48), gateway to Shēnzhèn; a spur runs from Tai Wai to Wu Kai Sha.

Light Rail Fares HK$4.10 to HK$6.50; routes in western New Territories between Tuen Mun and Yuen Long, and feeds the West Rail.

Largo do Senado, Macau
MANFRED GOTTSCHALK/GETTY IMAGES ©

West Rail From Hung Hom station to Tuen Mun (HK$20) via Yuen Long.

Tram

Hong Kong's century-old trams are the only all double-decker wooden-sided tram fleet in the world. They operate on six overlapping routes running east–west along the northern side of Hong Kong Island.

Taxi

Hong Kong is served by taxis of three colours:

Blue Serving Lantau; HK$17 flag fall, then HK$1.40 for every 200m.

Green Serving the New Territories; HK$18.50 flag fall, then HK$1.40 for every 200m.

Red Serving Hong Kong Island and Kowloon; HK$22 flag fall for the first 2km, then HK$1.60 for every additional 200m.

MACAU

♪ 853 / POP 549,500

Mainlanders can't get enough of this once Portuguese-administered backwater-turned-gambling megaresort. Such has been its explosive growth since 2002 that it is commonplace to refer to Macau as the Vegas of the East. It might be more appropriate to put that the other way round, since Macau has eclipsed its American rival in gambling income. And there are many other things that Macau does better. Beyond the gaming halls, it offers cobblestoned streets punctuated with Chinese temples and baroque churches, pockets of (natural) greenery, a historic centre of Unesco World Heritage status and balmy beaches.

History

Portuguese galleons first visited southern China to trade in the early 16th century, and in 1557, as a reward for clearing out pirates endemic to the area, they obtained a leasehold for Macau and were allowed to establish a tiny enclave here. However, after the Opium Wars between the Chinese and the British, and the subsequent establishment of Hong Kong, Macau went into a long decline.

In 1999, under the Sino–Portuguese Joint Declaration, Macau was returned to China and designated a Special Administrative Region (SAR).

⊙ Sights

For a small place (just 29 sq km), Macau is packed with important cultural and historical sights, including eight squares and 22 historic buildings, which have collectively been named the Historic Centre of Macau World Heritage Site by Unesco.

CENTRAL MACAU PENINSULA

Running from Avenida da Praia Grande to the Inner Harbour, Avenida de Almeida Ribeiro – or San Ma Lo (新馬路; New Thoroughfare) in Cantonese – is the peninsula's main thoroughfare and home to the charming **Largo do Senado**, a black and white tiled square close to major sights.

297

Monte Fort
Fort

(大炮台, Fortaleza do Monte; ⏱7am-7pm; 🚌7, 8, disembark at Social Welfare Bureau) Just east of the ruins of the Church of St Paul, Monte Fort was built by the Jesuits between 1617 and 1626 as part of the College of the Mother of God. Barracks and storehouses were designed to allow the fort to survive a two-year siege, but the cannons were fired only once, during the aborted attempt by the Dutch to invade Macau in 1622. Now the ones on the south side are

If You Like...
Macau Architecture

If you liked the Ruins of the Church of St Paul and Mandarin's House, there's an invigorating selection of building styles in Macau, ranging from handsome libraries to art deco classics.

1 SIR ROBERT HO TUNG LIBRARY
(何東圖書館; 3 Largo de St Agostinho; ⏱10am-7pm Mon-Sat, 11am-7pm Sun; 🚌9, 16, 18) This charming building founded in the 19th century was the country retreat of the late tycoon Robert Ho Tung who purchased it in 1918. The colonial edifice featuring a dome, an arcaded facade, Ionic columns and Chinese-style gardens, was given a modern extension by architect Joy Choi Tin Tin not too long ago. The new four-storey structure in glass and steel has Piranesi-inspired bridges connecting to the old house and a glass roof straddling the transitional space.

2 PIER 8
(8號碼頭; Rua do Dr Lourenco Pereira Marquez; 🚌5, 7) A stunner in grey 50 paces south of Macau Masters Hotel (162 Rua das Lorchas); best views from the **South Sampan Pier** next door.

3 EAST ASIA HOTEL
(東亞酒店; cnr Rua do Guimares & Rua da Madeira; 🚌5, 7) Not much of a hotel perhaps, but what a building! This green structure in a Chinese art deco style stands out in its modest-looking neighbourhood. But too bad that there's not enough space around it to get a good photo of it.

trained at the gaudy Grand Lisboa Casino like an accusing finger.

Mandarin's House
Historic Building

(鄭家大屋, Caso do Mandarim; 📞2896 8820; www.wh.mo/mandarinhouse; 10 Travessa de Antonio da Silva; ⏱10am-5.30pm Thu-Tue; 🚌28B, 18) **FREE** Built around 1869, the Mandarin's House with over 60 rooms, was the ancestral home of Zheng Guanying, an influential author-merchant whose readers had included emperors, Dr Sun Yatsen and Chairman Mao. The compound features a moon gate, tranquil courtyards, exquisite rooms and a main hall with French windows, all arranged in that labyrinthine style typical of certain Chinese period buildings.

St Lazarus Church District
Neighbourhood

(瘋堂斜巷, Calcada da Igreja de Sao Lazaro; www.cipa.org.mo; 🚌7, 8) A lovely neighbourhood with colonial-style houses and cobbled streets. Designers and independents like to gather here, setting up shop and organising artsy events, such as the weekly **Sun Never Left – Public Art Performance** (黃昏小叙-街頭藝術表演; www.cipa.org.mo; Rua de Sao Roque; ⏱3-6pm Sat & Sun; 🚻; 🚌7, 8). **Tai Fung Tong Art House** (大瘋堂藝舍; 📞2835 3537; 7 Calcada de Sao Lazaro; ⏱2-6pm Tue-Sun; 🚌7, 8), **G32** (📞2834 6626; 32 Rua de Sao Miguel; ⏱free guided tours 2.30-5pm Sat & Sun; 🚌7, 8) and the **Old Ladies' House** are also here.

St Joseph's Seminary & Church
Church

(聖若瑟修院及聖堂, Capela do Seminario Sao Jose; Rua do Seminario; ⏱church 10am-5pm; 🚌9, 16, 18, 28B) St Joseph's, which falls outside the tourist circuit, is one of Macau's most beautiful models of tropicalised baroque architecture. Consecrated in 1758 as part of the Jesuit seminary (not open to the public), it features a white and yellow facade, a scalloped entrance canopy (European) and the oldest dome, albeit a shallow one, ever built in China. The most interesting

WIBOWO RUSLI/GETTY IMAGES ©

★ Don't Miss
Ruins of the Church of St Paul

A gateway to nowhere in the middle of the city is all that remains of the Church of St Paul, considered by some to be the greatest monument to Christianity in Asia. The church was designed by an Italian Jesuit and built in 1602 by Japanese Christian exiles and Chinese craftsmen. In 1835 a fire destroyed everything except the facade. Behind the ruins, there's a small **Museum of Sacred Art** (天主教藝術博物館和墓室, Museu de Arte Sacra e Cripta; Rua de São Paulo; ⊗9am-6pm) FREE, and a crypt and ossuary.

NEED TO KNOW
大三巴牌坊, Ruinas de Igreja de São Paulo; Travessa de São Paulo; 🚌8A, 17, 26; disembark at Luís de Camões Garden FREE

---

feature, however, is the roof that features Chinese materials and building styles.

Leal Senado   Historic Building
(民政總署大樓; Map p300; ☎2857 2233; 163 Avenida de Almeida Ribeiro; ⊗9am-9pm Tue-Sun; 🚌3, 6, 26A, 18A, 33, disembark at Almeida Ribeiro) Facing Largo do Senado is Macau's most important historical building, the 18th-century 'Loyal Senate', which houses the Instituto para os Assuntos Cívicos e Municipais (IACM; Civic and Municipal Affairs Bureau). It is so-named because the body sitting here refused to recognise Spain's sovereignty during the 60 years that it occupied Portugal. In 1654, a dozen years after Portuguese sovereignty was re-established, King João IV ordered a heraldic inscription to be placed inside the entrance hall, which can still be seen today.

Macau Peninsula

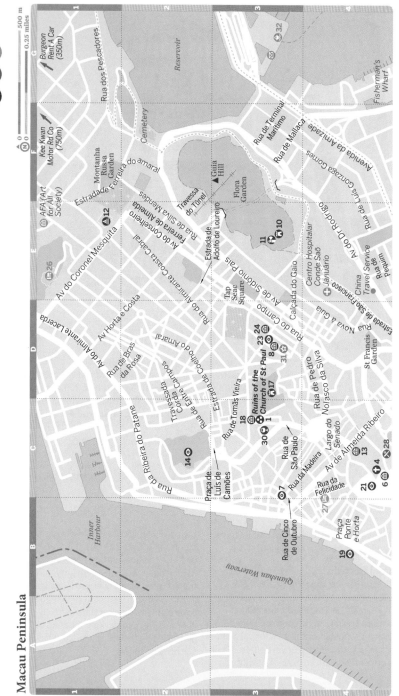

Inner Harbour

Qiansham Waterway

Reservoir

Cemetery

Montanha Russa Garden

AFA (Art for All Society)

Burgeon Rent A Car (350m)

Kee Kwan Motor Rd Co (750m)

Rua dos Pescadores

Estradade Ferreira do amaral

Av do Coronel Mesquita

Av do Almirante Lacerda

Rua da Ribeira do Patane

Av Horta e Costa

Rua de Bras da Rosa

Travessada Corda Caral

Rua de Entre Campos

Estrada de Coelho do Amaral

Rua da Almirante Costa Cabral

Av do Conselheiro Ferreira de Almeida

Rua de Silva Mendes

Travessa do Túnel

Estrada de Adolfo de Loureiro

Guia Hill

Flora Garden

Av de Sidónio Pais

Tap Seac Square

Rua do Campo

Calçada do Gaio

Centro Hospitalar Conde Saõ Januário

Rua Nova à Guia

Av do Dr Rodrigo

Estrada de São Francisco

China Travel Service

Rua de Pequim

St Francis Garden

Rua de Luís Gonzaga Gomes

Avenida da Amizade

Rua de Terminal Marítimo

Rua de Mallaca

Fisherman's Wharf

Praça de Luís de Camões

Rua de Tomás Vieira

Rua de São Paulo

Rua da Madeira

Rua da Felicidade

Rua de Cinco de Outubro

Praça Ponte e Horta

Rua de Pedro Nolasco da Silva

Largo do Senado

Av de Almeida Ribeiro

Ruins of the Church of St Paul

26
12
11 10
14
7
19
18 1 17
30 1
23 24
8
31
13
4
28
21 6
27
32

500 m
0.25 miles

N
0

Macau Peninsula

SOUTHERN MACAU PENINSULA

The southern Macau peninsula features a number of old colonial houses and baroque churches that are best visited on foot.

Macau Museum of Art   Museum

(澳門藝術博物館, Museu de Arte de Macau; ☏8791 9814; www.mam.gov.mo; Macau Cultural Centre, Avenida Xian Xing Hai; adult/child MOP$5/2, Sun free; ⏰10am-6.30pm Tue-Sun; 🚌1A, 8, 12, 23) This excellent five-storey museum has well-curated displays of art created in Macau and China, including paintings by Western artists like George Chinnery, who lived in the enclave. Other highlights are ceramics and stoneware excavated in Macau, Ming- and Qing-dynasty calligraphy from Guǎngdōng, ceramic statues from Shíwān (Guǎngdōng) and seal carvings. The museum also features 19th-century Western historical paintings from all over Asia, and contemporary Macanese art.

A-Ma Temple   Taoist Temple

(媽閣廟, Templo de A-Ma; Rua de São Tiago da Barra; ⏰7am-6pm; 🚌1, 2, 5, 6B, 7) A-Ma Temple was probably already standing when the Portuguese arrived, although the present structure may date from the 16th century. It was here that fisherfolk once came to replenish supplies and pray for fair weather. A-Ma, aka Tin Hau, is the Goddess of the Sea, from which the name Macau is derived. It's believed that when the Portuguese asked the name of the place, they were told 'A-Ma Gau' (A-Ma Bay). In modern Cantonese, 'Macau' (Ou Mun) means 'gateway of the bay'.

NORTHERN MACAU PENINSULA

The northern peninsula is quite a good area to just wander around in.

Guia Fort & Guia Chapel   Fort, Church

(東望洋炮台及聖母雪地殿聖堂, Fortaleza da Guia e Capela de Guia; ⏰chapel 9am-5.30pm; 🚌2, 2A, 6A, 12, 17, 18 Flora Garden stop) As the highest point on the peninsula, Guia Fort affords panoramic views of the city and, when the air is clear, across to the islands and China. At the top is the stunning Chapel of Our Lady of Guia built in 1622 and retaining almost 100% of its original features, including some of Asia's most valuable frescoes. Next to it stands the oldest modern **lighthouse** (旅遊局東望洋燈塔分局; Map p300; ☏2856 9808; ⏰9am-1pm & 2.15-5.30pm) on the China coast – an attractive 15m-tall structure that is closed to the public.

Luís de Camões Garden & Grotto

Gardens

(白鴿巢公園, Jardim e Gruta de Luís de Camões; Praça de Luís de Camões; ⏰6am-10pm; 🚌8A, 17, 26) This relaxing garden with dappled meandering paths is dedicated to the one-eyed poet Luís de Camões (1524–80), who is said to have

A-Ma Temple
CHRISTINE PEMBERTON/GETTY IMAGES ©

MANFRED GOTTSCHALK/GETTY IMAGES ©

⭐ Don't Miss
Colonial Macau

From Avenida de Almeida Ribeiro, follow Calçada do Tronco Velho to the **Church of St Augustine** (聖奧斯定教堂, Igreja de Santo Agostinho; No 2, Largo de St Agostinho; ⊙10am-6pm; 🚌3, 4, 6, 26A), dating from 1814. Facing the church is China's first Western theatre, the **Dom Pedro V Theatre** (崗頂劇院, Teatro Dom Pedro V; 📞2893 9646; Calçada do Teatro, Largo de St Agostinho; ⊙10am-6pm Wed-Mon; 🚌3, 4, 6A, 8A, 19). This 19th-century pastel-green building is not open to the public. Next up is the **Church of St Lawrence** (聖老楞佐教堂, Igreja de São Lourenço; Rua de São Lourenço; ⊙10am-5pm Tue-Sun, 1-2pm Mon; 🚌9, 16, 18, 28B) with its magnificent painted ceiling. Walk down Travessa do Padré Narciso to the pink **Government House** (特區政府總部, Sede do Governo; cnr Avenida da Praia Grande & Travessa do Padré Narciso; 🚌3, 6A, 9, 9A,16), the headquarters of the Macau SAR government. The oldest section of Macau is a short distance southwest of here, via the waterfront promenade **Avenida da República** (🚌6, 9, 16). Along this stretch you'll see several colonial villas and civic buildings. These include the **Residence of the Portuguese consul-general** (葡國駐澳門領事官邸; Consulado-Geral de Portugal em Macau; Rua do Boa Vista), which was once the Hotel Bela Vista, one of the most storied hotels in Asia.

written part of his epic *Os Lusíadas* in Macau, though there is little evidence that he ever reached the city. You'll see a bronze bust (c 1886) of the man here. The wooded garden attracts a fair number of chess players, bird owners and Chinese shuttlecock kickers. The **Sr Wong Ieng**

Kuan Library (白鴿巢公園黃營均圖書館, Praça de Luís de Camões; Map p300; 📞2895 3075; ⊙8am-8pm Tue-Sun) is also here.

Kun Iam Temple   Buddhist Temple
(觀音廟, Templo de Kun Iam; 2 Avenida do Coronel Mesquita; ⊙7am-5.30pm; 🚌1A, 10, 18A,

303

stop Travessa de Venceslau de Morais) Macau's oldest temple was founded in the 13th century, but the present structures date back to 1627. Its roofs are embellished with porcelain figurines and its halls are lavishly decorated. Inside the main one stands the likeness of Kun Iam, the Goddess of Mercy; to the left of the altar is a statue of a bearded arhat rumoured to represent Marco Polo. The first Sino-American treaty was signed at a round stone table in the temple's terraced gardens in 1844.

THE ISLANDS

Connected to the Macau mainland by three bridges and joined together by an ever-growing area of reclaimed land called Cotai, Coloane and, to a lesser extent, Taipa are oases of calm and greenery. By contrast, the Cotai Strip is development central, with megacasinos sprouting up.

Taipa   Island
(氹仔, Tam Chai in Cantonese) Traditionally an island of duck farms and boat yards, Taipa is rapidly becoming urbanised and now houses hotels, a university, a racecourse, a stadium and an airport. But a parade of baroque churches, temples, overgrown esplanades and lethargic settlements mean it's still possible to experience the traditional charms of the island.

Coloane   Island
(路環, Lo Wan in Cantonese) A haven for pirates until the start of the 20th century, Coloane, considerably larger than Taipa, is the only part of Macau that doesn't seem to be changing at a head-spinning rate, which is a relief.

All buses stop at the roundabout in Coloane village on the western shore, which overlooks mainland China across the water. The main attraction in the village is the **Chapel of St Francis Xavier** (聖方濟各教堂, Capela de São Francisco Xavier; Rua do Caetano, Largo Eduardo Marques, Coloane; ⊙10am-8pm; 🚌15, 21A, 25, 26A), built in 1928 and which contains a relic of the saint's arm bone. The village has some interesting temples, including the

Tam Kong Temple (譚公廟; Avenida de Cinco de Outubro, Largo Tam Kong Miu; ⊙8.30am-5.30pm; 🚌15, 21A, 25, 26A), where you'll find a dragon boat made of whale bone. To the north of the village on Estrada da Lai Chi Vun are photogenic **old junk-building sheds**, which have been the centre of a development-versus-preservation debate.

🏃 Activities

Macau Formula 3
Grand Prix   Sports
(🕿2855 5555; www.macau.grandprix.gov.mo) Macau's biggest sporting event of the year is held in the third week of November.

HIKING

Macau's hiking trails are not difficult and you can quickly get to a road to flag down a taxi if necessary. The longest one is the 8100m **Coloane Trail**, which begins in the mid-section of Estrada do Alto de Coloane and winds around the island.

🛏 Sleeping

Most of Macau's hotels are aimed at mon-eyed visitors rather than budget travellers. Rates shoot up on Friday or Saturday, while during the week you can find some incredible deals at travel agencies, hotel websites and specialist sites such as www.macau.com, and booths at Hong Kong's **Shun Tak Centre** (信德中心; Map p282; 200 Connaught Rd, Central, Hong Kong) from where the Macau ferries depart, and the arrivals hall of the Macau Ferry Terminal.

MACAU PENINSULA

Mandarin
Oriental   Luxury Hotel $$$
(文華東方; 🕿8805 8888; www.mandarinoriental.com/macau; Avenida Dr Sun Yat Sen, Novos Aterros do Porto Exterior; r MOP$2088-4000, ste MOP$4788-6588; ⊖🌸@🛜🏊) A great high-end option, the Mandarin has everything associated with the brand – elegance, superlative service, comfortable rooms and excellent facilities. Though relatively small, it's a refreshing contrast to the glitzy casino hotels.

Chapel of St Francis Xavier

MANFRED GOTTSCHALK/GETTY IMAGES ©

San Va Hospedaria   Guesthouse $
(新華大旅店; ☎8210 0193 reservations,
2857 3701; www.sanvahotel.com; 65-67 Rua da
Felicidade; d MOP$190-220, tw MOP$320-360, tr
MOP$380; ☒3, 6, 26A) Built in 1873, San Va,
with its green partitions and retro tiles, is
about the cheapest and most atmospheric
lodging in town – Wong Kar-wai filmed
parts of *2046* here. However, it's also very
basic, with shared bathrooms and no air-
conditioning (just fans).

Pousada de Mong Há   Inn $$
(澳門望廈迎賓館; ☎2851 5222; www.ift.edu.
mo; Colina de Mong Há; r MOP$700-1300, ste
MOP$1300-1800; ☒✳@☎; ☒5, 22, 25)
Sitting atop Mong Há Hill near the ruins
of a fort built in 1849 is this Portuguese-
style inn run by students at the Institute
for Tourism Studies. Rooms are well
appointed, with some having computers,
and the service is attentive. Rates include
breakfast. Discounts of 25% to 40% midweek and off season.

Pousada de
São Tiago   Historic Hotel $$$
(聖地牙哥古堡; ☎2837 8111; www.saotiago.
com.mo; Fortaleza de São Tiago da Barra,

Avenida da República; ste MOP$3000-5400;
☒✳@☎☒; ☒6, 9, 28B) Built into the
ruins of the 17th-century Barra Fort, the
landmark São Tiago is the most romantic
place to stay in Macau. No other hotel
has such a rich history. All 12 rooms are
elegantly furnished suites. Discounts of
up to 35% in off season. The restaurant La
Paloma is here.

Eating

Browse a typically Macanese menu and
you'll find an enticing stew of influences
from Chinese and Asian cuisines, as well
as from those of former Portuguese colo-
nies in Africa, India and Latin America.

Alfonso III   Portuguese $$
(亞豐素三世餐廳; ☎2858 6272; 11a Rua
Central; meals MOP$300; ⏱11.30am-2.30pm
& 6-9.30pm; ☒; ☒3, 6, 26A) A short stroll
southwest of Leal Senado is this tiny,
family-run restaurant that has won a
well-deserved reputation among Macau's
Portuguese community. Service is patchy,
but no one seems to mind. Tables are often
in short supply, so phone ahead.

António
Portuguese $$$

(安東尼奧; ☎2899 9998; www.antoniomacau.
com; 7 Rua dos Clerigos, Taipa; meals MOP$350-
1200; ⏰noon-10.30pm; ☐22, 26) The cosy
mahogany-framed dining room, the meticu-
lously thought-out menu and the entertain-
ing chef, António Coelho, all make this the
go-to place for traditional Portuguese food.
If you can only try one Portuguese restau-
rant in Macau, make it this one.

Tim's Kitchen
Chinese $$$

(桃花源小廚; ☎8803 3682; www.hotelisboa.
com; Shop F25, East Wing, Hotel Lisboa, 2-4 Avenida de Lisboa, Praia Grande; meals MOP$300-
1500; ⏰noon-2.30pm & 6.30-10.30pm; ☐3, 6,
26A) At Tim's, with one Michelin star, fresh
ingredients are meticulously prepared
using methods that preserve or highlight
their original flavours, resulting in dishes
that look simple but taste divine – a giant
'glass' prawn shares a plate with a sliver
of Chinese ham; a crab claw lounges on
a cushion of winter melon surrounded by
broth.

Restaurante Fernando
Portuguese $$

(法蘭度餐廳; ☎2888 2264; 9 Hác Sá beach;
meals MOP$150-270; ⏰noon-9.30pm; ☐;
☐21A, 25, 26A) Possibly Coloane's most
famous restaurant, Fernando's easy-
breezy atmosphere makes it perfect for a
protracted seafood lunch by the sea, as its
devoted customers would agree. The bar
stays open till midnight.

🍷 Drinking

Macau's unique and atmospheric drinking
places are far removed from the glitz of the
Outer Harbour.

Macallan Whisky Bar & Lounge
Bar

(☎8883 2221; www.galaxymacau.com; 203, 2nd
fl, Galaxy Hotel, Cotai; ⏰5pm-1am Mon-Thu, to
2am Fri & Sat; ☐25, 25X) Macau's best whisky
bar is a traditional affair featuring oak pan-
els, Jacobean rugs and a real fireplace. The
400-plus whisky labels include representa-
tives from Ireland, France, Sweden and
India, and a 1963 Glenmorangie.

⭐ Entertainment

Macau's nightlife may be dominated by the
ever-expanding casino scene, but a num-
ber of interesting live-music venues
have also sprung up about town.

Macau Soul
Bar

(澳感廊; ☎2836 5182; www.
macausoul.com; 31a Rua de São
Paulo; ⏰3-10pm Sun, Mon
& Thu, to midnight Fri & Sat;
☐8A, 17, 26) An elegant
haven in wood and
stained glass, where
twice a month, a jazz
band plays to a packed
audience. On most
nights though, Theloni-
ous Monk fills the air as
customers chat with the
owners and dither over

Sir Robert Ho Tung Library (p298)
TOM COCKREM/GETTY IMAGES ©

their 430 Portuguese wines. Opening hours vary; phone ahead.

🔒 Shopping

Browsing through the shops in the old city, specifically on crumbly **Rua dos Ervanários** and **Rua de Nossa Senhora do Amparo** near the ruins of the Church of St Paul, can be a great experience.

ℹ Information

The Macau Government Tourist Office (MGTO) distributes the excellent (and free) *Macau Tourist Map*, with tourist sights and streets labelled in Portuguese and Chinese.

Medical Services

Centro Hospitalar Conde Saõ Januário (山頂 醫院; ☎ 2831 3731; Estrada do Visconde de São Januário) Southwest of Guia Fort.

Money

ATMs are everywhere, with half a dozen just outside the Hotel Lisboa.

You can change cash and travellers cheques at the banks (🕘9am-5pm Mon-Fri, to 1pm Sat) lining Avenida da Praia Grande and Avenida de Almeida Ribeiro.

Hong Kong bills and coins (except the HK$10 coins) are accepted everywhere in Macau, but your change will be returned in patacas.

Tourist Information

Macau Government Tourist Office (☎ 2835 8444; 🕘10am-6pm) has themed leaflets on Macau's sights and bilingual maps at its outlets:

MGTO-Macau Maritime Ferry Terminal (旅遊局 外港碼頭分局; ☎ 8790 7039; 🕘9am-10pm)

ℹ Getting There & Away

Air

Macau International Airport (☎ 2886 1111; www.macau-airport.com) Macau's airport is located on Taipa Island, 20 minutes from the city centre. Frequent services to destinations including Bangkok, Chiang Mai, Kaohsiung, Kuala Lumpur, Manila, Osaka, Seoul, Singapore, Taipei and Tokyo. There are also regular flights to Běijīng, Hángzhōu, Nánjīng, Níngbō, Shànghǎi and Xiàmén and less frequent flights to Chéngdū, Chóngqìng, Fúzhōu and Wǔhàn.

Sky Shuttle (☎ in Hong Kong 2108 9898; www.skyshuttlehk.com) Runs a 15-minute helicopter shuttle between Macau and Hong Kong up to 27 times daily.

Boat

Macau is linked directly to Hong Kong International Airport by **TurboJet** (p295) which has eight ferries operating between 10am and 10pm. It costs MOP$233/178/126 per adult/child/infant and takes 45 minutes. However, please note that this ferry service is for transit passengers only. It is not applicable to passengers originating in Hong Kong.

CotaiJet (☎ 2885 0595; www.cotaijet.com.mo) Every half-hour from 7am to 1am; runs between Taipa Ferry Terminal and Hong Kong's Hong Kong–Macau Ferry Terminal. A feeder shuttle bus service drops off at destinations on the Cotai Strip. Check the website for services to Hong Kong International Airport.

Bus

Macau is an easy gateway into China. Simply take bus 3, 5 or 9 to the Border Gate (關閘; Portas do Cerco; open 7am to midnight) and walk across. Cotai Frontier Post (9am to 8pm) on the causeway linking Taipa and Coloane allows visitors to cross Lotus Bridge by shuttle bus (HK$3) to Zhūhǎi; buses 15, 21, 25 and 26 drop you off at the crossing. Buses from the Macau International Airport Bus Terminal run to Guǎngzhōu and Dōngguǎn (both MOP$155, four hours).

Kee Kwan Motor Rd Co (歧關車路有限公司; ☎ 2893 3888; Underground bus terminal near Border Gate; 🕘7.15am-9pm) Has buses going to Guǎngzhōu (MOP$80, four hours, every 15 minutes from 8am to 9.40pm) and to Zhōngshān (MOP$23, 90 minutes, every 20 minutes from 8am to 8pm).

ℹ Getting Around

To/From the Airport

The airport bus AP1 (MOP$4.20) leaves the airport and zips around Taipa before heading to the Macau Maritime Ferry Terminal and the border gate. The bus stops at a number of major hotels en route and departs every five to 12 minutes from 6.30am to midnight. Other services run to Praça de Ferreira do Amaral (MT1 and MT2) and Coloane (bus 26).

A taxi from the airport to town centre is about MOP$40.

Bicycle

Bikes can be rented in Taipa village. You are not allowed to cross the Macau–Taipa bridges on a bicycle.

Car

Burgeon Rent A Car (2828 3399; www. burgeonrentacar.com; Shops O, P & Q, Block 2, La Baie Du Noble, Avenida Do Nordeste) Hires Kia cars with the cheapest model starting at MOP$450 for the first nine hours. The cheapest car with chauffeur costs MOP$230 per hour, with a minimum of two hours.

Public Transport

Routes Macau has about 50 public bus and minibus routes running from 6am to midnight.

Fares MOP$3.20 on the peninsula, MOP$4.20 to Taipa, MOP$5 to Coloane village, MOP$6.40 to Hác Sá Beach.

Information Macau Transmac Bus Co (www. transmac.com.mo), Macau TCM Bus Co (www.tcm. com.mo) and Reolian (www.reolian.com.mo) have info on routes and fares.

Useful services Buses 3 and 3A go between the ferry terminal and city centre. Buses 3 and 5 go to the Border Gate. Bus 12 goes from the ferry terminal past Hotel Lisboa to Lou Lim loc Garden and Kun lam Temple. Buses 21, 21A, 25 and 26A go to Taipa and Coloane.

Taxi

Flag fall is MOP$15 for the first 1.6km and MOP$1.50 for each additional 230m. There is a MOP$5 surcharge to go to Coloane; travelling between Taipa and Coloane is MOP$2 extra. For yellow radio taxis, call 2851 9519 or 2893 9939.

THE SOUTH

....

Guǎngzhōu 广州

020 / POP 12 MILLION

Guǎngzhōu, known to many in the West as Canton, is China's busiest transport and trade hub. You are likely to pass through it at least once to get to other parts of the country.

HONG KONG & THE SOUTH GUǍNGZHŌU

Sleeping

Guǎngzhōu's choices in the budget and lower midrange are dreary. For those who want to splurge, there are plenty of excellent top-end and upper midrange hotels.

Garden Hotel
Hotel $$$

(花园酒店; Huāyuán Jiǔdiàn; ☑8333 8989; www.thegardenhotel.com.cn; 368 Huanshi Donglu; 环市东路368号; r/ste from ¥3200/5200; ✳@☎☂; MLine 5, Táojīn) One of the most popular luxury hotels in Guǎngzhōu with waterfalls and lovely gardens in the lobby and on the 4th floor. The rooms are just as classy. Bookings essential.

Guǎngzhōu Youth Hostel
Hostel $

(广东鹅潭宾馆; Guǎngdōng Étán Bīnguǎn; ☑8121 8298; www1.gzyhostel.com; 2 Shamian Sijie; 沙面四街2号; dm/s/tr ¥60/240/390, d ¥260-320; @) For the cheapest beds on Shāmiàn Island, head to this nondescript hostel. Backpacker ambience is non-existent, but rooms are moderately clean.

Eating

Guǎngzhōu is home to some superb Cantonese restaurants.

Pànxī Restaurant
Dim Sum $$

(泮溪酒家; Pànxī Jiǔjiā; ☑8172 1328; 151 Longjin Xilu; dishes from ¥40; ☉7.30am-midnight; MChángshòu Lù) Set in a majestic garden and embracing another one within its walls, Pànxī is the most representative of Guǎngzhōu's garden-restaurants. Corridors and courtyards are brought together to give the effect of 'every step, a vista' (一步一景). Elderly diners are known to get up and sing an operatic aria or two when the mood is right. You'll need to queue for a table after 8.30am.

ℹ Information

Medical Services

Guǎngzhōu First Municipal People's Hospital
(广州第一人民医院; Guǎngzhōu Dìyī Rénmín Yīyuàn; ☑8104 8888; 1 Panfu Lu) Medical clinic for foreigners on the 1st floor.

Money

ATMs available, most 24 hours, throughout Guǎngzhōu.

Bank of China (中国银行; **Zhōngguó Yínháng**; ☎8334 0998; 686 Renmin Beilu; ⏰9am-5.30pm Mon-Fri, to 4pm Sat & Sun) Most branches change travellers cheques.

ⓘ Getting There & Away

Air

China Southern Airlines (中国南方航空; Zhōngguó Nánfāng Hángkōng; ☎95539; www. cs-air.com; 181 Huanshi Xilu; ⏰24hr) The office of the major airline serving Guǎngzhōu is southeast of Guǎngzhōu railway station. Frequent flights to major cities in China include Guìlín (¥660), Shànghǎi (¥1280) and Běijīng (¥1700); also numerous international destinations.

Bus

Some useful stations:

Tiānhé passenger station (天河客运站; Tiānhé Kèyùnzhàn; ☎3708 5070; www.tianhebus. com; Yanling Lu; 燕玲路; MTiānhé Kèyùnzhàn) Most frequent departures to destinations in Guǎngdōng; accessible by metro.

Fāngcūn passenger station (芳村客运站; Fāngcūn Kèyùnzhàn; ☎3708 5070; www. fangcunbus.com; Huadi Dadao; 华地大道; MKēngkǒu) Accessible by metro.

Guǎngzhōu Dōngzhàn coach station (广州东站汽车客运站; Guǎngzhōu Dōngzhàn Kèyùnzhàn; Linhe Xilu) Behind Guǎngzhōu east train station.

Guǎngdōng long-distance bus station (广东省汽车客运站; Guǎngdōng Shěng Qìchē Kèyùnzhàn; Huanshi Xilu) To the right of the train station.

Destinations include:

Guìlín ¥160, 10 hours, eight daily from Guǎngdōng long-distance bus station (8.30am to 11.30pm)

Xiàmén ¥220, nine hours, every 45 minutes from Tiānhé passenger station.

Deluxe buses ply the Guǎngzhōu–Shēnzhèn freeway to Hong Kong. Buses (¥100 to ¥110) leave from Hotel Landmark Canton near Hǎizhū Sq station every 30 minutes.

Buses through Zhūhǎi to Macau (¥75, 2½ hours) leave frequently from Tiānhé passenger station (7.40am to 8pm).

Train

Guǎngzhōu's three major train stations serve destinations all over China. China Travel Service, next to Hotel Landmark Canton, books train tickets up to five days in advance for ¥10 to ¥20.

From **Guǎngzhōu main train station** (广州火车总站; Guǎngzhōu Zhàn; Huanshi Xilu; MLine 2, Guǎngzhōu Huǒchēzhàn) trains depart for:

Shàoguān ¥38, 2½ hours, frequent services

High-speed trains leave from **Guǎngzhōu south station** (广州火车南站; Guǎngzhōu Nánzhàn; Shibi, Pānyú) in Pānyú to:

Shēnzhèn North Station ¥75, 45 minutes

Wǔhān ¥464, four hours, frequent

Light rail goes to **Zhūhǎi** (¥34, one hour).

From **Guǎngzhōu east station** (广州火车东站; Guǎngzhōu Dōngzhàn; MLine 1, Guǎngzhōu Dōngzhàn) trains depart for:

Běijīng ¥250 to ¥450, 22 hours, one daily (4.11pm)

Shànghǎi ¥220 to ¥380, 16 hours, one daily (6.06pm)

The station is used more for bullet trains to Shēnzhèn (¥80, 1½ hours, every 15 minutes, 6.15am to 10.32pm) and a dozen direct trains to Hong Kong (¥190/HK$190, 2 hours, 8.19am to 9.32pm).

ⓘ Getting Around

The metro is the speediest way to get around.

To/From the Airport

Báiyún International Airport (p408) is 28km north of the city. Airport shuttle buses (¥17 to ¥32, 35 to 70 minutes, every 20 to 30 minutes, 5am to 11pm) leave from half-a-dozen locations, including Garden Hotel and Tiānhé bus station. A taxi to/ from the airport will cost about ¥150.

Metro line 2 links the airport's south terminal (Airport south station; Jīchǎng Nán) and Guǎngzhōu east station. The ride takes 40 minutes (¥7, from 6.10am to 11pm).

Metro

Guǎngzhōu has 10 metro lines in full service, all with free maps available.

Transit passes (羊城通; yáng chéng tōng) are available at metro stations from ¥70 (deposit ¥20 included). The deposit is refundable at designated stations, including Tiyu Xilu and Gōngyuán Qián. This pass can be used on all public transport, including yellow taxis. There are also one-day (¥20) and three-day (¥50) metro passes.

Taxi

Flag fall is ¥10 for the first 2.3km, ¥2.60 for every additional kilometre, with a ¥1 fuel surcharge.

....

Guìlín 桂林

📞 0773 / POP 826,640

Whether you're going north to the highlands, or south to Yángshuò and beyond, Guìlín is where you're likely to spend a night or two.

◎ Sights

Sun & Moon Twin Pagodas   Pagoda

(日月双塔; Rìyuè Shuāng Tǎ; admission ¥45; ⏲8am-10.30pm) Elegantly embellishing the scenery of **Shān Lake** (杉湖; Shān Hú), the Sun and Moon Twin Pagodas, beautifully illuminated at night, are the highlight of a stroll around Guìlín's two central lakes. The octagonal, seven-storey **Moon Pagoda** (月塔; Yuè Tǎ) is connected by an underwater tunnel to the 41m-high **Sun Pagoda** (日塔; Rì Tǎ), one of the few pagodas with a lift.

Solitary Beauty Peak   Park

(独秀峰; Dúxiù Fēng; 1 Wangcheng; 王城1号; admission ¥130; ⏲7.30am-6pm; 🚌1, 2) This park is a peaceful, leafy retreat from the city centre. The entrance fee for the famous lone pinnacle includes admission to an underwhelming 14th-century Ming prince's mansion (oversold as a 'palace'). The 152m peak affords fine views of Guìlín.

Just west of Solitary Beauty Peak is **Wave-Subduing Hill** (伏波山; Fúbō Shān; admission ¥25; ⏲7am-6pm), which offers more great views as well as the chance to see Song- and Tang-dynasty Buddhist carvings etched into the walls of a cave. A short walk further north is **Folded Brocade Hill** (叠彩山, Diécǎi Shān; admission ¥35; ⏲7am-6pm), where you can find arguably the best views of the city and a collection of Buddhist sculptures. Just south of the city centre is **Elephant Trunk Hill** (象鼻山, Xiàngbí Shān; admission ¥75; ⏲7am-6.30pm), perhaps best viewed from one of the bamboo rafts that float down the Lí River.

Seven Stars Park   Park

(七星公园; Qīxīng Gōngyuán; admission ¥75, Seven Star Caves ¥60; ⏲park 6am-9.30pm, caves 8am-5.30pm; 👪) The 137-hectare park makes for some pleasant strolls if you have the time, though children may like it here more than adults – there are makeshift play areas and a pond where you can feed fish with a milk bottle. The illuminated caves are artificial looking and

Sun & Moon Twin Pagodas, Guìlín
POLA DAMONTE/GETTY IMAGES ©

forgettable. **Crescent Restaurant** (月牙楼; Yuèyá Lóu), famous for its vegetarian fare, is inside the park.

To get here, walk, cycle or catch bus 10 or 11 from the train station. From the park, free bus 58 runs to Wave-Subduing Hill, Folded Brocade Hill and Reed Flute Cave.

🖝 Tours

The popular **Lí River trip** from Guìlín to Yángshuò lasts about 4½ hours and includes a wonderfully scenic boat trip to Yángshuò, lunch and a bus ride back to Guìlín. Expect to pay ¥350 to ¥450 for a boat with an English-speaking guide or ¥245 for the Chinese version.

🛏 Sleeping

Riverside Hostel   Inn $$
(九龙商务旅游酒店; Jiǔlóng Shāngwù Lǚyóu Jiǔdiàn; ☑ 258 0215; www.guilin-hostel.com; 6 Zhumu Xiang, Nánmén Qiáo; 南门桥竹木巷6号;

s & d ¥150-300; ❄ @ 🛜) This cosy inn by the Táohuā River (桃花江) comes highly recommended by travellers (especially couples) for its attentive staff and pleasant rooms. Advance booking is essential.

White House   Boutique Hotel $$$
(白公馆; Bái Gōngguǎn; ☑ 899 9888; www.glbgg.com; Bldg 4, 16 Ronghu Beilu; 榕湖北路16号4栋; d ¥1380-1780, ste ¥2380; ➦ ❄ @ 🛜) The White House is decked out in all manner of art deco–inspired trappings to honour the building it's in – part of the former residence of General Bai Chongxi (白崇禧), a powerful regional Guǎngxī warlord and father of the Taiwanese writer Kenneth Pai Hsien-yung (白先勇). The spacious guestrooms are lavishly appointed, featuring, among other luxuries, a mini-spa and high-thread-count bedding. Photos of General Bai (literally 'white') and his era grace the corridors, and vintage artefacts are displayed in the lobby.

Left: Karsts near Guìlín; **Below:** Monkey, Seven Stars Park (p311)

(LEFT) HELMINADIA/GETTY IMAGES ©; (BELOW) SEAN GALLAGHER/GETTY IMAGES ©

The hotel is ¥12 by cab from the main bus station, and ¥120 from the airport.

🍴 Eating

Local specialities include Guìlín *mǐfěn* (桂林米粉; Guìlín rice noodles), *píjiǔ yā* (啤酒鸭; beer duck) and Guìlín *tiánluó* (桂林田螺; Guìlín snails), while the ubiquitous *chǎoguō fàn* (炒锅饭; claypot rice dishes; from ¥6) make a great snack.

Chóngshàn Rice Noodle Shop
Noodles $

(崇善米粉店; Chóngshàn Mǐfěn Diàn; 📞282 6036; 5 Yiren Lu, near junction with Zhengyang Lu, Qixing District; noodles ¥3-5; ⏰6.30am-midnight) Wildly popular Guìlín noodle shop with branches all over town. Order at the front, take your docket to the cook and retrieve your food from a window. The slippery rice noodles come with a variety of ingredients, but the Guìlín speciality (also the tastiest) is with stewed vegetables (卤菜粉; *lǔcài fěn*).

🍷 Drinking

Guìlín's streets are dotted with trendy little cafes, while Zhengyang Lu has a short stretch of bars with outdoor seating. Binjiang Lu has a slew of cute cafes and bars, most with free wi-fi.

Róng Coffee
Cafe

(榕咖啡; Róng Kāfēi; Bldg 5, Rónghú Hotel, 16 Ronghu Beilu; coffee & tea ¥18-188, cake ¥24-28; ⏰1-11pm; 📶) Looking like a greenhouse with colourful armchairs, this peaceful cafe by the picturesque Róng Lake offers a lovely getaway. It's even got a tiny garden with a couple of tables and a garden swing.

ℹ️ Information

Bank of China (中国银行; Zhōngguó Yínháng) Branches on Zhongshan Nanlu (near the main bus station) and Jiefang Donglu change money, give credit-card advances and have 24-hour ATMs.

Guìlín Tourist Information Service Centre (桂林旅游咨询服务中心; Guìlín Lǚyóu Zīxún Fúwù Zhōngxīn; ☏280 0318; South Gate, Ronghu Beilu; ☺8am-10pm) These helpful centres dot the city. There's a good one by the South Gate on Róng Lake.

People's Hospital (人民医院; Rénmín Yīyuàn; 70 Wenming Lu) This large, well-equipped hospital is a designated International SOS service provider, and the teaching hospital of several universities in Guǎngxī.

Public Security Bureau (PSB; 公安局; Gōng'ānjú; ☏582 3492; 16 Shijiayan Lu; ☺8.30am-noon & 3-6pm Mon-Fri) Visa extensions. Located by Xiǎodōng River and 500m south of the Seven Stars Park. A taxi from downtown will cost around ¥18.

ℹ Getting There & Away

Air

Air tickets can be bought from the **Civil Aviation Administration of China** (CAAC; 中国民航; Zhōngguó Mínháng; ☏384 7252; cnr Shanghai Lu & Anxin Beilu; ☺7.30am-8.30pm).

Bus

Guìlín's **main bus station** (桂林汽车客运总站; Guìlín Qìchē Kèyùn Zǒngzhàn; ☏386 2358; 65 Zhongshan Nanlu; ☐3, 9, 10, 11, 16, 25, 51, 88, 91, 99) has regular buses to the following destinations:

Guǎngzhōu ¥180, 9½ hours, eight daily

Lóngshèng ¥40, two hours, five daily (8am, 8.30am, 9.30am, 1pm and 3pm)

Sānjiāng ¥43, four hours, hourly

Train

Few trains start in Guìlín, so it's often tough to find tickets, especially for sleepers.

Direct services include:

Běijīng ¥446, 23 hours, four daily (1.57am, 1.05pm, 3.40pm and 6.55pm)

Guǎngzhōu ¥230, 12 hours, two daily (6.28pm and 9.18pm)

Shànghǎi ¥360, 22 hours, four daily (11.58am, 3pm, 5.13pm and 7.11pm)

ℹ Getting Around

To/From the Airport

Guìlín's **Liǎngjiāng International Airport** (两江国际机场; Liǎngjiāng Guójì Jīchǎng) is 30km west of the city. Half-hourly shuttle buses (¥20) run from the CAAC office between 6.30am and 9pm. A taxi costs about ¥120 (40 minutes).

Bicycle

Guìlín's sights are all within cycling distance. Many hostels rent out bicycles (about ¥20 per day).

Bus

Buses numbered 51 to 58 are all free but run very infrequently. Regular buses cost ¥1 to¥2.

Dragon's Backbone Rice Terraces 龙脊梯田

☏0773

This part of Guǎngxī boasts stunning views of terraced paddy fields, and the clear standout is **Dragon's Backbone Rice Terraces** (龙脊梯田; Lóngjǐ Tītián; adult ¥80). The rice fields rise up to 1000m high and are an amazing feat of farm engineering on hills dotted with minority villages. The best time to visit is after the summer rains in May, which leave the terraces shimmering with reflections. The fields turn golden just before harvesting (October), and become snow-white in winter (December). Avoid early spring (March), when the mountains are shrouded in mist.

There are several villages to visit. **Píng'ān** (平安), a sprawling 600-year-old Zhuang village, is the biggest settlement and the most popular among tourists.

Further along is **Dàzhài** (大寨), a laid-back Yao village that has an idyllic rural allure with a bubbling stream. Continue uphill to the village of **Tiántóuzhài** (田头寨) atop the mountain. It's a sublime place to marvel at the panoramic views of the terraces, the sunrise or the starry night sky.

Most locals here are Zhuang or Yao, but you'll also find Dong and Miao people in the area.

As all of the villages are perched on hills, bring a daypack and leave your luggage at the hotel in Guìlín or at left luggage in the main ticket office. Otherwise porters can help lug your luggage up for ¥40. There's nowhere in this area to change money.

🎯 Activities

The four- to five-hour hike between the villages of Dàzhài and Píng'ān, passing through the villages of Tiántóuzhài and Zhōngliù (中六), is highly recommended.

🛏 Sleeping

You can stay in traditional wooden homes of minority villagers (¥30 to ¥40 for a simple bed), but three in particular – Dàzhài, Tiántóuzhài and Píng'ān – are set up for tourists.

PÍNG'ĀN

Lìqíng Hotel Hotel **$**
(丽晴饭店; Lìqíng Fàndiàn; 📞138 7835 2092; www.liqinghotel.com; d ¥100, tw ¥120-200, tr ¥280, ste ¥398; ❄@🛜) This excellent-value hotel offers simple but comfortable rooms with different feature combos to suit different wallets. The friendly, English-speaking staff will explain the

details to you. Lìqíng is a 20-minute climb from the village parking lot, but villagers will carry your bags for ¥40 apiece.

DÀZHÀI

Minority Cafe & Inn Guesthouse **$**
(龙脊咖啡店; Lóngjǐ Kāfēidiàn; 📞758 5605; r ¥100) Perched above Dàzhài village on the trail leading up to Tiántóuzhài, this small guesthouse has a terrace. It's about a 20-minute walk (1km) uphill from the village's main gate.

TIÁNTÓUZHÀI

Méijǐnglóu Inn **$**
(美景楼; 📞758 5678; r ¥120-150; ❄@) This welcoming guesthouse is located above Tiántóuzhài. Rooms at the front have unobstructed views to the fields. After you leave Tiántóuzhài village, take the path up to the right. From there it's another 800m. There are steps leading up to the entrance.

ℹ️ Getting There & Away

Hotels in Dàzhài and Tiántóuzhài arrange direct shuttle service from Dàzhài to Guìlín (10am, 1pm and 4pm), and from Guìlín to Dàzhài (8am,

Dragon's Backbone Rice Terraces

NISA AND ULLI MAIER PHOTOGRAPHY/GETTY IMAGES ©

10.30am and 2pm) for their guests. The price is ¥50 per person. They also take other passengers if seats are available. Reservations are a must. All hotels in Píng'ān provide a similar service.

For public transport, head to Guìlín's Qíntán bus station via public bus 1. From there, take a bus to Lóngshèng (龙胜; ¥24 to ¥35, 1½ hours, every 40 minutes, 7am to 7pm) and ask to get off at Hépíng (和平). From the road junction (or the ticket office three minutes' walk away), minibuses trundle between Lóngshèng and the rice terraces, stopping to pick up passengers to Dàzhài (¥9, 1 hour, every 30 minutes, 7am to 5pm) and Píng'ān (¥7, 30 minutes, every 20 minutes to 1 hour, 7am to 5pm).

Guìlín's main bus station also has buses to Dàzhài and Lóngjǐ (Píng'ān; ¥50, 3 hours, 8.30am, 9am and 2pm).

Yángshuò 阳朔

 0773 / POP 310,000

Seasoned travellers to Guǎngxī spend as little time in Guìlín as possible, preferring to make Yángshuò their base, though many of these veterans will gripe about Yángshuò's lack of authenticity – 'too many tourists', they complain.

Outside of town, however, Yángshuò's dramatic karst landscape is surreal and the stuff of Chinese landscape paintings. Take a leisurely bamboo-raft ride or cycle through the dreamy valleys and you'll see.

🏃 Activities

Yángshuò is one of the hottest climbing destinations in Asia. There are eight major peaks in regular use, already providing more than 250 (and climbing!) bolted climbs.

Insight Adventures
Yángshuò   Rock Climbing
(☏ 881 1033; www.insight-adventures.com; 12 Fu Rong Lu; ⏱ 9am-9pm) Offers local advice for experienced climbers and fully guided, bolted climbs for beginners. Prices start at ¥350 per person for a half-day climb. Kayaking and other activities are also organised.

Bike Asia   Cycling
(☏ 882 6521; www.bikeasia.com; 42 Guihua Lu; 桂花路42号; ⏱ 9am-6pm) Bike Asia has the best equipment and advice on trips. Bikes are ¥70 per day (deposit ¥300), including safety helmet and map. English-speaking guides (from ¥300 per day) are available.

🛏 Sleeping

Yángshuò is overrun with hotels run by English-speaking staff, and all provide internet access.

Yángshuò

Bamboo rafts on the Lí River

ATA MOHAMMAD ADNAN/GETTY IMAGES ©

Secret Garden
Boutique Hotel **$$$**

(秘密花园酒店; Mìmì Huāyuán Jiǔdiàn; ☑ 877 1932, 138 0773 5773; www.yangshuosecret garden.com; Jìuxiàn Village; 旧县村; r ¥420-460, ste ¥560-580; ☀ @ ☎) A South African designer nicknamed 'Crazy One' by the locals has turned a cluster of Ming-dynasty houses in the village of Jìuxiàn into a gorgeous Western-style boutique hotel with 18 rooms. A taxi to town from here costs ¥50.

Tea Cozy Hotel
Boutique Hotel **$$$**

(水云阁; Shuǐyún Gé; ☑ 135 0783 9490, 881 6158; www.yangshuoteacozy.com; 212 Báishā Zhèn, Xiàtáng Village, 白沙镇下塘村212号; r ¥480, ste ¥528-880; ☀ @ ☎) What makes Tea Cozy a true winner is not the 12 ethnic-style balcony rooms (though these are wonderful in themselves), but the exceptional service by the English-speaking staff. Also laudable are the culinary skills of the restaurant staff (mains ¥18 to ¥108). The hotel has shuttle buses daily to Yángshuò and back, or you can take a taxi for ¥30.

Green Forest Hostel
Hostel **$**

(瓦舍; Wǎshě; ☑ 888 2686; greenforest_ yangshuo@yahoo.com; 3rd fl, Zone A, Business St, Chéngzhòngchéng, Diecui Lu, 叠翠路, 城中城, 城南商业街A区3楼; dm ¥40, r ¥200; ☀ @ ☎) A hostel whose attractiveness is highlighted by the rundown building it's in. Rooms are painted white with colourful accents and earth-toned furnishings; communal areas are flooded in natural light. From the bus station, turn right and walk along Diecui Lu, past Guihua Lu. At the junction with Chengzhong Lu, turn right and look for 99 Shopping Centre (99超市).

🍴 Eating & Drinking

From wood-fired pizza to that most famous of fast foods, you'll now find it in and around Xijie.

317

Pure Lotus Vegetarian Restaurant
Chinese, Vegetarian $$

(暗香蔬影素菜馆; Ànxiāng Shūyǐng Sùcàiguǎn; ☏881 8995; www.yangshuomagnolia.com/pure lotus.htm; 7 Diecui Lu; dishes ¥18-48; ☺10am-10.30pm; ❄🍴♿) A Zen-like atmosphere created by Buddhist music, antique furniture and a cast of quiet, industrious staff prepares you for an innovative vegetarian meal. Prominently displayed wine bottles are an unexpected surprise in a place you wouldn't expect to serve alcohol.

☆ Entertainment

Impressions Liú Sānjiě
Performing Arts

(印象刘三姐; Yìnxiàng Liú Sānjiě; ☏881 7783; tickets ¥200-680; ☺7.30-8.30pm & 9.30-10.30pm) The busiest show in town is directed by filmmaker Zhang Yìmóu, who also directed the opening ceremony at the Běijīng Olympics and acclaimed films such as *Raise the Red Lantern*. Six hundred performers take to the Lí River each night with 12 illuminated karst peaks serving as a backdrop. Book at your hotel for discounts and transport to/from the venue (1.5km from town).

ℹ Information

Travel agencies are all over town, while backpacker-oriented cafes and bars, as well as most hotels, can often dispense good advice.

Bank of China (中国银行; Zhōngguó Yínháng; Xijie; 西街; ☺9am-5pm) Foreign exchange and 24-hour ATM for international cards.

People's Hospital (人民医院; Rénmín Yīyuàn; 26 Chengzhong Lu) English-speaking doctors available.

Public Security Bureau (PSB; 公安局; Gōng'ānjú; Chengbei Lu; ☺8am-noon & 3-6pm summer, 2.30-5.30pm winter) Has several fluent English speakers. Doesn't issue visa extensions. It's 100m east of People's Hospital.

ℹ Getting There & Away

Air
The closest airport is in Guìlín. Your hotel should be able to organise taxi rides directly to the airport (about ¥240, one hour).

Bus
Direct bus links:

Guìlín ¥20, one hour, every 15 to 20 minutes (6.45am to 8.30pm)

Xīngpíng ¥8, one hour, every 15 minutes (6.30am to 6pm)

ℹ Getting Around

Bicycles can be rented at almost all hostels, and from streetside outlets for ¥10 to ¥25 per day.

Around Yángshuò

The countryside of Yángshuò offers weeks of exploration by bike, boat, foot or any combination thereof.

The villages in the vicinity of Yángshuò, especially Xīngpíng, come alive on **market days**, which operate on a three-, six- and nine-day monthly cycle.

XĪNGPÍNG & AROUND 兴坪

Xīngpíng (兴坪), the location of the photo on the back of ¥20 banknotes, is more than 1000 years old and houses a number of historic residences.

The HI-affiliated **This Old Place** (老地方; Lǎo Difang; ☏870 2887; www.topxingping.com; 5 Rongtan Lu; 榕潭街5号; dm ¥50-80, s ¥100-120, d ¥140-380; ☺cafe noon-9.30pm; ❄@🛜) is an excellent place to stay, with a cosy, large lounge area, helpful English-speaking staff and great wood-fired pizza. Stay in the new wing or ask for the balcony room 305 in the old wing.

You can hike the mountain behind Xīngpíng, past pomelo and orange groves, to the sleepy old **Fish Village** (鱼村; Yúcūn). A bus from Yángshuò to Xīngpíng takes 40 minutes (¥7, every 15 minutes, 6am to 7pm).

YÙLÓNG RIVER 遇龙河

The scenery along this smaller, quieter river, about 6km southwest of Yángshuò, is breathtaking. There are a number of great swimming spots and countless exploring possibilities. Just rent a bike and get out here.

One option is to aim for **Dragon Bridge** (遇龙桥; Yùlóng Qiáo), about

YVES ANDRE/GETTY IMAGES ©

10km upstream. This 600-year-old stone arched bridge is among Guǎngxī's largest and comes with higgledy-piggledy steps and sides that lean inwards with age.

You can also get here by taking the bus to Jīnbǎo (金宝); get off at Dragon Bridge (¥6, 35 minutes), just after Báishā (白沙).

Fènghuáng 凤凰

📞 0743

Fènghuáng was once a frontier town, marking the boundary between the Han civilisations of the central plains and the Miao (苗), Tujia (土家) and Dong (侗) minorities of the southwest mountains. Its diverse residents built a breathtaking riverside settlement of winding alleys, temples and rickety stilt houses.

◎ Sights & Activities

Wandering aimlessly is the best way to experience the charms of **old town Fènghuáng** (凤凰古城; Fènghuáng gǔchéng).

Much of Fènghuáng can be seen for free, but the **through ticket** (tōngpiào; 📞322 3315; ¥148) allows two days' access to major sights and a half-hour boat ride

from the North Gate Tower down the Tuó River (Tuó Jiāng).

INSIDE THE CITY WALL

City Wall Historic Site
(城墙, Chéngqiáng) Restored fragments of the city wall lie along the south bank of the Tuó River. Carvings of fish and mythical beasts adorn the eaves of the **North Gate Tower** (北门城楼; Běimén Chénglóu), one of four original main gates. Another, the **East Gate Tower** (东门城楼; Dōngmén Chénglóu; admission with through ticket), is a twin-eaved tower of sandstone and fired brick.

Hóng Bridge Bridge
(虹桥, Hóng Qiáo; through ticket for upstairs galleries) In the style of the Dong minority's wind and rain bridges.

Yáng Family Ancestral Hall Historic Site
(杨家祠堂, Yángjiā Cítáng; admission with through ticket) West of East Gate Tower. Built in 1836, its exterior is covered with slogans from the Cultural Revolution.

Tiānhòu Temple Temple
(天后宫, Tiānhòu Gōng) Off Dongzheng Jie, dedicated to the patron of seafarers.

319

Fènghuáng

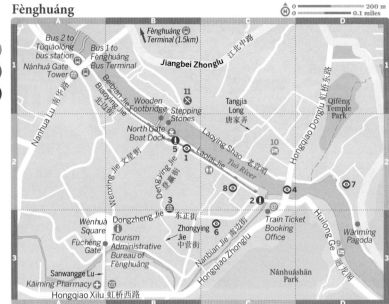

Fènghuáng

Gǔchéng Museum   Museum

(古城博物馆, Gǔchéng Bówùguǎn; Dengying Jie; admission with through ticket; ⊙6.30am-6pm) A survey of the old town's history.

OUTSIDE THE CITY WALL

The north bank of the river offers lovely views of Fènghuáng's *diàojiǎolóu* (吊脚楼; **stilt houses**). Cross by *tiàoyán* (跳岩; **stepping stones**), best navigated when sober, or the *mùtóu qiáo* (木头桥; **wooden footbridge**).

Wànshòu Temple   Historic Site

(万寿宫, Wànshòu Gōng; admission with through ticket) Built in 1755 by Jiāngxī arrivals, this assembly hall north of Wànmíng Pagoda houses a minority culture museum.

Southern Great Wall   Architecture

(南方长城, Nánfāng Chángchéng; admission ¥45) The Ming-dynasty defensive wall, 13km from town, once stretched to Guìzhōu province. Take bus 2 from Nánhuá Gate Tower to its terminus at Tǔqiáolǒng bus station (土桥垅车站; Tǔqiáolǒng chēzhàn), from where you can catch a bus here.

🛏 Sleeping

Inns are easy to find in Fènghuáng. In July and August, rates triple and rooms go quickly, so book ahead.

A Good Year
Guesthouse $

(一年好时光; Yī Nián Hǎo Shíguāng; ☎322 2026; 91 Huilong Ge, 迴龙阁91号; r¥100-130; ❄❧) There are just 10 rooms in this sweet, wood-framed inn on the river; all have balconies, showers and TVs but six have fantastic river views (¥130). Air-con is ¥20 extra.

Phoenix Jiāngtiān Holiday Village
Hotel $$$

(凤凰江天旅游度假村; Fènghuáng Jiāngtiān Lǚyóu Dùjiàcūn; ☎326 1998; Jiangtian Sq, 虹桥路江天广场; r from ¥588, discounted to ¥288; ❄@❧) The only proper hotel by the old town, Phoenix has decent, good-sized rooms, but bathrooms are small and there are no river views.

Eating & Drinking

There are woefully few mellow watering holes. Bars wake up with a shout at nightfall along **Laoying Shao** (老营哨; Lǎoyíng Shào) on the river's north bank, and opposite along Beibian Jie and the north end of Huilong Ge.

Miss Yang Restaurant
Hunan $$

(杨小姐的餐厅; Yángxiǎojiede Cāntīng; 45 Laoying Shao; 老营哨45号; mains ¥30-80; ⏰11am-9pm) Specialising in local cuisine, particularly that of the Miao and the Tujia people, this intimate restaurant serves some truly tasty delights, including Fènghuáng's most famous dish, Fènghuáng xuèbāyā (凤凰血粑鸭; duck-blood cakes). Trust us: it's much nicer than it sounds.

Information

The main bank branches are on Nanhua Lu. **China Construction Bank** (中国建设银行; Zhōngguó Jiànshè Yínháng) has a currency exchange and 24-hour ATM.

Getting There & Around

Buses from **Fènghuáng bus terminal** (凤凰汽车客运总站; Fènghuáng Qìchē Kèyùn Zǒngzhàn) include the following:

Huáihuà ¥40, three hours, hourly, 8am to 6pm

Jíshǒu ¥22, one hour, frequent, 6.30am to 7.30pm

Zhāngjiājiè ¥80, 4½ hours, hourly, 8.30am to 5pm

There's no train station in Fènghuáng; book tickets at the **train ticket booking office** (火车代票处, Huǒchē Dàipiàochù; ☎322 2410; Hongqiao Zhonglu; ⏰8am-10pm) south of Hóng Bridge.

Xiàmén 厦门

☎0592 / POP 668,000

With its quaint historical buildings, neat streets and charming waterfront district, you can understand why Xiàmén, also known to the West as Amoy, is a popular holiday destination for Chinese flashpackers.

The highlight of Xiàmén is to stay on the tiny island of Gǔlàng Yǔ, once the old colonial roost of Europeans and Japanese.

HISTORY

Xiàmén was founded around the mid-14th century in the early years of the Ming dynasty, when the city walls were built and the town was established as a major seaport and commercial centre. In the 17th century it became a place of refuge for the Ming rulers fleeing the Manchu invaders.

In August 1841 a British naval force of 38 ships carrying artillery and soldiers sailed into Xiàmén harbour, forcing the port to open. Xiàmén then became one of the first treaty ports. Japanese and Western powers followed soon after, establishing consulates and making Gǔlàng Yǔ a foreign enclave.

Sights

The most absorbing part of Xiàmén is near the western (waterfront) district, directly opposite the small island of Gǔlàng Yǔ.

Nánpǔtuó Temple
Buddhist

(南普陀寺, Nánpǔtuó Sì; Siming Nanlu; ⏰8am-6pm) FREE This Buddhist temple complex on the southern side of Xiàmén is one of the most famous temples among the Fujianese, and is also considered a pilgrimage site by dedicated followers from Southeast Asia. The temple has been repeatedly destroyed and rebuilt. Its latest incarnation dates to the early 20th century, and today it's an active and busy temple with chanting monks and worshippers lighting incense.

🛏 Sleeping

Xiàmén is a popular, year-round destination in China, so making a reservation well in advance is essential.

Yue Hotel Boutique Hotel **$$**
(悦雅居酒店, Yuèyǎjū Jiǔdiàn; ☑206 7518; www.yuehotel.com; 21 Nanhua Lu, 南华路21号; r¥340-560; ❄@📶) Identifiable by two blocks of red-brick houses, this boutique hotel has a dozen well-presented rooms. Ask for one with balcony. The hotel is just a stone's throw from Xiàmén University and Nánpǔtuó Temple.

Hotel Indigo Xiàmén Harbour Hotel **$$$**
(厦门海港英迪格酒店, Xiàmén Hǎigǎng Yīndígé Jiǔdiàn; ☑226 1666; www.hotelindigo.com; 16 Lujiang Dao, 鹭江道16号; d¥2600-3600; ➸❄@) This chain hotel at the water-front district has found a balance between funky and kitschy in its design and decor. Both business travellers and tourists will appreciate the central location and the generous number of rooms with sweeping harbour views. Staff are attentive. Discounts of around 50% are available.

🍴 Eating

Seaview Restaurant Dim Sum **$$**
(鹭江宾馆观海厅, Lùjiāng Bīnguǎn Guānhǎitīng; 7th fl, 54 Lujiang Dao, 鹭江道54号; meals from ¥80; ⏱10am-10pm) What's better than sipping tea and enjoying freshly made dim sum on a sun-kissed terrace with sweeping harbour views? This rooftop restaurant in **Lùjiāng Harbourview Hotel** (鹭江宾馆, Lùjiāng Bīnguǎn; ☑202 2922; www.lujiang-hotel.com; s¥670-730, sea-view d¥929-1040; ❄@) is a choice place to savour Fujianese street snacks in a comfy setting. No English dim sum menu, but you can pick what you want from the cooking stations.

ℹ Information

Bank of China (中国银行, Zhōngguó Yínháng; 6 Zhongshan Lu) The 24-hour ATM accepts international cards.

City Medical Consultancy (来福诊所, Láifú Zhěnsuǒ; ☑532 3168; 123 Xidi Villa Hubin Beilu; ⏱8am-5pm Mon-Fri, to noon Sat) English-speaking doctors; expat frequented. Telephone-operated 24 hours.

Public Security Bureau (PSB; 公安局; Gōng'ānjú; ☑226 2203; 45-47 Xinhua Lu) Opposite the main post and telephone office. The **visa section** (出入证管理处, chūrùjìng guǎnlǐchù; open 8.10am to 11.45am and 2.40pm to 5.15pm Monday to Saturday) is in the northeastern part of the building on Gongyuan Nanlu.

Nánpǔtuó Temple (p321)
THOMAS ROETTING/LOOK-FOTO/GETTY IMAGES ©

What's On Xiamen (www.whatsonxiamen.com) Up-to-date information on Xiàmén.

Getting There & Away

Air

Air China, China Southern, Xiàmén Airlines and several other domestic airlines operate flights to/from Xiàmén to all major domestic airports in China. There are international flights to/from Bangkok, Hong Kong, Jakarta, Kuala Lumpur, Los Angeles, Manila, Osaka, Penang, Singapore and Tokyo.

Boat

There are ferry services to Kinmen (Jīnmén) in Taiwan (¥150, one hour, hourly).

Bus

Buses to the following destinations leave from **Húbīn long-distance bus station** (湖滨长途汽车站, Húbīn chángtú qìchēzhàn; 58 Hubin Nanlu) and tickets can also be bought two days in advance at the ticket booth in the local bus terminal adjacent to Xiàmén University at the end of Siming Nanlu:

Guǎngzhōu ¥227, nine hours, two daily

Lóngyán ¥75, three hours, eight daily

Nánjīng (in Fújiàn) ¥28, two hours, 11 daily

Yǒngdìng ¥75, four hours, nine daily

Train

Xiàmén's main train station is on Xiahe Lu. All trains stop at Xiàmén north station 25km north of the city centre. Tickets can be booked through the **train ticketing booth** (☎ 203 8565; cnr Xinhua Lu & Zhongshan Lu) behind the Gem Hotel (金后酒店; Jīnhòu Jiǔdiàn).

Hángzhōu ¥282 to ¥357, seven hours

Shànghǎi ¥328 to ¥413, 7½ hours

Getting Around

To/From the Airport

Xiàmén airport is 15km from the waterfront district. Taxis cost around ¥45.

Gǔlàng Yǔ   鼓浪屿

☎ 0592

The small island of Gǔlàng Yǔ is the trump card of Xiàmén. Just a five-minute boat ride away, you'll find yourself on a breezy islet with warrens of backstreets, set in the architectural kaleidoscope of more than 1000 colonial villas, imposing mansions and ancient banyan trees.

The foreign community was well established on Gǔlàng Yǔ by the 1880s, with a daily English newspaper, churches, hospitals, post and telegraph offices, libraries, hotels and consulates. In 1903 the island was officially designated an International Foreign Settlement, and a municipal council with a police force of Sikhs was established to govern it.

Sights

Consulate Inn   Historic Building
(永顺卡斯特宾馆; Yǒngshùn Kǎsītè Bīnguǎn; ☎ 206 0920; 14-16 Lujiao Lu; r ¥466) A three-storey Victorian-style building, formerly the British Consulate and currently running as a hotel.

Ecclesia Catholica   Church
(鼓浪屿天主堂, Gǔlàngyǔ Tiānzhǔtáng; 34 Lujiao Lu) A magnificent snow-white Gothic-style church built in 1917.

Former Spanish Consulate   Historic Building
(西班牙领事馆, Xībānyá lǐngshìguǎn) A historic 19th century building, standing next to Ecclesia Catholica.

Former Japanese Consulate   Historic Building
(日本领事馆, Rìběn lǐngshìguǎn; 26 Lujiao Lu) A handsome red-brick building located to the southwest of Gǔlàng Yǔ.

Huáng Róngyuǎn Villa   Performance Venue
(黄荣远堂; Huángróngyuǎn Táng; ☎ 257 0510; 32 Fujian Lu; admission ¥118; ⏰8.30am-5pm, seven shows daily) A marvellous pillared building that now houses the Puppet Art Centre.

Sānyī Church   Church
(三一堂, Sānyī Táng; 67 Anhai Lu) A protestant church built in 1934.

Organ Museum   Museum
(风琴博物馆, Fēngqín Bówùguǎn; 43 Guxin Lu, 鼓新路43号; admission ¥20; ⏰8.40am-5.30pm) Housed in the highly distinctive Bāguà Lóu (八卦楼) building is the Organ Museum,

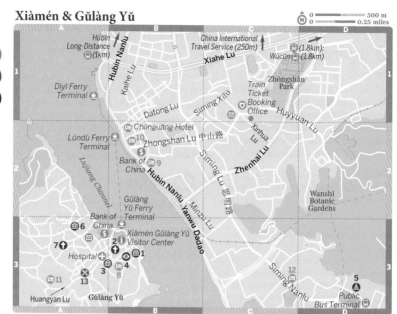

Xiàmén & Gǔlàng Yǔ

⊙ Sights

1	Consulate Inn	B3
2	Ecclesia Catholica	B3
3	Former Japanese Consulate	A3
	Former Spanish Consulate	(see 3)
4	Huáng Róngyuǎn Villa	B3
5	Nánpǔtuó Temple	D3
6	Organ Museum	A3
7	Sānyī Church	A3

⊟ Sleeping

8	Gǔlàng Yǔ Lù Fēi International Youth Hostel	B3
9	Hotel Indigo Xiàmén Harbour	B2
10	Lùjiāng Harbourview Hotel	B2
11	Miryam Boutique Hotel	A3
12	Yue Hotel	C3

⊗ Eating

	Seaview Restaurant	(see 10)
13	The Chu Family Coffee	A3

with a fantastic collection including a Norman & Beard organ from 1909.

🛏 Sleeping

There's a plethora of accommodation choices in Gǔlàng Yǔ; however, its popularity means booking in advance is a must. Cars aren't allowed on the island, so it's a good idea to book a hotel closer to the ferry terminal if you are bringing a lot of luggage.

Gǔlàng Yǔ Lù Fēi International Youth Hostel
Hostel $

(鼓浪屿鹭飞国际青年旅舍, Gǔlàng Yǔ Lù Fēi Guójì Qīngnián Lǚshè; ☏208 2678; www.yha14f. cn; 20 Guxin Lu, 鼓新路20号; dm ¥65, s & d ¥260-380; ✳ @ 🛜) Rooms are cute and sparklingly clean, and each has a theme. We love its pastel hues and wrought-iron beds. It's 400m west of the ferry terminal.

Miryam Boutique Hotel
Boutique Hotel $$$

(Miryam老别墅旅馆, Miryam Lǎo Biéshù Lǚguǎn; ☏206 2505; www.miryamhotel.com; 70 Huangyan Lu, 晃岩路70号; r ¥688-1688; ✳ @ 🛜) Miryam is located right below Sunlight Rock and is housed in an opulent Victorian-era mansion. Rooms are ultra-spacious, with antique bits and pieces of furniture to give them character. The food served in the attached restaurant is as dreamy as the surroundings.

✕ Eating

The Chu Family Coffee   Cafe $$
(褚家园咖啡馆, Chǔjiāyuán Kāfēiguǎn; ☎206 3651; 15 Zhonghua Lu; meals from ¥60; ⊙11am-9pm) Behind the red-brick wall is this sleek cafe with a very nice, leafy alfresco area. Caffeine addicts can find their *real* cup of coffee here. The tiramisu is a delight, too.

ℹ Information

Bank of China (中国银行, Zhōngguó Yínháng; 2 Longtou Lu; ⊙9am-7pm) Forex and 24-hour ATM.

Hospital (Yīyuàn; 60 Fujian Lu) Has its own miniature ambulance for the small roads.

Xiàmén Gǔlàng Yǔ Visitor Center (Xiàmén Gǔlàng Yǔ Yóukè Zhōngxīn; Longtou Lu) Left luggage ¥3 to ¥5.

ℹ Getting There & Around

Ferries for the five-minute trip to Gǔlàng Yǔ leave from **Lúndù ferry terminal** (轮渡) just west of Xiàmén's Lùjiāng Harbourview Hotel. The round-trip fare is ¥8 (getting on the upper deck costs an additional ¥1). Boats run between 5.45am and midnight.

Fújiàn Tǔlóu 福建土楼

☎0597 / POP 40,200

Scattered all over the pretty, rolling countryside in southwestern Fújiàn, the remarkable *tǔlóu* (roundhouse; 土楼) are vast, fortified earthen edifices that have been home to both the Hakka and the Mǐnnán (Fujianese) people since the year dot.

Since Unesco status was conferred on 46 *tǔlóu* in 2008, the local government has been in a flap revamping.

◎ Sights

The most notable of the 3000-odd *tǔlóu* are lumped into various clusters, and they are in the vicinity of two main counties: Nánjìng (南靖) and Yǒngdìng (永定). Only the three most developed clusters: Hóngkēng, Tiánluókēng and Yúnshuǐyáo

are accessible by public transport. However, bus services are neither frequent nor punctual. Booking a tour or hiring a vehicle is recommended if you want to venture off the beaten path and see more.

HÓNGKĒNG TǓLÓU CLUSTER   洪坑土楼群

Cluster admission is ¥90.

Zhènchéng Lóu   Tǔlóu
(振成楼) This most visited *tǔlóu* is a grandiose structure built in 1912, with two concentric circles and a total of 222 rooms. The ancestral hall in the centre of the *tǔlóu* is complete with Western-style pillars. The locals dub this *tǔlóu wángzǐ* (土楼王子), the prince *tǔlóu*.

Kuíjù Lóu   Tǔlóu
(奎聚楼) Near Zhènchéng Lóu, this much older, square *tǔlóu* dates back to 1834.

Rúshēng Lóu   Tǔlóu
(如升楼) The smallest of the roundhouses, this late-19th-century, pea-sized *tǔlóu* has only one ring and 16 rooms.

Fúyù Lóu   Tǔlóu
(福裕楼) Along the river, this five-storey square *tǔlóu* boasts some wonderfully carved wooden beams and pillars. Rooms are available here from ¥100.

TIÁNLUÓKĒNG TǓLÓU CLUSTER   田螺坑土楼群

A pilgrimage to the earthen castles is not complete if you miss Tiánluókēng (田螺坑), which is 37km northeast of Nánjìng and home to arguably the most picturesque cluster of *tǔlóu* in the region. The locals affectionately call the five noble buildings 'four dishes with one soup' because of their shapes: circular, square and oval.

There's one direct bus (¥47, 3½ hours) to the cluster from Xiàmén, leaving at 8.30am. Cluster admission is ¥100.

YÚNSHUǏYÁO TǓLÓU CLUSTER   云水谣土楼群

The cluster, 48km northeast of Nánjìng, is set in idyllic surrounds with rolling hills, verdant farms and babbling streams. There are six buses (¥20) to Yúnshuǐyáo (云水谣) that leave from the bus station in Nánjìng. The admission is ¥90.

🛏 Sleeping & Eating

There are many hotels in Yǒngdìng and Nánjìng, but neither town is attractive. We recommend you base yourself in a *tǔlóu*, which will give you a glimpse of a vanishing dimension of life in China. Bring a flashlight (torch) and bug repellent. Most families can cook up meals for you.

You will be able to find a room in most of the *tǔlóu* you visit as many families have now moved out. Some *tǔlóu* have upgraded their rooms with modern facilities, but most are still very basic – a bed, a flask of hot water and a fan. You might also find that the toilets are on the outside, and the huge gates to the *tǔlóu* shut around 8pm.

Most *tǔlóu* owners can also organise a pick-up from Xiàmén and transport for touring the area.

Fúyù Lóu Chángdì Inn Tǔlóu **$**
(福裕楼常棣客栈; Fúyù Lóu Chángdì Kèzhàn; 📞 553 2800, 1379 9097 962; www.fuyulou. net; Hóngkēng Tǔlóu Cluster; d incl breakfast ¥100-150; 📶) Rooms are basic but comfy. Doubles complete with fan and TV. The owners are friendly and speak some English.

ℹ Getting There & Away

Bus
Nánjìng From Xiàmén long-distance bus station, take a bus headed to Nánjìng (¥32, two hours, 12 daily between 7am and 5.30pm).
Yǒngdìng Xiàmén has seven daily buses to Yǒngdìng (永定县; ¥75, four hours) from 7.10am to 4pm. From there, there are infrequent buses to Gāoběi Tǔlóu Cluster. Yǒngdìng can also be accessed by bus from Guǎngdōng and Lóngyán (¥20, one hour, regular).

Train
Ten high-speed D trains link Xiàmén and Lóngyán via Nánjìng (¥27, 35 minutes) daily. Local buses 1 and 2 link the train and bus stations in Nánjìng.

ℹ Getting Around

The easiest way to see the *tǔlóu* is to book a tour, or hire a vehicle either from Xiàmén, Nánjìng or Yǒngdìng. You'll find taxi drivers in Yǒngdìng and Nánjìng offering their services for around ¥400 a day (¥700 if you hire for two days), setting off early morning and returning late afternoon. Expect to see two clusters per day.
Amazing Fujian Tulou (www.amazing fujiantulou.com) and Discover Fujian (www. discoverfujian.com) can organise English-speaking guided tours.

Tǔlóu
TUUL AND BRUNO MORANDI/GETTY IMAGES ©

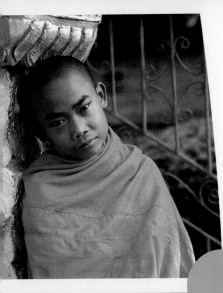

The Best of the Rest

Yúnnán (p328)
Lìjiāng and Dàlǐ are two of China's most attractive ancient towns, embedded in a fantastic landscape that includes the dramatic Tiger Leaping Gorge.

Sìchuān (p336)
Home of China's spiciest cuisine and a mountainous frontier with Tibet, Sìchuān is also the habitat of the reclusive Giant Panda.

Silk Road (p340)
China's ancient Silk Road – running through Gānsù and Xīnjiāng – passes by the astonishing Mògāo Caves and the dramatic Great Wall fort of Jiāyùguān.

Top: Buddhist monk outside temple; **Bottom:** Walking along the Silk Road

(TOP) AUSTIN BUSH/GETTY IMAGES ©; (LEFT) MATTHIEU PALEY/GETTY IMAGES ©

Yúnnán

HIGHLIGHTS

① **Dàlǐ** Funky Bai town surrounded by stunning scenery.

② **Lìjiāng** (p331) Extraordinary Naxi town with riveting ethnic textures.

③ **Yùlóng Xuěshān** (p332) One of China's most stunning mountains.

④ **Tiger Leaping Gorge** (p333) Yúnnán's – and possibly China's – greatest trek.

Temple overlooking rice terraces, Yúnnán
CHINAFACE/GETTY IMAGES ©

DÀLǏ 大理
📞0872 / POP 40,000

Dàlǐ, the original funky banana-pancake backpacker hang-out in Yúnnán, was once *the* place to chill, with its stunning location sandwiched between mountains and Ěrhǎi Lake (Ěrhǎi Hú).

Over the past decade the Chinese tourist market discovered Dàlǐ and the scene changed accordingly. Still, Dàlǐ has not succumbed to the tourist mania that infected nearby Lìjiāng and remains a reasonably relaxed destination, with the local population still a part of daily life.

◎ Sights

Three Pagodas   Pagoda
(三塔寺, Sān Tǎ Sì; adult incl Chóngshèng Temple ¥121; ⊙7am-7pm) Absolutely *the* symbol of the town/region, these pagodas, a 2km walk north of the north gate, are among the oldest standing structures in southwestern China. The tallest of the three, **Qiānxún Pagoda**, has 16 tiers that reach a height of 70m. It was originally erected in the mid-9th century by engineers from Xī'ān. It is flanked by two smaller 10-tiered pagodas, each of which are 42m high.

✺ Festivals & Events

Third Moon Festival   Cultural
Merrymaking – along with endless buying, selling and general horse-trading (but mostly partying) – takes place during the third moon fair (*sānyuè jié*), which begins on the 15th day of the third lunar month (usually April) and ends on the 21st day.

Torch Festival   Cultural
The torch festival (*huǒbǎ jié*) is held on the 24th day of the sixth lunar month (normally July) and is likely to be the best photo op in the province. Flaming torches are paraded at night through homes and fields. Locals throw pine resin at the torches causing minor explosions everywhere. According to one local guesthouse owner, 'it's total madness'.

🛌 Sleeping

Jade Emu   Hostel $

(金玉缘中澳国际青年旅舍, Jīnyùyuán Zhōng'ào Guójì Qīngnián Lǚshè; ☏0872 267 7311; www.jade-emu.com; West Gate Village, 西门村; 4-bed dm with bathroom ¥40, 6-bed dm without/with bathroom ¥25/35, d/tw ¥150-180; @ 🛜) Smack in the shadow of Cāng Shān (a five-minute walk from the old town), the Jade Emu sets the standard for hostels in Dàlǐ and elsewhere with its attention to detail. There's an in-house VPN for access to social media sites banned in China, while the dorm beds are more comfortable than most and the staff efficient and friendly.

Jim's Tibetan Hotel   Hotel $$

(吉姆和平酒店, Jímǔ Hépíng Jiǔdiàn; ☏0872 267 7824; www.china-travel.nl; 13 Yuxiu Lu, 玉秀路13号; s/d ¥300; ✳@🛜) The rooms here are some of the most distinctive in Dàlǐ, coming with Tibetan motifs and packed with antique Chinese-style furniture. The bathrooms too are a cut above the competition, while there's a garden, rooftop terrace, restaurant and bar. Travel services and tours can be booked.

🍴 Eating

Good Panda   Yunnan $

(妙香园, Miàoxiāng Yuán; 81 Renmin Lu, 人民路81号; dishes from ¥18; ⏱9am-10pm) Surrounded by Western-style restaurants, this is a more local joint and a good

introduction to classic Dàlǐ dishes like sizzling beef (*tiěbǎn niúròu*) and crispy carp (*jiànchuān gānshāo yú*), plus Yúnnán and Sìchuān food. There's a limited English menu, but you can point at the vegetables that look best. The patio is an excellent spot for people-watching.

ⓘ Information

On hikes around Cāng Shān there have been several reports of robbery of solo walkers.

Bank of China (中国银行, Zhōngguó Yínháng; Fuxing Lu) Changes cash and travellers cheques, and has an ATM that accepts all major credit cards.

Public Security Bureau (PSB, 公安局, Gōng'ānjú; ☎0872 214 2149; Dàlǐ Rd, Xiàguān; ☺8-11am & 2-5pm Mon-Fri) Note that visas cannot be renewed in Dàlǐ; you have to go to Xiàguān.

ⓘ Getting There & Away

The golden rule: most buses advertised to Dàlǐ actually go to Xiàguān. Coming from Lìjiāng,

Xiàguān-bound buses stop at the eastern end of Dàlǐ to let passengers off before continuing on to the Xīngshèng bus station.

From Kūnmíng's west bus station there are numerous buses to **Dàlǐ** (¥138, four to five hours, every 20 minutes from 7.20am to 8pm).

Heading north, it's easiest to pick up a bus on the roads outside the west or east gates; buy your ticket in advance from your guesthouse or a travel agent and they'll make sure you get on the right one.

From the old town (near West Gate Village) you can catch a 30-seat bus to **Kūnmíng** for ¥110, it runs four or five times a day, departing 9am, 10.30am, 11.30am, 1.30pm and 4.30pm.

ⓘ Getting Around

From Dàlǐ, a taxi to Xiàguān airport takes 45 minutes and costs around ¥100; to Xiàguān's train station it costs ¥50.

Buses (¥3, 30 minutes, marked 大理) run between the old town and Xiàguān from as early as 6.30am; wait along the highway and flag one down. Bus 8 runs between Dàlǐ and central Xiàguān (¥2, 30 minutes) on the way to the train station every 15 minutes from 6.30am.

Left: Black Dragon Pool Park, Lìjiāng;
Below: Regional-style shoes on display
(LEFT) FENG WEI PHOTOGRAPHY/GETTY IMAGES ©; (BELOW) PICTUREGARDEN/GETTY IMAGES ©

BEST OF THE REST YÚNNÁN

LÌJIĀNG
丽江

📞 0888 / POP (OLD TOWN) 40,000

A Unesco World Heritage Site since 1997, Lìjiāng is a city of two halves: the old town and the very different and modern new town. The old town is where you'll be spending your time and it's a jumble of lanes that twist and turn.

◎ Sights

Note that a ¥80 'protection fee' is sold at most guesthouses and provides free entry to Black Dragon Pool.

Old Town   Historic Site
(古城) The old town is centred around the busy and touristy **Old Market Square** (四方街; Sìfāng Jiē). The surrounding lanes are dissected by a web of artery-like canals that once brought the city's drinking water from Yuquan Spring, on the far outskirts of what is now Black Dragon Pool Park. Several wells and pools are still in use around town (but hard to find). Where there are three pools, these were designated into pools for drinking, washing clothes and washing vegetables.

Black Dragon Pool Park   Park
(黑龙潭公园, Hēilóngtán Gōngyuán; Xin Dajie; admission free with ¥80 town entrance ticket; ⏰ 7am-7pm) On the northern edge of town is the Black Dragon Pool Park; its view of **Yùlóng Xuěshān** (Jade Dragon Snow Mountain) is the most obligatory photo shoot in southwestern China. The **Dōngbā Research Institute** (东巴文化研究室, Dōngbā Wénhuà Yánjiūshì; ⏰ 8am-5pm Mon-Fri) is part of a renovated complex on the hillside here. You can see Naxi cultural artefacts and scrolls featuring a unique pictograph script.

🛏 Sleeping

Throw a stick and you'll hit a Naxi guesthouse in the old town. In peak seasons

331

(especially holidays), prices double (or more).

Blossom Hill Joyland
Boutique Hotel $$$

(花间堂, Huājiān Táng; ☎ 400 076 7123; www.blossomhillinn.com; 55 Wenhua Xiang, Wuyi Jie; 五一街文华巷55号; d/tw ¥880-1586; ❄ 🛜) There are only 18 rooms, all individually decorated in very tasteful and comfortable fashion, at this boutique inn in the heart of the old town. Bathrooms are modern and large, while each room comes with its own collection of antiques and wood furnishings. Staff are helpful and there's a small common area with a library. It's essential to book ahead.

🍴 Eating

Āmāyì Nàxī Snacks
Yunnan $$

(阿妈意纳西饮食院, Āmāyì Nàxī Yīnshí Yuàn; ☎ 0888 530 9588; Wuyi Jie; dishes from ¥28; ⏰ 11am-9.30pm) The name doesn't do justice to the small but select and very authentic selection of Naxi cuisine on offer at this calm courtyard restaurant. There are fantastic mushroom dishes, as well as *zhútǒng fàn*, rice that comes packed in bamboo. It's down an alley off Wuyi Jie, close to the Stone Bridge.

⭐ Entertainment

Nàxī Orchestra
Live Music

(纳西古乐会, Nàxī Gǔyuè Huì, Nàxī Music Academy; Xinhua Jie, 新华街; tickets ¥120-160; ⏰ performances 8pm) Attending a performance of this orchestra inside a beautiful building in the old town is a good way to spend an evening in Lìjiāng. Not only are all two dozen or so members Naxi, but they play a type of Taoist temple music (known as *dòngjīng*) that has been lost elsewhere in China.

ℹ️ Information

Bank of China (中国银行, Zhōngguó Yínháng; Yuyuan Lu; ⏰ 9am-5pm) This branch has an ATM and is convenient for the old town. There are many ATMs in the old town, too.

Public Security Bureau (PSB, 公安局, Gōng'ānjú; ☎ 0888 518 8437; 110 Taihe Jie, Xianghelicheng District; ⏰ 8.30-11.30am & 2.30-5.30pm Mon-Fri) Reputedly speedy with visa extensions. Located on the west side of the Government Building. A taxi here will cost ¥15 from the city centre.

ℹ️ Getting There & Away

Air

Lìjiāng's airport is 28km east of town. Tickets can be booked at **Civil Aviation Administration of China** (CAAC; 中国民航, Zhōngguó Mínháng; cnr Fuhui Lu & Shangrila Dadao; ⏰ 8.30am-9pm).

Bus

The main **long-distance bus station** (客运站, kèyùnzhàn) is south of the old town; to get here, take bus 8 or 11 (¥1; the latter is faster) from along Minzhu Lu.

Train

There are six trains daily to **Dàlǐ** (¥34, two hours, 7.39am to 10.55pm) and eight trains to **Kūnmíng** (hard sleeper ¥147, nine hours, 7.39am to 11.20pm).

ℹ️ Getting Around

Buses to the **airport** (¥20) leave from outside the CAAC office, 6.30am to 10pm.

Taxis flagfall is ¥8, although you will struggle to get drivers to use their meters. Taxis are not allowed into the old town. Bike hire is available at most hostels (¥40 per day).

AROUND LÌJIĀNG

Yùlóng Xuěshān 玉龙雪山

Also known as Mt Satseto, **Yùlóng Xuěshān** (玉龙雪山, Jade Dragon Snow Mountain; adult ¥105, protection fee ¥80) soars to some 5500m.

Buses from Lìjiāng arrive at a parking area where you can purchase tickets for the various cable cars and chairlifts that ascend the mountain. This is also where the **Impression Lìjiāng** (admission ¥190-260; ⏱daily 1pm) show is held, a megasong and dance performance. Note that if you are going to the performance you will also have to pay the park admission fees. Close to the parking area is **Dry Sea Meadow** (干海子; Gānhǎizi), a good spot for photographing the mountain.

A cable car (¥185) ascends the mountain to an elevation of 4506m, from here you can walk up another 200m to a viewing point to see the glacier near the peak. It can often get chilly near the top so bring warm clothes. You will also have to pay ¥20 for the bus ticket to the base of the cable car.

Minibuses (¥30) leave from opposite Mao Square. Returning to Lìjiāng, buses leave fairly regularly but check with your driver to find out what time the last bus will depart.

Tiger Leaping Gorge 虎跳峡

📞0887

Gingerly stepping along a trail swept with scree to allow an old fellow with a donkey to pass; resting atop a rock, exhausted, looking up to see the fading sunlight dance between snow-shrouded peaks, then down to see the lingering rays dancing on the rippling waters 1km away; feeling utterly exhilarated. That pretty much sums up **Tiger Leaping Gorge** (虎跳峡; Hǔtiào Xiá; admission ¥65), the unmissable trek of southwest China.

One of the deepest gorges in the world, it measures 16km long and is a giddy 3900m from the waters of the Jīnshā River (Jīnshā Jiāng) to the snowcapped mountains of Hābā Mountain (Hābā Shān) to the west and Yùlóng Xuěshān to the east, and, despite the odd danger, it's gorgeous almost every single step of the way.

The gorge hike is not to be taken lightly. The path constricts and crumbles; it certainly can wreck the knees. When it's raining (especially in July and August), landslides and swollen waterfalls can block the paths, in particular on the low

road. (The best time to come is May and the start of June, when the hills are afire with plant and flower life.)

A few people – including a handful of foreign travellers – have died in the gorge. During the past decade, there have also been cases of travellers being assaulted on the trail. As always, it's safer in all ways not to do the hike alone.

Check with cafes and lodgings in Lìjiāng or Qiáotóu for trail and weather updates. Make sure you bring plenty of water on this hike – 2L to 3L is ideal – as well as plenty of sunscreen and lip balm.

 **Activities**

HIKING

There are two trails: the higher (the older route) and the lower, which follows the new road and is best avoided unless you enjoy being enveloped in clouds of dust from passing tour buses and 4WDs. While the scenery is stunning wherever you are in the gorge, it's absolutely sublime from the high trail.

It's six hours to Běndìwān, eight hours to Middle Gorge (Tina's Guesthouse), or nine hours to Walnut Garden. By stopping overnight at one of the many guesthouses along the way, you'll have the time to appreciate the magnificent vistas on offer at almost every turn of the trail.

Ponies can be hired (their owners will find you) to take you to the gorge's highest point for ¥200; it's not uncommon to see three generations of a family together, with the oldies on horseback and the young ones panting on foot behind them.

The following route starts at **Jane's Guesthouse**. Walk away from **Qiáotóu** (桥头), past the school, for five minutes or so, then head up the paved road branching to the left; there's an arrow to guide you. After about 2.5km on the road the gorge trail proper starts and the serious climbing begins.

The toughest section of the hike comes after **Nuòyú** (诺余) village, when the trail winds through the 28 agonising bends, or turns that lead to the highest point of the gorge. Count on five hours at normal pace to get through and reach **Yāchà** (牙叉) village. It's a relatively straightforward walk on to **Běndìwān** (本地湾). About 1½ hours on from there, you begin the descent to the road on slippery, poor paths.

After the path meets the road at **Tina's Guesthouse**, there's a good detour that leads down 40 minutes to the middle rapids and **Tiger Leaping Stone**, where a tiger is once said to have leapt across the Yangzi River, thus giving the gorge its name. From one of the lower rest points another trail (¥10) heads downstream for a one hour walk to **Walnut Garden** (核桃园).

Most hikers stop at Tina's, have lunch, and head back to Qiáotóu. Those continuing to Walnut Garden can take the trail along the river or use an alternative trail that keeps high where the path descends to Tina's, and crosses a stream and a 'bamboo forest' before descending into Walnut Garden. If you are deciding where to spend the night, Walnut Garden is more attractive than Tina's.

🛌 Sleeping

QIÁOTÓU

Jane's Guesthouse
Guesthouse $

(峡谷行客栈, Xiágǔ Xíng Kèzhàn; ☏0888 880 6570; 4-bed dm ¥30, d or tw without/with bathroom ¥60/120; @🛜) This friendly place with tidy, clean rooms is where many people start their trek. The breakfasts here make for good walking fuel and it has left-luggage facilities (¥5 a bag).

IN THE GORGE

Naxi Family Guesthouse
Guesthouse $

(纳西雅阁, Nàxī Kèzhàn; ☏0888 880 6928; dm ¥30, d/tw ¥120; @🛜) Taking your time to spend a night here instead of double-timing it to Walnut Garden isn't a bad idea. It's an incredibly friendly, well-run

place (organic vegies and wines), set around a pleasant courtyard.

Come Inn
Guesthouse $

(下一客栈; Xiàyī Kèzhàn; ☏181 8385 3151; 4-bed dm ¥50, d/tw ¥200) Huge dorms with bathrooms and sliding doors that open out onto a vast wooden terrace with super views are on offer at this brand-new guesthouse near the entrance to Běndìwān village. Private rooms are in tip-top condition.

Tina's Guesthouse
Guesthouse $

(中峡旅店, Zhōngxiá Lǚdiàn; ☏0888 820 2258; 2625441148@qq.com; dm ¥30, d/tw ¥120-280; @🛜) Almost a package-holiday operation, with travellers funneled to and from the gorge, Tina's lacks the charm of its competitors. But it's efficiently run, has plenty of beds and the location is perfect for those too knackered to make it to Walnut Garden. Pricier rooms have excellent views. There are daily buses from here to Lìjiāng and Shangri-la (¥55, 3.30pm).

Halfway Guesthouse
Guesthouse $$

(中途客栈, Zhōngtú Kèzhàn; ☏139 8870 0522; Běndìwān; 10-bed dm ¥40, d/tw ¥120-200) Once a simple home to a guy collecting medicinal herbs and his family, this is now a busy-busy operation. The vistas here are awe-inspiring and perhaps the best of any lodging in the gorge; the view from the communal toilets is worth the price of a bed alone.

Sean's Spring Guesthouse
Guesthouse $$

(山泉客栈, Shānquán Kèzhàn; ☏0888 820 2223, 158 9436 7846; www.tigerleapinggorge. com; r ¥60-80, with bathroom ¥160-380; @🛜) One of the original guesthouses on the trail, and still the spot for lively evenings, the eponymous Sean is a true character and one of the few locals seriously concerned with the gorge's environmental well-being. There are 28 rooms here, including a couple of cheapies, and the best have great views of Yùlóng Xuěshān (see p332).

❶ Getting There & Away

From Lìjiāng's long-distance bus station there are two direct buses a day to **Qiáotóu** (¥29, 2¼ hours, 8.30am and 9am). Otherwise, catch any bus to **Shangri-la** (¥40, 2¼ hours, every 40 minutes, 7.30am to 3.30pm) and get off at Qiáotóu.

Most travellers get a minivan (¥35) to the start of the walking track, organised through their guesthouse in Lìjiāng. The minivan can deliver extra luggage to the guesthouse of your choice (usually Tina's or Jane's).

Returning to Lìjiāng from Qiáotóu, buses start passing through from Shangri-la at around 10am. The last one rolls through at around 8pm.

At the time of writing, there were no buses to Báishuǐtái from Lìjiāng.

Sìchuān

HIGHLIGHTS

① **Éméi Shān** Awe-inspiring mountain scenery and sacred Buddhist place of pilgrimage.

② **Grand Buddha** (p337) Buddhist China's most colossal historic statue.

③ **Jiǔzhàigōu National Park** (p339) Idyllic landscape of lakes forests, waterfalls and mountains.

GIANT PANDA BREEDING RESEARCH BASE 大熊猫繁育基地

One of Chéngdū's most popular tourist attractions, this **wildlife reserve** (大熊猫繁育基地, Dàxióngmāo Fányù Jīdì; ☎ 8351 0033; www.panda.org.cn; 1375 Xiongmao Dadao; adult/student ¥58/29; ◷ 8am-5.30pm), 18km north of the city centre, is the easiest way to catch a glimpse of Sìchuān's most famous residents outside of a zoo.

Home to nearly 120 giant and 76 red pandas, the base focuses on getting these shy creatures to breed; March to May is the 'falling in love period', wink, wink. If you visit in autumn or winter, you may see tiny newborns in the nursery. Try to visit the base in the morning, when the pandas are most active.

Catch bus 49 (¥2, 40 minutes) and transfer at Zhāojué Hénglù stop (昭觉横路站) to bus 87 or 198 (¥2, 20 minutes) to the Panda Base stop (熊猫基地站, Xióngmāo Jīdì). Alternatively, from North Train Station take bus 9 (¥2, 60 minutes) to the Zoo stop (动物园站, Dòngwùyuán) and switch to bus 198 (¥2, 20 minutes). Hostels run trips here, too. Metro line 3 will run directly here when it is completed.

ÉMÉI SHĀN 峨眉山

☎ 0833

A cool, misty retreat from the Sìchuān basin's sweltering heat, stunning **Éméi Shān** (峨眉山; ☎ 0883 552 3646; adult/student & seniors ¥185/90, in winter ¥110/55; ◷ 6am-6pm) is one of China's four most famous Buddhist mountains (the others are Pǔtuóshān, Wǔtái Shān and Jiǔhuá Shān).

Sleeping

ON THE MOUNTAIN

Almost all the temples on the mountain (with the notable exception of Jīndǐng Temple at the summit) offer cheap lodgings in dormitory-style accommodation

Giant panda

with shared bathrooms but usually no showers.

Xiānfēng Temple Monastery $

(仙峰寺, Xiānfēng Sì; ☎ 189 8131 0142; dm & tw without bathroom ¥50-240, tw with bathroom ¥600; 🛜) This remote temple hidden in a forest backed by rugged cliffs has a good range of rooms, from dorms to pricey twins with showers. There's even wi-fi in the common space. Approximate walking time from base/summit is about six/four hours.

IN BÀOGUÓ VILLAGE

Teddy Bear Hotel Hostel $$

(玩具熊酒店, Wánjùxióng Jiǔdiàn; ☎ 559 0135, manager 138 9068 1961; www.teddybear.com. cn; 43 Baoguo Lu, next to bus station; dm ¥40, r ¥80-260; ❄ @ 🛜) If you can get past the theme (bears, bears, everywhere), this very clean backpacker hostel offers nice rooms and an English-speaking staff that provides solid, hostel-style travel services plus decent coffee and Western food. The left-luggage service is free, as are walking sticks, crampons, maps, and pick up from Éméi town (call Andy, the manager).

ℹ️ Information

Agricultural Bank of China (农业银行, Nóngyè Yínháng; 🕙9am-5pm) Has a foreign-exchange desk and a foreign-card–friendly ATM. The ATM by Bàoguó village bus station also accepts foreign cards.

ℹ️ Getting There & Away

The town of Éméi (峨眉山市; Éméi Shān Shì) is the transport hub and lies 6.5km east of the park entrance. Most buses terminate at Éméi Shān central station (峨眉山客运中心; Éméi Shān kèyùn zhōngxīn), directly opposite Éméi Railway Station (峨眉火车站; Éméi Huǒchēzhàn). If you ask, some drivers will go all the way to the more convenient Bàoguó village bus station (报国汽车站) – which confusingly is also known as the Éméi Shān tourist bus station (峨眉山旅游客运中心; Éméi Shān lǚyóu kèyùn zhōngxīn) – for ¥10 more. A taxi from Éméi town to Bàoguó village is about ¥25.

Buses from Bàoguó village bus station include:

Chéngdū ¥50, 2½ hours, frequent services from 8am to 6pm

Chóngqìng ¥140, six hours, 8.30am

Lèshān ¥11, 45 minutes, every 20 minutes from 8am to 5pm

Train

Chéngdū K-class ¥24, 2½ hours, seven daily (3.16am to 10.25am, then 6.36pm and 9.15pm)

Kūnmíng K-class seat/hard sleeper ¥124/223, 17 hours, four daily (3.23pm, 4.37pm, 5.19pm and 9.42pm)

Lèshān K-class ¥8, 16 minutes, three daily (7.27am, 10.25am and 6.36pm)

Xī'ān K-class hard/soft sleeper ¥231/364, 20 hours, 10.25am

ℹ️ Getting Around

Buses from Bàoguó village bus station travel to three depots on the mountain: Wǔxiǎngǎng (五显冈; 30 minutes, round trip ¥40), about a 20-minute walk below Qīngyīn Pavilion; Wànnián (万年; 45 minutes; round trip ¥40), below Wànnián Temple; and Léidòngpíng (雷洞坪; 1½ hours, round trip ¥90), a few minutes' walk from Jīn Dǐng cable car. If you return via a different depot, you may have to pay a small surcharge.

Buses run frequently from around 6am to 5pm (7am to 4pm in winter). The last buses head down the mountain at 6pm (5pm in winter).

LÈSHĀN 乐山

🎵0833 / POP 156,000

With fingernails bigger than the average human, the world's largest ancient Buddha draws plenty of tourists to this relaxed riverside town.

◉ Sights

Grand Buddha Buddhist Statue

(大佛, Dàfó; adult ¥90, students & seniors ¥50; 🕙7.30am-6.30pm Apr-early Oct, 8am-5.30pm early Oct-Mar) Lèshān's serene, 1200-year-old Grand Buddha sits in repose, carved from a cliff face overlooking the confluence of three busy rivers: the Dàdù, Mín, and Qīngyì. The Buddhist monk

Haitong conceived the project in AD 713, hoping that Buddha would protect the boats and calm the lethal currents.

🛏 Sleeping

Jīntáoyuán Dàjiǔdiàn　Hotel **$$**
(金桃源大酒店; ☎0833 210 7666; 136 Binjiang Lu, 滨江路南段136号; d from ¥158-218; ❄@🛜) Smart, clean and across the street from the river. The river-view rooms are a good deal at ¥188. No English sign.

ℹ️ Information

Bank of China (中国银行, Zhōngguó Yínháng; 16 Renmin Nanlu) Answers all your money-changing needs.

Public Security Bureau (PSB, 省公安厅外事科, Gōng'ānjú; ☎0833 518 2555; http://lsscrj.gotoip1.com; 548 Fenghuang Lu Zhongduan, 3rd fl; 凤凰路中段548号; ⏰9am-noon & 1-5pm Mon-Fri) Visa extensions in five days. Take bus 6 (¥1) from the centre.

ℹ️ Getting There & Around

Bus

Buses from Chéngdū's Xīnnánmén station usually arrive at Xiàobà bus station (肖坝车站; Xiàobà chēzhàn), the main tourist station. The central bus station (乐山客运中心车站; Lèshān kèyùn zhōngxīn chēzhàn) and Liányùn bus station (联运车站; Liányùn chēzhàn) are also useful.

Note, if you're heading to Éméi Shān, it's better to use Xiàobà bus station, as buses from there go all the way to **Bàoguó village bus station** (¥11, 45 minutes, every 30 minutes from 7.30am to 5pm).

Other services from Xiàobà bus station include:

Chéngdū ¥47, two hours, every 30 minutes from 7am to 7pm

Chóngqìng ¥138, six hours, 10.40am

Éméi town ¥8, 30 minutes, every 30 minutes from 7.30am to 6pm

JIǓZHÀIGŌU NATIONAL PARK 九寨沟风景名胜区

☑0837 / POP 62,000

The stunning Unesco World Heritage Site of **Jiǔzhàigōu National Park** (Jiǔzhàigōu Fēngjǐng Míngshèngqū; 九寨沟风景名胜区; ☑0837 773 9753; www.jiuzhai.com; admission incl bus adult/concession 1 May–15 Nov ¥310/200, Nov 16–Apr 31 ¥170/130; ⏱7am-7pm May–mid-Nov, 8am-6pm mid-Nov–Apr, last tickets 3hr before closing) is one of Sìchuān's star attractions. More than two million people visit the park every year to gawp at its famous bluer-than-blue lakes, its rushing waterfalls and its deep green trees backed by snowy mountains.

🛏 Sleeping

There's an almost endless supply of hotels around Péngfēng Village (彭丰村; Péngfēng Cūn), so don't worry if your preferred option is full. Staying inside the park is not allowed.

Zhuo Ma's   Homestay **$**

(卓玛, Zhuómǎ; ☑135 6878 3012; www.zhuoma jiuzhaigou.hostel.com; per person ¥200) A genuine Tibetan homestay, this pretty wood cabin in a tiny village about 10km up the valley from the main park has six simple rooms and a wonderfully accommodating family. There's a common bathroom with shower, and prices include three meals and pick-up from the bus station (otherwise it's around ¥60 in a taxi).

❶ Information

An ATM (自动柜员机; Zìdòng Guìyuán Jī) at the park entrance accepts foreign cards, as does the China Construction Bank (near the bus station) and Agricultural Bank of China (in Pengfeng Village), where you can also change cash.

❶ Getting There & Around

Air

More than a dozen daily flights link Chéngdū with Jiǔzhàigōu Airport (officially called Jiǔhuáng Airport). Other direct flights include Běijīng, Shànghǎi, Hángzhōu, Chóngqìng, Kúnmíng and Xī'ān.

Buses to Jiǔzhàigōu (¥50, 1½ hours) meet arriving flights. A taxi from the airport is about ¥300.

Bus

Buses leaving from Jiǔzhàigōu bus station (汽车站; qìchēzhàn) include those listed below:

Chéngdū ¥149, 10 hours, four daily (6am, 7am, 8am and 10am)

Chóngqìng ¥230, 12 hours, 7.30am

Silk Road

HIGHLIGHTS

1 **Labrang Monastery** (p341) Vast Tibetan Buddhist monastery and inspiring places of devotion.

2 **Jiāyùguān Fort** (p342) Sublime Great Wall fort framed by snow-capped mountains.

3 **Mògāo Caves** (p343) China's most astonishing collection of Buddhist cave art.

4 **Kashgar** (p344) The Silk Road's most distinctive Uighur town.

Kora (pilgrim path) encircling Labrang Monastery, Xiàhé

MARTIN MOOS/GETTY IMAGES ©

LÁNZHŌU 兰州

🎵 0931 / POP 2.17 MILLION

Roughly at China's cartographic bullseye, Gānsù's elongated capital marks the halfway point for overlanders hiking across the country.

🛏 Sleeping

Jǐnjiāng Inn   Hotel **$$**
(锦江之星; Jǐnjiāng Zhīxīng; 🎵 0931 861 7333; 182 Tianshui Nanlu, 天水南路182号; tw ¥229-289; ❄ 🛜) Neat and tidy express business-style hotel around 1km north of the train station with unfussy, compact and well-maintained rooms and snappy service.

ℹ Information

Bank of China (中国银行; Zhōngguó Yínháng; Tianshui Lu; ⏱ 8.30am-noon & 2.30-5.30pm Mon-Fri) Has an ATM and changes travellers cheques on the 2nd floor.

Public Security Bureau (PSB; 公安局; Gōng'ānjú; 🎵 0931 871 8610; 482 Wudu Lu; ⏱ 8.30-11.30am & 2.30-5.30pm Mon-Fri) The foreign-affairs branch is on the 2nd floor. Visa extensions take several days; one photo required.

ℹ Getting There & Away

Air

Lánzhōu has flights to Běijīng (¥1460), Dūnhuáng (¥1466), Jiāyùguān (¥1576), Kūnmíng (¥1902), Shànghǎi (¥1750) and Xī'ān (¥480).

Bus

The **main long-distance bus station** (长途车站; Chángtú Chēzhàn; Pingliang Lu) is now just a ticket office outside which you catch a shuttle bus 30 minutes before departure for the **east bus station** (汽车东站; Qìchē Dōngzhàn; 🎵 0931 841 8411; Pingliang Lu).

For journeys to the south of Gānsù head to the **south bus station** (汽车南站; Qìchē Nánzhàn; Langongping Lu).

The following services depart from the south bus station:

Xiàhé ¥76.50, 3½ hours, five daily (7am to 3pm)

Train

Lánzhōu is the major rail link for trains heading to and from western China. For Dūnhuáng make sure to get a train to the town itself and not Liǔyuán, a time-wasting 180km away.

There are frequent trains to the following:

Dūnhuáng Hard/soft sleeper ¥244/398, 13 hours (two per day direct to Dūnhuáng at 5.50pm and 7.10pm; the rest go to Liǔyuán)

Jiāyùguān Hard/soft seat ¥103/160, seven to eight hours; hard/soft sleeper ¥179/275, 11 hours

Xī'ān Hard/soft sleeper ¥164/252, eight to nine hours

XIÀHÉ   夏河

 0941 / POP 70,000

The alluring monastic town of Xiàhé attracts an astonishing band of visitors, from backpack-laden students, insatiable wanderers, shaven-headed Buddhist nuns, Tibetan nomads in their most colourful finery, camera-toting tour groups and dusty, itinerant beggars.

◉ Sights

Labrang Monastery   Buddhist
(拉卜楞寺; Lābǔléng Sì; Renmin Xijie; tour ¥40) With its endless squeaking prayer wheels (3km in total length), hawks circling overhead and the throb of Tibetan longhorns resonating from the surrounding hills, Labrang is a monastery town unto itself. Many of the chapel halls are illuminated in a yellow glow by yak-butter lamps, their strong-smelling fuel scooped out from voluminous tubs.

🛏 Sleeping

Overseas Tibetan Hotel   Hotel $
(华侨饭店; Huáqiáo Fàndiàn; ☎ 0941 712 2642; www.overseastibetanhotel.com; 77 Renmin Xijie; 人民西街77号; dm ¥50, d ¥200-300; 🛜) A well-run and bustling place, mid 2014 saw the final renovations of the guesthouse including wi-fi that reaches every corner, and solar power to ensure 24/7 hot water. The modern doubles are the best value

Xiàhé

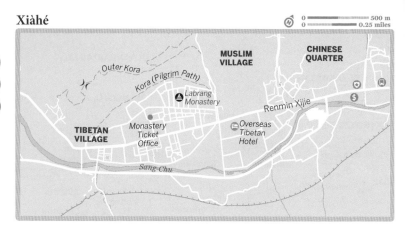

0   500 m
0   0.25 miles

Outer Kora

Kora (Pilgrim Path)

MUSLIM VILLAGE

CHINESE QUARTER

Labrang Monastery

Renmin Xijie

TIBETAN VILLAGE

Monastery Ticket Office

Overseas Tibetan Hotel

Sang-Chu

in town with clean enclosed showers (proper glass doors!), flat-screen TVs and the cushiest thick mattresses in Xiàhé. Discounts of 20% in quiet periods.

ℹ️ Information

Industrial & Commercial Bank of China
(ICBC; 工商银行; Gōngshāng Yínháng; 98 Nanxiahe Jie, 南下河街98号; ⏱8.30am-4pm daily) Has an ATM and changes US dollars but not travellers cheques.

ℹ️ Getting There & Away

Air

The Gānnán Xiàhé Airport (GXH; Gānnán Xiàhé Jīchǎng; 甘南夏河机场) opened in early 2014 with flights to Xī'ān (¥1130), dodging the uninspiring Lánzhōu–Xiàhé bus journey, and Lhasa (¥1760), with Běijīng and Chéngdū to come. There is no airport bus, but OT Travels & Tours (☎1390 9419 888; amdolosang@ hotmail.com; 77 Renmin Xijie, 人民西街77号; ⏱8am-9pm daily) can arrange a private taxi to the airport for ¥400.

Bus

The following bus services depart from Xiàhé:
Lángmùsì ¥72.50, 3½ hours, one daily (7.40am)
Lánzhōu ¥77, 3½ hours, four daily (6.30am, 7.30am, 8.30am and 2.30pm)

JIĀYÙGUĀN & AROUND 嘉峪关

☎0937 / POP 170,000

You approach Jiāyùguān through the forbidding lunar landscape of north Gānsù. It's a fitting setting, as Jiāyùguān marks the symbolic end of the Great Wall, the western gateway of China proper and, for imperial Chinese, the beginning of the back of beyond.

As one of the defining points of the Silk Road, a Ming-dynasty fort was erected here in 1372.

◎ Sights

Jiāyùguān Fort   Fort
(嘉峪关城楼; Jiāyùguān Chénglóu; Xinhua Nanlu; admission ¥120; ⏱8am-6pm) One of the classic images of western China, the fort guards the pass between the snow-capped Qílián Shān peaks and the Hēi Shān (Black Mountains) of the Mǎzōng Shān range.

Built in 1372, it was christened the 'Impregnable Defile Under Heaven'. Although the Chinese often controlled territory far beyond the Jiāyùguān area, this was the last major stronghold of imperial China – the end of the 'civilised world', beyond which lay only desert demons and the barbarian armies of Central Asia.

🛏 Sleeping

Kānghūi Hotel
Hotel $$

(康辉宾馆, Kānghūi Bīnguǎn; ☎0937 620 3456; 1599 Xinhua Zhonglu; 新华中路1599号; tw/tr ¥208/288; ❄@🛜) Wide windows, high ceilings and very spacious rooms (and bathrooms) are highlights at this tidy business hotel in the centre of town. Renovations finished in 2013 yet prices remained the same, making its excellent location on the tree-lined street hard to beat. Discounts of 30% are typical.

ℹ Information

The Bank of China (中国银行; Zhōngguó Yínháng) south of the Lanxin Xilu intersection on Xinhua Zhonglu has an ATM and can change money.

ℹ Getting There & Away

Jiāyùguān has an airport with flights to Běijīng, Shànghǎi and Lánzhōu but most people arrive by bus or train.

Bus

Jiāyùguān's bus station (汽车站; qìchēzhàn) is by a busy four-way junction on Lanxin Xilu, next to the main budget hotels. Doubling as a billiards hall, the station has buses to:

Dūnhuáng ¥73, five hours, four daily (9am to 2.30pm)

Lánzhōu ¥160, 12 hours, three daily sleepers

Train

Most trains to Dūnhuáng stop at Liǔyuán (180km away). Direct trains are few and not well scheduled.

Jiāyùguān's train station (火车站) is southwest of the town centre. Services include:

Lánzhōu Hard/soft seat ¥103/160, seven to eight hours; hard/soft sleeper ¥179/275, nine hours

MÒGĀO CAVES 莫高窟

The Mògāo Caves (Mògāo Kū) are, simply put, one of the greatest repositories of Buddhist art in the world. At its peak, the site housed 18 monasteries, more than 1400 monks and nuns, and countless artists, translators and calligraphers. Wealthy traders and important officials were the primary donors responsible for creating new caves, as caravans made the long detour past Mògāo to pray or give thanks for a safe journey through the treacherous wastelands to the west. The traditional date ascribed to the founding of the first cave is AD 366.

The caves fell into disuse after the collapse of the Yuan dynasty and were largely forgotten until the early 20th century, when they were 'rediscovered' by a string of foreign explorers.

Entrance to the **caves** (莫高窟; Mògāo Kū; low/high season ¥100/180; ⏲8.15am-6pm May-Oct, 9.15am-5.30pm Nov-Apr, tickets sold till 1hr before closing) is strictly controlled – it's impossible to visit them on your own.

The general admission ticket grants you a two-hour tour (display great interest at the start as your guide has the discretion to make this longer) of around 10 caves, including the infamous Library Cave (No 17) and a related exhibit containing rare fragments of manuscripts in classical Uighur and Manichean. Excellent English-speaking guides are available (and included in the admission price) at 9am, noon and 2pm, and you should be able to arrange tours in other languages as well.

Of the 492 caves, 20 'open' caves are rotated fairly regularly, so recommendations are useless, but tours always include the two big Buddhas, 34.5m and 26m tall, respectively. It's also possible to visit some of the more unusual caves for ¥100 to ¥500 per cave.

Photography is strictly prohibited everywhere within the fenced-off caves area. And if it's raining, snowing or sand storming, the caves will be closed.

ℹ Getting There & Away

The Mògāo Caves are 25km (30 minutes) southeast from Dūnhuáng. A green minibus (one way ¥8) leaves every 30 minutes from 8am to 5pm from outside Charley Johng's Cafe (风味餐馆, Fēngwèi Cānguǎn; ☎0937 388 2411; Mingshan Lu; dishes ¥6-36; ⏲8am-10pm); buses return every 30 minutes 9am to 6pm to

Shāzhōu Night Market (沙洲夜市, Shāzhōu Yèshì; btwn Yangguan Donglu & Xiyu Lu; ⊙morning-late)'s north end.

A return taxi costs ¥100 to ¥150 for a day, or try finding a taxi willing to take you back to Dūnhuáng from the caves for ¥40.

KASHGAR 喀什

☏0998 / POP 350,000

Locked away in the westernmost corner of China, physically closer to Tehran and Damascus than to Běijīng, Kashgar (Kāshí) has been the epicentre of regional trade and cultural exchange for more than two millennia.

The roads, rail and planes that now connect the city to the rest of China have brought waves of Han migrant workers, and huge swathes of the old city have been bulldozed in the name of economic 'progress'.

Yet, in the face of these changes, the spirit of Kashgar lives on. Uighur craftsmen and artisans still hammer and chisel away in side alleys, traders haggle over deals in the boisterous bazaars and donkey carts still trundle their way through the suburbs.

◎ Sights

Grand (Sunday) Bazaar
Market

(大巴扎; Dàbāzhā; Yengi Bazaar; Aizirete Lu, 艾孜热特路; ⊙daily) Kashgar's main bazaar is open every day but really kicks it up a gear on Sunday. Step carefully through the jam-packed entrance and allow your five senses to guide you through the market; the pungent smell of cumin, the sight of scorpions in a jar, the sound of *muqam* music from tinny radios, the taste of hot *samsas* (baked mutton dumplings) and the feel of soft sheepskin caps are seductive, and overwhelming.

Sunday Livestock Market
Market

(动物市场, Dòngwù Shìchǎng, Mal Bazaar; ⊙8am-6pm Sun) No visit to Kashgar is complete without a trip to the Livestock Market, which takes place once a week on Sunday. The day begins with Uighur farmers and herders trekking into the city from nearby villages. By lunchtime just about every sellable sheep, camel, horse, cow and donkey within 50km has been squeezed through the bazaar gates. It's dusty, smelly and crowded, and most people find it wonderful, though the treatment of the animals often leaves something to be desired.

Old Town   Old Town
The Chinese government spent the past two decades knocking the Old Town down, block by block, and building a replacement. Many travellers still enjoy exploring the new areas but to see some of the last remaining alleys check out the neighborhood near Donghai Lake in the east part of the city. Sprawling on both sides of Jiefang Lu there are also alleys

lined with Uighur workshops and adobe houses right out of an early-20th-century picture book.

Id Kah Mosque   Mosque
(艾提尕尔清真寺; Ài Tígǎ'ěr Qīngzhēn Sì; Id Kah Sq; admission ¥30) The yellow-tiled Id Kah Mosque, which dates from 1442, is the spiritual and physical heart of the city.

Enormous (it's the largest mosque in China), its courtyard and gardens can hold 20,000 people during the annual Qurban Baiyram. Also known as Eid, or Id, celebrations fall in September for the next few years.

Non-Muslims may enter, but not during prayer time. Dress modestly, including a headscarf for women. Take off your shoes if entering carpeted areas and be discreet when taking photos.

🛌 Sleeping

Eden Hotel
Hotel $$

(海尔巴格大饭店; Hǎiěrbāgé Dàfàndiàn;
☏ 0998 266 4444; 148 Seman Lu; tr with
breakfast ¥188; 🛜) The quiet rooms and
excellent location of this midrange hotel
make it good value. The staff speak some
English and there's a superb attached
Turkish restaurant.

🍴 Eating

Ōu'ěr Dáxīkè Night Market
Market $

(欧尔达稀克夜市; Ōu'ěr Dáxīkè Yèshì; Ou'er
Daxike Lu; meals from ¥10; ⏱ 8pm-midnight
Xīnjiāng time) The night market across
Jiefang Beilu from the Id Kah Mosque is
a great place to sample local fare. Among
the goodies are fried fish, chickpeas,
kebabs, fried dumplings known as
hoshan and bubbling vats of goat's head
soup. Top off a meal with a glass of tart
pomegranate juice or freshly churned
vanilla-scented ice cream.

ℹ️ Information

Travellers have lost money or passports to
pickpockets at the Sunday Market, so keep
yours tucked away.

Kashgar is the most conservative corner of
Xīnjiāng and the one place where you will see
women's faces obscured by headscarves or
veils. Some foreign women walking the streets
alone have been sexually harassed.

Public Security Bureau (PSB; 公安局;
Gōng'ānjú; 111 Youmulakexia Lu; ⏱ 9.30am-
1.30pm & 4-8pm) Visa extensions take three to
four days, dependent on the political climate.

Money

Bank of China (中国银行; Zhōngguó Yínháng;
People's Sq; ⏱ 9.30am-1.30pm & 4-7pm)
Changes travellers cheques and cash and has
a 24-hour ATM. You can also sell yuan back into
US dollars at the foreign-exchange desk if you
have exchange receipts; this is a good idea if you
are headed to Tashkurgan, where the bank hours
are erratic.

ℹ️ Getting There & Away

When you buy tickets in Kashgar it's imperative
to verify which time the ticket is for. It should be
Běijīng time, but this isn't always the case.

Id Kah Mosque (p345), Kashgar

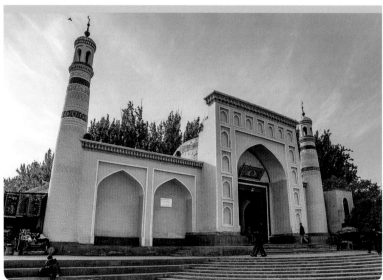

FENG WEI PHOTOGRAPHY/GETTY IMAGES ©

Air

More than one dozen daily flights depart for Ürümqi (¥1100).

Bus

Domestic buses use the **long-distance bus station** (地区客运站, **Dìqū Kèyùnzhàn; Tiannan Lu**).

Sleeper buses depart from the international bus station (国际汽车站) on Jiefang Beilu for: **Ürümqi** ¥265 to ¥280, 24 hours, eight buses per day between 9am and 10pm.

Train

Ürümqi hard/soft sleeper ¥182-342/338-527, 25 to 31 hours, three daily (8.01am, 12.52pm and 9.41pm)

ℹ Getting Around

To/From the Airport

The airport is 13km northeast of the town centre. A taxi costs ¥15 to ¥20 but drivers often ask for double this. Bus 2 (¥1) goes directly to the airport from People's Square and Id Kah Mosque.

Taxi

Taxis are metered and the flag fall is ¥5.

China

In Focus

Miao girls in traditional costume
KEREN SU/GETTY IMAGES ©

China Today

Lama Temple, Běijīng (p72)

China today is as multifaceted as its challenges are diverse.

belief systems
(% of population)

70
Atheist

22
Buddhist

4
Christian

1-2
Taoist

1-2
Muslim

if China were 100 people

92 would be Han Chinese

8 would be ethnic minorities, eg Zhuang, Manchu, Uighur etc

population per sq km

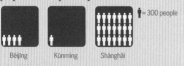

♦ ≈ 300 people

Běijīng   Kūnmíng   Shànghǎi

A highly idiosyncratic mix of dyed-in-the-wool Marxists, can-do entrepreneurs, inward-looking Buddhists, overnight millionaires, leather-faced farmers, unflagging migrant workers and round-the-clock McJobbers, China today is as multifaceted as its challenges are diverse. From the outside, China's autocratic decision-making may suggest national uniformity, but things are actually more in a state of controlled, and not-so-controlled, chaos.

New Superpower or the Next Japan?

Tipped to overtake the US economy sometime before 2020, China can readily seem to be assuming the mantle of superpower. The rash of books trumpeting China's ascendancy echoes the glut of titles in the late 1980s that celebrated the rise of its island neighbour. While the Chinese economy effortlessly streaked past Japan's in 2010 and today gradually fills the United States' rear-view mirror, the unstoppable juggernaut of the Chinese economy

1976. Carrying the Yutu (玉兔, Yùtù, Jade Rabbit) lunar rover, the mission also marked China's coming of age as a space power. Rivalries notwithstanding – India's unmanned Mars probe achieved Martian orbit in 2014 – China wants to show the world it has both the ambition and the sophistication to pull a (jade) rabbit from its hat. The space program also casts China as an exploratory power that is willing to take risks, in an arena littered with noble failures. China also has a working space station – the Tiangong-1, a precursor to a much larger station in the pipeline – and plans to put a man on the moon and land a rover on Mars.

KYLIE MCLAUGHLIN/GETTY IMAGES

could be hitting some hefty potholes, if not nearing the end of the road. Some financial analysts foresee China slewing into a long era of stagnation similar to that which depressed Japan after its asset bubble burst in the early 1990s. A combination of bad debt accumulation, imbalanced growth, downward property prices, a burdensome overcapacity and over-dependence on exports could commence a persistent squeeze to the brakes on economic growth. Resolving bad debt and sorting out the shaky banking sector and the deeply under-capitalised financial system may be central to any long term resolution. However, a real estate slump could limit options, while inequality in China remains among the most severe in the world.

To Boldly Go

In December 2013 the Chang'e 3 probe landed on the surface of the moon, marking the first lunar landing since

Troubled Waters and Restive Borderlands

China's dazzling economic trajectory over the last two decades has been watched with awe by the West and increasing un-ease by the Middle Kingdom's neighbours. By virtue of its sheer size and population, a dominant China has been ruffling some East Asian feathers. A growing – and seemingly intractable – spat over the contested and uninhabited Diaoyu Islands (Senkaku Islands to the Japanese) has soured relations between China and Japan. Occasionally, violent anti-Japanese protests in China have been the result. A festering dispute has also seen growing tensions between China and Vietnam, the Philippines and other nations over the control of waters, islands, reefs, atolls and rocky outcroppings in the South China Sea. While keeping an eye on maritime issues, at home, President Xi Jinping has to deal with growing unrest in Xīnjiāng province, which has led to terror attacks in both Yúnnán and in front of the Gate of Heavenly Peace in Běijīng, as well as a spate of brazen bombings and attacks in Xīnjiāng itself.

History

Lion guarding the Gate of Heavenly Peace, Běijīng (p77)

MANFRED GOTTSCHALK/GETTY IMAG

The epic sweep of China's history paints perhaps a deceptive impression of long epochs of peace periodically convulsed by break-up, internecine division or external attack. Yet for much of its history China has been in conflict, either internally or with outsiders. Although China's size and shape has also continuously changed – from tiny beginnings by the Yellow River (Huáng Hé) to the subcontinent of today – an uninterrupted thread of history links its earliest roots to the full flowering of Chinese civilisation.

From Oracle Bones to Confucius

The earliest 'Chinese' dynasty, the Shang, was long considered apocryphal; however, archaeological evidence (unearthed cattlebones and turtle shells used for divination – called 'oracle bones' – covered in mysterious scratches, recognised as an early form of Chinese writing) proved that a society known as the Shang developed in central China from around 1766 BC.

c 4000 BC
Archaeological evidence for the first settlements along the Yellow River (Huáng Hé).

Sometime between 1050 and 1045 BC, a neighbouring group known as the Zhou conquered Shang territory. The Zhou was one of many states competing for power during the next few hundred years, but developments during this period created some of the key sources of Chinese culture that would survive to the present day. A constant theme of the first millennium BC was conflict, particularly the periods known as the 'Spring and Autumn' (722–481 BC) and 'Warring States' (475–221 BC).

From this disorder surfaced the thinking of Confucius (551–479 BC), whose system of thought and ethics underpinned Chinese culture for 2500 years. Confucius' desire for an ordered and ethical world seems a far cry from the warfare of his age.

Early Empires

The Warring States period ended decisively in 221 BC when the Qin kingdom conquered other states in the central Chinese region and Qin Shi Huang declared himself emperor. Later histories portrayed Qin Shi Huang as particularly cruel and tyrannical, but Qin Shi Huang also oversaw vast public-works projects, including defences built by some 300,000 men, connecting fortifications into what would become the Great Wall. He unified the currency, measurements and written language, providing the basis for a cohesive state.

The Qin dynasty was overturned by a peasant, Liu Bang, who rose up and founded the Han dynasty, a dynasty so important that the name Han still refers to ethnic Chinese. Critical to the centralisation of power, Emperor Wu (140–87 BC) institutionalised Confucian norms in government. Promoting merit as well as order, he was the first leader to experiment with examinations for entry into the bureaucracy, but his dynasty was plagued by endemic economic difficulties and the inability to exercise control over a growing empire, which led to the collapse of the Han.

Disunity Restored

Between the early 3rd and late 6th centuries AD, north China witnessed a succession of rival kingdoms vying for power, while a potent division formed between north and south. Riven by conflict, the north was controlled by non-Chinese rule, most successfully by the Northern Wei dynasty (386–534). A succession of rival regimes followed until nobleman Yang Jian (d 604) reunified China under the fleeting Sui dynasty (581–618). His son Sui Yangdi contributed greatly to the unification of south and north through the construction of the Grand Canal, which was later extended and remained the empire's most important communication route between south and north until the late 19th century. After instigating three unsuccessful incursions onto Korean soil,

551 BC

The birth of Confucius. His thoughts were collected in *The Analects* – deeply influential ideas of an ethical, ordered society.

214 BC

Emperor Qin indentures thousands of labourers to link existing city walls into one Great Wall.

c 100 BC

Buddhism first arrives in China from India.

The Best...
Confucius Temples

1 Confucius Temple, Qūfù (p170)

2 Confucius Temple, Běijīng (p81)

3 Confucius Temple, Píngyáo (p152)

resulting in disastrous military setbacks, Sui Yangdi faced revolt on the streets and was assassinated in 618 by one of his high officials.

The Tang

The Chinese nostalgically regard the Tang (618–907) as their cultural zenith. The output of the Tang poets is still regarded as China's finest, as is Tang sculpture, while its legal code became a standard for the whole East Asian region.

The Tang was founded by the Sui general Li Yuan, his achievements consolidated by his son Taizong (626–49). Cháng'ān (modern Xī'ān) became the world's most dazzling capital, with its own cosmopolitan foreign quarter, a population of a million, a market where merchants from as far away as Persia mingled with locals and an astonishing city wall that eventually enveloped 83 sq km.

Taizong was succeeded by Chinese history's sole reigning female emperor, Wu Zetian (625–705). Under her leadership the empire reached its greatest extent, spreading well north of the Great Wall and far west into inner Asia. Her strong promotion of Buddhism, however, alienated her from the Confucian officials and in 705 she was forced to abdicate in favour of Xuanzong.

Xuanzong appointed minorities from the frontiers as generals, in the belief that they were so far removed from the political system and society that ideas of rebellion or coups would not enter their minds. Nevertheless, it was An Lushan, a general of Sogdian-Turkic parentage, who took advantage of his command in north China to make a bid for imperial power. The fighting lasted from 755 to 763, and although An Lushan was defeated, the Tang's control over China was destroyed forever.

In its last century, the Tang withdrew from its former openness, turning more strongly to Confucianism, while Buddhism was outlawed by Emperor Wuzong from 842 to 845. The Tang decline was marked by imperial frailty, growing insurgencies, upheaval and chaos.

Open Markets

Further disunity – the fragmentary Five Dynasties or Ten Kingdoms period – followed the fall of the Tang until the Northern Song dynasty (960–1127) was established. The Song dynasty existed in a state of constant conflict with its northern neighbours, being eventually driven from Kāifēng to its southern capital in Hángzhōu for the period of the Southern Song (1127–1279).

874 AD

The Huang Chao rebellion breaks out, which helps reduce the Tang empire to chaos and leads to the fall of the capital in 907.

1215

Genghis Khan conquers Běijīng as part of his creation of a Eurasian empire under Mongol rule.

Hall of Preserving Harmony, Běijīng

The age was culturally rich and economically prosperous. The full institution of a system of examinations for entry into the Chinese bureaucracy was brought to fruition during the Song. Young Chinese men sat tests on the Confucian classics, obtaining office if successful. The economy thrived during Song times, as cash crops and handicraft products became far more central to the wealth of the nation.

Mongols to Ming

Genghis Khan (1167–1227) began his rise to power, turning his gaze on China; he took Běijīng in 1215, destroying and rebuilding it; his successors seized Hángzhōu, the Southern Song capital, in 1276. The court fled and, in 1279, Southern Song resistance finally expired. Kublai Khan, grandson of Genghis, now reigned over all of China as emperor of the Yuan dynasty. Under Kublai, the entire population was divided into categories of Han, Mongol and foreigner, with the top administrative posts reserved for Mongols, even though the examination system was revived in 1315. An innovation was the use of paper money, although overprinting created a problem with inflation.

The Mongols ultimately proved less able at governance than warfare, their empire succumbing to rebellion within a century and eventual vanquishment. Ruling as Ming emperor Hongwu, Zhu Yuanzhang established his capital in Nánjīng, but by the early 15th century the court had begun to move back to Běijīng where a hugely ambitious reconstruction project was inaugurated by Emperor Yongle (r 1403–24), building the Forbidden City and devising the layout of the city we see today.

In 1405 Yongle launched the first of seven great maritime expeditions. Led by the eunuch general Zheng He (1371–1433), the fleet consisted of more than 60 large vessels and 255 smaller ones, carrying nearly 28,000 men. The fourth and fifth expeditions departed in 1413 and 1417, and travelled as far as the present-day Middle East. The emperors after Yongle however, had little interest in continuing the voyages, and China dropped anchor on its global maritime explorations.

The Great Wall was re-engineered and clad in brick while ships also arrived from Europe, presaging an overseas threat that would appear from entirely different directions. Traders were quickly followed by missionaries, and the Jesuits, led by the formidable Matteo Ricci, made their way inland and established a presence at court.

The Ming was eventually undermined by internal power struggles and rebellion. Natural disasters, including drought and famine, combined with a menace from the north. The Manchu, a nomadic warlike people, saw the turmoil within China and invaded.

The Qing: the Path to Dynastic Dissolution

After conquering just a small part of China and assuming control in the disarray, the Manchu named their new dynasty the Qing (1644–1911). Like the Mongols before them, the conquering Manchu found themselves in charge of a civilisation whose government they had defeated, but whose cultural power far exceeded their own. They

---

1406

Ming emperor Yongle begins construction of the 800 buildings of the Forbidden City.

1644

Běijīng falls to peasant rebel Li Zicheng. Last Ming emperor Chongzhen hangs himself in Jǐngshān Park; Qing dynasty is established.

1842

The Treaty of Nánjīng ends the first Opium War. China is forced to hand over Hong Kong island and open five ports to foreign trade.

The Best... Ruins

1 Ruins of the Church of St Paul, Macau (p299)

2 Jiànkòu Great Wall, (p115)

3 Old Summer Palace, Běijīng (p93)

4 Ming City Wall Ruins Park, Běijīng (p84)

enforced strict rules of social separation between the Han and Manchu, and tried to maintain – not always very successfully – a culture that reminded the Manchu of their nomadic warrior past. The Qing flourished best under three emperors who ruled for a total of 135 years: Kangxi, Yongzheng and Qianlong.

Much of the map of China that we know today derives from the Qing period. Territorial expansion and expeditions to regions of Central Asia spread Chinese power and culture further than ever.

War & Reform

For the Manchu, the single most devastating incident was not the Opium Wars, but the far more destructive anti-Qing Taiping War of 1856–64, an insurgency motivated partly by a foreign credo (Christianity). The Qing eventually reconquered the Taiping capital at Nánjīng, but upwards of 20 million Chinese died in the uprising.

The events that finally brought the dynasty down, however, came in quick succession. Foreign imperialist incursions continued and Western powers nibbled away at China's coastline. Hong Kong was a British colony and Macau was administered by the Portuguese. Attempts at self-strengthening – involving attempts to produce armaments and Western-style military technology – were dealt a brutal blow by the Sino-Japanese War of 1894–95. Not only was Chinese influence in Korea lost, but Taiwan was ceded to Japan.

One of the boldest proposals for reform, which drew heavily on the Japanese model, was the program put forward in 1898 by reformers including the political thinker Kang Youwei (1858–1927). However, in September 1898 the reforms were abruptly halted, as the Dowager Empress Cixi, fearful of a coup, placed the emperor under house arrest and executed several of the leading advocates of change. In a major misjudgement, the dynasty declared in June that it supported the Boxers (anti-Christian rebels opposed to the foreign presence in China) in their uprising. Eventually, a multinational foreign army forced its way into China and defeated the uprising that had besieged the foreign Legation Quarter in Běijīng. The imperial powers then demanded huge financial compensation from the Qing.

The Cantonese revolutionary Sun Yatsen (1866–1925) remains one of the few modern historical figures respected in both China and Taiwan. Sun and his Revolutionary League made multiple attempts to undermine Qing rule in the late 19th century, raising sponsorship and support from a wide-ranging combination of the Chinese diaspora, the newly emergent middle class and traditional secret societies.

1904–05

The Russo-Japanese War is fought entirely on Chinese territory. Japan's victory is the first by an Asian power over a European one.

1911

Revolution spreads across China as local governments withdraw support for the dynasty, and instead support a republic.

1925

The shooting of striking factory workers by foreign-controlled police (the 'May 30th Incident') fires nationalism.

The end of the Qing dynasty arrived swiftly. A local uprising in the city of Wǔhàn in October 1911 was discovered early, leading the rebels to take over command in the city and declare independence from the Qing dynasty. Within a space of days, then weeks, most of China's provinces did likewise. Provincial assemblies across China declared themselves in favour of a republic, with Sun Yatsen (who was not even in China at the time) as their candidate for president.

The Republic: Instability & Ideas

The Republic of China lasted less than 40 years on the mainland with the country under threat from what many described as 'imperialism from without and warlordism from within'. There was breathing room for new ideas and culture, yet the period was marked by repeated disasters.

Sun Yatsen returned to China and only briefly served as president, before having to make way for militarist leader Yuan Shikai. In 1912 China held its first general election, and it was Sun's newly established Kuomintang (Nationalist; Guómíndǎng, literally 'Party of the National People') party that emerged as the largest grouping. Parliamentary democracy did not last long, as the Kuomintang itself was outlawed by

Great Wall, Jīnshānlǐng (p116)

1937
On 7 July the Japanese and Chinese clash at Wanping, sparking conflict between China and Japan which only ends in 1945.

1946
Communists and the Kuomintang fail to form a coalition government, plunging China back into civil war.

1949
Mao Zedong stands on the Gate of Heavenly Peace on 1 October to announce the creation of the People's Republic of China.

Yuan and Sun fled to exile in Japan. However, after Yuan's death in 1916 the country split into rival regions ruled by militarist warlord-leaders. Also, in reality, the foreign powers still had control over much of China's domestic and international situation. The city of Shànghǎi became the focal point for the contradictions of Chinese modernity. The racism that accompanied imperialism was visible every day, as Europeans kept themselves separate from the Chinese. Amid the glamour of modernity, its inequalities and squalor also inspired the first congress of the Chinese Communist Party (CCP).

Double-dealing by the Western Allies and Chinese politicians who had made secret deals with Japan led to some 3000 students gathering in central Běijīng in 1919 and marching to the house of a Chinese government minister closely associated with Japan. Once there, they broke in and destroyed the house. This event, over in a few hours, became a legend.

The student demonstration came to symbolise a much wider shift in Chinese society and politics. The May Fourth Movement, as it became known, was associated closely with the New Culture. In literature, a May Fourth generation of authors wrote works attacking the Confucianism that they felt had brought China to its current crisis, and explored new issues of sexuality and self-development while the CCP was founded in the intellectual turmoil of the movement.

The Northern Expedition & the Long March

After years of vainly seeking international support for his cause, Sun Yatsen found allies in the newly formed Soviet Russia. The Soviets ordered the fledgling CCP to ally itself with the Kuomintang. Their alliance was attractive to Sun: the Soviets would provide political training, military assistance and finance. From their base in Guǎngzhōu, the Kuomintang and CCP trained together from 1923, in preparation for their mission to reunite China.

Sun died of cancer in 1925. Under Soviet advice, the Kuomintang and CCP prepared for their 'Northern Expedition', the big 1926 push north that was supposed to finally unite China. The most powerful military figure turned out to be an officer from Zhèjiāng named Chiang Kaishek (1887–1975). Chiang moved steadily forward and finally captured Shànghǎi in March 1927. Using local thugs and soldiers, Chiang organised a lightning strike by rounding up CCP activists and union leaders in Shànghǎi and killing thousands of them.

Chiang Kaishek's Kuomintang government officially came to power in 1928 through a combination of military force and popular support. Marked by corruption, it ruthlessly suppressed political dissent. Yet Chiang's government also kick-started a major industrialisation effort, greatly augmented China's transport infrastructure, and successfully renegotiated what many Chinese called 'unequal treaties' with Western powers.

A major centre of CCP activity was the base area in impoverished Jiāngxī province. However, by 1934, Chiang's previously ineffective 'Extermination Campaigns' were

1962

Mass starvation from the Great Leap Forward; Liu Shaoqi and Deng Xiaoping reintroduce market reforms leading to condemnation.

1966

The Cultural Revolution breaks out. The movement is marked by a fetish for violence as a catalyst for transforming society.

1972

US President Richard Nixon visits China, marking a major rapprochement and the start of full diplomatic relations.

making the CCP's position in Jiāngxī untenable. The CCP commenced their Long March, travelling over 6400km. Four thousand of the original 80,000 communists who set out eventually arrived, exhausted, in Shaanxi (Shǎnxī) province in the northwest.

Events came to a head in December 1936, when the militarist leader of Manchuria (General Zhang Xueliang) and the CCP kidnapped Chiang. As a condition of his release, Chiang agreed to an openly declared United Front: the Kuomintang and communists would put aside their differences and join forces against Japan.

War & the Kuomintang

The Japanese invasion of China, which began in 1937, was merciless, with the notorious Nanjing Massacre just one of a series of war crimes committed by the Japanese Army. The government had to operate in exile from the far southwestern hinterland of China as its eastern seaboard was lost to Japanese occupation.

In China itself, it is now acknowledged that both the Kuomintang and the communists had important roles to play in defeating Japan. Chiang, not Mao Zedong, was the internationally acknowledged leader of China during this period, and despite his government's many flaws, he maintained resistance to the end. The communists had an important role as guerrilla fighters, but did far less fighting in battle than the Kuomintang.

The real winners from WWII, however, were the communists. By the end of the war with Japan the communist areas had expanded massively, with some 900,000 troops in the Red Army, and party membership at a new high of 1.2 million.

The Kuomintang and communists plunged into civil war in 1946 and after three long years the CCP was victorious, prompting Nationalist troops to retreat to Taiwan. On 1 October 1949, Mao ascended the Gate of Heavenly Peace in Běijīng and declared the establishment of the People's Republic of China.

Mao's China

Mao's China desired, above all, to exercise ideological control over its population.

The US refused to recognise the new state at all. The 1950s marked the high point of Soviet influence on Chinese politics and culture. However, the decade also saw rising tension between the Chinese and the Soviets, fuelled in part by Khrushchev's condemnation of Stalin (which Mao took, in part, as a criticism of his own cult of personality).

Mao's experiences had convinced him that only violent change could shake up the relationship between landlords and their tenants, or capitalists and their employees, in a China that was still highly traditional. The first year of the regime saw some 40% of the land redistributed to poor peasants. At the same time, some one million or so people condemned as 'landlords' were persecuted and killed.

As relations with the Soviets broke down in the mid-1950s, the CCP leaders' thoughts turned to economic self-sufficiency. Mao, supported by Politburo colleagues,

1976
Mao Zedong dies, aged 83. The Gang of Four are arrested by his successor and put on trial.

1989
Student demonstrations in Tiān'ānmén Sq end, resulting in the deaths of hundreds of people. Statue, Tiān'ānmén Square (p76), Běijīng

proposed the policy known as the Great Leap Forward (Dàyuèjìn), a highly ambitious plan to harness the power of socialist economics to boost production of steel, coal and electricity.

However, the Great Leap Forward was a monumental failure. Its lack of economic realism caused a massive famine and at least 20 million deaths.

Cultural Revolution

In 1966 Mao decided that a massive campaign of ideological renewal, in which he would attack his own party, had to be launched.

Still the dominant figure in the CCP, Mao used his prestige to undermine his own colleagues. Top leaders suddenly disappeared from sight, only to be replaced by unknowns, such as Mao's wife Jiang Qing and her associates, later dubbed the 'Gang of Four'. Meanwhile, an all-pervasive cult of Mao's personality took over. One million youths at a time, known as Red Guards, would flock to hear Mao in Tiān'ānmén Sq. Immense violence permeated throughout society: teachers, intellectuals and landlords were killed in their thousands.

Worried by the increasing violence, the army forced the Red Guards off the streets in 1969. While the early 1970s saw a remarkable rapprochement between the US and China. Secretive diplomatic manoeuvres led, eventually, to the official visit of US President Richard Nixon to China in 1972, which began the reopening of China to the West. Slowly, the Cultural Revolution began to cool down.

Reform

Mao died in 1976, to be succeeded by the little-known Hua Guofeng (1921–2008). Within two years, Hua had been outmanoeuvred by the greatest survivor of 20th-century Chinese politics, Deng Xiaoping. Deng enlisted a policy slogan originally invented by Mao's pragmatic prime minister, Zhou Enlai – the 'Four Modernisations'. The party's task would be to set China on the right path in four areas: agriculture, industry, science and technology, and national defence.

The first, highly symbolic move of the 'reform era' (as the post-1978 period is known) was the breaking down of the collective farms. Farmers were able to sell a proportion of their crops on the free market, and urban and rural areas were also encouraged to establish small local enterprises. As part of this encouragement of

1997
Hong Kong is returned to the People's Republic of China.

2001
China joins the World Trade Organization, giving it a seat at the top table that decides global norms on economics and finance.

2008
Běijīng hosts the 2008 Summer Olympic Games and Paralympics, burnishing China's image overseas.

entrepreneurship, Deng designated four areas on China's coast as Special Economic Zones (SEZs).

The new freedoms that the urban middle classes enjoyed created the appetite for more. After the death in April 1989 of relative liberal Hu Yaobang, Tiān'ānmén Sq was the scene of an unprecedented demonstration. At its height, nearly a million Chinese workers and students, in a rare cross-class alliance, filled the space in front of the Gate of Heavenly Peace. On the nights of 3 and 4 June the military was enlisted to quell the demonstration, which ended tragically with the deaths of possibly hundreds of civilians.

For some three years, China's politics were almost frozen, but in 1992 Deng undertook what Chinese political insiders called his 'southern tour', or *nánxún*. By visiting Shēnzhèn, one of the SEZs, Deng indicated that the economic policies of reform were not going to be abandoned.

21st-Century China

From 2002, the leadership made efforts to deal with growing regional inequality and the poverty scarring rural areas. The question of political reform, however, found itself shelved, partly because economic growth was bringing prosperity to so many, albeit in uneven fashion. For many, the first decade of the 21st century was marked by spectacular riches for some – the number of dollar billionaires doubled in just two years – and escalating property prices. This period coincided with the greatest migration of workers to the cities the world has ever seen.

Vice-president from 2008, Xi Jinping replaced Hu Jintao as president in 2013. Pledging to root out corruption, Xi has also sought to instigate reforms, including a relaxation of the one-child policy and the abolition of the *láojiào* (re-education through labour) system. These reforms, however, were matched by a growing zeal for internet and social media controls and a domestic security budget that sucked in more capital than national defense.

Xi Jinping inherited a China that was a tremendous success story, but one that remained beset with problems. Despite resilient and ambitious planning (massive expansion of the high-speed rail network, a space program setting itself bold targets, some of the world's tallest buildings), the Chinese economy was still fundamentally imbalanced. Skewed towards the export industry and high-investment projects, growth needed to derive more from domestic demand to create sustainability, a challenge that his predecessor had left on the back burner but which requires Xi's increasing attention today.

2009
July riots in Ürümqi leave hundreds dead as inter-ethnic violence flares between Uighurs and Han Chinese.

2010
The largest ever World Expo is held in Shànghǎi in spring.

2013
China's lunar lander *Chang'e 3* touches down on the moon in December, the first spacecraft to soft-land on the moon since 1976.

Family Travel

Children with umbrellas, Sìchuān

KEREN SU/GETTY IMAGES

China is full of promise as a family travel destination, but this potential remains largely unrealised. As parents, an adventurous spirit is crucial and you should treat any journey to China with your children as a learning curve, in more ways than one. If you expect to find the kind of kid-friendly service that you find in the West, you will arrive unprepared.

The Basics

Foreign children will feel more at home in the large cities of Hong Kong, Macau, Běijīng and Shànghǎi, where there is a service industry (hotels, restaurants and sights) attuned to the needs of parents, but in smaller towns and rural areas, little provision is made.

Travelling long distances with children in China has its own challenges. Hiring a car is problematic and remains an unrealistic way of travelling, partly because the car-hire network remains undeveloped, you cannot drive everywhere and China is simply massive. Trains (especially sleepers) are great fun, but can get crowded; on long-distance trains, food options are limited. Long-distance buses are also crowded and seatbelts often not provided. Many taxis in provincial towns only have seatbelts in the front.

Food is another challenge. While larger towns will have Western restaurants, outside of fast food, smaller towns may only have serve local food (fine for adults, not necessarily for young kids).

Sightseeing also needs to be varied. Teenagers may not share your enthusiasm for China's ancient sights, but they may fall for the great scenic outdoors. China may not have many famous beaches, but your children will enjoy balmy Qīngdǎo (p172). There are also some fantastic museums – especially in the large cities – and Shànghǎi, Běijīng, Hong Kong and other large towns have plenty of amusements to keep children occupied, from theme parks to high-altitude observation decks, ice skating rinks, aquariums, acrobatics shows, zoos and much more.

Safety

The Chinese love children and pay them a lot of attention; expect your children to receive even more attention for the colour of their hair or eyes.

China is generally very safe for non-Chinese children. Trafficking in Chinese children in China does occur and is a source of anxiety for Chinese mothers, but non-Chinese-looking children are generally left alone. Your biggest concerns may be what your children eat and keeping an eye on them when they cross the road.

The Best...
For Children

1 Star Ferry, Hong Kong (p286)

2 Shànghǎi World Financial Center Observation Deck (p202)

3 Acrobatics show, Shànghǎi Centre Theatre (p218)

4 Yángshuò (p316)

5 Qīngdǎo's beaches (p175)

6 Peak Tram, Hong Kong (p279)

Practicalities

For train travel, children shorter than 1.4m can get a hard sleeper for 75% of the full price or a half-price hard seat. Children shorter than 1.1m ride free, but you have to hold them the entire journey.

Many sights and museums have children's admission prices, which usually apply to children under 1.3m in height. Infants under the age of two fly for 10% of the full airfare, while children between the ages of two and 11 pay half the full price for domestic flights and 75% of the adult price for international flights.

Strollers are hard to come by, and you may wish to take your own. If so, prepare for the inconvenience of uneven pavements. Escalators at metro stations are often up only.

Always ensure that your child carries a form of ID and a hotel card in case they get lost.

Baby food and milk powder are widely available in supermarkets, as are basics like nappies, baby wipes, bottles, medicine, dummies and other paraphernalia. Few restaurants have highchairs or kids' menus, and finding baby-changing rooms is next to impossible. Hotels with cots are also rare.

Ask a doctor specialising in travel medicine for information on recommended immunisations for your child.

363

The People of China

Family outside their home

Despite being the world's most populous nation – stamping ground of roughly one-fifth of humanity – China is often regarded as homogenous. This is perhaps because the Han Chinese – the predominant ethnic type in this energetic and bustling nation – constitute more than 90% of the population. But as with China's mystifying linguistic babel, you only have to pop your travelling shoes on to discover a vibrant mix of diverse ethnicities.

Ethnic Make-up

Han Chinese (Han zu) – the largest clan in China and the nation's 56th recognised ethnic group – make up the lion's share of China's people, 92% of the total figure. When we think of China – from its writing system to its visual arts, calligraphy, history, literature, language and politics – we tend to associate it with Han culture.

The Han Chinese live throughout China but are generally concentrated along the Yellow River, Yangzi River and Pearl River basins. A glance, however, at a map of China reveals that these core heartland regions of Han China are fragments of contemporary China's vast expanse. The colossal regions of Tibet, Qīnghǎi, Xīnjiāng, Inner Mongolia and the three provinces of the northeast (Manchuria) are all historically non-Han regions, areas of which remain essentially non-Han today.

Many of these regions are peopled by some of the remaining 8% of the population: China's 55 other ethnic minorities, known collectively as *shǎoshù mínzú* (少数民族; minority nationals). The largest minority groups in China include the Zhuang (壮族), Manchu (满族), Miao (苗族), Uighur (维吾尔族), Yi (彝族), Tujia (土家族), Tibetan (藏族), Hui (回族), Mongolian (蒙古族), Buyi (布依族), Dong (侗族), Yao (瑶族), Korean (朝鲜族), Bai (白族), Hani (哈尼族), Li (黎族), Kazak (哈萨克族) and Dai (傣族). Population sizes differ dramatically, from the abundant Zhuang in Guǎngxī to meagre numbers of Menba (门巴族) in Tibet. Ethnic labelling can be reasonably fluid: the Hakka (客家) were once regarded as a separate minority, but are today considered Han Chinese.

China Demographics

Population 1.35 billion

Birth rate 12.25 births per 1000 people

Percentage of people over 65 years of age 9.4%

Urbanisation rate 2.85%

Sex ratio (under age of 15) 1.17 (boys to girls)

Life expectancy 75 years

China's minorities tend to cluster along border regions, in the northwest, the west, the southwest, the north and northeast of China, but are also distributed unevenly throughout the land. Some minority peoples are found in one area alone (such as the Hani in Yúnnán); others, such as the Muslim Hui, are scattered across China.

Wedged into the southwest corner of China between Tibet, Myanmar (Burma), Vietnam and Laos, fecund Yúnnán province alone is home to over 20 ethnic groups, making it one of the most ethnically diverse and culturally rich provinces in the country.

The Chinese Character

Shaped by Confucian principles, the Chinese of today's China are thoughtful and discreet, but also highly pragmatic and practically minded. Conservative and somewhat introverted, they favour dark clothing over bright or loud colours while their body language is reserved and undemonstrative, yet attentive.

The Chinese (apart from the Shanghainese, some Chinese insist) are particularly generous. Don't be surprised if a Chinese person you have just met on a train invites you for a meal in the dining carriage. They will insist on paying, in which case do not try to thwart their efforts. The Chinese also simply adore children and delight in showing them affection.

Particularly diligent, the Chinese are inured to the kind of hours that may prompt a workers' insurrection elsewhere. This is partly due to a traditional culture of hard work, but it is also a response to inadequate social security safety nets and an expression of anxiety regarding economic and political uncertainties. The Chinese impressively save much of what they earn, emphasising the virtue of prudence. Despite this restraint, however, wastefulness can be astounding when 'face' is involved: mountains of food are often left on restaurant dining tables, particularly if important guests are present.

The Chinese are also an exceptionally dignified people. They are proud of their civilisation and history, their written language and of their inventions and achievements. This pride rarely comes across as arrogance or self-assurance, however, and may be tinged with a lack of confidence. The Chinese may, for example,

be very gratified by China's newfound world status, but might squirm at the mention of food safety and hygiene.

The modern Chinese character has been shaped by recent political realities, and while Chinese people have always been reserved and circumspect, in today's China they can appear even more prudent. Impressive mental gymnastics are performed to detour contentious domestic political issues, which can make the mainland Chinese appear complicated, despite their reputation for being straightforward and down-to-earth.

Women in China

Chairman Mao once said that women hold up half the sky, and when Liu Yang became the first Chinese woman in space in 2012, his words took on a new meaning.

Women in today's China officially share complete equality with men; however, as with other nations that profess sexual equality, the reality is often far different. Chinese women do not enjoy strong political representation and the Chinese Communist Party (CCP) remains a largely patriarchal organisation. Iconic political leaders from the early days of the CCP were all men and the influential echelons of the party remain a largely male domain. For example, only a handful of the great scientists celebrated in a long photographic mural at Shànghǎi's Science and Technology Museum are women.

High-profile, successful Chinese businesswomen are very much in the public eye, but the relative lack of career opportunities for females in other fields also indicates a continuing bias against women in employment. Women in today's China enjoy more freedom than ever before, but sexual discrimination in the workplace continues to survive.

In traditional China, an ideal woman's behaviour was governed by the 'three obediences and four virtues' of Confucian thought. The three obediences were submission to the father before marriage, husband after marriage and sons in the

Bai women, Yúnnán
DAMIEN SIMONIS/GETTY IMAGES ©

case of widows. The four virtues were propriety in behaviour, demeanour, speech and employment.

After 1949, the Communist Party tried to outlaw old customs and place women on equal footing with men. As a result it abolished arranged marriages and encouraged women to get an education and join the workforce. Women were allowed to keep their maiden name upon marriage and leave their property to their children. In its quest for equality during this period however, the Communist Party seemed to 'desexualise' women, fashioning instead a kind of idealised worker/mother/peasant paradigm.

China's One-Child Policy

The 'one-child policy' (in effect a misnomer) was railroaded into effect in 1979 in a bid to keep China's population to one billion by the year 2000 (a target it failed to meet); the latest government estimate claims the population will peak at 1.5 billion in 2033.

The policy was harshly implemented at first but rural revolt led to a softer stance; nonetheless, it generated much bad feeling between local officials and the rural population.

All non-Han minorities are exempt from the one-child policy; Han Chinese parents who were both single children could have a second child and in a new policy initiative from 2013, this has been expanded to include couples, if at least one of them is a single child. Rural families are allowed to have two children if the first child is a girl, but some have upwards of three or four kids. Additional children often result in fines and families having to shoulder the cost of education themselves, without government assistance.

Official policy opposes forced abortion or sterilisation, but allegations of coercion continue as local officials strive to meet population targets. In 2014, the film director Zhang Yimou was fined US$1.2m for breaking the one-child policy.

Families who abided by the one-child policy often went to great lengths to make sure their child was male. In parts of China, this resulted in a serious imbalance of the sexes – in 2010, 118 boys were born for every 100 girls. In some provinces the imbalance has been even higher. By 2020, potentially around 35 million Chinese men may be unable to find spouses.

Another consequence of the one-child policy was a rapidly ageing population, with more than a quarter of the populace predicted to be over the age of sixty-five by 2050.

As women can have a second child abroad, which has led to large numbers of mainland women giving birth in Hong Kong (where the child also qualified for Hong Kong citizenship). The Hong Kong government has used new legislation to curb this phenomenon, dubbed 'birth tourism', as government figures revealed that almost half of babies born in the territory in 2010 were born to mainland parents. In 2013, the Hong Kong government prohibited mainland women from visiting Hong Kong to give birth, unless their husband is from the territory.

Women's improved social status today has meant that more women are putting off marriage until their late 20s or early 30s, choosing instead to focus on their education and career opportunities.

This has been enhanced by the rapid rise in house prices, further encouraging women to leave marriage (and having children) till a later age. Premarital sex and cohabitation before marriage are increasingly common in larger cities and lack the stigma they had several years ago.

As in other areas, a strong rural-urban divide exists and all is not well down on the farm. Urban women are far more optimistic and freer, while women from rural areas, where traditional beliefs are at their strongest, fight an uphill battle against discrimination. Rural China is heavily weighted against girls, while a marked preference for baby boys over baby girls endures. This has resulted in an imbalance between China's population of men to women, a consequence of female foeticide, selective abortions and even infanticide. China's women are more likely to commit suicide than men (bucking the global trend), while rural Chinese women are up to five times as likely to kill themselves.

When one considers the fact that most of the Chinese population lives in rural areas, the problem comes into frightening perspective.

Some Chinese women are making strong efforts to protect the rights of women in China, receiving international attention in the process. In 2010 the Simone de Beauvoir prize for women's freedom was awarded to Guo Jianmei, a Chinese lawyer and human rights activist, and filmmaker and professor Ai Xiaoming. Guo Jianmei also received the International Women of Courage Award in 2012.

Who's in the Middle?

China's middle class (zhōng chǎn jiējí) is a controversial subject. For starters, no one can agree on how it should be defined. China's State Information Centre takes a numbers approach, identifying the middle class as those whose annual income is between US$7300 and US$73,000 (¥50,000 to ¥500,000). International banks and market research groups tend to raise the bar slightly higher, identifying the minimum cut-off at US$10,000 (¥68,382) and looking at factors such as whether or not households own a car, apartment, eat out regularly and so on.

Other economists, however, are less enthusiastic. Dragonomics, which publishes the China Economic Quarterly, believes that 'middle class' is a misleading term; many Chinese described as such are in fact considerably poorer than their counterparts in developed countries. Their study argues that the country consists of 'consuming China' – 110 million people living in the Běijīng, Shànghǎi and Guǎngzhōu metropolitan areas – and 'surviving China' – everyone else. But however you define it, everyone does agree that the middle class – or the consumers – are on the rise.

According to official figures, over half of China's urban population will have an annual income of more than $7300 by 2025.

Lifestyle

Economic liberalisation measures mean that the people of China today enjoy a far more diverse array of lifestyles than at any other time in their history. Young, ambitious Chinese are presented with a totally modern and sophisticated set of urban living choices. Unlike the West, very few young Chinese are idealists driven by anti-establishment goals, so the generation may appear brash and materialistic. This mindset is not their fault, but a reflection of government policy to create – through propaganda and education – a generation that is largely in agreement with its mandate.

Beyond ethnic differences, the big divide is between the city and the countryside. The culture of the big city – with its bars, white-collar jobs, desirable schools, dynamism and opportunities – stands in marked contrast to rural China, where little may have changed in the past three decades.

Further polarisations include the generation gap. An absence of sympathy exists between youngsters and their parents, and in particular their grandparents', generation.

This misunderstanding can, in a Western context, be explained by youthful rebellion and nonconformity. Chinese youths, however, are generally more conformist than their Western counterparts; what is more evident is the juxtaposition of two completely opposing political cultures and generations, one that was communist and the other which is staunchly materialist and more egocentric.

Muslim boys in Xī'ān's Muslim Quarter (p139)
GREG ELMS/GETTY IMAGES ©

Chinese Cuisine

Cuisine plays a central role in both Chinese society and the national psyche. When Chinese people meet, a common greeting is 'Nǐ chī fàn le ma?' – 'Have you eaten yet?'. Work, play, romance, business and the family all revolve around food. Meals are occasions to clinch deals, strike up new friendships and rekindle old ones. All you need to explore this tasty domain is a visa, a pair of chopsticks, an adventurous palate and a passion for the unexpected.

Real Chinese Food

Because the nation so skilfully exported it cuisine overseas, your very first impressions of China were probably via your taste buds. Chinatowns the world over teem with the aromas of Chinese cuisine, ferried overseas by China's versatile and hard-working cooks.

But what you see – and taste – at home is usually just a wafer-thin slice of a very hefty and good-looking pie. Chinese cuisine in the West is culled from the cookbook of an emigrant community largely drawn from China's southern seaboard. So although you may be hard pressed to avoid dim sum and *cha siu* in your local Chinatown, discovering more 'obscure' specialities from Yúnnán, the northeast or Xīnjiāng can be a tough (fortune) cookie.

Remember that China is not that much smaller than Europe. Although Europe is a patchwork of different nation states, languages, cultural traditions and climates, China is also a smorgasbord of dialects, languages, ethnic minorities and often dramatic geographic and climatic differences. Eating your way around China is one of the best ways to journey the land, so pack a sense of culinary adventure along with your travelling boots!

Regional Cooking

The development of China's varied regional cuisines has been influenced by the climate, abundance of certain crops and animals, the type of terrain, proximity to the sea and last, but not least, the influence of neighbouring nations and the importation of ingredients and aromas. Naturally fish and seafood is prevalent in coastal regions of China, while in Inner Mongolia and Xīnjiāng there is a dependence on meat such as beef and lamb.

Many Chinese regions proudly lay claim to their own culinary conventions, which may overlap and cross-fertilise each other. The cooking traditions of China's ethnic minorities aside, Han cooking has traditionally been divided into **eight schools** (中华八大菜系; *zhōnghuá bādàcàixì*):

Chuān 川 (Sìchuān cuisine)
Huī 徽 (Ānhuī cuisine)
Lǔ 鲁 (Shāndōng cuisine)
Mǐn 闽 (Fújiàn cuisine)
Sū 苏 (Jiāngsū cuisine)
Yuè 粤 (Cantonese/Guǎngdōng cuisine)
Xiāng 湘 (Húnán cuisine)
Zhè 浙 (Zhèjiāng cuisine)

Although each school is independent and well defined, it is possible to group these eight culinary traditions into **Northern**, **Southern**, **Western** and **Eastern** cooking.

A common philosophy lies at the heart of Chinese cooking, whatever the school. Most vegetables and fruits are yin foods, generally moist and soft, possessing a cooling effect while nurturing the feminine aspect. Yang foods – fried, spicy or with red meat – are warming and nourish the masculine side. Any meal should harmonise flavours and achieve a balance between cooling and warming foods.

Northern School

With Shāndōng cooking (鲁菜; *lǔcài*) – the oldest of the eight regional schools – at its heart, northern cooking also embraces Běijīng, northeastern (Manchurian) and Shānxī cuisine, creating the most time-honoured and most central form of Chinese cooking.

In the dry, north Chinese wheat belt an emphasis falls on millet, sorghum, maize, barley and wheat rather than rice (which requires lush irrigation by water to cultivate). Particularly well suited to the harsh and hardy winter climate, northern cooking is rich and wholesome. Filling breads – such as *mántou* (馒头) or *bǐng* (饼; flat breads) – are steamed, baked or fried, while noodles may form the basis of any northern meal (although the ubiquitous availability of rice means it can always be found). Northern cuisine is frequently quite salty, and appetising *jiǎozi* (饺子; dumplings) are widely eaten, usually boiled and sometimes fried.

> Of their various cooking schools, the Chinese traditionally say '南甜北咸东辣西酸' or 'Sweet in the south, salty in the north, hot in the east and sour in the west'. It's a massive generalisation, but as with most generalisations, there's more than a grain of truth.

As Běijīng was the principal capital through the Yuan, Ming and Qing dynasties, imperial cooking is a chief characteristic of the northern school. Peking duck is Běijīng's signature dish, served with typical northern ingredients – pancakes, spring onions and fermented bean paste.

With China ruled from 1644 to 1911 by non-Han Manchurians, the influence of northeast cuisine (*dōngběi cài*) has naturally deeply permeated northern cooking, dispensing a legacy of rich and hearty stews, dense breads, preserved foods and dumplings.

The nomadic and carnivorous diet of the Mongolians also infiltrates northern cooking, most noticeably in the Mongolian hotpot and the Mongolian barbecue.

Hallmark northern dishes include the following:

Běijīng kǎoyā	北京烤鸭	Peking duck
jiāo zhá yángròu	焦炸羊肉	deep-fried mutton
qīng xiāng shāo jī	清香烧鸡	chicken wrapped in lotus leaf
shuàn yángròu	涮羊肉	lamb hotpot
mántou	馒头	steamed buns
jiǎozi	饺子	dumplings
ròu bāozi	肉包子	steamed meat buns
sān měi dòufu	三美豆腐	sliced bean curd with Chinese cabbage

Southern School

The southern Chinese – particularly the Cantonese – historically spearheaded successive waves of immigration overseas, leaving aromatic constellations of Chinatowns around the world.

Typified by **Cantonese** cooking (粤菜; *yuècài*), southern cooking lacks the richness and saltiness of northern cooking, instead coaxing more subtle aromas to the fore. It's an article of faith to the Cantonese that good cooking requires little flavouring: it is the *xiān* (natural freshness) of the ingredients that mark a truly high-grade dish. Hence the near obsessive attention paid to the freshness of ingredients in southern cuisine.

The hallmark Cantonese dish is dim sum (点心; Mandarin: *diǎnxīn*). Dishes – often in steamers – are wheeled around on trolleys so you can see what you want to order. Well-known dim sum dishes include *guōtiē* (a kind of fried dumpling), *shāomài* (a kind of open pork dumpling), *chāshāobāo* (pork-filled bun) and *chūnjuǎn* (spring rolls).

Hitting the Hot Spot

The Sìchuān hotpot sets foreheads streaming and tummies aquiver all over China, from sultry Hǎinán Island to the frigid borderlands of Hēilóngjiāng. It is a fierce and smouldering concoction, bursting with fire and boiling with volcanic flavour.

The Mongolian hotpot is a very different and more subtle creature indeed. Mutton or lamb is the principal meat in a Mongolian hotpot, with scalded strips of meat rescued from the boiling soup and doused in thick sauces, especially *zhīmajiàng* (芝麻酱; sesame sauce). Vegetables – cabbage, mushrooms and potatoes – are also cast into the boiling froth and eaten when soft. The hotpot dates to when Mongolian soldiers would use their helmets as a pot, cooking them up over a fire with broth, meat, vegetables and condiments.

Fújiàn cuisine (闽菜; *mǐncài*) is another important southern cooking style, with its emphasis on light flavours and seafood. Hakka cuisine from the disparate and migratory Hakka people (Kèjiāzú) is another feature of southern Chinese cooking as is the food of Cháozhōu in eastern Guǎngdōng.

Rice is the primary staple of southern cooking. Sparkling paddy fields glitter across the south; the humid climate, plentiful rainfall and well-irrigated land means that rice has been farmed in the south since the Chinese first populated the region during the Han dynasty (206 BC–220 AD).

Southern dishes include the following:

bái zhuó xiā	白灼虾	blanched prawns with shredded scallions
mì zhī chāshāo	密汁叉烧	roast pork with honey
háoyóu niúròu	蚝油牛肉	beef with oyster sauce
kǎo rǔzhū	烤乳猪	crispy suckling pig
shé ròu	蛇肉	snake
tángcù páigǔ	糖醋排骨	sweet and sour spare ribs

Western School

The cuisine of landlocked western China, a region heavily dappled with ethnic shades, hogs the fierier end of the culinary spectrum. The trademark ingredient of the western school is the fiercely hot red chilli, a potent firecracker of a herb that deluges dishes with spiciness. Adding pungency and bite, aniseed, coriander, garlic and peppercorns are tossed in for good measure.

The standout cuisine of the western school is fiery **Sìchuān** (川菜; *chuāncài*) food, one of China's eight regional cooking styles, renowned for its eye-watering peppery aromas. One of the herbs that differentiates Sìchuān cooking from other spicy cuisines is the use of 'flower pepper' *(huājiāo),* a numbing peppercorn-like herb that floods the mouth with an anaesthetising fragrance in a culinary effect termed *málà* (numb and hot). The sweltering Chóngqìng hotpot is a force to be reckoned with but must be approached with a stiff upper lip (and copious amounts of liquid refreshment).

Another of China's eight regional schools of cooking, dishes from **Húnán** (湘菜; *xiāngcài*) are similarly pungent, with a heavy reliance on chilli. Unlike Sìchuān food, flower pepper is not employed and instead spicy flavours are often sharper and fiercer.

Dishes from the western school include the following:

gōngbào jīdīng	宫爆鸡丁	spicy chicken with peanuts
shuǐ zhǔ niúròu	水煮牛肉	spicy fried and boiled beef
suāncàiyú	酸菜鱼	sour cabbage fish soup
shuǐzhǔyú	水煮鱼	fried and boiled fish, garlic sprouts and celery
dāndan miàn	担担面	spicy noodles
huíguō ròu	回锅肉	boiled and stirfried pork with salty and hot sauce
Chóngqìng huǒguō	重庆火锅	Chóngqìng hotpot
yú xiāng ròusī	鱼香肉丝	fish-flavour pork strips
bàngbàng jī	棒棒鸡	shredded chicken in a hot pepper and sesame sauce
málà dòufu	麻辣豆腐	spicy tofu

Eastern School

The eastern school of Chinese cuisine belongs to a fecund region of China, slashed by waterways and canals, dotted with lakes, fringed by a long coastline and nourished by a subtropical climate. Jiāngsū province itself is the home of Jiāngsū cuisine (苏菜; sūcài) – one of the core regions of the eastern school – famed as the 'Land of Fish and Rice', a tribute to its abundance of food and produce. The combination of wealth and bountiful food has created a culture of epicurism and gastronomic enjoyment.

South of Jiāngsū, Zhèjiāng cuisine (浙菜; zhècài) is another cornerstone of Eastern cooking. The Song dynasty saw the blossoming of the restaurant industry here; in Hángzhōu, the southern Song-dynasty capital, restaurants and teahouses accounted for two-thirds of the city's business during a splendidly rich cultural era. With a lightness of flavour, Ānhuī cuisine (徽菜; huīcài) – one of China's eight principal culinary traditions and firmly in the eastern cooking sphere – puts less emphasis on seafood.

Generally oilier and sweeter than other Chinese schools, the eastern school revels in fish and seafood, in reflection of its watery geography. Fish is usually qīngzhēng (清蒸; steamed) but can be stirfried, panfried or grilled. Hairy crabs (dàzháxiè) are a Shànghǎi speciality between October and December. Eaten with soy, ginger and vinegar, and downed with warm Shàoxīng wine, the best crabs come from Yángchéng Lake.

As with Cantonese food, freshness is paramount and sauces and seasonings are only introduced to augment essential flavours. Stirfrying and steaming are also used, the latter with Shànghǎi's famous xiǎolóngbāo, steamer buns filled with nuggets of pork or crab swimming in a scalding meat broth.

Dumplings in a bamboo steamer
GREG ELMS/GETTY IMAGES ©

Famous dishes from the eastern school include the following:

jiāng cōng chǎo xiè	姜葱炒蟹	stirfried crab with ginger and scallions
xiǎolóngbāo	小笼包	steamer buns
mìzhī xūnyú	蜜汁熏鱼	honey-smoked carp
níng shì shànyú	宁式鳝鱼	stirfried eel with onion
qiézhī yúkuài	茄汁鱼块	fish fillet in tomato sauce
qīng zhēng guìyú	清蒸鳜鱼	steamed Mandarin fish
sōngzǐ guìyú	松子鳜鱼	Mandarin fish with pine nuts
yóubào xiārén	油爆虾仁	fried shrimp
zhá hēi lǐyú	炸黑鲤鱼	fried black carp
zhá yúwán	炸鱼丸	fish balls

Ordering Essentials

rice	báifàn	白饭
noodles	miàntiáo	面条
salt	yán	盐
pepper	hújiāo	胡椒
sugar	táng	糖
soy sauce	jiàngyóu	酱油
chilli	làjiāo	辣椒
egg	jīdàn	鸡蛋
beef	niúròu	牛肉
pork	zhūròu	猪肉
chicken	jīròu	鸡肉
lamb	yángròu	羊肉
vegetables	shūcài	蔬菜
potato	tǔdòu	土豆
broccoli	xīlánhuā	西兰花
carrots	húluóbo	胡萝卜
sweet corn	yùmǐ	玉米
green peppers	qīngjiāo	青椒
soup	tāng	汤
chopsticks	kuàizi	筷子
knife	dāozi	刀子
fork	chāzi	叉子
spoon	sháozi	勺子
hot	rède	热的
ice cold	bīngde	冰的

Home Style Dishes

Besides China's regional cuisines, there is a tasty variety of *jiāchángcài* (home-style) dishes you will see all over the land, cooked up in restaurants and along food streets.

gōngbào jīdīng	宫爆鸡丁	spicy chicken with peanuts; kung pao chicken
háoyóu niúròu	蚝油牛肉	beef with oyster sauce
hóngshāo páigǔ	红烧排骨	red-braised spare ribs
hóngshāo qiézi	红烧茄子	red-cooked aubergine
hóngshāo yú	红烧鱼	red-braised fish
huǒguō	火锅	hotpot
húntùn tāng	馄饨汤	wonton soup
jiācháng dòufu	家常豆腐	'homestyle' tofu
jiǎozi	饺子	dumplings
jīdànmiàn	鸡蛋面	noodles and egg
qīngjiāo ròupiàn	青椒肉片	pork and green peppers
shāguō dòufu	沙锅豆腐	bean curd casserole
suānlàtāng	酸辣汤	hot and sour soup
tiěbǎn niúròu	铁板牛肉	sizzling beef platter
xīhóngshì jīdàntāng	西红柿鸡蛋汤	egg and tomato soup
yúxiāng qiézi	鱼香茄子	fish-flavoured aubergine

Dining: the Ins & Outs

Chinese Restaurants

Restaurants in China serve scrumptious food, but finding eateries with any sense of warmth or charm can be a real task outside the big cities. With their huge round tables and thousand-candle-power electric lights, large banqueting-style restaurants are impersonal with little sense of intimacy or romance. At the lower end of the scale are the cheap Chinese restaurants, where diners leave chicken bones on the tabletop, loudly slurp their noodles, chain-smoke and shout into mobiles. At each extreme, the food is the focal point of the meal and what diners are there for. Many restaurants charge for the prepacked moist tissues which may be handed to you; you are not charged if you refuse them.

Dining Times

The Chinese eat early. Lunch usually commences from around 11.30am, either self-cooked or a takeaway at home, or in a street-side restaurant. Rushed urban diners may just grab a sandwich, a fast-food burger or a lunchbox. Dinner usually kicks off from around 6pm. Reflecting these dining times, some restaurants open at around 11am to close for an afternoon break at about 2.30pm before opening again at around 5pm and closing in the late evening.

Table Manners

It is good form to fill your neighbours' teacups or beer glasses when they are empty: show your appreciation to the pourer by gently tapping your middle finger on the table. To serve yourself tea or any other drink without serving others first is bad form.

It's best to wait till someone has announced a toast before drinking your beer; if you want to get a quick shot in, propose a toast to the host.

Smokers can light up during the meal, unless you are in the nonsmoking area of a restaurant. If you are a smoker, ensure you hand around your cigarettes to others as that is standard procedure.

Last but not least, never insist to the last on paying for the bill if someone is tenaciously determined on paying – usually the person who invited you to dinner. By all means offer but then raise your hands in mock surrender when resistance is met; to pay for a meal when another person is determined to pay is to make them lose face.

Chinese toothpick etiquette is similar to that found in other Asian nations: one hand excavates with the toothpick, while the other hand shields the mouth.

Street Food

Snacking your way around China is a fine way to sample the different flavours of the land while on the move. Most towns have a *yèshì* (夜市; street market or a night market) for good-value snacks and meals so you can either take away or park yourself on a wobbly stool and grab a beer.

Vegetarianism

If you'd rather chew on a legume than a leg of lamb, it can be hard going trying to find truly vegetarian dishes. China's history of famine and poverty means the consumption of meat has always been a sign of status and symbolic of health and wealth.

You will find that vegetables are often fried in animal-based oils, while vegetable soups may be made with chicken or beef stock, so simply choosing vegetable items on the menu is ineffective. In Běijīng and Shànghǎi you will, however, find a generous crop of vegetarian restaurants to choose from.

Out of the large cities, you may be hard pressed to find a vegetarian restaurant. Your best bet may to head to a sizeable active Buddhist temple or monastery, where you could well find a Buddhist vegetarian restaurant that is open to the public. Buddhist vegetarian food typically consists of 'mock meat' dishes created from tofu, wheat gluten, potato and other vegetables.

If you want to say 'I am a vegetarian' in Chinese, say 我吃素 (wǒ chī sù).

Making noodles

Arts & Architecture

Ceramics stall, Pānjiāyuán Market (p106), Běijīng

MANFRED GOTTSCHALK/GETTY IMAGES

China is custodian of one of the world's richest cultural and artistic legacies. Until the 20th century, China's arts were deeply conservative and resistant to change, but in the last hundred years revolutions in technique and content have fashioned a dramatic transformation. Despite this evolution, China's arts – whatever the period – remain united by a common aesthetic that taps into the very soul and essence of the nation.

Aesthetics

In reflection of the Chinese character (p365), Chinese aesthetics have traditionally been marked by restraint and understatement, a preference for oblique references over direct explanation, vagueness in place of specificity and an avoidance of the obvious in place of a fondness for the veiled and subtle.

For millennia, Chinese aesthetics were highly traditionalist and, despite coming under the influence of occupiers from the Mongols to the Europeans, defiantly conservative. It was not until the fall of the Qing dynasty in 1911 and the appearance of the New Culture Movement that China's great artistic traditions began to rapidly transform. In literature the stranglehold of classical Chinese loosened to allow breathing space for *báihuà* (colloquial Chinese) and a progressive new aesthetic began to flower, ultimately leading to revolutions in all of the arts, from poetry to painting, theatre and music.

Painting

Traditional Painting

As described in Xie He's 6th century AD treatise, the *Six Principles of Painting*, the chief aim of Chinese painting is to capture the innate essence or spirit *(qì)* of a subject and imbue it with vitality. As a general rule, painters were less concerned with achieving outward resemblance (that was the third principle) than with conveying intrinsic qualities.

Early painters dwelled on the human figure and moral teachings, while also conjuring up scenes from everyday life. By the time of the Tang dynasty, a new genre, known as landscape painting, had begun to flower. Reaching full bloom during the Song and Yuan dynasties, landscape painting meditated on the environment around man. Towering mountains, ethereal mists, open spaces, trees and rivers, and light and dark were all exquisitely presented in ink washes on silk.

On a technical level, the success of landscapes depended on the artists' skill in capturing light and atmosphere. Blank, open spaces devoid of colour create light-filled voids, contrasting with the darkness of mountain folds, filling the painting with *qì* and vaporous vitality. Specific emotions are not aroused but instead nebulous sensations permeate. Painting and classical poetry often went hand in hand, best exemplified by the work of Tang-dynasty poet/artist Wang Wei (699–759).

Modern Art

After 1949, classical Chinese techniques were abandoned and foreign artistic techniques imported wholesale. Washes on silk were replaced with oil on canvas and China's traditional obsession with the mysterious and ineffable made way for concrete attention to detail and realism.

By 1970, Chinese artists had aspired to master the skills of socialist-realism, a vibrant communist-endorsed style that drew from European neoclassical art, the lifelike canvases of Jacques Louis David and the output of Soviet Union painters. The entire trajectory of Chinese painting – which had evolved in glacial increments over the centuries – had been redirected virtually overnight.

It was only with the death of Mao Zedong in September 1976 that the shadow of the Cultural Revolution – when Chinese aesthetics were conditioned by the threat of violence – began its retreat and the individual artistic temperament was allowed to re-emerge. Painters such as Luo Zhongli employed the realist techniques gleaned from China's art academies to depict the harsh realities etched in the faces of contemporary peasants. A voracious appetite for Western art introduced fresh concepts and ideas while the ambiguity of exact meaning in the fine arts offered a degree of protection from state censors.

Much post-1989 Chinese art dwelled obsessively on contemporary socio-economic realities, with consumer culture, materialism, urbanisation and social change a repetitive focus. Meanwhile, many artists who left China in the 1990s have returned, setting up private studios and galleries.

Cynical realists Fang Lijun and Yue Minjun fashioned grotesque portraits that conveyed hollowness and mock joviality, tinged with despair. Born just before the Cultural Revolution in 1964 and heavily influenced by German expressionism, Zeng Fanzhi explored the notions of alienation and isolation – themes commonly explored by Chinese artists during this period – in his *Mask* series from the 1990s.

Ai Weiwei, who enjoys great international fame partly due to his defiant stand, best exemplifies the tense overlap between artistic self-expression, dissent and conflict with the authorities in China today. Arrested in 2011 and charged with tax evasion, Ai Weiwei gained further publicity for his temporary *Sunflower Seeds* exhibition at London's Tate Modern, which featured millions of handpainted porcelain seeds. In 2012, he also jointly won the inaugural Vaclav Havel Prize for Creative Dissent from the Human Rights Foundation, along with Myanmar's Aung San Suu Kyi.

Working collaboratively as Birdhead, Shànghǎi analog photographers Ji Weiyu and Song Tao record the social dynamics and architectural habitat of their home city in thoughtful compositions. Běijīng-born Ma Qiusha works in video, photography, painting and installations on themes of a deeply personal nature. In her video work From No.4 Pingyuanli to No.4 Tianqiaobeili, the artist removes a bloody razor blade from her mouth after narrating her experiences as a young artist in China. Born in 1982, Ran Huang works largely in film but across a spectrum of media, conveying themes of absurdity, the irrational and conceptual. Shànghǎi artist Shi Zhiying explores ideas of a more traditional hue in her sublime oil paint depictions on large canvases of landscapes and religious and cultural objects. Also from Shànghǎi, Xu Zhen works with provocative images to unsettle and challenge the viewer. Xu's Fearless (2012), a large mixed-media work on canvas, is a powerful maelstrom of symbolism and the fragments of cultural identity. Xīnjiāng-born Zhao Zhao – once an assistant to Ai Weiwei – communicates provocative sentiments in his work. In an interview with Der Spiegel, Zhao Zhao observed: 'There are lines that you can't cross in this state. I try to resist being tamed as an artist'.

Literature

Classical Chinese novels evolved from the popular folktales and dramas that entertained the lower classes. During the Ming dynasty they were penned in a semi-vernacular (or 'vulgar') language, and are often irreverently funny and full of action-packed fights.

Probably the best-known novel outside China is *Journey to the West* (Xīyóu Jì) – more commonly known as *Monkey*. Written in the 16th century, it follows the misadventures of a cowardly Buddhist monk (Tripitaka; a stand-in for the real-life pilgrim Xuan Zang) and his companions – a rebellious monkey, lecherous pig-man and exiled monster-immortal – on a pilgrimage to India. In 2007 a Chinese director collaborated with Damon Albarn of the virtual band Gorillaz to transform the story into a circus opera that has played to considerable international acclaim.

The 14th-century novel *The Water Margin/Outlaws of the Marsh/All Men Are Brothers* (Shuǐhǔ Zhuàn) is, on the surface, an excellent tale of honourable bandits and corrupt officials along the lines of the stories of Robin Hood. On a deeper level, though, it is a reminder to Confucian officials of their right to rebel when faced with a morally suspect government (at least one emperor officially banned it).

Classical Chinese maintained its authority over literary minds until the early 20th century, when it increasingly came under the influence of the West. Torch-bearing author Lu Xun wrote his short story *Diary of a Madman* in 1918. Apart from the opening paragraph, Lu's seminal and shocking fable is written in colloquial Chinese. For Lu Xun to write his short story in colloquial Chinese was explosive, as readers were finally able to read language as it was spoken.

A growing number of contemporary voices have been translated into English, but far more exist in Chinese only. The 2012 Nobel Prize in Literature-winner Mo Yan (*Life and Death Are Wearing Me Out*; 2008), Yu Hua (*To Live*; 1992) and Su Tong (*Rice*; 1995) have written momentous historical novels set in the 20th century; all are excellent, though not for the faint of heart.

'Hooligan author' Wang Shuo (*Please Don't Call Me Human*; 2000) is one of China's best-selling authors with his political satires and convincing depictions of urban slackers. Émigré Ma Jian (*Red Dust*; 2004) writes more politically critical work; his debut was a Kerouacian tale of wandering China as a spiritual pollutant in the 1980s.

Controversial blogger Han Han (http://blog.sina.com.cn/twocold) catapulted himself into the literary spotlight with his novel *Triple Door*, a searing critique of China's educational system.

Winner of the Man Asian Literary Prize in 2010, Bi Feiyu's *Three Sisters* is a poignant tale of rural China during the political chaos of the early 1970s. In *Northern Girls*, Sheng Keyi illuminates the prejudices and bigotries of modern Chinese society in her story of a Chinese girl arriving as an immigrant worker in Shēnzhèn.

Film

The moving image in the Middle Kingdom dates to 1896, when Spaniard Galen Bocca unveiled a film projector and blew the socks off wide-eyed crowds in a Shànghǎi teahouse. Shànghǎi opened its first cinema in 1908; soon cinema owners would cannily run the film for a few minutes, stop it and collect money from the audience before allowing the film to continue.

The golden age of Shànghǎi film-making came in the 1930s when the city had more than 140 film companies, but China's film industry was stymied after the Communist Revolution, which sent film-makers scurrying to Hong Kong and Taiwan.

It wasn't until two years after the death of Mao Zedong that the Běijīng Film Academy, China's premier film school, reopened in September 1978. Its first intake of students included Zhang Yimou, Chen Kaige and Tian Zhuangzhuang – masterminds of the celebrated 'Fifth Generation'. Rich, seminal works such as *Farewell My Concubine* (1993; Chen Kaige) and *Raise the Red Lantern* (1991; Zhang Yimou) were garlanded with praise, winning standing ovations and netting major film awards.

Sixth Generation film directors eschewed the luxurious beauty of their forebears, and sought to capture the angst and grit of modern urban Chinese life.

Jia Zhangke has emerged as the most acclaimed of China's new film-makers. His meditative and compassionate look at the social impact of the construction of the Three Gorges Dam on local people, *Still Life* (2006), scooped the Golden Lion at the 2006 Venice Film Festival.

Historical *wuxia* (martial arts) cinema is enduringly popular in China and typified much film-making in the noughties, with films like *Hero* (2002; Zhang Yimou), *House of Flying Daggers* (2004; Zhang Yimou) and *The Banquet* (2006; Feng Xiaogang) leading the way. Epic historical war dramas such as *Red Cliff* (2008 & 2009; John Woo) and *The Warlords* (2007; Peter Chan) belong to a similar genre. The Hong Kong director Wong Kar-wai is particularly notable for seductively filmed classics such as *In the Mood for Love* (2000) and *2046* (2004).

Zhang Yimou's *The Flowers of War* (2011) gained considerable acclaim for its depiction of the horrific Rape of Nanking in 1937. Feng Xiaogang's popular *Aftershock* (2010) dealt with the traumatic events surrounding the devastating Tángshān earthquake of 1976. Grossing more than US$200 million at the Chinese box office, *Lost in Thailand* (2012; Xu Zheng) was a highly successful Chinese slapstick comedy, bringing a refreshing change to a cinematic landscape otherwise dominated by martial arts films, period dramas and historical blockbusters.

The Best... Art Museums

1 Shànghǎi Museum (p195)

2 Poly Art Museum, Běijīng's (p92)

3 Rockbund Art Museum, Shànghǎi (p191)

4 Hong Kong Museum of Art (p278)

Architecture

If modern architecture in China is regarded as anything post-1949, then China has ridden a roller-coaster ride of styles and fashions. In Běijīng, stand between the Great Hall of the People (1959) and the National Centre for the Performing Arts (2008) and weigh up how far China travelled in 50 years. Interestingly, neither building has clear Chinese motifs. The same applies to the complex form of Běijīng's CCTV Building, where a continuous loop through horizontal and vertical planes required some audacious engineering.

Many of the top names in international architecture – IM Pei, Rem Koolhaas, Norman Foster, Kengo Kuma, Jean-Marie Charpentier, Herzog & de Meuron – have all designed at least one building in China in the past decade. Other impressive examples of modern architecture include the National Stadium (aka the 'Bird's Nest'), the National Aquatics Centre (aka the 'Water Cube') and Běijīng south train station, all in Běijīng; and the art deco-esque Jīnmào Tower, the towering Shànghǎi World Financial Center, Tomorrow Square and the Shànghǎi Tower in Shànghǎi. In Hong Kong, the glittering 2 International Finance Centre on Hong Kong Island and the International Commerce Centre in Kowloon are each prodigious examples of modern skyscraper architecture. The planned Sky City in the Húnán capital of Chángshā will be the world's tallest building, if built. The company aiming to erect it – Broad Sustainable Building – says the job can be completed in just 90 days, although the go-ahead was still awaiting government approval at the time of writing. Opening in Chéngdū in 2013, the staggeringly large New Century Global Center is the world's largest freestanding building: big enough to swallow up 20 Sydney Opera Houses!'

Oriental Pearl TV Tower (p204), Shànghǎi

Religion & Beliefs

Writing Buddhist scriptures

BRADLEY MAYHEW/GETTY IMAGES ©

Ideas have always possessed a certain volatility in China. The Taiping Rebellion (1850–64) fused Christianity with revolutionary principles of social organisation, leaving 20 million dead in its bloody 20-year spasm. Communism itself is – or was – an ideology that briefly assumed immense authority over the minds of China's citizens. Today's Chinese may be more down-to-earth and pragmatic, but they are increasingly returning to religion after decades of state-orchestrated atheism.

Buddhism

Although not an indigenous faith, Buddhism (Fó Jiào) is the religion most deeply associated with China, Tibet and Chinatowns abroad. Many Chinese may not be regular temple-goers but they possess an interest in Buddhism; they may merely be 'cultural Buddhists', with a fondness for Buddhist civilisation.

Buddhism in China

Like other faiths such as Christianity, Nestorianism, Islam and Judaism, Buddhism originally reached China via the Silk Road. The earliest recorded Buddhist temple in China proper dates back to the 1st century AD at Luòyáng but it was not until the 4th century when a period of warlordism coupled with nomadic invasions plunged the country into disarray, that Buddhism gained mass appeal. Buddhism's sudden growth during this period

The Best... Buddhist Temples

1 Lama Temple, Běijīng (p72)

2 Labrang Monastery, Xiàhé (p341)

3 Pǔníng Temple, Chéngdé (p121)

4 Xiǎntōng Temple, Wǔtái Shān (p157)

5 Língyǐn Temple, Hángzhōu (p239)

6 Pǔtuózōngchéng Temple, Chéngdé (p120)

is often attributed to its sophisticated ideas concerning the afterlife (such as karma and reincarnation), a dimension unaddressed by either Confucianism or Taoism. At a time when existence was especially precarious, spiritual transcendence was understandably popular.

As Buddhism converged with Taoist philosophy (through terminology used in translation) and popular religion (through practice), it went on to develop into something distinct from the original Indian tradition. The most famous example is the esoteric Chan school (Zen in Japanese), which originated sometime in the 5th or 6th century, and focused on attaining enlightenment through meditation.

Buddhist Schools

Regardless of its various forms, most Buddhism in China belongs to the Mahayana school, which holds that since all existence is one, the fate of the individual is linked to the fate of others. Thus, Bodhisattvas, those who have already achieved enlightenment but have chosen to remain on earth, continue to work for the liberation of all other sentient beings.

Ethnic Tibetans and Mongols within the People's Republic of China (PRC) practise a unique form of Mahayana Buddhism known as Tibetan or Tantric Buddhism (Lǎma Jiào). Tibetan Buddhism, sometimes called Vajrayana or 'thunderbolt vehicle', has been practised since the early 7th century AD and is influenced by Tibet's pre-Buddhist Bon religion, which relied on priests or shamans to placate spirits, gods and demons. Priests called lamas are believed to be reincarnations of highly evolved beings; the Dalai Lama is the supreme patriarch of Tibetan Buddhism.

Taoism

A home-grown philosophy/religion, Taoism is also perhaps the hardest of all China's faiths to grasp. Controversial, paradoxical, and – like the Tao itself – impossible to pin down, it is a natural counterpoint to rigid Confucianist order and correctness.

Taoism predates Buddhism in China and much of its religious culture connects to a distant animism and shamanism, despite the purity of its philosophical school. In its earliest and simplest form, Taoism draws from *The Classic of the Way and its Power* (Dàodé Jìng), penned by the sagacious Laotzu (Laozi; c 580–500 BC).

The Classic of the Way and its Power is a work of astonishing insight and sublime beauty. Devoid of a godlike being or deity, Laotzu's 's writings instead endeavour to address the unknowable and ineffable principle of the universe which he calls dao (道; dào), or 'the way'. This way is the method by which the universe operates, so it can be understood to be a universal or cosmic principle.

Confucianism

Confucianism is based upon the teachings of Confucius (Kǒngzǐ), a 6th century BC philosopher who lived during a period of constant warfare and social upheaval. While Confucianism changed considerably throughout the centuries, some of the principal ideas remained the same – namely an emphasis on five basic hierarchical relationships: father-son, ruler-subject, husband-wife, elder-younger and friend-friend. Confucius believed that if each individual carried out his or her proper role in society (ie a son served his father respectfully while a father provided for his son, a subject served his ruler respectfully while a ruler provided for his subject, and so on) social order would be achieved. Confucius' disciples later gathered his ideas in the form of short aphorisms and conversations, forming the work known as *The Analects* (Lúnyǔ).

Christianity

Christianity first arrived in China with the Nestorians, a sect from ancient Persia which spilt with the Byzantine Church in AD 431, who arrived in China via the Silk Road in the 7th century. A celebrated tablet in Xī'ān's Forest of Stelae Museum (p133) records their arrival. Much later, in the 16th century, the Jesuits arrived and were popular figures at the imperial court, although they made few converts.

Some estimates point to as many as 100 million Christians in China. However, the exact population is hard to calculate as many groups – outside of the four official Christian organisations – lead a strict underground existence (in what are called 'house churches') out of fear of a political clampdown.

Islam

Islam (Yīsīlán Jiào) in China dates to the 7th century, when it was first brought to China by Arab and Persian traders along the Silk Road. Later, during the Mongol Yuan dynasty, maritime trade increased, bringing new waves of merchants to China's coastal regions, particularly the port cities of Guǎngzhōu and Quánzhōu. The descendants of these groups – now scattered across the country – gradually integrated into Han culture, and are today distinguished primarily by their religion. In Chinese, they are referred to as the Hui.

Other Muslim groups include the Uighurs, Kazaks, Kyrgyz, Tajiks and Uzbeks, who live principally in the border areas of the northwest. It is estimated that 1.5% to 3% of Chinese today are Muslim.

China's Landscapes

Three Gorges (p254)

VIEWSTOCK/GETTY IMAGES

The world's third-largest country – on a par size-wise with the USA – China covers a colossal 9.5 million sq km, only surpassed in area by Russia and Canada. Straddling natural environments as diverse as subarctic tundra in the north and tropical rainforests in the south, this massive land embraces the world's highest mountain range and one of its hottest deserts in the west, to the steamy, typhoon-lashed coastline of the South China Sea.

The Land

Mountains & Deserts

China has a largely mountainous and hilly topography, commencing in precipitous fashion in the vast and sparsely populated Qīnghǎi–Tibetan plateau in the west and levelling out gradually towards the fertile, well-watered, populous and wealthy provinces of eastern China.

Averaging 4500m above sea level, the Qīnghǎi–Tibetan region's highest peaks thrust up in the Himalayan mountain range along its southern rim, where mountains average about 6000m above sea level, with 40 peaks rising dizzyingly to 7000m or more. This vast high-altitude region (Tibet alone constitutes one-eighth of China's landmass) is home to an astonishing 37,000 glaciers, the third-largest mass of ice on the planet after the Arctic and Antarctic.

This mountain geology further corrugates the rest of China, continuously rippling the land into spectacular mountain ranges.

China also contains extensive – and growing – desert regions that occupy almost a fifth of the country's landmass, largely in its mighty northwest. These are inhospitably sandy and rocky expanses where summers are torturously hot and winters bone-numbingly cold. North towards Kazakhstan and Kyrgyzstan from the plateaus of Tibet and Qīnghǎi lies Xīnjiāng's Tarim Basin, the largest inland basin in the world. This is the location of the mercilessly thirsty Taklamakan Desert – China's largest desert and the world's second largest mass of sand after the Sahara Desert. China's most famous desert is of course the Gobi, although most of it lies outside the country's borders.

East of Xīnjiāng extend the epic grasslands and steppes of Inner Mongolia – China's largest production centre for mining rare earth metals and the nation's chief coal-producing region – in a huge and elongated belt of land that stretches to erstwhile Manchuria.

The Best... Mountains

1 Huángshān (p250)

2 Wǔtái Shān (p156)

3 Huà Shān (p143)

4 Mògānshān (p244)

5 Éméi Shān (p336)

6 Tài Shān (p166)

Rivers & Plains

The other major region comprises roughly 45% of the country and contains 95% of the population. This densely populated part of China descends like a staircase from west to east, from the high plateaus of Tibet and Qīnghǎi to the fertile but largely featureless plains and basins of the great rivers that drain the high ranges. These plains are the most important agricultural areas of the country and the most heavily populated.

China's longest river, the Yangzi (the 'Long River'), is one of the lengthiest rivers in the world. Its watershed of almost 2 million sq km – 20% of China's land mass – supports 400 million people. Dropping from its source high on the Tibetan plateau, it runs for 6300km to the sea, of which the last few hundred kilometres is across virtually flat alluvial plains.

About 5460km long and the second-longest river in China, the Yellow River (Huánghé) is touted as the birthplace of Chinese civilisation and has been fundamental in the development of Chinese society.

Fields & Agriculture

China's hills and mountains may sculpt a dramatic and sublime backdrop for travellers, but have long been a massive agricultural headache for farmers. Small plots of land are eked out in patchworks of land squashed between hillsides or rescued from mountain cliffs and ravines, in the demanding effort to feed 20% of the world's population with just 10% of its arable land.

Wildlife

China's vast size, diverse topography and climatic disparities support an astonishing range of habitats for a wide-ranging diversity of animal life. Scattered from steamy tropical rainforests in the deep southwest to subarctic wilderness in the far north, from the precipitous mountains of Tibet to the low-lying deserts of the northwest and the huge Yangzi River, China's wild animals comprise nearly 400 species of mammal (including some of the world's rarest and most charismatic species), more than 1300 bird species, 424 reptile species and over 300 species of amphibian. The Tibetan plateau alone is the habitat of more than 500 species of birds, while half of the animal species in the northern hemisphere can be found in China.

Almost every large mammal you can think of in China has crept onto the endangered species list, as well as many of the so-called 'lower' animals and plants. Deforestation, pollution, hunting and trapping for fur, body parts and sport are all culprits. The snow leopard, Indochinese tiger, chiru antelope, crested ibis, Asiatic elephant, red-crowned crane and black-crowned crane are all endangered.

Despite the threats, a number of rare animal species cling to survival in the wild. Notable among them are the Chinese alligator in Ānhuī, the giant salamander in the fast-running waters of the Yangzi and Yellow Rivers, the Yangzi River dolphin in the lower and middle reaches of the river (although there have been no sightings since 2002), and the pink dolphin of the Hong Kong islands of Sha Chau and Lung Kwu Chau. The giant panda is confined to the fauna-rich valleys and ranges of Sìchuān, but your best chances for sighting one is in Chéngdū's Giant Panda Breeding Research Base.

Plants

China is home to more than 32,000 species of seed plant and 2500 species of forest tree, plus an extraordinary plant diversity that includes some famous 'living fossils' – a diversity so great that Jílín province in the semifrigid north and Hǎinán province in the tropical south share few plant species. Many reserves still remain where intact vegetation ecosystems can be seen firsthand, but few parts of the country have escaped human impact. Deforestation continues apace in many regions and vast areas are under cultivation with monocultures such as rice.

Apart from rice, the plant probably most often associated with China and Chinese culture is bamboo, of which China boasts some 300 species. Bamboo grows in many parts of China, but bamboo forests were once so extensive that they enabled the evolution of the giant panda, which eats virtually nothing else, and a suite of small mammals, birds and insects that live in bamboo thickets.

Deciduous forests cover mid-altitudes in the mountains, and are characterised by oaks, hemlocks and aspens, with a leafy understorey that springs to life after the winter snows have melted. Among the more famous blooms of the understorey are rhododendrons and azaleas, and many species of each grow naturally in China's

Top Books on China's Environment

○ *When a Billion Chinese Jump* (2010) Jonathan Watts' sober and engaging study of China's environmental issues.

○ *The River Runs Black: The Environmental Challenge to China's Future* (2010; 2nd edition) Elizabeth Economy's frightening look at the unhappy marriage between breakneck economic production and environmental degradation.

○ *The China Price: The True Cost of Chinese Competitive Advantage* (2008) Alexandra Harney's telling glimpse behind the figures of China's economic rise.

○ *China's Water Crisis* (2004) Ma Jun rolls up his sleeves to examine the sources of China's water woes.

○ *Mao's War Against Nature* (2001) Judith Shapiro looks at the ideological clash between communism and the environment.

mountain ranges. At the very highest elevations, the alpine meadows grazed by yaks are often dotted with showy and colourful blooms.

The Urban Environment

China may be vast, but with two-thirds of the land either mountain, desert or uncultivable, the remaining third is overwhelmed by the people of the world's most populous nation. For social, economic and political reasons, China is experiencing its – and the world's – most rapid period of urbanisation in history. All this means the city can impinge in inescapable fashion. For the first time in its history, China's city dwellers began to outnumber rural residents in 2011, with an urbanisation rate set to increase to 65% by 2050. During the next 15 years, China is expected to build urban areas equal in size to 10 New York Cities.

A Greener China?

In 2010 China overtook the USA as the world's largest energy consumer; in the same year the nation replaced Japan as the world's second-largest economy and is tipped to overtake the USA by 2030 (some say by 2020). In 2012, China's per capita carbon dioxide emissions caught up with the European Union and China is now responsible for roughly a quarter of global emissions.

The World Bank calculates the annual cost of pollution alone in China at almost 6% of the national GDP; when all forms of environmental damage are incorporated, the figure leaps as high as 12%, meaning China's final environmental costs may overshadow economic growth.

China is painfully aware of its accelerated desertification, growing water shortages, shrinking glaciers, acidic rain, contaminated rivers, caustic urban air and polluted soil. There is strong evidence of ambitious and bold thinking: Běijīng is committing itself to overtaking Europe in investment in renewable energy by 2020, and has earmarked

Giant panda

a staggering US$140 billion for an ambitious program of wind farms from Xīnjiāng province to Jiāngsū province in the east, due for completion in 2020. Also China leads the world in the production of solar cells, and aims to reduce energy use per unit of GDP by more than 15% before 2015.

China's authoritarian system of governance allows it to railroad through bold initiatives, but it also encourages a heavy reliance on technological 'solutions' and huge engineering programs to combat environmental problems. For example, China seeks to engineer an answer for its water crisis by diverting Yangzi River waters to thirsty north China, when sustainable solutions to water use may be a more manageable policy.

One of China's main energy quandaries is coal. Coal is cheap, easy to extract and remains China's primary energy source, accounting for almost 70% of power requirements. China extracts more coal than any other nation and possesses the world's third largest deposits. Domestic demand for coal leapt almost 10% in 2011 alone, compared to an increase of 2.7% for crude oil in the same year. China's coal-fired growth also comes at a time when efforts to tackle global warming have become a major global priority. Experts predict China may hit 'peak coal' – the point of maximum production, after which the industry will fall into decline – as early as 2020, or even earlier.

Public protests – sometimes violent – against polluting industries have proliferated in recent years across China and have scored a number of notable victories, including the 2012 demonstrations in Shífāng (Sìchuān) which led to the cancellation of a planned US$1.6 billion copper smelting facility.

China Dialogue (www.chinadialogue.net) is a resourceful dual-language website that seeks to promote debate on China's immense environmental challenges.

Survival
Guide

Yúnnán woman at a food stall
MARK READ/CUMLUS LIBRARY/LP MAGAZINE ©

A-Z

Directory

● ● ●

Accommodation

From rustic homesteads, homestays, enterprising youth hostels, student dormitories, guesthouses, courtyard lodgings, snappy boutique hotels and elegant historic residences to metallic five-star towers and converted art deco apartment blocks, China's accommodation choice is impressive (on a national level). The choice varies enormously, however, between regions and cities. Top-tier draws such as Běijīng, Shànghǎi, Hángzhōu and Hong Kong sport a rich variety of accommodation options but other towns can have a poor supply, despite being inundated with visitors. Rural destinations are largely a patchwork of homesteads and hostels, with the occasional boutique-style choice in big ticket villages.

Rooms & Prices

Accommodation is divided by price category, identified by the symbols **$** (budget), **$$** (midrange) or **$$$** (top end); accommodation prices vary across China, so one region's budget breakdown may differ from another. We list the rack rate, which generally reflects the most you are ever expected to pay. However, at most times of the year discounts are in effect which can range from 10% to 60%.

Rooms come with private bathroom or shower room, unless otherwise stated. Rooms are generally easy to procure, but phone ahead to reserve a room in popular tourist towns (such as Hángzhōu), especially for weekend visits.

Most rooms in China fall into the following categories:

○ **Double rooms** (双人房、标准间; *shuāng rén fáng* or *biāozhǔn jiān*) In most cases, these are twins, ie with two beds.

○ **One-bed rooms/single** (单间; *dānjiān*) This is usually a room with one double-sized bed.

○ **Large-bed rooms** (大床房; *dàchuáng fáng*) Larger than a one-bed room, with a big double bed.

○ **Suites** (套房; *tàofáng*) Available at most midrange and top-end hotels.

○ **Dorms** (多人房; *duōrénfáng*) Usually, but not always, available at youth hostels (and at a few hotels).

○ **Business rooms** (商务房; *shāngwù fáng*) Usually equipped with computers.

Restrictions

The majority of hotels in China still do not have the authorisation to accept foreigners. This can be a source of frustration when you find yourself steered towards pricier midrange and top-end lodgings. All hotels we list accept foreign guests. To see if a hotel accepts foreign guests, ask: *zhège bīnguǎn shōu wàiguórén ma?* (这个宾馆收外国人吗?).

Booking

Booking online can help you secure a room and obtain a good price, but remember you should be able to bargain down the price of your room at hotel reception (except at youth hostels and the cheapest hotels) or over the phone. To secure accommodation, always plan ahead and book your room in advance during the high season. Airports at major cities often have hotel-booking counters that offer discounted rates.

Ctrip (☏ 400 619 9999; www.english.ctrip.com) Excellent hotel booking, air and train ticketing website, with English helpline. Useful app available.

Book Your Stay Online

For more accommodation reviews by Lonely Planet authors, check out http://hotels.lonelyplanet.com. You'll find independent reviews, as well as recommendations on the best places to stay. Best of all, you can book online.

Hotel Discounts & Tips

Always ignore the rack rate and ask for the discounted price or bargain for a room, as discounts usually apply everywhere but at youth hostels (except for hostel members) and the cheapest accommodation; you can do this in person at reception, or book online. Apart from during the busy holiday periods (the end of April and first few days of May, the first week of October and Chinese New Year), rooms should be priced well below the rack rate and are rarely booked out. In some towns (such as Hángzhōu), there may be a pricier weekend rate (Friday and Saturday). Discounts of 10% to 60% off the tariff rate (30% is typical) are the norm, available by simply asking at reception, by phoning in advance to reserve a room or by booking online at Ctrip (http://english.ctrip.com). Some tips:

○ The standard of English is often better at youth hostels than at midrange or some high-end hotels.

○ Your hotel can help with ticketing, for a commission.

○ Almost every hotel has a left-luggage room, which should be free if you are a guest in the hotel.

○ Always bargain for a room.

○ Ask your hotel concierge for a local map.

Elong (☎ 010-8457 7827, 400 617 1717; www.elong.net) Hotel and air ticket booking, with English helpline.

Travel Zen (☎ 400 720 3355; www.travelzen.com) Air and hotel bookings. English helpline.

Checking In

At check-in you will need your passport; a registration form will ask what type of visa you have. For most travellers, the visa will be L (travel visa). A deposit (押金; *yājīn*) is required at most hotels; this will be paid either with cash or by providing your credit-card details. International credit cards are generally only accepted at midrange hotels

or chain express hotels and top-end accommodation; always have cash in case. If your deposit is paid in cash, you will be given a receipt and the deposit will be returned to you when you check out.

Courtyard Hotels

Largely confined to Běijīng, courtyard hotels have rapidly mushroomed. Arranged around traditional *sìhéyuàn* (courtyards), rooms are on ground level. Courtyard hotels are charming and romantic, but are often expensive and rooms are small, in keeping with the dimensions of courtyard residences. Facilities will be limited so don't expect

a swimming pool, gym or subterranean garage.

Budget Business Chain Hotels

Dotted around much of China, budget business chain hotels can sometimes be a decent alternative to old-school two- and three-star hotels, with rooms around the ¥180 to ¥300 mark. In recent years, however, their once-pristine facilities have sometimes come to resemble the threadbare clunkers they aimed to replace. Still, their sheer ubiquitousness means you can usually find accommodation (but look at the rooms first). They often have membership/loyalty schemes which make rooms cheaper. Chains include:

Home Inn (☎ 400 820 3333; www.homeinns.com)

Jinjiang Inn (☎ 400 820 9999; www.jinjianginns.com)

Guesthouses

The cheapest of the cheap are China's ubiquitous guesthouses (招待所; *zhāodàisuǒ*). Often found clustered near train or bus stations but also dotted around cities and towns, not all guesthouses accept foreigners, and Chinese skills may be crucial in securing a room. Rooms (doubles, twins, triples, quads) are primitive and grey, with tiled floors and possibly a shower room or shabby bathroom; showers may be communal.

Other terms for guesthouses:

○ 旅店 (*lǚdiàn*)

○ 旅馆 (*lǚguǎn*)

o 有房 means 'rooms available'

o 今日有房 means 'rooms available today'

o 住宿 (zhùsù; 'accommodation')

Hotels

Hotels vary wildly in quality within the same budget bracket. The star rating system employed in China can also be misleading: hotels may be awarded four or five stars when they are patently a star lower in ranking. The best rule of thumb is to choose the newest hotel in each category as renovations can be rare. Deficiencies may not be immediately apparent, so explore and inspect the overall quality of the hotel; viewing the room up front pays dividends.

China has few independent hotels of real distinction, so it's generally advisable to select chain hotels that offer a proven standard of international excellence. Shangri-La, Marriott, Hilton, St Regis, Ritz-Carlton, Marco Polo and Hyatt all have a presence in China and can generally be relied upon for high standards of service and comfort.

Note the following:
o English skills are often poor, even in some five-star hotels.

o Most rooms are twins rather than doubles, so be clear if you specifically want a double.

o Virtually all hotel rooms, whatever the price bracket, will have air-conditioning and a TV.

o Very cheap rooms may have neither telephone nor internet access.

o Wi-fi is increasingly common in hostels and midrange and top-end hotels (but might be only in the lobby).

o Late-night telephone calls or calling cards from 'masseurs' and prostitutes are still common in budget and lower midrange hotels.

o All hotel rooms are subject to a 10% or 15% service charge.

o Practically all hotels will change money for guests, and most midrange and top-end hotels accept credit cards.

o A Western breakfast may be available, certainly at four-star establishments.

o The Chinese method of designating floors is the same as that used in the USA, but different from, say, that used in Australia. What would be the ground floor in Australia is the 1st floor in China, the 1st is the 2nd, and so on.

In China, hotels are called:
o bīnguǎn (宾馆)

o dàfàndiàn (大饭店)

o dàjiǔdiàn (大酒店)

o fàndiàn (饭店)

o jiǔdiàn (酒店)

Temples & Monasteries

Some temples and monasteries (especially on China's sacred mountains) provide accommodation. They are cheap but ascetic, and may not have running water or electricity.

Activities

Grab copies of expat magazines in Běijīng, Hong Kong, Guǎngzhōu and Shànghǎi for information on activities such as golf, running, horse riding, cycling, football, cricket, hiking and trekking, swimming, ice skating, skiing, skateboarding, waterskiing and rock climbing.

Children

More comfortable in the large cities of Hong Kong, Běijīng and Shànghǎi, children are likely to feel out of place in smaller towns and in the wilds. With the exception of Hǎinán, China is not famous for its beaches. Ask a doctor specialising in travel medicine for information on recommended immunisations for your child.

Practicalities

o Baby food, nappies and milk powder: widely available in supermarkets.

o Restaurants: few have baby chairs.

o Train travel: children shorter than 1.4m can get a hard sleeper for 75% of the full price or a half-price hard seat. Children shorter than 1.1m ride free, but you have to hold them the entire journey.

Climate

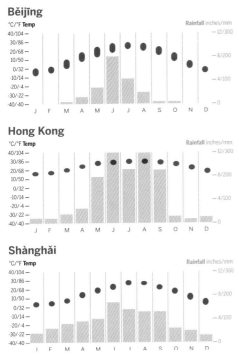

Běijīng

°C/°F **Temp**   Rainfall inches/mm
40/104 —   — 12/300
30/86 —
20/68 —   — 8/200
10/50 —
0/32 —
-10/14 —   — 4/100
-20/-4 —
-30/-22 —
-40/-40 —   — 0
        J F M A M J J A S O N D

Hong Kong

°C/°F **Temp**   Rainfall inches/mm
40/104 —   — 12/300
30/86 —
20/68 —   — 8/200
10/50 —
0/32 —
-10/14 —   — 4/100
-20/-4 —
-30/-22 —
-40/-40 —   — 0
        J F M A M J J A S O N D

Shànghǎi

°C/°F **Temp**   Rainfall inches/mm
40/104 —   — 12/300
30/86 —
20/68 —   — 8/200
10/50 —
0/32 —
-10/14 —   — 4/100
-20/-4 —
-30/-22 —
-40/-40 —   — 0
        J F M A M J J A S O N D

o Air travel: infants under the age of two fly for 10% of the full airfare, while children between the ages of two and 11 pay half the full price for domestic flights and 75% of the adult price for international flights.

o Sights and museums: many have children's admission prices, for children under 1.1m or 1.3m in height.

o Always ensure your child carries ID in case they get lost.

●●● Customs Regulations

Chinese customs generally pay tourists little attention. 'Green channels' and 'red channels' at the airport are clearly marked. You are not allowed to import or export illegal drugs, or animals and plants (including seeds). Pirated DVDs and CDs are illegal exports from China – if found they will be confiscated. You can take Chinese medicine up to a value of ¥300 when you depart China.

You're allowed to import the following duty-free allowances:

o 400 cigarettes or the equivalent in tobacco products.

o 1.5L of alcohol.

o 50g of gold or silver.

As well:

o Importation of fresh fruit and cold cuts is prohibited.

o There are no restrictions on foreign currency (but declare any cash exceeding US$5000 or its equivalent in another currency).

Objects considered antiques require a certificate and a red seal to clear customs when leaving China. Anything made before 1949 is considered an antique, and if it was made before 1795 it cannot legally be taken out of the country. To get the proper certificate and red seal, your antiques must be inspected by the **State Administration of Cultural Heritage** (Guójiā Wénwù Jú; ☎ 010-5679 2211; www.sach.gov.cn; 83 Beiheyan Dajie) in Běijīng.

●●● Discount Cards

Seniors over the age of 65 are frequently eligible for discounts and 70-and-overs get free admission, so make sure you take your passport when visiting sights as proof of age. An International **Student Identity Card** (ISIC; www.isic.org; €12) can net students half-price discounts at many sights (but you may have to insist).

Electricity

220V/50Hz

220V/50Hz

Gay & Lesbian Travellers

Greater tolerance exists in the big cities than in the more conservative countryside, but even in urban areas, gay and lesbian visitors should be quite discreet. You will often see Chinese same-sex friends holding hands or putting their arms around each other, but this usually has no sexual connotation.

Spartacus International Gay Guide (Bruno Gmunder Verlag; www.spartacusworld. com/en) Best-selling guide for gay travellers; also available as an iPhone App.

Utopia (www.utopia-asia.com/tipschin.htm) Tips on travelling in China and a complete listing of gay bars nationwide.

Health

China is a reasonably healthy country to travel in, but some health issues should be noted. Pre-existing medical conditions and accidental injury (especially traffic accidents) account for most life-threatening problems, but becoming ill in some way is not unusual. Outside of the major cities, medical care is often inadequate, and food and waterborne diseases are common. Malaria is still present in some parts of the country, and altitude sickness can be a problem, particularly in Tibet.

In case of accident or illness, it's best just to get a taxi and go to hospital directly.

The following advice is a general guide only and does not replace the advice of a doctor trained in travel medicine.

Before You Go

o Pack medications in their original, clearly labelled containers.

o If you take any regular medication, bring double your needs in case of loss or theft.

o Take a signed and dated letter from your physician describing your medical conditions and medications (using generic names).

o If carrying syringes or needles, ensure you have a physician's letter documenting their medical necessity.

o If you have a heart condition, bring a copy of your ECG taken just prior to travelling.

o Get your teeth checked before you travel.

o If you wear glasses, take a spare pair and your prescription.

In China you can buy some medications over the counter without a doctor's prescription, but not all, and in general it is not advisable to buy medications locally without a doctor's advice. Fake medications and poorly stored or out-of-date drugs are also common, so try to take your own.

Insurance

o Even if you are fit and healthy, don't travel without health insurance – accidents happen.

o Declare any existing medical conditions you have (the insurance company *will* check if your problem is pre-existing and will not cover you if it is undeclared).

o You may require extra cover for adventure activities such as rock climbing or skiing.

o If you're uninsured, emergency evacuation is expensive; bills of more than US$100,000 are not uncommon.

o Ensure you keep all documentation related to any medical expenses you incur.

Vaccinations

Specialised travel-medicine clinics stock all available vaccines and can give specific recommendations for your trip. The doctors will consider your vaccination history, the length of your trip, activities you may undertake and underlying medical conditions, such as pregnancy.

o Visit a doctor six to eight weeks before departure, as most vaccines don't produce immunity until at least two weeks after they're given.

o Ask your doctor for an International Certificate of Vaccination (otherwise known as the 'yellow booklet'), listing all vaccinations received.

o The only vaccine required by international regulations is yellow fever.

Proof of vaccination against yellow fever is only required if you have visited a country in the yellow-fever zone within the six days prior to entering China. If you are travelling to China directly from South America or Africa, check with a travel clinic as to whether you need a yellow-fever vaccination.

In China

Availability of Health Care

Good clinics catering to travellers can be found in major cities. They are more expensive than local facilities but you may feel more comfortable dealing with a Western-trained doctor who speaks your language. These clinics usually have a good understanding of the best local hospital facilities and close contacts with insurance companies should you need evacuation.

If you think you may have a serious disease, especially malaria, do not waste time – get to the nearest quality facility. To find the nearest reliable medical facility, contact your insurance company or your embassy. Hospitals are listed in the Information sections in cities and towns throughout the guide.

Infectious Diseases

DENGUE

This mosquito-borne disease occurs in some parts of southern China. There is no vaccine so avoid mosquito bites. The dengue-carrying mosquito bites day and night, so use insect-avoidance measures at all times. Symptoms include high fever, severe headache and body ache. Some people develop a rash and diarrhoea. There is no specific treatment – just rest and paracetamol. Do not take aspirin.

HEPATITIS A

A problem throughout China, this food-and-waterborne virus infects the liver, causing jaundice (yellow skin and eyes), nausea and lethargy. There is no specific treatment for hepatitis A; you just need to allow time for the liver to heal. All travellers to China should be vaccinated.

Health Advisories

It's usually a good idea to consult your government's travel-health website before departure, if one is available.

Australia (www.dfat.gov.au/travel)

Canada (www.travelhealth.gc.ca)

New Zealand (www.mfat.govt.nz/travel)

UK (www.gov.uk/foreign-travel-advice) Search for travel in the site index.

USA (www.cdc.gov/travel)

HEPATITIS B

The only sexually transmitted disease that can be prevented by vaccination, hepatitis B is spread by contact with infected body fluids. The long-term consequences can include liver cancer and cirrhosis. All travellers to China should be vaccinated.

JAPANESE B ENCEPHALITIS

A rare disease in travellers; however, vaccination is recommended if you're in rural areas for more than a month during summer months, or if spending more than three months in the country. No treatment available; one-third of infected people die, another third suffer permanent brain damage.

MALARIA

Malaria has been nearly eradicated in China; it is not generally a risk for visitors to the cities and most tourist areas. It is found mainly in rural areas in the southwestern region bordering Myanmar (Burma), Laos and Vietnam, principally Hǎinán, Yúnnán and Guǎngxī. More limited risk exists in the remote rural areas of Fújiàn, Guǎngdōng, Guìzhōu and Sìchuān. Generally, medication is only advised if you are visiting rural Hǎinán, Yúnnán or Guǎngxī.

To prevent malaria:

○ Avoid mosquitoes and take antimalarial medications (most people who catch malaria are taking inadequate or no antimalarial medication).

○ Use an insect repellent containing DEET on exposed skin (natural repellents such as citronella can be effective, but require more frequent application than products containing DEET).

○ Sleep under a mosquito net impregnated with permethrin.

○ Choose accommodation with screens and fans (if it's not air-conditioned).

○ Impregnate clothing with permethrin in high-risk areas.

○ Wear long sleeves and trousers in light colours.

○ Use mosquito coils.

○ Spray your room with insect repellent before going out for your evening meal.

Recommended Vaccinations

The World Health Organization (WHO) recommends the following vaccinations for travellers to China:

○ Adult diphtheria and tetanus (ADT)

○ Hepatitis A

○ Hepatitis B

○ Measles, mumps and rubella (MMR)

○ Typhoid

○ Varicella

The following immunisations are recommended for travellers spending more than one month in the country or those at special risk:

○ Influenza

○ Japanese B encephalitis

○ Pneumonia

○ Rabies

○ Tuberculosis

Pregnant women and children should receive advice from a doctor who specialises in travel medicine.

RABIES

An increasingly common problem in China, this fatal disease is spread by the bite or lick of an infected animal, most commonly a dog. Seek medical advice immediately after any animal bite and commence postexposure treatment. The pretravel vaccination means the post-bite treatment is greatly simplified.

If an animal bites you:

o Gently wash the wound with soap and water, and apply an iodine-based antiseptic.

o If you are not prevaccinated, you will need to receive rabies immunoglobulin as soon as possible, followed by a series of five vaccines over the next month. Those who have been prevaccinated require only two shots of vaccine after a bite.

o Contact your insurance company to locate the nearest clinic stocking rabies immunoglobulin and vaccine. Immunoglobulin is often unavailable outside of major centres, but it's crucial that you get to a clinic that has immunoglobulin as soon as possible if you have had a bite that has broken the skin.

SCHISTOSOMIASIS (BILHARZIA)

This disease occurs in the central Yangzi River (Cháng Jiāng) basin, carried in water by minute worms that infect certain varieties of freshwater snail found in rivers, streams, lakes and, particularly, behind dams. The infection often causes no symptoms until the disease is well established (several months to years after exposure); any resulting damage to internal organs is irreversible. Effective treatment is available.

o Avoid swimming or bathing in fresh water where bilharzia is present.

o A blood test is the most reliable way to diagnose the disease, but the test will not show positive until weeks after exposure.

TYPHOID

Typhoid is a serious bacterial infection spread via food and water. Symptoms include headaches, a high and slowly progressive fever, perhaps accompanied by a dry cough and stomach pain. Vaccination is not 100% effective, so still be careful what you eat and drink. All travellers spending more than a week in China should be vaccinated.

Environmental Hazards

AIR POLLUTION

Air pollution is a significant and worsening problem in many Chinese cities. People with underlying respiratory conditions should seek advice from their doctor prior to travel to ensure they have adequate medications in case their condition worsens. Take treatments such as throat lozenges, and cough and cold tablets.

HYPOTHERMIA

Be particularly aware of the dangers of trekking at high altitudes or simply taking a long bus trip over mountains. Progress from very cold to dangerously cold can be rapid due to a combination of wind, wet clothing, fatigue and hunger, even if the air temperature is above freezing. Dress in layers; silk, wool and some artificial fibres are all good insulating materials. A hat is important, as a lot of heat is lost through the head. A strong, waterproof outer layer (and a space blanket for emergencies) is essential. Carry basic supplies, including food containing simple sugars, and fluid to drink.

Symptoms of hypothermia are exhaustion, numb skin (particularly the toes and fingers), shivering, slurred speech, irrational or violent behaviour, lethargy, stumbling, dizzy spells, muscle cramps and violent bursts of energy.

To treat mild hypothermia, first get the person out of the wind and/or rain, remove their clothing if it's wet, and replace it with dry, warm clothing. Give them hot liquids – not alcohol – and high-calorie, easily digestible food. Early recognition and treatment of mild hypothermia is the only way to prevent severe hypothermia, a critical condition that requires medical attention.

Important Numbers

Ambulance ☎120
Fire ☎119
Police ☎110
Country code (China/Hong Kong/Macau) ☎86/852/853
International access code ☎00
Directory assistance ☎114

●●●
Insurance

Carefully consider a travel-insurance policy to cover theft, loss, trip cancellation and medical eventualities. Travel agents can sort this out for you, although it is often cheaper to find good deals with an insurer online or with a broker. Worldwide travel insurance is available at www.lonelyplanet.com/travel-insurance. You can buy, extend and claim online any-time – even if you're already on the road.

Some policies specifically exclude 'dangerous activities' such as scuba diving, skiing and even trekking. Check that the policy covers ambulances or an emergency flight home.

Paying for your airline ticket with a credit card often provides limited travel accident insurance – ask your credit-card company what it's prepared to cover.

You may prefer a policy that pays doctors or hospitals directly rather than reimbursing you for expenditures after the fact. If you have to claim later, ensure you keep all documentation.

●●●
Internet Access

Wi-fi accessibility in hotels, cafes, restaurants and bars is generally good. The best option is to bring a wi-fi equipped smartphone, tablet or laptop or use your hotel computer or broadband inter-net connection.

The Chinese authorities remain mistrustful of the internet, and censorship is heavy-handed. Around 10% of websites are blocked; sites like Google may be slow, while social-networking sites such as Facebook and Twitter are blocked (as is YouTube). Gmail is often inaccessible, as is Google Drive, so plan ahead. Newspapers such as the *New York Times* are also blocked, as is Bloomberg. Users can get around blocked websites by using a VPN (Virtual Private Network) service such as **Astrill** (www.astrill.com).

Many internet cafes only accept customers with Chinese ID, barring foreigners. In large cities and towns, the area around the train station generally has internet cafes.

The internet icon (@) in hotel reviews indicates the presence of an internet cafe or a terminal where you can get online; wi-fi areas are indicated with a wi-fi icon (🛜).

●●●
Legal Matters

China does not officially recognise dual nationality or the foreign citizenship of children born in China if one of the parents is a People's Republic of China (PRC) national. If you have Chinese and another nationality you may, in theory, not be allowed to visit China on your foreign passport. Dual-nationality citizens who enter China on a Chinese passport are subject to Chinese laws and are legally not allowed consular help. If over 16 years of age, carry your passport with you at all times as a form of ID.

Gambling is officially illegal in mainland China. Distributing religious material is also illegal in mainland China.

China's laws against the use of illegal drugs are harsh; trafficking in more than 50g of heroin can lead to the death penalty. Foreign-passport holders have been executed in China for drug offences. The Chinese criminal justice system does not ensure a fair trial and defendants are not presumed innocent until proven guilty. If arrested, most foreign citizens have the right to contact their embassy.

Anyone under the age of 18 is considered a minor; the minimum age for driving a car is 18. The age of consent in China is 14; in Hong Kong and Macau it is 16. The age of consent for marriage is 22 for men and 20 for women. There is no minimum age restricting the consumption of alcohol or use of cigarettes.

●●●
Money

The Chinese currency is the rénmínbì (RMB), or 'people's money'. The basic unit of RMB is the yuán (元; ¥), which is divided into 10 jiǎo (角), which is again divided into 10 fēn (分). Colloquially, the yuán is referred to as kuài and jiǎo as máo (毛). The fēn has so little value these days that it is rarely used.

The Bank of China issues RMB bills in denominations of ¥1, ¥2, ¥5, ¥10, ¥20, ¥50 and ¥100. Coins come in denominations of ¥1, 5 jiǎo, 1 jiǎo and 5 fēn. Paper versions of the coins remain in circulation.

Hong Kong's currency is the Hong Kong dollar (HK$). The Hong Kong dollar is divided into 100 cents. Bills are issued in denominations of HK$10, HK$20, HK$50, HK$100, HK$500 and HK$1000. Copper coins are worth 50c, 20c and 10c, while the HK$5, HK$2 and HK$1 coins are silver and the HK$10 coin is nickel and bronze. The Hong Kong dollar is pegged to the US dollar at a rate of US$1 to HK$7.80, though it is allowed to fluctuate a little.

Macau's currency is the pataca (MOP$), which is divided into 100 avos. Bills are issued in denominations of MOP$10, MOP$20, MOP$50, MOP$100, MOP$500 and MOP$1000. There are copper coins worth 10, 20 and 50 avos and silver-coloured MOP$1, MOP$2, MOP$5 and MOP$10 coins. The pataca is pegged to the Hong Kong dollar at a rate of MOP$103.20 to HK$100. In effect, the two currencies are interchangeable and Hong Kong dollars, including coins, are accepted in Macau. Chinese rénmínbì is also accepted in many places in Macau at one-to-one. You can't spend patacas anywhere else, however, so use them before you leave Macau. Prices quoted are in yuán unless otherwise stated.

ATMs

Bank of China and the Industrial & Commercial Bank of China (ICBC) 24-hour ATMs are plentiful, and you can use Visa, MasterCard, Cirrus, Maestro Plus and American Express to withdraw cash. All ATMs accepting international cards have dual-language ability. The network is largely found in sizeable towns and cities. If you plan on staying in China for a few weeks or more, it is advisable to open an account at a bank with a nationwide network of ATMs, such as the Bank of China or ICBC. HSBC and Citibank ATMs are available in larger cities. Keep your ATM receipts so you can exchange your yuán when you leave China.

The exchange rate on ATM withdrawals is similar to that for credit cards, but there is a maximum daily withdrawal amount. Note that banks can charge a withdrawal fee for using the ATM network of another bank, so check with your bank before travelling.

To have money wired from abroad, visit Western Union or **Moneygram** (www.moneygram.com).

Credit Cards

In large tourist towns, credit cards are relatively straightforward to use, but don't expect to be able to use them everywhere, and always carry enough cash; the exception is in Hong Kong, where international credit cards are accepted almost everywhere (although some shops may try to add a surcharge to offset the commission charged by credit companies, which can range from 2.5% to 7%). Check to see if your credit card company charges a foreign transaction fee (usually between 1% and 3%) for purchases in China.

Where they are accepted, credit cards often deliver a slightly better exchange rate than banks. Money can also be withdrawn at certain ATMs in large cities on credit cards such as Visa, MasterCard and Amex.

Moneychangers

It's best to wait till you reach China to exchange money as the exchange rate will be better. Foreign currency and travellers cheques can be changed at border crossings, international airports, branches of the Bank of China, tourist hotels and some large department stores; hours of operation for foreign-exchange counters are 8am to 7pm (later at hotels). Top-end hotels will generally change money for hotel guests only. The official rate is given almost everywhere and the exchange charge is standardised, so there is little need to shop around for the best deal.

Australian, Canadian, US, UK, Hong Kong and Japanese currencies and the euro can be changed in China. In some backwaters, it may be hard to change lesser-known currencies; US dollars are still the easiest to change. Lhasa has ATM-style currency exchange machines that can change cash in several currencies into rénmínbì 24 hours a day, with your passport.

Keep at least a few of your exchange receipts. You will need them if you want to exchange any remaining RMB you have at the end of your trip.

Tipping

Almost no one in China (including Hong Kong and Macau) asks for tips. Tipping used to be refused in restaurants, but nowadays many midrange and top-end eateries include their own (often huge) service charge; cheap restaurants do not expect a tip. Taxi drivers throughout China do not ask for or expect tips.

Travellers Cheques

With the prevalence of ATMs across China, travellers cheques are not as useful as they once were and cannot be used everywhere, so always ensure you carry enough ready cash. You should have no problem cashing travellers cheques at tourist hotels, but they are of little use in budget hotels and restaurants. Most hotels will only cash the cheques of guests. If cashing them at banks, aim for larger banks such as the Bank of China or ICBC.

Stick to the major companies such as Thomas Cook, Amex and Visa. In big cities travellers cheques are accepted in almost any currency, but in smaller destinations, it's best to stick to big currencies such as US dollars or UK pounds. Keep your exchange receipts so you can change your money back to its original currency when you leave.

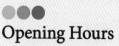

Opening Hours

China officially has a five-day working week. Saturday and Sunday are public holidays.

Practicalities

○ The standard English-language newspaper is the (censored) *China Daily* (www.chinadaily.com.cn). China's largest circulation Chinese-language daily is the *People's Daily* (Rénmín Rìbào). It has an English-language edition on http://english.peopledaily.com.cn. Imported English-language newspapers can be bought from five-star hotel bookshops.

○ Listen to the BBC World Service or Voice of America; however, the websites can be jammed. Chinese Central TV (CCTV) has an English-language channel – CCTV9. Your hotel may have ESPN, Star Sports, CNN or BBC News 24.

○ China officially subscribes to the international metric system, but you will encounter the ancient Chinese weights and measures system that features the *liǎng* (两; tael; 50g) and the *jīn* (斤; catty; 0.5kg). There are 10 *liǎng* to the *jīn*.

○ Banks, offices and government departments open Monday to Friday (roughly 9am until 5pm or 6pm), possibly closing for two hours in the middle of the day; many banks are also open Saturday and maybe Sunday.

○ Post offices are generally open seven days a week.

○ Museums generally stay open on weekends and may shut for one day during the week.

○ Travel agencies and foreign-exchange counters in tourist hotels are usually open seven days a week.

○ Department stores, shopping malls and shops are open daily from 10am to 10pm.

○ Internet cafes are typically open 24 hours, but some open at 8am and close at midnight.

○ Restaurants open from around 10.30am to 11pm; some shut at around 2pm and reopen at 5pm or 6pm.

○ Bars open in the late afternoon, shutting around midnight or later.

Passports

You must have a passport (护照; hùzhào) on you at all times; it is the most basic travel document and all hotels will insist on seeing it for check-in. It is now mandatory to present your passport when buying train tickets; you will also need it for using internet cafes that accept foreigners.

The Chinese government requires that your passport be valid for at least six months after the expiry date of your visa. You'll need at least one entire blank page in your passport for the visa.

Take an ID card with your photo in case you lose your passport and make photocopies of your passport;

your embassy may need these before issuing a new one. You must report the loss to the local Public Security Bureau (PSB), who will issue you with a 'Statement of Loss of Passport'.

Long-stay visitors should register their passport with their embassy.

Public Holidays

The People's Republic of China (PRC) has a number of national holidays. Some of the following are nominal holidays that do not result in leave. It's not a great idea to arrive in China or go travelling during the big holiday periods as hotels prices reach their maximum and transport can become very tricky.

New Year's Day 1 January

Chinese New Year 19 February 2015, 8 February 2016, 28 January 2017; a week-long holiday for most.

International Women's Day 8 March

Tomb Sweeping Festival First weekend in April; a popular three-day holiday period.

International Labour Day 1 May; for many it's a three-day holiday.

Youth Day 4 May

International Children's Day 1 June

Dragon Boat Festival 20 June 2015, 9 June 2016, 30 May 2017

Birthday of the Chinese Communist Party 1 July

Anniversary of the Founding of the People's Liberation Army 1 August

Mid-Autumn Festival 27 September 2015, 15 September 2016, 4 October 2017

National Day 1 October; the big one, a week-long holiday.

Safe Travel

Crime

Travellers are more often the victims of petty economic crime, such as theft, than serious crime. Foreigners are natural targets for pickpockets and thieves – keep your wits about you and make it difficult for thieves to get at your belongings.

High-risk areas in China are train and bus stations, city and long-distance buses (especially sleeper buses), hard-seat train carriages and public toilets.

Women should avoid travelling solo. Even in Běijīng, single women taking taxis have been taken to remote areas and robbed by taxi drivers.

Loss Reports

If something of yours is stolen, report it immediately to the nearest Foreign Affairs Branch of the **Public Security Bureau** (PSB; 公安局; Gōng'ānjú). Staff will ask you to fill in a loss report before investigating the case.

A loss report is crucial so you can claim compensation if you have travel insurance. Be prepared to spend many hours, perhaps even several days, organising it. Make a copy of your passport in case of loss or theft.

Scams

Con artists are widespread. Well-dressed girls flock along Shànghǎi's East Nanjing Rd, the Bund and Běijīng's Wangfujing Dajie, asking single men to photograph them on their mobile phones before dragging them to expensive cafes or Chinese teahouses, leaving them to foot monstrous bills. 'Poor' art students haunt similar neighbourhoods,

Government Travel Advice

The following government websites offer travel advisories and information on current hot spots.

Australian Department of Foreign Affairs & Trade (📞 1300 139 281; www.smarttraveller.gov.au)

British Foreign & Commonwealth Office (📞 0845-850-2829; www.gov.uk/foreign-travel-advice)

Canadian Department of Foreign Affairs & International Trade (📞 800-267 6788; http://travel.gc.ca/travelling/advisories)

US State Department (📞 888-407 4747; http://travel.state.gov)

press-ganging foreigners into art exhibitions where they are coerced into buying trashy art.

Taxi scams at Běijīng's Capital Airport are legendary; always join the queue at the taxi rank and insist that the taxi driver uses his or her meter. Try to avoid pedicabs and motorised three wheelers wherever possible; we receive a litany of complaints against pedicab drivers who originally agree on a price and then insist on an alternative figure (sometimes 10 times the sum) once you arrive at the destination.

Be alert at all times if you decide to change money or buy tickets (such as train tickets) on the black market, which we can't recommend.

Always be alert when buying unpriced goods (which is a lot of the time): foreigners are frequently ripped off. Always examine your restaurant bill carefully for hidden extras and if paying by credit card ensure there are no extra charges.

Transport

Traffic accidents are the major cause of death in China for people aged between 15 and 45, and the World Health Organization (WHO) estimates there are 600 traffic deaths per day. On long-distance buses, you may find there are no seatbelts or the seatbelts are virtually unusable through neglect, or inextricably stuffed beneath the seat. Outside of the big cities, taxis are unlikely to have rear seatbelts fitted.

Your greatest danger in China will almost certainly be crossing the road, so develop 360-degree vision and a sixth sense. Crossing only when it is safe to do so could perch you at the side of the road in perpetuity, but don't imitate the local tendency to cross without looking. Note that cars frequently turn on red lights in China, so the green 'walk now' man does not mean it is safe to cross.

Telephone

Mobile Phones

A mobile phone should be the first choice for calls, but ensure your mobile is unlocked for use in China if taking your own. If you have the right phone (eg Blackberry, iPhone, Android), **Skype** (www.skype.com) and **Viber** (www.viber.com) can make calls either very cheap or free with wi-fi access. Also consider buying a data SIM card in China for constant network access away from wi-fi hotspots; plans start at under ¥70 for 300mb of data, 50 minutes of China calls, and around 240 free local SMS per month. If buying 3G SIM cards, China Unicom offers almost twice as much data as China Mobile. China Mobile or China Unicom outlets can sell you a standard SIM card (note that numbers with eights in them are more expensive, numbers with fours are cheaper) which cost from ¥60 to ¥100 and include ¥50 of credit. When this runs out, top up by buying a credit-charging card *(chōngzhí kǎ)* from outlets. Cards are also available from newspaper kiosks and shops displaying the China Mobile sign.

Buying a mobile phone in China is also an option as they are generally inexpensive. Make sure the phone uses W-CDMA, which works on China Unicom and most carriers around the world, and not TD-SCDMA, which works only on China Mobile and not international carriers. Cafes, restaurants and bars in larger towns and cities are frequently wi-fi enabled. Consider investing in a USB portable power bank for charging your phone and other devices while on the road.

Landlines

If making a domestic call, look out for very cheap public phones at newspaper stands (报刊亭; *bàokāntíng*) and hole-in-the-wall shops (小卖部; *xiǎomàibù*); you make your call and then pay the owner. Domestic and international long-distance phone calls can also be made from main telecommunications offices and 'phone bars' (话吧; *huàbā*). Cardless international calls are expensive and it's far cheaper to use an internet phone (IP) card. Public telephone booths are rarely used now in China but may serve as wi-fi hot spots (as in Shànghǎi).

Phonecards

Beyond Skype or Viber, using an IP card on your mobile or a landline phone is much cheaper than calling direct, but they can be hard to find outside the big cities. You dial a local number, punch in your account number, followed by a pin number and finally the number you wish to call. English-language service is usually available. Some IP cards can only be used locally, while others can be used nationwide, while still others are no good for international calls, so it is important to buy the right card (and check the expiry date).

Visas

Applying for Visas

For China

Apart from visa-free visits to Hong Kong and Macau and useful 72-hour visa-free transit stays (for visitors from 51 nations) to Běijīng, Shànghǎi, Guǎngzhōu, Xī'ān, Guìlín, Chéngdū, Chóngqìng, Dàlián and Shěnyáng (although you won't be permitted to leave transit cities during your three-day stay), you will need a visa to visit China. Citizens from Japan, Singapore, Brunei, San Marino, Mauritius, the Seychelles and the Bahamas do not require a visa to visit China. There remain a few restricted areas in China that require an additional permit from the PSB. Permits are also required for travel to Tibet, a region that the authorities can suddenly bar foreigners from entering.

Your passport must be valid for at least six months after the expiry date of your visa (nine months for a double-entry visa) and you'll need at least one entire blank page in your passport for the visa. For children under the age of 18, a parent must sign the application form on their behalf.

At the time of writing, the visa application process had become more rigorous and applicants were required to provide the following:

- a copy of flight confirmation showing onward/return travel

- for double-entry visas, flight confirmation showing all dates of entry and exit

- if staying at a hotel in China, confirmation from the hotel (this can be cancelled later if you stay elsewhere)

- if staying with friends or relatives, a copy of the information page of their passport, a copy of their China visa and a letter of invitation from them

At the time of writing, prices for a standard single-entry 30-day visa were as follows:

- UK£30 for UK citizens

- US$140 for US citizens

- US$30 for citizens of other nations

Visa Types

There are 12 categories of visas (for most travellers, an L visa will be issued).

TYPE	ENGLISH NAME	CHINESE NAME
C	flight attendant	chéngwù 乘务
D	resident	dìngjū 定居
F	business or student	fǎngwèn 访问
G	transit	guòjìng 过境
J	(J1) journalist (more than six months)	jìzhě1 记者1
J	(J2) journalist (less than six months)	jìzhě2 记者2
L	travel	lǚxíng 旅行
M	commercial and trade	màoyì 贸易
Q	(Q1) family visits (more than six months)	qīnshǔ1 亲属1
Q	(Q2) family visits (less than six months)	qīnshǔ2 亲属2
R	talents/needed skills	réncái 人才
S	(S1) visits to foreign relatives/private (more than six months)	sīrén1 私人1
S	(S2) visits to foreign relatives/private (less than six months)	sīrén2 私人2
X	(X1) student (more than six months)	xuéxí1 学习1
X	(X2) student (less than six months)	xuéxí2 学习2
Z	working	gōngzuò 工作

Double-entry visas:

o UK£45 for UK citizens

o US$140 for US citizens

o US$45 for all other nationals

Six-month multiple-entry visas:

o UK£90 for UK citizens

o US$140 for US citizens

o US$60 for all other nationals

A standard 30-day single-entry visa can be issued in four to five working days. In many countries, the visa service has been outsourced from the Chinese embassy to a **Chinese Visa Application Service Centre** (www. visaforchina.org), which levies an extra administration fee. In the case of the UK, a single-entry visa costs UK£30, but the standard administration charge levied by the centre is an additional UK£36 (three-day express UK£48, postal service UK£54). In some countries, such as the UK, France, the US and Canada, there is more than one service centre nationwide. Visa Application Service Centres are open Monday to Friday.

A standard 30-day visa is activated on the date you enter China, and must be used within three months of the date of issue. Sixty-day and 90-day travel visas are harder to get. To stay longer, you can extend your visa in China.

Visa applications require a completed application form (available from the embassy, visa application service centre or downloaded from its website) and at least one photo (normally 51mm x 51mm). You generally pay for your visa when you collect it. A visa mailed to you will take up to three weeks. In the US and Canada, mailed visa applications have to go via a visa agent, at extra cost. In the US, many people use the **China Visa Service Center** (📞 in the US 800-799 6560; www.mychinavisa.com), which offers prompt service. The procedure takes around 10 to 14 days. **CIBT** (www.uk.cibt. com) offers a global network and a fast and efficient turnaround.

Hong Kong is a good place to pick up a China visa. **China Travel Service** (CTS; 广州中国旅行社; Zhōngguó Lǚxíngshè) will be able to

obtain one for you, or you can apply directly to the **Visa Office of the People's Republic of China** (Map p288; 📞 852 3413 2300; www. fmcoprc.gov.hk/eng; 3rd & 4th fl, China Resources Building, 26 Harbour Rd, Wan Chai; ⏰ 9am-noon & 2-5pm Mon-Fri).

Be aware that American and UK passport holders must pay considerably more for their visas. You must supply two photos. Prices for China visas in Hong Kong are as follows:

o **Standard visa** One-/two-/three-day processing time HK$500/400/200

o **Double-entry visa** One-/two-/three-day processing time HK$600/500/300

o **Multiple-entry six-month visa** One-/two-/three-day processing time HK$800/700/500

o **Multiple-entry one-, two-or three-year visa** One-/two-/three-day processing time HK$1100/1000/800

You can buy a five-day, Shēnzhèn-only visa (¥160 for most nationalities, ¥469 for Brits; cash only) at the **Luóhú border** (Lo Wu; ⏰ 9am to 10.30pm), **Huánggǎng** (⏰ 9am-1pm & 2.30-5pm) and **Shékǒu** (⏰ 8.45am-12.30pm & 2.30-5.30pm). US citizens must buy a visa in advance in Macau or Hong Kong.

Three-day visas are also available at the **Macau–Zhūhǎi border** (¥168 for most nationalities, ¥469 for British; US citizens excluded; 8.30am to 12.15pm, 1 to 6.15pm & 7 to 10.30pm). US citizens have to buy a visa in advance in Macau or Hong Kong.

Be aware that political

Visa-Free Transits

Citizens from 51 nations (including the US, Australia, Canada, France, Brazil and the UK) can now stay in Běijīng and Shànghǎi for 72 hours without a visa as long as they are in transit to other destinations outside China, have a third-country visa and an air ticket out of Běijīng or Shànghǎi. Similarly, citizens from the same nations can also transit through Guǎngzhōu, Xī'ān, Guìlín, Chéngdū, Chóngqìng, Dàlián and Shěnyáng for 72 hours visa-free, with the same conditions. Visitors on such three-day stays are not allowed to leave the transit city.

events can suddenly make visas more difficult to procure or renew.

When asked about your itinerary on the application form, list standard tourist destinations; if you are considering going to Tibet or western Xīnjiāng, just leave it off the form. The list you give is not binding. Those working in media or journalism may want to profess a different occupation; otherwise, a visa may be refused or a shorter length of stay than that requested may be given.

For Hong Kong

At the time of writing, most visitors to Hong Kong, including citizens of the EU, Australia, New Zealand, the USA and Canada, could enter and stay for 90 days without a visa. British passport holders get 180 days, while South Africans are allowed to stay 30 days visa-free. If you require a visa, apply at a Chinese embassy or consulate before arriving. If you visit Hong Kong from China, you will need a double-entry, multiple-entry or new visa to re-enter China.

For Macau

Most travellers, including citizens of the EU, Australia, New Zealand, the USA, Canada and South Africa, can enter Macau without a visa for between 30 and 90 days. British passport holders get 180 days. Most other nationalities can get a 30-day visa on arrival, which will cost MOP$100/50/200 per adult/child under 12/family. If you're visiting Macau from China and plan to re-enter China, you will need to be on

a multiple- or double-entry visa.

Visa Extensions

For China

The Foreign Affairs Branch of the local PSB deals with visa extensions.

First-time extensions of 30 days are usually easy to obtain on single-entry tourist visas; a further extension of a month may be possible, but you may only get another week. Travellers report generous extensions in provincial towns, but don't bank on this. Popping across to Hong Kong to apply for a new tourist visa is another option.

Extensions to single-entry visas vary in price, depending on your nationality. At the time of writing, US travellers paid ¥185, Canadians ¥165, UK citizens ¥160 and Australians ¥100. Expect to wait up to five days for your visa extension to be processed.

The penalty for overstaying your visa in China is up to ¥500 per day. Some travellers have reported having trouble with officials who read the 'valid until' date on their visa incorrectly. For a one-month travel (L) visa, the 'valid until' date is the date by which you must enter the country (within three months of the date the visa was issued), not the date upon which your visa expires.

For Hong Kong

For tourist-visa extensions, inquire at the **Hong Kong Immigration Department** (☏ 852 2852 3047; www.immd. gov.hk; 2nd fl, Immigration Tower, 7 Gloucester Rd, Wan

Chai; ⊙ 8.45am-4.30pm Mon-Fri, 9-11.30am Sat). Extensions (HK$160) are not readily granted unless there are extenuating circumstances such as illness.

For Macau

If your visa expires, you can obtain a single one-month extension from the **Macau Immigration Department** (☏ 853 2872 5488; ground fl, Travessa da Amizade; ⊙ 9am-5pm Mon-Fri).

Transport

Getting There & Away

Flights, cars and tours can be booked online at www.lonely planet.com/bookings.

Entering China

No particular difficulties exist for travellers entering China. Chinese immigration officers are scrupulous and highly bureaucratic, but not overly officious. The main requirements are a passport that's valid for travel for six months after the expiry date of your visa, and a visa. Travellers arriving in China will receive a health declaration form and an arrivals form to complete.

Air

Airports

Hong Kong, Běijīng and Shànghǎi are China's principal international air gateways; Báiyún International Airport in Guǎngzhōu is of lesser, but growing, importance.

Báiyún International Airport (白云国际机场; CAN; Báiyún Guójì Jīchǎng; ☏ 020-3606 6999; www.baiyunairport.com) In Guǎngzhōu; receiving an increasing number of international flights.

Capital Airport (PEK, Shǒudū Jīchǎng; ☏ 96158; http://en.bcia.com.cn) Běijīng's international airport; three terminals.

Hong Kong International Airport (HKG; ☏ 2181 8888; www.hkairport.com) The futuristic passenger terminal consists of eight levels, with check-in on level seven, departures on level six and arrivals on level five.

Hóngqiáo Airport (SHA; Hóngqiáo Jīchǎng; Map p194; ☏ 021-6268 8899, 3659) In Shànghǎi's west; domestic flights, and some international connections.

Pǔdōng International Airport (PVG; Pǔdōng Guójì Jīchǎng; ☏ 021-96990) In Shànghǎi's east; international flights.

Land

China shares borders with Afghanistan, Bhutan, India, Kazakhstan, Kyrgyzstan, Laos, Mongolia, Myanmar (Burma), Nepal, North Korea, Pakistan, Russia, Tajikistan and Vietnam; the borders with Afghanistan, Bhutan and India are closed. There are also official border crossings between China and its special administrative regions, Hong Kong and Macau.

Lonely Planet *China* guides may be confiscated by officials, primarily at the Vietnam–China border.

Kazakhstan

Border crossings from Ürümqi to Kazakhstan are via border posts at Korgas, Ālāshànkǒu, Tǎchéng and Jímùnǎi. Ensure you have a valid Kazakhstan visa (obtainable, at the time of writing, in Ürümqi, or from Běijīng) or China visa. Apart from Ālāshànkǒu, which links China and Kazakhstan via train, all other border crossings are by bus; you can generally get a bike over, however. Two trains weekly (32 hours) run between Ürümqi and Almaty, and one train per week runs to Astana.

Remember that borders open and close frequently due to changes in government policy; additionally, many are only open when the weather permits. It's always best to check with the **Public Security Bureau** (PSB; Gōng'ānjú) in Ürümqi for the official line.

Kyrgyzstan

There are two routes between China and Kyrgyzstan: one between Kashgar and Osh, via the Irkeshtam Pass; and one between Kashgar and Bishkek, via the dramatic 3752m Torugart Pass.

Laos

From the Měnglà district in China's southern Yúnnán province, you can enter Laos via Boten in Luang Nam Tha province (from Móhān on the China side), while a daily bus runs between Vientiane and Kūnmíng and also from Jǐnghóng to Luang Nam Tha in Laos.

On-the-spot visas for Laos are available at the border, the price of which depends on your nationality (although you cannot get a China visa here).

Mongolia

From Běijīng, the Trans-Mongolian Railway trains and the K23 train run to Ulaanbaatar. There are also trains and regular buses between Hohhot and the border town of Erenhot (Èrlián). Mongolian visas on the Chinese side can be acquired in Běijīng, Hohhot or Erenhot.

Myanmar (Burma)

The famous Burma Road runs from Kūnmíng in Yúnnán province to the Burmese city of Lashio. The road is open to travellers carrying permits for the region north of Lashio, although you can legally cross the border in only one direction – from the Chinese side (Jiěgào) into Myanmar; however, at the time of writing the border was not open to foreign travellers and flying in from Kūnmíng was the only option. Myanmar visas can only be arranged in Kūnmíng or Běijīng.

Nepal

The 865km road connecting Lhasa with Kathmandu is known as the Friendship Highway, currently only traversable by rented vehicle (for foreign travellers). It's a spectacular trip across the

Tibetan plateau, the highest point being Gyatso-la Pass (5248m).

Visas for Nepal can be obtained in Lhasa, or at the border at Kodari.

When travelling from Nepal to Tibet, foreigners still have to arrange transport through tour agencies in Kathmandu. Access to Tibet can, however, be restricted for months at a time without warning.

North Korea

Visas for North Korea are not especially hard to arrange although it is not possible to travel independently so you will need to be on a pre-planned tour. Those interested in travelling to North Korea on tours from Běijīng should contact Nicholas Bonner or Simon Cockerell at **Koryo Tours** (010-6416 7544; www.koryogroup.com; 27 Beisanlitun Nan, Běijīng).

Four international express trains (K27 and K28) run between Běijīng train station and Pyongyang.

Pakistan

The exciting trip on the Karakoram Hwy, said to be the world's highest public international highway, is an excellent way to get to or from Chinese Central Asia. There are buses from Kashgar for the two-day trip to the Pakistani town of Sost via Tashkurgan when the pass is open. Pakistani visas are no longer available to tourists on arrival (and visas are difficult to get in Běijīng), so the safest option is to arrive in China with a visa obtained in your home country. Check the current situation as this could change.

Russia

The train from Hā'ěrbīn East to Vladivostok is no longer running but you could take the train to Suífēnhé and take an onward connection there.

The Trans-Mongolian (via Erenhot) and Trans-Manchurian (via Hā'ěrbīn) branches of the Trans-Siberian Railway run from Běijīng to Moscow.

There are also border crossings 9km from Mǎnzhōulǐ and at Hēihé.

Tajikistan

At the time of writing, the Qolma (Kulma) Pass, linking Kashgar with Murghab, was not yet open to foreign travellers.

Vietnam

Visas are unobtainable at border crossings; Vietnam visas can be acquired in Běijīng, Kūnmíng, Hong Kong and Nánníng. Chinese visas can be obtained in Hanoi.

China's busiest border with Vietnam is at the **Friendship Pass**, an obscure Vietnamese town of Dong Dang, 164km northeast of Hanoi. The closest Chinese town to the border is Píngxiáng in Guǎngxī province, about 10km north of the actual border gate. Seven Hanoi-bound buses run from Nánníng via the Friendship Pass; twice-weekly trains (T5 and T6) connect Běijīng and Hanoi (via Nánníng) while a daily train (T8701 and T8702) links Hanoi with Nánníng.

The **Hékǒu–Lao Cai** border crossing is 468km from Kūnmíng and 294km from Hanoi. At the time of

writing, the only way to reach Vietnam via Hékǒu was by bus from Kūnmíng.

A third, but little-known border crossing is at **Mong Cai** in the northeast corner of Vietnam, just opposite the Chinese city of Dōngxīng and around 200km south of Nánníng.

 Sea

Japan

There are weekly ferries between Osaka and Kōbe and Shànghǎi. There are also twice-weekly boats from Qīngdǎo to Shimonoseki. The weekly ferry from the Tiānjīn International Cruise Home

Climate Change & Travel

Every form of transport that relies on carbon-based fuel generates CO_2, the main cause of human-induced climate change. Modern travel is dependent on aeroplanes, which might use less fuel per kilometre per person than most cars but travel much greater distances. The altitude at which aircraft emit gases (including CO_2) and particles also contributes to their climate change impact. Many websites offer 'carbon calculators' that allow people to estimate the carbon emissions generated by their journey and, for those who wish to do so, to offset the impact of the greenhouse gases emitted with contributions to portfolios of climate-friendly initiatives throughout the world. Lonely Planet offsets the carbon footprint of all staff and author travel.

International Train Routes

In addition to the Trans-Siberian and Trans-Mongolian rail services, the following routes can be travelled by train:

- Hung Hom station in Kowloon (Jiǔlóng; Hong Kong; www.mtr.com.hk) to Guǎngzhōu, Shànghǎi, Běijīng

- Pyongyang (North Korea) to Běijīng

- Almaty (Kazakhstan) to Ürümqi

- Astana (Kazakhstan) to Ürümqi

- Běijīng to Ulaanbaatar (Mongolia)

- Běijīng to Hanoi (Vietnam)

Port to Kōbe (神户; Shénhù) had been suspended indefinitely at the time of writing.

Check in two hours before departure for international sailings.

South Korea

International ferries connect the South Korean port of Incheon with Wēihǎi, Qīngdǎo, Yāntái, Dàlián and Dāndōng. The ferry to Incheon from the Tiānjīn International Cruise Home Port was suspended at the time of research, but should be up and running again.

Tickets can be bought cheaply at the pier, or from **China International Travel Service** (CITS; Zhōngguó Guójì Lǚxíngshè) for a very steep premium.

Taiwan

Daily ferries ply the route between Xiàmén and Kinmen Island in Taiwan, from where you can fly to other major cities in Taiwan. You can also catch a ferry from Fúzhōu's Máwěi ferry terminal to Taiwan's archipelago of Matzu, from where there are boats to Keelung and flights to other cities in Taiwan.

Getting Around

✈ Air

China's air network is extensive and growing. The civil aviation fleet is expected to triple in size over the next two decades, up to 70 new airports were planned for construction by 2015 alone and 100 more were to be expanded or upgraded. Air safety and quality have improved considerably, but the speed of change generates its own problems: a serious shortage of qualified personnel to fly planes means China needed a reported 18,000 new pilots by 2015. When deciding between flying and using high-speed rail, note that flight delays in China are the worst in the world, according to travel industry monitor FlightStats (while trains almost always leave on time).

Shuttle buses usually run from **Civil Aviation Administration of China** (CAAC; Zhōngguó Mínháng) offices in towns and cities throughout China to the airport, often running via other stops. For domestic flights, arrive at the airport at least one hour before departure.

Remember to keep your baggage receipt label on your ticket as you will need to show it when you collect your luggage. Planes vary in style and comfort. You may get a hot meal, or just a small piece of cake and an airline souvenir. On-board announcements are delivered in Chinese and English.

Tickets

Except during major festivals and holidays, tickets are easy to purchase, with an oversupply of airline seats. Purchase tickets from branches of the CAAC nationwide, airline offices, travel agents or the travel desk of your hotel; travel agents will usually offer a better discount than airline offices. Discounts are common, except when flying into large cities such as Shànghǎi and Běijīng on the weekend, when the full fare can be the norm. Fares are calculated according to one-way travel, with return tickets simply costing twice the single fare. If flying from Hong Kong or Macau to mainland China, note that these are classified as international flights; it is much cheaper to travel overland into Shēnzhèn, Zhūhǎi or Guǎngzhōu and fly from there.

You can use credit cards at most CAAC offices and travel agents. The departure tax is included in the ticket price.

🚲 Bicycle

Bikes (自行车; zìxíngchē) are an excellent method for getting around China's cities and tourist sights. They can also be invaluable for exploring the countryside and surrounding towns such as Yángshuò.

Hire

Hángzhōu has the world's largest bicycle sharing network with docking stations dotted around the town, however its success (and foreigner-friendly ease of use) has only been fitfully replicated elsewhere in China. Generally, the best places to try are youth hostels which rent out bicycles, as do many hotels, although the latter are more expensive.

Bikes can be hired by the day or by the hour and it is also possible to hire for more than one day. Rental rates vary depending on where you find yourself, but rates start at around ¥10 to ¥15 per day in cities such as Běijīng.

Touring

Cycling through China allows you to go when you want, to see what you want and at your own pace. It can also be an extremely cheap, as well as a highly authentic, way to see the land.

You will have virtually unlimited freedom of movement but, considering the size of China, you will need to combine your cycling days with trips by train, bus, boat, taxi or even planes, especially if you want to avoid particularly steep regions, or areas where the roads are poor or the climate is cold.

A basic packing list for cyclists includes a good bicycle-repair kit, sunscreen and other sun protection, waterproofs, fluorescent strips and camping equipment. Ensure you have adequate clothing, as many routes will be taking you to considerable altitude. Road maps in Chinese are essential for asking locals for directions.

BikeChina (www.bikechina. com) arranges tours and is a good source of information for cyclists coming to China.

🚢 Boat

Boat services within China are limited, especially with the growth of high-speed rail and expressways. They're most common in coastal areas, where you are likely to use a boat to reach offshore islands such as Pǔtuóshān or Hǎinán, or the islands off Hong Kong. The Yāntái–Dàlián ferry will probably survive because it saves hundreds of kilometres of overland travel, although a super-long undersea tunnel is on the drawing board. There's also a ferry every other evening to Dàlián from the **Tiānjīn International Cruise Home Port** (天津国际游轮母港; Tiānjīn Guójì Yóulún Mǔgǎng; ☎ 022-2560 4137).

The best-known river trip is the three-day boat ride along the Yangzi River (Cháng Jiāng) from Chóngqìng to Yíchāng. The Lí River (Lí Jiāng) boat trip from Guìlín to Yángshuò is a popular tourist ride.

Hong Kong employs an out-and-out navy of vessels that connects with the territory's myriad islands, and a number of boats run between the territory and other parts of China, including Macau, Zhūhǎi, Shékǒu (for Shēnzhèn) and Zhōngshān.

Boat tickets can be purchased from passenger ferry terminals or through travel agents.

🚌 Bus

Long-distance bus (长途公共汽车; chángtú gōnggòng qìchē) services are extensive and reach places you cannot reach by train; with the increasing number of intercity highways, journeys are getting quicker.

Buses & Stations

Routes between large cities sport larger, cleaner and more comfortable fleets of private buses, some equipped with toilets and hostesses handing out snacks and mineral water; shorter and more far-flung routes still rely on rattling minibuses into which as many fares as possible are crammed. Buses often wait until they fill up before leaving, or (exasperatingly) trawl the streets looking for fares.

Sleeper buses (卧铺客车; wòpù kèchē) ply popular long-haul routes, costing around double the price of a normal bus service. Bunks can be short, however, and there have been several fatal fires in recent years.

Bus journey times should be used as a rough guide only. You can estimate times for bus journeys on nonhighway routes by calculating the distance against a speed of 25km per hour.

All cities and most towns have one or more long-distance bus station (长途汽车站; chángtú qìchēzhàn), generally located in relation to the direction the bus heads in. Most bus stations have a left-luggage counter. In many cities, the train station forecourt doubles as a bus station.

Tickets

Tickets are getting more expensive as fuel prices increase but are cheaper and easier to get than train tickets; turn up at the bus station and buy your ticket there and then. The earlier you buy, the closer to the front of the bus you will sit, although you may not be able to buy tickets prior to your day of travel. At the time of writing, ID was required for the purchase of bus tickets in restive Xīnjiāng.

Tickets can be hard to procure during national holiday periods.

Dangers & Annoyances

Breakdowns can be a hassle, and some rural roads and provincial routes (especially in the southwest, Tibet and the northwest) remain in bad condition. Precipitous drops, pot holes, dangerous road surfaces and reckless drivers mean accidents remain common. Long-distance journeys can also be cramped and noisy, with Hong Kong films and cacophonous karaoke looped on overhead TVs. Drivers continuously lean on the horn (taking an MP3 player is crucial for one's sanity). Note the following when travelling by bus:

○ Seat belts are a rarity in many provinces.

○ Take plenty of warm clothes on buses to high-altitude destinations in winter. A breakdown in frozen conditions can prove lethal for those unprepared.

○ Take a lot of extra water on routes across areas such as the Taklamakan Desert.

🏍 Car & Motorcycle

Hiring a car in China has always been complicated or impossible for foreign visitors and in mainland China is currently limited to Běijīng and Shànghǎi, cities that both have frequently gridlocked roads. Throw in the dangers, complexity of Chinese roads for first-time users and the costs of driving in China and it makes more sense to use the subway/metro system and taxis, both of which are cheap and efficient in Běijīng and Shànghǎi. Hiring a car with a driver from your hotel is possible, but it's generally far cheaper and more convenient to hire a taxi for the day instead.

Driving Licence

To drive in Hong Kong and Macau, you will need an International Driving Permit (IDP). Foreigners can drive motorcycles if they are residents in China and have an official Chinese motorcycle licence. International driving permits are generally not accepted in China.

Hire

Běijīng Capital Airport has a **Vehicle Administration Office** (车管所, Chēguǎnsuǒ; ☏ 6453 0010; 1st fl, Terminal 3; ⊙ 9am-6pm) where you can have a temporary three-month driving licence issued (an international driver's licence is insufficient). This will involve checking your driving licence and a simple medical exam (including an eyesight test). You will need

this licence before you can hire a car from **Hertz** (☏ 400 888-1336; www.hertzchina.com), which has branches at Capital Airport. Check out the **Hertz office** (☏ 021-6085 1900; Terminal 2; ⊙ 8am-8pm Mon-Fri & 9am-6pm Sat-Sun) at Shànghǎi's Pǔdōng International Airport for how to obtain a temporary licence in Shànghǎi. There are also branches in both central Běijīng and Shànghǎi. Hire cars from Hertz start from ¥230 per day (up to 150km per day; ¥20,000 deposit). **Avis** (☏ 400 882 1119) also has a growing network around China, with car rental starting from ¥200 per day (¥5000 deposit).

Road Rules

Cars in China drive on the right-hand side of the road. Even skilled drivers will be unprepared for China's roads: in the cities, cars lunge from all angles and chaos abounds.

🚆 Train

Trains are the best way to travel long distance around China in reasonable speed and comfort. Colossal investment over recent years has put high-speed rail at the heart of China's rapid modernisation drive.

Train Types

Chinese train numbers are usually (but not always) prefixed by a letter, designating the category of train.

The fastest, most luxurious and expensive intercity trains are the streamlined, high-speed C (*chéngjì*; 城), D (*dòngchē*; 动车) and G (*gāotiě*; 高铁) trains, which rapidly shuttle between major cities.

D-class temperature-regulated 1st-class carriages have mobile and laptop chargers, seats are two abreast with ample legroom and TV sets. Second-class carriages have five seats in two rows.

G-class trains are faster than D-class trains, but have limited luggage space. Less fast express classes include the overnight Z-class trains (zhídá; 直达), while further down the pecking order are older and more basic T (tèkuài; 特快) and K (kuàisù; 快速) class trains.

Tickets

It is possible to upgrade (补票; bǔpiào) your ticket once aboard your train. If you have a standing ticket, for example, find the conductor and upgrade to a hard seat, soft seat or hard sleeper (if there are any available).

SOFT SLEEPER

Soft sleepers are a very comfortable. Tickets cost much more than hard-sleeper tickets and often sell out, however, so book early. Tickets on upper berths are slightly cheaper than lower berths. Expect to share with total strangers. If you are asleep, an attendant will wake you to prepare you to disembark so you will have plenty of time to ready your things.

Soft sleeper carriages contain the following:
o four air-conditioned bunks (upper and lower) in a closed compartment

o bedding on each berth and a lockable door to the carriage corridor

o meals, flat-screen TVs and power sockets on some routes

o a small table and stowing space for your bags

o a hot-water flask, filled by an attendant (one per compartment).

HARD SLEEPER

Hard sleepers are available on slower and less modern T, K and N class trains, as well as trains without a letter prefix.

There is a small price difference between the numbered berths, with the lowest bunk (下铺; xiàpù) the most expensive and the highest bunk (上铺; shàngpù) the cheapest.

Hard-sleeper tickets are the most difficult of all to buy; you almost always need to buy these a few days in advance. Expect:
o doorless compartments with half a dozen bunks in three tiers

o sheets, pillows and blankets on each berth

o a no-smoking policy

o lights and speakers out at around 10pm

o a hot-water flask, filled by an attendant (one per compartment)

o trolleys passing by selling food and drink

o a rack above the windows for stowing your baggage.

SEATS

First-class (一等; yīděng) and 2nd-class (二等; èrděng) soft seats are available in D, C and G class high-speed trains. G class trains also offer business class and/or VIP seats, which include a hot meal and added comfort.

First-class comes with TVs, mobile phone and laptop charging points, and seats arranged two abreast. Second-class soft seats are also very comfortable. Overcrowding is not permitted and power points are available. On older trains, soft-seat carriages are often double-decker, and are not as plush as the faster and more modern high-speed express trains.

Hard-seat class is not available on the faster and plusher C, D and G class trains, and is only found on T and K class trains, and trains without a number prefix; a handful of Z class trains have hard seats. They generally have padded seats, but it's hard on your sanity; often unclean, noisy and very busy, and painful on the long haul. If seats have sold out, ask for a standing ticket, which gets you on the train, where you may find a seat or can upgrade; otherwise, you will have to stand in the carriage or between carriages (with the smokers).

Buying tickets

The Achilles heel of China's overburdened rail system, buying tickets can be a pain. Most tickets are one way only, with prices calculated per kilometre and adjustments made depending on the class of train, availability of air-con, type of sleeper and bunk positioning.

Some tips on buying train tickets:
o Never aim to get a sleeper ticket on the day of travel – plan and purchase ahead.

o Most tickets can be booked 18 days in advance of your departure date when booking

Internet Resources

- **The Man in Seat 61** (www.seat61.com/china.htm)
- **Travel China Guide** (www.travelchinaguide.com)
- **China Tibet Train** (www.chinatibettrain.com)

in person at ticket offices, and 20 days when booking online.

- Buying tickets for hard-seat carriages at short notice is usually no hassle, but it may be a standing ticket rather than a numbered seat.

- You can only buy tickets with cash or bank cards that are part of the Chinese UnionPay network.

- You will need your passport when buying a ticket (the number is printed on your ticket) at all train ticket offices.

- All automated ticket machines (eg at Shànghǎi Train Station) require Chinese ID (ie your passport will not work); you will need to queue at the ticket window.

- As with air travel, buying tickets around the Chinese New Year, 1 May and 1 October holiday periods can be very hard.

- Tickets on many routes (such as to Lhasa) can be very hard to get in July and August; consider flying to distant destinations.

- Expect to queue for up to half an hour or more for a train ticket at the station; ticket offices outside of the station are often less busy.

- Avoid black market tickets: your passport number must be on the ticket.

- Refunds for lost train tickets are arduous and involve

purchasing a new ticket and getting a refund at the other end once it has been proved no one occupied your seat.

- If you miss your D- or G-class train, you will be allowed to take the next available train on the same day only, at no charge. For all other trains, your ticket is forfeited (unless your connecting train was late).

Ticket Offices & Buying Online

Ticket offices (售票厅; *shòupiàotīng*) at train stations are usually to one side of the main train station entrance. Automated ticket machines operate on some routes but never accept foreign passports as ID. At large stations there should be a window manned by someone with basic English skills.

Alternatively, independent train ticket offices usually exist elsewhere in town where tickets can be purchased for a ¥5 commission without the same kind of queues; we've listed these where possible. Larger post offices may also sell train tickets. Your hotel will also be able to rustle up a ticket for you for a commission, and so can a travel agent.

You can buy tickets online at www.12306.cn but the website is Chinese-language only and you will need a Chinese bankcard. It's

cheaper to buy your ticket at the station, but tickets can be bought online at the following (China DIY Travel is the cheapest):

China DIY Travel (www.china-diy-travel.com; commission $10 per ticket)

CTrip (📞 400 619 9999; www.english.ctrip.com)

China Trip Advisor (www.chinatripadvisor.com)

For trains from Hong Kong to Shànghǎi, Guǎngzhōu or Běijīng, tickets can be ordered online at no mark-up from **KCRC** (www.mtr.com.hk), however for Běijīng or Shànghǎi a faster alternative is the high-speed trains from Shēnzhèn to Shànghǎi (D train) and Běijīng (G train), which take around 10 hours compared to 20 to 24 hours for departures from Hong Kong. You can also find English-language train time-tables on these websites.

To get a refund (退票; *tuìpiào*) on an unused ticket, windows exist at large train stations where you can get from 80% to 95% of your ticket value back, depending on how many days prior to the departure date you cancel.

Local Transport

Long-distance transport in China is good, but local transport is less efficient, except for cities with metro systems. The choice of local transport is diverse but vehicles can be slow and overburdened, and the network confusing for visitors. Hiring a car is often impractical, while hiring a bike can be inadequate. Unless the town is small, walking is often too tiring. On the plus side, local transport is cheap, taxis are usually ubiquitous and affordable, and metro systems continue to rapidly expand in large tourist towns.

Bus

With extensive networks, buses are an excellent way to get around town, but foreign travellers rarely use them. Ascending a bus, point to your destination on a map and the conductor (seated near the door) will sell you the right ticket. The conductor will usually tell you where to disembark, provided they remember. In conductor-less buses, you put money in a slot near the driver as you embark.

o Fares are very cheap (usually ¥1 to ¥2) but buses may be packed.

o In cities such as Běijīng, Shànghǎi and Hong Kong, a locally purchased transport card can be used on the buses.

o Navigation is tricky for non-Chinese speakers as bus routes at bus stops are generally listed in Chinese, without Pinyin (Romanised Chinese).

o In Běijīng and Shànghǎi and other large tourist towns, stops will be announced in English.

o Always have change ready if there is no conductor on the bus.

o Buses with snowflake motifs are air-conditioned.

o Traffic can make things slow.

Subway, Metro & Light Rail

Going underground or using light rail is fast, efficient and cheap; most networks are either very new or relatively recent and can be found in a rapidly growing number of cities, including Běijīng, Shànghǎi, Sūzhōu, Xī'ān, Hángzhōu, Tiānjīn, Chéngdū, Shēnzhèn, Wǔhàn, Kūnmíng, Chóngqìng and Hong Kong.

Taxi

Taxis (出租汽车; *chūzū qìchē*) are cheap and easy to find. Taxi rates per kilometre are clearly marked on a sticker on the rear side window of the taxi; flag fall varies from city to city, and depends upon the size and quality of the vehicle.

Most taxis have meters but they may only be switched on in larger towns and cities. If the meter is not used (on an excursion out of town, for example, or when hiring a taxi for the day or half-day), negotiate a price before you set off and write the fare down. If you want the meter used, ask for *dǎbiǎo* (打表). Also ask for a receipt (发票; *fāpiào*); if you leave something in the taxi, the taxi number is printed on the receipt so it can be located.

Note that:

o Congregation points include train and long-distance bus stations, but usually you can just flag taxis down.

o Taxi drivers rarely speak any English so have your destination written down in characters.

o If you have communication problems, consider using your mobile to phone your hotel for staff to interpret.

o You can hire taxis on a daily or half-day basis, often at reasonable rates (always bargain).

o To use the same driver again, ask for his or her card (名; *míngpiàn*).

o In many provinces, taxis often cover long-distance bus routes. They generally charge around 30% to 50% more but are much faster. You need to wait for four passengers.

Other Local Transport

A variety of ramshackle transport options exist across China; always agree on a price in advance (preferably have it written down).

o **Motor pedicabs** are enclosed three-wheeled vehicles (often the same price as taxis).

o **Pedicabs** are pedal-powered versions of motor pedicabs.

o **Motorbike** riders also offer lifts in some towns for what should be half the price of a regular taxi. You must wear a helmet – the driver will provide one.

a b c

Language

To enhance your trip with a phrasebook, visit **lonelyplanet.com**. Lonely Planet iPhone phrasebooks are available through the Apple App store.

Mandarin

In this section we've provided Pinyin (the official system of writing Mandarin in the Roman alphabet) next to the Mandarin script. The tones are indicated by accent marks on vowels: high (ā), rising (á), falling-rising (ǎ) and falling (à). Keep in mind that 'ü' is pronounced like 'ee' with pursed lips; 'c' as the 'ts' in 'bits'; 'q' as the 'ch' in 'cheese'; 'x' as the 'sh' in 'ship'; 'z' as the 'ds' in 'suds'; and 'zh' as the 'j' in 'judge'.

Basics

Hello./Goodbye.
你好。/再见。 Nǐhǎo./Zàijiàn.
Yes./No.
是。/不是。 Shì./Bùshì.
Excuse me.
劳驾。 Láojià.
Sorry.
对不起。 Duìbùqǐ.
Please ...
请…… Qǐng ...
Thank you.
谢谢你。 Xièxie nǐ.
You're welcome./That's fine.
不客气。 Bù kèqi.
How are you?
你好吗？ Nǐhǎo ma?
Fine. And you?
好。你呢？ Hǎo. Nǐ ne?
Do you speak English?
你会说英文吗？ Nǐ huìshuō Yīngwén ma?
I don't understand.
我不明白。 Wǒ bù míngbai.

How much is this?
多少钱？ Duōshǎo qián?

Accommodation

Do you have a single/double room?
有没有单人/ Yǒuméiyǒu dānrén/
套房？ tào fáng?
How much is it per night/person?
每天/人多少钱？ Měi tiān/rén duōshǎo qián?

Eating & Drinking

I'd like ..., please.
我想吃…… Wǒ xiǎng chī ...
That was delicious.
真好吃。 Zhēn hǎochī.
The bill/check, please.
买单。 Mǎidān.
I'm allergic to (nuts).
我对(果仁)过敏。 Wǒ duì (guǒrén) guòmǐn.

I don't eat ...
我不吃…… Wǒ bùchī ...
  fish 鱼 yú
  poultry 家禽 jiāqín
  red meat 牛羊肉 niúyángròu

Emergencies

I'm ill.
我生病了。 Wǒ shēngbìng le.
Help!
救命！ Jiùmìng!
Call a doctor!
请叫医生来！ Qǐng jiào yīshēng lái!
Call the police!
请叫警察！ Qǐng jiào jǐngchá!

Directions

Where's a/the ...?
……在哪儿？ ... zài nǎr?
  bank 银行 Yínháng
  market 市场 Shìchǎng
  museum 博物馆 Bówùguǎn
  post office 邮局 Yóujú
  restaurant 餐馆 Cānguǎn
  toilet 厕所 Cèsuǒ
  tourist office 旅行店 Lǚxíng diàn

Cantonese

If you read our pronunciation guides, provided in this section next to the Cantonese script, as if they were English, you'll be understood fine. The tones are indicated by accent marks on 'n' and on vowels: high (à), high rising (á), low falling (à), low rising (á) and low (a). Note that 'au' is pronounced like the 'ou' in 'out'; 'eu' as the 'er' in 'fern'; 'ew' as in 'blew' (with tightened lips); 'iu' as the 'yu' in 'yuletide'; and 'ui' as the French word *oui* (or the English 'we'). Also, the 'ng' sound can appear at the start of a word, and the words ending with 'p', 't' and 'k' must be clipped in Cantonese. You can hear this in English as well – say 'pit' and 'tip' and listen to how much shorter the 'p' sound is in 'tip'.

Basics

Hello.
哈佬 。 hàa·ló

Goodbye.
再見 。 joy·gin

Yes.
係 。 hai

No.
不係 。 ǹg·hai

Excuse me.
對唔住 。 deui·ǹg·jew

Sorry.
對唔住 。 deui·ǹg·jew

Please ...
唔該…… ǹg·gòy ...

Thank you.
多謝 。 dàw·je

You're welcome./
That's fine.
唔駛客氣 。 ǹg·sái haak·hay

How are you?
你幾好啊嗎 ? láy gáy hó à maa

Fine.
And you?
幾好 。 gáy hó
你呢 ? láy lè

Do you speak English?
你識唔識講 láy sìk·ǹg·sìk gáwng
英文啊 ? yìng·mán aa

I don't understand.
我唔明 。 ngáw ǹg mìng

How much is this?
幾多錢? gáy·dàw chín

Accommodation

Do you have a (single/double) room?
有冇 (單人/ yáu·mó (dàan·yàn/
雙人)房 ? sèung·yàn) fáwng

How much is it per (night/person)?
一 (晚/個人) yàt (máan/gaw yàn)
幾多錢 ? gáy·dàw chín

Eating & Drinking

I'd like ..., please.
我想食…… ngáw séung sik ...

That was delicious.
真好味 。 jàn hó·may

I'd like the bill/check, please.
唔該我要埋單 。 ǹg·gòy ngáw yiu màai·dàan

I'm allergic to (nuts).
我對 (果仁) ngáw deui (gwáw·yàn)
過敏 。 gaw·mán

I don't eat ...
我唔吃…… ngáw ǹg sik ...
  fish 魚 yéw
  poultry 雞鴨鵝 gài ngaap ngàw
  red meat 牛羊肉 ngàu yèung yuk

Emergencies

I'm ill.
我病咗 。 ngáw beng·jáw

Help!
救命 ! gau·meng

Call a doctor!
快啲叫醫生 ! faai·dì giu yì·sàng

Call the police!
快啲叫警察 ! faai·dì giu gíng·chaat

Directions

Where's a/the ...?
……喺邊度? ... hái bìn·do
  bank
  銀行 Ngàn·hàwng
  market
  街市 Gàai·sí
  museum
  博物館 Bawk·màt·gún
  post office
  郵局 Yàu·gúk
  restaurant
  酒樓 Jáu·làu
  toilet
  廁所 Chi·sáw
  tourist office
  旅行社 Léui·hàng·sé

Behind the Scenes

Author Thanks

Damian Harper

Thanks to Dai Min, Dai Lu, Alvin and Chengyuan, Edward Li, John Zhang, Jimmy Gu and Liu Meina. Much gratitude also to Jiale and Jiafu for everything, as always, plus immense gratitude to the people of China for making this nation such a joy to explore.

Acknowledgments

Climate map data adapted from Peel MC, Finlayson BL & McMahon TA (2007) 'Updated World Map of the Köppen-Geiger Climate Classification', *Hydrology and Earth System Sciences*, 11, 163344.

Illustrations pp68-9 and pp196-7 by Michael Weldon.

Cover photographs: Front: Black Dragon Pool Park, Lìjiāng, Yúnnán, Henry Westheim Photography/Alamy ©; Back: Sūzhōu Creek towards Wàibáidù Bridge and Pǔdōng New Area, Shànghǎi, Alan Copson/AWL ©.

This Book

This 3rd edition of *Discover China* was coordinated by Damian Harper and researched and written by Damian Harper, Piera Chen, Chung Wah Chow, David Eimer, Tienlon Ho, Robert Kelly, Shawn Low, Emily Matchar, Daniel McCrohan and Phillip Tang. This guidebook was commissioned in Lonely Planet's London's office, and produced by the following:

Destination Editor Megan Eaves

Coordinating Editors Kate Mathews, Amanda Williamson

Senior Cartographers David Kemp, Julie Sheridan

Book Designer Jennifer Mullins

Assisting Editors Jenna Myers

Cover Researcher Naomi Parker

Language Content Branislava Vladisavljevic

Thanks to Sasha Baskett, Ignacio Esteban, Ryan Evans, Elizabeth Jones, Alison Ridgway, Angela Tinson, Saralinda Turner, Samantha Tyson

Index

798 Art District 96

A

Aberdeen village 277
accommodation 49, 392-4,
  see also individual locations
  language 416, 417
activities 42-5, 394, *see
  also* birdwatching, cruises,
  cycling, hiking, *individual
  locations*
air travel 408, 410
airports 408, *see also
  individual locations*
  Capital Airport, Běijīng 111
  Hong Kong International
    Airport, Hong Kong 294-5
  Hóngqiáo International
    Airport, Shànghǎi 223-4,
    226
  Macau International
    Airport 307
  Nányuàn Airport, Běijīng 111
  Pǔdōng International
    Airport, Shànghǎi 223-4,
    226
animals 387-8
archeological sites
  Army of Terracotta
    Warriors 13, 126, 141
  Bànpō Neolithic
    Village 142
architecture 56, 264, 378,
  382, *see also* historic

buildings, notable buildings,
  individual locations
colonial 303, 323
diàojiǎolóu (stilt houses)
  24, 320
Macau 298
modern 14, 85-87, 195, 382
tǔlóu 20, 325-6
area codes 399
Army of Terracotta
  Warriors 13, 126, 141
art galleries, *see* museums
  & galleries
arts 378-81
  film 381
  literature 380-1
  music 47
  painting 379-80
ATMs 48, 401

B

Bādálǐng 117
Bai people 43, 328-30
Bank of China Tower 275
Bànpō Neolithic Village 142
beaches
  Hong Kong 277
  Qīngdǎo 175
Běijīng 51-112, **64-5**, **70**, **74-5**,
  82, **86-7**, **89**, **93**, **94**, **101**
  accommodation 93-7
  activities 93
  architecture 14, 56
  drinking & nightlife 17,
    99-102
  entertainment 102-5
  food 13, 56, 97-9
  Forbidden City 12, 54,
    66-76, **70**
  highlights 53-5, **53**
  history 62-3
  hútòng 27, 54, 60-1, 78-9,
    98, **60**
  information 108
  internet resources 57

itineraries 58-9, 60-1, **60**, **58**
  museums 63
  planning 57
  safety 57, 107
  scams 107, 109
  shopping 29, 57, 105-7
  sights 66-93, 96, 105, 106
  Summer Palace 55, 90-3, **94**
  Temple of Heaven 55, 83-4,
    101
  travel to/from 57, 108-10
  travel within 57, 111-12
  views 56
Bell Tower, Běijīng 80-1
Bell Tower, Xī'ān 133
bicycle travel, *see* cycling
Big Goose Pagoda 133
bilharzia 399
Bird's Nest (National
  Stadium) 85, 87
birdwatching 294
Bìshǔ Shānzhuāng 118-19
boat travel 409-10, 411, *see
  also* cruises
books 47, 388
border crossings 408-9
Buddhism 383-4
Buddhist culture 128
Buddhist statues
  Grand Buddha 337-8
  Lama Temple 72
  Lóngmén Caves 149-50
  Mògāo Caves 21, 343-4
  Po Lin Monastery &
    Big Buddha 280-1
  Shuānglín Temple 23
  Yúngāng Caves 29, 127,
    162-3
  Xiǎntōng Temple 157
Buddhist temples
  & monasteries 18, 384
  Big Goose Pagoda 133
  Hanging Monastery 162
  Huáyán Temple 160
  Jade Buddha Temple 201
  Jìng'ān Temple 201

000 Map pages

N

000 Map pages

How to Use This Book

These symbols will help you find the listings you want:

◎	Sights	🅖	Tours	🍷	Drinking
🏖	Beaches	🎉	Festivals & Events	☆	Entertainment
➕	Activities	🛏	Sleeping	🔒	Shopping
🔄	Courses	✖	Eating	ℹ	Information/ Transport

Look out for these icons:

FREE No payment required

🍃 A green or sustainable option

Our authors have nominated these places as demonstrating a strong commitment to sustainability – for example by supporting local communities and producers, operating in an environmentally friendly way, or supporting conservation projects.

These symbols give you the vital information for each listing:

☏	Telephone Numbers	🛜	Wi-Fi Access	🚌	Bus
⊙	Opening Hours	🏊	Swimming Pool	⛴	Ferry
P	Parking	🥗	Vegetarian Selection	M	Metro
⊖	Nonsmoking	📖	English-Language Menu	S	Subway
❄	Air-Conditioning	👪	Family-Friendly	🚋	Tram
@	Internet Access	🐾	Pet-Friendly	🚆	Train

Reviews are organised by author preference.

Map Legend

Note: Not all symbols displayed appear on the maps in this book

Sights
- 🏖 Beach
- 🐦 Bird Sanctuary
- ⚫ Buddhist
- 🏰 Castle/Palace
- ✝ Christian
- ☯ Confucian
- 🕉 Hindu
- ☪ Islamic
- ⚫ Jain
- ✡ Jewish
- ⬤ Monument
- 🏛 Museum/Gallery/ Historic Building
- ⊗ Ruin
- ⛩ Shinto
- ☸ Sikh
- ☯ Taoist
- 🍷 Winery/Vineyard
- 🐾 Zoo/Wildlife Sanctuary
- ⬤ Other Sight

Activities, Courses & Tours
- 🏄 Bodysurfing
- 🤿 Diving
- 🛶 Canoeing/Kayaking
- • Course/Tour
- ♨ Sento Hot Baths/Onsen
- ⛷ Skiing
- 🤿 Snorkelling
- 🏄 Surfing
- 🏊 Swimming/Pool
- 🚶 Walking
- 🏄 Windsurfing
- ➕ Other Activity

Sleeping
- 🛏 Sleeping
- 🏕 Camping

Eating
- ✖ Eating

Drinking & Nightlife
- 🍷 Drinking & Nightlife
- ☕ Cafe

Entertainment
- ☆ Entertainment

Shopping
- 🔒 Shopping

Transport
- ✈ Airport
- ⊗ Border crossing
- 🚌 Bus
- 🚠 Cable car/Funicular
- 🚲 Cycling
- ⛴ Ferry
- Ⓜ Metro/MRT/MTR station
- 🚝 Monorail
- P Parking
- ⛽ Petrol station
- Ⓢ Skytrain/Subway station
- 🚕 Taxi
- 🚉 Train station/Railway
- 🚋 Tram
- Ⓤ Underground station
- • Other Transport

Information
- 🏦 Bank
- 🏛 Embassy/Consulate
- ➕ Hospital/Medical
- @ Internet
- 👮 Police
- ✉ Post Office
- ☎ Telephone
- 🚻 Toilet
- ℹ Tourist Information
- • Other Information

Geographic
- 🏖 Beach
- 🗼 Lighthouse
- 👁 Lookout
- ▲ Mountain/Volcano
- 🏝 Oasis
- 🌳 Park
-)(Pass
- ⛱ Picnic Area
- 💧 Waterfall

Population
- ☆ Capital (National)
- ◉ Capital (State/Province)
- ● City/Large Town
- • Town/Village

Boundaries
- International
- State/Province
- Disputed
- Regional/Suburb
- Marine Park
- Cliff; Wall

Routes
- Tollway
- Freeway
- Primary
- Secondary
- Tertiary
- Lane
- Unsealed road
- Plaza/Mall
- Steps
- Tunnel
- Pedestrian overpass
- Walking Tour
- Walking Tour detour
- Path/Walking Trail

Hydrography
- River, Creek
- Intermittent River
- Canal
- Water
- Dry/Salt Lake
- Reef

Areas
- Airport/Runway
- Beach/Desert
- Cemetery (Christian)
- Cemetery (Other)
- Glacier
- Mudflat
- Park/Forest
- Sight (Building)
- Sportsground
- Swamp

Tienlon Ho

Shāndōng, Sìchuān Tienlon was born and raised in Worthington, Ohio, where the best Chinese food was always at her house. She moves around a lot but mostly keeps to San Francisco and other places where people eat thoughtfully and passionately, and mangosteens are readily available. This is her second round with the *China* guide, and she has also worked on Lonely Planet's *Southwest China* and *California* guides. Read more at http://tienlon.com.

Robert Kelly

Xīnjiāng As a long-term resident of Taiwan, Robert appreciated being asked to cover another of China's 'rebel provinces'. For this edition, he had his hands full navigating a frontier with such a confounding history and culture. But the chance to delve into the subtleties of Islamic pilgrimage, the variations of Persian influence on Buddhist cave art and the origins of Uighur resistance to Han rule was a welcome challenge. A freelance writer since the early 2000s, Robert is contributing to Lonely Planet's *China* for the fourth time.

Shawn Low

Shānxī Shawn grew up in hot, humid, food-crazy Singapore but later

Read more about Shawn at: lonelyplanet.com/members/shawnlow

made his way further south to less hot, less humid, food-crazy Melbourne (Australia, not Florida). He's spent the last eight years working for Lonely Planet: as an editor, commissioning editor, author, TV host and travel editor. Shawn's fourth foray into China for LP saw him explore the lush Inner Mongolian grasslands and some of the more remote northerly provinces bordering North Korea and Russia. Hey, it's a hard job, but someone's gotta do it, right? He's on Twitter @shawnlow.

Emily Matchar

Hong Kong Emily has contributed to some two dozen Lonely Planet

Read more about Emily at: lonelyplanet.com/members/emilymatchar

guides, and she writes for newspapers and magazines all over the world. A native of North Carolina in the southern USA, she currently lives near the top of the world's longest outdoor escalator in Hong Kong.

Daniel McCrohan

Běijīng, The Great Wall, Húnán, Jiāngxī, Tiānjīn & Héběi Daniel has been living in China for more than a decade, and he has been working

Read more about Daniel at: lonelyplanet.com/members/danielmccrohan

in China, India and beyond for much of that time. This is his 22nd Lonely Planet guidebook and his fourth successive stint on the *China* guide. Away from guidebooks, Daniel is the creator of the iPhone app Běijīng on a Budget and co-host of the TV series *Best in China*. He also builds personalised itineraries for travellers to China, India, Mongolia and Bangladesh. Find out more at http://danielmccrohan.com, where you can also watch the videos he makes while on the road for Lonely Planet.

Phillip Tang

Gānsù, Shaanxi (Shǎnxī) Phillip first visited China in 1998 to put

Read more about Phillip at: lonelyplanet.com/members/philliptang

to use his Chinese degree and a love of potent cigarettes. He's fascinated with China's transformation. His return trips can be signposted through witnessing VCD stores morph into DVD parlours and then mobile-phone emporiums. Phillip lives between Mexico City, London and Sydney. He no longer smokes. Find Phillip's China photos on Instagram @mrtangtang-tang, tweets @philliptang and more tips on the Middle Kingdom and elsewhere at http://philliptang.co.uk.

Our Story

A beat-up old car, a few dollars in the pocket and a sense of adventure. In 1972 that's all Tony and Maureen Wheeler needed for the trip of a lifetime – across Europe and Asia overland to Australia. It took several months, and at the end – broke but inspired – they sat at their kitchen table writing and stapling together their first travel guide, *Across Asia on the Cheap*. Within a week they'd sold 1500 copies. Lonely Planet was born.

Today, Lonely Planet has offices in Melbourne, London, Oakland and Delhi, with more than 600 staff and writers. We share Tony's belief that 'a great guidebook should do three things: inform, educate and amuse'.

Our Writers

Damian Harper
Coordinating Author, Shànghǎi, Hénán, Jiāngsū, Zhèjiāng, Ānhuī

Read more about Damian at:
lonelyplanet.com/members/damianharper

After graduating with a degree in Chinese in the days when it was still an unfashionably exotic choice, Damian relocated to Hong Kong to see out the last year of British rule. Since undertaking a leg-busting nine-province journey for the sixth edition of Lonely Planet's *China* in 1997, Damian has tumble-weeded his way around China, working on multiple editions of *China*, *Shanghai* and *Beijing*, contributing to *Hong Kong* and *China's Southwest* and road-testing incalculable hotel beds, hole-in-the-wall menus and wayside watering holes.

Piera Chen
Guǎngdōng, Guǎngxī, Macau Hong Kong native Piera first travelled to China to visit relatives as a child. It's where she learned how to

Read more about Piera at:
lonelyplanet.com/members/pierachen

smoke, ride a bike and coax a water leech away – skills that came in handy during dozens of subsequent sojourns in different parts of the country, including research trips for this book. Piera also pays frequent visits to Macau for food, friends and her favourite secret places. Piera has worked on several editions of *Hong Kong* and *China*.

Chung Wah Chow
Fújiàn Born and raised in Hong Kong, Chung Wah first visited the home of her ancestors in China when she was four. Since then, she

Read more about Chung Wah at:
lonelyplanet.com/members/xcwchow

has been returning to China to visit relatives in Guǎngdōng, study graves in Fújiàn and trek in the wilderness in Xīnjiāng. Chung Wah contributed to the previous three editions of this book and has co-authored other Lonely Planet titles, including *Hong Kong* and *Taiwan*.

David Eimer
Cruising the Yangzi, Yúnnán David first came to China in 1988, when cars and foreigners were both in short supply. After spells as a journalist in LA and in his native London, David

Read more about David at:
lonelyplanet.com/members/davideimer

spent seven years living in Běijīng. His travels have taken him to almost every province in the Middle Kingdom. David has co-authored the last four editions of both the *China* and *Běijīng* guides. Now based in Bangkok, he contributes to a variety of newspapers and magazines in the UK.

← More Writers ....

Published by Lonely Planet Publications Pty Ltd
ABN 36 005 607 983
3rd edition – July 2015
ISBN 978 1 74321 405 3
© Lonely Planet 2015 Photographs © as indicated 2015
10 9 8 7 6 5 4 3 2 1
Printed in Singapore